大河文明旅游报告

TOURISM DEVELOPMENT REPORT ON RIVER VALLEY CIVILIZATION

世界旅游联盟
WORLD TOURISM ALLIANCE

中国旅游出版社

前　言

目前，旅游业已成为全球经济中规模最大和发展势头最为强劲的产业之一。旅游业在社会发展中的产业地位、经济作用逐步增强，对经济的拉动性、社会就业的带动性以及对文化与环境的促进作用日益显现。大河流域地区是人类生存发展、文明进步的源头，具有丰富的自然、文化资源，旅游发展潜力巨大，因此，大河文明旅游也是旅游开发的热点。在此背景下，2018年9月27日，由世界旅游联盟（WTA）、山西省旅游发展委员会、中共临汾市委、临汾市人民政府主办的"首届大河文明旅游论坛"在山西省临汾市召开，300余名文化旅游领域政界、业界、学界嘉宾出席此次盛会，共话"流向未来的大河"主题，一同追寻世界大河文明印迹，谋划大河文明旅游发展大计。首届大河文明旅游论坛为中华民族文明与世界大河文明搭建了对话平台，从全球旅游视角聚焦大河文明的传承利用与创新发展，探讨大河流域的未来旅游发展方向，对促进大河文明在世界范围实现共同发展具有重要战略意义。

为了更好地促进世界大河文明的交流互鉴，世界旅游联盟（WTA）、山西省临汾市文化和旅游局与南开大学旅游与服务学院联合撰写了《大河文明旅游报告》。该报告共包括三个部分，在大量研读国内外大河文明相关资料和实地走访调研基础上，从三个不同方面对大河文明旅游发展进行了深入剖析。第一部分围绕大河文明与旅游的主题，阐释了世界主要大河文明旅游的起源与发展、大河文明旅游的需求与市场分析、大河文明旅游开发效益与挑战等内容；第二部分对大河文明旅游发展模式进行了系统探究，通过对一手和二手资料的分析，归纳出以大河古文明、大河水利工程、大河景观文化、大河沿岸民俗等为核心吸引力的文旅融合发展模式，以及以增长极模式、点—轴模式、线性开发模式为主的空间推进模式；第三部分对大河文明旅游发展经验与对策进行了探究，报告选取了世界范围内的代表性河流——黄河、莱茵河、泰晤士河、密西西比河，分别从旅游规划、产品开发、发展模式等方面剖析了上述河流的旅游发展经验与对策。

在加强生态文明建设、推进消费升级、促进文旅融合的时代背景下，大河文明旅游迎来了崭新的发展机遇。本报告通过对世界大河流域及我国黄河流域内生态、文化、经济、旅游发展的深入剖析，一是有助于推动我国大河流域社会经济及文化旅游的发展，为活化大河流域文明、保护流域生态环境、促进大河旅游可持续发展等提供切实的指导与帮助。二是有助于促进大河流域的文明与旅游发展，推动文化与旅游的进一步融合与文旅产业转型升级，从而推动地区经济社会的发展。三是有助于充分发挥旅游对大河流域所承载优秀传统文化的保护、利用和传承作用，在活化利用唤醒其当代价值、重塑大河文明等方面具有重要的战略意义和实践参考价值。

Preface

Tourism industry has become one of the largest industries in the global economy with rapid developmental momentum. It has prominent industrial status in accelerating economic growth, driving employment, as well as promoting cultural and environmental development. Great river basin is not only a complete, independent and self-contained hydrological unit, the natural area where it is located is also an important social place for all human activities of economy, culture and tourism. Therefore, tourism development on great river civilization becomes a hotspot in the industry. Under this context, World Tourism Alliance (WTA), Shanxi Tourism Development Council, Municipal Party Committee of Linfen and Linfen Government jointly hosted 'The First Great Rivers Civilization Forum on Tourism' at Linfen, Shanxi on September 27th, 2018. More than 300 delegates from tourism politics, industry, and academia participated in this forum and discussed the topic of 'The River to the Future', which traces back the ancient great rivers civilization in the world and conceives the future development of great rivers civilization on tourism. 'The First Great Rivers Civilization Forum on Tourism' launches a dialogue platform connecting Chinese civilization and great rivers civilization in the world. From a global perspective of inheritance and creative development, this forum discussed the future directions and promoted a collective effort on developing great rivers civilization tourism throughout the world.

In order to enhance the communication of management experiences on great rivers civilization tourism, World Tourism Alliance (WTA), LinFen Culture & Tourism Bureau, Shanxi and College of Tourism and Service Management in Nankai University jointly write the report of 'Tourism Development Report on River Valley Civilization'. Based on extensive literature review and field research, this report comprises three parts and uses different angels to analyze tourism development on river valley civilization. The first part elaborates the origin and development of the major ancient river civilizations in the world, introduces the demand and market analysis, as well as the economic benefits and challenges of river valley civilization tourism. The second part systematically elucidates tourism development models of river valley civilization, departing from both primary and secondary data. It concludes a range of development models including culture-tourism integration model driven by water projects, river landscape and folk arts along the riversides; and spatial models, namely, growth pole model, point-axis model and linear development model. The third part explores the strategies and experiences of river valley civilization tourism, taking world's typical river valley civilizations as examples, such as Yellow River, Rhine River, the Thames and the Mississippi.

In the era of reinforcing ecological civilization construction, promoting consumption upgrading and deepening the integration of culture and tourism sectors, great rivers civilization on tourism is embracing its new opportunities of development. This report makes significant implications for such development. First, it offers effective guidance for rejuvenating river valley civilizations, protecting ecological environment and accelerating the overall sustainable development of great river basins in China. Second, it sheds light on the development of great river civilization tourism and the promotion of culture-tourism integration, thereby driving the regional social and economic development. Lastly, it highlights the role of tourism industry in protecting, transmitting and inheriting the traditional culture and customs along the riversides, which is of strategic significance and practical value to reshape the contemporary great river civilization.

目录 · CONTENTS

大河文明旅游报告

第一篇 大河文明与旅游

第一章 大河与文明 / 4
第一节 大河及其流域 / 4
　　一、河流与大河 / 4
　　二、大河流域 / 4
第二节 大河文明 / 6
　　一、大河文明概念界定 / 6
　　二、大河文明特性和价值 / 7
　　三、大河流域及其文明 / 8
第三节 大河文明与旅游发展 / 14
　　一、大河文明与旅游发展的关系 / 14
　　二、大河文明旅游概念界定 / 15

第二章 大河文明旅游与开发 / 17
第一节 大河文明旅游活动起源与发展 / 17
　　一、亚马孙河文明旅游活动的起源与发展 / 17
　　二、尼罗河文明旅游活动的起源与发展 / 19
　　三、莱茵河文明旅游活动的起源与发展 / 20
　　四、密西西比河文明旅游活动的起源与发展 / 22
　　五、黄河文明旅游活动的起源与发展 / 23
　　六、长江文明旅游活动的起源与发展 / 25

第二节　大河文明旅游产业的开发形势 / 27
　　　　一、旅游规划和法律先行 / 28
　　　　二、流域管理和功能定位 / 29
　　　　三、资源开发和产品优化 / 30
　　第三节　大河文明旅游需求与市场 / 32
　　　　一、大河文明旅游游客需求分析 / 32
　　　　二、大河文明旅游市场供给分析 / 33

第三章　大河文明旅游开发效益与挑战 / 35
　　第一节　大河文明旅游开发的效益 / 35
　　　　一、大河文明旅游开发的社会效益 / 35
　　　　二、大河文明旅游开发的经济效益 / 36
　　第二节　大河文明旅游开发面临的挑战 / 37
　　　　一、文化遗产保护与传承 / 37
　　　　二、大河文明生态环境 / 38
　　　　三、大河文明旅游规划与开发 / 40
　　　　四、管理和政策 / 40

第二篇　大河文明旅游发展模式

第一章　文旅融合模式 / 44
　　第一节　以大河古代文明为核心吸引力的融合模式 / 44
　　　　一、考古发现 / 44
　　　　二、历史传说 / 47
　　　　三、历史事件 / 49
　　第二节　以大河水利工程为核心吸引力的融合模式 / 51
　　　　一、水利发电工程 / 51
　　　　二、治水工程 / 56
　　第三节　以大河景观文化为核心吸引力的融合模式 / 61
　　　　一、自然景观文化 / 61
　　　　二、人文景观文化 / 66

第四节　以大河沿岸民俗为核心吸引力的融合模式 / 70
　　　　一、民间艺术 / 70
　　　　二、岁时节庆活动 / 77

第二章　空间推进模式 / 81

第一节　增长极模式 / 81
　　　　一、河流旅游增长极的形成 / 81
　　　　二、河流旅游增长极辐射作用的发挥 / 83
　　　　三、长江流域的旅游增长极发展模式 / 84

第二节　点—轴模式 / 88
　　　　一、河流旅游点—轴模式的形成 / 88
　　　　二、长江流域的旅游点—轴发展模式 / 89

第三节　线性开发模式 / 93
　　　　一、线性空间 / 93
　　　　二、生态景观型廊道 / 96
　　　　三、遗产保护型廊道 / 99
　　　　四、旅游开发型廊道 / 103

第三篇　大河文明旅游发展经验与对策

第一章　中国黄河文明旅游发展经验 / 110

第一节　黄河文明旅游发展经验 / 110
　　　　一、发布《中国黄河旅游发展指数报告》/ 110
　　　　二、举办黄河旅游大会，打造交流合作平台 / 111
　　　　三、设立沿黄旅游产业发展基金促进共同发展 / 111
　　　　四、成立沿黄城市旅游产业联盟创新合作机制 / 112

第二节　山西省黄河文明旅游发展模式 / 112
　　　　一、临汾黄河文明旅游资源 / 112
　　　　二、临汾黄河文化旅游发展模式 / 118

第三节　山西省临汾黄河旅游发展经验与对策 / 131
　　　　一、黄河文明旅游发展经验 / 131

二、未来发展建议 / 136

第二章　世界典型河流文明旅游发展经验 / 143

第一节　莱茵河旅游发展经验 / 143
  一、莱茵河沿岸风光 / 143
  二、莱茵河整体发展模式 / 143
  三、莱茵河旅游产业空间布局 / 144
  四、莱茵河主要旅游产品形式 / 146
  五、莱茵河旅游发展经验 / 146

第二节　泰晤士河旅游发展经验 / 148
  一、泰晤士河沿岸风光 / 148
  二、泰晤士河旅游活动的发展历程 / 149
  三、泰晤士河沿岸旅游空间布局 / 150
  四、泰晤士河主要旅游产品类型 / 150
  五、泰晤士河旅游发展经验 / 151

第三节　密西西比河旅游发展经验 / 153
  一、密西西比河流域旅游开发 / 153
  二、密西西比河整体发展模式 / 154
  三、密西西比河主要旅游产品形式 / 154
  四、密西西比河旅游发展经验 / 155

Tourism Development Report on River Valley Civilization

Part I　River Valley Civilization and Tourism

Chapter One　The Great River and Its Civilization / 160

Section 1　Great Rivers and Their Basins / 160
  1. Rivers and Great Rivers / 160
  2. Great River Basin / 161

Section 2　River Valley Civilization / 163

　　1. The Definition of River Valley Civilization / 163

　　2. Characteristics and Values of River Valley Civilization / 164

　　3. Great River Basin and its Civilization / 167

Section 3　River Valley Civilization and Tourism Development / 175

　　1. The Relationship between River Valley Civilization and Tourism Development / 175

　　2. The Conceptualization of River Valley Civilization Tourism / 176

Chapter Two　Tourism on River Valley Civilization and Development / 178

Section 1　Origin and Development of River Valley Civilization Tourism / 178

　　1. The Origin and Development of Tourism Activities of Amazon Civilization / 178

　　2. The Origin and Development of Nile Civilization Tourism / 181

　　3. Origin and Development of Civilization Tourism Activities in the Rhine River / 183

　　4. Origin and Development of Civilization Tourism in the Mississippi River / 185

　　5. Origin and Development of Civilization Tourism in the Yellow River / 187

　　6. Origin and Development of Civilization Tourism in the Yangtze River / 190

Section 2　Development of Great Rivers Civilization Tourism Industry / 194

　　1. Tourism Planning and Regulation Taking Priority / 194

　　2. Watershed Management and Functional Positioning / 197

　　3. Resource Development and Product Optimization / 199

Section 3　Demand and Market of the Great River Civilization Tourism / 201

　　1. Analysis of Tourist Demand of Great River Civilization Tourism / 202

　　2. Analysis on the Supply of Great River Civilization Tourism Market / 202

Chapter Three　Benefits and Challenges of River Valley Civilization Tourism Development / 205

Section 1　Benefits of Developing River Valley Civilization Tourism / 205

　　1. Social Benefits of Developing River Valley Civilization Tourism / 205

　　　　　　2. Economic Benefits of Developing River Valley Civilization Tourism / 207
　　Section 2　Challenges in the Process of Developing River Valley Civilization Tourism / 208
　　　　　　1. Protection and inheritance of Cultural Heritage / 208
　　　　　　2. Ecological Environment of the River Valley Civilization / 210
　　　　　　3. Planning and Development of River Valley Civilization Tourism / 212
　　　　　　4. Management and Policies / 213

Part II Tourism Development Model of River Valley civilization

Chapter One　Integration of Culture and Tourism / 218
　　Section 1　Integration Driven by the Core Attraction of Ancient River Valley Civilization / 218
　　　　　　1. Archaeological Discovery / 218
　　　　　　2. Historical Legends / 223
　　　　　　3. Historical Events / 225
　　Section 2　Integration Driven by the Core Attraction of Water Project / 228
　　　　　　1. Water Projects for Power Generation / 228
　　　　　　2. Projects of Water Management / 236
　　Section 3　Integration Driven by the Core Attraction of River Landscape / 243
　　　　　　1. Culture of Natural Landscape / 244
　　　　　　2. Culture of Humane Landscape / 251
　　Section 4　Integration Driven by the Folk Customs along the Riversides / 258
　　　　　　1. Folk Art / 258
　　　　　　2. Seasonal and Festival Activities / 268

Chapter Two　Spatial Promotion / 273
　　Section 1　Promotion in the Growth Pole Model / 273
　　　　　　1. The Formation of Growth Pole in River Valley Tourism / 273
　　　　　　2. The Radiation Effect of Growth Pole in River Valley Tourism / 276
　　　　　　3. Growth Pole Development of Tourism in the Yangtze River / 277
　　Section 2　Point-Axis Model / 284

  1. The Formation of Point-Axis Model in River Tourism / 284

  2. The Development of Point-Axis Model in the Yangtze River Valley / 286

Section 3 Linear Development / 292

  1. Linear Space / 292

  2. Corridor of ecological landscape / 295

  3. Corridor for Heritage Protection / 300

  4. Corridor of Tourism Development / 307

Part Ⅲ Experience and Strategy of Great River Civilization Tourism Development

Chapter One Experience and Strategy of Civilization Tourism in the Yellow River / 314

Section 1 Experience on the Development of the Yellow River Civilization Tourism / 314

  1. Report on Tourism Development Index of the Yellow River in China / 315

  2. Holding the Yellow River Tourism Conference to Build a Platform for Exchange and Cooperation / 315

  3. Promoting Mutual Development by Establishing Tourism Industry Development Fund along the Yellow River / 316

  4. Innovative Cooperation Mechanism of Tourism Industry Alliance along the Yellow River / 317

Section 2 The Development Model of the Yellow River Civilization Tourism in Shanxi Province / 317

  1. The Yellow River Civilization Tourism Resources of Linfen / 318

  2. Linfen Yellow River Cultural Tourism Development Model / 326

Section 3 Experiences and Countermeasures of Tourism Development of the Yellow River in Linfen, Shanxi Province / 348

  1. Experience in the Development of Yellow River Civilization Tourism / 348

  2. Suggestion and Recommendation for the Future / 357

Chapter Two　Development Experience of The World's Typical River Civilization Tourism / 368

Section 1　Experiences of Rhine River Tourism Development / 368

　　1. Scenery along the Rhine River / 368

　　2. Development Model of Rhine River / 369

　　3. The Spatial Distribution of the Rhine River Tourism Industry / 369

　　4. Main Forms of Tourism products of the Rhine River / 372

　　5. Experiences in the Development of Rhine Tourism / 373

Section 2　Tourism Development Experience from the Thames / 376

　　1. Landscape along the Thames / 376

　　2. Tourism Development along the Thames / 376

　　3. Tourism Spatial Layout alongside the Thames / 378

　　4. Major Tourism Products over the Thames / 378

　　5. Tourism Development Experiences of the Thames / 380

Section 3　Tourism Development Experiences from the Mississippi / 382

　　1. Tourism Development in the Mississippi / 382

　　2. The Development Model of the Mississippi / 383

　　3. The Main Forms of Tourism Products / 383

　　4. Tourism Development Experiences from the Mississippi / 384

参考文献 / 386

大河文明
旅游报告

第一篇
大河文明与旅游

第一章　大河与文明

河流孕育了人类文明，是人类文明和城市的诞生地。人类早期"逐水而居"的生存方式，以及河流得天独厚的生存条件，造就河流成为人们生存的命脉。世界四大古文明都发源于大河流域，如中国的黄河流域、埃及的尼罗河流域、幼发拉底河和底格里斯河两河流域，以及印度的恒河流域。本章首先对河流、大河以及大河流域的概念进行界定；其次，对大河文明的概念进行界定，指出大河文明的特性和价值，并分析大河流域的四大古文明；最后，对大河文明与旅游发展的关系进行剖析，给出大河文明旅游的概念界定。

第一节　大河及其流域

本小节主要对大河及大河流域的概念进行界定，并分析了大河流域的特性。人类的生存发展、人类文明的进步都离不开大河的哺育，因此，要想深刻了解大河文明和大河文明旅游，首先应该了解什么是大河，以及什么是大河流域。

一、河流与大河

所谓河流，是指由降水或地下涌出地表的水汇集在地面低洼处，在重力作用下经常性或周期性地沿着狭长凹地流动的水流。河流是地球上水循环的重要路径，是泥沙、盐类和化学元素等进入湖泊、海洋的通道，是地球生命的重要组成部分，也是人类生存和发展的基础。

河流在我国的称谓很多，较大的称江、河、川，较小的称溪、涧、沟、渠等，每一条大的河流，都是由一条主流和若干条支流组成，同时支流又由更小的水流组成。所谓大河，广义上而言，就是指流域面积很大的河流。然而，河流流域面积的大小与河流流量、总水量密切相关，一般来讲，流域面积越大，河流流量和总水量越大，所以大河的界定标准不应仅限于流域面积，还需要考虑河流流量、总水量，以及河流长度等指标，基于此，我们认为狭义上的大河指的是流域面积、河流流量和总水量都比较大，河流长度较长的河流。

二、大河流域

（一）大河流域概念

流域又称"集水区"，是一个水文概念，是地表水及地下水分水线所包围的集水区域的总称，分为地面集水区和地下集水区两类。每条大河都有自己的流域，一个大流域可以按照水系等级分成数个小流域，小流域又可以分成更小的流域等。很明显，大河流域中最主要的要素是水，没有水，也就无所谓流域，但流域毕竟是一个集水区域，因此流域概念还应包括水流经的土地、土地上的植被、土地和森林中的矿藏、水中以及水流经土地的生物等。大河流域中的水体、地貌、土壤和植被等各因素都是一个紧密相关的整体。

其实，大河流域不但是一个从河源到河口的完整、独立、自成系统的水文单元，其所在的自然区域也是人类经济、文化等一切活动的重要社会场所，从这个层面看，流域已经超出了地理水文意义，成为一个自然—人类复合系统，由自然封闭的区域转化为与人类活动密切相关的开放复合的区域。人类为了生存，必须开发利用流域中的各种自然资源，包括水、土地、矿藏、植被、动物等。同样，流域中人类的社会生活，包括风俗习惯、文化背景、社会人口状况等，也对流域资源和环境产生影响。可以说，大河流域是在其边界范围内由于水的自然流动而形成的一个十分重要的自然—经济—社会复合生态系统，这一系统之内的各种自然要素之间、自然要素与经济要素和社会要素之间、流域上下游、干支流之间都在不断地进行着物质能量、信息的交换及资金、人员的交流，一个因素发生变化，整个流域的其他因素都会受其影响。

（二）大河流域特性

根据大河流域的概念，可以把其特性归纳为以下几个方面：

1. 整体性

大河流域是一个天然的集水区域，流域中最主要的因子是水，正是由于水的流动导致了流域内地理上的关联性及环境资源的联动性，也决定了流域成为一个统一完整的生态系统。流域的上中下游、左右岸、支流和干流、河水和河道、水质与水量、地表水与地下水等，都是该流域不可分割的组成部分，具有自然整体性。同时，以水体为媒介，流域中的土壤、森林、矿藏、生物等也组成了一个紧密相关的整体，该整体中的任一要素发生变化都会对整个流域产生重大的影响。此外，流域又是人们经济、社会生活的重要场所，流域内人们的社会、经济活动会对流域生态系统产生极大的影响。流域的整体性特点要求流域管理应该根据上、中、下游地区的社会经济情况、自然资源和环境条件，以及流域的物理和生态方面的作用和变化，从流域生态系统整体出发来考虑其开发、利用和保护方面的问题，这无疑是最科学、最适合流域可持续发展客观需要的一种选择。

2. 公共性

大河流域资源是一种公共资源，它具有公共资源的一般属性，如有限性、外部性和使用的分散性，相互依存性与不可分性。作为共同财富和公共产品，对流域资源的使用必须是集体行动，个体对公共资源的自由选择与利用和社会对公共资源的分散管理，必将产生破坏性竞争。根据决策理论，在公共管理中，管理主体越多越分散，管理责任就会越趋于松弛，对资源的保护就越是无力，资源的状况就越坏。反之，权力越统一，责任就越大，权力越集中并趋向单一中心，责任就越明确，权力主体之间的破坏性竞争和摩擦就越小。因此，大河流域的公共性要求流域管理应该设定一个统一的流域机构实行整体管理和调控。

3. 复杂性

大河流域通常经度和纬度跨度较大，上中下游表现出明显的区段性和差异性，这就导致上下游、左右岸和干支流在自然条件、地理位置、经济技术基础和历史背景等方面有所不同，因此，流域生态系统覆盖了不同的自然地理单元，具有多样性的自然景观、森林植被和气候特征。同时，人类开发利用流域资源的方式多种多样，从农业生产活动到城市生态系统，从矿产资源开发到工矿业加工，由此所产生的生态环境影响也是复杂多样的。

4. 生态的不可逆性

流域生态系统内任何人类生产活动所产生的生态效应都是不可逆的，生态系统一旦遭到破坏，不会自行恢复到原来的生态面貌。

第二节　大河文明

本小节在对大河文明进行概念界定的基础上，阐释了大河文明的价值和特征，同时又对世界大河流域的四大文明进行了介绍。地球上几乎所有的文明都起源于河流，古印度文明起源于印度河及恒河，古埃及文明起源于尼罗河，古中国文明起源于长江和黄河……无论是西方文明的源头还是东方文明，都是依托河流兴起。

一、大河文明概念界定

河流是地球多样生态系统中最基本的存在形式之一，历史上人类及其社会生态系统的发展与河流密不可分，人类社会文明起源于河流文化，人类社会发展积淀河流文化，河流文化作为一种人类文明类型，被人们认知已经经历了很长的历史时期。

狭义上，大河文明也叫农耕文明，根基是大河流域，那里沃野千里、灌溉便利，有独特的农耕环境，为人类的生存创造了良好的条件，人类古代居民很早便在大河流域生产劳动、生息繁衍，形成了以农耕经济为基本形态的大河文明。古代大河流域以农耕文明为特征，农业是这些地区最主要的生产部门，也是这些地区国家形成和发展的经济基础，古埃及、古巴比伦、古印度和古中国这四大文明古国，就是在农业经济的基础上建立和发展起来的，并表现出自己的文明特征。

河流不仅产生生命，关系到陆地、水生生物的繁衍、生息和生态稳态，而且也直接影响人类在长期历史传统中形成的对河流、人以及社会休戚相关的精神信仰、心灵形象和品味象征意义。因此，广义上而言，大河文明不局限于农耕文明，而是应该既包括大河流域居民在采集和制作食物时所表现出来的智慧，同时也包括社会发展到较高阶段时，大河流域居民所创造出来的推动社会发展的更高层次的文明，如贸易和制造业、文字、先进的技术、科学、社会习俗、文化和宗教等。

二、大河文明特性和价值

（一）大河文明的特性

1. 稳定性

大河文明系统的稳定性是由相应的地理环境决定的，以中国古代大河文明而论，中国的黄河、长江等主要河流，历史上虽然发生过改道等变动，但是其基本的河流系统不变、格局不变，大体上还是以前的样子，黄河、长江仍是黄河、长江，并没有从中国转移到欧洲或世界上其他地方去。在相当长的时空内，河流的历史远比人类的历史更为持久，这就是地理环境的稳定性。稳定的地理环境提供了稳定的生产方式和生活方式，也造就了相应的文明系统，并使该文明系统拥有了地理环境的特性——稳定性。

此外，农民作为大河农业文明的直接创造者，"日出而作，日落而息"是他们最基本的生活规律。早上走出定居之所，在固定（稳定）的耕地上种植庄稼，晚上又睡在定居之所。他们不仅春种、夏锄、秋收、冬贮，一年四季都劳作于相对稳固的耕地上，生活于相对稳固的居所内，而且于此养育儿女，繁衍后代，培养农业文明的继承人，如此一年又一年，一代又一代，生生不息地固守在耕地上和居所中。尽管由于战乱等原因，农民也有背井离乡的时候，但古代农民的生产方式和生活方式却并未因此而大变，这就是大河农业文明系统稳定性的根本。

2. 丰富性

大河文明的丰富性也是受自然环境（或地理条件）所支配的。大河流域内包含有主流、支流、湖泊、沼泽、水渠、流域、地形、温度、土质、物产、地势、气候等诸多元素，这些元素在不同的地方具有不同的特征。例如中国的黄河，在其发源地青海省的综合地理条件，与其中下游地区如河南、山东的综合地理条件就很不相同。可以说，不同的自然环境（地理条件）造就了相互差异、多姿多彩的具体文化，这就是大河文明系统丰富性的根源所在。

当然，大河文明的丰富性是以其稳定性为前提的，是大河文明稳定性的活力显现，尽管大河文明稳定性较强，但其内部的丰富性又显示了特定的活力特征或开放性。大河文明的丰富性表现在许多方面，如表现在所有子系统中，如物产丰富性、地理条件丰富性等。

在中国古代文明系统中，中国北方游牧经济多次被中原的农业文明吸引或溶化，中国北方的游牧业文明是中国古代文明系统极其重要的一个子系统，一方面它显示了中国古代文明系统的丰富性，另一方面又以其经济优势补充了农业文明，从而促使古代文明系统更加久远。

（二）大河文明对人类社会的价值

1. 古代农耕文明发育的初始摇篮

水是地球生命之源，自诞生之日起，人类便将江河流域视为天赐养育之母，作为淡水资源的关键载体，大河流域始终是人类文明发育的摇篮，是人类早期文明的发源地。人类史上的第一种文明形态——农耕文明，就是发源于大河流域。农耕文明本质上需要顺天应命，需要守望田园，需要辛勤劳作，主要表现为男耕女织、规模小、分工简单，不用于商品交换。原始农业和原始畜牧业、古人类的定居生活等的发展，使人类从食物的采集者变为食物的生产者，实现第一次生产力的飞跃，人类进入农耕文明。农耕文明一直延续到工业革命之前，此间，人们以农业为主，政治体制一般实行君主制或君主专制，社会结构呈现为金字塔形。

农耕文明的生产和发展得益于优越的自然环境，需要良好的气候、资源等条件作支撑，而大河流域凭借其优势条件，如：气候温和，适合人类居住；河流两岸土地肥沃，益于农耕；河流水源充足，不仅方便灌溉，而且便于牲畜饮用；河流物产丰富，有大量的水产和禽鸟；且乘船可前往沿海各地，交通、运输较为方便等，为农业文明提供了便利的生产条件。可见，大河流域完全能够适应于农业的生产和人类的居住，因此成为农耕文明的重要发源地。

2. 现代工业文明发展的核心基地

农耕文明是工业文明的摇篮，尽管农耕文明也不都是田园牧歌，也有争斗和战乱，但较之于游牧文明和工业文明，具有质的不同。农耕文明相对于游牧文明的好处体现为能大幅度提高生产力，这样一来才激发一些解决了温饱问题的人去做温饱之外的事情，如研发科技、发展文化等，从而促进了工业文明的产生。

大河流域不仅哺育了农耕文明，而且也是现代工业文明发展的核心基地。如作为世界四大文明古国之一和人口最多的国家——中国，在其现代工业文明发育之初，长江与黄河两大流域的开发在国家社会经济中占有极为重要地位。20 世纪 60~70 年代，随着国家工业化的全面推进，长江与黄河两大流域的开发在全国社会经济，特别是经济发展中的地位开始呈现较为明显的下降趋势。到 1970 年，两大流域 GDP 在全国的比重下降到了 52.6%，较 1952 年时减少了 5 个百分点。而改革开放以后，沿海沿江开放和西部大开发政策的实施，加快了长江和黄河两大流域开发的速度，到 2010 年，两大流域 GDP 占全国的比重已重新攀升至 59.0%，显示了两大流域在国家现代工业文明发展中的地位和作用。[1]

三、大河流域及其文明

（一）尼罗河流域古埃及文明

1. 古埃及文明的起源

尼罗河流域是世界文明发祥地之一，该流域人民创造了灿烂的文化，在科学发展的历史长河中做出了杰出的贡献，突出的代表就是古埃及文明。

古埃及文明的产生，首先得益于大自然为人类造就的较为优越的地理环境，即古埃及文明首先是尼罗河流域的先民适应自然环境的产物。从公元前 5700 年前起，干燥的气候促使生活在大草原上以畜牧为生的人们为寻求水源和草料，开始向尼罗河河谷移动和集结，自此，人们就在蜿蜒如带

---

[1] 张雷，鲁春霞，李江苏. 中国大河流域开发与国家文明发育 [J]. 长江流域资源与环境，2015，24（10）.

的尼罗河两岸繁衍生息。在古埃及所处的地理环境中，适合种地也是唯一能够种地的只有尼罗河沿岸，这片土地非常肥沃，周期性的河水泛滥会给沿岸带来大量富含肥料的泥沙，很容易种植出大量粮食作物，逐渐地，尼罗河沿岸就集聚了大量部落。公元前 4500 年左右，先民利用尼罗河河水泛滥后的肥沃泥土，开始从事小麦、大麦等农作物的种植，从而进入了农业文明时代。

2. 古埃及文明的发展

古埃及文明的产生和发展与尼罗河密不可分，正如古希腊历史学家希罗多德所言："埃及是尼罗河的赠礼。"古埃及时期，尼罗河几乎每年都会泛滥，淹没农田，同时也使被淹没的土地成为肥沃的耕地。此外，古埃及文明之所以延绵数千年，另一个原因是其与外部世界相对隔绝的地理环境，北面和东面分别是地中海和红海；西面是杳无人迹的沙漠；南面是尼罗河的上游，有一系列飞流直下的大瀑布；只有东北部有一个通道通往西亚。这种地理环境虽然阻断了古埃及人与外部世界的联系，造成埃及与世隔绝的局面，但也使得外族人不容易进入古埃及，为古埃及提供了天然的保护屏障。古埃及人生活在这样得天独厚的环境里，长期免于外来侵略之患，因而产生了一种优越的安全感。

古埃及的居民是由北非的土著居民和西亚的塞姆人融合形成的，在公元前 4000 年后半期逐渐形成了国家，至公元前 343 年为止，共经历了前王朝时期、早王朝时期（1~2 王朝）、古王国时期（3~6 王朝）、第一中间期（7~10 王朝）、中王国时期（11~12 王朝）、第二中间期（13~17 王朝）、新王国时期（18~20 王朝）、第三中间期（21~25 王朝）和后王朝时期（26~31 王朝）9 个时期 31 个王朝的统治，其中古埃及在十八王朝时（前 15 世纪）达到鼎盛。古埃及有自己的文字系统、完善的政治体系和多神信仰的宗教系统，其丰富的历史文化遗产，如金字塔、木乃伊、尼罗河盛产的纸草、行驶在尼罗河上的古船等，都标志着古埃及数千年文明发展的历程。

3. 古埃及文明的衰落

公元前 12 世纪，古埃及国力大衰，频频遭受野蛮民族的入侵。第 20 王朝以后，一系列的奴隶起义导致国力衰竭，其间经历被利比亚人、努比亚人和亚述人的统治。自第 26 王朝进入古埃及后期，最终在公元前 525 年被波斯阿契美尼德帝国征服，文化从此一蹶不振，古埃及时代结束了。波斯人在古埃及建立第 27 王朝和第 31 王朝，古埃及第 26 王朝后裔反抗波斯人成功，建立了短暂的第 28、第 29 和第 30 王朝。公元前 332 年，古埃及又被亚历山大大帝所统治，亚历山大死后，其部将托勒密占领古埃及，建立托勒密王朝，也被称为法老，但当时的古埃及已经是彻底在外族人的统治下。随后，古罗马崛起，成为地中海世界大国，古埃及也被其占领。之后在 7 世纪，阿拉伯人再次入侵古埃及，古埃及原有的文明在这一过程中被阿拉伯文明所取代，而逐渐消失。

（二）印度河和恒河流域古印度文明

1. 古印度文明的起源

印度是四大文明古国之一，古印度最早的文明诞生在南亚最长河流——印度河的河谷，印度河流域每年泛滥两次，给两岸带来了非常厚的淤泥，土地肥沃，适合孕育文明，因此成为古印度文明的最早起源地。

古印度文明历史可追溯到公元前 2500 年左右，这一时期，印度河流域诞生了哈拉帕文明。哈拉帕文明是由邻近地方或古时的村庄演变而来，产生的先决条件是适宜农牧业生产和人类生产生活的、稳定的气候条件的出现。但哈拉帕文明存在时间并不长，公元前 1750 年左右，印度河文明遭到毁灭，短短 500 多年时间，哈拉帕文明就突然消失，直到 20 世纪通过考古发掘才展现出来。

2. 古印度文明的发展

印度河文明消亡后，有数百年之久，那里的城市文化是死寂的，令古印度文明出现了七八百年的断层。而在这个断层的早期，公元前 1500 年左右，世界上最早的游牧民族之一——雅利安人乘虚而入，落脚于印度河上游五河地区，与北印度土著不断融合，从约公元前 1000 年开始，有了恒河文明。

公元前 6 世纪，印度历史进入了"列国时代"，印度北部尤其是恒河流域列国林立，各城邦之间为了兼并土地、争夺霸权不断进行战争，最终摩揭陀国战胜其他强国，逐渐统一了北印度。公元前 518 年，印度河流域被波斯帝国占领，波斯人统治印度西北部近两个世纪。公元前 4 世纪后期，马其顿王亚历山大率军侵入印度西北部，并派总督和驻军进行统治。公元前 324 年，旃陀罗笈多领导印度河流域人民反抗马其顿取得胜利后，自立为王。接着挥师东进，灭了难陀王朝，建立了印度历史上第一个统一帝国——孔雀帝国，帝国版图扩展到除印度半岛最南端以外的整个南亚次大陆。公元前 187 年，孔雀帝国灭亡，印度陷于分裂状态，印度的分裂给外族入侵以可乘之机。从公元前 2 世纪以后的 200 年间，先后有大夏的希腊人、安息人、塞种人、贵霜人侵入印度，其中，只有贵霜人曾在印度西北部建立了稳固的政权。到 3 世纪，贵霜帝国分裂成若干小公国。4 世纪初，笈多王朝兴起，其极盛时期的版图主要在北印度，并未包括整个半岛。5 世纪中叶，哑哒人自中亚侵入印度，占领印度北部和中部大部分地区。6 世纪 20 年代，北印度各王公的联军打败哑哒人，但笈多王朝经哑哒人打击后，内部各小邦纷纷独立，陷入分裂混战之中。7 世纪初，戒日帝国兴起，戒日王统一了北印度。

古印度是一个多宗教教派的社会。吠陀教、婆罗门教、耆那教、佛教、印度教、锡克教等宗教，均起源于印度，其他较小的宗教和各教中的众多派别更是不胜枚举。此外，主要的世界宗教如伊斯兰教、基督教、犹太教和琐罗亚斯德教等在印度都有自己的信徒。印度宗教之多，是古代世界其他各国难以比拟的，被称为"宗教博物馆"。[1]

3. 古印度文明的衰落

古印度文明的第一期——印度河文明，最终走向消失，而至于消失的原因，历史学家给出了 3 种可信的推测：一是外族（很可能是雅利安人）入侵。因为根据考古发现，哈拉帕文明的 1500 多处遗址中，几乎没有发现战争的痕迹和制造的武器，说明城市间很少发生冲突，这一文明爱好和

---

[1] 张永秀. 论古印度文明的特性［J］. 潍坊学院学报，2011，11（1）.

平，很容易被外族征服。二是地震说。地震破坏了原有地形，很多印度河支流因此干涸，建在一旁的城市人民缺少足够的灌溉用水，人们只好抛弃这里。三是破坏环境，自取灭亡。不管哪种说法，印度河文明是确实消失了。

尽管印度河文明没有摆脱衰落的命运，但古印度文明的第二期——恒河文明却得以延续下来。古印度的黄金时代——笈多王朝帝国（4世纪初）延续了230年后终于崩溃，其后又过了半个多世纪，北印度迎来了戒日王朝（7世纪初），戒日王朝垮台后，北印度陷入混乱。13世纪起，从阿富汗来的穆斯林先后在北印度建立了德里苏丹国和莫卧儿帝国，再后来是西方列强（包括葡萄牙人、法国人和英国人）的殖民，直到1947年印度最终获得独立。可见，有着3000多年历史的恒河文明与中华文明、犹太文明一样，都没有遭到灭绝式的打击而延续至今，这为曾经中断的古印度文明，增添了一份与时俱进的魅力。

（三）两河流域（底格里斯河和幼发拉底河）苏美尔文明

1. 苏美尔文明的起源

文字记载的两河流域文明大致可以划分为两个阶段：第一阶段是从乌鲁克Ⅳ到古巴比伦帝国建立，被称为"苏美尔文明"；第二阶段是从古巴比伦帝国的建立到波斯帝国的灭亡，被称为"巴比伦—亚述文明"。苏美尔文明是目前所知世界历史上最为古老的文明，它植根于幼发拉底河和底格里斯河下游冲积平原，是古代两河流域文明的发端，构成了古代两河流域文明的主体，并深刻地影响了之后的巴比伦文明和亚述文明。苏美尔文明具体被界定为，是指公元前4500~前2000年在两河流域冲积平原南部兴起的古代文明，它跨越乌鲁克时代、早王朝时期、阿卡德王国、乌尔第三王朝及伊新第一王朝五个时代，是古代两河流域文明进入有史时代的第一个文明发展阶段。

苏美尔这个名词源自地名，指两河流域冲积平原的南部区域，生活在这个地区的古代居民也被称为苏美尔人。苏美尔人及两河流域南部冲积平原居民共同创造了人类历史上最古老的文明。这个文明创造了多种原生文明的要素，主要体现在农业的产生和定居生活的开始，城市的出现与社会组织的日益复杂化，国家的形成，文字、科技、艺术等文化要素的发展等多个方面，这一切都发生在公元前4500~前2900年。①

2. 苏美尔文明的发展

苏美尔文明在存在的几千年历史中，做出了许多伟大的贡献，被冠以诸多的"第一"。第一个发明文字——楔形文字；第一个创造了带轮的马车；第一个绘画星象图，与现代几乎一样；第一个拥有完善的城市排水系统，包括汲水吊杆、运河、水渠、堤坝、堰和水库，同时还具有发达的贸易业、农业、牲畜业、手工业，如纺织、制陶、印刷、酿酒、造船等；创造了啤酒，将是否会喝啤酒视为未开化人与文明人之间的分界线，并且还拥有自己的啤酒女神；能计算15位数字，而被称为西方文明摇篮的希腊，到了2500年前才能计算到万位；发明了12单位与60单位度量划分；将一

---

① 刘健. 苏美尔文明基本特征探析［J］. 外国问题研究，2016（2）.

年分为12个月，一周分为7天；拥有多学科教育的规范学校，当中的学科包括神学、植物学、动物学、矿物学、地理学、算术学和语言学等；最早的军阵也是出自苏美尔。

苏美尔文明简直是天外飞来，不可一世。苏美尔几乎没有资源，包括森林、矿藏甚至石头，但尽管如此，苏美尔人不仅了解地质学，知道如何获得矿石和其他方面的工艺，而且还制造出世界上第一种合金和青铜。通过这些发明创造，可以发现苏美尔人的文明程度不是一个原始民族能够发展起来的，虽然苏美尔文明可能是目前最有证据的世界上最古老的文明，但苏美尔人来自何处至今是个谜。

3. 苏美尔文明的衰落

苏美尔文明本身就是由数个独立的城市国家组成的，在公元前3000年，苏美尔地区出现了12个国家，这些国家用运河和界石划分，每个国家的中心是该城市的保护神或保护女神的庙，每个国家由一个主持该城市的宗教仪式的祭司或国王统治，这些国家因水权、贸易道路和游牧民族的进贡等事务进行了持久的互相争战。

苏美尔人这种内部不团结的劣根性，给了亚述人进攻的天赐良机，他们于公元前1800年左右大举发动扩张战争，占领了美索不达米亚北部和中部，好不容易复兴起来的苏美尔民族，眨眼间又处在了亡国灭种的险境。公元前1792年，汉漠拉比大帝在巴比伦即位，美索不达米亚平原上新的统一战争开始了；公元前1763年，最后一位苏美尔民族的君主瑞穆辛的首都拉尔萨城被巴比伦军队攻陷，从此以后，苏美尔人便在历史上销声匿迹了，苏美尔文明也消失在了历史长河中。

（四）黄河、长江流域的中华文明

1. 中华文明的起源

中国是世界上最古老的文明古国之一，长江和黄河一起并称为中国的"母亲河"，两大流域珠联璧合，成为中华农业文明的保障基地，以及中华文明的重要发祥地。中华文明的摇篮在新石器时代，中华民族的初始阶段在华夏。早在距今约7800年，黄河下游的磁山就孕育了裴李岗文化，6000多年前又孕育了"半坡文化"。距今约8000年，长江中游的彭头山也孕育了城背溪文化，与半坡文化几乎同时期，长江流域孕育了河姆渡文化。年代最早的文字出现在黄河流域，而作为文字萌芽的刻画符号在黄河流域和长江流域都有，最早的铜器出现在黄河流域，但铜器离不开铜源，而铜和锡、铅等有色金属的成矿带大半在长江流域。黄河流域和长江流域都发现了一些新石器时代的城址。可见，黄河文化与长江文化互相联系，相互交流，相互促进，共同孕育了早期文明要素。

2. 中华文明的发展

公元前3000年前后的炎黄时代，是中华文明的起源期与生成期。在黄河、长江两河流域，出现了古典农业、多元文化、综合创新，出现了文明时代的四大标志"金属工具、书面文字、原始城市、原始国家"。公元前1000年前后的殷周之际，是中华文明的雏形期，主要贡献有：①殷代后期把中国青铜时代文明发展到高峰阶段，同时也把中华文明形成的四大标志发展到一个大大高于炎黄时代起源期的新水平。②西周之初的周公改革，强调家国同构的宗法制度、人伦精神、六艺教育，为中华古典文明的总体框架奠定了雏形。③《易经》《诗经》《尚书》这三大中华文化元典都在这个历史转变时代应运而生。公元前500年前后的春秋战国之际到秦汉之际，是中华文明的定型期，在此时期，中华文明有着五大经济支柱：①后来居上的铁器革命。②最先走向精耕细作的农业革命。③早熟形态的古代交通革命。④超越早期原始城市的古代城市革命。⑤城市的五大飞跃（规模、数量、功能、结构和体系）。公元1000年前后的唐、宋、元时代，尤其是两宋时代，是中华文明的转型期。它以宋代商业革命为经济基础，推动了儒、释、道三大文化的综合创新，产生了火药、活字印刷术和指南针三大发明及一系列科学创新。①

在自身的发展过程中，中华文明同其他文明一样，也曾多次面临落后的游牧文明的强力冲击，中华帝国也曾多次出现经济文化的倒退和国家的短暂分裂。但中华文明却没有像其他古文明和大帝国那样衰败或崩溃，而是通过各民族的融合使国家再次统一，不仅没有因为其他文明的冲击被削弱，反而在这种民族交往中不断得以发展，虽然也有跌宕起伏，却从未发生断裂，像一条从未断流的大河，保持了别具一格的发展延续性。

3. 中华文明的时代价值

黄河和长江二者合成一个摇篮，是中华文明莫大的幸运。与古埃及、古印度等文明相比较，中华文明以其民族、历史、地理、伦理等支撑了文明的独特持续性，至今尚然独存，并且在历史发展的长河里贡献出了一份力量。

从科技方面看，中华民族的创造力，为人类文明的发展贡献了不少技术与发明成果，可以说，中国的四大发明在一定程度上推动了世界的进步：近代化的开端、新航路的开辟，离不开指南针；思想解放、文艺复兴、启蒙运动离不开造纸术和印刷术。

从文化方面看，中华文明历史悠久，从先秦子学到宋明理学，经历了数个学术思想繁荣时期，在历史长河中，中华民族产生了儒、道、墨等各家学说，涌现了老子、孔子、庄子、孟子、荀子等一大批思想大家，留下了浩如烟海的文化遗产，为古人认识世界、改造世界提供了重要依据，也为人类文明做出了重大贡献。

从交通方面看，海陆丝绸之路的开辟，连接了亚欧，促进了各地的交流，不仅为世界输送了实用的商品，还将整个欧亚大陆（包括北非）联系了起来，对人类文明的交流发展起到了大动脉作用，而中国就近乎是这动脉系统中的心脏，并且几乎持续了2000年之久。

从经济方面看，虽然封建经济的特点是自给自足，但是不能说中国古代对世界经济是没有积极影响的，中国是世界上最早种植水稻的国家，水稻种植的传播极大地促进了其他地区农业的发展，养活了更多的人口，而且中国拥有高度发达的农耕文明，作为农业文明时代的巅峰，发展出许多农业与手工业产品，成为全世界的生产中心。

---

① 王东. 中华文明的文化基因与现代传承（专题讨论）中华文明的五次辉煌与文化基因中的五大核心理念[J]. 河北学刊，2003（5）.

从对外交往方面看，中华文明历来崇尚"以和邦国""和而不同""以和为贵"，几千年来，和平融入了中华民族的血脉中，刻进了中国人民的基因里。如郑和下西洋时倡导的不欺寡、不凌弱、友好相处、共享太平，为亚非国家间的交往确立了不成文的准则，对后世影响深远。

当然，在长期演化过程中，中华文明也从与其他文明的交流中获得了丰富营养，独学而无友，则孤陋而寡闻，文明之间需要相互学习借鉴。因此，对人类社会创造的各种文明，无论是古代的埃及文明、两河文明、印度文明，还是现在的亚洲文明、非洲文明、欧洲文明、美洲文明、大洋洲文明等，都应该采取学习借鉴的态度，都应该积极吸纳其中的有益成分，使人类创造的一切文明中的优秀文化基因与当代文化相适应、与现代社会相协调，把跨越时空、超越国度、具有当代价值的优秀文化精神弘扬起来。

第三节 大河文明与旅游发展

本节将对大河文明与旅游发展的关系，以及大河文明旅游的概念进行阐释。文化是旅游业的灵魂，旅游活动归根结底是一种文化活动，而体验不同的文化也是旅游者的出发点和归宿点，二者相辅相成。大河文明旅游是依托其独特的水文化、自然景观、民俗文化等旅游资源，以满足游客体验大河文化内涵的一种旅游形式，融知识性、文化性和趣味性为一体。

一、大河文明与旅游发展的关系

（一）旅游发展诠释大河文明

随着社会的发展，旅游业已成为全球经济中发展势头最为强劲和规模最大的产业之一。旅游业在社会经济发展中的产业地位、经济作用逐步增强，旅游业对经济的拉动性、社会就业的带动力以及对文化与环境的促进作用日益显现。与此同时，原生态的大河文化可以作为大河流域旅游的主要吸引物，大河文明旅游也成为开发的新热点。

大河流域地带的城市、乡村中遗留有丰富的历史文化资源，可以通过旅游开发对这些资源进行挖掘、保护、活化和整合，构建具有显著特色文化吸引力，且能与区域经济社会发展相融合的特色旅游文化，使得大河文化得到新的诠释，并通过旅游活动的开展获得快速的文化认同与文化传播。另外，大河所流经地区的相对独立性使得不同地区旅游资源形成了差异性和独特性，一条大河凝聚了流域不同的历史文化和世事沧桑，可以通过旅游开发对大河流域不同文化和民俗情感进行挖掘，满足人们探求历史文化和亲近自然的双重功效。而且通过河流旅游发展把流域内分散的历史文化及民俗串联在一起，能够增加大河文化的完整和谐感及动态真实性。

（二）大河文明哺育旅游文化

由于大河流域独特的自然条件和历史演变，各类文化和自然旅游资源得天独厚，旅游开发潜力巨大，具有广阔的旅游发展空间。大河流域孕育了灿烂的文明，在大河流域形成了具有鲜明特色的文化，具有巨大的感召力和显著的标识性，为旅游文化的形成奠定了基础。大河所流经地区类型多样、文化内涵深厚、自然和人文景观优美，形成了丰富且体验独特的旅游活动，世界上许多大河旅游景点都吸引了大量旅游者，如巴黎的塞纳河、伦敦的泰晤士河等，以及我国的长江三峡、黄河等。

一方面，河流是人类早期文明发展的摇篮，作为人居环境重要的分布区域，为当地文明的起源和发展提供了良好的自然条件，一些著名的早期文明都诞生于河流地区，例如：我国的黄河流域、埃及的尼罗河流域、幼发拉底河、底格里斯河等，世界四大文明的发源地都是在大河流域，河流以其得天独厚的生存条件，孕育了人类文明，形成了独具特色的旅游文化；另一方面，由于大河流域地区具有丰富的自然、文化资源，旅游活动丰富、体验独特等特点，使得这些地区的旅游业非常发达，具有巨大的发展潜力，在我国，长江、黄河等大河孕育了中华的大河文化，各大河流域地区都已成为或正在成为旅游热点地区。这些各具特色的河流文明及其流域丰富的自然与人文景观的存在，为开展一系列旅游活动提供了必要的基础条件。

二、大河文明旅游概念界定

（一）大河文明旅游概念

大河文明旅游似乎是一个人们早已熟知的概念，是一种重要的旅游活动类型。事实上，大河文明旅游的价值早已被人所知，对大河自然风景的欣赏、文化的体验，以及围绕其所开展的丰富多样的旅游活动也早已存在。在原国家旅游局提出的《旅游资源分类标准》中，"风景河段"是其中重要的亚类，包括了观光游憩河段、暗河河段及古河道段落3种基本类型。在中国现有5A级景区、世界遗产和国家级风景名胜区中，以河流为核心吸引物的景区占了一定比重。在首批66处5A级景区中占了8处，达12.1%。至2015年，在48处世界遗产中占了2处（云南"三江并流"自然景观、中国大运河），达4.2%。至2015年，在先后八批225家国家级风景名胜区中占了约36处，达16.0%。[①]

大河文明旅游本质上属于文化旅游的一种形式，是依托独特的大河文化资源和自然资源，以体验大河文化内涵为主要目的一种旅游形式。大河文明旅游是人们离开自己惯常居住地，暂时前往异地大河流域去接触、体验大河文明及其自然风光的一种活动，不但可以扩充知识、开阔眼界，同时还能获得许多乐趣，满足人们精神生活的需求。如大河除了能提供人类赖以生存的水源外，大河文明旅游能给人以灵性，近水亲水的活动对于人的情绪和心理有调节作用，能给人以愉悦、放松之感。

（二）大河文明旅游的特殊性

大河文明旅游相对于传统的旅游来说是一个创新的旅游概念，它更多的是为体验大河文化和自

---

① 鲍捷，陆林. 河流旅游：缘起、内涵及其研究体系——一个本体论的诠释［J］. 地理科学，2017，37（7）.

然景观而形成的旅游形式，以了解大河流域旅游目的地的文化与历史知识，学习、研究、考察、欣赏特定的大河人文与自然景观。大河流域特殊的地理环境，使得大河文明旅游资源具有稀缺性、特殊性、发展潜力大等特点。大河文明旅游也具有其他文化旅游的传承性、独特性等特征，并且具有可以开发成不同类型旅游活动的文化内涵和价值。大河地区独特的山水、文化、民俗、建筑等资源相结合，就会形成独特的旅游景观，成为大河文明旅游的特色吸引物。

第二章 大河文明旅游与开发

旅游业被誉为 21 世纪的朝阳产业、无烟工业，旅游功能也是现代河流开发中的一大重要功能。世界早期的河流旅游活动中，乘船观光是一个重要的旅游活动类型，而随着时代进步与市场发展，早期河流旅游活动已经无法适应现阶段旅游需求，因此，大河文明旅游开发不得不做出改善之举。本章首先介绍了大河文明旅游活动的起源和发展历程；其次，对大河文明旅游产业现阶段发展形势进行综合阐述；最后，分析了大河文明旅游的游客需求及当前面临的市场状况。

第一节 大河文明旅游活动起源与发展

要想了解大河文明旅游产业形势以及旅游市场的发展状况，就必须首先厘清大河文明旅游活动的缘起。因此，本节主要针对大河文明旅游活动的起源及发展历程进行阐释。大河流域的动植物、矿产等自然资源不但具有非常重要的商业价值，而且也有很高的娱乐和旅游价值，大河文明旅游活动就是在这些自然资源的基础上，依托人类在长期社会发展中积淀的历史文化资源而发展起来的。

一、亚马孙河文明旅游活动的起源与发展

（一）文化与生态旅游资源特色

亚马孙河流域有全球面积最大的热带雨林地区，被誉为"地球之肺"。热带雨林蕴藏着世界上最丰富的生物资源，珍贵动植物资源均居世界首位，同时，亚马孙河流域还蕴藏丰富的矿产资源，如煤炭、金属、石油等。无论从流域面积还是资源财富程度来说，亚马孙河都可称为世界第一大河。

亚马孙森林中存在一些原始部落，自 14 世纪初葡萄牙人登上巴西大陆直到现在，巴西政府已经在亚马孙中发现了 67 个印第安人部落，这 67 个部落大都依旧保持着原始的生活状态，都沿袭着各自不同的传统，吸引众多游客到此参观。此外，亚马孙河流域还存在多样生态景观，如上游的黑河和索利芒斯河交汇形成的最美的"黑白双色河"景观，以及世界自然奇观——亚马孙潮等，其中，亚马孙潮可与中国的钱塘江大潮媲美，巴西人把亚马孙海潮称为"波波罗卡"，涌潮时游人争相前往，每逢涨潮，场面极为壮观。

(二)亚马孙河文明旅游活动的起源

亚马孙河的名字与一个希腊神话有关,相传,在黑海高加索一带有个叫亚马孙的女人王国,王国里的妇女勇敢强悍。在早期西班牙殖民主义者来到现在的亚马孙河时,发现该流域的居民像古时亚马孙女人王国的妇女一样勇敢强悍,不甘屈服,且这条河也神秘莫测,难以驯服,因此他们将这条河称为亚马孙河。

亚马孙河流域最早的主人是印第安人,早在1970年,考古学家就在该流域发现了古印第安人居住过的十几个洞穴,如今的亚马孙地区依然居住着几十万印第安人,且相当一部分仍处于原始的刀耕火种阶段,称为"被遗忘的人",长期以来一直吸引着很多旅游者到此游览。亚马孙流域较早开展旅游活动的地区是巴西,但早期巴西亚马孙地区尽管资源丰富,却一直不发达,以自给性小农生产为主,商品经济落后,劳动力缺乏,交通闭塞。巴西政府为了改变亚马孙地区贫困落后的状态,于20世纪40年代中期启动亚马孙河流域地区的开发治理。1966年成立了"亚马孙地区开发管理局",1970年又制定了《全国一体化规划》,到70年代,开发亚马孙地区步伐加快,成为巴西重点开发地区。

(三)亚马孙河文明旅游发展历程

亚马孙河上游的港口城市伊基托斯,是亚马孙地区商业中心,建城已有130多年的历史。在20世纪初,这里是种植园主和巨商大贾挥霍和娱乐之地,一些雕栏画壁的欧式建筑至今仍保留着当年的风姿。秘鲁政府从20世纪60年代起,在这里实行特殊政策,现在已有4000多种商品可以免税进口,使它成为半自由港,吸引了大量欧美的商品。为了游览和购买廉价商品,此地每年涌来不少游客,促进了当地经济的发展。

亚马孙河中游内格罗河汇入的马瑙斯市,是巴西西部新兴的工商业城市,也是整个亚马孙河流域的第一都市。16世纪时它还只是印第安人的一个小村落,现在已经发展成为巴西著名的旅游胜地和重要的机械、电子、石化等工业基地。马瑙斯最早是葡萄牙人为掠夺亚马孙流域财富设立的一个据点。1968年,巴西政府设立了马瑙斯自由贸易区,区内进出口自由。如今马瑙斯已成为巴西著名的旅游胜地,其美丽的自然风光吸引了世界各地的游客,在旅行者心目中,马瑙斯代表一种文化,城市很大,虽显破旧但富有魅力,有旧式船坞区、繁忙的商业中心以及热闹的夜生活等。

亚马孙河中游地区的小镇——派廷斯也是巴西重要的旅游目的地,是巴西黄麻工业中心,亚马孙河口地区的贝伦,是亚马孙流域最大的港口城市,也是亚马孙地区农产品的集散地。1978年,亚马孙流域八国外长就在巴西首都签署了"亚马孙合作条约",经过十几年的努力,亚马孙流域各国正在共同努力、合理开发亚马孙地区的旅游资源,建立和完善这一地区基础设施和服务设施,保持生态平衡,不断改善卫生条件,为旅游发展提供良好的前提条件。[①]

[①] 王素霞. 世界第一河——亚马孙河[J]. 水利天地,2006(12).

(四)亚马孙河流域旅游发展现状

亚马孙河流域经过多年开发,目前已经改善了区域交通条件,崛起了现代工业,发展了农牧业、旅游业,初步改变了亚马孙流域经济贫困落后的面貌。但其开发过程却导致了热带雨林的毁损,没有实现环境与经济协调发展,导致环境质量大为下降。因此,亚马孙流域在开发过程中还需要做出一些改善:

第一,开发前的谨慎研究。主要表现在制定权威性的法规保障,了解亚马孙热带雨林的生态规律,开发过程要考虑到雨林的生态敏感性和脆弱性,做到因地制宜,不能导致生态系统的恶化。第二,开发过程中要重视环境保护。巴西亚马孙河流域的开发要把生态环境保护与建设作为根本任务和指导思想,不能走牺牲环境生态效益来发展经济的不可持续发展之路,而是要保证环境与经济协调发展,走可持续发展之路。第三,亚马孙地区开发中应当注重科学研究和普及教育。在利用各种木材前,应该研究如何利用新技术才能综合平衡利用各种木材资源,以减少对雨林的毁损。

二、尼罗河文明旅游活动的起源与发展

(一)文化与生态旅游资源特色

尼罗河流域流经多个国家,支撑数百万人口的生计,流域内生物多样,拥有众多特有物种,著名的有罗非鱼、大尼罗河鱼、鳄鱼、软壳龟和巨蜥等,尼罗河三角洲还是世界最重要的鸟类迁徙必经路线。尼罗河两岸风光旖旎,古迹众多,最突出的代表在古埃及。提到古埃及的文化遗产,首先会想到尼罗河畔耸立的金字塔、盛产的纸草和神秘莫测的木乃伊,它们不仅标志着古埃及数千年文明发展的历程,同时也是推动埃及旅游业快速发展的重要力量。

(二)尼罗河文明旅游活动的起源

尼罗河流域旅游开发最具代表性的地区是埃及,埃及大部分都是黄沙滚滚的沙漠,只有尼罗河冲刷过的地方是绿带。尽管埃及拥有几千年的文明古迹,其旅游市场开发得也很早,但其实在早期,对于大多数旅游者来说,他们对埃及的印象只是沙漠、骆驼和金字塔,认为埃及人的生活还停留在几个世纪前的落后状态,并以为埃及游就是历史古迹游,埃及的旅游产品都是文化类旅游产品,导致当时到埃及的游客有80%都是冲着开罗的金字塔、卢克索的神庙和法老陵墓来的,而一些有消费能力的人但素质还达不到"认识"埃及的程度,也就不会选择出游。而随着旅游部门对于埃及的宣传,以及少数游客到来后发现埃及不仅有历史古迹、文化旅游,还有漫长的海岸线和休闲旅游资源,此后才逐渐开始对埃及有了新的认知,来埃及旅游的游客才逐渐增多。[①]

(三)尼罗河文明旅游发展历程

作为尼罗河流域重要旅游地——埃及,最先是凭借其历史古迹开展文化旅游,但随着时间的推移,文化旅游出现萎缩趋势,埃及开始寻找新的增长点,开始推广旅游产品的"选择多样性",并

---

① 孙海燕,李关云. 埃及旅游业:新休闲主义的"黄与蓝"[J]. 21世纪商业评论,2005(5).

发展起了休闲度假旅游，大量休闲旅游产品在埃及出现，休闲成为埃及旅游业的主导方向。埃及的国土虽然90%以上都是沙漠，但它濒临红海和地中海，拥有漫长的海岸线，一年四季都温暖舒适，为发展休闲度假旅游提供了资源和条件。

2003年，埃及完全放开汇率，埃镑对于美元的大幅贬值使得旅游产品的价格更具竞争力，带动埃及旅游业迅速发展。俄罗斯和东欧诸国大批新兴的中产阶级对于休闲的渴求，给埃及输送了大量客源。并且随着埃及休闲旅游业的兴旺，推动了该领域的投资热潮，近年来，旅游投资项目占到埃及国内投资总项目的10%以上，且投资大部分来自于私人资本。

在休闲旅游的新形势下，尼罗河上游的卢克索和阿斯旺等文化游重镇也在努力开掘自己的休闲潜力，它们利用自身所处尼罗河上游，河水完全没有受过污染，甚至比海水还要湛蓝的优势，开展休闲度假旅游，在那里游客完全可以不必理会那些沉重的古迹，只是享受充足的阳光、纯净的空气和河上扬帆的滋味。

（四）尼罗河文明旅游发展现状

尼罗河流域是人类古文明的发祥地，其开发历史相当悠久，丰富的旅游资源极大地促进了旅游业的发展，近年来，旅游业一跃成为尼罗河流域一些国家（如埃及）的支柱产业。

随着旅游业的发展，一些负面影响也随之而来，如环境问题、文物破坏等，但各国政府高度重视这些问题，积极采取各种措施保护文化遗产和环境，努力实现旅游的可持续发展。然而，就整个尼罗河来看，由于沿河地区民族矛盾、种族仇视等原因使其旅游发展依然存在一些不尽如人意，许多潜力巨大的景点还有待进一步开发，许多历史文物古迹还未开发和完全呈现在人们面前，尚没有成为旅游产品。如何做好尼罗河各区段的河道治理、旅游规划以及各个国家相互协调工作是当前开发尼罗河旅游资源潜力的重要途径。

三、莱茵河文明旅游活动的起源与发展

（一）文化与生态旅游资源特色

莱茵河流域拥有独特的生态景观，从瑞士的巴塞尔到德国的波恩为河流中游，该地区河道蜿蜒曲折，两岸重峦叠嶂，沿途有无数的古堡，景观独具特色。同时，中游还流经了诸多大城市和标志性建筑，如科隆旧城、德国煤田的首要商业中心杜塞尔多夫等。从河源到瑞士的巴塞尔为河流上游，河水自南向北流淌，形成瑞士和列支敦士登的天然国界，列支敦士登以其优美的自然风光、古老的城堡、精湛的艺术品和稀世的邮票，每年吸引着数万的游人。

莱茵河具有悠久的历史文化传统，莱茵河畔是国际无产阶级革命导师马克思、荷兰著名画家伦勃朗，以及音乐大师贝多芬的诞生地，也是原子结构秘密被揭开的地方。马克思的故居——特利尔是德国最古老的城市，每年都有无数世界各地的游客前来参观。贝多芬故居——德国伯恩小巷号，1989年被开辟为博物馆，陈列着音乐家生前的原物。此外，莱茵河曾经历过长达一个世纪的战争，长时间的战乱给如今的游客留下了许许多多值得寻思的古战场。

（二）莱茵河文明旅游活动的起源

莱茵河是欧洲重要的水运通道，也是流域内工业、生活用水的重要水源，多年来一直以航运和工业著称于世，因此被定位为著名的航运河和工业河。然而事实上，莱茵河除了具有无可替代的航运和工业价值外，也以旅游业发达而闻名遐迩，因此，也被定位为景观河、旅游河、文化河。

莱茵河中游全部在德国境内，数百年以来河流中游形成了一段陡峭的崖壁，这就是宾根与科布伦茨两个城市之间的河谷，旅游者到此看到的有漫山遍野的葡萄园、梯田，有绿如地毯的牧场，有满山的茂密森林，优美的自然景观吸引了越来越多的旅游者，旅游业由此发展起来。

（三）莱茵河文明旅游发展历程

莱茵河流经国家把大力发展旅游业作为综合治理莱茵河、加快产业转型、促进国民经济增长的重要途径，主要采取措施如：打造复合多元的旅游产品、建立高效的旅游管理模式、构建水环境综合治理模式、制定紧密一体的规划体系、建设便捷通畅的交通网络等，这些措施促使旅游产业发展获得巨大成功。

莱茵河也曾在20世纪中期受到沿岸的工业污染。20世纪80年代，德国、法国、卢森堡、荷兰、瑞士以及欧洲联盟决定调整内河经济带，20世纪末，这些国家共同在鹿特丹签署了《莱茵河保护公约》，此后，欧洲国家还成立了"保护莱茵河国际委员会"，开展了持续的"拯救莱茵河"行动，如今的莱茵河河水清澈，波光粼粼。可以说，莱茵河旅游发展离不开沿岸各国出台的相关政策和相关规划，尽管流域各国没有统一的旅游产业发展规划，但却各自根据自身资源禀赋，制定了适合自身旅游产业发展的相关规划。以德国为例，黑森州在全州经济发展规划中制定了专门的旅游产业发展规划，同时为了支持旅游产业发展，在文化体育方面还专门制定了专项发展规划。此外，交通是旅游产业发展的基础，莱茵河自源头至入海口，构建起了沿岸及周边城镇的，包括航运交通、水上交通、陆上交通以及休闲交通在内的，多元化、通畅、方便快捷的立体交通网络。

（四）莱茵河文明旅游发展现状

莱茵河流域在近两个世纪的不断开发中，取得了举世瞩目的社会、经济、环境综合发展效益，成为世界上河流旅游开发的成功典范，为其他河流开发提供了宝贵的经验借鉴。莱茵河旅游开发的成果主要体现在以下几个方面。

1. 全流域发展规划

作为一条国际河流，流域各国在开发过程中也曾一度缺乏统一规划，各自为政在所难免，但由于共同利益的驱动，增强了沿岸各国流域经济荣损与共的整体意识，使各国十分认真地搞好不同历史阶段全流域发展规划的协调和合作，并切实贯彻执行。

2. 强烈的环境保护意识

莱茵河流域各国经济发展水平尽管不同，但实施莱茵河流域可持续管理的认识是相同的。莱茵河流域管理行动计划要求跨国和跨部门间的密切合作，因为它不是以某一个地方局部或单项管理措施为指导，而是以整个莱茵河流域可持续管理为最终目标。因此莱茵河流域开发基本上走的是一条开发与保护相结合、发展与环境相协调的路子。

3. 完备的基础设施和服务设施

莱茵河沿岸建设了码头、机场、沿岸的公路、铁路，发展水陆交通，形成了立体式综合交通运输网络，为旅游产业发展、产业集聚奠定了重要基础。此外，在德国公开出版的从美茵茨到科布伦茨莱茵河风光带的各种各样导游图中，标记有很多露营地和青年旅舍，露营地平均每10千米有1.44个，青年旅舍平均每10千米有1.11个，普通旅馆的密度更大，在每个村镇上都有度假旅馆。[①]

4. 复合多元的旅游产品

莱茵河作为一个整体旅游区，其旅游产品呈现整体性、多元化特征，具体可分为莱茵河上游、中游、下游产品结构：一是上游湖泊休闲度假旅游，主要形式为冬季滑雪旅游、夏季避暑旅游；二是中游历史文化遗产旅游，主要形式是邮轮旅游、山地徒步旅游等；三是下游工业与工业遗产旅游。

四、密西西比河文明旅游活动的起源与发展

（一）文化与生态旅游资源特色

密西西比河是北美洲流程最长、流域面积最广的水系，拥有丰富多样的能源、矿产资源和便捷的航运资源。同时，密西西比河还是美国最重要的粮食产区，拥有得天独厚的农业资源，流域内拥有面积约120万平方千米的黑土地，是世界三大黑土区之一，是美国小麦、玉米、大豆、棉花的最大产地。美国能够成为世界上最主要的农作物以及肉、蛋、奶等畜产品的生产国，绝大部分归功于密西西比河流域得天独厚的农业资源。

密西西比河还是美国国家文化和娱乐休闲的宝库，每年仅旅游、捕鱼和休闲娱乐三项产业的产值就能达到200多亿美元。密西西比河是一个巨大的钓场，在河流北部有巨大的河坝和回水区，春季河道水流湍急，鱼种很多。

（二）密西西比河文明旅游活动的起源

密西西比河中游密苏里河携带大量泥沙，在下游河口处堆积成世界上最大的鸟足状三角洲——密西西比河三角洲。在20世纪初期，由于历史、种族、教育等问题，密西西比河三角洲地区经济发展相对缓慢，是美国最贫穷的地方之一。为改变落后现状，促进密西西比河三角洲地区发展，该地区开始大力发展旅游业，充分利用一切资源做好旅游开发，如美国南方的象征——橡树大道和庄园建筑，《汤姆叔叔的小屋》《飘》等著作以及风靡全球的蓝调、爵士乐和其他音乐资源。其中，尤以布鲁斯蓝调旅游最受欢迎，不仅在黑人音乐中占有重要地位，也是美国黑人文化甚至是美国文化遗产的重要组成部分，在不断发展中融入了主流音乐的行列，逐渐影响世界流行音乐的发展轨迹。

（三）密西西比河文明旅游发展历程

密西西比河现以美丽、宏伟和多样性而著称，美国对密西西比河的整治始于19世纪70年代，

---

① 翟辅东. 湘江风光带开发与莱茵河风光带对比研究［J］. 旅游学刊，2001，16（3）.

先后成立"陆军工程兵团""密西西比河委员会"等开发治理机构，并制定专门的法律法规。在整治过程中，美国政府在密西西比河干支流两岸选择了一大批城镇作为对外开放的窗口，把整个密西西比河作为一种产品进行营销，带动国外资金和人员的进入，从而提高旅游的收入。

20世纪30年代以后，大规模综合治理和运渠化工程的实施，使密西西比河基本消除了洪灾，且干流和支流都按现代化的先进技术标准进行治理，积极顺应河流自然过程，建立起一张以干流为纲、以支流及湖海为目的、标准统一的现代化航运网和经济带，为其水运旅游做了很好的铺垫。

20世纪90年代以后，为保护密西西比河沿岸的珍贵资源，展现密西西比河独特迷人的风采，美国政府开始实施自北向南贯通全美的大河路国家风景道计划，这是美国最长的一条风景道，是体验密西西比河奇观的必经之路，按沿途所呈现的景观特征的不同，分为源头段、上游段、中游段、下游段四段。

（四）密西西比河文明旅游发展现状

超前的环保意识使密西西比河生态资源保存完好。美国在河流开发过程中，对环保和生态平衡考虑非常细致，如项目实施和完成后，必须设置专门的野生动物保护区，甚至施工过程中对周围居民的影响（包括噪声）亦应考虑适当的补偿和措施等。正是由于采取了诸多积极有效的环保措施，密西西比河至今依然环境优美，生态资源完好。

科学而且具有法律效力的规划为密西西比河旅游开发奠定了基础。密西西比河流域有一个明确的开发与管理机构，它是一个具有一定权力的实体机构，拥有较为独立的自主管理权，其主要目的是研究密西西比河的开发治理规划。在密西西比河的旅游开发历程中，该管理机构制定的有关密西西比河开发的总体构想、开发程序和实施步骤等规划起着关键作用，正是因为有了这些权威的规划和严格的管理，密西西比河的旅游开发才有了现在的成果。

五、黄河文明旅游活动的起源与发展

（一）文化与生态旅游资源特色

黄河流域历史悠久，地域辽阔，旅游资源极为丰富，全国八大古都黄河沿线有4个，全国三大石窟艺术宝库都散布在黄河流域；全国五岳名山在黄河沿线有4个，黄河沿线4A级旅游景区有105个[1]，丰富的旅游资源为旅游发展奠定了坚实的基础，具体而言，黄河流域旅游资源可分为下述类型：

首先，是以名山大川为中心的生态旅游资源。从东岳泰山到西岳华山，从黄河而西的三门峡、壶口瀑布到宁夏平原的青铜峡、甘肃刘家峡以及青海黄河源头，其间还包括许多著名的自然风景区，如山西黄河壶口瀑布、宁夏的沙湖、青海的青海湖旅游区等。

其次，是以文物古迹、宗教寺院为中心的古文化旅游资源，表现为一大批举世闻名的名胜古迹，如古都西安、开封，秦始皇兵马俑，以及各大宗教留下的宗教文化和艺术圣地，如甘肃敦煌莫

---

[1] 王开泳，张鹏岩，丁旭生. 黄河流域旅游经济的时空分异与R/S分析[J]. 地理科学，2013，34（3）.

高窟，陕西西安大雁塔、宝鸡法门寺，河南洛阳白马寺，山西忻州五台山等。

最后，是以少数民族宗教、风土人情为中心的民族风情旅游资源。黄河流域西部是我国少数民族聚居区，各民族在其繁衍发展过程中形成了各自独特的民族文化。如新疆维吾尔族语言、服饰、舞蹈，宁夏回族的伊斯兰风情，蒙古族的"那达慕"和大草原风情，青海的藏族风情和藏传佛教等。这些民族文化不但使整个中华民族的文化艺术事业呈现出色彩斑斓的局面，同时也为发展民俗文化旅游提供了条件。

（二）黄河文明旅游活动的起源

黄河流域是中华民族五千年文明的摇篮，发展旅游具有得天独厚的优势，主要体现在：首先，黄河流域是中华文明的发祥地，保留了完整的华夏文化遗存，这种文化背景对游客具有强烈的吸引力，给开发旅游提供了雄厚的资源和市场。其次，该地带自然地理环境独特，生态系统复杂，拥有名山大川、大漠盆地、高山雪域，为开发旅游提供了良好的生态资源条件。最后，黄河流域古往今来是众多民族栖息和发展的地方，不同时代的游牧、农耕民族都留下了丰富而又极富个性的文化遗存，独特的民俗风情和传统特征异彩纷呈，为开发旅游准备了独特的民俗文化条件。

20世纪80年代是黄河流域旅游业发展的雏形阶段，在该阶段，流域内多个地区开始尝试性地确定部分旅游点。比如，当时工业文明带来的一系列社会和环境问题，使城市居民普遍产生逃避喧嚣、回归自然的心理认同，生态旅游超越了古迹观光旅游成为首选，而恰好黄河三角洲地区——东营市的资源特色与这个主题相吻合，所以东营市在当时就开始借助资源优势打造生态旅游，确定了重点建设的五大旅游区。与此同时，滨州市也开始成立地区旅游局，组织整理和修复部分旅游点和文物，并尝试性地确定部分旅游点。但由于当时人们思想观念、开发条件等因素的限制，这一阶段的旅游开发还不成熟，尚处于初始阶段，旅游产品层次低、数量少，存在很大发展空间。

（三）黄河文明旅游发展历程

20世纪80年代之后，随着改革开放的不断深入，黄河中上游的旅游事业得到了空前发展。各地政府充分认识到旅游事业不但能给经济振兴、社会发展增添新的活力和增长点，而且对于宣传本地区和增进国际、国内的经济社会交往有重要作用。因此，这一带都开始在旅游上做文章，如河南打造的以古（历史文化）、河（黄河）、拳（少林拳、陈氏太极拳和郑州国际少林武术节）、根（寻根觅祖）、花（洛阳牡丹花会）为特色的旅游活动；陕西西安打造"古文化艺术节"等。

进入2000年以来，黄河流域很多地区旅游发展的整体思路基本形成，基本实现旅游业的跨越式发展。经过多年的连续开发建设，黄河流域旅游业发展迅速，目前已逐步形成了一系列有特色的旅游产品，流域内游客接待规模和旅游收入也持续增长，旅游配套设施建设较快，并逐渐趋向完善。

（四）黄河文明旅游发展现状

1. 黄河文明旅游方兴未艾，呈蒸蒸日上的发展趋势

无论是旅游外汇收入，还是接待旅游人数近年来都有所增加（表1.1），旅游线路和旅游景点开发日益增多，服务功能日臻完善，地区旅游服务设施配套齐全，交通通信设施也逐渐接近国际水平，总体而言，这一地带的旅游已由过去的"接待型"向"经济型"转变，并展现出良好的发展势头。

表 1.1 黄河三角洲旅游收入和接待游客情况

年份	接待游客		旅游收入	
	入境（万人次）	国内（万人次）	入境（亿美元）	国内（亿元）
2010	28.47	4243.70	2.03	324.60
2011	36.92	5189.50	2.57	411.70

资料来源：杨文娟. 黄河三角洲历史文化资源的旅游开发研究［D］. 苏州：江苏师范大学，2013.

2. 黄河文明旅游市场前景广阔，但与国际旅游事业还存在一些差距

黄河文明旅游市场发展势头良好，但与国际旅游实践还存在差距，尤其是西北地区尚有潜力未进一步发挥。所以，黄河文明旅游开发还需认真学习和借鉴国外先进的开发经验，进一步开拓市场，使旅游开发在该地带的经济发展中占有更大的比例，发挥更重要的作用。

六、长江文明旅游活动的起源与发展

（一）文化与生态旅游资源特色

长江流域资源极为丰富，自古以来就是中国最重要的农业经济区。这里地貌类型丰富，有高山、有丘陵，也有平原和湖泊（表1.2），形成了多姿的地理景观，而且流域经、纬度跨度大，气候多样，形成多样性的局地气候特征区。复杂的地质地理条件和多样的气候特征，孕育了长江流域的生物多样性，流域内分布了全国2/3的生物资源，为旅游开发提供了巨大资源优势。[①]

长江流域在经历了历代王朝漫长岁月后，也积累了大量文化资源。如长江流域的第一座商代古城——武汉市黄陂区盘龙城；中国发现年代最早、规模最大且保存最完好的古铜矿——大冶铜绿山古铜矿；长江下游重要商代遗址——江西清江的吴城遗址等，此外还有大量青铜器、玉器、陶器等，以及扬名中外、无比壮丽的长江三峡等，这些都足以体现我国的社会文明，对于了解长江流域文化具有非常高的科学价值，同时也成为旅游开发的特色资源。

表 1.2 长江流域生态旅游资源

山名	地点	特点及评价
武当山	湖北省	有着中国保存最完整、规模最大、等级最高的，并已列入世界文化遗产的明代道教建筑群。
张家界	湖南省	是中国第一个国家森林公园，与相邻的索溪峪自然风景区、天子山自然保护区共同构成的武陵源风景名胜区，是国家级风景名胜区，又是联合国批准的世界自然遗产之一。
九山	湖北省	"九天仙山"，既有江南山峰的奇秀，又具塞北岭岳的雄伟，雄、奇、秀、险集于一身。

---

① 黄德林，黄道明. 长江流域水资源开发的生态效应及对策［J］. 水利水电快报，2005，26（18）.

续表

山名	地点	特点及评价
庐山	江西省	1996年，联合国教科文组织世界遗产委员会批准庐山作为"世界文化景观"被列入《世界遗产名录》。
三清山	江西省	道教七十二福地之一，国家级风景名胜区。前人赞它为"高凌云汉江南第一仙峰，消绝尘嚣天下无双福地"。
井冈山	江西省	1991年被评为中国旅游胜地四十佳。
黄山	安徽省	"中国第一奇山"，国家级风景名胜区，亦是世界级的旅游胜地。
天柱山	安徽省	国家风景名胜区，被誉为江淮大地第一名山。
琅琊山	安徽省	自古有"皖东第一名胜"之赞誉，是我国二十四座文化名山之一。
鄱阳湖	江西省	中国第一大淡水湖，湖上名山秀屿比比皆是，九江市旅游局已将鄱阳湖上的各景点通过游船连成一线。
洞庭湖	湖南省	中国第二大淡水湖，自古以来，洞庭湖就以湖光山色吸引游人，历代著名文学家为之倾倒，洞庭湖是楚文化的摇篮。
太湖	江苏省	中国第三大淡水湖，苏州太湖国家旅游度假区是1992年10月国务院批准建立的首批国家旅游度假区之一。
洪泽湖	江苏省	中国第四大淡水湖，水生资源丰富，螃蟹也远近驰名，其莲藕、菱角在历史上享有盛名。
巢湖	安徽省	中国第五大淡水湖，巢湖风景区是皖中著名的旅游胜地。

资料来源：陈胜军．长江水运旅游发展研究［D］．武汉：武汉理工大学，2003.

（二）长江文明旅游活动的起源

人类的祖先在长江流域的活动在100多万年前就开始了，因为其深厚的文化、独特的自然景观，使得长江历来就受到人们的关注，成为游山玩水的一个重要场所。历史上许多名人骚客都曾经游历过长江，并留下了动人的篇章，在那时长江就已经开始作为文人们游览山河的一个景点了，可以说，长江旅游自古有之。

近代长江流域旅游开发以三峡为典型代表，1978年10月至1979年7月，邓小平同志专门讲话，要求尽快发展旅游业。邓小平同志关于加强旅游宣传促销，重视环境保护，搞好配套设施建设、人才培养，管理、改革分配制度，提高服务质量，旅游商品开发等一系列旅游经济思想成为新时期中国旅游业的发展指南，长江三峡旅游正是在这一宏观经济背景下才发韧、发展起来的。1982年，长江三峡被国务院批准为第一批国家重点风景名胜区。1990年，成立了长江上第一家专业旅游船公司——长江轮船海外旅游总公司，标志着长江旅游进入了一个专业化、系统化的阶段，旅行社加船东的企业形式开了长江旅游大发展的先河。

（三）长江文明旅游发展历程

自1990年长江旅游进入专业化阶段，在此后的十年间，由于受经济、政治、自然以及三峡工程建设等诸多因素影响，长江旅游发展并非一帆风顺，但正是这种曲线发展的状况，使长江旅游在不断摸索中从无到有、从小到大，从初级阶段逐渐走向稳定和成熟。

长江旅游在发展过程中有几点明显的变化：一是旅游服务设施有所丰富。比较典型的有，长江旅游发展之初，旅游船较少，基本上没有形成发航周期，而目前游船数量不断增多、各地方基础建设逐步加强。二是客源市场经主动拓展渐趋多元。长江旅游发展初期，除少量欧美游客以外，主要客源地在中国台湾、东南亚、日本等地，从事旅游的公司基本上不具备很强的旅游销售能力，而在目前长江旅游的客源市场中，中国台湾、东南亚游客仍占相当比例，欧美市场则有显著增长，日本、韩国、澳洲市场也有增量。三是旅游产品结构进一步完善，游船旅游、移民旅游、历史文化旅游、自然生态旅游、都市旅游、节事会展旅游等旅游产品不断丰富，多样化旅游产品体系形成。

（四）长江文明旅游发展现状

长江流域旅游近年来虽然取得了很大的进步，但仍然需要进一步完善：

1. 需要建立科学的旅游规划

旅游市场的活跃和旅游资源的合理开发等都需要有科学的规划来指导。旅游业要想保持快速健康和可持续发展，就必须制定科学、精确的旅游发展规划，旅游业要发展，规划要先行，这已成为旅游业界的共识。缺乏总体的旅游规划，制约了长江旅游的整体发展，品牌就更无法形成。

2. 西部地区开发需进一步提升

长江由西向东横跨中国，长江下游是中国富饶的东部，中游是小富即安的中部地区，而源头和上游地区是资源丰富但却相对贫穷的西部。虽然在国家和地方政策的支持下，中西部经过20多年开发，也形成了诸如长江三峡、九寨沟等国际旅游热点目的地，但在交通、管理、设施建设等多方面与东部发达地区相比还存在一些差距，未来还需要进一步提升。

3. 加强对外宣传，打造整体形象

长江横贯八个省、两个直辖市和一个自治区，其中长江三峡为湖北省和重庆市共有，虽然开发较成熟，但其功能作用远不如杭州对于浙江、西安对于陕西的作用之大，这不但是旅游资源分布和总体开发设计的原因，更重要的是在对外宣传上不够完整，因此长江流域地区在未来旅游开发中需要加强协同合作和对外宣传，打造整体旅游形象，实现共同发展。

第二节 大河文明旅游产业的开发形势

本节将对现阶段大河文明旅游产业的开发形势进行综合阐述，随着经济社会快速发展和旅游市场需求的转变，大河旅游开发当前正处在重大的转型和调整之中，开始重视旅游规划和法规的建设，强调空间环境的有效利用和河流功能的完善，不断调整旅游产品结构，将休闲度假作为主题，在早期观光游的基础上注入新元素，进行新一轮的产品深度开发。

一、旅游规划和法律先行

（一）更加重视法律保障和权威的规划指导

健全的法律和权威的旅游规划是大河文明旅游建设发展具体化、形象化的顶层设计，旅游开发理应做到规划先行，做到计划性、有序性、合理性。一项完整权威的旅游规划之所以重要，一方面在于它有利于处理好大河旅游开发建设与环境保护的关系，处理好旅游业发展与功能分区、部门协调等之间的关系，既根据大河自然景观和文化景观特点确定大河主要功能，保留和发挥其个性特点，又符合生态保护和整体协调的原则，形成一个良好的区域旅游整体。另一方面，旅游规划还利于体现各区域旅游发展的优势，形成特色互补，协调岸线国家和地区的发展，避免无序开发。

当前旅游规划在国外大河旅游开发过程中的重要性已经凸显，旅游开发前就制定出明确的规划制约，如密西西比河畔杰弗逊·帕里斯娱乐总体规划。规划中明确提出期限内要实现的目标，包括基础设施建设、环境保护、预防自然灾害等，任何环境管理部门、旅游开发和经营者，都必须遵循并共同努力实现计划制订的目标。其次规划中还会明确旅游项目的开发，根据各个地区的区域特色，开发符合特色的旅游项目，避免盲目雷同开发，使大河旅游更具竞争力和生命力。[1]

（二）旅游规划更加注重生态保护和区域合作

大河旅游首先是建立在大河生态环境系统上的旅游，大河流域生态系统具有典型的脆弱性，任何对自然环境和生态系统的干扰，都会对大河旅游长期稳定发展产生严重后果，因此，生态保护原则是大河旅游开发所应遵循的总原则。这一点在国内河流旅游开发中开始逐渐受到重视，一些大尺度流域旅游规划越来越关注生态保护。如一些河流旅游地生态管理从规划阶段就已开始，在规划时进行项目建设环境影响评价，包括对各环境要素的影响评价（大气、水、土壤、噪声、生物环境影响评价），以及视觉景观影响评价、社会经济影响评价和环境影响综合评价。同时，在河流岸线分配与划分旅游功能区时，更加平等兼顾各类岸线的公共利用，如规划供市民游憩的岸线，能够充分体现以人为本的原则，立足长远，有序开发，保护旅游区内特殊的环境特色，合理高效开发利用、保持岸线的再生机制。

此外，河流旅游区域合作，谋求共同发展也已经普遍达成共识，河流岸线的各个国家、各个城市充分协调各部分关系，使其在岸线利用上相得益彰、共同发展，保持岸线利用的动态平衡。在河流岸线旅游开发利用中，做到统筹资源、集中营销，实现一体化宣传营销，实现信息共享、平台共建的大格局。

---

[1] 王守书. 河流旅游功能构建与产品开发研究［D］. 上海：上海师范大学，2009.

案例 1.1
田纳西河流域的科学发展规划[①]

科学的发展规划是大河流域综合开发的基础，田纳西河流域正是通过科学发展规划的制定与实施，成为全球欠发达地区摆脱贫困的范例。

田纳西河位于美国东南部，发源于阿巴拉契亚山脉的西坡，是密西西比河的二级支流，俄亥俄河的一级支流。历史上，田纳西河是一条"害河"：植被破坏，水土流失严重，洪水时常泛滥；水深不足、无法通航；环境污染，流域内传染病盛行；老棉花带衰落，农民负债严重，人均收入水平及人均农作物产出只有全国平均水平的2/5。

为了改善该流域的落后面貌，同时也为了摆脱全国性的大萧条，罗斯福政府决定开展田纳西河流域的综合开发治理工程。1933年5月18日，美国国会批准成立田纳西河流域管理局（Tennessee Valley Agency，TVA），负责制定并实施田纳西河流域的综合开发规划。规划主要涉及6个方面：生态保护和洪水控制、改善航运、发展电力、改善沿岸土地利用、在流域内必要的地区植树造林、改善流域内人民的经济社会条件。

科学的发展规划使田纳西河流域的经济发展步入了健康的轨道。廉价的水电为国家提供了充足的电力，改善的航运条件也吸引了火电站和核电站的建设，大耗电工业开始布局到河谷地区，制造业、渔业和旅游业蓬勃发展，水土保持成效显著，农业的产量增长了三倍。田纳西这个昔日以落后形象出现的州，如今成长为南方的工业大州，不仅如此，田纳西河流域综合治理的成果还惠及周围的6个州，从而成为美国区域经济发展史上的里程碑。

田纳西河流域正是由于制定了科学的发展规划才摆脱了落后的面貌，走出昔日萧条的泥潭，充分体现出规划先行对于河流流域开发的重要性。

二、流域管理和功能定位

（一）国际河流跨界流域管理工作逐渐完善

一般而言，大河跨界区域通常蕴藏着丰富的水电、森林、矿产、渔业等资源，对多种类型的大农业发展，以及各种矿产资源及金属的开发有着得天独厚的优势，且跨界河流大多占据重要的地理位置，一直以来都是流域内外各国竞相涉足和开发的重要资源。

如澜沧江—湄公河是亚洲最重要的跨界水系，其发源于中国，流经缅甸、老挝、泰国、柬埔寨、越南。近年来，在亚洲开发银行的协助下，六国共同成立了澜沧江—大湄公河次区域合作组织，负责统筹协调各国之间的利益，共谋经济之发展。此外，还有一些大河通过采取制定空间流域规划的方式来解决跨界河流开发问题。可见，跨国界、跨区县界河流的治理和管理能更好地服务于

[①] 夏骥，肖永芹. 密西西比河开发经验及对长江流域发展的启示[J]. 重庆社会科学，2006（5）.

域内国家与地区的经济、政治、社会等各方面发展，这一现象已经得到许多国家的共识，国外对跨界流域管理的实践探索也更加深入醇熟。[①]

（二）河流空间功能呈现多元化及生活化

根据河流属性不同，可分为不同的空间功能，河流空间功能是河流自然、生态和社会属性的效用体现，是河流系统发挥的有利作用，明确划分河流空间功能是规范和引导河流开发与保护的基础。不同的国家地域，在不同的历史时期，对河流旅游开发就会有不同的功能区划，以往对于河流的功能区划多是从生态功能的角度，以生态保护为主要目的，如我国长江干流河段的生态功能划分等。但目前来看，随着河流旅游的发展、生活条件的改善，以及旅游需求的转变等因素出现，河流在旅游开发过程中更加注重空间功能的多元化及生活化，更加着重于公共性设施建设，特别是商业、游览设施的开发等，通过不同旅游功能的空间呈现，来满足不同服务对象的需求。

（三）河流功能定位更注重与城市发展相伴而行

早期的河流功能定位仅仅是无专门旅游规划的开发，产品也仅是简单的游船观光，而随着我国城市化进入加速期，河流开发更大程度上是在经济全球化、快速城市化时期，以及在工业化和信息化带来发展机遇与挑战的时期，所进行的经济社会转型、空间形态重构和文化特色重塑的一种普遍性反映。因此，河流开发更加注重与城市发展战略制定，以及城市快速扩张等战略性活动相伴而行，河流功能定位也开始考虑城市的整体结构和发展，关注城市整体结构重构。这种情况下，河流开发不但担负了提升城市河流综合竞争力、振兴流域经济的作用，同时也承担起塑造城市特色形象的使命。

对于穿越城市中心的滨水区，在功能定位时更加关注城市生活的整体性，充分利用商业设施和各种商业手段，着眼于城市功能的复活。如巴尔的摩内港开发，20世纪初，巴尔的摩港口航运及工业渐渐衰落，成了一个充满破旧码头、仓库的地区，失业率、犯罪率上升，物质环境和社会环境恶劣。1965年，开始内港的改造与更新，目标定位为利用位于城市中心的滨水条件，把中心区与内港连接为一体，建成将商业、办公、娱乐等功能融为一体的充满活力的城市生活中心。经过十余年的操作，摩内港终于形成了世界贸易中心、国家水族馆、内港广场、体育娱乐设施、滨水步行道等主要功能区，在创造税收、吸引游客、提供就业岗位及带动市中心的开发方面，取得了巨大的效益。[②]

三、资源开发和产品优化

（一）强调水资源的综合利用与开发

旅游规划开发离不开水，由于水在人类生活中的不可或缺性，以及人类与生俱来的亲水性特

---

① 沈皆希，赵又霖，郭利丹. 跨界河流空间信息服务模型研究：以湄公河为例 [J]. 武汉理工大学学报（信息与管理工程版），2017（3）.

② 高永宏. 沈阳市浑河滨水区开发战略研究 [D]. 东北大学，2005.

征，决定了水对旅游者有极强的吸引力和亲和力。在旅游规划与开发中做好水资源的规划设计，具有极强的经济价值和社会价值，一方面，水资源具有极强的包容性，易与其他元素融合，可为旅游规划提供诸多素材；另一方面，水可以通过洗浴、疗养、娱乐等各种方式融入休闲度假活动中，为游客提供休闲游憩空间。当前，越来越多国家和地区在开发大河旅游时开始重视水资源的有效利用，借助水资源开发各种各样的休闲体验活动，激发游客参与体验的热情。对于河流旅游开发而言，水就是生命，如果能将水的文章做好，无疑会给河流旅游增光添彩。

欧洲国家就十分重视水资源的开发，注重水资源的综合利用，并开发与水有关的历史文化要素，充分挖掘水文化的潜力。如莱茵河流域制订的"三角洲计划"，就是为了全面开发、综合利用水资源，包括航运、防洪、供水、旅游、发电、灌溉、渔业等，充分体现了多层次、多方位的效益相兼顾，还利于环境保护和自然生态平衡。并且流域各国都能够紧密结合各河段的实际，以梯级开发为中心，实行干支流并举的综合开发方针，优先开发水能资源和水运资源，为河流水资源的综合利用提供了经验借鉴。[1]

（二）产品开发更加重视多样化和功能优化

求新求异是旅游者外出旅游的拉动力之一，单一的观光功能区和旅游线路很难吸引游客重游，因此旅游产品在开发设计上应尽量走特色化、多元化道路，凸显自己的特色，不断优化休闲游憩功能，唯有此才能在众多的同类旅游地中脱颖而出，不断地吸引更多旅游者。

我国河流旅游产品开发已经逐渐摆脱单一旅游项目开发形式，开始更加注重产品的多样化和丰富化开发，细致划分旅游者不同需求的产品类型及不同功能分区，不断革新并设计出更多功能优化的产品，在提升趣味性的同时还增加了游客的参与性，满足了更多旅游者的需求。如河流度假旅游产品在开发规划时，既考虑游客对宁静幽雅的环境需求，也考虑游客的娱乐和运动需要，所以度假区内接待设施不但达到舒适的服务标准以及私密性、隔离感要求，还提供了多项具有安全保证的休闲和游憩设施，供游客参与娱乐。

案例1.2
巴黎塞纳河：打造浪漫休闲的文化型河流[2]

塞纳河是法国北部大河，其旅游开发是1989年根据巴黎城市规划进行的，据统计，塞纳河每年的旅游收入大于巴黎旅游总收入的10%。塞纳河旅游开发突出的理念和特点在于：

第一，有效的景观保护及文化底蕴的强大支持。塞纳河将巴黎最精华的旅游资源串联在一起，同时注重文化遗产的保护。完善的立法保护、详细的文化景观资源普查、有效的管理体制，以及全

---

[1] 刘健. 莱茵河流域的开发建设及成功经验[J]. 世界农业，1998（2）.
[2] 沈虹，冯学钢. 都市文化型河流旅游开发研究——以上海苏州河为例[J]. 桂林旅游高等专科学校学报，2006（5）.

民的保护参与都为其提供了卓有成效的保护。

第二，水陆互动良好结合，游船节目丰富，河道突出亲水特点。塞纳河旅游设计是开放性的，水陆联动突出，水、岸遍布休闲场所。其游船功能齐备，节目丰富，每经过一个典型景观，游船的解说系统都会配以相应的解说词和相关的文学、艺术作品，充分调动游客感官。

第三，与巴黎城市气质协调一致的都市形象功能。塞纳河是法国巴黎的代言人，处处散发出悠闲的氛围、艺术的气息，以及浪漫的情韵。从功能上说，它集运输、旅游、娱乐、休闲于一身；从历史上看，它是巴黎的发源地，塞纳河留下了不同时期的印记，代表着巴黎的发展；从氛围角度，塞纳河充满了浪漫和闲适。这些都是巴黎典型的气质，这样的契合使塞纳河成了巴黎浪漫都市的典型代表，获得了巨大的增值效应。

塞纳河首先是巴黎之河，其旅游发展的成功离不开河流与城市相互依存的关系，也离不开水资源的有效利用，更离不开河流生态景观的保护以及在此基础上进行的产品深度开发。

案例来源：沈虹，冯学钢. 都市文化型河流旅游开发研究——以上海苏州河为例［J］. 桂林旅游高等专科学校学报，2006（5）：542-545.

（本研究根据上述来源归纳整理）

第三节　大河文明旅游需求与市场

本节主要针对大河文明旅游发展的游客需求和市场概况进行分析。游客需求可能会因时尚潮流的变化而发生兴趣转移，从而引起客源市场的变化，在当前文化旅游的时尚潮流下，大河文明旅游的市场地位得到提升，各国家和地区也因势利导，发展大河文明旅游的积极性变得空前高涨。

一、大河文明旅游游客需求分析

（一）旅游者产品消费偏好转变

随着我国经济改革的日益深化，科技文化水平的不断提高，人们生活质量的日趋完善，游客对旅游产品的消费偏好也有了显著的改变，需求种类呈现多样化，品位也在不断提升，由传统项目向现代娱乐时尚项目转移。传统河流旅游产品的开发理念明显跟不上如今强调产品个性化、功能多样化、追求刺激等旅游消费市场的需求；相反，一些带有些许体验要素的河流旅游产品在市场上初露端倪，颇为走俏，如异域民俗文化体验、温泉疗养、演艺娱乐等相较于传统的垂钓和游泳等展现出较高的热度，可见，未来大河文明旅游若想开发出高质量的旅游产品，必然离不开深度体验这一主题。

（二）旅游者对大河文明旅游的认同度提升

随着知识经济时代的到来，以及游客需求的转变和旅游品位的提升，现阶段旅游者已经不仅仅局限于对优美自然风光的单纯欣赏,"了解异地的文化和生活方式"成为出游的一大动机,由此推动了文化体验旅游成为旅游业的热点。而大河文明旅游说到底是一种文化游和体验游,承载着体验大河流域民俗文化和人文风情的使命和价值,象征着大河文化和旅游体验的深度融合,与现阶段游客需求及旅游市场发展趋势正相吻合,成为旅游市场中吸引旅游者的重要力量。因此,大河文明旅游在旅游市场中的地位和作用越来越重要,游客对其认同度也在不断提升。

二、大河文明旅游市场供给分析

（一）客源市场开发范围逐步扩增

早期大河旅游客源市场开发主要以国内市场为主、海外市场为辅,目前随着大河旅游热度提升,旅游产品设计不断成熟,以及旅游交通越来越便利等利好性因素增加,大河旅游市场开始进一步发育,国际游客数量逐渐增加。当前,一些大河流域的国家和地区在发展旅游时,针对的目标市场已经不局限于国内范围,而是开始延伸至国际范围,如埃及旅游市场。近年来埃及不断推出跨国旅游线路,大力开拓国外旅游市场,从而使得到埃及旅游的国外游客数量快速增加,同时客源国覆盖范围也不断扩大（图1.1）。

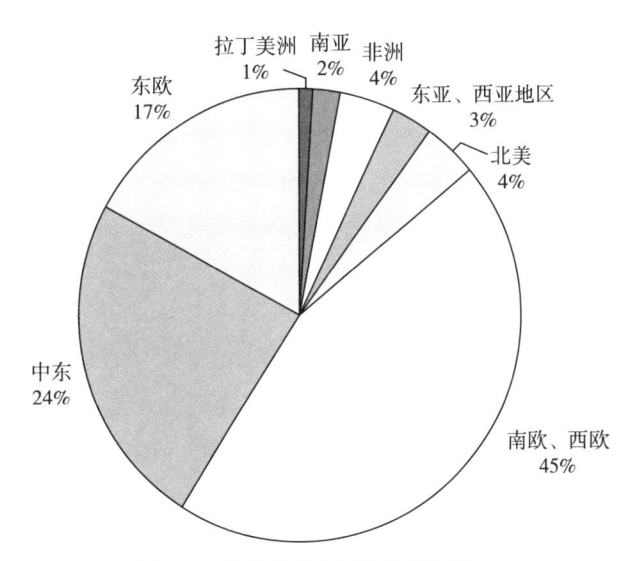

图 1.1 埃及旅游主要海外客源地区

资料来源：孙海燕, 李关云. 埃及旅游业：新休闲主义的"黄与蓝"[J]. 21世纪商业评论, 2005 (5): 119–123.

然而,在客源市场开拓过程中,如何能够持续吸引国际客源,不断提升市场规模也是一个十分关键的问题,这就要求地区旅游部门加大宣传和营销力度,同时还要在产品开发上下功夫,只有开发出更多具有创新性和吸引力的旅游产品,才能持续提升国外游客的出游兴趣。

（二）客源市场层次划分重要性凸显

伴随大河旅游市场范围和规模的扩大,市场层次划分显得尤为必要,因为在一个河流流域中必然会存在不同类型、不同层次的旅游产品，既包括观光休闲、度假型生态旅游产品，同时也包括具有一定专业性的文化旅游产品。其中，观光、度假类旅游主要是通过感受意境、体会心态来满足人们的休闲、放松需求，而文化旅游则是人们带有某种求知的目的进行的旅游活动，因此，不同类型旅游产品对应的目标市场应该是有所不同的，这就要求大河旅游在营销过程中做到将恰当的产品形式奉献给恰当的目标游客。如对于文化专业性程度较高文化类旅游产品，其针对的目标群体应该是具有一定文化素养，对大河文化和文明比较认同，同时也热衷于推崇文化保护和研究的客源市场，而不是针对完全泛化的大众旅游市场。

第三章　大河文明旅游开发效益与挑战

大河文明是一个国家精神、一个民族文化的重要载体之一，在当前大力发展河流旅游业的背景下，大河文明旅游开发已经成为保护水资源环境、流域文明、风俗等的重要途径之一。以旅游产业复兴大河文明可以促进其实现可持续发展，实现区域旅游形式多样化，提升流域经济的发展水平等。本章将对大河文明旅游开发的效益、大河文明旅游开发面临的挑战进行深入阐述。

第一节　大河文明旅游开发的效益

旅游业是 21 世纪的无烟产业，旅游功能也是河流现代开发中一大重要功能，世界早期的旅游活动中，乘船进行河流观光是一个重要的旅游活动类型。在经济和科技日新月异的今天，如何让大河文明可持续地发展，继续发挥它的巨大作用，就必须对大河的功能和开发给予良好的定位。开发大河文明旅游资源，形成各具特色的大河文明旅游产品，对带动旅游经济的发展、大河文明的可持续发展具有重要价值。

一、大河文明旅游开发的社会效益

（一）符合文旅融合新时代产业发展方向

在文旅融合发展、旅游产业转型升级的背景下，大河文明旅游有利于整合流域沿线丰富的文化和旅游资源；有利于满足广大游客对于高品质文化旅游产品的需求；有利于通过旅游传播博大精深的中华文明，为世界提供认识中国传统大河文化和现代生活的空间载体。把文旅融合作为弘扬大河文化、旅游产品开发的核心，为借助国家推进黄河文明旅游带建设的历史机遇、探索文化和旅游有机融合的有效路径提供了新舞台，也符合文旅融合新时代产业发展方向。此外，通过大河文明旅游的开发，不仅有助于推动优秀传统大河文化的保护与传承，同时也有利于促进跨区域创新融合协调发展，推动大河流域形成合作共赢新局面，在流域旅游经济发展过程中将逐步形成大河观光旅游产品、研学旅游产品、休闲度假产品等，真正使大河的文化功能、旅游功能、经济功能、社会功能得到充分发挥。

（二）促进世界多元文明交流与协同发展

在全球经济一体化的今天，加强区域间的合作是时代的需要和发展的趋势。大河不仅有人们赖以生存的宝贵水资源，大河在历史发展的过程中也形成了独特的大河文明与文化。不同时期、各具特色的自然和文化景观，如河流沿岸的传统民俗、古老建筑、特色街道等构成了大河沿岸独特的文化景观带。大河文明旅游在不同国家、不同文化里都有开展，拥有大河文明的国家也很重视对大河水资源、文化资源等的保护开发。尤其是大河文明旅游对于推动世界各民族的团结、共同繁荣进步具有积极的意义，能进一步促进世界多元文明交流与协同发展。

具体来说：一是，通过对大河文明旅游的开发，不仅加强对水资源和文化的尊重和保护意识，还能促使经济可持续发展。二是，通过大河文明旅游的开发促进不同地区之间的文化交流与合作让游客体察、了解、感知不同大河流域地区人民的生活方式、民俗文化、特色建筑、非物质文化遗产等，大河文明旅游也成为人民寻求文化享受和加强民间交流的渠道。三是通过大河文明旅游开发，促进文化和旅游业的联动发展，不同地区通过不同形式的交流、合作能够实现资源互补、市场互享、营销互动、合作双赢的目标。

（三）促进大河流域旅游的可持续发展

随着人们的环境保护意识越来越强，大河作为一个重要的环境要素必然成为关注的热点和研究的主体。而大河文明旅游的开发研究，强调在生态原理基础上保护周围自然景观、水体、文化、民俗等资源，也是以环境保护为前提，对人与自然融合需求的重视，为大河文明的可持续发展提供了实践的指导，从而促进大河文明旅游的可持续发展。在中国，黄河流域地区把文化旅游和生态旅游结合起来发展，以此丰富旅游产品体系，增加新的经济增长点和多样的旅游方式。而且通过大河文明旅游引导人们对大河文化的了解，尊重保护与大河相关的自然与人文资源。

二、大河文明旅游开发的经济效益

（一）有利于推动大河流域旅游经济的发展

旅游业是一个关联性、带动性特别强的行业，大河文明旅游的发展促进大河流域内第一产业、第二产业、第三产业等方面实现广泛的融合，从而推动大河流域经济的发展，以及大河旅游目的地的旅游经济繁荣。大河是不同地理单位以河流为纽带连接在一起的自然和经济联合体。大河文明流域内资源有许多共性，其所具有的资源基础、文化内涵、交通等成为连接区域内人们沟通的优势条件，促进大河文明旅游的发展，从而使得许多大河流域成为发达的经济发展区域。通过对大河流域地区的文化与自然资源的开发，形成完善和具有特色的旅游产品体系，能带动大河流域地区商业、农业等行业的发展，有利于促进旅游经济的大作，增加劳动就业机会实现旅游致富，也能通过旅游扶贫促进大河流域贫困地区脱贫致富。伴随着我国旅游业加快发展的大趋势，大河文明旅游也面临良好的发展机遇。如欧洲的莱茵河流域、塞纳河流域，南美洲的亚马孙河流域，国内的长江三角洲、黄河三角洲等都是发达的经济圈，流域旅游经济圈的发展日益繁荣，并且相继成为世界旅游经济的热点板块和增长极。

（二）为河流型旅游目的地提供开发模式借鉴

伴随着我国旅游业加快发展的大趋势，通过对世界上大河流域地区的文明与旅游发展的深入剖析，并对国内外大河旅游发展的比较，有助于借鉴典型案例的优秀做法，为不同区域大河流域文明和旅游资源的开发与旅游模式的构建提供建议与对策，同时也为其他河流型旅游目的地提供开发模式经验的借鉴。如山西省专门对黄河流域进行了专项发展规划，通过大河文明旅游不仅能够保护黄河流域地区丰富的自然资源和文化资源，还能促进沿岸地区的旅游经济发展，打造全域旅游的开发模式，进而推动大河流域内旅游经济的发展。

（三）为政府部门提供大河旅游开发的建议与对策

通过对国内外的大河文明旅游开发的总结、分析和比较，能更好地为政府制定相关政策与规划服务，以及制定大河流域经济、文化与旅游开发措施提供理论指导，寻找一种全新的适合自身的大河文明旅游发展模式，促进大河流域地区的文明与旅游发展，推动文化与旅游的进一步融合与文旅产业转型升级，最终推动整个旅游经济的发展。

第二节　大河文明旅游开发面临的挑战

大河流域地区的生态环境往往较为脆弱，人们的生产、生活，以及旅游开发、旅游活动等都会对大河的水资源、动植物资源、文化资源等造成破坏，并且在一定程度上已经阻碍大河文明旅游的可持续发展。如何在开发利用大河自然与文化旅游资源的同时，又能够保护大河流域的各类旅游资源、生态环境、历史文化、水资源等，从而实现可持续发展是大河文明旅游发展面临的重要挑战。

一、文化遗产保护与传承

（一）文化遗产的保护

世界上许多著名的城市都有一条著名的河流与之相伴，人的生存离不开水。因此，人类的每一段文明都离不开大河的哺育。古巴比伦、古埃及、古印度、古中国，这些相继出现的文明，与其说是人类智慧的结晶，不如说是大河的成就。大河被认为是古代文明的发祥地，但更是文化遗产的集聚地，经过几千年甚至几万年的发展，如今的大河流域已经积累了丰富的文化遗产资源。

大河流域文化遗产资源能否得到有效的开发和利用，关系到人类文明的可持续发展，而文化遗产开发的第一步则是遗产的保护，保护是开发过程的重中之重，没有保护就无法进行良好的开发。但当前大河流域很多国家及城市依然尚未意识到大河文化遗产保护的重要性。因此，大河流域各界应积极采取措施保护大河流域的文化遗产，促进文化与自然、文化与社会发展的和谐共生。可以采取的具体措施如：建立国际性的文化遗产合作和创新平台；共享大河流域文化资源管理、开发、保护和利用的经验；构筑大河流域城市间沟通交流的桥梁，加强城际协作创新，促进文化遗产与旅游、科技等产业的融合发展，促进大河文化遗产的传承与保护，进而实现大河文明的可持续发展。

（二）文化遗产的传承

文化是旅游的灵魂，是区别不同区域的重要"识别码"，旅游是文化的载体，是提升文化魅力的重要依托。大河文明旅游从本质上来讲也是一种文化旅游，大河文化遗产是人类文明发展的见证，也是人类知识、智慧、创造的结晶，大河文明旅游的主要特色和优势体现在对大河文化遗产的传承和开发上。文化遗产是历史的产物，而我们面对的是一个现代化社会，因此，一方面，要使文化遗产存活于当代、适应于当代，就需要做好传承过程的"转化"工作，创新大河文化遗产的传承形式、传承载体等；另一方面，我们还要保证文化遗产活态传承，不能过度更改，要保持大河文化遗产的原真性，在了解大河文化遗产的价值、属性及特征的基础上，尊重大河文化遗产的原貌，在向现代社会"转化"时要适度、合理，保证大河文化真实性，只有这样，才能确保大河文化遗产在旅游开发中，实现经济价值和社会价值的可持续增长。

（三）文化遗产的开发

大河文化遗产是人类文明的结晶，往往能够代表人类文明的发展历程，对游客具有潜在吸引力，因此，利用大河文化遗产开展旅游活动，将大河流域的文化遗产与沿岸的人文景观、自然景观、民俗文化、传统文化、科技文化等旅游资源联结起来进行旅游开发，具有突出的历史和社会文化价值。但当前国际上很多地区在大河文化遗产开发过程中，由于存在开发方式不当、缺乏规划和有效监管等问题，导致大河文化遗产的旅游价值和文化价值并未得到有效彰显。大河文化遗产旅游开发不是一蹴而就的，而是要注意开发的方式与方法，以满足当前和未来旅游需要为目标，制订合理的开发方案，既要尊重原有的文化内涵，在形式和内涵上尊重文化的原貌，不能随意更改，又要在尊重文化内涵的基础上去开发新的河流旅游产品，如开发历史文化、文学艺术、音乐等类型的大河文化遗产旅游产品，只有如此才能广泛适应市场需求，发挥大河流域突出的经济、历史文化价值，特别是无形的文化内涵。

二、大河文明生态环境

坚持人与自然和谐共生，保护生态文明是人类永续发展的千年大计。保护生态环境不仅是人类生存发展的需要，良好的自然生态环境和原生态的文化也是旅游业发展繁荣的基础。因此，必须树立和践行"绿水青山就是金山银山"的理念，坚持可持续发展的宗旨与原则，实行严格的生态环境保护制度，形成绿色发展方式和生活方式，实现大河文明旅游的可持续发展。

（一）水环境污染

千百年来，河流为人类文明的发展做出了重大贡献，但过去人类对河流往往索取多于贡献。在与人类活动最为密切的河流中，由于人为等各方面原因，导致水体环境污染加剧乃至失去正常河流功能的情况已是屡见不鲜，更有些水体鱼类绝迹，丧失了景观价值，造成环境质量的下降，影响人们游览、娱乐和修养等。绝大部分的水污染物质是人们在生产生活过程中将生活污水和工业废水排进水体所造成的，因此，要严格对排入河流中的水进行控制，从工业生产、居民生活、农业生产等方面加强对河流水污染源头的控制，保证控制和治理后能够有效地保持河流水体的长期健康。

国际上也有很多河流在经过认真治理之后又恢复了昔日碧波荡漾、清澈澄净的面貌。如莱茵河，起初由于河流上游旅游景点的深入开发，外来旅游人员的不断增多，高山畜牧业的调整和阿尔卑斯山区自然环境的破坏程度加剧等，导致上游水质遭到直接影响。为了保护莱茵河水质，维护原始地貌，瑞士各级政府和专业职能部门做出了巨大的努力。先后颁布了《森林法》《环境保护法》《特殊垃圾回收与运输规定》《水资源保护法》《环保法》等数10部涉及保护水体的法律、法规。并且规定企业不准将未经处理的工业和生活用水直接排放到附近的任何水体，就连濒河建筑物上的雨水也必须经屋檐排水槽引入地下，再经过处理后才准排入水体。由于实施了严格的水体环境保护法，不仅莱茵河源头，包括整个瑞士的数十条河流、上千个湖泊的水体至今常年清澈透明，所有水质全部达到饮用水标准。莱茵河流域的9个国家制定了一个莱茵河日常养护"国际公约"，并成立了由12人组成的保护莱茵河国际委员会，委员会主席由成员国部长轮流担任，多年来，莱茵河流域国家基本上是在自觉地养护各自的河段。

（二）洪涝灾害

由于自然因素和人类活动的影响，如降水量的强度和季节变化，流域内气候水文条件、地形条件等自然因素，以及滥砍滥伐造成植被减少，在坡地上农业耕种等人类活动的影响，导致河流流域频发规模和影响较大的自然灾害，尤以洪涝灾害的影响最为显著。一方面，洪涝灾害给人类生产生活以及社会经济的发展带来了巨大破坏，如不仅冲毁房屋、直接造成人员大量伤亡，致使农田、城郭和水利建筑毁坏，还带来了严重的难民问题，引发经济波动等；另一方面，洪涝灾害也为河流旅游的开发带来较大的负面影响，如直接破坏旅游景观和旅游设施、制约河流旅游市场需求、阻碍旅游交通、危及游客人身安全等。因此，河流旅游的发展应当建立相应的预防洪涝灾害的措施，如完善洪涝灾害预警防范系统、建立洪涝灾害安全避难所、保障旅游者人身安全。此外，还需要做好环境保护工作，减少森林砍伐，适宜地开垦土地，提高森林覆盖率，减少自然灾害发生的频率。

（三）森林退化

大河流域地区对大河沿岸的大规模开发利用，会危及大河系统自身的生存发展，其中，林木过度砍伐导致森林退化，破坏生态系统稳定就是一个典型例子。森林是大河流域重要的生态保护带和生物栖息地，一旦采伐过度，就会导致生物多样性被破坏、生态系统恶化和生态功能下降等，甚至还会带来一系列自然灾害，危及大河流域的生产、生活和生存。同时，大河流域的旅游开发也离不开良好的森林资源，借助森林资源开展休闲游憩活动是大河旅游发展的重要方式之一，因此，大河流域森林资源的退化也将会不可避免地制约河流旅游开发。

亚马孙河流域就是森林退化的典型案例，由于过度采伐，导致植被破坏、森林退化，造成水土流失、水量减少、输沙量增大、河道淤塞。并且森林退化导致热带雨林作用减弱，对地球这个人类家园也会造成严重影响。为了保护亚马孙河流域，厄瓜多尔已经启动了资源保护项目，致力于减缓森林砍伐和气候变化，保护这个世界上最具有生物多样性的地区，以及在这里生活着的原始土著。

三、大河文明旅游规划与开发

(一) 产品缺少文化特色

旅游产品不但要从表现形式上去探索、去创新，还需要从文化意义上去挖掘、去创造。大河文明旅游产品，作为人类文明的体现形式，一定要是外在表达方式与内在文化内涵的最协调的呈现。然而，在实际大河旅游发展中，大河流域的旅游产品开发在一定程度上存在产品类型单一、缺乏地域特色和文化内涵，这不仅直接导致大河旅游资源的吸引力下降，河流旅游的价值得不到发挥，而且也会在一定程度上降低游客的期望值，造成河流旅游市场需求降低。河流旅游产品不应当仅仅流于形式，而应该深刻呈现河流文化内涵，体现河流文化特色，让旅游产品在河流文化与旅游者之间起到"纽带"作用，将河流的文化属性广泛传播给旅游者，使旅游者在游玩过程中能体验到河流文化的魅力，激发情感共鸣，从而传递游客对人类文明的认同感和自豪感。

(二) 旅游产品开发缺少有机组合

尽管近年来国内外河流旅游产品开发方式在不断改善和创新，但目前在国际范围的河流旅游产品开发中，依然存在大量河流旅游产品碎片化开发问题，不少河流旅游产品依然是粗糙的、简陋的、碎片化的，缺少有机组合。这种分散蔓延的产品开发方式是低效的、浅层次的，容易造成旅游发展低效重复、旅游者体验差、旅游生态空间破碎等多种问题，不利于河流旅游深度发展。因此，要从规划源头上杜绝碎片化产品开发情况的发生，构建完善的河流旅游产品体系。做到在综合分析大河旅游目的地资源、市场需求以及竞争环境的基础上，对大河旅游产品进行有机整合，同时强调体现大河地域文化特征，突出大河文明旅游形象定位，推动大河旅游产品间的协调发展，形成主次结合、内容丰富、文化深厚的大河流域产品体系，实现对大河旅游的高效、深度开发。

(三) 旅游产品开发层次低

大河旅游产品承载着厚重的大河文化，是大河文明的呈现和传播，产品开发理应受到严格要求和高度重视。目前，大河旅游产品在开发过程中存在品种单一、缺乏创意、没有突出旅游资源特色等诸多问题，旅游产品开发档次低，对游客的吸引力不大，没有呈现出理应呈现的经济价值和社会价值。针对这种情况，河流旅游管理部门应当给予关注，重视对旅游产品的提质升级，改善产品品质不高的问题。随着河流旅游市场的迅速发展和旅游需求的扩大，河流旅游产品开发需要立足于细分市场，在旅游资源整合和旅游市场识别的基础上进行创新，深度挖掘资源特色，开发高品质的、具有文化内涵的旅游产品。比如可以开发以文化旅游、水上旅游、生态体育旅游、民俗旅游、遗产旅游等为主题的旅游产品，呈现品质化、多元化特色，提升对旅游者的吸引力。

四、管理和政策

(一) 多头管理

世界上存在很多国际河流，由于其资源的丰富性、战略利益的利害关系，以及国际河流权益的共享性特点，导致河流开发问题错综复杂。开发过程中往往涉及多个利益相关者，且类型各不相同，具体可分为地域主权政府组织、域外政府组织、非政府组织及当地民众等。各利益主体在河流管理过程中所扮演的角色、拥有的权利和应承担的责任各不相同，且域外势力往往根据自身战略利益对流域规划管理进行干涉，造成多头管理的局面，使得域内国家的自主管理权变得被动。这种管理的多元化状态不但容易因利益冲突而引发各种争端，阻碍大河流域旅游开发建设，而且多个政府职能部门共同参与规划管理，也容易造成职能交叉重复，难以实现河流开发的互补效益。

（二）资源分配

跨界河流往往蕴藏着丰富的资源，且大多占据重要的地理位置，因此是流域内外各国竞相涉足和开发的重要旅游资源，但由于流域内外各国的国家战略差异，各国利益诉求不一，资源需求不尽相同，导致跨界河流资源的开发环境变得复杂。其实，无论是河流资源开发问题，还是各国利益协调问题，归根结底都是资源所有权分配的问题，由于跨界河流资源分配不明确、资源服务对象模糊，导致资源开发变得复杂，阻碍了流域各国间的交流合作以及河流资源的共享。此外，由于河流资源的分配尚不明确，导致河流资源管理和保护工作也难以有序健康地实施，部分跨界河流流域各国为获取现时利益对河流资源进行竭泽而渔式的开发，一方面造成了河流水位异常变化、河堤受侵蚀加剧、鱼类减少等生态问题，不利于周边环境的稳定和水、土地等资源的可持续利用；另一方面也增加了河流旅游开发的经济成本，影响河流资源的可持续利用。

（三）法规制定

国际河流的开发涉及流域内国家关系，国家经济和社会的发展，也涉及生态环境的保护等问题，国际河流的开发如处理不善，常常会引起双方或多方的国际纠纷，甚至地区不稳定。因此，为解决国际河流开发中的矛盾与争端，国际河流法规建设是必要的，健全的法律体系是河流开发管理成功的保障。虽然国际间的一些非政府组织和联合国有关机构，从21世纪初以来，就已经着手探讨和制定河流相关法规，如《日内瓦公约》《人类环境宣言》《联合国水利会议报告（附件）》等，但这些法规大多不具有官方所签订的公约效力，在开发利用国际河流水资源时，上述国际法条文及其他文件仅供参考，并未成为各流域国必须共同遵守的法规，所以目前并没有一部各国公认的有关国际河流的国际法。因此，国际河流法规建设问题仍然是世界各国需要完善的一个重要课题，没有法律、法规的制约，国际河流开发问题就难以解决，各国矛盾争端也将难以平息。

第二篇
大河文明旅游发展模式

第一章　文旅融合模式

大河沿线有着深厚的历史文化沉淀与巨大的旅游开发潜力，大河的自然风光与人文旅游资源优势推动了大河文明与旅游融合的新业态。文化与旅游的融合发展既是对大河文明的传承与创新，也为大河沿岸的旅游发展带来了新的机遇。促进文旅融合，可从文化遗产与旅游品牌建设、博物馆型旅游目的地的开发、流域沿岸联合发展等角度分析大河文旅融合的共赢模式，进而探索文旅融合的创新发展路径。本章分别从大河古代文明、水利工程、景观文化、沿岸民俗四方面分析大河的核心吸引力，探讨大河文旅融合模式。

第一节　以大河古代文明为核心吸引力的融合模式

本节将对以大河古代文明为核心吸引力的融合模式进行阐述。丰富多彩的历史遗迹、从古至今流传下来的历史传说、著名的历史事件是大河文化的重要载体，也是以大河古代文明为核心吸引力的旅游资源基础，两者的融合发展对于大河古文明的可持续发展有十分重要的意义。

一、考古发现

考古发现是考古人员以田野调查发掘工作为基础，通过对古代遗存发掘和研究，结合史料和辅助手段（现代科技），发现的古代人类活动遗留下来的实物或文化传统。考古发现的主要对象是文化遗产，包括物质文化遗产和非物质文化遗产。物质文化遗产包括所有具有文化价值的某种物质化体现的资产，如历史城镇、建筑、考古遗址、文化风景、文化实物、收藏及博物馆，非物质文化遗产包括被视为文化遗产的各种实践、表演、知识、技能及有关的工具、实物、工艺品和文化场所。[1]

（一）大河古代文明的考古发现与类型

大河古代文明的考古发现主要体现在遗址的发现，考古遗址是最具代表的文物形式，同时也是弥足珍贵的文化遗产，具有重要的文物价值和社会价值，是大河文化源远流长的见证。通过遗址的发掘能够推演出大河文明的演进过程，帮助人类充分理解各文明在农业生产、政治制度、军事活动、科技文化等方面的起步、发展、繁荣及衰败。如尼罗河流域发掘的各个遗址展示了南部

---

[1] Hilary du Cros，Bob Mckercher. Cultural Tourism［M］. 第二版. 朱路平，译. 北京：商务印书馆，2017.

埃及崛起的地方权贵是如何借助先进的生产工艺，通过对剩余产品的积累和奢侈品的垄断来彰显自己的身份，并且用文字和实物建构了一系列表征他们地位和权力的模式[①]；黄河中下游仰韶、龙山、大汶口等新石器文化遗址，以及安阳殷墟等商周故城的发掘确证了黄河流域是中华文化发祥地；再如在南埃及尼罗河流域发现了迄今所知世界最早的农耕文化遗址——瓦迪·库巴尼亚涧润农耕遗址。[②]

大河古代文明的考古遗址按类型可分为古城址、古墓葬、古文化遗址、石刻石碑等。考古发现的文化遗产按可否转移又可分为可移动文化遗产和不可移动文化遗产。可移动文化遗产代代相传，各类文物分布在大河文明各地的博物馆中，如塞纳河北岸的卢浮宫博物馆、泰晤士河畔的大英博物馆、尼罗河东岸的埃及开罗博物馆都储藏着丰富的大河文物；不可移动的文化遗产散布在世界各地，如埃及的金字塔、狮身人面像，印度河流域的梅赫尔格尔文明遗址，长江流域的河姆渡文化遗址、良渚文化遗址、古城遗址等（图2.1）。

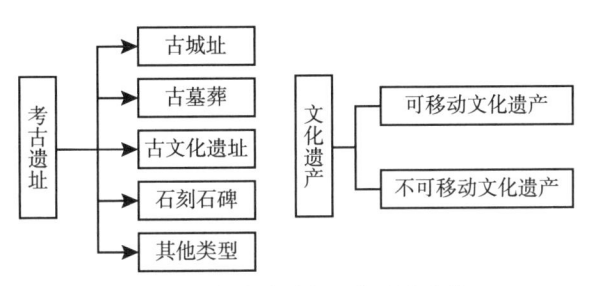

图2.1　考古遗址和文化遗址分类

资料来源：本研究整理。

（二）以大河考古发现为核心吸引力的文旅融合模式

1. 建设以遗址博物馆和遗址公园为形式的旅游目的地

为实现考古遗址保护和文化传播共享，引导公众走近遗址、热爱遗址，很多大河文明都在开展考古遗址的保护与开发工作，通过建设遗址博物馆、遗址公园来展示考古遗址丰富的文化内涵和历史底蕴。遗址博物馆或遗址公园应有鲜明的主题、多样化的展示方式和丰富的互动体验，如圆明园遗址公园，以遗址为主题，已经形成了凝固的历史与充满蓬勃生机的园林气氛相结合的独特的旅游景观。遗址公园兼具考古、教育、游憩等综合功能，如美国国家历史公园作为美国文化遗产类国家公园的代表，致力于对文化遗产的整体性保护利用，其伙伴关系包括美国国家宪法中心、费城会议旅游局、东方国家协会、大费城旅游营销公司等13个公共和私营部门，合作进行公园的保护、教育、讲解、旅游开发等活动。"发现历史"是国家历史公园的核心使命，旨在通过保护和阐释具有重要历史意义的文化遗产，使人们深入了解和积极探索美国历史，国家公园管理局将"发现历史"

[①] 金寿福. 内生与杂糅视野下的古埃及文明起源［J］. 中国社会科学，2012，（12）.

[②] 郑若葵. 埃及发现世界最早的农耕文化遗迹［J］. 农业考古，1987（1）.

界定为四点——美国故事、保护地点、教育培训、遗产旅游，以此为基础已经形成了以保护功能为核心，涵盖研究、展示、教育、休闲等功能的综合性体系。[①]

2. 开发具有共同文化背景的跨区域合作旅游项目

当今具有较高市场价值的文化旅游线路，其价值会随着其国际范围的扩大而增加，通过与邻国整合旅游产品形成的市场网络，可能会增加外国游客数量。早在1987年，欧盟委员会（Council of Europe）就推出了旨在以"时间范畴"与"空间范畴"上的旅游为手段，展示欧洲不同国家和文化背景下的文化遗产是怎样构成一个有共同文化背景的整体的文化线路——欧盟第一条文化线路遗产"圣地亚哥·德·孔波斯特拉—西班牙段"，此线路也是一张朝圣线路网，朝圣者跟随标识和地图指引的线路前行，在终点可以索取由天主教会颁发的证书做纪念，法国与西班牙边界两侧的省级政府承担旅游宣传职责，该线路也被列入《世界遗产名录》。塞尔维亚将多瑙河文化遗产作为国家旅游发展的战略重点，塞尔维亚文化部在2009年启动了"文化之路——多瑙河上的堡垒"（Cultural route—Fortresses on the Danube）试点旅游项目，并于2010年在贝尔格莱德（Belgrade）成立多瑙河能力中心——区域旅游合作组织（Danube Competence center-Regional Tourism Cooperation），有来自克罗地亚（Republic of Croatia）和黑海之间的6个国家22名成员参与，该组织的目的是将多瑙河地区的旅游利益相关者联系起来，以加强彼此间的旅游合作，促进多瑙河历史文化资源的开发利用。[②] 大河古文化遗产的分布较为集中，可以借鉴成功经验，将聚集的众多古建筑、遗址视为整体和连续的实体，规划不同主题的文化旅游线路。

3. 构建大河古文化遗产廊道

遗产廊道是国际遗产保护领域受到认可的遗产保护新模式，在遗产保护与开发中具有重要价值。遗产廊道的概念始于美国，是其保护本国较大范围内历史文化遗产时所采取的措施，以保护具有线性特征的河流峡谷、运河、道路的廊道式遗产资源为主。遗产廊道既注重对廊道沿线和辐射区内的文化遗址和历史遗迹的保护，也注重资源的开发利用，发展旅游也是其重要功能之一。[③] 美国建设较为成熟的遗产廊道有约翰·H.采菲黑石河峡谷国家遗产廊道（John H. Chafee Blackstone River Valley National Heritage Corridor）、凯恩河国家遗产区域（Cane River National Heritage Area）等。大河流域大尺度、跨区域及线性遗产资源丰富，美国遗产廊道的实践对大河古文明遗产资源的保护有极大的实用性与适用性，已有学者提出通过建设三峡遗产廊道来实现长江三峡文物考古成果的旅游转化，将龙骨坡遗址等古遗址、杨粲墓等古墓葬作为重要文化旅游资源纳入廊道，并提出构建设想。

---

① 王京传. 美国国家历史公园建设及对中国的启示［J］. 北京社会科学，2018（1）.

② Aleksandra TERZIĆ, Nevena ĆURČIĆ. Culture Resources in fuction of regional development and international cooperation-Danube Region, Serbia［J］. Geographica Timisiensis，2016（1）.

③ 龚道德，袁晓园，张青萍. 美国运河国家遗产廊道模式运作机理剖析及其对我国大型线性文化遗产保护与发展的启示［J］. 城市发展研究，2016，23（1）.

4. 挖掘古文化的现代价值

（1）文创产品。大河古文明的可移动考古文物很多储藏在博物馆中，近年来，世界著名的博物馆逐步将旅游业和文化相结合，利用馆藏资源开发文化创意商品。一方面，将文化资源转化为经济效益；另一方面，将收入用于文物保护，改善展厅设计，促进博物馆的良性发展。比较著名的是大英博物馆，将镇馆之宝——古埃及罗塞塔石碑作为创作灵感来源，设计马克杯、护照夹、鼠标垫等69件文创产品，还结合馆内藏品推出了一套小黄鸭纪念品，将鸭子装扮成古埃及狮身人面像、日本武士、古罗马战士、维京海盗等。应深入挖掘大河文化的现代价值，充分利用多样化的互联网新媒体传播媒介与形式，大力开发基于互联网、移动终端等载体的大河文创产品，促进大河文化品牌资源的多渠道推送、多平台展示。

（2）节庆与盛事。包括节庆活动、体育赛事、展览等。世界各地大河流域都开展着丰富的文化节庆活动，有传统的节庆如埃及法老集会节、印度太阳神节，还有新创立的节庆活动如新奥尔良爵士音乐节与遗产节（New Orleans Jazz & Heritage Festival），作为一个真正的传承音乐节，自从1970年成立以来，每年都会庆祝新奥尔良和路易斯安那州独特的文化和遗产，并将大面积的场地投入到独有的文化和历史活动中：大舞台（The Grandstand）给参加节庆的人深入了解路易斯安那州充满活力的文化、美食和艺术的机会，民俗村展示着来自路易斯安那州许多土著部落的传统土著工艺品，例如编织篮子、木雕和珠饰，可以一边品尝传统的美国本土食物，一边欣赏传统的"战俘舞"；文化交流馆（CEP）用以纪念新奥尔良的文化血统；儿童艺术作坊成为外地孩子接触其文化的有效途径，节庆期间除了爵士表演艺术外，也促进了视觉艺术与当地文化。①

二、历史传说

历史传说是一种富有魅力的非物质旅游资源。它以现实为原型，通过想象，借助人与神之间或人与人之间的悲欢离合来演绎人们心中的真善美，具有极高的艺术价值。历史传说作为一种古老的文化样式，在当今的社会发展中具有丰富的经济文化价值，同时由于它与各民族的文化习俗、各地的风景名胜有着广泛的联系，它使旅游景点的文化内涵更加丰富，本身也是一种重要的旅游资源。

（一）大河古代文明的主要历史传说

大河古代文明深受宗教神话影响。歌颂神明、英雄与国王、创世神话与洪水传说等形成了一个大的神话系统，盛行于古代。如以下流传较广的历史传说。

1. 多瑙河传奇故事

在布达佩斯的多瑙河一段有九座桥，据说当船穿行过桥下时人的祈祷就会灵验。游客可以做出九个这样的祈求，九座桥中被称为"布达佩斯的象征"的链子桥最为有名，相传过去的人们在下雨

---

① 案例整理自 New Orleans Jazz & Heritage Festival 官网 http://www.nojazzfest.com/

的时候，把链子桥推入城堡山的隧道，以免雨水把它淋湿。①

2. 黄河的大禹治水传说

传说在尧帝时期，黄河流域经常发生洪水，为了制止洪水泛滥，保护农业生产，尧帝曾召集部落首领会议，征求治水能手来平息水害。鲧被推荐来负责这项工作，鲧接受任务后，用堤阻水，作三切之城，九年而不得成功，最后被放逐羽山而死。舜帝继位以后，任用鲧的儿子禹治水，禹总结父亲的治水经验，改"疏围堵障"为"疏顺导滞"的方法，把洪水引入疏通的河道、洼地或湖泊，然后合通四海，从而平息水患。中国人为了纪念大禹，把整个中国大陆称为"禹迹"，意思是大禹的足迹所到之处，治水之功惠泽之处，尊大禹为神禹。

（二）以大河历史传说为核心吸引力的文旅融合模式

1. 旅游景观建造模式

神话人物留下了众多活动遗迹和纪念古迹，这些遗址古迹既是神话传说的承载者，又是开发旅游不可或缺的物质基础。历史传说可以成为当代的一种文化资源，如提供民间读物的原材料、庙宇等恢复重构以及旅游景观建造的文化依托。自20世纪80年代以来，大禹庙得到大规模的重新修建，其中以禹州拉王庙、河津大禹庙最为典型。典型的旅游景观建造案例是埃及的"法老村"，它坐落在开罗市区尼罗河中的雅各布岛上，是由埃及著名学者拉加布博士开辟的仿古旅游点，完全按照史书记载的古埃及风格建造。"法老村"的人们过着远古时代的生活，他们熟谙古埃及历史，身着法老时代的衣饰，手持仿造的古埃及时期的劳动工具，男人从事农耕、放牧、吊水、制陶，女人则从事收割、加工、纺织，并且侍候客人和为客人表演弹唱等。② 在小岛四周矗立着许多神像雕塑，是根据埃及神话故事还原的，有尼罗河神像、埃及著名神话故事中的人物奥西里斯和妻子伊西丝、伯斯神像等。以历史传说为主题的空间复兴和人文旅游景观的新造，为地方经济与文化的建构提供了新的资源与途径。

2. 艺术改编模式

电视剧、电影对大河地域文化旅游的拉动作用影响显著，影视剧是对历史传说所在地的间接宣传，人们被故事化、形象化、通俗化的影视作品吸引，进而萌生出游览的意愿。当今有很多神话故事改编的影视作品，如：印度神话剧《众神之王》《除障者伽内什》；埃及神话剧《第七卷轴》、神话电影《埃及诸神》；中国神话剧《封神榜》《王屋下的传说》等。此外，越来越多景区积极开发旅游文化资源，通过实景演出表演传达鲜明的旅游主题和形象，进而弘扬当地文化，带动旅游产业发展。如威海华夏城景区推出的《神游华夏》通过声光电现代化科技手段，使观众观赏到与众不同的女娲传说、羿射九日、月宫仙女等中国古典传说，充满地方特色的舞蹈演绎和精彩的表演手段抓住了游客的观赏兴致，也提高了景区的知名度。

---

① 赵乾坤，鲁特，洪毅，等. 大河：穿行世界文明的经络［J］. 中国三峡，2009,（2）.
② 戴惠坤. 仿古旅游地——埃及"法老村"［J］. 世界知识，1990（22）.

3. 节庆旅游（公共关系）模式

把握时机节点，利用好大型活动和事件的活动效应开展旅游宣传，独特的节事活动对旅游者有特殊的吸引力，有助于游客体验真实的文化氛围。充分挖掘民间传说的文化内涵，能让更多游人参与到活动中来，以此提高大河旅游的知名度、扩大影响力。旅游节庆活动是当今旅游业十分青睐的一种旅游宣传推介的手段，借助"旅游文化节"广泛的影响力，能够突出特色，形成规模放大效应并激活市场。

三、历史事件

历史事件是指历史上发生过的，被当时或后来的历史学家看作具有一定历史作用的事件。这类事件往往延续一定的时间，活动范围或大或小，由若干位领袖人物领导，被广大群众参与或响应，对当代或后代产生了重大的历史影响。

（一）大河古代文明的重要历史事件类型

在世界大河古文明的演进发展中，有一些决定性的历史事件影响了文明的走向和进程。如商鞅变法使秦国的经济得到发展，军队战斗力不断加强，逐渐发展成为战国后期最富强的集权国家；古巴比伦王国强盛时期，汉谟拉比颁布《汉谟拉比法典》，它代表了古东方文明的伟大成就，其确立的一些原则，特别是有关债权、契约、侵权行为、家庭以及刑法等均对后世立法具有重大影响。大河古代文明的历史事件可大致分为以下几类。

1. 战争类

在大河古文明的演进中，出现了很多重要的战争，有的影响了朝代的更迭，有的则直接导致了文明的衰败及灭亡。古巴比伦有阿摩利人入侵、消灭亚述帝国等战争；古印度著名战役有波斯帝国入侵、马其顿入侵等；古埃及有赫梯战争，利比亚人、波斯人入侵等；古代中国著名的战争有春秋战国时期诸侯争霸，秦时期陈胜吴广起义、巨鹿之战、楚汉之争，东汉时期官渡之战、赤壁之战，东晋时期淝水之战，唐朝安史之乱等。

2. 变革类

大河文明经历了一系列政治经济文化变革，最终在人类文明史上留下了重要的一笔。如汉谟拉比制定了世界上第一部较为完备的成文法典——《汉谟拉比法典》；古埃及建立了君主专制制度，法老作为国家权力的象征和代表，严格控制着国家经济；从公元前7世纪的"管仲变法""四民分业"思想和盐铁专营政策到公元前4世纪的"商鞅变法"，从土地私有化、户籍制、军爵至上到秦始皇确立郡县制、统一货币、度量衡、汉字，再到"汉武帝变法"，围绕产业、流通、货币及财税核心问题的体制改革，以及"罢黜百家，独尊儒术"的思想大一统……变革是古代中国的永恒命题。

3. 科技文化类

科技文化类历史事件包括手工业如纺织、制陶技术的发明突破，也包含文字、数学、天文学、物理学、建筑学等的出现和进步。楔形文字是两河流域苏美尔人的一大发明；古埃及的科技文化成就极高，数学家、几何学家已经能够计算等腰三角形、长方形、梯形和圆形的面积，古埃及人拥有相当水准的天文学知识，还发明了水钟、日晷、犁、汲水器和渠道等，世界上第一张由芦苇制成的纸也在古埃及出现；古代张衡发明地动仪、蔡伦改进造纸术、贾思勰《齐民要术》的出版、京杭大运河的开通等历史事件推动了古代中国经济发展和文明的进步。

（二）以大河历史事件为核心吸引力的文旅融合模式

1. 建设重大历史事件遗址旅游地

历史上的重大事件吸引着文人、研究者、游客的探索兴趣，以历史事件为旅游吸引源，建设以历史事件为核心主题的旅游目的地是融合的模式之一。建设古战争遗址旅游地的项目最多，比较典型的是三国赤壁古战场景区。三国赤壁古战场位于长江中游南岸，长江黄金水道从此境流过，是我国古代"以少胜多、以弱胜强"的七大战役中唯一尚存原貌的古战场遗址，承载了世人对三国历史的经典记忆。[①] 整个景区将古战场遗址和仿汉代建筑群融为一体，铸有诸葛亮、周瑜等历史人物的雕像，还原了赤壁山、南屏山、金銮山等历史事件发生地，还建设有赤壁大战陈列馆、赤壁碑廊、赤壁塔等数十处人文景观。三国赤壁古战场景区开发有"研学营地"、拓展训练基地"水兵校场"，以及再现三国风情和地方特色的大型实景戏演出等旅游项目。历史事件遗址旅游地兼具观光览胜、度假休闲、科学考察、历史考古、科普教育等功能，是文旅融合的有效实践。

2. 以历史事件为主题进行文化旅游创意研发

大河古代文明出现了许多重大历史事件，深度挖掘具有代表性的历史事件，并对其进行创意研发，可衍生出丰富多彩的文化旅游产品表现形式。如方特欢乐世界推出华夏五千年360°环幕立体电影，以华夏五千年历史为主要内容，讲述了炎黄传说时期开始，直至当代中国七个阶段的众多重大历史事件，影片总时长20分钟。观众佩戴特制眼镜观看立体电影，影片播放时，环形的荧幕包围观众，使观众产生身临其境之感。[②]

3. 建立历史事件和历史名人纪念建筑（墓、馆、碑、祠等）

为纪念历史事件和与历史事件相关联的文化名人，世界很多地方都建有纪念建筑，可以结合数字化时代的科技，通过全景VR互动技术、多媒体交互技术等使游客获得浸入式体验，并开展丰富的体验式活动提高游客的游览兴致。如为纪念蔡伦改进造纸术这一卓越历史贡献，耒阳市蔡侯祠内建有蔡伦纸文化博物馆和蔡伦纪念馆，除展示陈列外，游客也可以在互动体验区亲身感受造纸技术；如在位于梅夫拉那苦行僧木屋的鲁米（Rumi是一位生活在13世纪的诗人、神秘主义者，是旋转舞苦行派的创始人）墓前每星期都会举行旋转舞表演，以表达对鲁米的纪念，旅游者只要心怀敬意，也可参与其中。

---

① 三国赤壁古战场官网 http://www.chinachibi.com/intro/1.html
② 大同方特欢乐世界官网 http://datong.fangte.com/

第二节　以大河水利工程为核心吸引力的融合模式

本节将首先对大河水利工程中的水利发电工程与治水工程进行简介，继而对围绕大河水利工程进行文化旅游开发的模式进行阐释。大河水利工程的功能多样，具备着巨大的社会效益、经济效益以及广阔的应用前景，大河的水利工程往往因为其出色的工程建筑、丰富的景观类型以及内部蕴藏的丰厚人文精神与思想，而成为标志性景观建筑，并且推动着大河流域的文化旅游发展。

一、水利发电工程

（一）大河水利发电工程

1. 简介与现状

水能是一种取之不尽、用之不竭、可再生的清洁能源。但为了有效利用天然水能，需要人工修筑能集中水流落差和调节流量的水工建筑物，如大坝、引水管涵等。水利发电工程投资大、建设周期长，但水力发电的优点在于效率高、发电成本低、机组启动快、调节容易。水力发电的基本原理是利用水位落差，配合水轮发电机产生电力，也就是利用水的位能转为水轮的机械能，再以机械能推动发电机，而得到电力。科学家以此水位落差的天然条件，有效地利用流力工程及机械物理等，精心搭配以达到最高的发电量，供人们使用廉价又无污染的电力。而低位水通过吸收阳光进行水循环分布在地球各处，从而恢复高位水源。

水电资源作为一种清洁的可再生能源，在世界各国得到了普遍的重视和较大规模的开发。在以煤炭、天然气、石油为代表的传统能源逐渐枯竭，同时传统能源的消耗又造成巨大环境压力以及对于环境保护的呼吁的背景之下，清洁的水电资源逐渐受到了各国的重视，并进行开发。很多大河流域，都建设或开始建设水利发电工程。早在1878年，法国就已建成世界第一座水电站。再到随后的美国胡佛大坝以及如今建立在长江上游的当前世界第一大的水电工程三峡大坝水电站等，可以看到，世界范围内水利发电工程的数量在日益增多。

如今的大多数水利发电工程属于现代大型水利工程，很多具有综合开发治理的特点，故常称"综合利用水利枢纽工程"。它往往兼顾了所在流域的防洪、灌溉、发电、通航、河道治理和跨流域的引水或调水等多重效益，有时甚至还包括养殖、给水或其他开发目标，优化水资源配置，构成水资源综合利用体系。

2. 意义与影响

首先毋庸置疑的是，水电工程以提供电能的形式带来直接显著的经济效益，同时还通过促进相关产业发展、拉动就业、增加税收等形式带来间接经济效益。并且水力发电是再生能源，对环境冲击较小。此外，除可提供廉价电力以及相较于其他能源开发最大化降低对于环境的影响外，水利发电工程的建设还有以下优点：在生态方面如控制洪水泛滥、减少干旱等自然灾害、改善局部气候、减少环境污染等；在生产生活方面如提供灌溉用水、改善河流航运；此外，工程还可改善该地区的交通、电力供应和经济，特别可以发展旅游业及水产养殖等。以例证之，如美国田纳西河的综合发展计划就是一项大型的水利工程，带动了整体的经济发展[①]；再如1959~1970年，耗时11年，耗资10亿美元，埃及所修建的举世闻名的阿斯旺高坝。阿斯旺高坝控制了尼罗河每年的洪水，保护了居民和农作物，使千万亩农田得到灌溉，改善了上下游通航能力，提供了大量的电力。最为重要的是阿斯旺水库有效地防治了埃及的旱涝灾害。[②]

诚然，水电工程的建设能给人们带来多种益处，如提供了清洁且大量的电能，并且降低了洪水危险等，但也不可避免地带来一些负面的影响。水电工程的建设在对江河、湖泊以及附近地区的自然面貌、生态环境，甚至对区域气候，都会产生不同程度的影响。

3. 开发要求

并不是每条河流的每段流域都适合于开发水电工程，同样工程建设也并不能拍脑门决定。工程的建设需要考虑很多因素，下面即为开发建设的要求：

（1）水力发电是水资源综合开发、治理、利用系统的一个组成部分。因此，在进行水电工程规划时要从水资源的充分利用和河流的全面规划角度，综合考虑发电、防洪、灌溉、通航、漂木、供水、水产养殖、旅游等各方面的需要，统筹兼顾，尽可能充分满足各有关方面的要求，取得最大的效益。

（2）要考虑社会因素。水电工程在开发和建设时，必须保障多方权益，为保障水电工程的可持续发展，必须赋予当地人合法的权利并且直接使受影响的人们受益。水电项目开发的目标是保证受其影响的所有个人和社区都能获得持续性的收益，如在移民工程设计上妥善安置移民生活，在别处兴建房屋并修建相应配套设施等。

（3）要考虑生态因素。在建设前期，要对建设水电工程对生态可能造成的影响进行评估，在尽可能减小生态负面影响的情况下进行开发。

（4）大型水电工程建设与运营所涉及的影响面还包括当地旅游业、流域防洪情势、流域水资源空间分配情况、河道航运条件等，需要综合考虑这些影响因素，进行统筹兼顾，协调开发。

总之，水利发电工程的建设离不开大河流域的规划，在进行水电工程的开发建设时，要综合考虑各方面的利弊影响，无论是经济效益、社会效益、生态效益等，都需要对这些影响进行充分估计，尽可能多地发挥水力发电工程的积极作用，尽可能消除或减少其可能带来的消极影响。在衡量过程中不仅要看到水电工程建设的综合效应，也要看到其对于生态环境及其他方面所带来的可能的负面影响。在对每条河流进行开发、每一个水电工程进行设计规划时，都要坚持开发与保护并存的

---

① 陈雪钧. 世界库坝旅游开发的经验与启示［J］. 消费经济，2013，29（1）.
② 罗美洁. 三峡工程与国外水利工程的文化比较——以胡佛、大古力、阿斯旺、伊泰普为例［J］. 三峡论坛（三峡文学·理论版），2014（2）.

原则，将可持续发展理念贯彻于设计到建设的全过程，实现人口、资源、环境的协调发展，使水电工程既满足于防洪、灌溉、通航、漂木、供水、水产养殖、旅游等各方面的需要，同时又达到生态环境、自然及文化景观多方面的保护的双赢开发目标。

4. 资源构成要素及其旅游价值

水利发电工程以水库和水电站（大坝）为主体，是人工建筑和自然山水相结合的复合体。相关旅游的构成要素主要包括水体、水生生物、库岸（盆）和相关建筑物[①]等。

（1）水体及其旅游价值。水体是进行各种水上娱乐活动的重要场所。作为水电工程中的一部分，水库水体表面狭长，呈树枝状。根据水库形态结构和吞吐流特征，水库水面由入水口到大坝可依次分为河流区、过渡区和湖泊区。河流区位于水库入水口处，此处水面窄浅，河水流速最快，水力滞留时间最短。河流区有许多狭窄、幽深的库汊港湾，这些地方是进行划船、游泳、垂钓等活动的最佳场所。相对于河流区，过渡区结构上宽而深，水流流速进一步减缓，这里是悬浮物沉积的主要区域，浮游植物的生物量及其生长率最高，适宜进行水产养殖。湖泊区靠近水库大坝处，是水库最宽、最深的区域。其宽阔的水面可设置水上摩托艇、水上飞机、水上滑水、水上高空滑翔伞等大型水上娱乐活动项目。

（2）水生生物及其旅游价值。水生生物包括各种水生动物、植物、微生物等。水生动物是旅游活动中比较重要的观赏对象。各种体形优美、色彩艳丽或较为奇特的鱼类会引起游客的观赏兴趣。同时，包括鱼类、甲壳类（如蟹、虾）、龟鳖类（如龟、鳖）、软体类（如蚌）在内的各种水生或两栖类动物为旅游者提供了观赏、垂钓、捕捞、采集的娱乐机会。另外，大规模的水产捕捞、鱼群洄游活动也是游客观光的对象之一。水生（含浮叶、挺水、沉水）植物，如睡莲、荷花、金鱼藻等也是广受赞誉（尤其是我国）的传统观赏植物。

（3）水库库岸及其旅游价值。作为工程的组成水库而言，水库库岸是进行各种户外游憩活动的重要场所之一。水库一般建造于河谷中，水库岸线发展系数相对于湖泊更大。库岸包括水库河流的河漫滩、岸坡和水库四周的山地等。水库库岸的旅游价值在以下3个方面：①丰富了景观类型。秀水为青山增添了一丝妩媚，青山则为秀水增加了几分雄浑，山水结合相得益彰。另外，包括人文景观在内的各类水库周边旅游资源更是丰富了水库景观的层次和结构。②提供了旅游活动场所。库岸的河漫滩包括沙地、草地等，往往是游客进行各类休闲及户外游憩活动的绝佳场所。③拓展了旅游活动空间。水库库岸的山地为登山、森林旅游等活动提供了场所，完成了旅游空间从水面向陆地的拓展。

（4）人工建筑物及其旅游价值。围绕着水利发电工程，该类建筑物主要包括拦河大坝、发电设施、专用建筑物等。其体型庞大、气势恢宏，代表着人类伟大成就的现代建筑物，也成为了重要的旅游资源。大坝是水电工程的核心建筑物和重要标志，也是重要的观光对象之一。

---

① 张西林，傅蓉，曾宪文. 水库旅游开发研究初探［J］. 中南林学院学报，2003（6）.

其他水力发电设施包括进水口、调压设施、压力管道、电站厂房和挡土墙等。水库泄水建筑物包括溢流坝、溢洪道、泄洪洞、坝身泄水孔、闸门、水流消能与防冲设施等。水库泄洪时，咆哮着直冲而下的水流似银河飞瀑，其磅礴的气势远远胜过奔腾的千军万马，带给游客无与伦比的强烈震撼。另外，由于大量的水流倾泻而下后形成大范围的人工水雾，在阳光照射下容易形成美妙而又壮丽的彩虹景观。

其他的一些专用建筑物还有过坝（木、鱼）建筑物、通航建筑物（含船闸、升船机）等。其中船闸和升船机的整个运作过程对大多数游客来说比较新奇，具有很强的吸引力，带来观赏价值。

（二）以水利发电工程为核心吸引力的文旅融合模式

1. 基于自然生态环境，推出生态观光型旅游

现代工业的发展对城市生活环境造成了严重的污染，它带来的热辐射、光辐射、放射性辐射、有害的装饰及建筑材料等对人体身心健康造成一定危害，人们对于清新无尘的空气、清洁纯净的水质和自然风光优美的居住环境的寻求与渴望日益强烈。而大河流域一般自然生态资源丰富，自然风光迤逦，有许多奇特的自然景观，水域（水体）及相关联的岸地、岛屿、林草等能对人产生吸引力的自然景观，比如，大量的水生生物资源为旅游者提供了观赏、垂钓、捕捞、采集的观光与娱乐的机会。因此，水电工程可以结合自身与所在河流资源，根据季节性和工程特有的景观打造生态观光型旅游产品，并在开发中坚持"以人为本"，营造健康优美的生态环境；"以可持续发展为本"，建设低污染和良好的生态环境，吸引游客前来观光旅游。

2. 以工程景观为内核，打造水电工程风景线

水力发电工程的建设在破坏原有自然或者文化景观的同时，也在创造新的旅游景观，带来新的景观价值。工程建设本身的特色也是或者可以用来开发成为旅游景观。

纵观古今中外，著名的水电工程都已经建设或者正在建设成为著名的旅游景点。美国的胡佛大坝本身就是知名的建筑，目前已被定为国家历史名胜和国家土木工程历史名胜，1994年，美国土木工程学会把它列为美国七大现代土木工程奇迹之一。自从1935年胡佛大坝对外开放以来，已经有超过3500万的游客来此观光。游客首先在大坝的顶部参观，之后乘坐电梯向下520英尺（约158.5米）直接到达大坝的底部。大坝内部有一些20世纪30年代典型的建筑风格，各种艺术装饰以及精简现代的设计；此外还有独具风格的美洲土著居民所设计的图案地板。在水坝的底部，游客可以参观一个拥有17台水力发电机组的发电厂房，这17台发电机组每年输送大约35亿千瓦时的电能。从那里继续向下深入水坝内部，可以看到巨大的导流洞。这些导流洞是在水坝施工期间用于分流大坝周围的水源所用。回到水坝的顶部，在位于内华达州境内的部分（水坝横跨内华达—亚利桑那边境），游客中心展示着整个科罗拉多河的水流系统以及水坝的历史。

以三峡大坝景观为基础的5A级景区——三峡大坝旅游区位于湖北省宜昌市境内，以世界上最大的水利枢纽工程——三峡工程为依托，其水电站特色景观以及高峡平湖等人文景观的产生，全方位地展示了工程文化和水利文化，为游客提供游览、科教、休闲、娱乐为一体的多功能服务，将现代工程、自然风光和人文景观有机结合，成为国内外游人向往的旅游胜地。

除工程本身之外，水电工程建成后，可以孕育新的人文景观，推动着旅游的发展。胡佛大坝，孕育了新兴的城市拉斯维加斯，可以说胡佛大坝是拉斯维加斯之母。如今，在胡佛大坝附近，还能找到残墙断垣、破败凄冷的小村庄，那里写着"Old Las Vegas"（拉斯维加斯旧城），那就是建造水坝时工人们的宿营地。拉斯维加斯就是从一个沙漠小村发展起来的。① 由此例可见，水利发电工程自身及其对于周边的"破坏性建设"所带来的新的景观，都可以是旅游资源，都可以围绕此进行旅游开发，打造水电工程风景线路。

3. 挖掘工程文化资源，进行衍生文化与 IP 开发

水电工程本身的建设就是一种精神的传承与象征。如修建于美国经济大萧条时期的胡佛和大古力水坝，本身彰显的就是美国"西部开发"中勇于开拓的"西部牛仔"精神的延续与体现，其自身的文化价值不言而喻，工程建设本身就是最好的文化宣传。再如阿斯旺水利工程的曲折而又艰难的建设过程，使得其本身也成为了埃及民族文化的象征。

除此之外，作为知名建筑与地标性景观，文人墨客留下的笔墨，相关纪录片与书籍的彰显，以及最为标志性的相关影视作品基于此地的拍摄，都带动了旅游的发展。仍然以胡佛大坝为例，《末日崩塌》《变形金刚》《宇宙战士》《10.5级大地震》《毁灭之日》等多部知名影视作品中都出现了胡佛大坝的身影，尤其是影片中很多经典场面都在此发生，这就进一步带动了大坝的知名度和旅游价值，吸引着影视作品迷和其他类型的游客前往参观。因此，衍生文化与 IP 的开发，对于水电工程起到了良好的传播与推广，并在一定程度上带动了旅游的发展，吸引着游客的到来。

4. 综合利用工程功能，打造一条龙观光线路

水利发电工程的建设，极大地促进了航运的发展，而航运的发展为旅游提供了坚实的交通条件，因此，基于工程所在河流流域客观条件，可以连通工程所在上下游，开发全线一条龙式的航运旅游。如长江上游三峡大坝的建设，使得高峡平湖的景观出现，而高峡出平湖又极大地改善了长江航运条件，这对于开发航运，结合三峡周边资源，进行开发游轮旅游是一极佳的条件。这就带动了休闲游轮旅游的发展。并且，除连通上下游进行航运旅游开发外，还可以进一步联动陆运交通，形成交通网络，进行一条龙的旅游观光线路的打造。

5. 整合自然与人文景观，形成区域（流域）联动旅游发展

大河流域源远流长，所跨区域众多，水力发电设施数量也较多，因此也是发展水利旅游的优势区。工程所在的水利旅游开发条件优越的地区，可与区域（流域）内部资源进行整合，形成联动效应。

例如，三峡旅游区的建设与打造。三峡旅游区拥有着一系列高品位的新型自然景观和人文景观，不仅规模宏大、价值和品位极高、吸引力巨大，而且类型齐全、数量众多、垄断性强。同时三

---

① 张志会. 世界经典大坝——美国胡佛大坝概览［J］. 中国三峡，2012（1）.

峡景观由长江一线向长江为中轴线的两岸纵深、腹地延展，使三峡旅游资源范围扩大，除了长江主航道上的传统旅游资源，也增加了长江两翼纵深处水路可达景点。并且，三峡大坝等水电工程的建设还带来了高峡出平湖及峡谷风光、三峡大坝工程景观、长江文化、移民文化与水电工程文化的景观组合。丰富、多样和品质高的旅游资源，为三峡旅游区发展独具特色的观光旅游、休闲度假旅游、生态旅游、科学考察与探险旅游、传统文化旅游、民族文化欣赏与民族风情体验旅游及其他特种旅游等，提供了得天独厚的条件，是三峡地区旅游业发展最基础的优势之一。[①]

在 2004 年，原国家旅游局就颁布了《长江三峡区域旅游发展总体规划》，这是我国第一个由国家组织的跨区域旅游规划。规划中明确提出将三峡旅游建设成以新三峡为品牌，以自然生态观光和人文览胜为基础，以休闲度假和民俗体验为主体，以科考探险和体育竞技为补充，融生态化、个性化和专题化为一体，打造具有国际影响力、竞争力和可持续发展的世界级旅游目的地。

在美国，大多数的水电库坝都建成了风景区，美国田纳西流域的水电群通过成功的旅游开发获得了巨大的旅游综合收益。美国的田纳西河全长 1050 千米，是美国的第五大河流。1918 年开始修建威尔逊大坝和水电站。1933 年根据罗斯福总统的建议，美国国会通过了《田纳西流域管理局法》，组建了田纳西流域管理局（简称"TVA"）。这一管理模式有效地促进了田纳西流域水电产业以及农业、林业、渔业，尤其是旅游业的全面发展，使得该流域成为美国最富裕的地区之一。目前流域内已建成 310 个风景区、110 个宿营地和俱乐部、24 个野生动物保护区。这些旅游和休息场所每年吸引游客超过 6500 万人次。[②]

二、治水工程

（一）大河治水工程

1. 概念及内涵

一条河流，大到洪涝灾害、小到水源污染，都可与治水工程相关联。水利发展事关人类生存、经济发展、社会进步，因此，小则影响人民的生产生活，大则影响社稷安危的治水工程贯穿于人类社会漫长的历史。治水工程，指的是对自然界的地表水和地下水进行控制和调配，以达到除水害和兴水利目的而修建的工程。治水工程在时间上重新分配水资源，做到蓄洪补枯，以防止洪涝灾害和发展灌溉、发电、供水等事业；同时改善水域环境，疏浚航道，建造码头，以利于水上运输；为防止水质污染、维护生态平衡，要因地制宜地修建一系列的水利工程。

治水工程的内涵与功能性是多样化的，又根据不同时期与不同流域的治水工程而呈现出不同。伴随着现代"资源水利"思想，如今的治水工程不仅包括灌溉、防洪、发电、航运等功能，还包括对水资源安全、水环境安全和水生态安全的保障等功能。反映了现代水利先进性（发展程度）、科

---

① 刘名俭，黄猛. 旅游目的地空间结构体系构建研究——以长江三峡为例［J］. 经济地理，2005（4）.
② 陈雪钧. 世界库坝旅游开发的经验与启示［J］. 消费经济，2013，29（1）.

学性（治水战略）、可持续性（社会效益）、高效性（开发、利用和回用）、安全性（抗风险能力）、公平性（行业服务）、规范性（管理制度）和创新性（建设潜力）等多方面的特点。

人类发展到现在，世界各国人民及治水人物发挥勤劳智慧，管水、治水、改水、用水，修建了无数大大小小的水利工程，促进了农业及经济的发展。治水工程是人民发展水利的必然产物，同时也是水利事业发展的载体，在古代就已建成了不少规模巨大、设计精巧、设计水平和使用功能堪称世界一流的治水工程。

以我国的治水工程为例，从传说中的大禹治水到先秦时期的郑国渠、都江堰，到秦汉时期的灵渠、秦渠、六辅渠、白渠，再到三国两晋南北朝时期的通渠灌溉。从隋唐开始，大一统帝国就开始围绕着贯通南北的大运河做文章①。这些大型治水工程无不散发出古代劳动人民优良的工程技术，也是体现中华民族杰出智慧的优秀文化遗产。时至今日，随着水利事业的发展和科技的进步，一些古代时期用于抗洪、灌溉、航运等作用的水利工程已经失去了功能性，而有些水利工程凭借自身强大的功能性以及周边的自然资源仍旧发挥着作用，甚至发挥了旅游观赏等更多的作用。例如战国时期李冰所主持修建的都江堰、隋唐时期隋炀帝主持开凿的京杭大运河等，现如今不仅在水利功能性当中仍发挥着重要的作用，而且自身也兼具水利景区旅游功能，促进了本地经济等多方面的发展。

2. 影响因素

不同大河流域的治水工程所呈现出的差别主要受两类因素的影响②。第一类因素是自然因素，指气候、地形、地势、河流、土壤、植被、条件、规律等有关方面。不同大河流域间的气候、降水等方面的自然因素都各有差异，所以，不同河流流域的治水工程因河而异，有所不同。

第二类因素是社会因素，指政治、经济、文化等多种因素。政治因素包括国家出台的水资源管理制度及水利发展方针、水利法制建设、跨国家河流安全情况等，它是符合国家发展目的的一种人为控制因素，直接关系到国家和社会发展的方向。在古代主要表现在国家为了战略需要或者带动地方经济而修建的渠系、运河等，而在现代则体现在战略部署、社会安全、能源开发、农业保障等方面。经济因素关系到经济制度和经济状况，如经济发展速度与水资源供给平衡关系、人民生活用水状况等。文化因素是指水文化教育、水利科技、水文化普及度、节水观念、风俗习惯等，如是否有先进的技术以及优秀的水利人才以支持治水工程的开发与建设等。因此，在开发与建设治水工程中，要综合考虑两类因素的影响。

3. 开发要求

治水工程历史悠久，它指导着我们现今进一步探寻水的自然规律和内在属性，帮助我们概括和总结治水的悠久历史、丰富经验和伟大成就，对促进人水和谐，保证水资源的可持续利用和经济社

---

① 吴士勇. 古代治水、开河与通漕的历史逻辑 [J]. 深圳大学学报（人文社会科学版），2018，35（2）.
② 韩春辉，左其亭，宋梦林，罗增良. 我国治水思想演变分析 [J]. 水利发展研究，2015，15（5）.

会的可持续发展,指导当今和未来水利事业发展有着重大的意义[①]。人类在探索水利发展的道路上,创造和积累了丰富的治水思想及方法。各大河流流域的治水工程都在发展中不断进步。现代的治水工程与理念在不断丰富与完善,同时,伴随着对于生态环境保护的需求,对于可持续发展的呼吁,在未来治水工程的建设中,要保护与开发并存,在创造效益与生态保护中寻求平衡,综合考虑多方因素,全面发挥大河流域水系的资源功能、环境功能以及生态功能,进行开发建设。

4. 蕴含的文化资源

在治水工程的文化旅游开发中,需倚重的文化既包括水利工程自身的文化,也包括与水利共生的水文化,同时还有资源所属的地域文化,三者共同构成水利旅游资源文化体系[②]。

(1)源远流长的水文化。大河孕育了生命,创造了文明。探究世界文明的源起,会发现所有的文明都与水结缘。人类社会文明起源于河流文化,人类社会发展积淀河流文化,河流文化生命推动社会发展。大河文明与人类文明息息相关,是人类文明的源泉和发祥地。河流与人类文明的相互作用,造就了河流的文化生命。因此,大河自身具有的源远流长的水文化是极其重要的旅游资源。

(2)层面齐全的治水工程文化。①坚实的水利物质文化。水利建设离不开各种形式的水利设施。这些设施为发展水利旅游提供了物质基础。古代的设施如春秋战国时期秦国郡守李冰兴建的都江堰工程、郑国修建的郑国渠(现在的泾惠渠前身)、楚国修建的芍陂等,至今仍然存在,经过扩建、改造和发展,继续为人民造福。现代更是创造了形式多样的水利工程服务人类,推进社会整体发展。当站在这些古代的、现代的水利旅游资源面前时,游人会由衷地感叹治水工程的伟大。②悠久的水利行为文化。在与水共生的历史中,以我国举例,就创造了许多具有中国特色的行为文化,据《洛阳记》载,"禹时有神龟,于洛水负文列于背,以授禹。文即治水文也"。致使后人在治水之前,均祭祀神龟,治水中,浇注大龟,以镇水妖,永保平安。在黄河下游两岸,各诸侯国自筑防洪堤防,"壅防百川,各以自利",以堤防保护本国,又以邻为壑,彼此"水攻"。直到公元前221年,秦始皇统一中国,才废止了"水攻",统一了全国水政。此外,中国民间为求免除水患困扰,多在江湖边铸铜牛以镇水,这一行为的起源有两种说法:一是大禹治水时为镇河患而设,二是战国时李冰治水,开凿都江堰时曾以牛为化身,征服了江神,故后人也以铜牛、铁牛镇水患。这样的具有特色的行为文化也是文化资源的一部分。③先进的水利科技文化。水利科技文化也构成了治水工程文化资源的一部分。以我国古代来说,都江堰的规划、设计和施工都具有比较好的科学性和创造性。"束水攻沙"理论是我国古代河流水文学的光辉成就,也是治黄和黄河大堤完善化的理论基础,在世界水文学史上占有重要地位。涪陵白鹤梁石鱼题刻断断续续记载了72个年份的枯水记录,是我国古代最早的"水位站"。由于航运、渔业、制盐、海战和潮灾预防等活动迫

[①] 毛春梅,陈苡慈,孙宗凤,等. 新时期水文化的内涵及其与水利文化的关系 [J]. 水利经济,2011,29(4).

[②] 丁枢,黄江涛. 水利旅游资源的文化内涵及开发思路 [J]. 中国水利,2009 (2).

切需要知道潮汐时间和强度，古代编制了不少潮汐表，其中又以唐代窦叔蒙的涛时图和宋代的四时潮候图最出名。

放至现代，现代治水工程从规划、设计、施工到运行管理都是科学与技术的综合应用，包含了建筑工程、机械工程、电气工程、管理工程、环境科学等众多科学知识。先进的技术是优秀治水工程共有的特性，也是水利旅游资源的关键看点所在。例如，黄河小浪底水利工程枢纽建设中，取得了一批重要科研成果，如大坝混凝土防渗墙施工技术、泄洪洞洞内孔板消能技术等。正是凭借这些科学技术含量极高的研究设计，才使得大量水利工程造福人类。

（3）多姿多彩的水利地域文化。遍布各地的治水工程因其不同的地域所属，各具不同的地域文化，表现出浓郁的地方特色，这一方面为全面发展水利旅游事业奠定了良好的基础，另一方面也为水利旅游的多样化提供了可能。越是具有当地特色的文化，越是能吸引旅游者的视线。把水利景观与所在地历史文化、风俗、饮食、商品结合起来，能创造出与众不同的、更具吸引力的水利景区。

（二）以治水工程为核心吸引力的文旅融合模式

1. 体现工程风采，建设水利风景区

随着时间的推移，早期一些治水工程在如今已经失去了功能性，但也形成了独特的文化遗产，而有些水利工程凭借自身强大的功能性以及周边的自然资源仍旧发挥着作用，这些彰显着人类智慧和勤劳的优秀文化遗产资源，通过后期加以休憩或者完善，如在原址上建造博物馆或者进行遗址修复等工作，可以通过优质的文化和精神内涵，吸引游客。

同时，相关的河流还可以立足于治水工程自身同时进行开发水域（水体）及相关联的岸地、岛均、林草、建筑等能对人产生吸引力的自然景观和人文景观等资源，形成风景区与旅游地。相关流域可以以治水水利工程为依托，在具有一定规模和质量的风景资源与环境条件的前提下，开发可供开展观光、娱乐、休闲、度假或科学、文化、教育活动的区域，形成水利风景区。水利风景区以培育生态、优化环境、保护资源、实现人与自然的和谐相处为目标，强调社会效益、环境效益和经济效益的有机统一。水利风景区在进行水利建设中要对现有或新建水利工程及其相连的水体，按照和谐、美观、实用的原则，综合分析社会与经济发展需求、生态与环境需求以及人文与历史需求等，进行景观化处理，从而形成具有一定文化与美学内涵的风景资源，使水利工程及其水体在满足基本的生产功能基础上，在更大的空间、更广阔的范围内发挥综合功能，供人们观光、娱乐、休闲或进行科学、文化、教育活动。

例如，由于小浪底水利枢纽工程的建设，现在的黄河小浪底水利风景区位于河南省洛阳市孟津县、济源市边界，它由小浪底大坝、荆紫山、八里峡、三门峡大坝四个片区，13个景区，113个景点组成。296平方千米的水域中湖汊河巷密布、岛屿半岛众多、自然景观荟萃[①]。

---

① 王会战. 小浪底水利风景区旅游可持续发展研究［D］. 青岛：青岛大学，2007.

2. 挖掘工程文化，开展科普旅游

主题旅游、知识旅游是当今旅游业发展的一个重要方向，科普宣传及阵地的建设已成为建设精神文明的重要内容，人们在旅游休闲过程中获得一定知识，受到文化熏陶，可增加旅游的意义。水利工程及其流域具有丰富的科普教育资源，是开展科普教育活动的理想场所。因此，可以以水利工程建造历史、水利工程知识文化普及为基础，基于历史和科学，发挥水利工程旅游的教育功能，延展旅游活动的精神内涵。例如，可以基于治水工程，打造研学基地，发挥科普教育作用。如都江堰所建设的水利博物馆以及依托于三峡水利工程所打造的三峡工程展览馆等。

3. 深挖水利文化资源，多样化展示

水利旅游资源文化内涵的挖掘，不能凭空想象，应该有的放矢，"的"是水，"矢"是文化，文化应围绕水大做文章。对于以现代科技手段为主的水利旅游资源，如水利工程枢纽、水土保持园等，可以通过文字、图示、模型等手法来展示工程的工作原理、工艺流程、整体布局等内容，使旅游者了解水利，认识水利，同时强化旅游者的水资源意识，全面促进人水和谐发展。水利旅游景区还可以用专题展览的形式，着重呈现与水相关的文学艺术作品，用来丰富景观构成。例如，屈原、杜甫、李白、王维、苏轼、陆游、欧阳修等中国文学史上诸多声名显赫的人物都与三峡有着不解的情缘，写下了许许多多叹咏三峡的诗句。三峡，在众多文化人的深情眷顾中，渐渐成为一种文学的景观，一种自然山水与人类文化和谐统一的境界。这些诗词歌赋都是水利旅游宝贵的无形资源，可以为水利风景区应用，加深游人的文化审美印象[①]。

4. 彰显治水精神，并进行衍生开发

从古到今的治水过程中涌现的治水人物、治水思想和治水精神，启示、影响和塑造着中华民族的精神世界，留下了丰富多彩的艺术瑰宝。大禹以水为师，带领百姓"疏川导滞"，其采取"疏导"的方法治水，对于后世关于堵塞与疏导关系的认识，产生了重大影响；李冰父子以自己的智慧和胆识带领人民开山凿渠，成功创建都江堰工程；明代治河专家潘季驯一生中四起四落，充满坎坷却痴情于治黄治淮，他总结出的"筑堤束水、以水攻沙"的治黄方略，对今天的黄河治理仍然有着十分重要的意义。水利先驱李仪址水利报国；林则徐把兴修水利、解民于困苦之中作为其人生理想……现代"万众一心、众志成城，不怕困难、顽强拼搏，坚韧不拔、敢于胜利"的抗洪精神和"献身、负责、求实"的水利精神为后代传承，丰富了水文化的内涵，并且也已成为普通群众与游客了解历史、追忆先人精神的重要线索，是一种具有独特性与地域性的异质文化资源，成为文化旅游的吸引力来源之一。[②]

除此之外，将治水工程中所涉及的相关人物、所彰显的治水思想加以开发和拓展，在电影、电视剧、戏曲等艺术形式的运用中，如大禹治水这一经典的上古洪荒神话传说，其不仅包含着丰富的

---

① 丁枢，黄江涛. 水利旅游资源的文化内涵及开发思路 [J]. 中国水利，2009（2）.
② 毛春梅，陈苡慈，孙宗凤，等. 新时期水文化的内涵及其与水利文化的关系 [J]. 水利经济，2011，29（4）.

自然人文景观，也蕴藏着深厚的精神文化内涵。基于大禹治水文化与传说资源的开发与挖掘，构建大禹文化博物馆、文化长廊等文化旅游产品，也是一种衍生开发模式。

再者，以黄河三门峡为例，三门峡黄河大坝是我国在黄河干流兴建的第一座大型水利枢纽工程，目前所建设的大坝风景区是一处依托三门峡大坝而建成的风景名胜和人造景观相结合的水库观光游憩类人文景观。三门峡枢纽具有广泛的知名度和丰厚的黄河三门峡文化，挖掘其中的内涵并通过景观、旅游产品等多种途径展示出来，可提升三门峡水利风景区的文化内涵，从而增加吸引力。[①]

第三节　以大河景观文化为核心吸引力的融合模式

本节对大河的自然景观与人文景观进行分类阐述，详细介绍磅礴大气的自然景观与风格各异的人文景观中所具备的独特的旅游吸引力，以及艺术家们与劳动人民赋予大河景观内在的文化底蕴，并进一步探讨了大河景观与文化旅游融合模式的经验借鉴，挖掘景观自身的审美价值潜力，突出旅游教育，打造开放式博物馆等。

一、自然景观文化

自然景观是指受到人类间接、轻微或偶尔影响而原有自然面貌未发生明显变化的景观，如极地、高山、大荒漠、大沼泽、热带雨林以及某些自然保护区等。大河的自然景观必然是以大河为中心，最重要的是流动的水体。其自然景观既包括大河自身形成的自然景观，如蜿蜒曲折的河道、起伏多变的河床、天然浅滩、深潭、沙洲以及水生动植物等，也包括大河沿岸的自然景观如河岸带的植被绿化等。

大河呈现给人们的变化多端、磅礴大气的自然景观。大河的自然生态系统具有强烈的美感和个性化的气质，这种景观本身作为一种独特的旅游吸引物，为旅游者的旅游活动提供了独特的空间。除此之外，大河的神秘感使其成为众多文人骚客审美寄情的重要载体，艺术家们往往会超越大河本身，运用才华描绘出理想中的大河之美，表达自己的思想，给予大河自然景观内在的文化感。例如在中国古代，黄河、长江往往是文人雅士们去国怀乡、发思古幽情之处。而莱茵河也一直都是诗人、画家、音乐家等寻求灵感的重要场所。

（一）大河自然景观文化类型

从旅游景观的角度来看，大河景观常被分为河源区、上游区、中游区、下游区、河口区。河源区情况根据地理位置不同而变化多端，湖泊、沼泽、冰川等景观各异；上游区往往山峦叠嶂、河面狭窄，瀑布、深涧等水流形态变化丰富；中游区的河床常由卵石和沙砾组成，常能见到沙洲和辫状

---

① 李明堂. 三门峡水利枢纽工程管理探索与实践［J］. 人民黄河，2017，39（7）.

水系；下游区水面宽阔、水流平稳，沿河风景常在水中形成倒影，水边常常可以看到大面积的芦苇景观；河口区河道平缓，水体流动缓慢，植被数量不多，绿化普遍比较简单。

1. 河源区

河源区是指大河的发源地，是其最重要且最具有生态活力的部分，形态各不相同，有湖泊、沼泽、冰川等。河源区纯天然的自然生态景观是吸引旅游者的重点所在。如长江、黄河、澜沧江—湄公河源头的三江源地区雪山连绵、沼泽密布、细草如毯，该地区以拥有大山、大江、大河、草原、雪山、湿地、动物乐园等原生态的自然景观；而密西西比河（Mississippi River）的源头则是明尼苏达州（mini sota）北部地区的伊塔斯卡湖（Lake Itasca），那里有上万个星罗棋布的湖泊，这些大大小小的湖泊像天然水库一样，对密西西比河的水源补给具有重要的调节意义。

河源区通常也是最为脆弱的部分，其生态环境往往极易遭到破坏。全球变暖、特大暴雨等自然环境的变化，还有人类不合理的开发利用均会影响河源区原有的生态平衡，进而影响大河原有水质与周边生存的部分物种，减少物种多样性，原有的生态景观也会随之改变甚至不复存在，因此在对河源区进行旅游开发时应当注意生态环境的保护。

2. 上游区

大河上游区的特点是落差大、水流急、河谷狭、流量小，河床中经常出现急滩和瀑布。同时大河往往在上游区分割山地，其支流如辫，弯弯曲曲，也因此形成了许多风景秀丽的峡谷。例如科罗拉多河（Colorado River）从落基山（Rocky Mountains）脉发源，最终进入墨西哥西北部，在科罗拉多高原上共切割出19条主要峡谷，其中最深、最宽、最长的一个就是科罗拉多大峡谷（the Grand Canyon）。科罗拉多大峡谷凭借其超乎寻常的体表和错综复杂、色彩丰富的地面景观而闻名，吸引了众多的旅游者前往；而南美洲的伊瓜苏河（Iguacu River）在与巴拉那河（La Plata Parana River）汇合前在经过一个U字形大拐弯时，从宽广的河道陡然跌入一条峡谷，形成了伊瓜苏瀑布。1984年，伊瓜苏瀑布被联合国教科文组织列为世界自然遗产，目前其在阿根廷境内的部分已被开辟为国家公园。

大河上游区的峡谷、瀑布等景观地带旅游资源丰富、物种丰富、地质地貌奇特。使其也成为许多IP的取景地之一，美国西部片里经常出现的牛仔骑马挎枪、骑马飞奔、寸草不生的红土地上的情景就是科罗拉多大峡谷地区的写照。但由于地形险峻、交通不便等问题，大河上游区旅游开发难度较大，投入有限，开发程度较低。同时峡谷、瀑布地区发生自然灾害的频率较高，生存环境也较为恶劣，因此大河上游区人口总数往往相对较少。

3. 中、下游区

大河中游区一般流经低山、丘陵地区，河流流速明显下降，流经地区形成较为宽阔的谷地平原；大河下游区的特点是河床宽、流速慢，从上游侵蚀了大量泥沙到了下游后因流速不再足以携带泥沙，结果这些泥沙便沉积在下游两岸，浅滩到处可见，冲积平原便也逐渐形成。此外，由于大河中下游区河流宽阔，航运便捷，这两个区段与上游区、河源区相比，人口分布与城市群通常较为密集，农工业发达，也是人类文明的发源地与繁盛地，著名的平原有亚马孙平原，长江中下游平原等。但也有例外，上文提到的位于亚马孙河中游地区的亚马孙平原热带雨林密布，动植物种类繁多，人口分布较少，农工业并不发达。

大河的中下游地区大部分地势平缓、交通便利，旅游的可进入性与可到达性都比较强。同时大河中下游区段独特的水文化也是其独特的旅游资源，其中下游区段往往流域面积较广，跨越不同的区域甚至不同国家，因此各国家、省市区域内的大河中下游区段的水文化也各不相同，不同地区借助本区域内的大河自然景观文化进行相应的旅游开发，开发方式与开发水平也都不尽相同。

4. 河口区

河口区是河流的终段，是大河与海洋相互作用的地方，按其地貌特征，河口分为溺谷型河口、峡湾型河口与沙坝型河口。溺谷型河口一般分布在中纬度地区，为沿海平原河的河口。当河流来沙较多时，泥沙沉积在河口区，便改变溺谷形态，发育成三角洲，如中国长江口和珠江口、美国密西西比河口；当河流来沙较少时，则保留或部分保留溺谷或河口湾的形态，如英国泰晤士河口、法国吉伦特河口、中国钱塘江河口；峡湾型河口仅分布于高纬度地区，冰川河槽受海侵后形成峡湾。其特点是在口门附近有高出水底约几十米的岩坝，岩坝之内水深可达数百米，向陆地可延伸几百千米。如挪威桑格纳峡湾、苏格兰埃蒂夫峡湾；沙坝型河口一般分布在热带地区或泥沙沉积活跃的沿海地区。

（二）以大河自然景观文化为核心吸引力的文旅融合模式

1. 审美价值潜力巨大，探险旅游未来可期

大河最直接的文化价值体现在审美上。大河从河源区至河口区，河流形态随地质地貌不断改变，造就了千姿百态的水体景观，具有声、形、色等诸种美的形态，成为旅游审美活动中的主要观赏对象，可以使旅游者充分领略大河自然景观的美感，获得最佳的旅游效果。旅游者面对同一江河景观，在不同时间、不同空间均会获得不同的审美体验。除此之外，大河及其周边形成的险峻的自然景观也吸引了不少的极限运动爱好者。在确保安全的情况下开展部分极限旅游项目，如激流皮划艇、障碍回旋、激流马拉松、漂流、皮艇球项目等，可以带给旅游者不一样的旅游体验。

较为有特色的大河自然景观有以下几类：

（1）峡谷景观，长江第一湾的虎跳峡、科罗拉多大峡谷、雅鲁藏布大峡谷等。

（2）河川清流，如广西"山青、水秀、洞奇、石美"的漓江风光、富春江等。

（3）飞瀑流泉，如黄河壶口瀑布、庐山香炉瀑布、杭州虎跑泉、贵州赤水河畔清泉等。

案例 2.1

黄河壶口瀑布自然景观与探险旅游

黄河奔腾至山西吉县与陕西宜川县交界处后，两岸石壁峭立，河口收束狭如壶口，形成世界上最大的黄色瀑布——壶口瀑布。壶口瀑布为两省共有旅游景区，是中国国家级风景名胜区，国家

4A级旅游景区。瀑布宽达50米，深约50米，最大瀑面3万平方米。滚滚黄河水从远方浩浩荡荡又铺天盖地地压来，惊涛怒泄，声若雷霆贯耳，急湍冲荡，状如水里生烟。[①]1992年壶口瀑布被评为"中国旅游胜地四十佳"之一，2002年被国土资源部评为国家地质公园及地质遗迹保护区，2008年被评为国家4A级旅游景区。[②]

壶口瀑布最佳观赏期分为两段，一是春季4~5月，正值农历三月间，漫山遍野的山桃花盛开，岸边冻结的冰崖消融，称为"三月桃花汛"；二是秋季9~11月雨季刚过去时，河边众多山泉小溪，汇集大量清流，阵阵秋风吹过，常有彩虹出现，叫作"壶口秋风"。这两个时期，水大而稳，瀑布宽度可达千米左右。主瀑难以接近，但远远望去，烟波浩渺，威武雄壮。大浪卷着水泡，奔腾咆哮，以翻江倒海之势，飞流而下。真是"水底有龙掀巨浪，岸旁无雨挂彩虹"。此情此景，实非笔墨所能形容。数九寒冬，壶口瀑布又换上了一派银装玉砌的景象，在那瑰丽的冰瀑面上，涌下清凉的河水，瀑布周围的石壁上挂满了长短、粗细不一的冰滴溜，配上河中翻滚的碧浪，更显示出一派北国特有的自然风光。

壶口瀑布景区主要游览内容有：黄河文化游、秦晋峡谷游、自然生态游、民俗风情游、地质考古游、爱国主义教育游。[③]景区属于河流侵蚀沉积岩系河床构成的自然风景区，这里黄河黄土交相辉映、峡谷高山相互衬托，体现出了南秀北雄的地域特色，是最能体现黄河黄土风情文化的旅游景点，而309国道吉壶段改线，高速公路直通壶口景区以及景区建设、管理等方面的提升，壶口瀑布景区具备了更好的迎客条件。据统计，2016年，壶口瀑布景区接待游客近百万人次，门票收入达到7600万元；2017年游客人数突破180万人次，2018年的11月25日就迎来了全年的第200万名游客。

除此之外，经过多年的发展，壶口瀑布景区也越来越受到极限旅游爱好者的青睐。1997年，台湾著名特技演员柯受良驾驶汽车成功飞跃壶口瀑布；1999年，黄河娃朱朝晖驾驶摩托车成功飞越黄河，使壶口名扬天下。

（本研究根据案例来源归纳整理）

2. 旅游式学习，全方位科普

在河源区与上游区可主要采用生态旅游与科普宣教相结合的模式，河源区独特的环境条件、上游区震撼的生态景观为旅游者提供了理想的度假休闲场所。第一，考虑到河源区与上游区生态系统的脆弱性，采用以"保护自然环境"为主题的生态旅游形式较为恰当；第二，在河源区和上游区，针对长距离旅游者可开展科普宣教的活动，重点关注河源区生态功能展示、河源区生态保护等方面，增强中下游区段居民"饮水思源"、保护河源区的意识。针对短距离旅游者可从大河的起源、

---

① 黄河魂——壶口瀑布. 临汾市文化和旅游局 http://wlj.linfen.gov.cn/contents/1217/364040.html
② 壶口瀑布. 陕西文化旅游网 http://www.sxtour.com/html/index.html
③ 壶口瀑布. 延安市地方志编纂委员会 http://fzbz.yanan.gov.cn/yats/fjmq/yicx/9143.htm

文化底蕴、历史上相关的神话传说等着手，增强其对于大河源头与上游的认识；也可面向全部旅游者进行地质地貌、物种知识的科普教育，使其了解大河源头区与上游区的文化生态，并进行跨文化解读，最终使旅游者全方位地获得深层文化教益。

位于美国亚利桑那州的科罗拉多大峡谷在1919年被开辟为"大峡谷国家公园"，迄今为止其成为美国游客众多且影响深远的国家公园之一。该峡谷公园旅游模式的开发便十分注重科学和生态教育功能，公园内介绍景点的解说牌和旅游手册中，注重传播科学知识，对游客进行地质学、生态学等科学教育。如画出游人所站地点所看到的岩层的剖面图，标出不同岩层的名称、特点、形成年代以及这些特定形状、颜色的成因等问题。帮助游人探求地质地貌的变化、了解自然界丰富信息，获取历史文化知识。管理人员培训也特别注重生态科普的教育。[①] 除此之外，大峡谷公园依据其自然景观雄奇、动植物生态分布丰富、以自然生态和探险运动旅游为主的特点，系统设计了以探险和科考旅游市场为主的特定客源解说系统，以人与自然和谐相处的理念作为大峡谷景区解说系统建设的出发点，在一定程度上发挥了旅游教育功能。

3. 营造文化环境，活化自然生态

一些哺育人类的名川大河，其形态气势常常在民族精神的塑造方面发挥着潜移默化的作用。江河的特质常常与人的精神品质相辅相成，例如中国的黄河、长江，千万年推沙负重、奔流不息，让人们感受到中华民族的源远流长和悠久历史。每条大河孕育出来的这种江河文化，对于旅游者而言，具有不可替代的吸引力。在这种前提下，大河的自然景观只是观光旅游的基础资源，而文化环境则是大河旅游的核心所在。每条大河各区段旅游资源丰富，但文化内涵的缺失往往是大部分大河旅游发展受限的关键所在。

在旅游开发时，应当做到尊重大河各区段的自然生态文化，合理地将大河自然生态文化活化。例如世界著名的峡谷文化旅游区——科罗拉多大峡谷中，为保护自然文化生态环境，景区内部不仅不设立人为景观，严格控制旅游者数量保护景区，并且提供旅游景区车通过聘用当地居民兼职司机与导游来限制私人汽车。除此之外，也可以在不破坏大河自然景观的前提下，采用恰当的形式和载体向旅游者展示大河自然生态文化的内涵，突出生态文化主题，发扬大河精神。如将山水诗画意象运用到大河旅游开发的基础设施设计当中，既可保留当地特色，又不会破坏其原本的自然景观。

4. 善用IP（知识产权）

从古至今以大河为载体的各类神话传说、历史名人传记等数不胜数，每条大河景观中往往拥有无比丰富的历史内涵，而这些也是其他大河无法复制的。近现代以来，大河以其独特的自然景观也吸引了众多电影、电视剧来此拍摄，介绍大河本身自然风光的各类纪录片也不断涌现……这些都成为大河可利用的IP，潜力巨大。对这些潜在IP进行开发运营，可以吸引原有IP粉丝并扩大粉丝群，

---

① 万津津，沙润，刘泽华. 美国科罗拉多大峡谷地质旅游管理特色及对我国的启示［J］. 生态经济，2017，33（10）.

推动产业化升级转型。例如目前长江流域内着手打造的《新三峡》纪录片项目，来记录长江三峡的生态之美、人文之美；除此之外，在嘉陵江的 IP 建设上，相关部门也提出了以纪录片为载体，通过全媒体思路和跨媒体行动"打造嘉陵江文化经济产业带和嘉陵江绿色经济走廊"的想法。[1]

二、人文景观文化

人文景观是人类通过自身的需要，在某个人居住的土地范围内，利用自然界的材料进行加工，在自然环境的基础上叠加出人类自己所创造的景观。人类在此特定的区域内繁衍生息，生活中特殊的痕迹给此区域留下了具象的景观，除此之外，此景观还赋予其人文、文化等非物质性的含义，形成与其他地域不同的景观。大河沿岸地带积累了不同历史时期、不同民族特色、不同地域风格的人文景观。

人类自古依水建城，逐水而居，河流为人类的生存与生活、农业的灌溉提供了不可或缺的重要水源，绝大多数的国家和城市都有哺育自己民族与人民、孕育自身灿烂文明的"母亲河"。如巴黎塞纳河沿岸、伦敦泰晤士河沿岸、开罗的尼罗河沿岸等，均因蕴含丰富多彩的民族人文景观而成为世界著名的都市人文景观带，显示出较高的历史文化价值和旅游价值。

（一）大河人文景观文化类型

大河的人文景观可分为以下三种类型：

1. 沿河城市人文景观

大河是许多沿河城市所特有且必不可少的资源，对很多沿河城市与跨河城市的发展、形态建构起着非常重要的作用。

第一，城市内部单个建筑物与水体交相辉映的人文景观。流动的水体可使得场景始终处于变化之中，为大河沿岸城市建筑景观带来活力。例如法国巴黎的塞纳河，贯穿整个巴黎，成为城市独特的景观，塞纳河上游一座座让人惊叹的桥梁，其两岸还有辉煌的宫殿、古老的教堂、高雅的雕塑等，如卢浮宫、巴黎圣母院、埃菲尔铁塔等。而顺着英国著名泰晤士河漂流而下，展现在眼前的是最古老、最隆重的英伦风格的建筑景观，大本钟、伦敦塔桥等世界名片历历在目。同时以贵族文化为主的建筑在泰晤士河畔一直源远流长，一些王公贵族的私人庄园和宅邸也保存至今。

第二，城市外围的防洪堤坝、人工堤岸等人文景观。防洪堤坝是建在大河流经的山地地貌城市的重要防洪建设。大河在流经山地时，河流两岸高低起伏，陡缓相间，水位变幅大，洪水陡涨陡落，特有的地貌形式与水流条件会使城市外围形成特殊的防洪模式与立体的人文景观界面，如由滨江路、防洪护岸、码头等要素构成沿江人文景观格局；[2] 而对于水流平缓地区的城市，往往会采取河道堤岸的工程措施，即在河流与城市的交界处种植植被，增加绿化面积，降低城市受江河水流、

---

[1] 袁瑞. 大型纪录片《嘉陵江》开机沿江 30 余区县发表绿色宣言. 中青在线 http://www.cyol.com/
[2] 刘平. 山地城市沿江防洪设施的景观化研究［D］. 重庆：西南大学，2017.

风浪的侵袭与冲刷的程度。这种绿化布置在增加河道稳定性与安全性的基础上，形成了赏心悦目的城市绿色人文景观，如植物墙等。这几类人文景观处于水域与陆域的交界处，靠近江河的最前端，也是人们除了在滩地之外进行亲水旅游活动的热门人文景观场地，沿河散步、跑步、骑行等亲水活动通常被自发开展。

第三，沿河城市整体的文化氛围。一般在历史悠久的沿河城市，大河往往是该城市生成与发展的动因，世界上大多数历史文化沉淀最为丰富的城市都建立在大江大河附近，例如南京"十里秦淮"的文化意象，就是以长江下游支流——秦淮河为核心，由两岸的历史人文景观为主题所构成的。城市整体作为人文景观，其文化形象因大河而具有强烈的识别特征。水的映射性可丰富城市的人文景观，而水位的变化也提供了变化多姿的景观。如浙江省钱塘江杭州湾部分，受河口形状、河床地貌、水文、气候等因素的综合影响，"钱江秋涛"闻名国内外，每年农历八月十八左右，钱塘江涌潮最盛，大量旅游者蜂拥而至，观赏钱塘江潮的盛况。

江河沿岸城市的人文景观本身就是极具文化底蕴的，旅游者行走其中，观赏沿岸建筑与水光融为一体的美景，漫步在河岸边，便自然而然可以感受到江河沿岸城市人文景观的独特魅力。许多对江河沿岸城市人文景观的旅游开发往往通过建造文化广场、景观公园来添加其文化底蕴，这类开发需要注意开发形式与原本景观文化、生态系统的侵略感与和谐性，否则一不小心便会起到画蛇添足的作用。因为当一个地区的文化气息已经达到一定程度后，过多的人为修建文化标识物可能会起到相反的效果。

2. 沿河村镇人文景观

江河水可用于灌溉农田与日常饮用，大河沿岸通常土壤肥沃、农业发达，优良的水环境是依靠农耕、渔猎为主的人类向大自然索取物质财富并赖以生存的理想定居地。此外由于大河的水陆交通便利，也为聚落的选址提供了动力，因此多数传统聚落的选址依存于河流。而依水而居的村镇与大河的关系从生存依赖慢慢发展到主动利用。加上人类的审美情趣，便在大河沿岸创造出一系列独特的村镇人文景观，主要有公共空间的人文景观与私人宅邸的人文景观。

江河沿岸村镇中公共空间的人文景观中包括村镇中的水街水巷、水榭水亭、临水楼阁、水口园林等人文景观。[①] 夹河而建的村镇往往以河道作为主要交通方式，由此而形成独特的景观——水街水巷，当地居民与旅游者乘船在水街水巷穿行中别有一番韵味。如威尼斯与我国苏浙一带的水乡村镇；水榭水亭、临水楼阁则是村镇中所建造的既有实用价值又具观赏价值的人文景观。既可作为供村民、游人休息之地，也可作为点缀景观与观赏美景之用。如雷峰塔、魁星阁与各色各样的水榭楼阁等；水口园林大多设在村边，并多伴随建有文昌阁、书院、庭园等公共建筑，行成独特的水景观。

江河沿岸村镇中私人宅邸的人文景观往往蕴含民居主人的个人审美特色，因此，每座私人宅邸

---

① 熊海珍. 中国传统村镇水环境景观探析［D］. 重庆：西南交通大学，2008.

的景观各不相同。中国江河沿岸村镇的私人宅邸建造中蕴含风水、等级制度、天人合一等思想，假山、泉水、游廊、漏窗等营造出的意境美使旅游者流连忘返。

3. 其他人文景观

桥梁。桥是跨越大河的一种有效的人工构筑物。它是水路、陆路交通的交汇处，也是休憩、观景的场所。同时桥梁景观以其流畅的形态，多姿多样的造型吸引着众多旅游者。部分桥梁还会有历史事件或人物的介入使其成为独特的人文景观。此外由桥梁延伸出来的桥亭、桥廊、桥屋、桥楼等，也是便于旅游者观赏风景的场所。有的桥楼中还供有神像，人们可以进香礼拜，祈求平安。

神祀庙宇。从古至今，宗教信仰是人文景观中并不少见的元素之一。几乎每一个地方、每一个行业都有其所信奉的神灵。依水而生、踏船而行的人们同样也有着非常深厚的信仰——水神。人们为表达自己的虔诚之心，往往在江河沿岸设立庙宇，祈求风调雨顺。例如我国的黄河、长江，从商代开始，几乎每届朝廷都会祭祀、立庙、赐封号等。

堰、坝。堰是一种横越河川的障碍设施，可以改变水流的特性，经常用来引水进入灌溉圳道、防范洪水、量测流量及增加水深以利于通航。水坝是建筑在溪流、河流和河口的屏障，用来防止洪水泛滥，生产水力发电，或是储水作饮食和灌溉之用。除上述作用外，堰和坝也因其大体量、大跨度的视觉震撼较容易成为所在自然环境中的地标，人类在建造时所投入的复杂感情和思想也会赋予它们更多的文化内涵，最终形成的综合景观会容易受到旅游者的青睐。著名的堰和坝有中国的都江堰、长江三峡大坝，建在科罗拉多河上的美国胡佛大坝等。

都江堰位于岷江由山谷河道进入冲积平原的地方，它灌溉着灌县以东成都平原上的万顷农田。岷江流经地势陡峻的山川上游后，一到成都平原，水速突然减慢，因而夹带的大量泥沙和岩石随即沉积下来，淤塞了河道。每年雨季到来时，岷江和其他支流水势骤涨，往往泛滥成灾，雨水不足时，又会造成干旱。公元前 256 年，李冰为蜀郡守时，在前人治水的基础上，依靠当地人民群众，在岷江出山流入平原的灌县建成了都江堰。都江堰水利工程体现出了古代建筑艺术之高超、选材之精妙，原本工程基本完好，让人不得不为之叹服，其历经 2000 年时光，依然屹立眼前，造福人类，使其成为游客到都江堰市后不得不前往瞻仰的一景。

（二）以大河自然景观文化为核心吸引力的文旅融合模式

1. 景观"活化"，人文精神的挖掘与传承

蜿蜒千年的江河沿岸所孕育出来的人文景观是一个时代风貌的浓缩，是人类洞悉历史、探究未来的宝藏。通过将城市的人文景观建筑与流经城市的河流结合，可深入挖掘沿河城市作为一个整体人文景观的文化内涵，使其文化形象鲜活起来，也能为旅游注入更加优质、更富传奇色彩的文化内容。同时也可借助每一类人文景观背后的文化内涵，开展各种主题游、体验游、研学游等旅游方式，打造独具特色的，具有人文精神的旅游精品。

案例 2.2

寿宁县廊桥旅游开发

福建省北部的寿宁县，溪峡密布、汇入赛江。先民为方便交通，越溪架桥，连通两岸，建立了各种各样的廊桥。寿宁县现存各种廊桥就有40多座，其中贯木拱廊桥19座，这19座卧藏于寿宁县内完整的贯木拱廊桥其数量、质量都居全国首位。寿宁以木拱廊桥年代系列最全、单拱跨度最长、收藏有全国仅见的造桥契约等特点，被誉为"世界贯木拱廊桥之乡"。[1]

寿宁廊桥既具有独特的风水文化与祭祀文化，又具有浓厚的乡土文化底蕴。关于风水文化，寿宁古廊桥的选址与中国风水相辅相成，其选址多在乡村溪流的上游或下游，建在下游，通常是用以补溪流形成的风口，保本村风水。建在上游的通常与下游形成一种相呼应的景象。目前寿宁19座廊桥中有4座建在上游，8座建在下游。[2]

近几年来，寿宁县依托历史悠久的廊桥文化，加强对19座木拱廊桥的保护修葺工作，并制定有关措施加强对桥匠技术传承与保护，打造廊桥建造团队，让建造技术不断层、不消逝，闽浙两省还建立统一协调的保护木拱廊桥机构，提请立法机关制定廊桥保护的法规，统筹保护与发展规划，实施有效保护，维护生态环境，科学合理利用，成立由闽浙两省相关部门、有关专家、木拱廊桥所在地参加并全力支持的木拱廊桥"申遗"机构。同时，进一步对廊桥文化进行挖掘、弘扬、传承，通过开展多种形式的廊桥主题活动，塑造廊桥文化品牌，传承地域工匠精神。同时，寿宁县也以度假游、养生养老游、乡村体验游为发展重点，持续开展旅游产品和服务创新，丰富业态，提升品质。[3]

除此之外，寿宁县也是福建省旅游投资发展集团打造多样化休闲旅游目的地和红色文化主题精品线路的重点区域。2018年7月，寿宁县与福建旅游投资集团合作建设"难忘下党"旅游项目。该项目计划用2年时间，在寿宁县下党乡，以党建带动旅游发展，整合周边乡村旅游、休闲农业、运动康体、梦龙文化等资源，通过多样化旅游产品的复合开发，面向大众旅游市场，连片打造集党性教育、研学教育、生态休闲等功能于一身的中国红色旅游新地标及全国新时期党性学习小镇。

（本研究根据案例来源归纳整理）

2. 旅游公共服务设施建设，深度体验景观文化底蕴

大河沿岸的人文景观往往沿着大河呈线状分布，旅游开发程度各不相同，各地的基础服务设施也良莠不齐。想要让旅游者可以长时间在人文景观处停留，深度体验其文化魅力所在，公共文化和

---

[1] 庄严，缪淑秀. 闽浙联手保护非物质文化遗产古廊桥[N]. 福建日报，2019.
[2] 何明春. 闽东周宁县木拱廊桥研究[D]. 福州：福建师范大学，2014.
[3] 赵巧红，吴通华. 寿宁深化文旅融合推进全域旅游发展：秀外慧中开新景. 闽江日报网. http://cmstop.ndsww.com/p/17875.html

旅游设施的建设必不可少。对于江河沿岸的村镇而言，这些村镇的人文景观旅游资源均十分丰富，多年来依水而居所形成的生活习惯与文化底蕴也是十分原生态的，通过推动基础设施全面化、公共服务一体化建设，拓展旅游服务功能，既可以增加旅游者的停留时间，又有利于当地村民发展庭院经济、特色渔业，实现文旅产业的纵深发展。

3. 沿河城区文旅融合共建，打造开放式大河博物馆

江河往往流经多个城市、多个区域，其沿岸人文景观文化相通相似，通过将各个城区之间的空间地域融合共建，既可以避免重复性建设，节约资源，也能使融合区域的经济和社会发展获得收益最大化。例如，浙江省绍兴市按照"天人合一，古今同源"理念，以"传承古越文脉，展示水乡风情"为主题，力图把大运河构筑成一条融历史、文化、生态为一体的历史文化风景线。而江苏省扬州市的目标则是大运河遗产全域游，计划利用城区遗产河道串联着诸多遗产点的优势，整合环水慢道系统、水上交通系统，再通过古城街巷的串联，将众多的遗产点串联成片，打造一个开放式的大运河博物馆。[1]

4. 文艺创作助力旅游，丰富景观文化内涵

推动文化艺术精品创作与旅游品质空间提升的融合，让文化创意赋予旅游业最生动鲜活的元素，使旅游具有持久的生命力。可以实景版旅游演艺、历史的艺术再现等形式，丰富江河沿岸人文景观的文化内涵。例如，万里长江源头的通天河因辑入《西游记》而名闻天下，其周围著名的文化便是晒经石，可通过在晒经石旁重演《西游记》片段为其注入新的活力，从而避免"有说头没看头"、到地"打卡游"的现象出现；除此之外，在某些江河沿岸的水神庙宇之地，可通过在某一特定时间点重演祭祀大典的方式，丰富人文景观的文化内涵。

第四节 以大河沿岸民俗为核心吸引力的融合模式

本节对大河沿岸丰富多彩的民间艺术与岁时节庆进行分类阐述，介绍了部分独具特色的大河沿岸民间艺术与岁时节庆活动，了解其文化价值与旅游发展现状，并提出以其为核心吸引力的文旅融合模式。大河沿岸民俗与旅游相融合，既可以为沿岸民俗的保护提供资金支持和社会关注度，也可以为大河沿岸地区带来可观的经济收入。此外，采用一些现代化的新媒体手段来展现和营销大河沿岸民俗活动也值得考虑。

一、民间艺术

民间艺术是针对学院派艺术、文人艺术的概念提出来的。[2] 民间艺术主要指物质民俗范畴中的

---

[1] 姜师立. 文旅融合打造大运河缤纷旅游带[N]. 中国文化报，2019-06-01（007）.

[2] 刘晓真. 从乡俗仪礼到民间艺术——当代山东商河鼓子秧歌文化功能的变迁与传承[J]. 北京舞蹈学院学报，2004（1）.

民间美术和手工艺，如民间绘画、纸艺、器皿、家具、玩具、织物及其他物品。[①]

江河流域都有民间艺术，依河而居的先人们创造了丰富多彩的民间文化。从邈远的史前时期，绵延数千年，这些民间文化植根在老百姓的日常，随同生活的变迁，有生长，有发展，也会有消亡，这是一种独具特色的文化资源。民间艺术含有丰厚的历史文化遗存，对游客具有天然的吸引力，只要被合理地开发就可成为富有吸引力的旅游产品。来自全国各地乃至全世界的游客往往具有不同的文化背景，在交流中会产生文化的碰撞与交融，这会促进本地民间艺术的传播与发展。除此之外，依托各类文化艺术节的举办、文化学术交流会的召开等文化与旅游交融的形式，为文化的交流与传播提供了重要的载体。

但同时，古老的民间艺术在现代文明的冲击下很容易受到破坏，它们自身产生的微弱的甚至为零的经济效益并不足以支持其传承保护，这就需要政府的资金投入。旅游业的发展，不仅能够为文化资源的保护提供资金支持，而且还可以为民间艺术带来可观的经济收入和社会关注度。[②]

（一）民间艺术类型

丰富多彩的民间艺术可以有多种角度的分类方法，按照制作技艺的不同，可将民间艺术分为染织绣类、塑作类、剪刻类、雕镂类、民间玩具、绘画类、编织类、扎糊类、表演类、其他方面等（图2.2）。

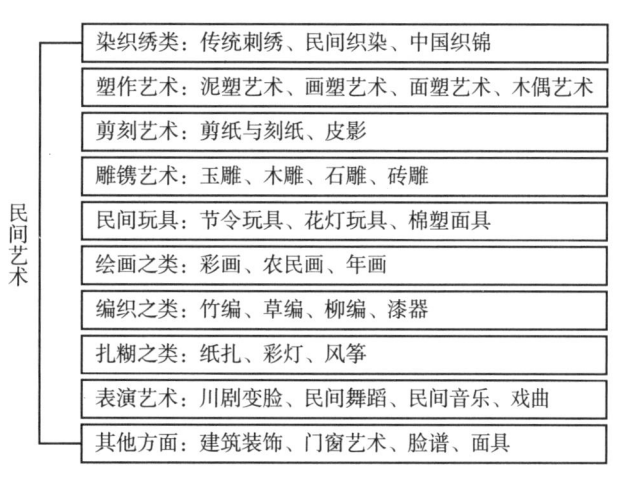

民间艺术
- 染织绣类：传统刺绣、民间织染、中国织锦
- 塑作艺术：泥塑艺术、画塑艺术、面塑艺术、木偶艺术
- 剪刻艺术：剪纸与刻纸、皮影
- 雕镂艺术：玉雕、木雕、石雕、砖雕
- 民间玩具：节令玩具、花灯玩具、棉塑面具
- 绘画之类：彩画、农民画、年画
- 编织之类：竹编、草编、柳编、漆器
- 扎糊之类：纸扎、彩灯、风筝
- 表演艺术：川剧变脸、民间舞蹈、民间音乐、戏曲
- 其他方面：建筑装饰、门窗艺术、脸谱、面具

图 2.2 民间艺术种类

资料来源：本研究整理。

1.染织绣类民间艺术包括印染、织锦、刺绣

染织绣艺术用一定的创造方式、表达手段来表达和完成的纺织产品之美。民间传统的染织绣艺术在效率、成本、精确性等方面虽比不上现代化工业所生产出来的产品，但其在技巧、气息、韵

[①] 李牧.民俗、艺术及审美经验——兼论季中扬《民间艺术的审美经验研究》[J].民族文学研究，2017，35（4）.

[②] 王霞.民间艺术融入文化旅游业发展[N].山西日报，2019-06-03.

味、纹样表达和色彩运用上都有着不可替代的独特魅力。我国海南省的黎族生活在热带雨林地区，植物染料资源十分丰富，几千年来，心灵手巧的黎族妇女凭借多种多样的植物类染料资源，不仅发明了先进的纺织技术，也成为最优秀的"调色师"。[1] 而存续3000年以上的黎族染织绣工艺，被誉为中国纺织史上的"活化石"，入选我国第一批国家级非物质文化遗产名录。

案例 2.3

黎族织锦

黎族，是中国最古老的民族之一，也是海南岛上最早的土著居民。在漫长的劳动生活岁月中，黎族人民积淀了丰富的传统文化，创造了许多宝贵的文化艺术财富。黎锦，就是黎族工艺奇葩中最绚烂的一支。黎锦是黎族纺、织、染、绣工艺的统称。今天在海南的五指山地区黎族村寨，黎族少女仍然使用原始的踞织腰机，综杆提花、断纬织绣，精心制作自己美丽的传统服饰[2]。

作为黎族文化的一个重要的组成部分，黎族织锦的价值并不单纯地在于其高超的织造技艺，其在艺术上的审美价值和所传达的社会文化价值越来越受到民族文化研究学者的重视。2006年6月，黎锦被列为国家级非物质文化遗产，标志着黎锦所传达的黎族原生态文化的价值与意义的被认可。与此同时，通过当地政府的重视及促进，黎锦的旅游观光价值也在逐渐被挖掘、开发和推广，使它与黎族人民的生活习俗、船形屋、民歌等一起成为黎族文化的显著标志。

黎锦在艺术上的选择以及创作特点，充分反映了黎族的生活、地理环境、民族审美情趣和特定的民族文化传统。例如，黎族服饰女装的图案或以黑色布为底，或直接织缀而成，多源于日常农耕生活及身处的山野、河流及动物、日月星辰、云彩，但又不是生活的照搬，而是抽象为直线、图形和几何形状的"花纹"。这种抽象性表现了黎族妇女惊人的观察力与想象能力、创造能力，因而具有极高的文化价值。在色彩的搭配上，因受色料采撷制作的局限，黎锦色调较为单纯，但单纯并非是呆板，通过织造者的别出心裁的处理，即使是简单的黑、红、黄、白，也编织出一片丰富而令人遐思的天地。

黎锦作为一种先进的纺织印染技术，代表了黎族在生产方面的技术创造和创新，集中体现了黎族人民的聪明才智，也对黎族地区的经济生活产生了促进作用。通过对这一非物质文化遗产的保护和宣传，有利于外界对黎族地区的了解，进而"筑巢引凤"，形成以旅游产品开发为主的经济产业，打造黎族地区旅游品牌，形成独特的文化产业，吸引海内外旅游观光客慕名而来，使之充分领略黎族文化之魅力，促进该地区经济的发展。[3]

（本研究根据案例来源归纳整理）

---

[1] 符少玲. 黎族非物质文化遗产资源开发对策研究——以黎族纺染织绣技艺为例 [J]. 大众文艺，2016（4）.
[2] 高丰，高昌. 海南民族民间工艺美术概述 [J]. 装饰，1999（3）.
[3] 周国耀，吴晓雯. 海南黎族织锦的艺术特点与文化价值 [J]. 改革与开放，2009（8）.

2. 塑作类民间艺术

塑作类民间艺术包括泥塑、面塑、画塑与木偶艺术。它是指以捏、塑、堆、纳等方法为主制作的民间艺术品。面塑的发源地就处于山西所在的黄河流域，在干燥的黄土地上，再普通不过的麦面馒头，摇身一变成了精致的工艺品，这其中凝注了山西人丰富而深厚的文化内涵。有花馍就有幸福，纯朴的山西人将好吃又好看的山西花馍普遍运用到当地居民的婚宴、寿宴和祭祀等重大活动中。山西民间花馍的造型样式自成一体，自古就有"山西花馍甲天下"美誉。[①] 山西闻喜花馍也于2008年被列入国家级非物质文化遗产。[②]

3. 剪刻类民间艺术

剪刻类民间艺术包括剪纸、刻纸、皮影。剪刻艺术整体简括、明快拙朴、顿挫有秩、对比强烈，具有极高的艺术价值。中国各地，均有剪纸习俗，风格迥异，做工良莠不齐，题材各有不同，剪纸材料千差万别。真正优秀的剪纸，当数江苏的扬州和天津杨柳青的单色剪纸，两地的剪纸，以造型优美、纸张考究、刀功犀利而著称。

4. 雕镂类民间艺术

雕镂类民间艺术包括玉雕、木雕、石雕、砖雕。雕与镂都是指在竹木、玉石、金属等介质上面进行的刻画方式。在雕刻类民间艺术上，非洲的木雕、欧洲的石雕等都是极具代表性的。除沙漠地区外，生活在尼罗河、尼日尔河流域的非洲人民在繁衍生息之际，创造出了多种多样的木雕艺术。除此之外，大河沿岸也经常出现立于河岸两侧的石碑、人像雕刻等。

5. 民间玩具

民间玩具包括节令玩具、花灯玩具、棉塑玩具、益智玩具等。中国的民间玩具种类繁多，制作精巧，件件都称得上是手工艺品。民间玩具作为中国民间工艺美术的一种独特艺术形式，也在漫长的发展过程中深受中国文化的影响，从而以其鲜明的娱乐性、趣味性和祈求性充实着百姓的生活。16~17世纪时，中国的民间玩具已流传至海外，同时也出现了受外来影响的玩具，如"洋片"和一些益智玩具。山西的民间玩具，是黄河流域传统文化的宝贵遗产和民族艺术发展的活化石。山西民间玩具由于地域性及各自依附的地理条件和生活习俗环境的差异而略有不同。晋南主要为黄河、汾河沿岸，地处河谷水道，沟壑纵横，加之古文化悠久，民间风俗古老，这一带民间玩具比较古朴雅拙；晋中地区处于平原地段，地理条件优越，经济文化繁荣，生活富裕，民间玩具比较秀丽雅致，精巧细腻；晋北地区多为山地丘陵、塞上高原，民间玩具比较雄浑豪放、粗犷质朴。

6. 绘画类民间艺术

绘画类民间艺术包括彩画、农民画、年画。民间绘画是相对于文人画、宫廷画、宗教画和现

[①] 薛雪. 面花装饰特色的比较研究——豫东沈丘顾家面花与山西花馍的比较研究[J]. 大众文艺，2017 (05).

[②] 楼兰. 晋城花馍：可以吃的民间艺术[J]. 中外文化交流，2014 (11).

代的学院派绘画而言的，其源头来自远古岩画、彩陶装饰画等原始艺术。民间绘画的特点是它有着强烈的地域色彩、民族色彩，与民间习俗相结合、有着很强的程式化色彩，造型古朴、夸张，色彩鲜明，既有工笔重彩之作，也有淡雅娟秀之作。民间年画的风格因地域不同而呈现出多种多样的面貌，如山西晋南一带的汉族流行的木版年画，主要产于山西临汾。木版年画是我国历史悠久的民间艺术，它源于上古岩画和祭祀，是伴随着年节民俗而产生的大众文化产物，也是百姓非常喜闻乐见的一种艺术形式。其中平阳（今临汾）木版年画以其风格严谨，雕镂精工，造型古朴秀丽的特色独树一帜，成为影响深远的民间艺术。平阳木版画是一个综合艺术，它将木版雕刻技法与绘画构图、色彩、线条、题材等结合融汇，是民间艺人智慧创造艺术的结晶，也是民俗文化、戏曲文化、历史文化等方面极其珍贵的形象资料。①

7. 编织类民间艺术

编织类民间艺术包括竹编、草编、柳编、漆器等。中国的竹、草、藤、柳、棕麻编织工艺品像其他工艺品一样，有着悠久的历史。草编主要产地是浙江、河南、山东、湖南、广东、广西等地。漆是取自漆树的一种天然胶质，是大自然赐予人类的珍贵材质，经过人工处理，提炼出漆泥，制成的各种器皿干后极为牢固并轻盈不变形。

8. 扎糊类民间艺术

扎糊类民间艺术包括纸扎、彩灯、风筝。扎糊是指以竹、木、铁丝等为骨架，以丝绸、纸等为外面，通过扎结、扣榫、糊裱等方法制作工艺品的方法。扎糊主要指的是纸扎类的作品，广义的纸扎包括彩门、灵棚、戏台、店铺门面装潢、匾额及人物、戏文、风筝、灯彩等项。

9. 表演艺术

表演艺术包括川剧变脸、民间音乐、民间舞蹈、戏曲、锣鼓艺术。民间艺术中大量的内容都是通过人的舞动、戏耍、操作、歌唱等形式来完成的，与这种表现方式有关的艺术门类都可称为表演类艺术。川剧变脸是运用在川剧艺术中塑造人物的一种特技，是揭示剧中人物内心思想感情的一种浪漫主义手法；民间音乐指与专业音乐创作方式、创作手法、创作风格、创作特征不同的，并形成于民间、流传于民间的歌舞音乐、器乐等各种音乐体裁；民间舞蹈是流传于民间、具有鲜明的地域特点和民族风格的舞蹈形式；戏曲是中国人喜闻乐见的艺术，它的历史源远流长，经历了孕育、形成、发展和兴盛等各个时期；锣鼓艺术是民间艺术中不可缺少的一部分，对于民间舞蹈、戏曲等的气氛渲染至关重要。山西临汾是锣鼓艺术的主要发祥地之一，古老的黄土高原文化，造就了经久不衰的民间锣鼓艺术。在众多的锣鼓艺术中，威风锣鼓是影响最大、流传最广的一种民间打击表演艺术，被老百姓俗称为"家伙"或"威风家伙"。②

---

① 石瑜. 平阳木版年画与赵大勇老人［J］. 文学界（理论版），2012（08）.
② 白英芳. 临汾威风锣鼓溯源初探［J］. 现代交际，2017（11）.

案例2.4

临汾威风锣鼓

威风锣鼓又称"锣鼓""家伙",相传,威风锣鼓起源于尧舜,普及于明代,兴盛于清代,这种锣鼓的演奏形式距今已有4000多年的历史,在晋南地区广为流行,中心地带为临汾地区的洪洞县、临汾市、汾西等地。临汾威风锣鼓气势恢宏、粗犷豪放、音域宽广、刚劲激昂、形式多变,深受大众的喜爱,其在乐器的配置、打法、表演队伍、演员着装和表演方面十分重视,每一个环节都要尽显威风。在临汾地区,威风锣鼓是一项重要的表演内容。早在尧舜时期,人们就用锣鼓表示欢庆,如今则是在每年的农历正月进行表演,并参加县市举办的娱乐比赛。威风锣鼓还曾多次在国内外的大型活动中表演,扬名中外。2006年被列为第一批国家非物质文化遗产。

临汾威风锣鼓的演奏由鼓、锣、钹、铙组成,四件乐器各有特色,将它们组合在一起,根据各自的特点,按一定的比例分声部演奏时,其音响效果浑厚、激昂,如雷贯耳。当击锣打鼓时,表演者的身体随着鼓点的节奏一曲一伸,做出张弛有度的律动,达到了音乐与身心的共鸣。威风锣鼓之所以威风,离不开好的乐曲,威风锣鼓的乐曲结构别具风格,常以对奏的形式来进行表演,演奏者之间一呼一应,多次重复,好似在对话。数千年来,从汾河东岸的羊獬到河西的历山,敲锣打鼓是沿途迎送时不可或缺的项目,因而产生了《西河滩》《四马投唐》《风搅雪》等诸多曲牌,并且各村有各村的曲牌,每个曲牌背后大都有一个故事或寓意,串连起来便形成了独具魅力的地域性锣鼓文化[1]。

随着威风锣鼓的不断发展与传承,它已经由祭祀祈雨活动发展为民间社火和喜庆节日的压轴表演节目。时代延续下的威风锣鼓表演方式千姿百态,它在自身发展中也有着多样的社会文化功能。如祭祀祈福、欢庆娱人、凝聚力量、交流沟通等。人们通过击鼓表演,在统一的节奏声中默契配合,感受心灵的共振,通过舞蹈与高亢的锣鼓声进行感情的交流与宣泄。这种形式的交流可以是同村亲朋的相聚祝福,也可以是村村之间的竞争联谊,但不论是交流还是比赛,人们之间的相互祝福是必不可少的,其中都饱含着人们的感情色彩与地域特色。

在漫长的历史发展中,临汾威风锣鼓汲取了各时代的艺术精髓,其表演体系也日趋完善。威风锣鼓表演中融入了音乐、舞蹈等多种艺术形式,丰富了表演内容,形成了自己独特的艺术风格和音乐内涵,不论音响、曲式还是舞动、场面,都尽显出威风锣鼓的威风之势,其所表现出的文化功能也让我们深深地感受到威风锣鼓深层的文化底蕴。[2]

(本研究根据案例来源归纳整理)

---

[1] 张李鹏. 铿锵鼓点里的坚守. 临汾日报. http://cnepaper.com/lfrb/html/2019-05/08/content_6_1.htm
[2] 张玥. 临汾威风锣鼓的表演特色及文化功能[J]. 当代音乐,2016(19):75-77.

其他方面的民间艺术有建筑装饰、门窗艺术、脸谱、面具等。建筑装饰的主要题材是具有镇宅、辟邪和迎吉纳祥功能的吉祥动物、花卉，或在民间广泛流行的传统戏曲画、历史故事、吉祥画等；中国古代门窗的文化内涵是由门窗纹饰与图案表现的，门窗的装饰也体现了房屋主人、官员、商人与文人迥异的审美情趣、身份地位和财富象征；脸谱可以上溯到远古时期原始人黥面文身的习俗，直接源头则是古代倡优女乐的脂粉装和俳优滑稽的粉墨装，是中国古老的化妆艺术；中国的面具历史悠久，品类丰富，最早广泛运用于原始初民的狩猎活动、图腾崇拜、部落战争和巫术仪式，之后随着社会的发展，宗教色彩减弱，娱乐色彩慢慢增加，民间的大头舞等面具的出现也极大地丰富了面具的文化。

（二）以大河沿岸民间艺术为核心吸引力的文旅融合模式

民间艺术是一种特有的文化资源，近几年来，随着民间艺术越来越受到重视以及旅游业的快速发展，民间艺术被越来越多的游客认知，特别是那些具有地方特色、传承时间较长的民间艺术给游客带来了强烈的吸引力。民间艺术也得到了更多文化创意性的开发、包装和市场化的运作，以更多元化的形式展现给旅游者。

1. 民间艺术的美学价值

民间艺术往往体现了人类对审美的本质性格，表现出人们对大自然纯天然的美的追求，同时也加入了人们对艺术追求的思想情怀，及对未来美好生活的期盼，以我国的民间艺术为例，古老的祖先在民间艺术中往往蕴含着对于"长寿、吉祥、求福、喜庆"等的美好祝愿。民间艺术丰富多彩的艺术表现形式和其具有的极大的审美价值，使得观赏、体验民间艺术活动也成为人们的一种审美活动，它涵盖了人们对于"美"的意愿，可使旅游者感到放松愉悦，也可以陶冶旅游者的审美情操。

除此之外，民间艺术也具有极大的研究价值，国内外有很多民间艺术研究者，多年一直致力于对民间艺术这一传统美学的研究，也会前往民间艺术的发源地进入深度考察与了解。例如，杨先让历时30多年，推出的《黄河十四走——黄河民艺考察记》，书中不仅详述了诸如安塞腰鼓、汉画像石、木版年画、剪纸、农民画、石刻等民间技艺，还分析了其艺术风格、反映了民俗风貌、折射了文化内涵等，并记录下当时优秀的民间艺人，如刘兰英剪纸、苏兰花剪纸、潘京乐皮影等，为黄河流域的民间艺术留下了珍贵的图文资料。

2. 民间艺术舞台化

将民间艺术舞台化是对旅游目的地进行塑造和建构的过程，将特定地域、特定群体的民间艺术有效地展示给旅游者观看，民间艺术舞台化内容涵盖民间艺术的各个方面，最为常见的是民间音乐、舞蹈戏曲等的舞台化。近年来，随着非遗文化保护项目的推进，越来越多的非物质文化遗产被列入民俗旅游的舞台化展演范畴。[①] 民间艺术的舞台化展演不仅带来了巨大的旅游经济效益，还促

---

① 李毓. 传承与创新：民俗文化的舞台化研究［D］. 广州：广东技术师范大学，2013.

进了民间艺术的传承与创新。但民间艺术舞台化的同时，也要注意一些潜在的问题，如浅层次的表象化展示而非具有历史深度的提炼和挖掘，为了满足游客的求新、求奇、求异的心理，不求历史内涵，但求轰动奇观效应等舞台化的文旅融合模式。想要成功地将民间艺术提炼后融入舞台作品中，首先，要走访民间，感受原生态的非遗民间艺术并了解其历史渊源，在学习交流过程中触发创作思维与灵感；其次，甄选与此类非遗民间艺术相契合的题材；最后，进行内容和形式的构思与编排，确保展演的形式最大限度地保留民间艺术的原真性。

3. 民间艺术+旅游新媒体

民间艺术向来安静、温润、小众、单一。然而在数字媒介快速发展的日子里，"酒香不怕巷子深"保守传播方式已行不通。借助互联网的传播优势，让民间艺术与新媒体旅游相结合，使用图像、文字、影像、语音等多种表现形式加以整合，从而发展全新的、综合性的文化旅游产业。例如，通过新媒体旅游大咖的镜头记录民间艺术的制作生产过程，创作一系列的图文与视频作品，在各种社交媒体网站上进行推介，对于民间艺术的传播与旅游目的地的营销具有极大的帮助作用；也可搭建"电商"营销平台，通过平台的运营，来实现旅游目的地民间艺术的宣传推广与旅游产品营销的结合，也可带动民间艺术电子商务衍生产业链的发展。将传统民间艺术与新媒体旅游相结合，也是一种对于优秀传统文化的继承与创新。

4. 旅游文创产品的设计

现阶段旅游纪念品千篇一律，无当地特色，已是旅游纪念品开发中的一大难题。旅游纪念品的特点之一在于其蕴含了旅游目的地的某种独特元素，在其他地方难以购买，而从人民日常生活中取材的民间艺术活动大多具有浓厚的民族地域性特点，例如：民间有八仙过海、鹊桥相会、女娲补天等神话故事，也有水浒人物、武松打虎、岳母刺字等民间故事，还有麻姑献寿、四季平安等具有浓厚的民俗特色的艺术形式，这些民间艺术均有着巨大的开发成为文创产品的潜力。

在意识到民间艺术品在旅游开发中独一无二的文化价值后，便可以将民间艺术与旅游相融合，既可以促进旅游者对于民间艺术的认识了解，又可以制造出具有目的地特色的旅游文化纪念品。目前已有一些地区利用当地民间艺术来开发旅游纪念品，且广受欢迎。例如苏州刺绣、蔚县剪纸、陇东布艺等。

二、岁时节庆活动

岁时节庆是民俗文化的一个重要组成部分，岁时节庆中的民间艺术反映了社会在时间运行和周而复始的循环过程中人们的观念与情感。大河沿岸往往是农业发达的地区，在漫长的几千年的文明历程中，岁时节庆中的各种农事节日和基于与农业生产有关的信仰而产生的各种节日，对大河沿岸民众的生活和艺术创作产生了巨大影响。

（一）中国岁时节庆活动

俗话说"十里不同俗"，因为地理环境、饮食等方面的差异，我国长江流域与黄河流域（也称

"南北方")的各种岁时节庆的民间习俗自然也会略有不同,下面列举了我国常见的几个岁时节庆基本习俗以及长江流域与黄河流域对于岁时节庆的习俗差异。

春节,俗称"过年",又叫阴历年,是一年当中最隆重、最富有特点的传统节日。在千百年的历史发展中,各地由于文化习惯不同,又各自形成了一些较为固定的民俗习惯和民俗活动。北方讲究吃饺子,取"新旧交替、更岁交子"的意思。又因为饺子的形状颇似元宝,煮熟后一盆盆端上桌象征着"新年大发财,元宝滚进来"的好兆头;南方则多数做年糕和汤圆,年糕谐音"年高",取吉祥如意的好兆头。汤圆也叫"团子""圆子",取"全家团圆"之意。

元宵节,农历正月十五,也称上元节。正月是农历的元月,古人称夜为"宵",所以称正月十五为元宵节。而十五日又是一年中第一个月圆之夜,又被称为上元节。元宵节是传统民俗大节,城乡居民盛行吃元宵,象征合家团圆。在闹元宵的方式上,北方过年会有扭秧歌、踩高跷等表演活动,南方则会表演舞龙舞狮。

端午节,农历五月五日为"端午节",又称"端阳节",有吃粽子的习俗。相传,有的是为纪念爱国诗人屈原;有的是有"吃了端午粽,一年不生病"的说法。端午节清晨,家家户户门窗上方有插艾蒿或柳条、小孩手脚腕有戴五色线绳之俗。长江流域盛行在端午插艾以避蚊驱邪,而河西走廊一带则盛行插柳枝用来祈求风调雨顺;同时黄河流域不像北方流域多大型湖泊,大部分地区水域缺乏,龙舟竞渡的娱乐形式较长江流域的少;除此之外,黄河流域端午的娱乐风俗除了射柳、吃粽子外,在西北地区还有"点高山"的习俗来驱狼抗旱。

辞灶,农历腊月二十三,俗称送灶君上天庭赴会的日子,故称"辞灶",人们对此节甚为重视,其隆重程度仅次于过大年,故有"小年"之称。小年在各地有不同的概念和日期,北方地区是腊月二十三,部分南方地区是腊月二十四。民间有用麦芽糖做成的糖瓜祭灶之俗,用糖瓜作供品、燃放鞭炮、烧纸钱、送灶君上天。

(二)西方大河沿岸岁时节庆活动

1. 巴黎沙滩节与塞纳河摇滚节

从2002年开始,巴黎市政府极具创意地推出巴黎沙滩节(Paris Plages),用细沙、棕榈树、游艇、折椅、吊床和遮阳伞等在塞纳河畔营造出了美丽的海岸风情,将沙滩搬到了巴黎街头。在每年7~8月的塞纳河畔,人造沙滩、几百棵棕榈树和各种沙滩运动设施,还有极具风格的小酒吧等一应俱全,整条塞纳河岸成为热闹非凡的巴黎沙滩,让众多无法远行旅游的巴黎人或前来巴黎游览的游客感受独特的城市沙滩。对于没有大海的巴黎来说,沙滩出现给这座城市带来别样的美丽风情。而自2003年以来的每个夏天,塞纳河摇滚节作为夏季狂欢的闭幕式,都会有上千人在巴黎圣·克鲁德国家公园举行为期3天的摇滚音乐节。这是巴黎地区最大的夏季音乐节之一,也是欧洲不可错过的文化节之一。在这几天,国际流行摇滚乐手、当代音乐代表人物以及初出茅庐的音乐新人都聚集在塞纳河畔,参与者可以在公园内五大演出场地全身心投入到音乐节中。

2. 狂欢节

狂欢节是欧美各国的传统节日。它起源于古罗马的农神节，发展于中世纪，盛行于当代。狂欢节的节期，各国不一，有的开始于元旦，有的开始于圣诞节或其他日子。但多数国家在二三月间气候宜人之时举行。意大利的海滨城市维亚雷焦是举世闻名的狂欢胜地之一。在莱茵河流域如科隆、杜塞尔多夫、亚琛、美因茨等地，狂欢节叫作 Karneval，而参加狂欢节的民众叫 Narr。这个地区的狂欢节是德国最热闹的，尤其是科隆的狂欢节举世闻名。

3. 泰晤士河节

这是伦敦最大型的免费户外艺术节，在每年的9月举行。该节日是一场户外庆祝活动，主旨是庆祝伦敦及泰晤士河的悠久历史，举办地点是位于伦敦眼和伦敦塔桥之间的露天公共场地。盛宴上的食物全部取材于英国最佳的可持续食品制造商。"河上船队巡游"是节日中一项著名的水上活动，一列由新旧不一的船只组成的船队将从伦敦塔桥一直航行至威斯敏斯特桥。泰晤士河畔节日经典活动将在圣凯瑟琳码头（St Katharine Docks）展出一批经典的木质帆船，而"驳船拉力赛"（Barge Pulling Race）活动将再现进入蒸汽时代之前水手们在泰晤士河上操作满载货物的驳船的场景。狂欢节期间，音乐节目和街头戏剧表演丰富多彩，引人注目。

（三）以大河沿岸岁时节庆活动为核心吸引力的文旅融合模式

1. 节庆旅游

节庆旅游是指以大河沿岸的自然景观资源与人文景观资源为依托，确立特定的主题，凭借一系列在岁时节庆中的特色民俗挥动来吸引旅游者的。在推广进行节庆旅游之时，要在节庆活动文化内涵建设上下功夫，强化节庆活动文化建设，提升文化内涵，形成独具特色的节庆文化。

除此之外，也可以对当地在校大学生进行招募培训，使他们作为节庆活动日开展时的志愿者，加快节庆旅游的发展速度[1]。对高校学生的培养，不仅有利于其自身能力的提高，也有助于以大学生为代表的青年群体创意思路、推动整体的节庆旅游活动，从而吸引更多的青年旅游者。

2. "浸入式"文化旅游体验

浸入式体验已经在娱乐、教育、商业等行业崭露头角。节庆文化旅游是一种体验经济，不只是满足顾客的物质需求，更重要的是为顾客带来了新鲜的生活体验和丰富的精神享受。在参与节庆活动过程中，游客融入情境中，在现场深度接触文化信息，使得他们对于文化活动的内涵在体验的基础上形成认同、接受、喜爱的情感，然后自发地再向更多的人传播，从而形成口碑效果。国外旅游业有很多节庆活动，如巴西圣保罗狂欢节、美国圣诞节、西班牙斗牛节、德国慕尼黑啤酒节、英国泰晤士河节等，每年节庆期间都产生不俗的经济效益[2]。

---

[1] 杨宇轩. 游客满意视角下的旅游节庆活动开发——以秦淮灯会为例［J］. 大众文艺，2019（8）.
[2] 张力. 用节庆文化牵引旅游体验经济［N］. 中国文化报，2019-06-22（007）.

案例 2.5

泰晤士河节

泰晤士河文化节也被称作泰晤士河狂欢节,是世界最大的免费户外艺术节之一,文化节的活动区域为伦敦塔桥与西敏士桥之间的泰晤士河畔南岸,自1997年创设以来,每年吸引世界近百个国家和地区参与,以多种形式展现不同国家地区和民族的文化、形象与魅力。

泰晤士河对于英国的重要性不言而喻,这条贯穿英格兰三个省份的"母亲河"是英国的重要象征之一,它和众多伦敦的地标建筑一起构成了闻名于世的景致。为了赞颂这条河,每年的整个9月份伦敦都会举办英国最大的户外艺术节——泰晤士河节(Totally Thames Festival)。在这一天,大约有170个激动人心的艺术文化活动在伦敦泰晤士河岸边举办,270多万人一同庆祝,这也是英国人和夏天告别、迎接秋天的仪式。

节日期间会有一小瓶来自泰晤士河的源头Kemble的河水被传递,搞笑市长Boris Johnson也参加过圣水传递仪式。节日开幕当天会有传统仪式,非常值得一看的是英国男人们会围成一圈跳一种叫作Morris Dance的民间舞蹈。仪式结束后后,这瓶水将像奥运圣火一样经过千千万万的志愿者通过游泳、划船、跑步等方式传递到伦敦,"圣水"到达伦敦后会被送进博物馆展览几天,之后节日期间再时不时地被拿出来展览。

同时The Great River Race比赛可以说是整个节日中最大型的活动。在这里,你可以看到各种奇葩的船齐聚泰晤士河一同比赛:龙舟、维京海盗船、夏威夷小船、鸭子船、铁架船……300艘形态各异的船可谓百花齐放!在Richmond与Ham House之间的河岸区域观看船赛,可以目睹冠军穿过终点线,礼炮齐鸣,随后沉浸在热烈的欢呼中。Tower Bridge附近的两岸也是绝佳围观地点。不想扎推的游客也可以选择塔桥两岸偏远一些的美食摊位,可以一边吃美食一边看划船比赛。

除了传统的船赛外,游客还有机会亲自体验现代的水上激情,London RIB Voyages公司推出的高速船艇,声称是泰晤士河上的火箭!和三五好友一起坐上船艇,全程15分钟在世界最著名的河上感受速度与激情。比较文艺和喜欢摄影的游客也可以去参观伦敦相片画廊举办的展览,这儿有来自世界各地新锐摄影师关于伦敦的摄影展。他们的拍摄主题就是泰晤士河或伦敦桥一带的景观。

案例来源:伦敦泰晤士河文化节首次邀请中国城市报名展示形象. 人民日报海外版 www.haiwainet.cn

(本研究根据案例来源归纳整理)

第二章 空间推进模式

大河流域面积广大，具有线性空间特征，呈带状分布，由此导致大河流域发展旅游需要采取空间推进的模式。本章以概念界定和具体实例来探索三种大河流域发展旅游的模式，分别是增长极模式、点—轴模式以及线性开发模式。其中，增长极模式选择合适的节点培育增长极，点—轴模式把节点的选择与发展轴的建设联动，线性开发模式针对线性空间或廊道进行开发，可以说是逐步推进地发展大河流域旅游。

第一节 增长极模式

增长极模式是大河流域旅游空间推进的重要模式，也是点—轴模式发展推进的基础前提。本节首先界定河流旅游增长极的内涵并分析其培育条件；其次，对河流旅游增长极辐射作用的发挥进行阐述；最后，以长江流域内旅游增长极发展模式为案例，深入解析如何具体培育河流旅游增长极和发挥其辐射作用。

一、河流旅游增长极的形成

（一）增长极的内涵

"增长极"概念，是法国发展经济学家佩鲁（Francois Perroux）在1950年发表在《经济学季刊》的"经济空间：理论与应用"一文中首次提出的。他认为："增长并非同时出现在所有地方，它以不同的强度首先出现在一些增长点或增长极上，然后通过不同的渠道向外扩散，并对整个经济产生不同的最终影响。"[1] 增长极可以是产业增长极，即经济空间上的某种有比较优势、竞争优势和较大关联度并有广阔市场前景的产业；也可以是城市增长极，即地理空间上的某个城市或城市群具有强有力的吸引、集聚或极化效应，扩展效应或涓流效应；并具有区位优势、资源优势和市场优势。[2]

（二）河流旅游增长极的内涵

河流是线性空间，呈带状分布，旅游资源较为分散且在流域内分布不均衡。有的地方旅游资源丰富，有的地方旅游资源却贫乏。河流流域旅游开发处于起步阶段时，宜采用增长极模式，就是要

---

[1] 安虎森. 增长极理论评述 [J]. 南开经济研究，1997（1）.
[2] 颜鹏飞，邵秋芬. 经济增长极理论研究 [J]. 财经理论与实践，2001（2）.

旅游资源丰富的地区先发展起来，然后带动旅游资源一般或贫乏的地区，从而使整个河流流域内的旅游发展得到全面提升。增长极模式为河流流域内旅游产业展开的空间形式之一。一般来说，河流旅游增长极的选择和培育，必须加强旅游业与地方性产业的融合，增强前后相关联效益，并逐步建立河流旅游增长极体系或系统，不断拓展增长极吸引辐射范围，借以全面振兴流域经济，并为下一时期实行点—轴开发打下基础。

所谓河流旅游增长极，是指河流流域内，某个旅游中心城镇或者某个旅游景区的发展规模和发展潜力超过其他旅游目的地，成为河流流域旅游中心。河流旅游增长极具有极化作用，能够促进河流流域旅游中心发展，并且以空间扩散机制对周边流域内旅游目的地产生支配、连锁、推动作用，引起游客在河流流域内流动和停留，从而引起旅游产业的集聚或扩散，带动周边流域旅游目的地发展。在增长极模式中，主要旅游企业、接待服务设施均集中于河流流域旅游中心，该旅游目的地同时作为旅游者进出的集散地和开展旅游活动的依托基地。①

（三）河流旅游增长极的培育

河流旅游增长极的形成，可以是通过自上而下的行政手段，直接选定河流流域内某些旅游目的地作为增长极；也可以通过自下而上的市场手段，例如流域内旅游资源丰富、交通条件优越的目的地自然形成增长极，目前我国这两种类型的河流旅游增长极都存在。选择和培育河流旅游增长极是依据一定条件的，不能靠主观意志脱离实际选择，选择的旅游增长极是要能够实现产业集聚、人才集聚、资本集聚、信息集聚、技术集聚的旅游目的地。

1. 资源先行

旅游资源的密集程度与特色条件是河流流域内旅游增长极形成的前提条件。旅游资源数量多，形成一定规模，就会具备较好的发展潜力；旅游资源质量高，对于旅游者的吸引力大，能够迎合市场需求，使有限的投资资金发挥最大的经济效益；旅游资源具有独特性，比周边地区同类资源相对重要程度高，具有较强的竞争力和资源的不可替代性，这些都是一个旅游目的地成为河流流域内旅游产业增长极的关键因素。

河流旅游资源一般被分为自然旅游资源与人文旅游资源两类。自然旅游资源主要是河流本身以及河流旅游地所依托的自然资源。人文旅游资源主要是依托河流产生的社会环境、人民生活、历史文物、文化艺术、民族风情和物质生产等具有旅游功能的事物和因素。

2. 基础先行

旅游设施包括河流流域内旅游目的地基础设施及旅游专用设施，例如住宿接待设施，包括各种餐饮设施、住宿设施；旅行设施，包括各种交通工具、停车场景区索道及通信设备；游览设施，包括各种标识、旅游者集散点、环境优化设施等；旅游安全及保健设施，包括景区保卫处、急救处等，旅游设施与旅游的发展是相互促进及制约的关系。旅游设施健全的河流流域内的旅游目的地能

---

① 樊信友. 区域旅游业空间布局研究［D］. 成都：四川大学，2004.

够产生较强的集聚能力，旅游设施滞后则会限制增长极的发展。因此，旅游设施健全是河流旅游增长极形成的基础条件。

其中河流流域内旅游目的地交通通达度尤为重要，它包括外部交通通达度和内部交通通达度。旅游交通的任务就是要解决旅游者在定居地与河流流域内旅游目的地之间的往返、从一个目的地到另外一个目的地，以及在一个目的地内的各地区间便利往来的问题。它不仅要解决往来不同地点间的空间距离问题，而且更重要的是要解决其中的时间距离问题。旅游交通不但是旅游者完成旅游活动的先决条件，它本身也是大河流域内旅游收入和旅游创汇的重要来源。[①]

3. 政策先行

由于我国大河流域内部分地区位置偏远，旅游发展水平较低，当地居民对于旅游的社会认知不足，人才匮乏等原因，政府的扶持对于增长极的快速成长仍至关重要，自上而下通过行政手段选择和培育的河流旅游增长极占据主导地位。从带动落后地区旅游业发展，促进河流全域旅游的角度考虑，培育的河流旅游增长极初期发展以极化功能为主，扩散功能较弱，带动范围较小，需政府采取适度有效措施扶持和引导增长极与周边落后地区的旅游人才交流、合作。

二、河流旅游增长极辐射作用的发挥

法国经济学家及增长极理论的提出者佩鲁认为，增长具有不均衡性，通常出现在一些增长点或增长极上，然后通过不同的渠道向外扩散。这也就是增长极的辐射作用机制。然而，缪尔达尔在《经济理论和不发达地区》等著作中，考察了增长极对周边地区的辐射能力，使用了"回波效应"和"扩散效应"来区分增长极对周边区域两种相反的作用力。[②]

对于河流旅游增长极来说，"回波效应"和"扩散效应"是指：一方面，流域内旅游发达地区可能对周边地区产生阻碍作用或不利影响，旅游产业投入、产出联系和知识溢出等因素导致旅游要素向流域内河流旅游增长极进一步聚集，从而扩大地区之间的旅游业发展水平差距和经济差距，即"回波效应"；另一方面，集聚会造成流域内河流增长极地区的土地成本上升、城市拥挤、旅游市场饱和以及超过当地旅游承载力等现象，河流旅游增长极地区的旅游要素，包括旅游企业和旅游人才等，会向周边地区扩散，推动周围贫困地区的旅游发展，逐渐缩小地区间旅游和经济发展差距，即"扩散效应"。

在大河旅游发展的初期，把有限的人力、物力和财力集中起来发展旅游资源丰富或者区位条件优越的旅游目的地是必然的。各种旅游资源和要素集中在河流旅游增长极后，使当地基础设施日益完善，旅游产业发展迅速，旅游人才不断聚集，游客人数逐年攀升，成为流域内旅游核心地区，产生极化效应，区域内旅游经济发展迅速。同时，对于河流旅游增长极周边地区，也会产生"回波效

---

① 陶云. 旅游产业增长极理论与应用研究 [D]. 合肥：安徽师范大学.
② 颜鹏飞，邵秋芬. 经济增长极理论研究 [J]. 财经理论与实践，2001（2）.

应"和"扩散效应"。避免"回波效应",增强"扩散效应",才能真正发挥增长极的辐射作用。

(一)衡量周边区域对于河流旅游增长极的承载能力

河流旅游增长极出现极化效应以后,周边地区与增长极的旅游发展就会出现不平衡现象。周边地区在一定时期内能够承受其与增长极之间的旅游发展差距增大所带来的压力,是增长极模式得以运用的一个必要条件。降低河流旅游增长极与周边地区的贸易成本,由易到难的顺序同旅游业不同部门合作,建立区域协调机制和补偿机制,对旅游发展落后的周边地区进行一定的经济补偿,促进旅游人才的交流和沟通。

(二)加强河流旅游增长极与周边地区之间的交通设施建设

交通一直都是旅游活动的一大重要因素,交通的通达性影响一个地区旅游业的发展。河流旅游增长极想要产生扩散效应,辐射周边地区旅游业的发展,需要健全的交通基础设施。不管是旅游产业的扩散,旅游人才的流动和交流,旅游信息技术的传播,游客的大量涌入,这些河流旅游增长极对周边地区的扩散效应都依赖于大河流域内的交通网络。

三、长江流域的旅游增长极发展模式

长江发源于"世界屋脊"——青藏高原的唐古拉山脉各拉丹冬峰西南侧。干流流经11个省、自治区、直辖市,于崇明岛以东注入东海,全长6300余千米,比黄河长800余千米,在世界大河中长度仅次于非洲的尼罗河和南美洲的亚马孙河,居世界第三位。[1]

长江三峡是长江流域内重要的河段,从四川奉节到湖北宜昌,全长约200千米,自西向东依次为瞿塘峡、巫峡、西陵峡。[2]2004年,原国家旅游局、国务院三峡办、国家发展改革委、国务院西部开发办、交通部、水利部等联合印发《长江三峡区域旅游发展规划纲要》,指出在旅游空间发展布局中,三峡旅游发展空间架构为"两极、三轴、三区、四带"。打造重庆都市旅游增长极和宜昌都市旅游增长极。三轴为以长江干线航道及沿线公路和铁路等为骨架,以重庆和宜昌为两大节点,包含传统三峡旅游线路的所有旅游吸引物的主干线发展轴线;以东北—西南走向的209国道为依托,辐射带动神农架、大宁河、恩施、张家界、湘西州、铜仁等地的"湘鄂陕"旅游发展轴;以西北—东南走向的乌江下游和渝怀铁路及区内公路为依托,辐射带动川东、渝西、赤水河等地的"川渝黔"旅游发展轴。三区为重庆大都市商务旅游片区、新三峡生态—文化旅游片区、两坝一峡—水电明珠旅游片区,是三峡区域旅游核心区。四带为赤水河旅游辐射带、乌江—梵净山旅游辐射带、清江旅游辐射带,是三峡区域辐射区的子区域。

金沙江是长江的上游河段,流域位于我国青藏高原、云贵高原和四川盆地的西部边缘。[3]金沙江下游流域跨越了云、贵、川3省,面积约为224712.3平方千米。近年来国家大型水电的开发建设

---

[1] 水利部长江水利委员会. 流域综述 [EB/OL]. http://www.cjw.gov.cn/zjzx/cjyl/lyzs/.
[2] 杨达源. 长江三峡的起源与演变 [J]. 南京大学学报(自然科学版),1988(3).
[3] 徐长江,范可旭,肖天国. 金沙江流域径流特征及变化趋势分析 [J]. 人民长江,2010,41(7).

极大地改善了该区域内的交通条件，选择和培育增长极带动整个区域发展显得尤为重要。由此，昭通和宜宾分别被选择为金沙江下游的河流旅游增长极，政府以及各界高度重视并大力支持两地发展。

（一）金沙江旅游增长极的培育

1. 资源先行

昭通和宜宾的旅游资源丰富，使其快速成为金沙江流域内的两大河流旅游增长极。昭通历史文化积淀深厚，是云南文化三大发源地之一，为中国著名的"南丝绸之路"的要冲，旅游资源类型多样。昭通市的"朱提文化"、大山包、小草坝、峡谷温泉、大关黄连河等资源特色鲜明、类型互补。宜宾拥有蜀南竹海、兴文石林、夕佳山古民居、李庄古镇国家4A级旅游区4处，另拥有国家级风景名胜区2处、省级风景名胜区5处，省级湿地公园2处。宜宾与云南省水富市交界处的向家坝水电站，坐拥着许多绮丽的旅游资源：峡谷风光、温泉，毗邻云南大山包、四川屏山县老君山、龙华古镇、书楼古镇，其库区旅游可能成为宜宾旅游的新增长极。宜宾和昭通丰富的旅游资源，使其与周边地区形成多方面的联系，对多种层次、多样化需求的市场具有多方面的影响力。

2. 基础先行

金沙江下游流域内的旅游增长极昭通和宜宾，其核心交通区位和可达性良好的交通环境不容忽视。昭通素有"咽喉西蜀，锁钥南滇"之称，位于国家规划的"攀西—六盘水经济开发区"腹心地带。近年来金沙江流域内的交通状况有了明显的改善并将有持续的提升。昭通作为连接云、贵、川三省的重要门户地位和交通枢纽作用日益凸显。在推进溪洛渡、向家坝、白鹤滩水电站的水电资源开发中，大量的建设与资源投入将极大地带动昭通相关地区交通沿线和附近城镇各行业的发展，交通设施和周边生态环境也会不断改善，可带来大量的投资机会。因此，连续十多年大型水电站的开发建设将是昭通千载难逢的历史发展机遇。

宜宾是四川省内以水、陆、空综合立体交通网络著称的区域中心城市。铁路方面已建成电气化铁路干线内昆铁路，2009年确定开工建设成贵高速铁路。高速公路已建成通车的有内宜高速、宜昆高速，宜乐高速、宜泸高速正在建设中。航空方面，已有一个4C级菜坝机场，2009年规划建设的4D级宗场国际机场已经开工建设。水运方面，长江干线叙泸航道于2007年整治开工，将达到3级航道的标准。

正是由于优越的交通区位和日益完善的交通设施，昭通和宜宾正逐渐成为金沙江下游流域旅游开发的核心腹地和投资力度最大的地区。

3. 政策先行

2001年，云南省委、省政府明确指出要加快滇东北旅游片区旅游业的发展，2004年正式批准了滇东北旅游区的旅游发展规划。2005年，昭通市明确将文化旅游作为重要产业纳入全市"十一五"规划，力争将旅游业打造成为昭通的一个新兴的经济增长点。近年来，昭通市又把旅游业作为"支柱产业"来抓。宜宾是四川四大旅游优先发展区之一、四川四条旅游精品线路的重要节点，政府对旅游发展提出"壮旅"战略，取得明显成效。2008年宜宾市经历年初低温雨雪、"5·12"汶川特大地震后,在"壮旅"战略的第二个年头,旅游总收入55.63亿元,同比增长19.8%,再创历史新高,跃居四川省市州第三名。[①]

4. 具体培育策略

除了具备以上河流旅游增长极形成的条件,还需制定和实施正确的培育策略,使之真正成长为大河流域内的旅游增长极。

(1)加强政府的整体调控职能,建立河流旅游增长极之间的长效合作机制。加强政府统一管理和宏观调控,可以密切大河流域内旅游业与社会经济其他产业要素的联系,例如未来经济走势、产业结构变化、旅游业发展自身条件与环境变化等,使之与流域内经济部门、其他产业、社会群体和谐发展。也可以发挥主导作用,建立流域内区域旅游合作机制,统筹规划、制定政策、协调利益、部署行动,从而为更好地培养河流旅游增长极打下基础。

宜宾与昭通旅游合作协议的签订,为金沙旅游圈增长极的两个极点的旅游合作提供了一个框架,如何切实推进核心区的区域旅游合作是一个现实课题。在区域旅游合作发展进程中,两市政府作为主导行为角色,其主要关注的作为空间应该集中在以下方面:一是坚持核心区内部的制度创新,推进旅游体验环境的质量建设;二是坚持致力于旅游基础设施建设,提供高质量的公共服务;三是坚持共同体的制度性活动,不断提升核心区的市场认知形象,建构起成熟的区域旅游合作机制。鉴于区域旅游经济合作发展的复杂性,实施区域旅游经济政策往往需要在相关的区域、经济部门、社会群体之间进行必要的协调,统一行动,一起来解决所面临的旅游经济发展问题。为此宜宾和昭通可以建立区域旅游经济政策协调机构,共同编制《区域旅游营销规划》《区域旅游线路规划》和重点景区重大项目的策划工作。这个协调机构既具有相应的行政协调权力,同时又有掌握两市政府为解决区域旅游经济发展问题所划拨的资金及其分配权,这样才能够有效地执行区域旅游经济政策,做好协调工作。

(2)吸引和拉动周围旅游要素趋向河流旅游增长极,树立增长极区域旅游形象。河流旅游增长极的极化效应是指迅速增长的旅游业吸引和拉动其他经济活动不断趋向增长极地区,不可避免地导致流域内地理上的极化,从而获得各种旅游聚焦,又进一步增强增长极地区极化的过程。发展河流旅游增长极,产生极化效应,不断增强其辐射能力和影响能力,对周边地区旅游发展起到示范作用。

首先,集中力量发展河流旅游增长极地区的社会经济。吸引民营资本和外部资本对当地旅游开发的资金注入,通过优惠制度的投资政策,拓展投融资渠道,集中资金大力发展河流旅游增长极地区的社会经济,完善增长极地区旅游配套设施,增强当地生活品质以及旅游吸引力。

其次,打造河流旅游增长极地区的旅游形象。打造河流旅游增长极地区良好的旅游形象,扩大旅游宣传,构建旅游推广网点,能够很好地突出当地特色,吸引旅游客源市场,宣传和弘扬大河文化。区域旅游形象是一个地区旅游业的灵魂。打造及推广良好的区域旅游形象是区域旅游市场营销

---

① 黄河. 基于增长极理论的金沙江下游旅游圈合作模式研究[J]. 生产力研究,2012(12):132~148.

中至为重要的战略模式选择。良好的市场形象有助于旅游区域突出自身特色，传播经营理念，建立顾客忠诚，最终实现营销目标。宜宾与昭通同处云、贵、川三省接合部，在长期的历史发展中，开展了广泛的交流，历史上曾有"搬不完的昭通，填不满的叙府"之说。据《史记》记载，秦始皇统一中国以后开凿五尺道，又称石门道，打通中原经道通往云南、贵州的道路。122年，汉武帝又派使臣到四川开辟从宜宾经云南昭通、昆明，最后到达缅甸、印度的"南夷道"，这就是有名的"南丝绸之路"。宜宾位于五尺道和"南丝绸之路"的起点，昭通位于五尺道和"南丝绸之路"的要冲，历史文脉相亲构成了宜宾—昭通树立区域旅游形象的资源基础。两市可以联手打造"南丝绸之路"的旅游品牌，并设计相关旅游线路，进行联合营销。

再次，突出河流旅游增长极地区的功能特色。明确流域内增长极地区发展旅游的特色，加强各项功能，集中力量开发当地特色旅游资源和旅游产品，增强核心竞争力。同时注重旅游创新，满足不断变化的、极具个性的旅游市场需求。

最后，培训旅游人才，吸引旅游企业。运用保障和激励措施，制定优惠的鼓励政策，吸引旅游企业进驻河流旅游增长极地区。注重对各类旅游人才的培养，对外来旅游人才有足够的保障措施和良好的待遇，营造当地良好的人才环境。建立旅游院校和旅游培训机构，加强旅游教育和培训，提高基层从业人员素质，完善高层管理人员能力，增加人才的研讨和交流，成为区域内旅游人才的聚集地。

宜宾和昭通河流旅游增长极吸引和拉动周围旅游要素，主要有以下四方面：第一，运用保障、激励措施和物质、精神鼓励相结合的方式来吸引旅游人才和旅游企业。第二，通过制度优惠的投资政策，积极采取各种投融资渠道，加大招商引资力度，吸引旅游资本注入。第三，集中力量有选择地开发和提升宜宾—昭通最具特色的旅游产品，重点突出精品旅游产品的生产和经营，提高要素配置的效益。第四，激活与创新旅游生产要素，如依托宜宾—昭通多样的地理环境和品质较高的生态资源开发生态、探险等特种旅游。

（3）发挥河流旅游增长极辐射作用，带动周边地区旅游大发展。宜宾—昭通应发挥核心交通区位优势，积极主动联系区域内的各地州市，建设与周边地区的交通联系，以旅游开发为窗口，扩大对外开放，加强各地间的旅游经济联系和协作，同时接受昆明等较发达地区的辐射，形成战略联盟，扩大自身增长极的规模，不断增强宜宾—昭通作为区域旅游增长极的辐射能力和影响力，以产生外部规模经济，发挥增长极的示范效应。在宜宾—昭通旅游增长极形成的基础上，发挥其扩散作用，将市内富余和优势的旅游要素向周围地区进行要素输出与配置，如通过输出旅游企业和资本以强化企业的经济辐射和扩散效应，特别是大中型旅游企业，通过多元化经营、资产重组和资本运营等方式将其用于扩大的资本输出至周边地区，进行旅游投资及开发，产生新的经济扩散效应，促进整个区域旅游的大发展。（资料来源：①② 本研究整理）

---

① 王静，罗明义，杜靖川. 试论金沙江下游流域旅游增长极的选择与培育[J]. 思想战线，2008（4）.
② 黄河. 基于增长极理论的金沙江下游旅游圈合作模式研究[J]. 生产力研究，2010（12）.

（二）金沙江所处的三江并流区域河流旅游增长极的培育

首届"三江并流"地区四州（市）十四县（市、区）旅游区域合作联席会上，怒江、大理、丽江、迪庆四个州市 14 县（区、市）部门负责人及有关旅游专家研究制定了《三江并流世界自然遗产地旅游规划纲要》，提出加快"三江并流"世界遗产地旅游发展，要以旅游市场需求为导向，以优势旅游资源为依托，以品牌旅游区为引导，以培育新供给、新动力为重点，借助丽江古城、香格里拉等旅游品牌效应和产业快速发展的态势，按照"一心三极八园十区三带"的空间发展布局，积极推进"三江并流"世界遗产地旅游发展。强化丽江旅游中心的引领作用，充分发挥丽江古城、玉龙县旅游品牌优势，着力打造成"三江并流"世界遗产地的旅游中心，辐射带动整个区域旅游加快发展。打造三大旅游增长极，将香格里拉市、泸水县、兰坪县打造成金沙江、怒江、澜沧江旅游带的游客集散中心和旅游增长极。为全面提升"三江并流"遗产地旅游可进入性和内部通达条件，构建"三江并流"遗产地旅游大交通网。

第二节　点—轴模式

点—轴模式是增长极模式的后续扩展，比增长极模式对于大河流域旅游发展的作用范围更大。例如，作为中华文明母亲河的黄河流域，在山西境内以运城、河曲、河津、吉县为重要节点，以黄河作为流域旅游重点开发轴线，将沿黄河的河曲黄河风光区、壶口瀑布景区、风陵渡景区以及鹳雀楼景区串联起来，辐射山西西部和南部以及河南、陕西等省的旅游发展。本节首先对点—轴模式、河流旅游节点和发展轴的内涵进行界定；其次，利用长江流域内部分支的旅游节点选择，探讨如何建设流域重点开发轴线，以图构建合理的河流旅游点—轴发展模式带来启示。

一、河流旅游点—轴模式的形成

（一）点—轴模式的内涵

新编经济金融字典定义"点—轴模式"为："增长极模式的扩展。由于增长极数量增多，增长极之间也出现了相互联结的交通线，两个增长极及其中间的交通线由此具有了高于增长极的功能，理论上称为发展轴。发展轴具有增长极的所有特点，而且比增长极的作用范围更大。"

（二）河流旅游节点和发展轴的内涵

对于河流旅游来说，点—轴模式中的"点"是大河流域内"轴线"上的旅游目的地，即旅游中心城市、核心旅游景区或者它们的组合。"轴线"一般是交通干线，包括水上交通和陆上交通。如长江流域内的三峡地区，它以长江沿岸三峡地区内著名的城市和景点为依托，带动了整个"轴线"旅游的发展。依据点—轴模式的理论，作为节点的核心旅游目的地与作为发展轴的交通线是具有等级的。不同等级的节点在发展轴上的地位和性质不一样，需要合理定位，整体协调规划；不同等级的发展轴也对周围区域具有不同强度的吸引力和凝聚力。对于大河流域旅游发展来说，分析和确定节点和发展轴的位置和等级是流域旅游开发非常重要的事情。

(三) 河流旅游点—轴模式的内涵

点—轴发展模式是大河流域旅游开发和发展中需要应用的模式，对其具有重要的价值，能够帮助大河流域提高旅游的交通可达性，发挥中心旅游城市或者旅游景区的辐射作用，实现流域内旅游的发展。河流旅游运用点—轴模式的步骤如下：

首先，根据旅游资源和城市的分布，在大河流域范围内确定若干具有发展潜力的交通路线经过的地带，作为"发展轴"予以重点开发。

其次，在各条发展轴上，确定若干个"点"，作为重点发展的城镇或旅游点，并且要明确各个重点发展城镇或景点在轴线上的地位、性质、发展方向和主要功能，以及它们的服务、吸引范围。

最后，确定"点"和"轴线"的等级体系，形成不同等级的点轴系统。在一定的流域范围内，应优先开发重点发展轴线和沿线地带高等级的点及其周边地区。以后随着发展轴及重点发展城镇或旅游点实力的增强，开发重心将逐步转移到级别较低的发展轴和点，并使发展轴逐步向不发达地区延伸，促进次级轴线和线上的点发展，最终形成由不同等级的发展轴及其发展中心组成的具有一定层次结构的点—轴系统，从而带动整个区域的发展。"发展轴"等级的确定，在一定程度上也是旅游线路等级的确定。点—轴布局模式在大河流域内旅游开发中的运用，要以可进入性为前提，并且沿线分布有不同等级的旅游城市和景点。[①]

二、长江流域的旅游点—轴发展模式

(一) 金沙江旅游点—轴发展模式的构建

金沙江是长江的上游，因江中沙土呈黄色得名。金沙江流域内选择宜宾、昭通作为两个节点，以内昆高速公路和铁路为发展轴，形成本区旅游发展的核心区域，通过核心区域带动整个区域。各区域旅游布局在由内向外扩展的圈层中，形成"市场—资源"共轭的旅游地体系，通过结构效应，实现区域板块的联动。

地处川滇边界的溪洛渡电站和向家坝电站的开工建设，促进了宜宾和昭通两市区域经济的联动。2008年8月，宜宾市与昭通市缔结友好城市并签订了合作框架协议，两市在交通、资源、旅游、库区经济等方面将全面合作。2008年9月，两市旅游部门签定了《宜宾市、昭通市构建无障碍旅游合作区》协议书。两市按照"自愿、平等、公正、共赢"的原则，达成了整合旅游资源，打造旅游精品，共同构建交通、服务、投诉"三无"障碍和资源、交通、基础设施、品牌、信息"五共享"无障碍旅游合作区协议。两市将联手开展旅游宣传促销，建立区域旅游合作保障机制。金沙江旅游圈增长极的点—轴系统已粗具雏形。由于本区的大多数州市缺乏旅游合作的经验，宜宾—昭通的旅游合作不仅可以促使点—轴系统的形成，同时具备示范效应，为整个旅游区域合作提供借鉴。（资

[①] 樊信友. 区域旅游业空间布局研究 [D]. 成都：四川大学，2004.

料来源：[①] 本研究整理）

（二）嘉陵江旅游点—轴发展模式的构建

嘉陵江是长江的上游支流，因流经陕西凤县东北嘉陵谷而得名。1999年，为渠化航道、发展航运、充分发挥嘉陵江的水资源优势，由交通、水利、水电部门共同规划编制了《嘉陵江渠化开发规划报告》。嘉陵江以航电结合方式实施的渠化开发，是一个集航运、发电、旅游、防洪等综合效益为一体的重大工程。渠化后将缩短航道里程56.2千米，全流域682.8千米的航道将达到三级、四级标准，2×500吨级船队可从广元直达上海。渠化后的嘉陵江将成为全国唯一的人工渠化内河航运线。嘉陵江丰富的水资源和渠化开发后形成的巨大运输通道，以及流域旅游资源的串珠分布，为选择嘉陵江作为流域旅游开发重点发展轴线提供了依据。

嘉陵江流域丰富的旅游资源为旅游开发提供了前提和基础，旅游业发展潜力巨大。随着流域内各级政府对旅游业的日益重视，嘉陵江流域旅游业有了较快发展。目前旅游开发已在较大范围内展开，形成了一批具有一定吸引力和影响力的旅游热点。综观嘉陵江流域旅游空间发展态势，旅游热点高度集中于重庆、广元、阆中等几个旅游中心城市，是流域旅游业发展的增长点。嘉陵江流域旅游发展表现出的这种"点"状特征，是流域旅游开发选择重点旅游发展点的客观依据。

由于旅游热点过于集中，许多品位高、质量好的旅游资源还没有开发，出现了一种优质的资源和落后的效益同时存在的现象。要解决上述问题必须优化流域旅游开发的空间布局，对旅游开发进行合理布局，促进流域旅游资源的全面开发，使其产生最大的经济效益、社会效益和生态效益。优化区域旅游空间布局的途径很多，结合嘉陵江流域旅游资源的"点"状和"线"状布局特征，实行"点—轴"发展是现实的选择。

1. 节点的选择

重庆是中国历史文化名城，曾是古代巴国的首都，历史悠久、文化积淀深厚。旅游资源表现出集山、水、林、泉、瀑、峡、洞等为一体的壮丽自然景色和熔巴渝文化、饮食文化、移民文化、"陪都"文化、都市文化于一炉的浓郁文化色彩。区内有旅游景点100余处，其中全国重点文物保护单位4处，省级重点文物保护单位20处，国家级风景名胜区2处，省级重点风景名胜区3处，已建自然保护区2处，森林公园14处。重庆的人文旅游资源以巴渝文化古迹、历史纪念地、城市园林和独特的建筑为主体，充分表现出多样化的特征。重庆旅游资源丰富、文化品位高，加之作为流域内的大城市，区位条件好、交通发达，理应成为流域内旅游重点发展点。要充分发挥重庆的交通地理优势，挖掘文化旅游资源优势，组合更有影响力的旅游产品推向市场，使重庆成为流域旅游的重点增长极。

南充正在努力构建川东北区域中心城市，打造南充成为川东北的政治、经济、文化中心需要经

[①] 黄河. 基于增长极理论的金沙江下游旅游圈合作模式研究[J]. 生产力研究，2010（12）.

济社会的全面发展，旅游业的发展即是一个重要方面。南充旅游景点最具吸引力和影响力的当数阆中古城无疑。阆中古城是全国四大古城之一，是嘉陵江流域旅游发展的亮点。目前古城旅游开发取得了较好的经济效益，将阆中作为流域重点旅游发展点，还需加快阆中与区域外的交通建设，形成立体交通网络，提高旅游的可进入性，推动阆中旅游的快速发展。

广元是四川的北部门户，旅游资源禀赋在流域内颇具优势，历史文化底蕴深厚。有全国重点文物保护单位皇泽寺、千佛崖和剑门蜀道国家级风景名胜区、明月峡、清风峡古栈道、剑门关国家森林公园等旅游景点。广元的节庆旅游在流域内也开展得较好，一年一度的"女儿节"吸引了众多游客参与，大大提高了城市的知名度和影响力。因此，考虑将广元作为流域重点旅游发展点有基础。但必须强调的是，广元作为一个中等城市，在城市功能、环境建设等方面还需加强，为广元的旅游加快发展奠定基础。

2. 发展轴的建设

嘉陵江渠化后形成的巨大航运能力，无疑将会大大促进区域经济的发展。因此，就流域旅游开发而言，以渠化后的嘉陵江作为流域旅游重点开发轴线是必然选择。同时，国道212线途经嘉陵江流域的广元、阆中、南充、广安、合川、重庆，将流域旅游中心城市串联在了一起，具备了良好的区域旅游的可达性。因此，在流域旅游开发中，要以嘉陵江干流和国道212线为主轴，重点开发那些资源特色鲜明、开发条件优越并对全流域旅游资源开发产生较大影响的各级增长点，并积极开拓次级发展轴线（国道318、国道210、南广高速、达成铁路），以此带动嘉陵江流域旅游的全面开发。（资料来源：[1] 本研究整理）

（三）三峡地区的旅游点—轴发展模式的构建

长江三峡是长江流域内重要的河段，从四川奉节到湖北宜昌，全长约200千米，两岸谷壁陡直，谷中水流浩荡，地貌上独具一格，自西向东依次为瞿塘峡、巫峡、西陵峡。[2]

原国家旅游局、国务院西部办、国家发改委、国务院三峡建设委员会、交通部、水利部六部委牵头，北京大学城市规划设计中心承担《长江三峡区域旅游发展规划》的制定，着手打造"大三峡旅游经济圈"，政府及各部门的行为极大地促进了"三峡旅游经济圈"的形成。

1. 节点的选择

从地缘因素及与长江三峡的关系来看，这个"三峡旅游经济圈"主要包括或者说其辐射范围有重庆、湖北、湖南、贵州四省市，更具体来说就主要包括鄂东、渝西、湘西、黔北等地区。建构三峡旅游经济圈，就是要在政府的主导下，首先重点培养旅游经济增长极，然后在其逐渐成熟之后，将注意力投向级别较低的旅游中心和旅游发展轴，从而形成地区的旅游综合开发网络优势，形成"点—轴"式发展格局，最终达到联合开发、互惠互利、协调发展的旅游产业带。

---

[1] 张明川. 基于"点—轴系统"理论的嘉陵江流域旅游开发研究[J]. 科技经济市场，2009（10）.
[2] 杨达源. 长江三峡的起源与演变[J]. 南京大学学报（自然科学版），1988（3）.

2. 发展轴的建设

"三峡旅游经济圈"的旅游经济发展轴可以由一条主轴和两条副轴构成。主轴即指由重庆市和宜昌市连接起来的长江主干旅游发展轴，发展副轴包括"湘鄂"三峡旅游发展副轴和"渝黔"三峡旅游发展副轴。不管是发展主轴还是副轴的形成，首先必须加强交通基础设施建设，围绕旅游办交通，跟进交通干旅游。四省市省际省内旅游线路除了黄金水线——长江以外，特别是对于副轴的形成，更重要的是陆路交通的完善。由于受到地形地质和资金的影响，公路和铁路在各省市之间的互通性并不是太好，陆路交通网络长期以来并不尽如人意。但近来各省市已意识到这一问题的严重性，各省市间高速公路的互通连接已初见成效。特别是在党中央、国务院实施西部大开发战略的十大标志工程之一的渝怀铁路（西起重庆，东至湖南怀化，途经渝、黔、湘三省市的长寿、涪陵、武隆、彭水、黔江、酉阳、铜仁等地区，全长 625 千米）的竣工，不仅结束了这一地段长期以来无铁路的历史，还对三峡旅游经济圈发展轴的形成及经济圈整体的协调发展，起到决定性的作用。

"三峡旅游经济圈"的发展主轴是经济圈的建设重点，它连接了经济圈内最重要的两个经济增长极城市，因此这个主轴发展的好坏将直接影响到整个经济圈的发展。"三峡旅游经济圈"两个旅游经济副轴———"湘鄂"旅游发展副轴和"渝黔"旅游发展副轴，对于整个旅游经济圈的最终形成和完善也起着很重要的作用。（资料来源：[①] 本研究整理）

（四）汉江走廊旅游点—轴发展模式的构建

陕南汉江走廊位于长江左岸最大的支流——汉江的中上游，发源于汉中市宁强县大安镇的汉王山（嶓冢山），沿途经勉县、汉中市区、城固县，东至洋县黄金峡，全长 110 千米，是一个狭长地带，是一条生态走廊和景观廊道。同时，陕南汉江走廊是地球上同纬度生态最好的地方，这片被巍峨秦岭和苍莽巴山环绕的盆地，被长江左岸最大的支流汉江滋养的秀土，虽然位于中国西部，但却拥有与江南同样的秀色，是一处得南北之利、兼南北之美的风水宝地。由于其气候温暖湿润，土地肥沃，物产丰饶，生态环境良好，旅游资源独特，人文自然相宜，具有广阔的旅游开发与发展潜力，亟待旅游业带动汉江走廊区域经济发展。

1. 节点的选择

点—轴模式中的"点"是带动区域发展的各级中心城镇，陕南汉江走廊旅游区包括三大主要城市，即汉中市、安康市和商洛市，三市的发展水平相近，以市区的旅游业发展最为繁荣，因此，汉中市、安康市和商洛市的市区就是旅游开发的基础。根据汉中市、安康市和商洛市旅游发展现状的分析结果来看，可以确定三个重点旅游增长点，即汉中市的汉台区、安康市的汉滨区和商洛市的商州区。

（1）一级旅游节点的选择与分析。汉中市的汉台区、安康市的汉滨区和商洛市的商州区是陕南

---

① 吕飞. 论"三峡旅游经济圈"构建中的"点—轴"式开发 [J]. 重庆职业技术学院学报，2006（6）.

三市的政治、经济和交通的中心，旅游区位优势明显，旅游资源集聚性强，旅游基础设施和服务功能比较齐全，旅游产业粗具规模，并且拥有本区最发达的交通运输条件，因此是本地区旅游开发的一级增长点。这三个一级增长点融合了陕南汉江走廊地区最有利的交通区位因素，可进入性强，游客集散便利，东、南、西、北连接各个下辖县区，通过区间交通可以顺利到达该市的所有重点景点，就像来陕西旅游，必须先来到西安市，再由西安市去往陕西的各个县市的景点一样，因此本地区旅游业的发展必须以这三点作为依托，这三点是来陕南地区旅游的必游之地。

（2）二级旅游节点的选择与分析。汉中市、安康市、商洛市下辖的25个县涵盖了陕南汉江走廊地区的重点旅游项目，但是由于交通的原因，一些景点的可进入性较差，且路况不好，只能保证进入景区的基本要求，县区和景区的基础设施建设不到位，虽然景点的游览价值很高，但是都要以汉台区、汉滨区和商州区作为依托来吸引游客，所以是本区的二级增长点。

2. 发展轴的建设

陕南汉江走廊地区的汉中、安康两地处于汉江的干流流域，商洛处于汉江的支流流域，在这三个地区，汉江是最重要的水系，但是由于地处河流的中上游，通航条件欠佳，三地的航空港规模小，运输能力和集散能力较差，因此，陕南汉江走廊地区的对外沟通主要依托的是公路交通和铁路交通，其中又以公路交通为主。（资料来源：[1] 本研究整理）

第三节 线性开发模式

本节主要介绍基于大河流域中具有丰厚自然资源和文化资源等的线性空间（廊道）进行开发的旅游模式，主要包括生态景观型廊道开发、遗产保护型廊道开发以及旅游开发型廊道开发。大河流域具有空间结构上的线型特征，并且有着丰富的功能与价值，是具有景观生态、遗产保护和休闲游憩等多种功能的空间类型。基于线性空间或廊道而对河流进行的开发模式，推动着大河流域的旅游发展。

一、线性空间

（一）线性空间内涵

在景观生态学中，通常用斑块、廊道、基质三个元素来描述景观的基本空间形态结构。其中，"廊道"是起分割或连通单元空间作用的特殊带状要素。Forman认为廊道在各种景观中均有渗透，并体现了交通、生态保护、审美等多方面的应用价值。[2] 这种功能多样、价值复合、学科交叉的特性使廊道研究从景观生态学逐渐扩展到遗产保护、文化地理、旅游开发等多个专业领域，由此也衍

---

[1] 李慧. 基于点—轴理论的陕南汉江走廊旅游开发模式研究 [D]. 西安：西安科技大学，2012.
[2] Forman RTT. Landscape Ecology [M]. New York, USA：Wiley, 1986.

生出了生态廊道、绿道、遗产廊道、文化线路、文化廊道、风景道、旅游走廊等多个内涵相似又相互区别的概念。对这些在形态上具有线型特征的可以统一归纳为线性空间或者廊道，基于线性空间或廊道而对河流进行的开发称为线性开发模式。此类线性空间包括河流周围的自然和人工空间环境，包括河流、水陆过渡区空间及周边陆域空间，其承载着丰富的自然资源要素和历史文化信息，强调自然界河流资源与人类社会的有机共生与可持续发展。

（二）线性空间分类

线性空间在空间上以河流（天然和人工）、山脉、古道、交通线、风景道路、线状构筑物，在时间上以主题性历史事件、历史人物等为依托，连接自然保护地、风景名胜区、历史遗产区及其他人类聚居区，是具有景观生态、遗产保护和休闲游憩等多种功能的空间类型。包括绿道（greenway）、生态/绿色廊道（ecological/green corridor）、遗产廊道（heritage corridor）、文化线路（cultural route）、风景道（parkway）等包罗概念[①]。

线性开放空间承载着丰富的自然资源要素和历史文化信息，具有典型的资源稀缺性和不可再生性；存在于不同空间尺度，且所涉及的空间尺度多超越行政边界，或更适合以自然地理单元的尺度与区域和城市及城市内部发生联系或相互影响。线性开放空间规划，应该是在保证资源可持续利用、保护生态系统完整性和满足人类其他社会心理需求基础上的多目标整合复杂工程，其成功与否对于大河流域的发展至关重要。

关于线性空间/廊道的分类，线性空间根据开发的侧重点，具体可分为遗产保护型线性空间、景观生态类线性空间以及旅游开发类线性空间。遗产保护类线性空间主要包括文化廊道、遗产廊道、文化线路，生态景观类线性空间主要包括绿道以及生态廊道，旅游开发类线性空间主要包括风景道、旅游线路、旅游走廊等，其分类与主要特点如表2.1所示。

表2.1　廊道的分类、细分及特点

分类	内容	特　点
生态景观型廊道	生态廊道	生态环境保护、有助于生态环境的可持续发展
	绿道	人居环境改善、连接人类居住环境与自然界
遗产保护型廊道	遗产廊道	文化、自然遗产保护、经济发展等多目标
	文化线路	人类文明轨迹的研究与保护
	文化廊道	历史文化线路的价值重现与开发
旅游开发型廊道	风景道	旅游者体验需求
	旅游线路	旅游产品的开发设计
	旅游走廊	注重旅游产业区域布局

资料来源：汪芳，廉华. 线型空间研究进展与发展趋势［J］. 华中建筑，2007（7）：88-91.；邱海莲，由亚男. 旅游廊道概念界定［J］. 旅游论坛，2015，8（4）：26-30.

---

① 李晓佳. 以线性空间理论解读富有城市特色的道路景观［D］. 北京：北京林业大学，2010.

(三)线性空间的特点

1. 作为一种线性的动态空间[①]

(1)交通性:由于各种线性空间的本质都是线型空间,交通是其所具备的最基础的功能,线是由点运动后所留下的轨迹,因此,流动性与动态性的交通属性构成最基本的特征。

(2)连接性:线性空间的形态可简化为线,这种简化而来的"线"实际上也具有宽度、面积等二维几何图形的几何度量。通过"线"的建设,连接各个功能区,同时连接一些重要的设施,满足各功能区之间的日常人流和物流空间转移的要求,是一个重要的轴线。

(3)连续性:线性空间中的各种序列形成了连续性,消除了断裂,保证了主体行为是连续的,形成运动中的秩序。

(4)方向性、引导性:视觉上的连续和心理上的连续感构成了线性休闲空间的有机整体,进而形成了一定的方向性,引导观察者向着某个目标前行。

(5)空间—时间性:运动着的活动者将各个时间点上的空间状态由心理记忆加以梳理、整合,得出整个线性空间的状态的主观印象。

(6)生长、延伸性:线"能够在视觉上表现出方向、运动和生长"。

(7)场所性:人们可以在其中进行活动和交往,能构成活动场所的线性空间需具备的重要条件是有适合的空间形式和适合的空间容量。

2. 作为使用者的活动场所

(1)多样性:人的活动的偶然性和生活的多元化使得作为人们活动场所的线性空间理应是一种具有多功能的场所。线性空间吸引人们共同生活在一起,需要通过适当的分区满足不同目的、不同阶层人们的不同的功能要求。多功能使用还表现在空间的利用有时间系列的变化。多样性的活动在不同时间内交错进行,使线性空间富有生气、使用率高而且安全。

(2)舒适性:线性空间以人的活动为主,具有适宜的尺度空间,使人感到亲切、有归属感。空间内设施的设计应符合人体工程学,具有舒适的人体尺度。

(3)可达性:对外交通的可达性鼓励多种交通方式的运用,使步行者、乘车者能方便地进入线性空间合理组织步道、广场、园林一体化多层次的步行系统,强调安全性、易达性、舒适性、连续性,保证步行系统的畅通。

(4)文化性:线性空间反映一定地区的文化特征。不同的文化类型,不仅可以反映到线性空间的形态上,也同时反映在人们活动的内容中。

3. 作为环境的生长空间

(1)景观性:线性空间的形式、色彩、尺度、纹理及细部设计,塑造了活动空间品格,决定了

[①] 李晓佳. 以线性空间理论解读富有城市特色的道路景观[D]. 北京:北京林业大学,2010.

不同空间类型的景观质量。

（2）生态性：线性空间不仅满足人们活动的要求，而且能够在一定程度上平衡生态环境。注重自然生态包括对气候的关注、对绿色植物的关注以及对水的关注。基于生态考虑的线性空间是有生命的、可持续发展的、充满活力和自然气息的休闲空间。

二、生态景观型廊道

（一）绿道

绿道是连接开敞空间、自然保护区和景观要素的绿色景观廊道，强调改善环境质量和提供户外娱乐的功能。以美国绿道管理与建设为例，1867年至今，美国完成了上千个绿道规划和建设项目。20世纪80年代，美国户外游憩总统委员会特别提出报告，指出绿道为居民带来了接近自然的机会。20世纪90年代至今，绿道运动已成为一项国际运动，世界上出现了从国际、国家到区域层次的绿道项目[1]。

从提出"绿道"这一概念的背景可以看出，绿道是在自然或人为廊道基础上，增加必要的休闲服务设施建设而成的廊道空间，其建设的主旨是为市民休闲游憩提供更多的自然空间。因此，与生态廊道相比较，绿道的人为性和实践性更强，在空间分布上多位于城市或人口密集的地区，起到连接城市与自然的作用。

（二）生态廊道

1. 生态廊道的概念及内涵

相较于绿道，生态廊道是着重体现生态服务功能的廊道类型。对于生态廊道的建设，关注点在于利用其分割景观格局、连通景观单元的结构特征，实现保护生态多样性。防风固沙、防止水土流失及阻隔污染物等生态保护功能。生态廊道概念是"廊道"概念最本源的面貌[2]。

生态廊道也称"绿色廊道"，引自欧美发达国家，是指在生态环境系统中呈线性或带状布局，能够沟通连接空间分布上较为孤立和分散的生态单元的生态系统空间类型，具有保护生物多样性、过滤污染物、防止水土流失、防风固沙、调控洪水等生态服务功能。生态廊道主要由植被、水体等生态性结构要素构成。经济高速发展的同时对于生态环境造成了严重的影响，在此基础上，生态廊道应运而生，其是解决当前人类剧烈活动造成的景观破碎化以及随之而来的众多环境问题的重要措施之一。

生态廊道作为景观元素之一，具有连通景观格局的作用，是生态流的通道；同时，也具有屏蔽、过滤和阻断某些生态流的负作用，对另一些生态功能有阻隔作用。因此，根据生态文明建设的需要，构建生态环境保护需要的生态廊道，对保护生物多样性、提升生态系统功能和维持区域生态

---

[1] 孙帅. 都市型绿道规划设计研究 [D]. 北京：北京林业大学，2013.
[2] 邱海莲，由亚男. 旅游廊道概念界定 [J]. 旅游论坛，2015，8（4）.

安全格局具有重要意义。

具体到河流的生态廊道，随着经济的快速发展，人类经济生产活动对河流以及河岸植被空间进行大量的人工改造，很大程度上破坏了河流的生态功能结构和生态系统自然循环过程，如：挤占河岸绿地、忽视河岸空间立体配植、景观绿地匀质化、景观廊道"断裂"等，部分河段植被生态系统迅速退化，生态服务质量较差，因此，就促成了河流生态廊道的建设。河流生态廊道在净化污染、提升生物生境质量、维持生物多样性、提高景观品质等方面起着重要的作用。基于生态廊道原理，河流廊道包括河流水体本身以及沿河流分布而不同于周围基质的植被带。其廊道的景观生态服务功能则主要依托河岸植被连续空间被体验感知。

2. 生态廊道的功能

20世纪中叶，生态廊道的功能主要是服务于审美休憩，为人们接近自然而将公园、保护区、文化景观或历史遗迹连通起来；20世纪末，随着景观破碎、生态环境破坏等生态问题的出现，人们开始重新审视生态廊道在解决生态问题上的潜力和能力，至此，生态廊道的功能被拓展至历史文化、娱乐以及生态环境保护等多个方面。在生态廊道的生态功能上可以概括为生物多样性保护、生态环境保护、生态安全格局建设、全球气候变化应对四方面[1]。

3. 生态廊道的分类

对于生态廊道的分类是多样化的，从结构上可以分为：①线状生态廊道（linear corridor）（如带状公园廊道、风景林带廊道、防护林带廊道）；②带状生态廊道（strip corridor）（如道路绿化廊道、林荫休闲廊道）；③河流廊道（stream corridor）（如滨河公园廊道、滨河绿带廊道和滨江绿带廊道）。其中，线状生态廊道是指全部由边缘种占优势的狭长条带；带状生态廊道是指有较丰富内部种的较宽条带；河流廊道是指河流两侧与环境基质相区别的带状植被，又称滨水植被带或缓冲带（buffer strip）；从空间尺度可以分为市级廊道、省级廊道、地区级廊道、国家级廊道；从功能上可以将廊道分为自然型生态廊道、娱乐型生态廊道、文化型生态廊道、综合型生态廊道等。

4. 生态廊道的旅游价值

生态廊道最为突出的生态资源，本身就是极为重要的旅游资源之一，具有的功能包括精神文化功能、审美观赏功能、生态娱乐功能、艺术启发功能、场所认同感、文化遗存功能、知识教育功能等。并且由于生态廊道的功能多样性，例如生态保护、娱乐休闲、历史文化保护等，发展旅游具有必然性与必要性的统一。一方面，生态廊道所在的区域，以点（包括自然保护区、森林公园、风景名胜区、国有林场等）、线（江河、公路、铁路、城乡道路、绿道、景观林带等）为基础而聚合而成的河流线型绿色廊道，自然资源禀赋高，生态优势明显，吸引着游客的到来；另一方面，旅游所带来的收益更加反过来促进生态廊道的保护，但需注意开发与保护的程度问题，坚持"发展与保护并重、水域与陆域共生、上中下游协调发展"的原则。

---

[1] 郑好，高吉喜，谢高地，等. 生态廊道[J]. 生态与农村环境学报，2019，35（2）.

5. 生态廊道的开发实践

（1）开发实践。在开展廊道研究时，要综合考虑区域间的相互影响和相互联系，在区域、国家及洲际层面构建大尺度生态廊道系统。一些国际生态环境保护组织较早意识到大型生态廊道对于景观连通性维护以及生物多样性保持的重要性，构建了若干国家级或洲际级的大型生态廊道系统，例如在里海区域蒸发强烈，生态环境脆弱，生物多样性降低，水质恶化严重的背景下，由关键生态系统合作基金（CEPF）组织发起，由俄罗斯、格鲁吉亚和伊朗三方合作的"高加索地区生物多样性热点"项目详细分析了研究区主要的生物物种及其栖息地，并以此为依据划定了10条大型生态廊道，分别为Kuma-Manych廊道、大高加索山脉廊道、里海海滨廊道、西小高加索廊道、Javakheti廊道、东小高加索廊道、Iori-Mingechaur廊道、南部高地廊道、Arasbaran廊道和Hyrcan廊道[①]。

在我国，生态廊道的建设最早可以追溯到20世纪70年代开展的三北防护林体系建设工程。随着生态问题的日益突出，生态廊道的建设也在不断被强调，党的十九大报告指出："优化生态安全屏障体系，构建生态廊道和生物多样性保护网络，提升生态系统质量和稳定性。"在河流生态廊道的实践方面，随着开发的进程，早期以各城市为主体的建设逐渐发展为流域内生态廊道构建，从微观的具体设计到宏观的区域战略规划。2010年2月，《珠江三角洲绿道网总体规划纲要》[②]指出，要在珠三角地区9个城市建设6条涵盖省级、城市和社区3个层次的区域绿色廊道，这也是我国首例在区域尺度下开展的多功能生态廊道建设工程（广东省人民政府，2010）。2016年10月，《长江经济带发展规划纲要》中要求严格保护一江清水，努力建成上中下游相协调、人与自然和谐发展的绿色生态廊道。

（2）启示借鉴。

第一，生态廊道的规划要求主要包括以下几方面：①连续性。由于人类的活动使自然景观被分割得四分五裂，景观的功能受到阻碍，故加强孤立斑块之间的联系是必需的。②数目原理。廊道是有利于生态系统运动和维持的，生态廊道的数目一般认为越多越好，使得各种生态流在其中流动，周围形成各种辐射区，廊道周边地块的环境得到改善。③构成原理。廊道本身应由乡土植物成分组成，并与所联系的斑块相近。④宽度原理。宽度对于廊道生态功能的发挥有着重要影响，不同类型的生态廊道应根据自身特点而给定不同的宽度以达到理想的生态调节功能。宽度原理也是这几个原理中最难掌握的一个。

第二，建设要求：目前，在一些生态廊道的建设中，生态廊道的多种生态功能并没有被充分认识及融入生态廊道的建设中，生态功能发挥受到限制，针对目前存在的生态廊道建设问题，可以从以下几个方面予以重视并加以解决：①注重生态廊道的生态功能。随着工业化和城镇化的发展，区域生态环境问题逐渐凸显，廊道的生态功能越来越受到重视。生态廊道构建不应仅局限于城市绿

---

① 郑好，高吉喜，谢高地，等. 生态廊道[J]. 生态与农村环境学报，2019，35（2）.
② 关于广东省绿道网建设总体规划（2011~2015年）的批复 http://www.gd.gov.cn/gkmlpt/content/0/140/post_140709.html

化、景观设计和文化休憩等方面，基于生物多样性保护、生态功能提升以及生态安全格局维护为主的生态廊道构建是未来的重要研究方向。②建立大尺度生态廊道。生态环境问题逐渐呈现区域化和全球化的趋势，景观连通性降低已成为不同地区和国家所面临的共同问题。因此，生态廊道构建需要从区域生态学出发，开展连续流域和山脉的区域层面、国家层面以及洲际层面的大型生态廊道建设，加强区域生态系统连通性和完整性，整体提升区域生态系统服务功能。在大型廊道规划和建设的过程中，需要全国各省、直辖市、自治区或各国政府提供跨界合作支持。③统筹考虑生态保护和生态通道建设。国际上大型生态廊道构建往往统筹考虑已有的生态保护工作基础。如20世纪90年代的欧洲绿带计划（The European Green Belt）[1]是欧洲绿色基础设施的重要基石和组成部分。由此可见，生态用地保护、植被带建设、生态规划等已有成果能够为大型生态廊道构建提供支持和保障，需要将廊道建设与生态保护基础和规划相统一、相衔接和相融合。

三、遗产保护型廊道

（一）文化线路

文化线路是指一种陆地道路、水道或者混合类型的通道，其形态特征的定型和形成基于它自身具体的和历史的动态发展和功能演变；它代表了众多的迁徙和流动，代表了一定时间内国家和地区内部或国家和地区之间人们的交往，代表了多维度的商品、思想、知识和价值的互惠和持续不断的交流；还代表了因此产生的文化在时间和空间上的交流与相互滋养，这些滋养长期以来通过物质和非物质遗产不断地得到体现[2]。

文化线路在选择和认定上更加严格，注重其文化意义，强调文化影响、交流和对话，是一种客观存在的遗产类型，那些通过不同遗产串联起来的、不具备历史文化意义的路线不能被认定为文化线路。

（二）遗产廊道

1. 遗产廊道的概念及内涵

从遗产廊道的发展脉络来看，它最初由绿道演变而来，即作为历史线路绿道与遗产保护相结合形成的区域化的遗产保护战略方法，而后逐渐发展成为独立的廊道形态。遗产廊道是集合了文化资源的带状景观，追求文化遗产保护和自然保护并举，同时兼顾经济发展、区域振兴、居民休闲和教育等多重目标。具体是指"拥有特殊文化资源集合的线性景观。通常带有明显的经济中心、蓬勃发展的旅游、老建筑的适应性再利用、娱乐及环境改善"。带状地貌如河流、峡谷、运河等，以及道路和铁路线等交通线路，都是遗产廊道的表现形式。它是历史文化保护向区域化发展的产物，是绿色廊道和遗产区域进行综合的遗产保护形式。

---

[1] 孙帅. 都市型绿道规划设计研究［D］. 北京：北京林业大学，2013.
[2] 陶犁. "文化廊道"及旅游开发：一种新的线性遗产区域旅游开发思路［J］. 思想战线，2012，38（2）.

遗产廊道首先是一种线性的遗产区域。它把文化意义提到首位，可以是河流峡谷、运河、道路以及铁路线，也可以指能够把单个的遗产点串联起来的具有一定历史意义的线性廊道。它们是人与自然长期共同发展、共同作用过程中形成的"人与自然的共同作品"。

2. 遗产廊道的功能

遗产廊道对遗产的保护采用区域而非局部点的概念，是一个综合保护措施，自然、经济、历史文化三者并举，是多目标的保护体系。

遗产廊道的内涵非常丰富，不仅强调遗产保护的文化意义，而且强调其生态和旅游经济价值。遗产廊道同时也可以成为战略性的生态基础设施（Ecological Infrastructure）。遗产廊道不仅保护了那些具有文化意义的线形遗产区域，而且通过适当的生态恢复措施和旅游开发手段，使区域内的生态环境得到恢复和保护，使得一些原本缺乏活力的点状遗产重新焕发青春，成为现代生活的一部分，为城乡居民提供游憩、休闲、教育等生态服务。这一点对于那些经济发展落后、人地关系危机严重的地区来说尤为重要。

3. 遗产廊道的特点

（1）是线性景观。遗产廊道属线性景观，这决定了遗产廊道同遗产区域的区别。一处风景名胜区或一座历史文化名城都可称之为是一个遗产区域，但遗产廊道是一种线性的遗产区域。它对遗产的保护采用区域而非局部点的概念，内部可以包括多种不同的遗产，可以是长达几千米以上的线性区域。

（2）尺度可大可小，但多为中尺度。这同绿色廊道很相似。它既可指某一城市中一条水系，也可大到跨几个城市的一条水系的部分流域。宾夕法尼亚州"历史路径"（The Historic Pathway）是一条长1.5英里的遗产廊道，而Los Cominosdel Rio Heritage Corridor 则有210英里长[1]。

（3）是一个综合保护措施。自然、经济、历史文化三者并举，不同于绿色廊道强调自然生态系统的重要性，它可以不具文化特性。遗产廊道将历史文化内涵提到首位，同时强调经济价值和自然生态系统的平衡能力。

4. 遗产廊道的开发实践

（1）开发要求。线性遗产由于其空间和时间上的跨度大、结构复杂、功能多样，对其保护和开发有一定难度和特殊性。同时，线性遗产的时空特征及系统功能，决定了对其旅游开发、遗产保护、价值挖掘等方面应有新的视角和方式。

（2）开发实践。在国外，伊利诺斯和密歇根运河于1984年被指定为第一条遗产廊道。此后黑石河峡谷国家遗产廊道、特拉华和莱通航运河国家遗产廊道及西班牙的桑地亚哥·德·卡姆博斯特拉朝圣路相继被列为遗产廊道[2]。

---

[1] 孙帅. 都市型绿道规划设计研究［D］. 北京：北京林业大学，2013.
[2] 王肖宇，陈伯超. 美国国家遗产廊道的保护——以黑石河峡谷为例［J］. 世界建筑，2007（7）.

美国的黑石河国家遗产廊道位于马萨诸塞和罗德岛内,其见证了人们定居工业化和环境退化的整个过程。在文化遗产系统利用方面,由于黑石河地区拥有大量的历史和考古资源以及工业遗存下来的厂房,规划中对历史工业建筑重新利用改造成新型工厂,同时将原先零散的文化遗产整合成区域性的整体,在遗产集中分布的区域规划主题组团。黑石河遗产廊道充分利用其自然生态系统,运用黑石河流域及支流地区已有的自然资源,如将湖泊、湿地等建设成为生态公园;原有的农田改造为田园式景观;峡谷等自然地形开发成森林探险、攀岩等旅游项目,并建设野生动植物保护区。除此之外,黑石河国家遗产廊道还建立了完善的支持系统,包括游憩系统、解说系统、公共服务设施系统以及管理系统,并鼓励在廊道上组织庆祝文化方面的活动。黑石河遗产廊道三位一体的保护规划体系,极大地促进了该地区文化、环境、经济的二次繁荣。

新加坡河是新加坡的命脉,早期的新加坡河港口贸易繁盛,频繁的交通量导致河道受到了严重污染而逐渐没落。新加坡运河在进行新一轮总体规划中对文化历史、自然生态等资源采用了主题分类开发的方法,将其划分为纪念性主题、宗教性主题、标志性主题三大类,针对主题特点进行形象包装体系的打造,建立了鱼尾狮公园、莱佛士登陆岸遗址、新加坡旧国会大厦、红灯码头等具有代表性的形象景点,并利用自然生态资源,建设新加坡河水上历史游览道和沿线自行车绿道系统。另外,新加坡运河配套了完善的支持系统增加其旅游体验感,如通过健全的慢行游憩系统对旅游资源进行串联,形成旅游廊道系统;设置多种文字的综合导向牌及互动体验式解说系统;构建具有历史特色的配套服务系统等。"遗产廊道"理念的引入,为保护新加坡河摆脱重重危机提供了新的思路和方法。

我国具有较为丰富的线形文化遗产,如古运河、长江三峡、丝绸之路、剑门蜀道等,目前也围绕着遗产廊道进行了一些相关的开发与保护措施。

(3)启示借鉴。①保护与可持续利用相结合,通过遗产廊道带动区域经济的复兴。慢行游憩系统的完善、解说系统的构建以及行之有效的市场与营销策略是遗产廊道对资源进行可持续利用的主要方法。②统筹与协调,建立以核心部门为纽带的广泛的合作伙伴关系实现共同管理。遗产廊道跨区域、多功能的属性决定了其管理工作需要经常协调不同行政区域和职能部门。因此,只有形成以具有执行力的核心管理部门为纽带,集各类政府机构及民间非营利组织为一体的合作伙伴关系进行统筹与协调,才能真正实现有效的沟通与管理,确保保护与管理等各项工作的顺利实施。

5. 遗产廊道与旅游开发

遗产廊道是始于美国的一种遗产区域保护方式,是指拥有特殊文化资源集合的线性景观,通常带有明显的经济中心、蓬勃发展的旅游、老建筑的适应性再利用、娱乐及环境改善等特点。作为绿色廊道和遗产区域结合的产物,遗产廊道不仅强调线性遗产保护的文化意义,而且强调其旅游价值、生态价值和经济价值。

(1)遗产廊道与旅游开发的关系。遗产廊道与旅游开发之间密切相关。一方面,从遗产廊道的视角进行旅游开发,是一种线性遗产区域旅游开发的新方式;另一方面,旅游开发是遗产廊道开发和保护的重要途径。主要依据如下：

第一，创新文化遗产区域保护和开发途径的需要。许多重要的自然和文化资源都集中于线性区域，河流沿岸有着丰富的线性遗产资源，最常见的形式是以历史时期人类迁徙和交流所形成的通道文化为基础的线性文化遗产。线性遗产除其固有的历史、文化价值外，往往还具有社会、生态、经济乃至政治价值，同时具有杰出的旅游开发价值。线性遗产由于其空间和时间上的跨度大、结构复杂、功能多样，对其保护和开发有一定难度和特殊性，必须创新文化遗产区域保护和开发的途径和方式。实践上，旅游是对文化遗产区域最直接的利用方式。

第二，发掘线性遗产区域多元价值的要求。遗产廊道的内涵和出发点不仅强调线路文化的"原真性""完整性"和文化遗产的保护，还同时将线路区域的整体开发及线路与环境、社区的关系放在重要位置。旅游活动具有经济和文化双重属性，具有最鲜明的系统性特征，是一种综合的发掘线路多元价值的方式。

第三，遗产廊道是一种对线性旅游产品较为深刻的表现形式。线性特征是大多数旅游产品的一个重要特征。遗产廊道可以成为旅游线路的灵魂，将单独的旅游景区景点、设施服务、城镇聚落、道路桥梁、环境生态通过跨越时空的故事联系起来，形成线状、带状和网状的旅游目的地特征，是一种对旅游产品最深刻的体验方式之一；廊道景观表达方式的"地方性"转变为旅游地的"地方性""标志性""可识别性"，并吸引旅游者，产生深刻的景观意向。

第四，遗产廊道的旅游开发可以创新旅游开发思路和模式。线性文化遗产的时空特征及系统功能，决定了对其旅游开发、遗产保护、价值挖掘等方面应有新视角和方式。遗产廊道的旅游开发体现了以下几方面的创新：①从以景点、景区为重点的旅游开发模式，到以线路为中心的开发模式，在更广范围内整合流域内线路资源，带动旅游温、冷点地区的开发；②从以决策为中心的旅游规划模式，回归到以文化为中心的规划重点，在更高层次上协调旅游、文化和环境的关系；③从以目的地品牌为重点的营销模式，到以线路文化品牌打造和管理为重点，实现全新的旅游品牌管理方式；④从对旅游交通物理属性的重视，上升到动态的、活态的、强调交流互动的具有"线路精神"的社会和心理层面。

（2）遗产廊道旅游开发的资源价值。

①文化价值。遗产廊道是一种特殊的文化景观遗产，以三峡为例，瞿塘峡以三国文化为支撑，巫峡以巴风巫韵的历史文化为内涵，西陵峡以三峡水利工程文化为重点。这些独特的文化底蕴正是其旅游业发展的灵魂。对于河流遗产廊道来说，其作为整体蕴含的文化价值远远大于各遗产点的旅游价值之和。因此，依托于遗产廊道的整体文化价值评价更具实际意义。打造不同文化遗产廊道线路，不仅对于遗产廊道保护具有重要意义，而且对河流廊道范围内旅游业发展也能起到推动作用。

②生态价值。一定尺度上的遗产廊道同时也可以成为战略性的生态基础建设工程。遗产廊道不仅保护了那些具有文化意义的线性遗产区域，而且通过适当的生态恢复措施和旅游开发手段，也可以使区域内的生态环境得到恢复和保护，使得一些原本缺乏活力的点状遗产重新焕发青春，成为现

代生活的一部分，为城乡居民提供游憩、休闲、教育等生态服务。这一点对于那些经济发展落后、人地关系危机严重的地区来说显得尤为重要。

遗产廊道的保护规划除了像一般的绿道规划强调景观生态过程，强调土地覆被、野生动物、栖息地和适宜性等因素以外，更重视的是对文化因素的保护和旅游开发的组织。就文化因素来讲，它强调对具有历史意义的植被如古树名木的保护，同时也注重历史气氛的烘托。

③游憩价值。遗产廊道区域往往拥有丰富的自然和文化旅游资源，生态与文化遗产旅游廊道游憩价值十分突出。对于河流遗产廊道而言，自行车道、游步道系统的设计提供了游憩活动可实现路径，廊道沿线文化和自然资源具有高质量的游憩价值。以生态保护、遗产保护和旅游开发为目的的遗产廊道本身就是一条旅游廊道，如若通过文化资源的整合，解说系统的构建，打造游憩线路，不仅能提升游客体验，而且能提升当地居民生活水平，其综合效益将惠及遗产廊道沿线地区。

④教育价值。遗产旅游廊道的教育价值可以体现为生态环境的保护、历史文化知识的普及、非物质文化遗产的保护与传承等。构建生态与文化遗产旅游廊道，有助于提升政府、当地居民和游客的环保意识。同时，遗产廊道大多拥有辉煌灿烂的历史文化，拥有丰富的非物质文化遗产，通过遗产廊道的核心解说系统可使人们了解遗产的历史、文化、美学价值等。

总体而言，建设遗产廊道，将使原先零散的文化遗产成为区域性的整体，通过系统的解说、游道组织，可以促进旅游业的发展，这一点已经被大量的事实所证实。在实践中美国很多地方遗产廊道带来的旅游业已经成为地方经济的亮点之一。建设遗产廊道，可以使得大量的文化遗产焕发活力，并且可以促进文化旅游的发展。

四、旅游开发型廊道

景观生态型廊道和遗产保护型廊道分别立足于生态和文化的视角进行廊道研究，两种类型的廊道都不可避免地涉及旅游游憩功能，因为生态景观品质高、文化资源价值高的线性空间本身就是开发潜力高的旅游资源，旅游开发型廊道由此产生[①]。

（一）旅游线路

旅游线路是旅游者从居住地出行到达一个或多个旅游目的地游憩并返回居住地所经历的空间线路。虽然旅游线路的空间模式呈现多样化特征，但旅游者从居住地到达目的地的空间位移轨迹则一定是线性的。旅游线路的概念弱化了旅游廊道的空间意义，强调旅游产品的组合与统筹安排，其追求的目标在于实现旅游时间安排的最优化方案。

（二）旅游走廊

旅游走廊常常被理解为旅游观光的通道，然而其所包含的内容并不仅仅在此。旅游廊道是以线型通道将旅游业所有要素进行联结聚合，实质是一种线型的旅游生产力空间布局形式。其具体实

---

① 邱海莲，由亚男. 旅游廊道概念界定［J］. 旅游论坛，2015，8（4）.

现形式是以交通干线或山脉河流等带状旅游吸引物为轴，聚合相互联系紧密的各类旅游资源区，并以城镇等旅游中心为增长极形成带状旅游系统。旅游走廊是"点轴理论"在旅游产业空间组织上的应用。

（三）风景道

1. 风景道的概念及内涵

风景道是旅游与交通功能相结合的景观道路，具有交通、景观、游憩、历史、文化、自然、文物等多重价值。在研究风景道及相关问题时，经常使用的概念有公园道（Parkway）、风景道（Scenic Byway）、文化线路（Culture Routes）、遗产廊道（Heritage Corridors）、风景公路（Scenic Highway）、风景驾车道（Scenic Drive）、风景线路（Scenic Routes）、风景路（Scenic Roads）、自然风景路（Natural Beauty Roads）、历史路（Historic Roads）、工程线路（Engineered Routes）等。总体上看，这些概念互有重复，有些含义略有不同，但均指"路旁或视域之内拥有审美风景、自然、文化、历史、游憩价值、考古学上值得保存和修复的景观道路"。对于风景道的定义，有广义和狭义之分：广义的是指兼具交通运输和景观欣赏双重功能的通道；狭义的则专指路旁或视域之内拥有审美风景的、自然的、文化的、历史的、考古学上的和（或）值得保存、修复、保护和增进的具游憩价值的景观道路。[①]

风景道（Scenic Byway）源起于欧美，是欧美国家百余年来注重生态环境、自然文化遗产保护和管理的延续及发展，反映了工程技术和生态保护、历史文化、景观环境、旅游游憩、社区经济等综合发展的新趋势。风景道是"生态文明"的一种发展，是综合交通运输发展的必然，也是当今自驾游时代和全域旅游时代发展的必然。

风景道现如今在保护生态环境、增加自然人文资源吸引力、满足审美游憩需求、优化城市、道路设计、拉动社区经济增长等多方面，正发挥着日益重要的作用。

滨水型风景道，即滨临河流、湖泊或者海洋等水体，且穿越的地区以水域为主体的风景道。从穿越的地区来看，风景道可分为三类：滨河型风景道即滨临江、河，且穿越的地区以河流为主体的风景道；滨湖型风景道即滨临湖泊，且穿越的地区以湖泊为主体的风景道；滨海型风景道即滨临海洋，且穿越的地区以海洋为主体的风景道。河流通常是人类与水最常接近的地方，与使用人群的关系最为密切，是风景道建设应重点投入的区域，而滨湖和滨海等形式由于其水域面积等因素，与人们的关系相对疏远。

2. 风景道的空间结构

廊道的实践发展表明，旅游廊道空间结构与一般廊道结构相似，具有轴线、节点和域面等空间组成元素。轴线是风景道的基本骨架，主要由公路交通线或具有旅游产业要素聚集能力的山脉、沟谷、河流等吸引物构成；如流经中国、缅甸、泰国、老挝、柬埔寨和越南6国的澜沧江—湄公河就是中国西南边境旅游开展的最重要旅游廊道。节点是旅游资源聚集区域和旅游集散中心与旅游服务

[①] 余青，吴必虎，刘志敏等. 风景道研究与规划实践综述[J]. 地理研究，2007（6）.

设施集中区域；域面是风景道辐射和影响的范围，这一范围以风景道轴线为中心，向两侧延伸，形成风景道空间范围。因此风景道是开放性的条带状空间，廊道的宽度和覆盖范围取决于轴线的集聚能力和风景道沿线内旅游产业发展的成熟程度。

3. 风景道的开发原则

风景道这一线性空间规划相对于点状和面状景点景区规划，最大的差别在于人们将公路廊道作为一个更广阔的人的价值的混合体，需要强化其在旅游者旅行途中的景观观赏功能、休闲游憩功能、体验教育功能和信息引导功能。在其开发建设中要遵循参考以下几个原则：

（1）自然生态原则。风景道沿线一般都是自然景观优美的地区，因此，在规划设计中要遵从自然，对于风景道路中新添加的景观与建筑也应起到良好的结合，同时，要保护生态系统的多样性，对自然环境和原始自然风貌予以保护，实现可持续发展。

（2）"四水"原则。具有旅游功能的风景道应该在开发时遵循亲水、赏水、戏水、玩水的原则，为游客提供充足的与水亲近的机会，从设施设计、游憩活动设计等多方面体现亲水性。

（3）陆、岸、水三类游憩活动的有机组合原则。河流的风景道独特之处，在于其连接了水体、岸带以及陆域三类地形，因此，可以以这三类要素为基础开发多种类型的游憩活动并进行科学有机的组合。其中，陆域要素包括滨水建筑、道路与游径系统、解说系统、游憩服务设施等；水体要素包括基于水体的游憩活动、水体设计等；岸带要素包括景观与植物配置、护岸、岸线设计等。

（4）文脉保护与延续原则。在风景道的开发与建设过程中，始终要注意历史文脉的保护与延续的原则，尊重历史，继承和保护历史文化遗产，提升风景道在历史文化方面的凝聚力和感召力。

（5）交通方式多样化、立体化原则。为了实现游憩活动的有机组合，可使游客以立体化的视角来体验风景道，交通方式的建设应以多样、立体的原则，采取多种交通方式进行组合，满足游客多样化的需求，以立体化的角度体验风景道。

4. 风景道的旅游特征

（1）旅游吸引物串联线索。从旅游资源的角度，景观生态型廊道和遗产保护型廊道的构成要素——自然景观与文化遗产都是旅游吸引物，这些旅游吸引物以一定的空间秩序串联起来形成旅游廊道的基础条件。每一条风景道应当拥有特定主题，以塑造独特的旅游形象，这一特定主题取决于旅游吸引物的内容。作为旅游吸引物串联线索，风景道体现了旅游线路的部分特点。

（2）游憩体验空间。风景道是区别于点、面的轴线型游憩空间，线性游憩空间使旅游者的观赏体验由静态转化为动态，对旅游吸引物形成整体连续的理解。这种线性游憩空间允许旅游者获得更丰富的旅行体验，在旅行过程中得到多种旅游交通形式的愉悦感受，如自驾车、徒步、自行车等都是风景道适宜开发的旅游产品形式。

（3）旅游产业聚集轴线。根据区域经济学的增长极理论和点轴理论，区域中具有资源优势的节点优先发展，发展势能沿发展轴向外延伸，形成产业带，最终带动整个区域的经济发展。旅游产业的发展需要同时具备旅游吸引物、旅游企业服务、旅游支持保障以及旅游客流，这些要素在风景道廊道区域内的流动和配置，廊道的交通线起聚合轴和发展轴的作用，成为廊道内旅游合作和客流运行的通道。各相对独立的旅游空间由交通线整合为完整带状旅游空间，激发旅游资源开发活力，同时保证产业要素的流动，从而促进整个带状区域旅游业的发展壮大。

5. 风景道的开发实践

在实践中，美国是风景道的发源地、主要实践地和研发基地。依据美国提出的保护和促进风景道发展的官方推广计划——国家风景道计划（National Scenic Byway Program），美国分别于1996年、1998年、2000年、2002年和2005年分5批共计评选出了32条泛美风景道和133条国家风景道，建立了由国家、州和地方级风景道构成的美国国家风景道体系。从主题划分上来看，国家风景道体系中的风景道包含了滨水型、山地型、生态型、遗产型、运动休闲型、民俗文化型等各种类型，不同主题型的风景道已在美国风景道的实践和理论中取得很大的实践和研究成果。滨水型风景道由于所占比例大，且大都位于经济社会发达地区，因此研究成果显著，特别是在实践中获得了巨大的推进与发展。

例如：美国的大河路（Great River Road）为著名的滨水自然、历史混合型风景道。大河路位于美国东部地区的密西西比河流域，自北向南，大河依次经过明尼苏达州、威斯康星州、艾奥瓦州、伊利诺伊州、密苏里州、肯塔基州、田纳西州、阿肯色州、密西西比州、路易斯安那州，总长将近3000英里（约4800千米），其中国家风景道的区段总长2069英里（约3329.7千米），是体验密西西比河奇观的必经之路。大河路（被指定为"国家风景道"的区段）按道路沿途密西西比河所呈现的景观特征的不同，可以分为四段密西西比河源头段、上游段、中游段与下游段[①]。

密西西比河和缓的源头段：源头段为大河路明尼苏达州段，即源头至圣保罗一段，河水清凉、舒缓，大河路沿线自然景色优美，有众多湖泊、沼泽与乡间低地。

上游滨水自然美景段：上游段从圣保罗至密苏里州圣路易附近密苏里河河口。此段流经石灰岩峭壁之间，景观壮美。美国土著文化突出，这一河段被当地印第安人称为"河流之父"。

中游滨水都市旅游段：自密苏里河汇入处至俄亥俄河河口为中游段。该段水流湍急，泥沙含量大。沿线有很多大都市，工业发达，城市旅游繁荣。

下游滨水游憩娱乐段：俄亥俄河在伊利诺州开罗汇入后，为密西西比河下游，该段河水丰满，河道宽广，两岸之间往往有公里之距，景观壮阔，游憩娱乐活动异常丰富。

相较于国外已对不同主题类型的风景道进行了研究与探讨，形成了较为成熟与完善的风景道体系，我国风景道的建设处于起步阶段，目前正在积极推进的过程中。我国领土广阔，河流、湖泊众多，水资源丰富，水网密布，尤其是大江大河蔚为壮观，为大河流域风景道开发与建设奠定了极好的资源条件，可以说，大河流域的风景道发展潜力巨大，前景广阔。例如，2018年6月25日，山

---

① 柳晓霞. 滨水型风景道规划设计研究 [D]. 北京：北京交通大学，2009.

西省旅游发展委员会对外公布《山西省黄河板块旅游发展规划》[①]，规划中明确提出要建设一条黄河风景道，即将沿黄 1225 公里公路建成"山西省黄河一号国家旅游专用公路"，形成板块南北畅通、旅游服务设施齐全、景观优美的国家级风景廊道。

总之，由国外发展而来的风景道具有的交通、景观、游憩、生态和保护等复合功能，所遵循的生态原则、景观原则和可持续发展原则，顺应了交通规划、景观设计、城市规划和旅游游憩发展趋势，受到了政府、投资商、旅游者和社区居民越来越多的重视和青睐，在交通、景观、城市建设、旅游游憩、环境保护和带动地方经济发展等方面正在发挥着重要的作用。

[①] 山西省人民政府办公厅关于印发山西省黄河、长城、太行三大板块旅游发展总体规划的通知_通知公告_新闻中心_山西省文化和旅游厅政务网 http://wlt.shanxi.gov.cn/sitefiles/sxzwcms/html/xwzx/tzgg/14977.shtml

第三篇
大河文明旅游发展经验与对策

第一章 中国黄河文明旅游发展经验

黄河自青藏高原起源，一路向东依次流过内蒙古高原、黄土高原和华北平原，最终汇入渤海。在不同的地理单元，黄河与当地自然环境融合，孕育了独特的地域文化。近年来，黄河沿线各省以开发和利用黄河文化为切入点，通过合作交流，共建黄河旅游发展平台，大力发展黄河文化旅游产业，推动地方经济转型已成为浪潮。其中，山西是最重要的沿黄流域省份，山西是黄河文明的发祥地，黄河文化同样也是山西文化旅游资源的重要组成部分，山西沿黄地区呈现出了独具魅力的自然景观，孕育了代表民族魂魄的黄河人文精神，形成了具有黄河文化标签的文化旅游目的地。

第一节 黄河文明旅游发展经验

黄河流域的省区通过开展一系列的合作，创新黄河旅游发展的合作机制与合作内容，并发布相关研究报告，对黄河旅游的发展进行分析，并从不同方面为未来的发展提供建议与对策。本节将对黄河文明旅游的发展经验进行深入阐释，通过相关经验的剖析，有利于为其他地区大河文明旅游的市场开发、产品设计、营销宣传等提供借鉴与启示。

一、发布《中国黄河旅游发展指数报告》

在 2018 年召开的中国黄河旅游大会上，发布了《中国黄河旅游发展指数报告》，该报告结合定性定量方法，通过网络舆情监测、国内外在线调查、深度访问等形式开展数据采集，涵盖美国、加拿大、日本、英国、阿联酋等 23 个国家和地区，覆盖 90% 以上的客源国。通过黄河旅游影响力指数、传播指数、品质旅游发展指数三大数据，专业分析了黄河旅游的可持续发展。在沿黄主要省区有关黄河旅游传播指数中，山西省排第二名，黄河壶口瀑布入围"中国黄河 50 景"代表景区，并受到较高的关注度[1]。

通过发布专业的数据研究报告，对黄河流域的旅游发展进行全面的分析，并从黄河旅游的影响力指数、传播指数、品质旅游发展指数三个方面进行专业的深入解读，让更多的旅游从业者、相关政府工作者等更加清楚地了解黄河旅游的发展现状，明晰了黄河文明旅游产业、各类旅游产品、市

---

[1] 2018 中国黄河旅游大会，《中国黄河旅游发展指数报告》成焦点 http://www.ctnews.com.cn/art/2018/9/21/art_126_25438.html

场开发与营销宣传的发展思路。通过发布该报告，也让更多的人了解了黄河丰富的旅游文化资源、旅游产品等，不仅扩大了黄河文明旅游的影响力、知名度等，也在一定程度上提升了沿黄地区的城市和景区的影响力。

二、举办黄河旅游大会，打造交流合作平台

黄河沿线地区的城市举办了不同类型的黄河旅游大会，打造黄河旅游带的交流合作平台，以此来加强黄河流域内不同地区的交流、沟通与合作。通过黄河旅游大会的举办，一是，有利于旅游专家学者、旅游行业从业者、相关政府管理人员共同研究探讨黄河文明、建设保护黄河流域地区的人文与自然生态环境、深入挖掘黄河不同类型的文旅资源；二是，展示黄河文明旅游的发展成果，有效地把沿黄各地旅游业紧紧相连在了一起，共同开发黄河旅游产品、做大黄河旅游产业规模、打造黄河文化旅游精品项目、提高黄河旅游品牌知名度和影响力以引导国内外游客认知黄河文明、畅游黄河风情，最终把黄河文明旅游带打造成为世界知名的旅游目的地；三是，通过黄河文明带动其沿线城市的全域旅游发展，推动黄河流域地区构建旅游产业新体系，这也已经成为我国旅游业进入新时代的发展特征和必由之路；四是，加强沿黄城市之间的互相交流和支持，共同开展黄河文明旅游的宣传推广，把黄河文化魅力讲给全世界，提高黄河文明旅游的品牌知名度；五是，进一步扩大了各城市之间的参与范围、合作领域，增加融合黏度，形成更大合力为黄河沿线旅游产业服务，打造世界级的中华文明之旅体验线，让黄河沿线旅游的好产品、好服务实现全民共同分享；六是，通过会议交流合作平台，有助于沿黄城市之相互学习、分享、交流各自在黄河旅游开发上的经验与做法，共同提升黄河旅游的开发能力，以及全域旅游综合治理能力，促进沿黄城市优质旅游的形成。

总而言之，通过召开不同的黄河旅游大会深入探讨黄河旅游合作与发展，为沿黄区域旅游产业搭建多种类型的沟通与合作平台，对促进黄河文明旅游发展和产业繁荣具有重要作用。

三、设立沿黄旅游产业发展基金促进共同发展

沿黄城市旅游产业联盟发展基金由陕西省旅游发展委员会和韩城市人民政府联合发起设立，基金吸引了华侨城集团公司、海航集团有限公司等多个知名投资机构，以及与平安银行、中信银行、浦发银行等多家银行达成合作，为将要投资的项目顺利建成搭建了良好的资本平台。基金总规模200亿元，首期出资20亿元，主要投资于沿黄区域旅游设施项目、旅游观光项目、文旅产业项目等沿黄优质旅游、文化项目，充分发挥政府资金带动作用。投资项目涉及"旅游+扶贫""旅游+文化""旅游+体育""旅游+科技""旅游+康养"等产业融合项目，可有效带动沿黄城市由传统旅游向产业化发展，丰富旅游产品体系、创新旅游产品的形式与内容，实现文旅融合，打造以黄河文明旅游为核心的河流型旅游目的地。为沿黄城市旅游产业联盟发展、全域旅游时代黄河流域产品开发以及大力推进产业融合发展提供重要支撑，加速黄河旅游向品质化、品牌化发展。

四、成立沿黄城市旅游产业联盟创新合作机制

为了更好地促进黄河文明旅游更好、更快地发展，黄河流域城市打破行政区划概念，冲破行业束缚，构建以黄河为纽带、以城市为载体、以产品为核心、以市场为导向、以互利合作为前提的沿黄河流域旅游发展共同体，沿黄城市旅游产业联盟乘势而为，应运而生。沿黄9省的旅游城市创建了该联盟，沿黄城市旅游产业联盟以搭建合作共赢平台、服务成员单位、实现优势互补、力促资源共享为己任，携手打造中国江河旅游合作新样板。以沿黄城市旅游产业联盟的成立为平台，创新合作机制与合作形式，合力打造黄河华夏文明旅游带的新亮点，把黄河文明旅游建设成为世界知名的旅游品牌和文化旅游带。各联盟成员将在政策咨询、旅游产业合作、黄河旅游产品开发、精品旅游线路设计、宣传营销、黄河旅游形象打造、黄河文明品牌包装、城市和企业之间的合作交流、经验分享上进行更多互动式合作，搭建更多交流合作大平台，以促进中国黄河文明旅游向产品系列化、服务品质化、市场规范化、交流常态化发展，努力把黄河旅游带推向国际。

第二节 山西省黄河文明旅游发展模式

在黄河流域的众多省份中，山西省黄河文明旅游资源丰富，具有鲜明的特色、形象突出。山西临汾古为帝尧之都，尧文化是中国原始社会后期向第一个阶级社会过渡时期的文化，是中华民族传统文化的主要源头，在中华文明的发展中具有承前启后的重要作用，上承原始社会文化，下启华夏文明。因此，山西临汾是黄河文明的发祥地，更有着"五千年文明看山西，黄河之魂在山西"的美誉。山西省资源蕴藏丰厚，特色鲜明，孕育和书写了黄河文明的华美篇章，山西素有华夏文明的"主题公园"、中国古代建筑博物馆、中国古代东方艺术宝库、中国古戏曲的摇篮、中国社会变革的"思想库"之美称。而在山西黄河段中，又以临汾黄河段的自然资源和文化资源最为多样，临汾素有"华夏第一都"的美称，是华夏民族文化的重要发祥地之一，也是黄河文明的摇篮，并形成了独特的发展模式。

一、临汾黄河文明旅游资源

山西黄河北起忻州偏关县关老牛湾，南至运城垣曲县马蹄窝，流经山西1081千米，包括19个县4市，其中有11个县为国家级重点生态功能区，同时为生态治理带，有4个县为国家级农产品主产区。山西黄河旅游资源丰富，有众多壮美的景观，沿途30多个传统旅游景点，有壶口瀑布自然壮丽的景观，还保存有一大批风光优美的自然村落，沿途还有尧、舜、禹等史前帝王活动遗迹，成为中华民族古老文明的发祥地之一。拥有历史悠久的黄河文明和丰富多彩的民俗文化、农耕文化、红色文化及名山大川，为山西黄河旅游发展奠定了良好的人文景观和自然景观基础。其中在山西黄河段，以临汾的黄河旅游文化和自然资源最为丰富，临汾是中华民族发祥地之一，《帝王世纪》

称："尧都平阳"，即今临汾。《禹贡》分天下为九州，平阳为冀州之地。冀州处九州之中央，故称"中国"，"中国"一词由此而来。

临汾是山西省最早开发黄河旅游的地市，黄河旅游是临汾"中国根·黄河魂"两大旅游品牌之一，是山西省黄河板块的主体区和核心区。壶口瀑布、乾坤湾等景区不仅是黄河板块上最具观赏价值的旅游景区，而且是黄河文明的核心、中华精神的地标。一句"所有旅行都是出发，到了临汾咱是回家"叩响着多少游子的故土情节。临汾市发展目标明确，步伐稳健，"平阳记忆""印象临汾"两大工程锻造城市新名片，"黄河、太岳、根祖"三大旅游板块叫响"中国根·黄河魂"旅游品牌。

（一）临汾市概况

1. 地理位置优越，交通便利

临汾市地处山西的西南部，黄河中游，汾河下游，现辖1区、2市、14县和两个经济技术开发区，总面积2.0275万平方千米。临汾市的地理位置优越，交通便利，处在京津地区、太原、郑州、西安等旅游热点中心，交通便捷，具有比较优越的旅游区位条件。临汾市区有火车站2座，分别是临汾站和临汾西站（大西高铁）。临汾市南北以全国铁路大动脉同蒲铁路、大西高铁纵贯，侯西线、侯月线横穿其东西区域，四大铁路干线在临汾境内所架构的铁路体系，纵横1835千米，并且有临汾乔李机场。临汾是中国东西走向的第二条大动脉和欧亚大陆桥的重要区间，其所辖的侯马市是华北铁路交通大枢纽、中国四大货运中心站之一。

2. 气候宜人，适宜旅游

临汾市地处半干旱、半湿润季风气候区，属温带大陆性气候，光照充足、热资源丰富、雨热同期的气候特点，气候宜人，人文文化浓厚，是旅游的理想地区。全市年内四季分明，春季气温回升迅速，夏季炎热多雨、雨热同季，秋季气候宜人、天高气爽，冬季干燥少雪，一年中的4~10月都是适宜旅游的月份；3月和11月虽为季节交换的过渡月份，但大部分县（区）的气候也是舒适，适宜旅游的。①

3. 社会环境优良

2017年12月，临汾入围2017中国特色魅力城市200强。中国特色魅力城市品牌不仅是城市生产、生活、宜居魅力的综合表征，而且也是城市融入现代化、国际化、智慧城市可持续发展的重要标志。该评选主要是由世界著名品牌大会（WFBA）对城市进行全面评估，重点调研9个方面的城市特色：历史风貌、生态文明、发展质量、民生幸福、法治化水平、创新活力、实体经济、"互联网+"、地域文化，同时重点调研15项指标：国际游客数量、生态环境质量、社区安全指数、人均公共绿地面积、居民可支配收入、民生满意度、政府管理效率、实体经济比重、森林覆盖率、互联网新经济比重、投资软硬环境、大数据平台建设、电商物流比重、技术进步贡献率、专利申请数量。根据

---

① 高明，贾海燕，申存良等. 临汾市旅游气候舒适度特征分析［C］// 第33届中国气象学会年会S5应对气候变化、低碳发展与生态文明建设. 2016.

候选城市各项指标的表现，通过独立公众问卷调查、统计数据分析、实地考察调研和权威专家函评等程序进行综合评价。临汾入围中国特色魅力城市说明其在以上各评价指标方面都有较高得分，也进一步说明其社会经济状况优良。[①]

此外，在2017年11月"世界厕所日暨中国厕所革命宣传日"活动中，临汾市荣获全国"厕所革命优秀城市奖"，这是临汾继获得"中国人居环境范例奖""迪拜国际最佳范例奖""中国公厕品牌示范城"称号后，在公厕文明建设中又一项最高荣誉。临汾市还在未来的厕所规划中融入绿色、环保、可循环、高科技理念，并结合社会老龄化的发展需求以及对婴幼儿的特殊照顾，设计"第三卫生间"，还将在城市厕所中增加自动存款机、报亭、便民书点、新能源汽车充电桩以及无线网络等便民设施，推动旅游厕所快速发展和提档升级。[②]

（二）文化与自然旅游资源多样

早在4000多年前，古帝尧王就在这里建都，因此有"华夏第一都"之称，也是中华民族生息繁衍的摇篮。临汾拥有较为丰富的自然景观、人文景观、非物质文化遗产等，以大河名山、根祖文化及多样的民俗风情旅游资源为特色。临汾有世界上最大的、被誉为"黄河的心脏"和"中华的灵魂"的黄色瀑布——黄河壶口瀑布；有全国著名的明代迁民遗址，以洪洞大槐树为标志的根祖文化旅游。临汾又是中国古文化的发祥地之一，以襄汾丁村遗址为代表的我国旧石器中期文化，"丁村人"和丁村文化反映了约10万年前旧石器中期人类文化的发展情况，丁村民俗博物馆又让人看到汉民族文化与民间风俗的丰富多彩，以及曲沃晋国博物馆、侯马晋国遗址为代表的晋文化等。

除此之外，还有与武当山齐名，中国古代著名的道教圣地云丘山；霍州州署是全国现存唯一的古代州级衙；有"华北绿肺"之称的七里峪太岳山国家森林公园等。可以说，在这里抓一把泥土，就可以攥出文明的汁液，华夏大半部的文明史都在这里浓缩。同时，临汾市非物质文化种类繁多，有蒲州梆子、威风锣鼓等多种民间艺术形式，被誉为"梅花之乡""剪纸之乡"和"锣鼓之乡"。

临汾在5000年的历史发展中形成了尧文化、根祖文化、黄河文化、民俗文化、红色文化等高品质的文化旅游资源，已经形成了中轴线寻根祭祖游、西线黄河风情游、东线生态休闲游三条精品线路，前两条线路已纳入全省六条精品线路中。临汾市目前拥有旅游景区（点）共计56处，其中，国家5A级旅游景区1处，国家4A级旅游景区12处，国家3A级旅游景区11处，国家2A级旅游景区2处，并且拥有国家级自然保护区2处、地质公园2处、风景名胜区1处、森林公园2处，国家级、省级生态农业旅游观光点10个，省级风景名胜区3处。由于历史文化悠久，临汾市博物馆的馆藏文物达4.6万余件。此外，还有全国重点文物保护单位43处、省级重点文物保护单位58处、各类文物单位3000余处，非物质文化遗产数量居全省首位，临汾的文化精髓和民俗特色值得步步回首、细细品读。

---

① 2017中国特色魅力城市200强出炉 http://china.cnr.cn/gdgg/20171224/t20171224_524073802.shtml
② 杜春春，临汾荣获全国"厕所革命优秀城市奖" http://www.xinhuanet.com/local/2017-11/24/c_129748314.htm

1. 自然景观资源

在自然景观资源方面，临汾有国家4A级旅游景区4处，分别是壶口瀑布风景区、汾河文化生态景区、云丘山风景区、人祖山风景区；国家3A级旅游景区4处：曲沃晋园、诗经山水景区、磨盘岭、翼城佛爷山，国家2A级旅游景区1处：曲沃荷塘月色景区；其他自然景区：姑射山景区、霍州七里峪景区、陶唐峪景区、襄汾龙澍峪景区、蒲县五鹿山、翼城历山舜王坪、永和乾坤湾、浮山尧山森林公园等（表3.1）。

表3.1 临汾市自然景观资源

景区类型	景点名称
国家4A级旅游景区	壶口瀑布风景区、汾河文化生态景区、云丘山风景区、人祖山风景区
国家3A级旅游景区	曲沃晋园、诗经山水景区、磨盘岭、翼城佛爷山
国家2A级旅游景区	曲沃荷塘月色景区
其他景区	姑射山景区、霍州七里峪景区、陶唐峪景区、襄汾龙澍峪景区、蒲县五鹿山、翼城历山舜王坪、永和乾坤湾、浮山尧山森林公园等。

资料来源：本研究整理。

2. 人文景观资源

在人文景观资源方面，有国家5A级旅游景区1处，即洪洞大槐树旅游景区；国家4A级旅游景区8处，分别是尧庙景区、华门景区、晋国博物馆、小西天景区、中国梨博园景区、牡丹文化旅游区、东岳庙景区、彭真故居；国家3A级旅游景区7处，分别是石桥堡、春秋晋国城、吉县克难坡、洪洞红军八路军纪念馆、广胜寺、朝阳沟、翼城古城；国家2A级旅游景区1处，分别是洪洞明代监狱；其他人文景观，如尧陵、尧居、牛王庙戏台、霍州署、铁佛寺、丁村遗址、丁村民居、陶寺遗址、师家沟古建筑群、蒲县东岳庙、大悲院（表3.2）。

表3.2 临汾市人文景观资源

景区类型	景点名称
国家5A级旅游景区	洪洞大槐树旅游景区
国家4A级旅游景区	尧庙景区华门景区、晋国博物馆、小西天景区、中国梨博园景区、牡丹文化旅游区、东岳庙景区、彭真故居
国家3A级旅游景区	石桥堡、春秋晋国城、吉县克难坡、洪洞红军八路军纪念馆、广胜寺、朝阳沟、翼城古城
国家2A级旅游景区	洪洞明代监狱
其他景区	尧陵、尧居、牛王庙戏台、霍州署、铁佛寺、丁村遗址、丁村民居、陶寺遗址、师家沟古建筑群、蒲县东岳庙、大悲院

资料来源：本研究整理。

3. 非物质文化遗产

临汾市是山西省非物质文化遗产的资源大市,截至目前,临汾市有国家级"非遗"项目21项,占山西省国家级"非遗"项目总数的20%,有省级"非遗"项目136项,有市级"非遗"项目300项。国家级"非遗"项目主要是晋南威风锣鼓、襄汾天塔狮舞、翼城花鼓、蒲州梆子、尧的传说、平阳木版年画、侯马布老虎、洪洞道情、翼城琴书、曲沃琴书、曲沃碗碗腔、云丘山中和节、尉村跑鼓车、晋南眉户、侯马麒麟采八宝、晋作家具制作技艺。其中代表性的是临汾威风锣鼓。

威风锣鼓是由锣、鼓、铙、钹四种乐器共同演奏的一种汉族传统打击乐艺术表演形式,因其表演时锣鸣镗镗、鼓声如雷,故名威风锣鼓。每逢过年过节、喜庆丰收、集会游行,便会出现在民间。威风锣鼓是古老的汉族民间艺术形式,这种锣鼓演奏形式开始于尧、舜时代,距今已有4000多年的历史。威风锣鼓融音乐、舞蹈、技艺于一体,展示了黄河文化的深沉厚重、体现了生活在黄土高原上的北方汉子粗犷豪放、不屈不挠、奔腾不羁的性格,是中国汉族传统艺术宝库中的精品。

戏剧历史悠久,源远流长。自金代戏剧到元曲最鼎盛时期,平阳府云集了中国戏剧最伟大的人物董解元、关汉卿、郑光祖、王实甫、白朴、石君宝……据史料记载,早在元代古平阳已成为和元大都北京齐名的全国戏曲中心,现存于广胜寺下寺水神庙中的元代戏曲壁画,画中生、旦、净、末、丑行当齐全,人物扮相俊丽、道具丰富逼真,形象地说明了当时平阳地区戏曲发展已经非常成熟。据史料记载,当时临汾戏曲的繁荣比戏剧中心北京还要早30年,全国最古老的元代戏台现存仅有8座,而临汾就有5座。浮山天圣宫镌刻唐代宫廷乐舞的石雕、侯马金墓出土的戏剧砖雕、襄汾丁村民居的戏剧木雕、明清的戏剧木版年画、民间刺绣和剪纸,都是中国戏曲演进的历史见证。

临汾现有蒲州梆子、晋南眉户、曲沃碗碗腔、洪洞道情、翼城琴书、浮山乐乐腔、侯马皮影戏、浮山木偶戏8个剧种。有25个戏曲演出团体,戏曲从业人员达1042人,新时期以来上演剧目598台,新编剧目273台。厚重的历史文化成就了临汾市地方戏曲文化持久馨香的艺术魅力。其中蒲剧(蒲州梆子)是梆子声腔中最古老的剧种,素有梆子戏剧种鼻祖之称,山西"四大梆子"之首。2006年被列入首批国家级非物质文化遗产保护名录。1984年中国戏剧首届梅花奖,临汾就捧回了两朵,蒲剧名家任跟心2000年又梅开二度,再获殊荣。而今,64朵大小梅花在平阳大地竞相开放,为了表彰临汾市在戏曲事业发展上的突出贡献,2005年中国戏剧家协会特别授予临汾市中国戏曲"梅花之乡"称号。

4. 节庆文化资源

除了有丰富的人文景观、自然景观和非物质文化遗产外,临汾还有丰富的节庆文化资源。目前,临汾已经形成了洪洞大槐树寻根祭祖节、黄河壶口文化旅游节、尧都文化旅游节、晋国古都文化旅游节等10余个节事旅游品牌。各具风格的旅游节庆活动、各具特色的传统文化、各具载体的人文与自然资源阐释了临汾节庆活动的多元化、多层次人文精髓,传递了华夏文明精神,在张扬中华民族源远流长的历史、文化和文明的同时,通过节庆旅游挖掘传统文化、弘扬时代精神、推动临汾文化旅游大繁荣、大发展(表3.3)。

表3.3 临汾市节庆文化旅游资源

旅游品牌	活动	主要内容
寻根祭祖游	寻根祭祖节	1991年，临汾举办了首次洪洞大槐树寻根祭祖节。在洪洞县移民遗址"古大槐树处"举办，节会期间主要举办主祭仪式，移民文化研讨会、书画会、民间艺术展、民风民俗表演、文艺演出等，同时举办物资交流大会，招商引资会等。
黄河风情游	黄河壶口国际旅游月	活动有腰鼓、唢呐、威风锣鼓等富有地方特色的文艺节目、书画摄影展、黄河文化研讨会、乡村休闲体验活动等。
唐尧文化游	尧庙根祖旅游月	突出景区观光游览、传统民俗巡游展演，游客可以逛庙会、游景区、拜先祖、赏民俗、中大奖、品美食、娱乐等，各种文艺表演、戏剧演出、文化展览、中秋赏月民乐晚会、明星演唱会、威风锣鼓选拔赛。
唐尧文化游	尧都文化旅游节	威风锣鼓、翼城花鼓、吉县唢呐等传统文化表演、尧文化高峰论坛、百家旅行社推介会、百家宗亲会长交流会、百名商界精英携手尧都活动、尧文化发展成就展、陶寺考古成果展等10项活动。
晋国文化游	古都文化节	古晋国文化研究、民间艺术展、菊花展、名优商品展、经贸洽谈、文艺晚会、戏曲表演、锣鼓大赛、晋宝斋新田古都艺术品展览及拍卖会等。
其他文化游	乡村风情桃花会	观光赏花、文艺展演、戏曲表演、特产展销、书法、茶艺表演、摄影大赛、农家美食等丰富多彩的活动，活动的内容从单纯的游园观花衍生出了民俗展示、儿童游戏、群众文体活动等很多项目。
其他文化游	古县牡丹文化旅游节	古县有"天下第一牡丹"的美誉。文化交流活动、戏曲晚会、民间文化表演、非物质文化遗产传承、美食展等。
其他文化游	云丘山"中和节"	云丘山"中和节"是国家级非物质文化遗产，是中和文化精神的传统载体。主要活动有祭祀大典、云丘中和花馍展、云丘山中和节庙会、云丘山传统民俗演艺（婚俗表演、皮影戏等节目）等，以及云丘山有机生态农业，云丘山古村落、云丘山二十四节气文化院、云丘书院、物候花径大道等旅游景点。
其他文化游	隰县"梨花节"	包括开幕式文艺演出、非遗文化展示、篝火晚会、"玉露香梨"发展专家论坛研讨会、果树定制认养专题会、特色农产品展、旅游推介会、书法展以及摄影写生比赛等活动内容，以梨花为媒，以文化为内涵，以系列活动为载体，做大做强旅游文化产业。
其他文化游	安泽荀子文化节	节庆期间通过祭荀大典、荀子文化高层论坛、"荀子故里、生态安泽"全国摄影大赛、荀子文化节书画笔会等丰富的活动内容，全景式展现荀子文化的恒久魅力。
其他文化游	安泽黄花旅游节	主要活动有文化旅游节开幕式、荀乡放歌、民俗舞蹈表演、黄花岭摄影比赛、中医养生讲座，以及上党鼓书、八音会演奏等。

资料来源：本研究整理。

二、临汾黄河文化旅游发展模式

（一）自然景区带动型发展模式

自然景区带动型发展模式，主要是指临汾市依托当地独有的龙头景区，将其打造成为吸引核和动力源，带动景区周边地区的发展。具体来说就是围绕龙头景区规划旅游产品、景点布局、旅游线路，完善旅游公共服务体系和旅游基础设施建设，依托龙头景区的辐射带动作用，推动区域旅游产业一体化发展，促进旅游产业与关联产业融合发展，实现区域社会与经济协同发展。切实发挥龙头景区在旅游品牌塑造、旅游空间结构优化、旅游宣传、游客集散中心建设等领域的引导作用，带动周边乡村、民俗文化、旅游商品等的发展。临汾市目前已经依托黄河壶口瀑布带动了周边旅游产业的发展，发挥了旅游业的带动作用，目前已经形成了以"黄河魂 + 华夏根 + 乡村旅游"景区带动型发展模式，以壶口瀑布为龙头，带动周边乡村旅游，突出黄河华夏文明，体现当地特色，建成集黄河文化、华夏文明、自然山水与民俗文化相结合的黄河精品旅游区。

1. 壶口瀑布概况

黄河壶口瀑布号称"黄河奇观"，是国家级风景名胜区、国家 4A 级旅游景区、国家级地质公园。壶口瀑布 2017 年被评选为"全国中小学生研学实践教育基地"、2018 中国黄河旅游大会上被评为"中国黄河 50 景"。壶口瀑布位于山西省临汾市吉县壶口镇，壶口瀑布是中国第二大瀑布，世界上最大的、唯一的黄色瀑布。黄河奔流至此，两岸石壁峭立，河口收束狭如壶口，故名壶口瀑布。瀑布上游黄河水面宽 300 米，在不到 500 米长距离内，被压缩到 20~30 米的宽度，飞流直下，骇浪翻滚，素有"不观壶口大瀑布，难识黄河真面目"的盛誉。1000 立方米 / 秒的河水，从 20 多米高的陡崖上倾注而泻，形成"千里黄河一壶收"的气概，此处河床形如一把巨大的茶壶，收尽奔腾不息的黄河之水，壶口因此得名。壶口瀑布极为壮观，滔滔黄水倾泻而下，瀑布高度在枯水期可达 15~20 米，夏、秋之际可达 45 米。

壶口瀑布是国内唯一的潜伏式的瀑布、移动式的瀑布、四季景色各异变化无常的瀑布、蕴涵丰富文化内涵的瀑布，以大自然的鬼斧神工造就了令世人震撼的动、静两大奇观——"动"是奔流不息、气势磅礴的壶口瀑布，"静"是千曲百回、蜿蜒柔美的乾坤湾，壶口瀑布是中华民族精神的重要象征，乾坤湾是中华文明的完美诠释。壶口瀑布不同的季节、不同的时间、不同的水流有着梦幻般的变化，形成了奇绝壮观的壶口十大景观：孟门夜月、卧镇狂流、十里龙槽、天河悬流、黄河惊雷、壶底生烟、彩虹飞渡、冰瀑银川、石窝宝镜、旱地行船。以壶口瀑布为中心的风景区，集黄河峡谷、黄土高原、古塬村寨为一体，展现了黄河流域壮美的自然景观和丰富多彩的历史文化积淀。壶口瀑布，以其深广的哲理内涵，吸引着炎黄子孙，人们视其为中华民族自强不息、昂扬奋发的精神象征，而这种精神正是中华民族的"民族魂"。

黄河旅游是临汾"中国根·黄河魂"两大旅游品牌之一，是山西省黄河板块的主体区和核心区。壶口瀑布、乾坤湾等景区不仅是黄河板块上最具观赏价值的旅游景区，而且是黄河文明的核心、中华精神的地标。

2. 代表性旅游项目与景点

临汾以壶口瀑布为核心，辐射带动周边旅游快速发展，集中打造临汾吉县旅游大循环圈、壶口和人祖山两个旅游小循环圈，倾力打造山水风光游、历史文化游、民俗风情游、考古寻根游、农业观光游、休闲度假游"六位一体"的多元发展，推进壶口景区景点与乡村旅游融合发展。除了黄河壶口瀑布这个核心景区，还发挥壶口景区的带动作用，主动联合克难坡和人祖山景区，塑造凸显艰苦奋斗、努力进取的中华精神。

（1）黄河文化旅游节。黄河文化旅游节以"黄河壶口文化原生态体验"和"黄土风情苹果观光采摘"为核心，集中展示"黄河文化、人祖文化、统战文化、苹果文化"四大旅游文化品牌，打造红色苹果、绿色生态、黄色瀑布"三色品牌"。活动推出"户外体验、经贸洽谈、乡村旅游"三大板块，举办"开幕盛典、特色农产品展、人祖山柿子滩出土文物展、秦晋之好书画摄影展、苹果采摘游、自驾游帐篷大会、经贸洽谈、旅游推介、民族歌舞邀请赛"等十大主题活动，展示"晋善晋美·大美壶口"的风采。

（2）依托苹果产业特色发展乡村旅游。临汾吉县按照"壶口龙头带动、苹果采摘支撑"的全域乡村旅游发展格局，已经实现了苹果采摘园、民俗体验园、农耕观光园、特色小吃等全面开花，悄然形成了自身鲜明的特色和独特的优势。临汾吉县海拔高、温差大、光照足，是原农业部确定的全国苹果最佳优生区，享有"中国苹果之乡"的美誉。吉县苹果因果形端正高桩、果面光洁细腻、着色鲜艳浓红、口感香脆甜爽，营养丰富、绿色安全、品质上乘，屡获大奖，曾获首届中国农博会苹果类唯一金奖，"第三届中国农博会名牌产品称号"等20多项国际国内大奖，被誉为"中华名果"。目前，全县苹果种植面积28万亩供游客采摘。吉县森林覆盖率达47.2%，优美的生态环境造就了宜人的"天然氧吧"，被誉为"吕梁山上的绿色明珠"，境内处处都是旅游人的"休闲公园""美丽家园""世外桃源"。

目前，吉县打造了集农业生产、农耕体验、文化娱乐、饮食文化、果品采摘、农产品销售于一体的民俗村、旅游度假村和休闲农业园区。上东村休闲农业园区设置了卡通人物、仿真苹果树造型、风车长廊，吸引了小孩们的眼球，"果二代"酒吧则让年轻人流连忘返。太度民俗村的美食一条街、农家乐让"吃货"们大饱口福，村民演出的乡土味道的文艺表演和婚俗表演引人注目。西岭村的"知青小屋"仿佛让人回到20世纪60年代，设置在森林中的徒步线路，让徒步爱好者们体验了在"天然氧吧"行走的乐趣。窑渠村设置的开心农场，为城里人提供了体验农耕、回归田园、休闲娱乐的天地。

（3）人祖山祭祖游。人祖山位于山西临汾市吉县，是全国唯一以"人祖"命名的大山。人祖山与壶口瀑布为邻，海拔高度1742.4米，景区面积203平方千米，核心面积45平方千米，是一座挺拔雄伟的名山。"人根之祖，出在吉州"的美丽传说，就出在此。人祖山有动物132种，植物400余种，保持了完好的原始生态。这里历史文化底蕴深厚，人文遗迹星罗棋布，主峰建有人祖庙，周围建有大小庙宇200余座，抗战时期的碉堡、战壕、工事保存完好。景区的开发目标是以自然资源为基础，以人文资源为支撑，以人祖文化为灵魂，以旅游资源为主导，打造出一个自然资源与人文资源交相辉映的旅游景区。人祖山美景名闻遐迩，是自然观光、休闲养性的绝佳胜境。

人祖文化是指2万~1万年前旧石器时代末期至新石器时代早期，即女娲伏羲时代，人类在创造婚配生育、定居用火、农耕畜养、观斗测日、历法八卦等新的生命延续方式、生存条件，形成新的认知意识的进程中所积淀的史前物质与精神文明的总和。它包括女娲文化和伏羲文化两个部分。人祖文化的核心体现了中华民族深远的宗族意识和寻根问祖的传统观念。改天换地、谋求生存的无畏精神，开拓进取、谋求发展的探索精神，安定民生、谋求和合的奉献精神，大公忘我、谋求福祉的牺牲精神。

山中历代庙宇、庙龛多达百余处，尤以人祖庙、玄天上帝庙、孔山寺、北斗七星庙最为著名。这里还有史前文明的活化石，柿子滩、造化坪、水獭坪万年前古人类遗址中出土的各类石器、陶片；中国现存最古老的"女娲岩画""伏羲岩刻"；人祖庙娲皇宫女娲塑像下发现的距今6200余年、明代人题记的"皇帝遗骨"，距今2100~900年的牛羊祭骨；风山、滚磨沟、穿针梁、洞房谷、造化坪等名地、村名；当地由来已久的祭祀人祖的风俗；广泛流传的关于人祖创世的美丽传说故事都对风姓神话人物女娲、伏羲做出了一种全新的诠释：女娲、伏羲是人不是神。人祖山也因此成为中华文明的一方发祥地，当之无愧的中华民族的根祖圣山。人祖山景区主要景点有：忘忧山庄、人祖庙、戏台庙、抗日烈士陵园、抗战文化体验园（真人CS游乐场）、玻璃彩虹鹊桥、祭祀广场、蔡家川森林公园等。人祖山是自然观光、休闲养生的绝佳圣地。

人祖庙，是中国现存最早的祭祀女娲、伏羲的场所遗址，是人祖山景区的核心景点，建在海拔高度1742.42米的人祖山主峰之巅。院内有伏羲殿、娲皇宫、地藏殿、唐代石碑等；娲皇宫悬崖下之伏羲岩建有十八罗汉廊，山壁嵌入十八罗汉浮雕；依山壁刻题建小庙一座，内奉玄武、观音。娲皇宫大门前有块天生巨石，有"卧云石""补天台""娲石"之称，上下两层，均有方圆石窝一组。有学者认为是伏羲仰观于天，俯察于地，产生"天圆地方"观念的表达。

（4）永和乾坤湾。乾坤湾位于晋陕峡谷中段，是个巨大的标准"S"形河湾景观，峻山凛冽中黄河迂迴，河水环抱下峰岛隽美，站在岸边山崖俯瞰，气势恢宏又不乏钟灵毓秀，酷似中国传统文化中的"太极阴阳图"，而"S"的两个湾里各有一个古老的村落，从总体上看，就像太极双鱼图的那两个"眼睛"。据清县志记载"伏义"就是"伏羲"的转音、转形，在伏义河村就有伏羲庙，庙前还有两棵千年古柏。河会里村有娘娘庙，娘娘庙的祖先即为"女娲"，因此两岸众多村落以"洼"命名。清县志记载：枣洼历代无枣，据考证，枣即女阴，洼即娲的转音，应为女娲。这种独特的山河地貌、十分奇巧的地名，在当地流传千年的古老传说以及近年一些专家的考察论证显示着永和县与伏羲、女娲密不可分的渊源关系。

2005年1月，通过山西省国土资源厅审查山西永和黄河蛇曲地质公园，并上报中华人民共和国国土资源部审批。2006年8月，经中华人民共和国国土资源部正式批准建立黄河蛇曲（山西永和）国家地质公园。公园位于山西省西南部，吕梁山西南端西翼，公园面积为210平方千米，主要地质遗迹分布面积152.64平方千米。黄河蛇曲（山西永和）国家地质公园地处晋陕峡谷的南部地段，公园内主要可供观赏的旅游景观为河流蛇曲曲流地貌景观。园区内有由河流地质作用形成的其他地质旅游资源及遗迹，如河心岛（鞋岛）、阶地、侧蚀洞穴、陡峭谷坡及化石遗迹等。除此之外，公园内历史上遗留的人文旅游资源比比皆是，对考察和研究黄河文化、黄土风情、近现代革命战争史等提供了不可多得的宝贵资料。

黄河蛇曲（山西永和）国家地质公园的旅游资源内容丰富。尤其是地学类旅游资源无论从宏观到微观景观遗迹都弥足珍贵，具有较高的教学、科研及旅游观赏价值。对这里地质公园的考证研究，能帮助我们深入了解黄河中游地壳的发育、演化史，黄土环境的变迁，以及黄河谷道的水力侵蚀模式具有重要意义。

（5）霍州市七里峪旅游景区。七里峪生态旅游景区位于山西省临汾市霍州东北一中镇霍山腹地，是太岳山国家森林公园的重要组成部分。景区距大运高速霍州出口仅5千米，依托大运高速90分钟可达太原机场，国道108、南同蒲铁路横贯市境南北，交通便捷。

景区拥有悠久的历史文化资源和丰富的自然景观资源，是山西省境内原生植被最好、景点最多的生态旅游资源集聚区域，植被覆盖率达90%以上，大气质量达国家一级标准，海拔800~2504.5米，年平均气温10℃，已查明的珍稀植物有670多种，野生珍贵动物70余种，可谓天然植物园和野生动物园。

七里峪景区分为三个小区，既霍红兆游览区、三眼窑游览区、黑龙峡游览区，拥有景点28个。主要景点有五龙壑、滴水崖瀑布、双乳峰、南天门、石人沟、牛老沟、石崖奇松、八仙洞、红兆烈士亭、金沟曼万亩落叶松人工林、黑龙峡等。目前，七里峪景区正在加紧建设，这里即将成为人们旅游观光、度假休闲、科研教学等为一体的避署胜地。

（6）翼城舜王坪。舜王坪位于山西省翼城、垣曲、沁水三县交界处历山自然保护区内，传说是上古时代舜帝耕作的地方。舜王坪是历山自然保护区的主峰，海拔2358米，是华北最高的亚高山草甸。草坪周围崇山峻岭，树木茂盛，是华北和黄河中下游唯一保存完好的原始森林。

舜王坪有5400余亩草地，绿草如茵。据当地老乡介绍，舜王坪生长着十几种中草药。牛吃后，既防病又上膘。每年春忙过后，周围村的农民就把牛赶上舜王坪，任牛群自由生活，无人管理。晚上，每个牛群聚集一方，公牛围成一圈，双角簇立，担任警卫，保护在圈内的母牛、小牛过夜，防止野兽袭击。秋忙时节，村民才赶牛下山，秋收秋种。

舜王坪的大小景点达百余处之多，大的有舜王坪亚高草甸，约260公顷，舜的传说与景点从这里开始。在舜王坪北面草坡上，有一排天然石头形成的石墙，高低参差不齐，其中有一块猴形石头十分显眼，当地人称此景为"群猴望月"。在舜王坪周围各县百姓中，至今还流传着许多关于舜帝种粟等古老故事，还有尧王访贤的望仙村。

(二)康养旅游发展模式

2016年5月,国家林业局在《林业发展"十三五"规划》中突出强调发展森林旅游休闲康养业,即要大力发展森林康养。2017年9月,山西省楼阳生省长首次明确提出要着力打造"夏养山西康养品牌"。楼阳生省长在《2018年山西省政府工作报告》中进一步指出:"实施康养产业带动……以养心、养生、养老为发展方向,开发全生命周期康养产品,发展融旅游、居住、康养、医疗、护理为一体的产业集群。重点发展乡村康养、森林康养、温泉康养、中医药康养和康养地产等新业态。加快建设一批康养旅游城市、康养小镇、康养产业园、康养度假区。"这充分说明康养旅游已经是一种重要的旅游方式,并受到政府部门的重视。康养旅游发展模式是通过养颜健体、营养膳食、修心养性、关爱环境等各种手段,使人在身体、心智和精神上都达到自然和谐的优良状态等各种旅游活动的总和。康养旅游的内涵包括三个层次:物候基础、康养需要和诗意地栖居。康养旅游作为一种新的旅游类型,是健康养生产品、资源与休闲度假旅游相结合的产物,满足人们对健康生活的追求,让人们在旅游中获得身心健康,这也能促进旅游业的转型升级。

临汾作为中华民族的发祥地之一,历史文化悠久,以云丘山为代表的风景区有着丰富的文化和康养旅游资源。云丘山以当地独有的根祖文化为特色,打造康养文化体验、康养教育休闲度假地。同时由于康养旅游"健康、可持续"的特点,发展康养旅游不仅能够促进临汾市旅游业的发展、升级、转型,还能够协同带动相关行业发展,带动当地的古村落游、森林游、农业种植、特色文化的发展等。

1. 云丘山概况

云丘山风景区属国家4A级旅游景区,是晋南根祖旅游核心景区,是中华农耕文明发源地之一,是华夏乡土文化的地理标志,是中和文化——非物质文化遗产的传承地,传递着浓浓的故乡深情。云丘山拥有丰富的自然资源、人文景观和文化遗产,是晋南地区少有的集旅游观光、休闲娱乐、度假养生、民俗体验、文化交流等功能于一体的综合性旅游风景区。云丘山特殊的喀斯特地貌和石山森林环。云丘山不仅自然景观奇特,而且文化底蕴深厚,是几千年来道家仙士的常游之所,享有"姑射最秀峰巅""河汾第一名胜"的美誉。一是,云丘山生态环境极佳、风景宜人,绿色养心。二是,云丘山承载着厚重的人文资源与文化底蕴。云丘山的文化脉络可追溯至远古文明,相传伏羲、女娲在此繁育华夏子孙;羲和观天测地在此订立二十四节气;后稷在此传承农耕技艺,中原农耕文明由此开始。三是,云丘山汇聚儒、释、道三教文化。道教全真教龙门派祖庭发源于此,与武当齐名,五龙宫、八宝宫等道观殿宇和云丘书院,多宝灵岩禅寺等儒释文化相融相生、和谐共存。四是,云丘山还完整保存有11座千年古村落,是罕见的晋南窑洞古村落群。现如今的塔尔坡,继承了当地的民俗、民风,瞬间让你感受到那种男耕女织、自给自足、婚丧嫁娶的世外桃源生活。在这里还能看到当地特有的花馍,一种山西省的汉族民俗艺术品。

2. 发展策略

2018年,山西省旅游发展委员会发布了《山西省黄河板块旅游发展总体规划》,该规划指出要充分利用云丘山峰岭翠叠的自然环境，深挖其原生态富氧养生和中和文化内涵，建设户外运动、康养度假、古村休闲、自驾旅游、拓展体验、登山祈福、儒释道共融文化体验和农耕文化体验等项目，提升建成5A级生态康养旅游区。以云丘山景区为核心，辐射带动周边的古村、民俗文化、特色种植等旅游快速发展，集中打造云丘山康养旅游度假区，推进云丘山的多元发展。

一是，拓展现有已经启动的国际文创基地建设规模，开展国际游客所钟爱的文化艺术原创活动，使之形成国际游客山西文化旅游目的地型旅游区。二是，以富氧养生为主旨，保护利用5个左右传统村落，发展山地康体养生度假，打造特色室外康养中心和中药材、有机蔬菜专业种植小区、花圃等。三是，提升建设现有的民俗文化体验街区，增加艺术商品和山野土特产售卖区。四是，建设融伏羲、女娲繁衍文化，羲和观天测地订立二十四节气，及后稷传承农耕技艺等文化于一体的农耕文化园。五是，开发保存较为完整的古村落，打造原汁原味的千年民居及院落，创建晋南民间版画和年画艺术村落。六是，提升每年3月份举办的中和文化节知名度，扩大表演规模和演出项目，将其打造成为山西省最重要的民间祭祀节庆活动。

3.代表性旅游项目与景点

（1）主题娱乐活动。围绕华夏文明起源、乡土文化、道教文化等进行文化挖掘、保护和传承，进行旅游产品的开发。目前，云丘山风景区已经形成了四大主题活动：民俗年、中和节、艺术节、红叶节。通过活动传递云丘印象与民俗民情，吸引游客参与其中，在体验中收获快乐与满足感。

云丘山设有多种娱乐项目。其中，最受欢迎的有全山西最高最长的鸳鸯桥（玻璃吊桥），鸳鸯桥悬于云丘山两座巨峰之间，身至桥上，可以全方位畅游梦幻般的云丘山仙界，俯瞰"近在咫尺"的千山万壑。云丘山高空玻璃桥整体长度219米、高度195米、宽度2米，为目前山西省最长+最高的全透明高空玻璃桥。风和日丽之时，踩在玻璃桥上，脚下峡谷裂隙尽收眼底，行走其上仿如御风而行，惊险无比；云深雾重之际，于桥上悬空赏景如漫步云端，如若"云中天桥"[①]。

云丘山冰洞群是世界三大冰洞奇观之一，也是目前国内发现规模最大的天然冰洞群。其围岩地层年龄在4亿年左右，所在区域地貌形成于300万年以前。全世界冰洞奇观主要分为三类，第一类是冰川型冰洞、第二类是气候型冰洞、第三类是地热负异常型冰洞。云丘山冰洞群属于制冷机制最为复杂的地热负异常型冰洞，全球权威专家至今无法破解其形成原理。因其成因复杂、规模最大、356天全年都有冰，所以云丘山冰洞群也成为具有科研价值和观赏价值的天然冰洞群。目前，冰洞已开发完成并向游客开放。

（2）旅游线路。第一，寻根觅祖（两日游）。云丘山是中国乡土文化地理标志，这里传承着华夏乡土的文脉，传递着浓浓的故乡深情。也许您来自远方，但这是我们共同的故乡。寻根觅祖线路带您领略云丘山——感受中华文明根脉中坚实的年轮。该线路包括参观晋南乡土文化标本村落，游古村、看民俗表演、体验道民共生的生活情趣，登山途经玉莲洞、一/二/三天门，欣赏最美云丘

---

① 游乐项目.山西云丘山旅游景区官网 http://www.yunqiushan.cn/about/?31.html#menuSub

山风景。第二天早上爬山登顶感受云丘山传承千年的中和文化、祈愿文化、生育文化。最后可选择体验滑翔翼、高空滑索、旱地滑雪等项目。（资料来源：山西云丘山旅游景区官网）

第二，周游云丘（一日游）。云丘山的优美风光和人文奇观岂是一日便可逛完。周游云丘线路串联景区主要景点，走马观花亦不会错过美景。景区内的摆渡大巴和缆车索道既能方便游客辗转景点之间，也可享受别样的沿途风景。该线路包含云丘山的精华景点，体验云丘山三教合一的祈福文化，挑战极限项目的心跳和刺激、感受道民共生的土著生活，喧嚣杂闹与聚凝心神过后，将经历精神上的满足。（资料来源：山西云丘山旅游景区官网）

第三，最秀峰巅（一日游）。云丘山素以道家文化著称，可与武当山齐名。最秀峰巅游线，主打"祈福朝拜，登山访仙"的特色，途经五龙宫、玉莲洞、祖师顶、玉皇顶等道家洞观仙境，还可参观2500年历史的塔尔坡古村，领略云丘山独特的"道民共生"文化，此条线路为云丘山登顶沿途风景最优美的线路。该线路可以听回荡山涧的燕语莺啼、看胜似蓬莱的云海翻腾。（资料来源：山西云丘山旅游景区官网）

第四，古村探秘（一日游）。云丘山境内有古村镇10余座，被誉为"华夏年轮 乡土文脉"。古村全新体验游线精选具有2500多年历史的塔尔坡古村供游客参观，以及云丘山全新体验项目玻璃桥、滑翔翼、滑索和旱地滑雪项目。游客不仅可在沧桑的石窟洞穴中体会时空穿越，还能品尝乡土水席，感受传承千年的婚俗、农耕文化，更能体验各种极限游乐项目。到千年古村塔尔坡听溪水潺潺、和风习习，品尝山西特色小吃，再亲手做一个云丘山花馍，全方位感受晋南乡土文化的魅力；再参与云丘山极限项目挑战，跨越山崖、水面滑索、滑翔翼俯瞰秀美山峰。（资料来源：山西云丘山旅游景区官网）

4. 云丘山中和文化节

在《山西省黄河板块旅游发展总体规划》中，"云丘山中和文化节"是黄河峡谷与红色文化旅游片区重点打造的十大节庆活动之一。云丘山中和文化节是一个传承了上千年的古老节日。唐贞元五年（789年）唐德宗李适钦点，中和节被正式确定为国家重要法定节日，朝廷行藉田之礼，百官上农书以示劝农，民间有祭祀勾芒以祈年谷等习俗。1200多年来，唯有云丘山把中和节传统完整保留下来，被誉为"中和节的活化石"。2011年，云丘山中和文化"中和节"被列入国务院公布的第三批国家级非物质文化遗产名录，该节庆项目传承1227年晋南乡土春祭大典。经过云丘山景区的精心打造和传承，中和节作为民间隆重的传统节日之一，已成为具有一定影响力的文化节、旅游节，已成为山西临汾展示其独特文化魅力的重要窗口、促进旅游与文化融合发展的重要平台。

上古时期云丘山就是官方、民间祭天场所、人们对天地的敬畏，通过祭天来表达对于天滋润赋予万物的感恩之情，以祈求皇天上帝保佑华夏子民没有天灾人祸、国泰民安、风调雨顺、五谷丰登，寓意"和谐共生，传承延续"。祈福法会作为一年一度中和节中最重要的活动，使所有来到云丘山的民众祈求云丘山诸位神灵保佑自己和家人身体健康、全家幸福，祈求一年的好运。云丘山的中和祭祀大典与众不同，这不仅是一个仪式，更是云丘人对中和节的传承，而云丘山作为中和节最后的传承地，对中和文化的发扬有着深深的责任感和使命感。

祭祀大典是中和节高潮环节，祭天敬祖、原始巫戏、众神抬阁巡游、大型文艺演出，精彩纷呈。在节庆期间，将举办数十项民俗文化活动，包括"祈愿中和——祭祀大典暨中和节开幕仪式""祈愿天成——万人祈愿中和节""福满云丘——云丘九境上上签""福照云丘——领福树，种福愿""云丘中和老庙会""云丘婚俗盛会——鞭杆挑花篮""云丘中和五福粥""云丘中和花馍展""云丘山冰洞群——冰点大挑战"等，带游客和群众感受中和文化之魅力。

祈福法会保平安。云丘山作为道教名山、全真教龙门派开山祖庭，中和节期间在五龙宫和八宝宫举办道教法会，通过系列法会，敬天奉祖，体悟大道天地自然的真理所在，同时为大众百姓祈福、消灾、保佑平安。

5. 塔尔坡古村落

云丘山塔尔坡古村，至今已有2500多年历史，原名榻耳坡，因老子李耳云游天下曾下榻于此地而得名。而后，道家闻名而至，和当地山民结邻而居，逐渐形成村落。塔尔坡古村更被称为"千年民居建筑的活化石"。塔尔坡整个村落依山傍水，古树掩映。村前的神仙峪里有从山上泉尔凹流下的清澈见底的山泉水，村后背依着高峻挺拔的云丘山主峰，玉莲洞道观雄踞古村之上的抱腹岩中。

塔尔坡古村落所有院落均是依山而建，建筑材料以石材为主。村落里有石拱顶的窑洞建构，现如今的塔尔坡，继承了当地的民俗、民风，瞬间让你感受到那种男耕女织、自给自足、婚丧嫁娶的世外桃源生活。当地村民还延承着先民的生殖崇拜、婚育、社祭、祈福等乡土文化习俗，始于唐代的"中和节"更是作为国家级非物质文化遗产传续至今。在这里还能看到当地特有的花馍，云丘山花馍是一种山西省的汉族民俗艺术品。

（三）人文景区旅游发展模式

人文景区旅游发展模式主要是指利用临汾黄河流域所具有旅游价值的遗址、遗迹、古代建筑等文化资源发展旅游。洪洞县历史悠久，文化灿烂，人文资源古老独特，民俗风情绚丽多彩。600多年来，"问我祖先在何处？山西洪洞大槐树"的民谣使洪洞大槐树成为大半个中国百姓魂萦梦牵的"根"。洪洞依托大槐树根祖文化发展文化旅游，目前已经形成了较为成熟的大槐树旅游景区和大槐树寻根祭祖节。

洪洞大槐树景区是临汾市"中线根祖文化游"的重点景区和洪洞县文化旅游产业"一核四带六大区"布局中的产业带动核心，为了更好地打造老家亲情品牌，建设根祖旅游新格局，洪洞大槐树寻根祭祖园以品牌带动服务、品牌带动管理、品牌带动发展的模式，为景区赢得良好的口碑，推动大槐树旅游事业高质量发展。

1. 大槐树景区概况

一部明代移民史，使洪洞大槐树成为大半个中国百姓魂牵梦萦的"根"。一种独特持久的文化现象背后，必然有一种独特的精神在支撑，这种精神就是大槐树精神。洪洞大槐树寻根祭祖园是国家5A级旅游景区、山西省重点文物保护单位，不仅是全国以"寻根"和"祭祖"为主题的唯一民祭圣地，也是全球华人寻根祭祖的圣地。几个世纪以来，一直被当作"家"、称作"祖"、看作

"根"。景区由"移民古迹区""祭祖活动区""民俗游览区""汾河生态区"四大主题板块组成，共60余处风景文化景点。洪洞大槐树寻根祭祖园独具特色的"祭祖习俗"是国家非物质文化遗产，并荣获"山西省十大旅游景区""美好印象山西十大旅游景区""山西旅游十大品牌企业""国家级旅游服务业标准化试点单位"等多项荣誉。

洪洞大槐树寻根祭祖园一直坚持多元化发展，已从单一的景区，发展成以景区、民俗饭店、旅行社三大经营板块为主体，集吃、住、行、游、购、娱为一体的综合旅游服务区，不但集中体现了深厚的移民文化内涵，为大槐树移民后裔营造了老家的氛围，同时还满足了广大移民后裔寻根祭祖、旅游观光、休憩、餐饮、购物的需求，是广大移民后裔进行深度文化体验，了解老家民俗的最佳选择。

2. 代表性旅游项目与景点

（1）移民古迹区主要景点有牌坊、第一代大槐树遗址、茶室、二代大槐树、三代大槐树、石经幢、古驿道、广济寺等。其中，石经幢是祭祖园中最古老的文物，也是现存明代迁民的唯一历史见证。经幢是古代佛教石刻的一种，创始于唐，由多块石刻堆建成柱状，柱上有盘盖，柱身刻陀罗尼经文及佛像，由广济寺大法师惠琎于金承安五年（1201年）所建，比移民还要早200多年，是广济寺的唯一遗物，也是典型的经幢作品，距今有800多年的历史。它由青石砌成，平面呈八角形，四层十五级，高9.4米，雕刻艺术古朴深厚，书法刚劲流畅，浮雕栩栩如生，是金代雕刻艺术的珍品。

（2）祭祖活动区主要景点有根雕大门、"根"字影壁、莲馨桥、槐香桥、鹳鸣桥、献殿、祭祀广场、祭祖堂、望乡阁、溯源阁等。祭祖堂是整个景区的核心，堂内供奉着已证实的1230个移民先祖姓氏牌位，是全国最大的平民祭祖祠堂，故称"天下民祭第一堂"。"根"字影壁造型独特、雕刻精美，是景区的标志性景观。影壁俗称照壁，在我国民间建筑中经常可以见到，像一般的四合院或大户人家的庭院都有照壁。根字影壁是大槐树景区的标志性建筑，它不是一般的平面结构，而是独特的八字形结构。上面的雕刻也非常精致，都是民间的吉祥图案。

（3）民俗游览区主要功能是观光、休憩，包括莲花塘、槐树庄、洪崖古洞等景点。其中，"洪崖古洞"是现在"洪洞"县名的由来，取县城城南"洪崖"，城北"古洞"而得名；"莲花塘"是当年洪洞县城别名——莲花城的象征，千百年来洪洞城四周蓄水植莲，夏季莲花盛开，情趣盎然，故称洪洞城为"莲花城"；槐树庄位于景区西轴线民俗体验区的中部，主要建筑包括特色民居、乡土菜园、古井台、老茶坊、传统作坊等，村中设有私塾、耕读园、水磨坊、土特产品作坊、打谷场、娱乐设施等各种活动场所，更有多种可供游客参与的活动，集文化展览、旅游观光、民俗体验于一体，使得老家的根祖文化魅力尽收眼底。

（4）汾河生态区是国家5A级旅游景区整体规划中的新建项目，于2015年免费开放，汾河生态区不但风景秀美而且人文荟萃，能够全面满足游客和当地居民休闲娱乐的需求。

3. 洪洞大槐树文化节

"洪洞大槐树文化节"，以清明节为主祭日，每届文化节都有数以万计的大槐树移民后裔云集于此，表达着对大槐树老家浓浓的爱、深深的情。洪洞大槐树文化节的举办推进了临汾市文化旅游产业融合发展、优质发展的重大举措。通过举办大槐树文化节，能够弘扬中华民族奉先思孝、报本溯源、敬宗忠国的家国情怀，能够弘扬优秀传统文化同国家级非物质文化遗产"大槐树祭祖习俗"紧密结合起来，带动文旅融合，强力打造具有地方特色、国家水准的"洪洞老家"文化旅游品牌。目前，祭祖园每年在清明节、中元节、寒衣节等节日都举行祭祖大典，吸引游子参祭。"洪洞大槐树祭祖习俗"也被列入国家级非物质文化遗产保护名录。

洪洞大槐树寻根祭祖园作为文旅融合发展的排头兵，始终以传承非遗、弘扬文化为己任，为进一步深化文旅融合发展，打响"老家"品牌而奋力出击。从第一届洪洞大槐树文化节举办至今，景区不仅将"洪洞大槐树祭祖习俗"完好地保留传承，还在全国掀起了"寻根热""祭祖热"，擦亮了大槐树5A级景区金字招牌。文化节期间还举办洪洞名优小吃节、传统戏曲表演、洪洞大槐树文化节寻根祭祖大典、洪洞大槐树移民文化研讨会、纪念革命先烈、百名金牌导游大赛等活动，弘扬祭祖文化，唱响"老家"品牌，走文化旅游融合发展道路。洪洞大槐树，已深深地扎根在中华儿女共同的精神家园中，承载着丰富的中华优秀传统文化内涵。

4. 洪洞大槐树寻根祭祖园研学实践教育基地

2018年10月，洪洞大槐树寻根祭祖园被教育部命名为全国中小学生研学实践教育基地。目前，洪洞大槐树寻根祭祖园结合景区现有资源优势、特点及全年研学项目计划，秉承"教育性、实践性、安全性、公益性"的研学实践教育原则，特制定了《关于全国中小学生研学实践教育基地工作推进的实施方案》，全面部署研学课程的开发和研学活动的开展，确保基地建设项目任务稳步推进。景区已确定将开发4门研学课程和多项研学活动，课程设计安排见表3.4。

表3.4 洪洞大槐树寻根祭祖园研学课程

课程名称	课程内容	课程地点
感悟华夏之根 抒发爱国情怀	红色教育体验 （缅怀、感知、继承）	烈士亭 文化革命院
弘扬根祖文化 彰显家国情怀	中华根祖祭祀文化 （非遗、传承、体验）	碑亭、献殿、祭祖堂移民实证展览馆
美丽中国根 魅力百家姓	中华根祖姓氏文化 （家风家训、传承弘扬）	祭祖堂、中华姓氏苑
多重实践 综合体验	教育与综合实践相结合 （探究精神、实践能力）	桃园、民俗村 研学耕地 大槐树民俗饭店

资料来源：洪洞大槐树官网。

5. 陶寺遗址

陶寺遗址位于襄汾县陶寺乡陶寺村南，分布面积约300万平方米，1988年被国务院公布为第三批全国重点文物保护单位。陶寺遗址既是国家"十一五""十二五"的大遗址保护工程，也是山西省"南部根祖文化旅游"最具价值的品牌,是"根祖文化"的直根、总根。陶寺遗址的保护、利用与开发,对实现转型发展具有重要意义,它是海内外华夏儿女寻根问祖的圣地,是山西省文化旅游产业发展最具潜力的项目,是弘扬"源远流长的廉政文化"的重要载体,其"尧都"和"中国"两个品牌价值无限,在全国独一无二。

从1978年开始,经过40年的考古发掘与研究,初步揭示出陶寺遗址是中国史前功能区划最完备的都城,兴建与使用年代距今4300~3900年。在这里发现了规模空前的城址、气势恢宏的宫殿区、观象祭祀区、独立的仓储区、工官管理下的手工业区、王族墓地、平民居住区等。出土了陶器、铜器、木器、玉石礼器等各类文物5500余件。其中,发现的鼍鼓是中国目前最早的鼓乐礼器、发现的铜铃是我国第一件金属乐器,表明了最早礼乐制度的形成;发现的观象台是世界上最早的观象台;发现了我国最早的文字、最早的木礼器等。

2015年6月18日,中国社会科学院、省委宣传部、临汾市委市政府在北京举行新闻发布会,证实了陶寺遗址是从时空上考古探索中华文明核心形成、最初中国诞生的重要节点,是中华文明的主脉。根据现有的发掘资料和研究成果,从年代、地望、等级、内涵和遗址性质看,陶寺遗址就是帝尧的都城遗址。

2018年5月28日,"中华文明起源与早期发展综合研究(简称'中华文明探源工程')成果发布会"在国务院新闻办公室举行,指出山西襄汾陶寺遗址的发现,是中华大地5000年文明的实证之一。陶寺遗址在中华文明形成过程中的地位极其重要,国家、省、市对陶寺遗址的保护利用工作极为重视,先后被国家文物局列入"十一五100处大遗址保护工程""大遗址保护'十二五'专项规划(150处)",并且成为中国社科院"哲学社会科学创新工程"和"中华文明探源工程"以及"国家大遗址考古计划"项目支撑。

6. 晋国博物馆

晋国博物馆位于曲沃县曲村镇,是依托全国重点文物保护单位"曲村天马遗址"而兴建的全省第一座以晋文化为主题的遗址类博物馆,于2014年国庆节正式对外开放。晋国博物馆是一座集文物收藏、保护、研究和文物遗迹展示为一体的山西省首座大型遗址博物馆,也是全国唯一一座完整展示晋国历史文化风貌的平台,对于传承和弘扬传统文化,彰显山西以晋文化为特色的地域文明,完善山西省旅游产业结构具有十分重要的意义。

晋国博物馆所在的"曲村天马遗址"规模宏大,东起翼城县天马村,西至曲沃县曲村镇,南起滏河岸,北达桥山坡。遗址东西长3800米,南北宽2800米,面积近11平方千米。经过北京大学和山西考古研究所连续十余次大规模勘探发掘,共揭露面积12000平方米,发掘墓葬1000余座,其中周代墓葬800余座。尤其是在该遗址的核心区域,发现了9组19座晋国早期国君及夫人墓葬,10座车马坑,发掘各类珍贵文物12000余件,其发掘成果为我国"夏商周断代工程"西周列王编年课题的解决提供了支撑,被列为1992年、1993年全国十大考古新发现之一,2001年又被评为中国20世纪一百项重大考古发现之一。

晋国博物馆，以晋文化为主题，打造了晋国史、发掘史、遗址展三个亮点。历史文化展厅以晋国历史为线索，通过晋侯墓地出土的大量珍贵文物，展示了晋国由公元前1040年左右叔虞封唐、燮父改唐为晋、文侯勤王、献公拓疆、文公称霸、六卿专政、三家分晋等一系列足以影响中国古代历史进程的重大事件。遗址发掘史展厅展示了北京大学考古文博学院和山西省考古研究所三代考古学人历尽艰辛、博览地书、寻觅求证的经过和考古发掘工作取得的一系列重大成果；遗址展厅则采用一处遗址一种展示方式的方法，重点展示了四组晋侯及夫人墓葬和三座车马坑，呈现给观众一幅两周时期邦国王侯墓葬的全景图画。

7. 蒲县东岳庙

东岳庙位于城东2.5公里的柏山之巅，为东岳天齐仁圣大帝黄飞虎的行宫。周围数十里茂林荫覆，山下有南川，景色十分优美，为蒲县旅游景点之首。东岳庙中的环形院落、二层回廊、窑楼建筑、品字戏台被誉为"庙中四绝"，又以千年古楸、八仙庆寿、金代石雕、木兰花慢、乐楼题记和晴雨碑、八音钟被称为"庙中七珍"。2001年被列为第五批全国重点文物保护单位。

东岳庙历史悠久，唐贞观年间已有规模，元代延祐五年即1318年重修，距今已有700多年历史。明清两代亦有修补增添，建筑风格集唐、宋、金、元、明、清建筑艺术大成。东岳庙为佛道混合型寺院，呈长方形组合群体，四合院式宫廷建筑，占地1万余平方米，建筑7000余平方米，共有殿堂楼阁280间。建筑以行宫大殿为中心，前有天堂楼，后有地府。四隅角楼高耸，院周楼廊环绕，组成一座规模宏敞、气势雄伟的宫廷式建筑群，主要由太尉庙、华池宫、行宫大殿、七十二司、地狱五部分组成，特别是明代所建地狱，内塑五岳大帝、十殿阎君、六曹判官及地府各种冥刑，共计150多尊塑像，大小与真人相仿，实为明代泥彩塑佳作。

（四）乡村旅游发展模式

乡村旅游发展模式主要是指利用临汾黄河流域所具有旅游价值的特色农业、农耕文化等资源发展旅游。大河流域的农耕地区都地处环境优美，山清水秀的地区，能够满足游客对于追求自然、健康养生的乡村文化旅游需求，根据当地文化和自然特色，可以发展乡村旅游、主题型旅游等多种形式的旅游活动。临汾市加强当地农业特色，将当地的梨果产业、自然资源与民族文化融合，创新发展一批"旅游+"产业，引领乡村旅游产业发展，建设特色乡村旅游目的地。如代表性的隰县依托当地特有的梨果产业，举办梨花节，发展乡村旅游，带动当地旅游产业的发展。

1. 隰县梨花节概况

隰县有丰富的旅游资源，梨园风光清纯秀美，紫荆山、石马沟景色怡人，五鹿山自然景区山峦叠嶂，小西天悬塑艺术精美绝伦、明代大观楼气势非凡，吸引着八方游客。最著名的景区是千佛庵，又名小西天，位于山西省隰县城西一里许的凤凰山巅，是一座佛教禅宗寺院，由明代东明禅师创建于明崇祯二年（1629）。初因大雄宝殿内有佛千尊而得名，后因重门额题"道人西天"，又为区别城南另一座明代寺院"大西天"而更名小西天。整个寺院依山叠造、浑然一体，特别是大雄宝殿内满堂木骨泥质悬塑艺术颇具特色，堪称中国雕塑艺术史上的"悬塑绝唱"，仅大雄宝殿的彩塑精品就占山西省明清彩塑作品的4%以上,而这些佳作仅塑于面积只有169.6平方米的小殿堂内,堪称佛教彩塑艺术之瑰宝。

隰县栽植梨果历史悠久,是闻名遐迩的"中国金梨之乡""中国大美梨"和"中国酥梨之乡"。隰县所产玉露香梨果有个大、可食率高、含糖量高等诸多优点,被国家梨产业体系专家公认为"中国第一梨"。

此外,临汾还有安泽黄花节、古县牡丹节、尧都桃花节、曲沃全域旅游推介、人祖山帐篷音乐节、蒲县四樵朝山节等。

2.代表性旅游项目与景点

隰县每年在该县午城镇阳德塬万亩梨园举办梨花节,为期一周。通过梨花节的举办,实现了由单纯卖梨果到观赏梨花、提升文化、壮大产业、梨果富民的新跨越,加快了农民增收致富达小康进程。梨花节通常包括开幕式、文艺演出、非遗文化展示、篝火晚会、招商引资洽谈及集中签约仪式、"玉露香梨"发展专家论坛研讨会、果树定制认养专题会、特色农产品展、旅游推介会、书法展以及摄影写生比赛等活动内容,旨在以梨花为媒,以文化为内涵,以系列活动为载体,整合旅游资源,打造清纯秀美的梨园风光,实现由单纯卖梨果到观赏梨花、提升文化、壮大产业,做大做强旅游文化产业,叫响该县玉露香品牌,加快农民增收致富达小康进程。同时,通过全方位、多元化宣传展示隰县梨果产业和旅游资源,以节扬名、以节交友、以节厚文、以节活县,进一步彰显魅力隰县新风采,奋力建设中国金梨之乡、山西绿色之州、晋西宜居之地、美丽幸福之都。

2019年第五届梨花节确定峪里村为乡村旅游示范村之一。一是营造特色农家旅游。围绕农家旅游,规划建设以桃、葡萄、桑葚、玉露香梨、苹果为主的采摘园;以休闲游玩为主的垂钓区;以农家饭菜为主的农家乐;以原生态农产品为主的"农展平台",形成具有个性特点的乡村旅游。二是形成融合发展试点。围绕产业融合发展进行综合打造。以玉露香产业为基,建基地、做示范、延链条,做强主导产业;坚持"绿水青山就是金山银山",以"石磨坊"为题,做记录、挖文化、搞专题,形成人文效应,扩大宣传范围,把峪里村打造成为一个微型的田园综合体,成为全县产业融合发展的示范村。

(五)文旅融合发展模式

非物质文化遗产作为文化保护传承的一项重要内容,能够为旅游业发展注入活力已成共识。为推动文旅融合向纵深发展,充分展示临汾市优秀的传统文化和旅游资源,临汾市创新发展思路,让"非遗"牵手"景区",启动非遗进景区活动,创建文旅融合示范基地,使景区"火"起来、"热"起来。

临汾市结合襄汾县荷花小镇的环境、区位优势,通过设立非遗现场体验区、非遗项目展演区、民俗活动演示区、商品展销区、非遗项目宣传区等,集中展示临汾市优秀非物质文化遗产,定期在小镇内开展非遗展演系列活动,真正做到非遗与景区在文旅融合中共同传承发展,并以此作为非遗与旅游融合的示范性园区进行打造,推动临汾市范围内开展非遗进景区工作,逐步打造一批文旅融合示范基地，全面推动文化与旅游融合发展工作，并带动相关文创产业的发展。

非遗驻景区，是临汾市积极践行"见人、见物、见生活"非遗保护理念的具体行动，对于全方位展示、宣传临汾丰富多彩的非物质文化遗产，提升旅游产业文化内涵，促进文旅深度融合发展大有裨益。通过非遗进景区让"非遗"与"旅游"牵手，让文旅活动与宣传营销相约，通过"诗"和"远方"的完美结合，让非遗"活起来"，让景区"火起来"、让游客"留下来"，让品牌"亮起来"，加快推进了临汾市文旅深度融合发展，创新了文旅融合的发展模式与路径。

第三节 山西省临汾黄河旅游发展经验与对策

临汾市以开发和利用黄河文化为切入点，大力发展文化旅游产业，推动地方旅游向高质量、高品质的方向发展，不仅促进了经济转型，还形成了具有黄河文化标签的文化旅游目的地。本部分将对临汾市的黄河旅游发展经验、未来发展的建议与对策进行深入阐述。

一、黄河文明旅游发展经验

本小节将对黄河文明旅游的发展经验进行深入阐释，通过相关经验的剖析，有利于为其他地区大河文明旅游的市场开发、产品设计、营销宣传等提供借鉴与启示。

（一）政府重视，打造三大板块规划

山西省旅发委主任盛佃清在2018年全省旅游发展工作会议上的讲话指出：山西省以满足人民日益增长的美好生活需要为导向，以发展全域旅游为战略要求，以推进旅游供给侧结构性改革为主线，坚持景区为王，路网先行，深化文旅融合，实施大项目建设、大企业运作、大活动引爆，着力锻造黄河、长城、太行三大旅游新品牌，加快构建山西文化旅游发展大格局升级版，编制了三大板块的旅游规划，分别是《山西省黄河板块旅游发展总体规划（2018~2025年）》《山西省长城板块旅游发展总体规划（2018~2025年）》《山西省太行板块旅游发展总体规划（2018~2025年）》。通过规划，进一步厘清山西省三大旅游资源的独特性，彰显文旅融合的主题特色；进一步明确具体的开发思路和工作目标，策划组织实施一批提升产品品质和服务功能的重点项目；进一步科学分析和预测旅游客源市场，引入定制化设计，满足全域旅游多层次消费需求。系统科学、务实有效的三大板块规划，必将使黄河、长城、太行三篇大文章焕发出无与伦比的独特魅力[①]。

"三大板块"旅游规划年限为近期2018~2020和远期2021~2025两个阶段，以沿黄河、长城、太行的核心区为主体区、辐射及相关地区为关联区，覆盖全省范围。规划内容主要包括规划背景、旅游资源分析与发展现状、目标定位与总体思路、功能分区和空间布局、旅游目的地公共服务体

---

① 山西三大板块旅游发展总体规划审议通过. 山西省人民政府门户网站 http://www.shanxi.gov.cn/yw/sxyw/201806/t20180625_457038.shtml

系、旅游形象和品牌、市场拓展与宣传推广、旅游资源保护、社会共享融合发展等。

1.《山西省黄河板块旅游发展总体规划（2018~2025年）》

黄河板块旅游发展以展现"黄河之魂在山西"为战略重点，打造水、陆、空全面发展的黄河旅游风景廊道，建设充分体现文旅融合、独具创意、具备国内外巨大影响力的旅游项目，使黄河板块旅游走出山设驱动的基础上，形成板块全域旅游发展的大格局、大趋势、大繁荣的跨越发展态势。

2.《山西省太行板块旅游发展总体规划（2018~2025年）》

太行山主体在山西，山西省太行板块山水风光雄奇秀丽、历史文化厚重、民俗风情浓郁，又是抗战圣地。太行板块旅游资源丰度大、密度高、整体性强、组合度好，全域旅游资源价值巨大。旅游资源特色鲜明、品位高，中国显性文化遗产高度集中。拥有五台山、平遥古城两处世界文化遗产，五台山景区、皇城相府景区、雁门关景区等国家5A级旅游景区，具有垄断性和国际性。太行板块旅游发展以纵贯南北的"山西省太行一号旅游公路"为连接和现有各类交通网络为支撑，形成一条连接沿线景区景点、旅游重点县、旅游城镇和重点旅游乡村的旅游风景道，打造形成沿太行山南北贯通的集旅游交通廊、文化景观廊、旅游经济发展廊和旅游体验廊于一体的国家级示范走廊。

3.《山西省长城板块旅游发展总体规划（2018~2025年）》

山西保留了战国到明朝等各个历史时期的长城遗址，见证了历史上匈奴、鲜卑、党项、沙陀等多个民族逐渐融合的过程，是山西作为民族熔炉的历史象征和文化地标，它既是祖先遗留下来的宝贵遗产，也是华夏文明的载体，是山西厚重文化底蕴的象征。山西长城包括墙体、关堡、敌楼、马面、马墙等多种建筑遗存，这些建筑遗存许多分布在险峻雄奇的地理环境之中，凝固了军事文化、边贸文化、民俗文化、地域文化等多种历史文化元素，通过深度挖掘山西长城的历史文化内涵，科学保护、维护管理与合理利用，凝练爱国主义、民族融合主题，结合晋中、晋北地区已有的五台山、平遥古城、云冈石窟三处世界级文化遗产，逐步将山西长城打造为世界级文化遗产旅游目的地。

长城板块旅游以"表里山河中华魂，长城博览在山西"的品牌形象，从山西省全域发展角度出发，深入调查山西长城的资源分布及文化特色。根据长城观赏及研究价值做主次区域划分；通过对山西省长城的背景、历史、文化、资源等的分类，以服务核、长城路、主题区、发展轴带等作为重点发展要素；通过对现有交通网络进行重新规划组织，带动旅游景区串联为整体；通过完善服务体系等级，提升游客体验。

（二）政策引领，优化环境

在《山西省黄河板块旅游发展总体规划》中明确了黄河旅游开发的政策保障与实施措施。一是加强组织领导。山西省设立由山西省旅游发展委员会牵头建立黄河板块各市联席会议制度，定期对黄河板块旅游发展情况进行沟通，实现信息共享、经验共享，及时协调解决黄河板块旅游发展中遇到的困难和问题。建立山西黄河板块城景联盟，即由板块的县（市）级旅发委和重要景区负责人建立的常设联席会议。联盟每年召开一次黄河板块大型旅游活动和节庆协调会，目的是在大型活动和节庆方面共同协商错位错时举行，以便使黄河板块时时有、处处有各类活动和节庆，让游客在南北长达1000千米的区带上，处处和时时都有玩头、有看头，强化黄河板块的整体旅游吸引力。二是强化规划引领。以"多规合一"为基本原则，针对景区、旅游项目、特色旅游村镇等需要编制相应的专项或详细规划来落实具体建设空间的控制，特别是特色旅游村镇方面。全面推进旅游规划与城乡、土地利用、道路交通、文物保护利用、环境保护、林业、农业、水利、体育等规划的协调衔接，提升规划的可操作性和落地性。

近年来，临汾在改善旅游发展的基础设施、环境卫生、产品开发、服务水平、发展模式上狠下功夫。一是在基础设施方面，临汾市下属的各县市都开始了开发、拓展和整修道路工程，并有了位居全省第一、全长超过10000千米的市公路通车里程。二是在环境保护方面，临汾积极开展环境治理，改变了传统的环境污染状况。三是重视旅游开发，对景区文化内涵的关注度越来越高，并大力打造文化底蕴丰厚、区域特色明显的旅游景区，并且出台了一系列包括《临汾市旅游发展总体规划》《临汾旅游奖励办法》等在内的政策、规划、方案。这都是临汾重视旅游发展的集中体现。

（三）规划先行，科学发展

从中央到地方政府都极为重视黄河文明旅游的开发，包括相应的旅游产业规划。在国家政府层面，2016年印发的《"十三五"旅游业发展规划》指出遵循景观延续性、文化完整性、市场品牌性和产业集聚性原则，依托线性的江、河、山等自然文化廊道和交通通道，串联重点旅游城市和特色旅游功能区；更是明确提出重点打造黄河华夏文明旅游带，为具有世界性特色大河流域的黄河旅游打开了新局面。在地方政府层面，2018年山西省旅游发展委员会制定了《山西省黄河板块旅游发展总体规划》，对山西省黄河旅游板块进行了详细的规划，结合山西省黄河旅游板块资源文化特性，打造"黄河魂·山西情"的品牌形象，并且对山西黄河旅游板块进行了总体定位、确定了总体的发展目标。

1. 建设黄河精品旅游带

山西省将依托独特的黄河自然资源、沿岸人文资源，以及特有的黄河精神和黄河文化，全力打造中国·山西黄河精品旅游带。落实国家《"十三五"旅游业发展规划》发展要求，以在建的山西省黄河一号国家旅游专用公路为轴，串接精品化建设的品牌景区和游线，拓展新产品，丰富新业态，发展特色旅游村镇，强固要素支撑，将山西黄河旅游板块建设成为"中国·山西黄河精品旅游带"。

2. 建设世界大河文明山西旅游目的地

山西将依托丰富的黄河文化旅游资源，打造世界大河文明山西旅游目的地。5000年山西历史文化发展，充分展现了世界四大流域文明唯一遗存的、连续不断的华夏大河文明，中华精神的魂和脉。结合当前我国"一带一路"的发展倡议，充分利用黄河孕育的厚重文化，打造世界文化旅游的卖点和品牌，将其建成"世界大河文明山西旅游目的地"。尤其是大河文明旅游论坛的召开，一方面搭建山西与全球交流互鉴、合作共赢的旅游高端平台，为山西打造一个规格高、影响大的旅游会议品牌；另一方面以"大河文明"为载体，助力山西抢占黄河的文化旅游价值高地，进一步提升世界级文化旅游目的地的形象。论坛的召开不仅能推动山西旅游与文化产业的融合发展，展现中国的文化自信、文化繁荣、文化软实力，还能助力山西加快打造和推出旅游产品，促进"黄河IP"的深度挖掘和创新营销，从而加快构建山西文化旅游发展大格局升级版，打造"世界大河文化旅游目的地"的黄金名片。

3. 打造国家级黄河文化旅游区

在《山西省黄河板块旅游发展总体规划》中，明确提出了黄河旅游板块的文化发展目标，凸显了山西省政府对黄河文明的重视。规划指出：黄河板块的文化开发要在创新、融合、特色之中建设讲好山西故事、演绎中国精神的国家级文化旅游区。其中包括策划和演出3台全国著名和具有世界影响的实景演艺和仪式性表演节目；大力保护和开发板块的非物质文化遗产，在民间戏曲、歌舞、音乐、特色饮食、特色手工艺品、特色旅游商品等方面下功夫，重点景区、旅游城镇和村庄要作为非物质文化遗产的主要展示地；挖掘黄河板块的历史文化，利用现代科技手段活化、显化、趣味化历史文化故事，使之成为发展观光、研学旅游的重要内容，让黄河板块的旅游凸显山西的历史文化和丰富多彩的民间文化优势。

山西省黄河板块旅游发展的总体目标是以山西省黄河一号国家旅游专用公路及相关道路为骨架，以资源整合提升、精致化建设等为手段，以将旅游业打造为牵动经济转型的战略型支柱产业为出发点，构建母亲黄河、龙腾黄河、多彩黄河、生态黄河的国家旅游精品线路，带动板块旅游整体的隆升发展，建成山西旅游的新高地、黄河旅游的新标杆、世界文化旅游的新视界。

（四）因地制宜，打造多样产品

根据《山西省黄河板块旅游发展总体规划》的相关内容，根据黄河不同区域的自然资源、文化资源，因地制宜突出特色，一是将黄河板块分为"西口文化与黄河古堡休闲片区、黄河峡谷与红色文化旅游片区、吕梁山生态康养休闲度假片区、黄河湿地和古中国文化休闲片区"四大功能片区。二是黄河主体区将建构"一条黄河廊道、四大旅游核心、四个旅游名县、六大主题游线、八大特色景区"的空间大格局。三是建设两大龙头项目、十大重点项目、十大特色项目以及55个县级重点项目。其中两个龙头项目是山西省黄河一号国家旅游专用公路项目、世界大河文明博览园项目。

1. 山西省黄河一号国家旅游专用公路项目

流经山西省的黄河全长约1008公里，规划建设的黄河一号国家旅游专用公路全长约1225千米，北起忻州万家寨，南至运城西，贯穿四市（忻州、吕梁、临汾、运城），连接14个A级及以上景区和75个非A级重要旅游资源。以建设山西黄河精品旅游带和世界大河文明山西旅游目的地为抓手，把沿黄1000多千米的主体公路建成南北畅通、旅游服务设施齐全、景观优美的风景廊道。该专用公路将打造成集母亲黄河、龙腾黄河、多彩黄河和生态黄河于一体的国家一级风景道，国内外知名的黄河文化观光、休闲廊道，串联景区和多种活动的特色线路旅游综合体。一路上，看不尽的黄河峡谷奇观、数不尽的历史文化遗存，成为旅游路、脱贫路、致富路。依托"黄河一号"旅游公路打造四片区：西口文化与黄河古堡休闲片区，黄河峡谷和红色文化旅游片区，吕梁山生态康养休闲度假片区以及主题区，黄河湿地和古中国文化休闲等片区。

其中临汾永和段，主线104千米、支线56千米，建成后串联20多个景点，有古村落、古渡口、古寺庙，有红军东征纪念馆，还有全国规模最大、最密集的河流蛇曲群"乾坤湾"。"天下黄河九十九道弯"，在乾坤湾段就拐了7个弯，乾坤湾试验段是旅游公路支线，形成湾湾相连、景景相通、快进慢游。此外，临汾市还全力打造了临汾沿黄扶贫旅游公路，该公路以"九曲黄河魂，峡谷风情线"为主题，融"交通+旅游+扶贫+文化+物联网"为一体，将连接起临汾市黄河沿岸乾坤湾、红军东征纪念馆、吉县人祖山、壶口瀑布、大宁二郎山、乡宁云丘山等40多处著名景点，带动沿黄旅游业的大发展[1]。

2. 世界大河文明博览园项目

依托世界大河古文明的彰显，结合我国"一带一路"的发展倡议，在黄河流域山西段建设以凸显黄河文明为主，集四大古流域文明于一体的世界大河文明博览园。山西是华夏文明重要发祥地之一，万荣县后土文化充分展现了黄河农耕文明曙光和华夏大地之母的特色，是黄河流域古文明的典型代表。因此，选择在万荣县黄河岸边建设世界大河文明博览园，打造5A级旅游景区。

3. 世界大河文明旅游论坛

山西在文旅融合发展的大潮中勇立潮头，深耕资源、创新产品、锻造品牌，进一步提升世界级文化旅游目的地形象。2018年，在临汾召开了首届世界大河文明旅游论坛，提升了山西省黄河旅游以及临汾旅游的国际知名度。《山西省黄河板块旅游发展总体规划》明确指出要打造世界大河文明论坛品牌，具体是策划举办世界大河文明论坛，建设世界大河文明论坛的永久会址。该论坛以远古时代著名的四大河流域文明文化研讨为主，广邀对世界大河流域文明进行研究的学者和历史、文化专业的青少年学生，以研讨、研学、学术交流及世界大河流域文明旅游发展为主题进行交流为主，致力于研究保护大河流域生态环境及建立经济—社会—环境可持续发展的大河流域合作机制，研究四大流域古文明的延续发展与我国"一带一路"战略的契合关系等。

通过世界大河文明旅游论坛，临汾还将进一步提升"中国根·黄河魂"旅游品牌的知名度和影响力，整合壶口瀑布、云丘山景区、洪洞大槐树、乾坤湾等旅游景区，规划建设沿黄生态文化旅游带，打造富有文化特色和时代精神的黄河文化走廊、生态走廊，推动临汾市黄河文化旅游快速发展。

（五）打造"黄河魂·山西情"的品牌和形象

"黄河魂"：九曲黄河在山西段是黄河流域地貌景观最出色的地段之一，也是黄河流域长达5000年华夏文化绵延不绝、承上启下最具代表性的地带。将黄河孕育的厚重文化、中华民族的根和脉打造为世界文化旅游的卖点和品牌，将会使进入山西黄河板块旅游的游客深深地体验和感悟到"黄河之魂在山西"。

---

[1] 山西临汾投资76.8亿元打造沿黄扶贫旅游公路[J]. 城市道桥与防洪，2018（2）.

"山西情"：山西黄河板块旅游可以为游客提供多重情感感知和想象力。将山西黄河板块建设成为山西黄河精品旅游带，不仅可以使游客在预期感知中得到"到山西黄河板块旅游可以在旅游过程中体验到友情和盛情"及"诚信为本的山西旅游"的心理暗示，而且在旅游实际过程中也会体验到山西人的友情、盛情款待和旅游享受。

形成了"河孕华夏，彩屏山西""晋之黄河，美哉山水""千里黄河览风光，百世山西积文脉"的宣传口号，这些宣传口号一是呈现山西的黄河是孕育华夏文明中国的核心区，二是直接点出黄河山西段的自然风光优美，突出山西段的山水风光有着与他处不同的美，值得来观光和游玩，三是展示黄河山西段长达1000多公里，沿途风光无限，显示了山西黄河地区文化和自然特色鲜明、丰富多彩，值得看和游。

（六）开发文创产品，带动乡村扶贫

临汾市除了拥有丰富的自然资源、人文资源、非物质文化遗产等旅游资源外，临汾市还研发了一系列独具特色的文创产品。临汾市通过开发乡村文创产品来推进乡村旅游扶贫，通过对农民进行技能培训，鼓励和扶持他们利用乡村的原材料，通过创意设计和加工制作，变成具有当地文化特色的旅游商品，帮助乡村农民就业和增收。

临汾市文化和旅游局下属尚尧文化艺术公司启动"乡村记忆，文创扶贫"，推出的"乡村记忆"系列文创产品受到市场的欢迎。尚尧文化艺术有限公司联合非遗保护单位及艺术院校大学生深入农村体验生活，采风调研，有针对性地设计推出"乡村记忆"系列近20种文创产品，以实际行动留住乡村记忆，力推文创扶贫。这些文创产品包括茶台、花盆、香插、砚台、文玩、蒲团、收纳盒、泥版画等，均取材于广大农村遍地皆是的废旧老砖、老麦草、老门板、老墙泥、老风化木以及部分废弃的生产材料，这些文创产品的加工不需要复杂的专业技术，对当地农民朋友稍加培训即可完成制作。

二、未来发展建议

目前，旅游已经成为人民群众日常生活的重要组成部分。自助游、自驾游成为主要的出游方式。游客对旅游产品的需求呈品质化趋势。游客的需求由传统的观光游向休闲度假转变，出行方式呈现自由化、个性化和散客化的发展趋势，对高品质的度假旅游产品的需求快速增长，对交通基础设施、公共服务、生态环境的要求越来越高，对个性化、特色化旅游产品和服务的要求越来越高，旅游需求的品质化和中高端化趋势日益明显。在这样的背景下，临汾在开发大河文明旅游时要做到以下一些方面。

（一）文旅融合，突出特色

文化是旅游的灵魂，旅游是文化的载体。随着文化旅游产业的发展，文化已经不再是旅游业的附属品，而是决定着旅游产业成败兴衰的关键要素。在旅游产品设计与开发中要充分利用和展示本土特色文化。旅游产品开发的本质是把文化内涵形象化，让游客能体验到文化内涵，可以让更多

的游客了解黄河文明、认同黄河文化，产生文化自豪感和认同感，彰显旅游的文化价值和社会价值。随着游客经济收入和受教育水平的不断提高，求知、求新、求异势必成为重要的旅游动机，他们对旅游地文化品质的要求也越来越高。对此，深入挖掘黄河文化旅游内涵需要在田野调查的基础上，发掘有形和无形的文化旅游资源，营造文化氛围，做到形神兼备，充分满足游客审美和求知的欲望（图3.1）。

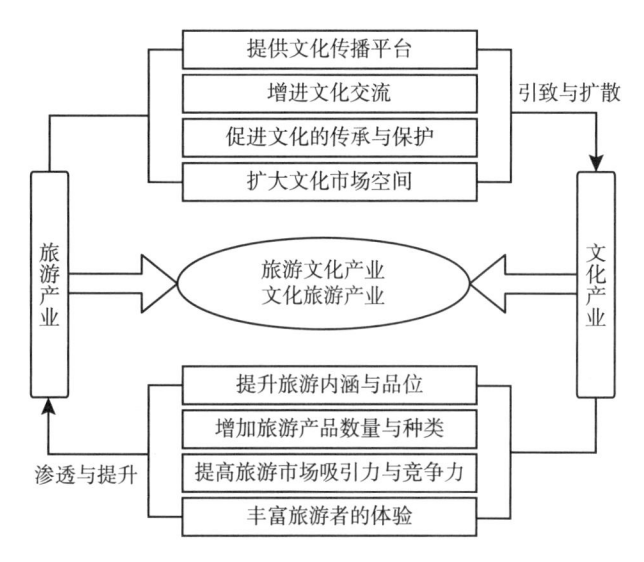

图 3.1 旅游产业和文化产业融合发展机制

资料来源：刘楚楚. 山西省文化产业与旅游产业融合发展研究［D］. 山西财经大学，2018.

因此，在开发黄河文明旅游项目和产品时，一定要充分挖掘黄河文化、黄河精神，以及黄河流域形成的历史文化、民俗文化、宗教文化、非物质文化遗产等，以独特的黄河文化和黄河精神增强旅游竞争力。黄河临汾流域文化和旅游资源特色鲜明，要充分挖掘黄河文化特色，做足水文章，整合文化、自然风光、湿地、民俗、非物质文化遗产等旅游资源。具体来说，以黄河流域沿线的非物质文化遗产、名人故里、历史遗存、特色建筑等为依托，开发特色文化休闲度假、民俗体验等旅游产品或者活动项目。策划举办系列黄河文明旅游文化节，充分展示临汾黄河流域深厚的历史文化底蕴。积极打造文化主题旅游品牌，以黄河历史文化为依托，打造黄河文明旅游回廊线路，建设名河旅游产品体系。尤其要充分挖掘临汾的名山、大河、人文、历史和都市的优质资源，依托黄河流域内的洪洞大槐树、壶口瀑布等，强化资源整合和区域协同开发，着力打造黄河临汾流域自然风光和生态旅游带。

（二）以旅游者需求为导向，创新产品

中国旅游研究院发布的《2018中国品质旅游发展报告》显示，游客更加关注市民休闲、生活方式、商业环境和公共服务，70%左右的游客出行选择的是非景区以及非核心城区，主客共享的生活空间已经逐步成为旅游的吸引物。目前国内旅游者的需求正在由观光向休闲度假转变。休闲旅游

的核心价值就在于旅游过程中旅游者能够广泛参与、深度体验。游客对于旅行内容、品质的要求已经提升，在旅行的过程中不仅仅是拍照，到此一游，他们更希望体验旅游目的地的一些细节，能够体会一把当地人的感觉，获得高品质的旅游体验。因此，临汾黄河旅游产品的开发要以旅游者需求为导向，在丰富文化内涵、强化旅游体验、延长旅游产业链上下功夫。因此，临汾市要增加休闲旅游产品的供给，增强产品特色和吸引力，形成供给结构合理的观光产品和能吸引游客的高质量休闲度假产品，满足旅游者对旅游产品休闲功能的需求。

1. 产品差异化与均衡化

第一，临汾市在开发黄河文明旅游产品时应避免产品同质化，只有产品差异化才能实现特色化。在产品体系、产品线路、产品服务上形成各自不同的特色，增强产品的吸引力，着力打造河流旅游产品、根祖游产品、乡村旅游产品、文化旅游产品、休闲度假旅游产品。第二，临汾市在黄河旅游产品开发上要突出层次性，形成由点（景区）、线（旅游线路）发展向面（旅游目的地）发展，发展全域旅游。黄河文明旅游产品开发应以水上旅游为主，以精品旅游区的打造为突破口，形成多元化发展，打造全域旅游目的地。第三，旅游产品设计坚持以人为本。相关旅游企业在产品设计时要坚持以人为本，把游客满意作为大河文明旅游业发展的根本目的，通过旅游促进人的全面发展，使大河文明旅游业成为提升人民群众品质生活的幸福产业。

2. 突出优势，强调特色

临汾市在现有的旅游开发中应突出黄河文化特色和田园、乡村、山水等生态特色，开发深度体验文化旅游产品和休闲度假产品，结合初步成熟的寻根祭祖旅游，打造具有临汾特色、黄河风情、根祖文化的旅游品牌和产品，通过旅游业的发展带动生态、文化、经济的全面发展，加快临汾黄河文明旅游的发展，在黄河流域旅游发展的格局中处于领先地位，成长为文化复合型的黄河文明旅游重要目的地和示范区。

大河旅游产品在供给上要有效地满足旅游者对旅游产品的多样化、品质化、特色化等需求，完善大河旅游产品的层级结构。因此，在旅游开发过程中，要对个性化、休闲度假产品进行更深度的开发与诠释，重点开发特色旅游和深度旅游产品。在突出优势、强调特色、巩固观光旅游的基础上，开发研学游、生态游、民俗游、休闲度假游、户外、现代时尚等特色旅游产品。

3. 深挖产品文化内涵

临汾市在旅游产品创新方面，要深度挖掘产品的文化特色，提高旅游产品质量与文化内涵。充分利用流域内的民族文化特色，突破单一的观光旅游形式，深入挖掘文化内涵，推进文化旅游开发，把民族文化与旅游创意开发完美结合，开发具有民族特色的黄河旅游产品，打造跨地域、跨国旅游精品线路，促进黄河文化旅游产品的转型升级。

4. 特色旅游线路和"线路套餐"布局

开辟"水上+陆地+空中"的旅游线路，将临汾黄河板块内的县域进行串联，360°全视角展示"华夏根、黄河魂"的品牌形象。通过旅游线路有机串联板块内的重要旅游景区、特色城镇、旅游景点、民俗文化、乡村风光、名人故居和各类旅游服务设施，通过"旅游+"形成特色突出的多产品、多业态组成的"旅游线路套餐"体系，为游客提供包括游览观光、休闲度假、民俗娱乐、康养、研学科考、商务会议以及生活补给等功能在内的多样化旅游产品供给，满足游客多种需求，建立立体化的旅游产品体系。

（三）打造品牌，强化营销

目前，临汾市依托其拥有的黄河自然与文化景观，以"中国根、黄河魂"为品牌形象，把临汾打造成为集绿色生态、文化遗产、现代农业、旅游文创等于一体的黄金生态文化旅游带。黄河是中华民族的"母亲河"，也是中华民族和东亚文明的主要发源地。强化资源整合和区域协同开发，着力打造黄河文明流域自然风光、文化旅游和生态旅游带，把黄河临汾流域建设成为旅游功能多样、文化特色鲜明、生态环境优越、基础设施完善、旅游服务优质的国际知名的黄河文明旅游目的地。此外，要不断提升现代旅游业服务营销水平，努力推进"中国根、黄河魂"旅游品牌的建设管理和推广，让"中国根、黄河魂"的旅游形象宣传取得实效。具体如下：

一是开展网络营销宣传与推广。随着网络移动信息技术的发展，消费者可以通过各种网络电子设备接收信息，因此临汾市要充分借助各类网络营销渠道，对旅游产品、旅游线路、旅游景点等进行宣传与推广。如可以充分利用当下流行的微信、抖音、网络直播等自媒体平台创造话题进行推广宣传。二是广告媒体宣传与推广。通过在电视、电台广播、网络、报纸、杂志等媒介上做广告对临汾市的旅游产品、旅游景点进行大力宣传。三是重视节庆对旅游形象的推广。如通过黄河文化旅游节、大河文明旅游论坛、大槐树文化旅游节等进行宣传推广，塑造"中国根，黄河魂""古尧都，新临汾"等鲜明的旅游形象，打造临汾旅游品牌。四是临汾市各区域要合作谋划宣传推广体系，构建目的地网络宣传营销推广平台，共享销售队伍、销售渠道来降低广告费用和销售成本，准确定位客源市场，实施网络精准营销。

（四）保护生态环境，实现可持续发展

牢固树立"绿水青山就是金山银山"的理念，将绿色发展贯穿到旅游规划、开发、管理、服务全过程，形成人与自然和谐发展的现代旅游业新格局。生态环境是黄河文明旅游开发的基础，生态环境关系到生存问题，是旅游开发最根本的问题。在旅游开发中，要注重黄河流域生态环境的保护，根据黄河临汾流域各地区的实际情况，做到适度开发、循序开发与保护开发的有机结合。

（五）培养人才，建立保障

黄河文明旅游发展对临汾市的旅游从业人员的数量、服务能力和服务质量等提出了更高的要求。旅游服务人才是临汾黄河文化旅游产品开发与经营管理的重要支撑，通过与知名旅游院校、旅游企业合作培训、进修等多种途径和方式提高从业人员的整体素质，满足市场对人才的要求。如旅游资源开发和旅游产品开发所需要的旅游规划与产品设计人才、高素质的服务人才、旅游景区管理人才等。

第一，旅游企业要开展常态化的职业培训，培养员工的职业技能、职业知识、职业素养，进而提高其服务能力、服务质量和服务水平，为游客创造良好的旅游服务体验。在培训过程中，既注重专家讲授，又安排现场操作体验，既为主讲者提供发挥空间，又为学员搭建参与互动交流对话平台。

第二，开展校企合作、产教融合，探索培养高素质旅游人才的机制。根据临汾市旅游市场对人才的需求，可以和当地的高校合作研发旅游课程体系、教学标准以及教材等，开展订单式人才培养。同时，也可以校企合作制订人才培养或职工培训方案，相互为学生实习实训、员工培训等提供支持。通过以上途径为临汾市黄河文明旅游发展提供高素质的人才。

第三，建立灵活的人才政策体系，吸引更多的高素质、懂经营和管理的旅游高水平人才到临汾创业，为加快发展临汾黄河文化旅游产业提供强大的人才支撑体系。

（六）抓住"一带一路"重大机遇，加强区域旅游合作

目前，很多国家、地区都把河流旅游业作为拉动内需、促进国民经济增长的一种产业，地区与地区之间、国家与国家之间流域旅游业的竞争是旅游企业、公司不可回避的难题。如黄河流域的沿线城市都在大力开发黄河文明旅游资源，打造黄河文明旅游带，开发多样化的黄河文明旅游精品产品，在一定程度上黄河流域的人文与自然旅游资源存在相似性，并且有些地区还都争夺相同的主要目标客源市场。在此背景下，临汾市要突出大河文明流域旅游区的资源特色、产品特色、文化特色，并实现与其他地区和景区的合作，实现优势互补。

"一带一路"也为临汾旅游的发展带来了重大机遇，尤其是入境旅游的发展。临汾市要抓住该机遇，一是，与黄河沿岸的其他城市建立黄河流域旅游发展联动机制，完善旅游市场体系。黄河流域沿线地区应遵循"保护生态环境、发扬黄河文化"的开发理念，统筹规划，协同开发利用流域内的优势资源，实现跨行政区域的文化和旅游生态系统开发、联动开发、完善旅游配套服务。二是，进一步加强城市合作，建立旅游协调发展合作机制。临汾市要与山西省内黄河沿岸地区加强合作，拓展旅游交流合作空间，建立区域内的旅游合作联盟，实现区域旅游繁荣。三是，加强区域行政合作，通过政策的制定，打破黄河文化旅游产品开发的空间限制和行政壁垒，充分联合黄河流域文化和旅游资源，加快推出集休闲度假、乡村旅游、文化旅游等为一体的多元化旅游精品线路，建设具有中国特色与文化内涵的黄河文化旅游产品体系，以增强旅游产品的国际竞争力。四是，处理好区域之间的利益分配，调动各方面的积极因素，推动区域之间的旅游协同发展，实现互利共赢。联合成立区域性协调组织，专项负责完成各种合作事务。这方面典型代表是"粤港澳珠江三角洲旅游推广机构"。五是，在提升旅游服务质量和旅游市场秩序方面，实现不同区域、不同部门的联合执法、共同监管，共同保障黄河旅游产品的质量，规范旅游市场秩序，构建旅游命运共同体。

在加强区域合作的过程中，可以构建以政府为主导，旅游企业等多方利益相关者参与的旅游合作机制。如图3.2所示，在政府的主导下，各利益主体共同合作，即政府与政府之间、政府与企业之间、企业与企业之间加强沟通、交流与合作，实现信息共享。推动临汾黄河流域信息、资本、人

才的交流，并构建利益分配与补偿机制，协调各方利益，保障区域内文化旅游健康发展；由政府提供相应的基础设施和旅游公共服务体系，由企业根据游客需求提供各类旅游产品（图3.2）。

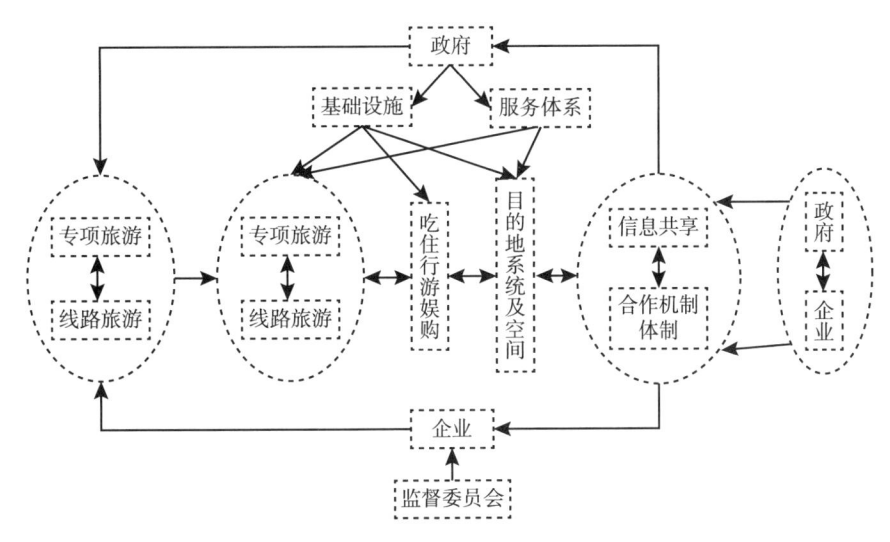

图 3.2　沿黄旅游区合作内容及机制

资料来源：刘敏，任亚鹏，王萍. 山西黄河文化：内涵、符号与旅游开发——基于晋西沿黄旅游景区比较研究 [J]. 晋中学院学报，2018，35（4）.

（七）产业联动，创新发展模式

在发展临汾黄河文明旅游的过程中，应做到产业联动。发挥旅游业的产业带动功能，与现代服务业、农业、工业、林业、商业和文化产业融合发展，形成"旅游+"的产业发展体系，打造临汾黄河文明流域旅游经济带，助力临汾旅游经济转型发展。如以10个国家级、省级生态农业旅游观光点为依托，大力发展临汾市的特色观光与休闲农业，充分发挥临汾市黄河流域的文化资源、自然资源、农业资源等优势，打造生态休闲农业的乡村旅游品牌形象，积极申报特色农产品地理标志、驰名商标等，加快形成乡村旅游品牌效应和规模效应。大力开发黄土高原的特色农产品，通过文化创意开发，形成有当地特色的旅游产品。

尤其是在文旅融合背景下，加快临汾当地文化产业和旅游产业的融合发展，探索大河文化与大河旅游产业的联动发展模式。如图3.3所示，应以政府为主导，企业、消费者、社区三方参与协调，为文化旅游产业联动发展提供保障与支撑，塑造具有鲜明特色的旅游形象品牌，推出具有文化旅游复合型特征的产品，采用多渠道的宣传方式，并在联合发展的过程中控制好政策实施、制度管理、危机处理、社会监督等问题，为两大产业联合发展提供内动力。如文化产业与现代科技产业联动发展，可以借助现代科技手段将非物质文化遗产融入其他景观，通过保护生态民俗村、建设相关主题公园以及大型实景展演等方式，不仅达到了对非物质文化遗产的整体性保护的目的，更为其提供了空间载体和消费市场，吸引更多青年群体的关注。通过与其他产业融合发展，使非物质文化遗产的可持续发展成为可能。

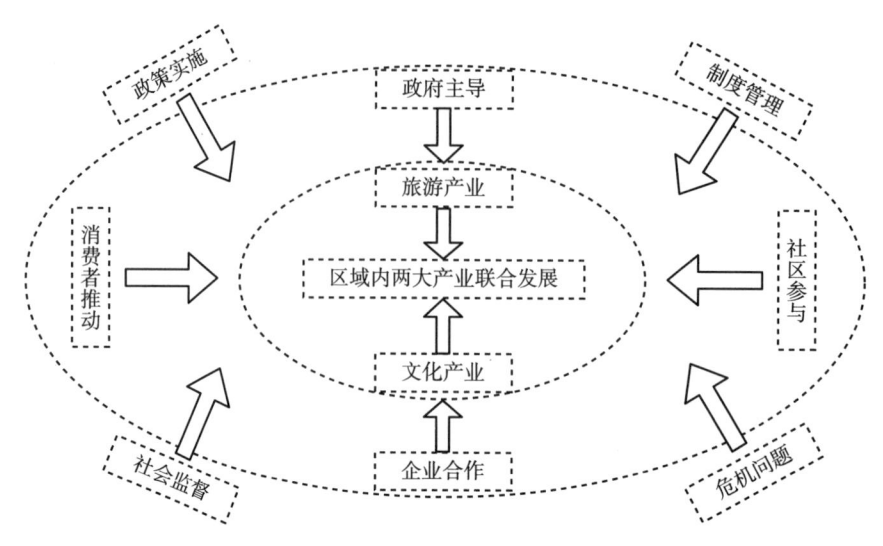

图 3.3　文化和旅游产业联动发展合作机制

资料来源：刘敏，任亚鹏，王萍. 山西黄河文化：内涵、符号与旅游开发——基于晋西沿黄旅游景区比较研究［J］. 晋中学院学报，2018，35（4）.

（八）完善旅游配套服务设施

临汾市由于地处黄土高原，四周环山，全境主要是山地、丘陵、盆地三大地形单元。一是，要加强对旅游景区的旅游交通建设，使得游客进入景区的道路环境更加便利，提高自由行、自驾游等游客的可进入性。二是，加强对景区内部的基础设施的整体规划建设，如游客中心、旅游标识系统等旅游公共服务设施布置，提高游客的旅游体验。三是，由市区到景区的直通车系统还不够完善，临汾市的大部分景区距离城市中心较远，因此要加强对旅游公交系统的完善，开通更多的旅游公交线路。四是，提升智慧旅游建设水平，做到景区的内部免费 Wi-Fi 实现区域全覆盖，完善景点随时定位智能语音讲解系统，升级电子售票、验票。

临汾已经制定出台相关政策，完善旅游配套服务设施。一是，提升旅游酒店接待能力和水平、加强旅游市场综合整治、推广旅游惠民一卡通等。二是，基础设施建设部分，包括实施旅游公路建设工程、旅游厕所建设工程、河道生态建设工程 3 项内容。三是，人居环境改善部分，包括加大环境卫生建设、园林城市建设、生态环境治理、城市设施保障、汾河景区提质 5 项内容。四是，文明素质提升部分，包括深化文明城市创建、文明旅游系列主题宣传、临汾形象整体宣传、"小手拉大手"文明共建四项内容。

第二章 世界典型河流文明旅游发展经验

第一节 莱茵河旅游发展经验

莱茵河作为贯通欧洲南北运输的大动脉之一，在过去曾一度是欧洲文化灵感的源泉，孕育了沿河的灿烂文化，是具历史意义的欧洲长河之一。莱茵河流经国家把大力发展旅游业作为综合治理莱茵河、加快产业转型、促进国民经济增长的重要途径。梳理和总结莱茵河流域旅游发展经验与做法，对我国大河流域治理与发展具有重要的借鉴意义。

一、莱茵河沿岸风光

莱茵河流域内总的地势自南向北倾斜，河流的南部（上莱茵河段）穿过黑森山林，以高山、雪峰、草场、湖泊、湿地、森林、瀑布为主要特色，包括著名的阿尔卑斯山、托马湖、日内瓦湖、康斯坦茨湖、莱茵河瀑布、黑森林等；中部（中莱茵河段）为丘陵地带，是该河景色最为壮丽的一段，以峡谷、丘陵为主，莱茵河从险峻的山坡之间流过，形成一段曲折而深邃的峡谷，两岸山坡上布满葡萄园和田园村镇，并分布着风格各异的古城堡、古城址，著名的四湖景也位于此；北部（下莱茵河段）为沿海低地，这里水量充足，工业发达，著名的工业中心鲁尔就位于此。

得益于莱茵河沿线丰富的人文环境和优美的自然景观，莱茵河沿线城镇每年吸引着众多旅游者，旅游业尤其发达。除古城堡、古城址、庄园外，还有大雪橇滑道、德意志角、"鼠塔"、普法战争纪念碑、荷兰风车等众多的旅游景点。其中最著名的沿河港口城市科隆，拥有3300多间酒吧、咖啡馆和餐馆，大量的画廊和博物馆向旅游者充分展示了城市历史和市民生活。另外，莱茵河流域每年还要举办各种节庆活动，包括巴塞尔狂欢节、德国科隆啤酒节等。[1]

二、莱茵河整体发展模式

莱茵河在重点开发与保护水资源的基础上，通过城市化与科技创新带动流域整体发展，积聚并形成了化工、钢铁、机械制造、旅游、金融保险等产业带。莱茵河流域经济的发展遵循经济空间结构的演变规律，优先发展港口城市作为经济增长的核心，对河道进行整治，开挖人工运河，建造堤

---

[1] 徐海峰，聂真，李媚. 莱茵河流域发展研究[J]. 四川建筑，2016，36（1）.

坝，使莱茵河航运成为世界上货运密度最大的内陆河流，带动了内陆经济的持续发展。继而布局航运网，接通河道腹地边缘地区以及连接河道上游地区，形成经济空间网络结构。发展港口及节点城市，仅在莱茵河干流上就建成近50座中等规模以上的城市，并具有各自的主导及特色职能和定位，如阿姆斯特丹为金融中心，斯特拉斯堡、海牙为行政中心，科隆为媒体业中心、香水之都和化工中心，埃森、多特蒙德、康斯坦茨为教育中心。各城市功能之间合作互补，城市化率急速提高，并使德国成为没有"大城市"的经济大国和全球城市化率最高的国家之一。[1]

三、莱茵河旅游产业空间布局

莱茵河从阿尔卑斯山发源以后往西北方向入海。基于其地貌类型特征，逐渐形成了上游、中游、下游各具特色的旅游产业空间结构。

（一）上游：湖泊休闲度假旅游

莱茵河上游以高山、亚高山、中低山地貌为主，遍布大量的湖泊，如博登湖、苏黎世湖等。这些湖泊成为莱茵河上游冬季滑雪旅游、夏季避暑旅游以及各种形式观光旅游的主要资源，形成了上游休闲度假旅游的空间布局。以博登湖为例，该区域位于德国、瑞士、奥地利三国交界处，面积540平方千米，是莱茵河上游的天然蓄水库。其独特的地理位置、美丽宜人的风光，形成水、陆、空等内容丰富、覆盖面广的旅游产品组合，使该区域成为欧洲知名的旅游度假胜地。

（二）中游：历史文化遗产旅游

莱茵河中游以低山峡谷地貌为主，核心部分是"莱茵中上游河谷"世界文化遗产，被公认为是莱茵河风景最美的一段。在2002年布达佩斯召开的世界遗产大会上，中莱茵河谷作为一直促进着地中海地区和欧洲北部地区之间的物质、文化交流的欧洲最重要的交通运输线路之一；作为一个人类杰出的、逐渐自发形成的文化景观的典范；以及作为位于狭窄河谷之中的传统生活方式和交流方法不断演化的典型代表这三点，被列入《世界遗产名录》。[2]

世界遗产委员会对其评价为：延绵65千米的中莱茵河河谷，和她沿途的古堡、历史小城、葡萄园生动地描述了一段同多变的自然环境相缠绕的漫长人类历史。这里发生了众多历史事件，演绎了许多传奇，几个世纪以来，为无数的作家、画家和音乐家提供了灵感。[3] 莱茵河中游的主要旅游资源为中世纪的古堡景观、上千年的葡萄耕作文化、葡萄酒酿造技术以及沿河古镇、峡谷自然风光。

1. 莱茵城堡

在中莱茵河河谷约65千米长的距离内，散布着约40座古城堡，这里城堡的数量和密度当数欧洲之最，其中大多是在公元11~13世纪时期建造起来的。如今这些城堡已经失去了其原有的军事防御和收取税金的功能，其中大多数保护较好或经过修葺的城堡已被改为酒店、青年旅舍和餐厅等，

---

[1] 马静，邓宏兵. 国外典型流域开发模式与经验对长江经济带的启示［J］. 区域经济评论，2016（2）.
[2] 张丹明. 中莱茵河谷：葡萄园—古堡—城镇—山河的奏鸣曲［J］. 中国文化遗产，2007（2）.
[3] 董波，杜雨辰. 国外运河遗产对中国大运河文化带建设的启示［J］. 发展规划研究，2019（5）.

是活着的、正在使用的文化遗产。

2. 葡萄园

中莱茵河河谷是德国四大葡萄酒产区之一。古罗马人在公元前2世纪时便将葡萄种植和葡萄酒酿造技术带到了莱茵河两岸，从那时起葡萄种植规模逐渐扩大，到公元12世纪时葡萄园梯田已经成为河谷的主要风景。中莱茵河地区的葡萄园，有85%位于山坡的台地上。这种陡坡、极陡的坡上的葡萄园对于莱茵河中游的人文景观而言是一个非常重要、不可或缺的因素；2000多年的葡萄种植历史在很多方面都影响和塑造着这里的景观，它是人们在长期生产实践中协调、适应复杂人地关系的结果。

3. 沿岸城镇

中莱茵河河谷沿岸有包括宾根、波帕德、布劳巴赫、科布伦茨等在内的30多个城镇，其中一些城镇的历史可以追溯到2000年前古罗马时期的聚落。宾根和布劳巴赫是典型的仍然保留着古罗马和中世纪时期生活环境的莱茵小镇，它们曾经都属于罗马时期最早建立要塞和堡垒的城镇和商品贸易场所的代表。许多城墙、防御设施等被较完整地保留了下来，布劳巴赫的小镇中心还保留着当年的集市广场。位于莱茵河和摩泽尔河交汇处的科伦布茨属于中莱茵河河谷中较大的城镇，城市内遗留了大量的文化遗迹与历史建筑。德意志角便是其中之一，德意志角上立着象征德意志和平统一的13个州和3个城市的州旗、州徽，以及完成德意志统一大业的威廉一世皇帝的骑像。[1]

中莱茵河河谷地区的主要旅游形式是游轮旅游、山地徒步行走、山地自行车运动等，并形成中游历史文化遗产旅游的区域旅游空间特征。

（三）下游：工业及工业遗产旅游

莱茵河下游的旅游资源主要是现代工业及工业革命后莱茵河及其支流鲁尔河流域形成的德国鲁尔工业区工业遗产。

鲁尔工业区位于德国西部，因鲁尔河（莱茵河支流）流过该区域而得名。19世纪上半叶大规模煤矿开采和钢铁生产，使鲁尔区逐渐成为世界上最著名的重工业区和最大的工业区之一。历经了约100多年的繁荣发展后，在20世纪60年代初鲁尔开始出现经济衰落，即所谓"逆工业化过程"，煤炭和钢铁工业尤为明显，如1957年有141个煤矿，49万煤矿工人，年产1.2亿吨原煤；到1995年只有13个煤矿，不足7万煤矿工人，年产原煤0.4亿吨。逆工业化过程导致大批工人失业、税收减少、污染得不到治理，区域形象恶化，转产、转型迫在眉睫。

面对工业化发展所引发的各种问题，鲁尔区打破常规思考模式，对工业化过程中留存的大量废弃工矿业、旧厂房和庞大的工业空置建筑和设施，重新发现其历史价值，将其视为工业文化遗产，进行工业遗产旅游和区域振兴等相结合的战略性开发与整治。经过了"否定与排斥""迷茫""谨慎尝试"三个阶段后，终于进入到"工业遗产旅游之路"的战略化阶段，以"博物馆""公共游憩空

---

[1] 张丹明. 中莱茵河谷：葡萄园-古堡-城镇-山河的奏鸣曲[J]. 中国文化遗产，2007（2）.

间""与购物旅游相结合"三种模式来实施。当年的厂房成了创意设计中心、车间成为大型剧场，昔日的产业工人成为导游解说员，并在此形成莱茵河旅游产业空间结构的工业及工业遗产旅游区。目前位于莱茵河畔的德国鲁尔区已成为世界上工业遗产旅游开展最好的典范。[①]

四、莱茵河主要旅游产品形式

从上述莱茵河旅游产业空间布局形态可以发现，因上、中、下游资源禀赋不同而形成特色各异的旅游产品，但是作为一个整体的旅游区，莱茵河的旅游产品同样具有整体性。

（一）水上旅游产品

莱茵河的水上旅游产品除了上游湖泊的帆船、帆板、短途环湖游船外，主要是内河游轮。这些游轮旅游产品的区别在于游程的长短和水陆旅游结合方式的差异。一般莱茵河内河游轮从阿姆斯特丹上船，沿途经过科隆、海德堡、德国黑森林、阿尔萨斯酒乡，最终达到巴塞尔。

（二）陆上旅游产品

随着信息技术的应用、经济的发展，消费者的消费习惯发生了变化，越来越多人选择自助游、自由行。政府在规划中，充分考虑到散客的旅游度假需求，在莱茵河两岸建有观光铁路，铁路的旁边各有一条高等级公路，公路的边上还专门辟有行人（自行车）车道。因此，旅游者除了参与常规的团队观光产品之外，还可以选择自驾游、房车旅游、自行车运动、徒步旅行和小镇葡萄酒文化体验游等。交通工具以汽车和火车为主，同时包括自行车等休闲交通工具。

（三）城市旅游产品

莱茵河两岸分布着许多重要城市，如美茵茨、科布伦茨、科隆等。因此，莱茵河流域的城市旅游产品非常受游客的欢迎，相关产品主要包括两个方面：一方面，是城市观光旅游者与莱茵河短途游轮相结合的旅游形式；另一方面，是通过莱茵河沿岸的交通、金融、商业、物流为主要依托的大中型城市发展的城市商务、会展旅游，如科隆、杜塞尔多夫等城市的城市旅游。

（四）空中旅游产品

空中旅游产品主要指的是低空旅游，是人们在低空空域依托通用航空运输、通用航空器和低空飞行器，所从事的旅游、娱乐和运动，直升机、热气球、滑翔伞、飞机跳伞、轻小型无人驾驶航空器等都属于这一范畴。莱茵河流域的低空旅游产品主要是重点旅游城镇开发的以城镇为依托，短时空中观赏莱茵河，直升飞机是主要的运载工具。同时，还包括乘坐热气球俯瞰莱茵河谷，滑翔伞以及私人定制旅程，比如搭乘私人飞机。

五、莱茵河旅游发展经验

河流是人类文明的摇篮，大河文明流淌着最丰富的人文情怀，每一条河流都有着自己的故事。

---

① 童潜明. 工业遗产旅游，另一种转型选择［J］. 经济问题探索，2012（7）.

欧洲的莱茵河，流经之地是欧洲文明的腹地和精华，因此莱茵河流域也成为欧洲重要的旅游胜地。尤其是对德国而言，莱茵河流域是德国最重要的旅游资源之一，旅游业在德国莱茵河流域经济中成为仅次于制造业的第二大产业。莱茵河的旅游发展对其他地区开展河流旅游具有重要的借鉴意义，解读他们的成功之处，可以发现主要是采取了以下措施。

（一）构建水环境综合治理模式

几十年来，莱茵河一个主要的问题就是水质。多年以来，来自城市和工业的大量废水未经加工处理就直接流入莱茵河，破坏了河流的生态系统。70年前河流里常见的大部分物种已经绝迹。为了治理莱茵河水污染，1963年，莱茵河流域各国与欧共体代表在保护莱茵河国际委员会范围内签订了合作公约，保护莱茵河国际委员会制定了相应法规，对排入河中的工业废水强行进行无害化处理；严格控制工业、农业、生活固体污染物排入莱茵河，违者重金处罚。2000年10月23日，欧洲议会和欧盟理事会又颁布了《欧盟水框架指令》，所有活动的制度基础为莱茵河流域各个区；起草并执行《莱茵河流域管理规划》和《行动计划》。通过几十年的治理与开发，莱茵河转变成了2000万人的饮用水源、周边国家最重要的旅游资源、著名的国际旅游目的地。

（二）制定紧密一体的规划体系

除莱茵河国际保护委员会统一制定《伯尔尼公约》《防治化学污染公约》《莱茵河行动计划》等相关政策外，各地都根据自身实际编制了旅游业发展规划。一是州域规划。以德国为例，莱茵河流经的黑森州编制了《黑森州旅游政策行动方案框架》《黑森州旅游业产业战略影响规划》《旅游合作企业的任务与结构——地方层面行动资助方案》等旅游专项规划和涉旅规划。二是州际规划。黑森州、莱茵兰—普法尔茨州、北莱茵—威斯特法伦3个州联合规划了沿莱茵河东岸全长320公里的徒步旅行道以及沿莱茵河谷的自行车道。三是国际规划。沿途6国还编制了统一的从瑞士河源地区到莱茵河口荷兰鹿特丹市的自行车道系统，该系统实现了跨国境的连接和统一的标识系统。

（三）建设便捷通畅的交通网络

一是航空交通。从上游到下游分别以苏黎世、阿姆斯特丹等国际著名空港实现了莱茵河地区与全球各地的空中连接与区域内的便捷中转。二是水上交通。构建了从瑞士巴塞尔到荷兰鹿特丹和阿姆斯特丹的水上客货运系统。三是陆上交通。沿岸全程形成了从铁路、高速公路到与城市交通和小城镇及旅游景点的便捷连接。特别是许多陆上交通方式都是沿河修建，使得陆上交通不但成为客流、物流通道，同时也成为景观通道。四是休闲交通。构建了沿江的全流域自行车道系统和徒步旅游道系统。

（四）打造复合多元的旅游产品

基于历史文化和自然资源禀赋，莱茵河基本形成了上游、中游、下游空间布局合理的产品结构：一是上游湖泊休闲度假旅游。主要旅游形式是冬季滑雪旅游、夏季避暑旅游以及各种形式的观光旅游。二是中游历史文化遗产旅游。主要旅游形式是游轮旅游、山地徒步旅行、山地自行车运动。三是下游工业及工业遗产旅游。同时，莱茵河作为一个整体旅游区，主要包括水上旅游产品、陆上旅游产品、城市旅游产品、空中旅游产品四大类，充分体现了旅游产品的特色性、差异性、整体性。

（五）建立高效的旅游管理模式

莱茵河旅游产业的管理以官方和半官方的形式实现。以德国黑森州为例，其旅游产业管理职能归属州政府经济部下的黑森促进局。旅游产业政策由经济部统一制定，黑森促进局是以国有的有限责任公司形式行使政府职能，负责旅游产业政策的落实和执行、旅游目的地的营销以及行业规范。同时，资讯服务是莱茵河旅游产业政府管理的重要职能，职能部门通过展会和网络提供给旅游投资商及运营商关于旅游目的地的有关资讯，并直接为旅游者提供旅游公共服务信息。[1]

第二节　泰晤士河旅游发展经验

泰晤士河是英国第二长河，流经英国10多座城市，是全世界水面交通最繁忙的都市河流和伦敦地标之一，滋养了沿岸灿烂的文明，是一部流动的英国历史。泰晤士河被公认为是伦敦最宝贵的天然财富，它不仅具有丰富的历史内涵，而且环境宜人，是休闲娱乐的好场所。[2]泰晤士河河流旅游发展相对成熟，对其他大河流域旅游发展有诸多经验可供借鉴。

一、泰晤士河沿岸风光

泰晤士河发源于英格兰西南部的科茨沃尔德丘陵地带，全长346千米，横贯英国首都伦敦与沿河的10多座城市，是英国工业化过程中地区贸易、经济发展的黄金水道。[3]泰晤士河流经之处，都是英国文化的精华所在，孕育和哺育了灿烂的英格兰文明。英国伦敦的主要建筑物大多分布在泰晤士河的两旁，尤其是那些有着上百年，甚至三四百年历史的老建筑，历经风雨，依然伫立在泰晤士河畔，宏大的威斯敏斯特大教堂、有象征胜利意义的纳尔逊海军统帅雕像、具有文艺复兴风格的圣保罗大教堂、曾经见证过英国历史上黑暗时期的伦敦塔、桥面可以起降的伦敦塔桥、议会大厦和伊丽莎白塔，每一幢建筑都堪称艺术的杰作，这些建筑虽历经沧桑，乃至第二次世界大战那样的战争洗礼，但仍然保持了固有的模样，直至今天还在为人们所使用。泰晤士河岸边，除了这些大名鼎鼎的历史建筑以外，比邻的还有数不胜数的现代化建筑，比如：高度309.6米的摩天大楼"碎片大厦"，号称北半球最高的摩天轮"伦敦眼"，为古老的泰晤士河沿岸增添了现代时尚的元素。在泰晤士河沿岸，还有许多名胜之地，诸如牛津等。

---

[1] 杨光荣. 欧洲莱茵河发展旅游业对湖南的启示[N]. 中国旅游报，2011（11）.
[2] 陆静依. 泰晤士河河岸改造工程的创意之作——新千年广场建设工程[J]. 国外科技，2000（1）.
[3] 高静. 大都市滨水区游憩化更新研究——基于伦敦与上海的比较案例[D]. 上海：华东师范大学，2015.

二、泰晤士河旅游活动的发展历程

河流流域是人类文明的发源地、是人类聚居的理想场所，世界上的著名城市也大多依水而建、依水而兴。历经岁月变迁，河流沿岸逐渐成为城市空间拓展的主轴线，承载着城市文化，呈现着城市形象，也为游客和居民提供了绝佳的休闲空间。

泰晤士河沿岸游憩活动发展历史非常悠久。其原因在于：第一，伦敦城诞生于泰晤士河畔，即在诞生伊始，泰晤士河即是伦敦人生产、生活、游憩的地方；第二，伦敦城市形态沿泰晤士河而展开，城市临水而生的特征非常突出；第三，在中世纪时代，伦敦的市政基础设施主要是利用自然的禀赋，大量的建筑最初沿河道而建，街道依地理空间而延伸，该公共服务与管理空间分布上的特征决定了泰晤士河滨水区在城市发展中具有举足轻重的地位；第四，皇宫、皇家公园及其他国家政治中心等沿泰晤士河而建，进一步提高了该地在国家生活中的地位；第五，进入16世纪英国出现了游乐园，17、18世纪时伦敦最大最知名的游乐园都分布在泰晤士河沿岸，如位于河南岸的沃克斯霍尔乐园、位于北岸的雷恩拉格公园等。

但随着工业革命的推进，在相当长时间内泰晤士河成为了一条死河。1858年6月，泰晤士河奇臭无比，以至于河边的议会大厦不得不在窗上挂起一条条消毒药水的被单。1878年，"爱丽丝公子"号游船在泰晤士河沉没，640多人因此死亡，但其中的多数人并非是因为溺水而死，而是因为污水中毒而丧命。事实上，直到第二次世界大战之后，泰晤士河的污染状况都是极其严重的，如在1951年的英国国庆节时，外国船只停泊在泰晤士河上，船体铅键层由于污水腐蚀而变黑，国际舆论一时哗然。环境的恶劣，必然会抑制泰晤士河流域游憩活动的发展。1955年以后，泰晤士河开展了大规模的治污活动，但直到1985年，政府才终于意识到旅游业在提供就业、创造经济产出、为当地小企业发展提供机会的潜力。

受住宿设施和吸引物集聚的影响，到20世纪90年代初时，伦敦的旅游观光活动还是主要集中在威斯敏斯特区、凯辛顿和切尔西区，以及伦敦城的卡姆登行政区，知名的旅游吸引物包括英国国会大厦、威斯敏斯特修道院、威斯敏斯特大教堂、泰特美术馆、图索夫人蜡像馆、唐宁街、牛津街、莱切斯特广场、科文特花园、大英博物馆、伦敦博物馆、白金汉宫、国家美术馆、圣保罗大教堂等。与泰晤士河北岸相比，南岸相关发展则较为落后，但从1993年开始，政府积极采取行动，在泰晤士河南岸投资了上亿英镑建设基础设施、旅游吸引物及旅游服务设施并形成了一个重点文化区，该文化区与班克塞得、伦敦池一起推动了南岸旅游观光业的发展。

为了推动泰晤士河休闲与旅游的发展，1990年，道克兰开发公司为码头区引入了艺术性活动，其目的是通过提供文化性基础设施吸引并留住核心技术工人，相关性活动还包括常规性的艺术活动，也包括为了提升环境质量的公共艺术、视觉艺术、音乐和表演艺术、艺术中心、艺术教育等。而水岸步道的发展、专业的购物商场、以水为基础的游憩活动，使码头区的发展更加融洽，同时，水上巴士和游船发展潜力逐渐凸显。[①]

三、泰晤士河沿岸旅游空间布局

泰晤士河沿岸景观空间的物质形态具有典型的游憩化特征，其沿岸的建筑空间富有吸引力，水系空间富有变化，视觉景观廊道得到有效控制。

泰晤士河从伦敦市中心穿过，大英帝国的精髓几乎都汇聚在泰晤士河畔，特别是北岸几乎就是文化的集聚地，相关的地标性建筑包括国会大厦、特拉法加广场、白金汉宫、威斯敏斯特大教堂、伦敦塔、塔桥、码头区、考文特花园、摄政公园等，这些富有中世纪特征的建筑不仅是伦敦的主要地标，也与周边建筑一起构成了泰晤士河沿岸富有变化与吸引力的景观空间。同时，泰晤士河拥有众多支流，这些支流与泰晤士河串联着众多公园、湿地和湖泊，共同形成了伦敦市重要的生态廊道，同时也极大增强了泰晤士河滨水区及相关区域提供游憩机会的可能性。

为保护伦敦的视觉廊道，伦敦当局曾制定多个规划案，如1991年发表的《区域规划纲要》确定了"战略眺望点保护"规则以管理伦敦的重要景观，发展到2005年时，大伦敦当局推出了《伦敦视觉管理框架草案》，泰晤士河沿岸的国会大厦、威斯敏斯特宫、白金汉宫、格林威治海军博物馆、圣保罗大教堂均纳入了"战略眺望点"的范畴，同时明确了对地标视觉廊道内发展高度的控制。在一系列措施的保障下，泰晤士河滨水区形成了优质的视觉通廊。

四、泰晤士河主要旅游产品类型

（一）低空旅游

低空旅游作为新兴旅游形式是促进交通运输与旅游融合发展的新经济代表性领域。低空旅游产业的兴起，有助于扭转旅游市场产品同质化的趋势，促进旅游市场转型升级。伦敦泰晤士河以航空为依托，将低空旅游产业作为提升旅游体验和丰富旅游资源的重要载体，直升机空中游览是泰晤士河热门旅游项目。

通过低空旅游项目将城市风光与旅游名胜地串联起来，并融入空中摆渡、野外探险等内容。其方便快捷、移位换景，受地形条件限制少等优势，可以摆脱常规步行、车辆等平面旅游方式，打破在陆地上观景的局限，把旅游者的视界从通常的平视和仰视中解脱出来，使旅游者以崭新的视角从空中俯瞰泰晤士河，体验到更高更美的视觉享受，满足高端或年轻旅游群体的高层次需求。伦敦泰晤士河的飞行线路侧重文化游，沿途景点包括圣保罗大教堂、伦敦桥、白金汉宫等著名景点。

（二）泰晤士河游船旅游

泰晤士河贯穿英国伦敦和沿河10多座城市，乘坐游船可以近距离、全面地欣赏沿岸景点，而且各种规格、不同档次的游船24小时不间断为游客提供服务，推出的娱乐产品包括：游河早餐、

[①] 高静. 大都市滨水区游憩化更新研究——基于伦敦与上海的比较案例[D]. 上海：华东师范大学，2015.

工作午餐、浪漫晚餐、选择性观光、通宵舞会等。[①] 因此，泰晤士河游船旅游产品深受市场欢迎。在泰晤士河上有几个较为著名的码头，比如威斯敏斯特码头、圣凯瑟琳码头等。沿河景点主要有威斯敏斯特教堂、议会大厦等。

（三）泰晤士河系列文化节庆活动

泰晤士河也以举办主题活动、采取以活动为主导的开发模式而闻名于世，两岸众多具有历史、文化、景观意义的建筑、公园、桥梁等，被广泛用于各种体育、娱乐、政治活动中。相关的主要活动项目有：

（1）剑桥牛津大学每年春天在泰晤士河上举行八人划小组赛艇比赛；在泰晤士河上也举行划船比赛，它是世界上最大的划船比赛，共有420多个八人组参与；每年7月在泰晤士河上举行的亨利赛艇会则是国际划船赛事。

（2）泰晤士河文化节也被称作泰晤士河狂欢节，是世界最大的免费户外艺术节之一。该节日是一场户外庆祝活动，主旨是庆祝伦敦及泰晤士河的悠久历史，节目活动精彩纷呈，包括音乐、舞蹈、合唱团表演、狂欢会、盛宴聚餐、河上比赛、街头艺术等。自1997年创设以来，文化节每年吸引世界近百个国家和地区参与，以多种形式展现不同国家地区和民族的文化、形象与魅力。

（3）英国皇家的仪式活动，突出了当地特有的文化历史，而且仪式体现的庄重与神圣丰富了泰晤士河的内涵。

上述文化节庆活动巧妙联系了泰晤士河及其两岸的资源，使整个观光和参与性活动融为一体，为文化性河流旅游提供了强大推动力，也提升了泰晤士河的知名度、丰富了伦敦的城市形象内涵。[②]

五、泰晤士河旅游发展经验

泰晤士河流经英国首都伦敦，沿岸保留了大量的令人向往的名胜古迹，是游人散步、休憩的绝佳胜地。依托泰晤士河开发的水上旅游项目已经成为伦敦一道独特的风景线，不仅产生了良好的经济效益，而且成为整个城市形象的有机组成部分。[③] 然而，100年前的泰晤士河几乎全被工业革命所破坏，大量的污染物充塞河道，各种水生生物濒临灭绝。泰晤士河大规模的综合整治始于第二次世界大战后英国的重建计划，经过30多年坚持不懈的努力，泰晤士河不但水变清了，恢复了往昔的生机，而且随着沿岸文化景观的保护与开发，美丽的泰晤士河已成为驰名世界的旅游观光带。回顾泰晤士河的发展历程，可以发现泰晤士河旅游发展主要采取了如下措施：

（一）保证沿岸景观的整体和谐

泰晤士河两岸分布着众多具有历史纪念意义、文化和景观意义的建筑、公园和桥梁等，这些具有历史文化意义的景观形成一个整体，成为伦敦乃至英国的象征。伦敦市认为两岸现有景观必须予

---

① 舒肖明．国外著名滨水城市水上旅游开发的实践与经验［J］．宁波大学学报（人文科学版），2008，21(3)．
② 高静．大都市滨水区游憩化更新研究——基于伦敦与上海的比较案例［D］．上海：华东师范大学，2015．
③ 舒肖明．国外著名滨水城市水上旅游开发的实践与经验［J］．宁波大学学报（人文科学版），2008，21(3)．

以保护，新建的景观必须与原有景观保持协调，突出整个景观的美感。①

（二）不断完善文化景观保护法规和法令

1882年，英国议会通过了第一个《古迹保护法》，但保护范围仅限于古堡及其构筑物。第二次世界大战后，又颁布了《城市规划法》（1947年）和《历史性建筑和纪念性构造物保护法》（1953年），并对古建筑进行登记注册，使第二次世界大战中受到损坏的古建筑得到及时修缮，免遭拆毁。1967年，英国政府颁布了《街区保护法》，首次提出了保护历史街区等文化景观。自1967年10月3日，斯坦福（Stamford）成为首块保护街区后，泰晤士河沿岸的查菲加广场、议会广场、圣保罗教堂先后被列为保护街区，使伦敦市的历史保护街区数成直线上升。

（三）鼓励利益相关者广泛参与

在泰晤士河旅游发展过程中，利益相关者的广泛参与和多方力量之间的制衡，对泰晤士河滨水区游憩化的发展也起到了一定积极作用。仅以伦敦南岸旅游功能区管理为例，运输和行政区域部分、旅游发展指导小组、岸边营销合营公司、南岸雇主委员会、伦敦池合营公司、萨瑟克遗产委员会、岸边商贸组织、岸边居民论坛和旅游官员等一起构成了旅游功能区管理的网络结构。在其中，伦敦池合营公司强调公共区域的改善，吸引内部投资，并为当地居民提供培训计划；岸边营销合营公司更加直接针对旅游业，关注旅游基础设施的改进并通过大型活动及旅游宣传册进行宣传营销；南岸雇主委员会主要是吸引国家政府投资并承担市场化的城市活动；运输和区域部门力图提高上述新合作关系的管理机制并给予参考性建议。同时，虽然当地的交易团体和小公司游离在政策发展和完善的外围，如岸边商贸组织和岸边居民论坛较难适应旅游发展的速度和规模的增长，但相关机制的存在确实为利益相关者提供了一定的对话通道，也为当地产业活动的合理拓展提供了柔性治理上的可能。②

（四）分区（段）保护与开发河流沿岸文化景观，构筑城市整体文化风貌

英国虽是近代城市规划的发源地，但它从没有诸如文化景观保护之类的单项规划，它是通过制定城市景观规划设计准则，达到对城市文化景观保护与开发的目的，这些准则贯彻落实到伦敦泰晤士河沿岸的建设、改造、更新和再开发过程中，使伦敦以泰晤士河为中轴形成风格有别、主题各异的五个文化景观保护开发段（区）。一是历史古城保护区。从白金汉宫到查菲加广场，集中了著名的王宫、议会和政府机构、商业和文化设施，不同时代古典建筑整齐划一，议会大厦和伊丽莎白塔为标志物，集中反映了伦敦历史和古城的景观特征。二是宗教与历史建筑保护区。从伦敦塔沿泰晤士河往西直到滑铁卢桥，以圣保罗大教堂为标志物。三是南岸近代建筑文化区。该区段建筑景观是伦敦近代历史的见证，以皇家节日大厅为标志物。四是科技文化功能区。即伦敦桥以东的格林尼治特别区，以皇家天文台旧址为标志物，包括国家海洋博物馆、军事科学院等文

---

① 阎水玉，王祥荣. 泰晤士河在伦敦城市规划中的功能定位、保证措施及其特征的分析［J］. 国外城市规划，1999（1）.

② 高静. 大都市滨水区游憩化更新研究——基于伦敦与上海的比较案例［D］. 上海：华东师范大学，2015.

化景观。五是道克兰现代滨水景观开发区。把原伦敦港废弃的码头区改造成现代商住区，实现沿岸用地功能转换，同时在泰晤士河岸边仍保留若干港口设施，包括码头、吊塔等，让人想起伦敦港昔日繁忙而辉煌的历史。

（五）政府设立保护补助费，吸引民间投资

文化景观保护在很大程度上属社会公益事业，投资规模大，回收期长，初期政府投资至关重要。英国政府采取政府补助的办法，吸引民间或社会团体资金。规定沿岸古迹保护或历史保护街区内所有与街路景观的维持和改善有关的项目，如街道的铺装、步行化、植树等与环境有关的项目，以及保护区内土地的购入等都可申请补助。不仅政府的有关部门可以申请，各种社会团体、个人都可以申请。由于英国政府 1981 年取消保护街区等级划分，所有保护街区都可以平等地申请补助。

从补助费发放情况看，伦敦接受修复和保护文物景观补助的保护街区从 1973 年度的 27 个街区，补助金额 10 万英镑发展到 1997 年 81 个街区 149 万英镑，累计发放补助 2.4 亿英镑，以此为基础，共吸收民间相关资金约 100 亿英镑，其中大部分投资集中在泰晤士河沿岸一带街区，道克兰滨水景观区开发就吸收民间资金 10 亿英镑。[1]

第三节　密西西比河旅游发展经验

密西西比河位于北美洲中南部，是世界第四长河，覆盖了美国东部和中部广大地区。它是美国的地缘核心，是美国早期经济崛起的关键基础，是美国长期繁荣宜居的地理基础，也是美国国家文化和娱乐休闲的宝库。通过梳理密西西比河旅游发展经验，对河流旅游开发具有重要价值。

一、密西西比河流域旅游开发

密西西比河是美国第一大河，是美国南北航运的大动脉，具有良好的水运旅游优势。美国对密西西比河的整治始于 19 世纪 70 年代，先后成立了"陆军工程兵团""密西西比河委员会""河流域管理局"等开发治理机构，并制定了专门的法律法规。20 世纪 30 年代以后实施大规模综合治理工程，其干流和支流都按现代化的先进技术标准进行治理，河道治理积极顺应河流自然过程，保护、借鉴和利用河流自然形成的各种地貌结构，使生态环境得到良好恢复，河流基本消除洪灾。提倡绿色航运，构建景观蓝脉，建立起标准统一的现代化航运网和经济带。这些措施为水运旅游奠定了很好的基础。同时该地区还充分利用《汤姆叔叔的小屋》《飘》等著作以及风靡全球的爵士乐和其他音乐的影响等进行旅游开发，使其成为国家文化和娱乐休闲的宝库。[2]

---

[1] 郑伯红，汤建中. 伦敦巴黎河岸景观带建设的实践与经验 [J]. 城市问题，2002（1）.
[2] 王守书. 河流旅游功能构建与产品开发研究——以海南万泉河为例 [D]. 上海：上海师范大学，2009.

二、密西西比河整体发展模式

密西西比河主要通过点轴开发，统一管理，使城市经济与流域经济互促发展。美国城市中超过10万人口规模的城市大约有150个，其中有131个位于流域周边，并且大部分城市分布在密西西比河的水系周边，加大城市之间的贸易往来，重点开发利用水资源，加强城市和城镇之间的水上运输联系，使一大批港口城市得以兴起。由于港口城市经济的迅速发展，基础设施的投入与建设大多集中于此并成为该区域的综合性的交通枢纽。随着周边各中小城市的发展与崛起，以港口城市为增长点，建立起了干支畅通、标准统一的现代化航运网。抓住科技创新带来的机遇，及时升级港口城市等经济较发达的老工业地区的产业结构，在这些地区大力发展新型制造业及服务业，河道流域经济得到了迅猛发展。

在管理上成立密西西比河流域委员会，这个机构在经济上完全自主，下设水利、电力、航运和工业发展、财务、环境保护、工程建设、农业和化学发展、森林和野生植物、渔业、旅游等10多个处，是一个具有官方权力与法律效力但按照民间企业管理的机构。该机构遵循流域经济一体化发展的理念，对密西西比河流域统一规划、灵活管理，提高流域经济发展质量。[1]

三、密西西比河主要旅游产品形式

（一）水上旅游产品

密西西比河是美国文化和娱乐休闲的宝库，河流沿岸处处是绿色的生态廊道，工业城镇星罗棋布。密西西比河的水上旅游产品丰富多样，有垂钓、漂流、滑水、游轮、房船等。密西西比河内河游轮的主要航程是新奥尔良和孟菲斯之间，也有圣路易斯和圣保罗密西西比河上游的行程。

（二）陆上旅游产品

密西西比河是孕育美国文化的灵魂之水，始终伴随大河的只有唯一一条纵贯南北的61号公路。61号高速公路由南向北连接新奥尔良和明尼苏达州，全长1400英里（2252千米），这条路除了被称为"大河之路"，也被誉为"布鲁斯（蓝调）公路"，被美国国家地理杂志评为"人生里必开的500条公路"之一。因此，沿密西西比河自驾旅行是该流域最著名的陆上旅游产品。沿着密西西比河自驾旅行，可以看到各类历史古迹、湖区、野生动物保护区、现代城市等。

（三）城市旅游产品

密西西比河流域范围很广，众多的支流联系着大半个美国的经济区域。因此，密西西比河沿岸城市旅游产品丰富，城市休闲观光旅游、商务旅游、会展旅游等应有尽有。比如密西西比河流域的出海门户新奥尔良，它是美国南方最主要的工业城市，旅游业兴盛，在城市经济中的地位仅次于运输业。

---

[1] 马静，邓宏兵. 国外典型流域开发模式与经验对长江经济带的启示[J]. 区域经济评论，2016（2）.

四、密西西比河旅游发展经验

同世界许多其他河流一样，密西西比河流域也经历了因过度开发而形成的生态环境恶化阶段。曾经是美国十大濒危河流之一的密西西比河，经过 100 多年的综合治理，如今河水透明清澈，已基本成为一条由人工控制的输水输沙廊道和航运大动脉，成为美国国家文化和娱乐休闲的宝库。一系列有效做法值得我国大江大河流域治理借鉴。

（一）不断健全法律体系

健全的法律体系是成功治理的保障。早在 1820 年，美国国会就开始讨论发展内河航运的法令。之后通过了多项法律法规，使水资源、水利、水电、水运工程建设与管理均有法可依，保障了内河开发有序进行。比如，20 世纪 60 年代，美国制定了《水资源规划法》。1972 年《清洁水法》颁布，通过实施国家污染物排放消除制度许可证项目，建立了以最佳可行技术的排放标准为基础的排污许可证制度。通过建设污水处理厂并实施排污许可制度，有效地降低了废水的生化需氧量，促进了流域水质的改善。除此之外，还设置了一系列的防洪、航运等法规。

（二）设置集中统一的管理机构

1879 年，美国国会设立密西西比河委员会，通过规划改造，最终形成了江、河、湖、海贯通，水深标准统一的内河航道网络。整个水系发展成为集航运、防洪、发电、供水、灌溉、娱乐、环保于一体的综合利用水系。1928 年制定的《防洪法》规定，由陆军部工程师团负责全国的防洪和航道整治管理。1997 年建立的富营养化工作组，参与部门包括美国环保局、农业部、内政部、商务部、陆军工程兵团和 12 个州的环保农业部门。此外，相关协调机构还包括密西西比河上游流域协会、密西西比河下游保护委员会等。

（三）制定联邦流域管理策略

20 世纪 80 年代，美国环保局逐渐认识到以流域为基本单元的水环境管理模式十分有效，开始在流域内协调各利益相关方力量以解决最突出的环境问题。1996 年，美国环保局颁布了《流域保护方法框架》，通过跨学科、跨部门联合，加强社区之间、流域之间的合作来治理水污染。框架实施过程中，结合排污许可证发放管理、水源地保护和财政资金优先资助项目筛选，有效地提高了管理效能。

（四）动态周密的资源调查与检测

动态周密的自然资源调查与监测是成功治理的基础。主要有四个任务：一是深入了解密西西比河的生态系统及其资源问题；二是监测河流生态系统的资源变化；三是寻求替代方案以更好地管理密西西比河系统；四是提供适当的监控信息管理。目标是为密西西比河多用途大型河流生态系统的管理和治理提供信息和决策支撑，主要包括地质灾害调查与检测、水位与水质监测、生物资源调查与检测等。[1]

---

[1] 张万益，崔敏利，贾德龙. 美国密西西比河流域治理的若干启示［J］. 中国矿业报，2018-07-03.

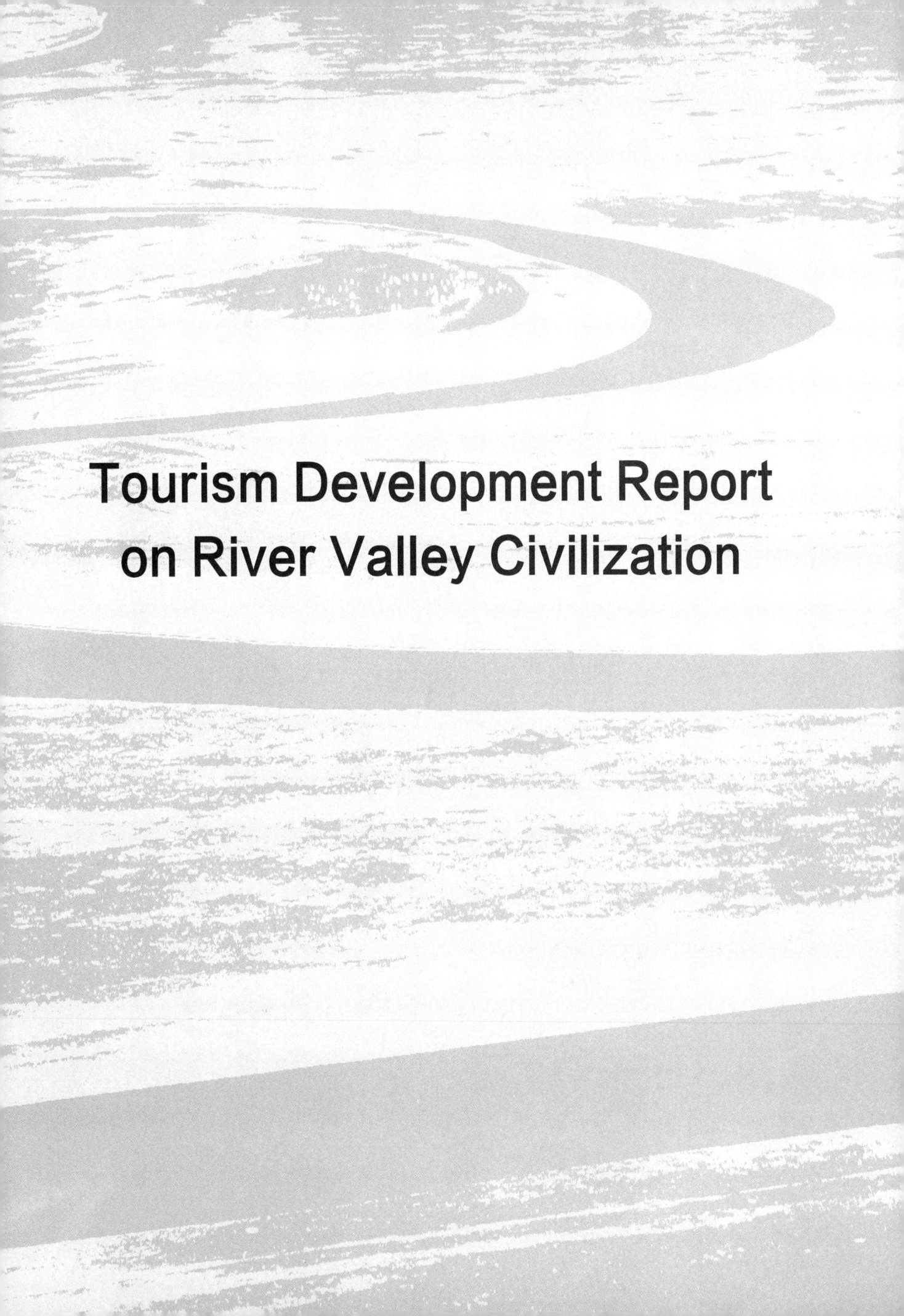

Tourism Development Report on River Valley Civilization

Part I
River Valley Civilization and Tourism

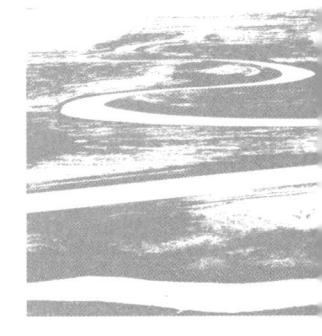

Chapter One　The Great River and Its Civilization

The river has nurtured human civilization, and given birth to the city, a form of human civilization. Besides, the river has become the lifeblood of survival for humans, due to the survival mode of early mankind living waterside and the unique blessed living conditions of the river. Four major ancient civilizations of the world are originated from the great river basins, namely, the Yellow River basin in China, the Nile River basin in Egypt, the Euphrates River and Tigris River basins, and the Ganges River basin in India. This chapter first defines the concepts of river, great river and great river basins; secondly, it introduces the definition of river valley civilization, points out the characteristics and values of river valley civilization, and analyzes the four ancient civilizations in the great river basins; finally, the relationship between river valley civilization and tourism development is analyzed, and the term of river valley civilization tourism is conceptualized.

Section 1　Great Rivers and Their Basins

This section mainly defines the concepts of the great river and the great river basin, and analyzes the characteristics of the great river basin. The survival as well as the progression of human civilization is inseparable from the nurturing of the great rivers. Therefore, we should firstly understand what a great river is and what a great river basin is, in order to deeply understand the great river valley civilization and the great river valley civilization tourism.

1. Rivers and Great Rivers

The so-called rivers refer to the flow of water that flows from the surface of the ground by precipitation or underground water, which is collected at the low point of the ground and flows along the narrow and concave ground under the action of gravity. Rivers are important paths for water circulation on the earth, and are channels for sediments, salts and chemical elements to enter into lakes and oceans. They are, as well, important parts of life on the earth and the basis for human survival and development.

There are many names for different kinds of rivers in the Chinese language. The larger ones are called JIANG, HE, CHUAN; the smaller ones are called XI, JIAN, GOU, QU, etc. Each large river is composed of a mainstream and several tributaries, while each tributary consists of several smaller streams of water. The so-called great river, in a broad sense, refers to rivers with a large basin area. Sometimes, the size of the river basin area is closely related to river flow and total water volume, and generally speaking, the larger the basin area is, the greater the river flow and total water volumes are. Therefore, the definition of great rivers should not be limited to the drainage area, but also other factors including river flow, total water volume and length of rivers. Based upon these, we believe that the great rivers, in the narrow sense, refer to rivers with large river basins, river flows, total water volumes, and river lengths.

2. Great River Basin

(1) The Definition of Great River Basin

The basin, also called the "catchment area", is a hydrological concept and it is the general term for the catchment area surrounded by surface water and groundwater separation lines. It is divided into two types: the ground catchment area and the underground catchment area. Each great river has its own basin. A large basin can be divided into several small basins according to the stream order, and the small basin can be divided into smaller basins. Obviously, the most important factor in the great river basin is water. Without water, there is no such thing as a basin. However, the basin is a catchment area in essence. Therefore, the concept of the basin should also include the land through which the water flows, the vegetation on the land, the land and the minerals in the forest, and the organisms living in water and land through which water flows, etc. The water body, landform, soil and vegetation in the great river basin are all closely related to form one single unit.

In fact, the great river basin is not only a complete, independent and self-contained hydrological unit from the headwater to the estuary, the natural area where it is located is also an important social place for all human activities of economy and culture. From this perspective, the basin has exceeded geographically hydrological significance and become a nature-human compound system that transformed from a naturally closed area into an open complex area closely connected to human activities. In order to survive, human beings must develop and utilize various natural resources in the basin, including water, land, minerals, vegetation, and animals. Similarly, the social life of human beings in the basin, including customs, cultural backgrounds, and social demographics, also has an impact on basin resources and the environment. In other words, the great river basin is a very important natural-economic-social complex ecosystem formed by the natural flow of water within its boundary. In this ecosystem, there are material energy exchange, information exchange, and flows of funds and personnel constantly being carried out among various natural elements, between natural and economic element and social element, the upstream and downstream of the basin, main stream and the tributaries. One factor changes, and other factors in the entire basin are affected.

(2) The Characteristics of Great River Basin

According to the concept of the great river basin, its characteristics can be generalized into the following ones:

a. Integrity

The great river basin is a natural catchment area and the most important factor in the basin is water. It is the water flow that causes the geographical correlation and the linkage of environmental resources and it is the water flow that determines the basin becomes a unified and complete ecosystem. The upper, middle and lower reaches of the basin, the left and right banks, the tributaries and main streams, the rivers and river channels, the water quality and quantity, the surface water and the groundwater are all inseparable components of the basin and have the natural integrity. Meanwhile, with the water body as the medium, the soil, forests, minerals and organisms in the basin also form a closely related whole unit. Any change in it will have a major impact on the whole river basin. In addition, the basin is an important place for people's economic and social life. The social and economic activities of people in the basin will have a great impact on the basin ecosystem. The characteristic of the wholeness of the basin requires that the basin management should take account of the socio-economic conditions, natural resources and environmental conditions of the upper, middle and lower reaches, as well as the physical and ecological aspects and changes of the basin to form the development, utilization and protection plan, which is undoubtedly the most scientific and most suitable choice for sustainable development in the basin.

b. Publicity

The resources of the great river basin are a kind of public resources, which has the general attributes of public resources, such as finiteness, externality and dispersion of use, interdependence and indivisibility. As a common wealth and public goods, the use of basin resources must be a collective action, and the individual's free choice and use of public resources and the decentralized management of public resources will inevitably lead to destructive competition. According to the theory of decision-making, in public management, the more dispersed the management subjects, the slacker the management responsibility, the weaker the protection of resources, and the worse the state of resources. On the contrary, the more unified the power, the greater the responsibility, the more concentrated the power and the single center, the clearer the responsibility, the less destructive competition and friction among the power subjects. Therefore, the publicity of the great river basin requires that the basin management should set up a unified basin organization to implement overall management and regulation.

c. Complexity

The great river basin usually has a large span of longitude and latitude, and the upper, middle and lower reaches show obvious segmentation and difference, which leads to differences between the upper and lower reaches, the left and right banks, the main stream and tributaries in terms of natural conditions, geographical location, economic and technical basis and historical background. Hence, the basin ecosystem covers different natural geographic units with diverse natural landscapes, forest vegetation and climatic characteristics. At the same time, human beings use a variety of ways to develop basin resources, from agricultural production activities to urban ecosystems, from mineral resources development to industrial and mining processing, and the results of ecological and environmental impacts are also complex and diverse.

d. Irreversibility of ecosystem

The ecological impacts of any human production activities in the basin ecosystem are irreversible. Once the ecosystem is destroyed, it will not return to its original ecological appearance by itself.

Section 2   River Valley Civilization

Based upon the conceptualization of the river civilization this section brings about, this section further explains the value and characteristics of river valley civilization, and introduces the four major civilizations of the world in terms of great river basins. Almost all civilizations on the earth originated from rivers, for example, ancient Indian civilization originated from the Indus River and Ganges River; ancient Egyptian civilization originated from the Nile River; ancient Chinese civilization originated from the Yangtze River and the Yellow River... no matter whether it is the source of Western civilization or Eastern civilization, they all rely on the rise of rivers.

1. The Definition of River Valley Civilization

Rivers are one of the most basic forms of existence in the diverse ecosystems of the earth. Historically, the development of humans and their social ecosystems is inseparable from rivers. Human civilization originated from river culture, human society developed river culture, and river culture, as a type of human civilization, has a long history.

In a narrow sense, river valley civilization is also called farming civilization and its foundation is the great river basin. There are vast fertile lands, convenient irrigation, and a unique farming environment, which creates good conditions for human survival. Ancient human residents produced labor in the river basin very early and lived from generation to generation, forming a river valley civilization with the farming economy as its basic form. The ancient great river basin is characterized by farming civilization. Agriculture is the most important production department in these areas, and it is also the economic foundation for the formation and development of these countries. The ancient civilizations of ancient Egypt, ancient Babylon, ancient India and ancient China are established and developed on the basis of the agricultural economy, and showed their own characteristics of civilization.

The river not only produces life, relating to the reproduction, living and ecological stability of land, aquatic life, but also directly affects the spiritual beliefs, spiritual image and symbolism of human beings in the long-term historical tradition. Therefore, in a broad sense, the great river valley civilization is not limited to farming civilization, but should also include the wisdom of the residents of the great rivers in collecting and producing food, as well as the higher levels of civilization of promoting social development, such as trade and manufacturing, writing, advanced technology, science, social customs, culture and religion.

2. Characteristics and Values of River Valley Civilization

(1) Characteristics of River Valley Civilization

a. Stability

The stability of the great river valley civilization system is determined by its corresponding geographical environment. Referring to ancient Chinese great river valley civilization, although the major rivers such as the Yellow River and the Yangtze River have undergone diversions in history, their basic river systems and patterns remain unchanged. The Yellow River and the Yangtze River still remain at the same place as before, and have not been transferred from China to Europe or other parts of the world. In a fairly long time and wide space, the history of a river is far more permanent than the history of mankind, which explains the stability of the geographical environment. A stable geographical environment provides stable production methods and lifestyles, creates a corresponding civilized system, and makes the civilized system possess the same characteristics of the geographical environment - stability.

In addition, as the direct creator of the great river valley agricultural civilization, the farmers follow their most basic rules of life, that is, working from sunrise to sunset day by day. In the morning, they walk out of the settlement, plant crops on fixed (stable) arable land, and sleep in the settlement at night. They work on relatively stable and arable land throughout the year, live in relatively stable homes, raise their children, breed offspring, and cultivate the heirs of agricultural civilization. They are constantly stuck in the cultivated land and in the home place year by year and generation by generation. Although the farmers also leave their homes due to war and other reasons, the production methods and lifestyles of the ancient farmers have not changed greatly. This is the basis for the stability of the river agricultural civilization system.

b. Abundance

The abundance of the river valley civilization is also governed by the natural environment or geographical conditions. The great river basin contains elements such as mainstream, tributaries, lakes, swamps, canals, basins, topography, temperature, soil, properties, topography, climate, etc. And these elements have different characteristics in different places. For example, the comprehensive geographical conditions of the Yellow River in China, in its origin, Qinghai Province, are very different from the comprehensive geographical conditions of the downstream areas such as Henan and Shandong. It can be said that different natural environments or geographical conditions create different and colorful specific culture, which is the origin of the abundance of the great river valley civilization system.

Clearly, the abundance of river valley civilization is based on its stability, and it shows the vitality of the stability. Although the stability of river valley civilization is obvious, its internal abundance shows specific vitality or openness. The abundance of river valley civilization is manifested in many aspects, including all subsystems, such as richness of products and rich geographical conditions.

In the ancient Chinese civilization system, the nomadic economy in northern China has many times been attracted to or dissolved by the agricultural civilization of the central plains. The nomadic civilization in northern China is an extremely important subsystem of the ancient Chinese civilization system. On one hand, it shows the abundance of ancient Chinese civilization system; on the other hand, it complements the agricultural civilization with its economic advantages, thus promoting a longer and lasting ancient civilization system.

(2) Values of River Valley Civilization

a. Cradle of Ancient Farming Civilization

Water is the source of life on the earth. Since the day of its birth, human beings have regarded the river basin as the mother of godsends. As a key carrier of freshwater resources, the river basin has always been the cradle of human civilization and the birthplace of early human civilization. The first form of civilization in human history is farming civilization, which originated in the great river basin. In essence, farming civilization needs to be accustomed to life, and should matchthe pastoral needs and requires hard work, mainly for males to do farming and women to do weaving and in a small scale, with simple division of labor, without being used for commodity exchange. The development of primitive agriculture and primitive animal husbandry, the settlement of ancient humans, etc., has enabled human beings to change from food collectors to food producers, achieving the first leap in productivity and entering farming civilization. The farming civilization has continued until the industrial revolution. At this time, people mainly relied on agriculture. The political system generally adopts monarchy and the social structure is pyramidal.

The production and development of farming civilization benefits from the superior natural environment, and requires good climate, resources and other conditions for support. The river basin relies on its advantageous conditions, such as, mild climate suitable for human habitation; fertile land on both sides of the river that is beneficial to farming; sufficient water supply which is not only convenient for irrigation but also convenient for livestock to drink; rich in products in rivers, so that there are a large number of aquatic products and birds; and convenient to travel and transport to the coastal areas by boat, which provides convenient production conditions for agricultural civilization. It can be seen that the great river valley basin can fully adapt to agricultural production and human habitation, and thus become an important source of agricultural or farming civilization.

b. Core Foundation of Modern Industrial Civilization

Farming civilization is the cradle of industrial civilization. Although farming civilization is not entirely a relatively idyllic pastoral experience as it has had struggles and wars, it is qualitatively different from nomadic civilization and industrial civilization. The advantage of farming civilization over nomadic civilization is reflected in the ability to greatly increase productivity, which in turn stimulates some people who have solved the problem of food and clothing to do things other than working for food and clothing, such as doing scientific research and developing culture, etc., thus promoting the emergence of industrial civilization.

The great river basin not only nurtures farming civilization, but also is the core basement for the development of modern industrial civilization. For example, as one of the world's four ancient civilizations and the most populous country, China, the development of the Yangtze River and the Yellow River basin has played an extremely important role in the national social economy at the beginning of its modern industrial civilization. In the 1960s and 1970s, with the comprehensive advancement of the country's industrialization, the development of the Yangtze River and the Yellow River basin began to show a relatively declining trend in the national social economy, especially in economic development. By 1970, the share of the two major river basins in the country had fallen to 52.6%, a decrease of 5 percentage from 1952. After the reform and opening up, the implementation of the coastal opening along the Yangtze River and the development of the western region accelerated the development of the two major river basins of the Yangtze River and the Yellow River. By 2010, the proportion of GDP in the two major river basins has risen to 59.0%, showing that the two great rivers play an important role in the development of the country's modern industrial civilization.[1]

---

[1] Zhang Lei, Lu Chunxia, Li Jiangsu. Development of China's Great River Basin and National Civilization Nurturing[J]. Resources and Environment of Yangtze River Basin, 2015, 24(10):1639-1645.

3. Great River Basin and its Civilization

(1) Ancient Egyptian Civilization in Nile Valley

a. The Origin of Ancient Egyptian Civilization

The Nile River basin is one of the birthplaces of world civilization. The people of the basin have created a splendid culture and made outstanding contributions in the long history of scientific development. The prominent representative is the ancient Egyptian civilization.

The creation of ancient Egyptian civilization benefited from the superior geographical environment created by nature for human beings in the first place, that is, the ancient Egyptian civilization was first and foremost the product of the ancestors of the Nile Valley adapting to the natural environment. From 5700 B.C., the dry climate prompted people living on the prairie to seek for water and forage, and began to move and assemble to the Nile Valley. Since then, people have been living and reproducing on the banks of the Nile. In the geographical environment of ancient Egypt, it is the only land suitable for planting. This land is very fertile, and the periodic flooding of rivers will bring a lot of fertilizer-rich sediment to the coast, which is easy to grow plants. A large number of food crops have been produced, and gradually a large number of tribes have been gathered along the Nile. Around 4,500 B.C., the ancestors began to engage in the cultivation of wheat, barley and other crops by using the fertile soil of the Nile River, and entered the era of agricultural civilization.

b. The Development of Ancient Egyptian Civilization

The emergence and development of ancient Egyptian civilization is inseparable from the Nile River, as the ancient Greek historian Herodotus said, "Egypt is a gift from the Nile." During the ancient Egyptian period, the Nile River flooded almost every year, flooding farmland and making the submerged land a fertile farmland at the same time. In addition, the reason why ancient Egyptian civilization has lasted for thousands of years is its relatively isolated geographical environment from the outside world. The north and east of Egypt are proximate to the Mediterranean sea and the Red sea respectively, the west is the untouched desert, the south is the upper reaches of the Nile, a series of large waterfalls that flow down, and only the northeast has a passage to West Asia. Although this geographical environment has blocked the connection between the ancient Egyptians and the outside world, resulting in the isolation of Egypt, it also made it difficult for foreigners to enter ancient Egypt and provided a natural protective barrier for ancient Egypt. The ancient Egyptians lived in such a unique environment and were protected from external aggression for a long time, thus creating a superior sense of security.

The inhabitants of ancient Egypt were formed by the fusion of indigenous peoples in North Africa and the Semites in West Asia. In the second half of 4,000 B.C., the country gradually formed, and until 343 B.C., it experienced the period of the former dynasty and the early dynasty (1-2 dynasty) , the ancient kingdom period (3-6 dynasty) , the first intermediate period (7-10 dynasty) , the middle kingdom period (11-12 dynasty) , the second intermediate period (13-17 dynasty) , the new kingdom period (18-20 dynasty), the third intermediate period (21-25 dynasty) and the post-dynasty period (26-31 dynasty) , the rule of 31 dynasties in 9 periods, including ancient Egypt in the 18th Dynasty (the first 15th century) reached the peak. Ancient Egypt has its own writing system, a perfect political system and a religious system of polytheistic beliefs. Its rich historical and cultural heritages, such as pyramids, mummies, paper grasses rich in the Nile River, and ancient ships on the Nile River, mark the course of the development of civilization in ancient Egypt for thousands of years.

c. The Decline of Ancient Egyptian Civilization

In the 12th century B.C., the ancient Egyptian power was in great decline, and it was frequently invaded by barbaric people. After the twentieth dynasty, a series of slave uprisings led to the defeat of national power, during which it was ruled by Libyans, Nubians, and Assyrians. Since the twenty-sixth dynasty, the late period of ancient Egypt, it was finally conquered by the Persian Achaemenid Empire in 525 B.C., and the culture has never recovered, which lead to the end of the ancient Egyptian era. The Persians established the twenty-seventh dynasty and the thirty-first dynasty in ancient Egypt. The descendants of the 26th dynasty of ancient Egypt resisted the Persians successfully and established the short-term twenty-eighth, twenty-ninth and thirties dynasties. In 332 B.C., ancient Egypt was ruled by Alexander the Great. After Alexander died, his ministry Ptolemy occupied the ancient Egypt and established the Ptolemy dynasty, also known as the Pharaoh. But the ancient Egypt was reigned completely by foreigners. Later, the rise of ancient Rome became a big country in the Mediterranean world, and ancient Egypt was occupied by it. And then, in the 7th century AD, the Arabs invaded ancient Egypt again. The original civilization of ancient Egypt was replaced by Arab civilization in this process, and ancient Egyptian civilization gradually disappeared.

(2) Ancient Indian civilization in the Indus and Ganges

a. The Origin of Ancient Indian Civilization

India is one of the four ancient civilizations. The earliest civilization in ancient India was born in the valley of the Indus, the longest river in South Asia. The Indus River is flooded twice a year, bringing very thick silt to the both banks. The land is fertile and suitable for breeding civilization, thus become the earliest origin of ancient Indian civilization.

The history of ancient Indian civilization dates back to around 2500 B.C. During this period, the Indus basin was born with the Harappan civilization, which was evolved from neighboring or ancient villages. The prerequisites for the civilization of Harappa were the emergence of stable and climatic conditions for the production of agriculture and animal husbandry and human living. However, Harappan civilization has not existed for a long time and around 1750 B.C., the Indus civilization was destroyed. In just about 500 years, Harappan civilization suddenly disappear, and it was not revealed through archaeological excavations until the last century.

b. The Development of Ancient Indian Civilization

After the disappearance of the Indus River civilization, the urban culture has been deadly quiet for hundreds of years, which has caused the ancient Indian civilization to have a fault of seven or eight hundred years. In the early days of this fault, around 1500 B.C., one of the world's first nomadic people, the Aryans, took advantage of the situation and they settled in the Wuhe area on the upper reaches of the Indus River and merged with the Native Americans of North India. From 1000 B.C., there was the beginning of the Ganges civilization.

In the 6th century B.C., the history of India entered the "era of the nations". In the north of India, especially the Ganges River, the cities and towns were divided. In order to merge the land and compete for hegemony, the cities and towns continued to wage war. In the end, Magadha kingdom won the victory over other powerful countries and gradually unified the northern India. In 518 B.C., the Indus basin was occupied by the Persian Empire, and the Persians ruled northwestern India for nearly two centuries. In the late 4th century B.C., Alexander the King of Macedonia led the army to invade northwestern India and sent the governor and the garrison to rule. In 324 B.C., Chandragupta led the people of the Indus basin to fight against Macedonia and became self-reliant. Then he marched eastward and destroyed the Nanda dynasty and he established the first unified empire in the history of India, the Peacock Empire. The empire's territory expanded to the entire South Asian subcontinent except the southernmost tip of the Indian peninsula. In 187 B.C., the Peacock Empire was ruined, and India was in a state of division. The split of India stimulated foreign invasions. In the 200 years after the 2nd century B.C., the Greeks, the Parthians, the Serbs, and the Kushans people of Bactria invaded India. Among them, only the Kushans established a stable political power in northwestern India. In the 3rd century, the Kushans Empire split into several small principalities. At the beginning of the 4th century, the dynasty of the Gupta Empire rose up. The territory of its epoch-making period was mainly in North India, and does not include the entire peninsula. In the middle of the 5th century, Arda people invaded India from central Asia and occupied most of northern and central India. In the 20s of the sixth century, the coalition forces of the princes of North India defeated the Arda people. However, after the dynasty Gupta was attacked by the Arda people, the small states within the country were independent and fell into a split and melee. At the beginning of the 7th century, the empire of the Harsha Empire rose, and the King of Harsha reunified northern India.

Ancient India is a multi-religious sect society. Religions such as Vedaism, Brahmanism, Jainism,

Buddhism, Hinduism, Sikhism, etc. all originated in India, and there are many other minor religions and many factions in various religions. In addition, major world religions such as Islam, Christianity, Judaism, and Zoroastrianism have their own believers in India. The various religions in India are unmatched by other countries in the ancient world and are called "religious museums".[①]

c. The Decline of Ancient Indian Civilization

The first phase of the ancient Indian civilization, the Indus River civilization, eventually disappeared, and for the reasons of the disappearance, historians gave three credible speculations. First, the invasion of foreigners (probably Aryans) caused this. According to archaeological findings, almost no traces of war and weapons were created in more than 1,500 sites of the Harappan civilization, indicating that there are few conflicts between cities. This civilization is peaceful and easy to be conquered by foreigners. The second is the earthquake. The earthquake destroyed the original terrain, and many of the Indus tributaries dried up. The urban people who built on the side lacked sufficient irrigation water, and had to abandon it. The third is destruction of the environment which led to the end of the civilization. Either way, the Indus civilization is indeed gone.

Although the Indus River civilization did not shake off the fate of decline, the second phase of the ancient Indian civilization, the Ganges civilization, was able to continue. The golden age of ancient India - the dynasty Gupta empire (early 4th century) finally collapsed after 230 years, and then more than half a century later, North India ushered in the dynasty Harsha empire (early 7th century) . After the fall of Harsha Empire, northern India fell into chaos. Since the 13th century, Muslims from Afghanistan have established the Sultanate of Delhi and the Mughal Empire in northern India, and later was colonized by Western powers (including Portuguese, French and British) , until India finally gained independence in 1947. It can be seen that the Gang River civilization, with more than 3,000 years of history, similar to the Chinese civilization and the Jewish civilization, has not been subjected to extinction attack, and it continues to nowadays, which adds a charm of advancing with the times for the ancient Indian civilization that was once interrupted.

(3) Sumerian Civilization in the two Rivers Basin (Tigris and Euphrates River)

a. The Origin of Sumerian Civilization

The two rivers civilizations recorded in the written text can be roughly divided into two stages. The first stage is from Uruk IV to the ancient Babylonian empire, known as the "Sumerian civilization" and the second stage is the establishment of the Babylonian Empire till the demise of the Persian Empire, called the "Babylon-Assyrian civilization." Sumerian civilization is the oldest civilization in the history of the world. It is rooted in the alluvial plains of the lower reaches of the Euphrates River and the Tigris River. It is the

---

① Zhang Yongxiu. On the Characteristics of Ancient Indian Civilization [J]. Journal of Weifang College, 2011, 11(1): 91-94.

origin of the civilization of the ancient two rivers and constitutes the main body of the ancient two rivers, and profoundly influenced the subsequent Babylonian civilization and Assyrian civilization. The Sumerian civilization is specifically defined as the ancient civilization that emerged in the southern part of the alluvial plains of the two river basins around 4500 B.C. to 2000 B.C.. It spans the Uruk era, the early Dynasty era, the Akkadian Kingdom, Ur III dynasty and the first dynasty of Yixin, and it was the first stage of civilization development in the ancient two rivers basin.

The term Sumer originates from the place name and refers to the southern part of the alluvial plains of the two rivers. The ancient inhabitants living in this area are also known as Sumerians. The Sumerians and the residents of the alluvial plains in the southern part of the two rivers have jointly created the oldest civilization in human history. This civilization has created a variety of elements of primitive civilization, mainly reflected in the emergence of agricultural production and settlement life, the emergence of cities and the increasing complexity of social organizations, the formation of the country, the development of cultural elements such as writing, science and technology, and so on. It all happened between 4500 B.C. and 2900 B.C..[1]

b. The Development of Sumerian Civilization

In the thousands of years of existence, the Sumerian civilization has made many great contributions and has been crowned with many "firsts". It includes the first invention of text, cuneiform writing; the first one to create a carriage with a wheel; the first painting astrological map, almost the same as modern; the first one to have a perfect urban launching system, including drowning booms, canals, water canals, dams and reservoirs, as well as developed trade, agriculture, livestock, handicrafts, such as textiles, ceramics, printing, wine making, shipbuilding, etc.; the first to create beer, whether to drink beer was considered as the dividing line with the civilized people and uncultivated, having its own beer goddess; the first one who can calculate 15 digits, and Greece, known as the cradle of Western civilization, could only calculate 4 digits 2,500 years ago; the first one invented 12 units and 60 units the measurement division; the first one who divide a year into 12 months, a week into 7 days; it regulates schools with multidisciplinary education, including theology, botany, zoology, mineralogy, geography, arithmetic and linguistics; besides, the earliest military array was also from Sumer.

Sumerian civilization is so great that people consider it simply flying outside the sky. Sumer has almost no resources, including forests, mineral deposits, and even stones. Despite this, the Sumerians not only understand geology, know how to obtain ore and other processes, but also create the world's first alloy and bronze. Through these inventions, it can be found that the Sumerian civilization is not developed by a

---

[1] Liu Jian. Analysis of the Basic Characteristics of Sumerian Civilization .Journal of Foreign Studies, vol. 2,2016, pp. 43-49,p. 118.

primitive nation. Although the Sumerian civilization is probably the most evidenced of the world's oldest civilization, where the Sumerian came from is a mystery to date.

c. The Decline of Sumerian Civilization

The Sumerian civilization itself is composed of several independent urban countries. In 3000 B.C., there were 12 countries in the Sumerian region. These countries are divided by canals and boundary stones. The center of each country is the protection God or the temple of the protected Goddess of the city, and each country is ruled by a priest or king who presides over the city's religious rituals. These countries have fought with each other for long-term battles to gain water rights, trade routes, and tributes from nomads.

The inferiority of the internal disunity of the Sumerians gave the Assyrians a good opportunity to attack. They launched a large-scale expansion war around 1800 BC, occupied the northern and central parts of Mesopotamia, and finally revived. The Sumerian nation was in danger of being destroyed soon. In 1792 B.C., Emperor Hammurabi was on the throne of Babylon, and a new united war began on the plains of Mesopotamia; in 1763 B.C., the capital Lalsa of the last king of the Sumerian nation, Rimousin, was captured by the Babylonian army. Since then, the Sumerians and the Sumerian civilization have disappeared in history.

(4) Chinese Civilization of Yellow River and Yangtze River

a. The Origin of Chinese Civilization

China is one of the oldest ancient civilizations in the world. The Yangtze River and the Yellow River together are called China's "Mother River". The two river basins are combined to become the support base for Chinese agricultural civilization and the important birthplace of Chinese civilization. The cradle of Chinese civilization was in the Neolithic Age. As early as about 7800 years ago, the magnetic mountain in the lower reaches of the Yellow River gave birth to the Peiligang culture, and the "Banpo Culture" was born more than 6,000 years ago. About 8,000 years ago, Pengtou Mountain in the middle reaches of the Yangtze River also gave birth to the Chengbeixi culture. At about the same time as Banpo culture, the Yangtze River basin gave birth to Hemudu culture. The earliest texts appeared in the Yellow River basin, and the sculpt symbols as the germination of the text were found in the Yellow River and the Yangtze River basin. The earliest bronzes appeared in the Yellow River basin, but the copper was inseparable from the copper source, while most of the metallogenic belts of the non-ferrous metals like copper, tin, and lead are in the Yangtze River basin. Some Neolithic sites have been discovered in the Yellow River and the Yangtze River basin. It can be seen that the Yellow River culture and the Yangtze River culture are interrelated, and jointly foster the necessary elements of early civilization.

b. The Development of Chinese Civilization

The Yanhuang era around 3000 B.C. was the period of origin and generation of Chinese civilization.

In the Yellow River and the Yangtze River, classical agriculture, multiculturalism, and comprehensive innovation emerged. The four major symbols of the civilized era were "metal tools, written texts, primitive cities, and primitive countries". The Yin and Zhou dynasties around 1000 B.C. were the embryonic period of Chinese civilization. The main contributions were as followings. First, the development of the Chinese Bronze age civilization was to the peak stage in the late Yin Dynasty, and the development of the four major symbols of Chinese civilization was to a higher level compared to the origin period of the Yanhuang era. Second, the reform of the Zhougong at the beginning of the western Zhou dynasty emphasized the patriarchal system, the spirit of humanity, and the education of the six arts, which laid the foundation for the overall framework of Chinese classical civilization. Third, the three major Chinese cultural symbols, such as Yijing, the Book of Songs and Shangshu, came into being in this era of historical transformation. Around the Spring and Autumn period and the Warring states period till Qin and Han period in 500 B.C., it was the formation period of Chinese civilization. During this period, the Chinese civilization had five major economic pillars: ① the Iron Revolution; ② the first agricultural revolution to intensive cultivation; ③ the ancient traffic revolution of early maturity; ④ the ancient urban revolution that transcended the early primitive cities; ⑤ the cities' five major leaps (scale, quantity, function, structure and system). The Tang, Song and Yuan eras around 1000 A.D., especially the Song dynasty, were the transition period of Chinese civilization. It took the commercial revolution of the Song dynasty as the economic foundation and promoted the comprehensive innovation of the three cultures of Confucianism, Buddhism and Taoism. It produced three inventions of gunpowder, movable printing and compass, and a series of scientific innovations.[①]

In the course of its own development, Chinese civilization, like other civilizations, has repeatedly faced the powerful impact of backward nomadic civilization. The Chinese empire has repeatedly experienced economic and cultural retrogression and short-term division of the country. However, the Chinese civilization has not decayed or collapsed like other ancient civilizations and empire and it has re-unified the country through the integration of all ethnic groups. Not only has it not been weakened by the impact of other civilizations, but it has continued to develop in such ethnic exchanges. Although there are ups and downs for Chinese civilization, there has never been a break, like a river that has never stopped flowing, maintaining a unique development continuity.

c. The Value of Chinese Civilization

The Yellow River and the Yangtze River combine to form a cradle which is a great fortune of Chinese civilization. Compared to civilizations such as ancient Egypt and ancient India, Chinese civilization

---

① Wang Dong. Cultural Genes and Modern Inheritance of Chinese Civilization (Panel Discussion) Five Great Brilliances of Chinese Civilization and Five Core Concepts in Cultural Genes[J]. Hebei Academic Journal,2003(05).

supports the unique continuity of civilization with its nationality, history, geography and ethics. It has survived so far and has contributed a lot to the historical development.

From the perspective of science and technology, the creativity of the Chinese nation has contributed a lot of technological and invention achievements to the development of human civilization. It can be said that China's four major inventions have promoted the progress of the world to a certain extent, the beginning of modernization, the opening of new route inseparable from the compass, the emancipation of the mind, the Renaissance, and the Enlightenment inseparable from papermaking and printing.

From the perspective of culture, the Chinese civilization has a long history. From the pre-Qin dynasty to the Song and Ming dynasties, it has experienced several periods of academic and ideological prosperity. In the long history, the Chinese nation has produced various theories such as Confucianism, Buddhism, Taoism and Mohism. A large number of thoughts such as Laozi, Confucius, Zhuangzi, Mencius and Xunzi have left enormous cultural heritage, which has provided an important basis for the ancient people to understand the world and transform the world, and has also made significant contributions to human civilization.

From the perspective of transportation, the opening of the sea-land Silk Road has connected Asia and Europe and promotes exchanges around the world. It not only transported practical goods to the world, but also connected the entire Eurasia (including North Africa) to human civilization. The development of communication has played a major role could be compared to the function of arteries, and China is almost the heart of this arterial system and has lasted for almost two thousand years.

From an economic point of view, although the feudal economy is characterized by self-sufficiency, it cannot be said that ancient China did not have a positive impact on the world economy. China is the first country in the world to grow rice. The spread of rice cultivation has greatly promoted agriculture in other regions. China has a highly developed farming civilization. At the peak of the agricultural civilization era, it has developed many agricultural and handicraft products and become the world's production center.

From the perspective of foreign exchanges, Chinese civilization has always advocated "to be harmonious with neighboring states", "promoting harmony while containing difference", and "harmony is highly valued". For thousands of years, peace has been integrated into the blood of the Chinese nation and engraved into the genes of Chinese people. For example, when Zheng He went to the Western Seas, he advocated not to deceive the minority, not to bully the weak, to be friendly, to be peaceful, which helps to establish unwritten rules for exchanges between Asian and African countries, and had far-reaching implications for future generations.

In the long-term evolution process, Chinese civilization has also gained nutrition from the exchanges with other civilizations. If you are independent and have no friends, you will be ignorant. The same is true for civilizations which need to learn from each other. Therefore, all kinds of civilizations created by human society, whether it is ancient Egyptian civilization, two river civilization, Indian civilization, or now Asian civilization, African civilization, European civilization, American civilization, Oceania civilization, etc., should learn from each other and should actively absorb the beneficial ingredients, so that the excellent cultural genes in all civilizations created by mankind can be adapted to contemporary culture, coordinate with modern society, and promote the excellent cultural spirit that transcends time and space, transcends the country boundary, and has contemporary values.

Section 3   River Valley Civilization and Tourism Development

This section will explain the relationship between river valley civilization and tourism development, as well as the concept of river valley civilization tourism. Culture is the soul of tourism and in the essence, tourism activities are a kind of cultural activities, and the experience of different cultures is also the starting point and destination of tourist activities. Both culture and tourism complement each other. River valley civilization tourism is a kind of tourism form that relies on its unique water culture, natural landscape, folk culture and other tourism resources to meet the tourist needs of experiencing great river valley culture, integrating knowledge, culture and interest in the tourism process.

1. The Relationship between River Valley Civilization and Tourism Development

(1) Tourism Development Interprets River Valley Civilization

Tourism has become one of the most powerful and largest industries in the global economy. The industrial status and economic role of tourism in social and economic development have gradually increased. The driving force of tourism to the economy, social employment, and the promotion of culture and the environment has become increasingly apparent. At the same time, the original great river valley culture can be used as the main attraction of tourism in the great rivers, and great river valley civilization tourism has become a new hot spot for development.

The cities and villages in the great river basins have rich historical and cultural resources, which can be excavated, protected, activated and integrated through tourism development, and have a distinctive cultural attraction and can be integrated with regional economic and social development. This has made a new interpretation to the great river valley culture and it helps to obtain rapid cultural identity and cultural communication through the development of tourism activities. In addition, the relative independence of the rivers flowing through the regions makes tourism resources in various regions different and unique. A large river condenses the different historical cultures and vicissitudes of the river basin, and it can excavate different cultures and folk customs through tourism development, which can meet the dual effects of people's exploration of history and culture as well as people's closeness to nature. Moreover, through the development of river tourism, the scattered historical culture and folk customs in the basin can be combined to increase the complete harmony and dynamic authenticity of great river valley culture.

(2) River Valley Civilization Nurtures Tourism Culture

Due to the unique natural conditions and historical evolution of the great river basin, various cultural and natural tourism resources are uniquely endowed with great potential and a broad space for tourism development. The great river basin has fostered a splendid civilization, and has formed a distinctive culture in the area. It has great appeal and remarkable identity, laying a foundation for the formation of tourism culture. The rivers flow through the region with diverse types, profound cultural connotations, and beautiful natural and cultural landscapes, forming a rich and unique experience of tourism. Many of the world's great river tourism attractions attract a large number of tourists, such as the Seine in Paris and the Thames in London, as well as the Three Gorges of the Yangtze River and the Yellow River in China.

On one hand, river is the cradle of the early development of human civilization. As an important distribution area of human settlements, it provides good natural conditions for the origin and development of local civilization. Some famous early civilizations were born in river areas, such as, the Yellow River basin in China, the Nile River basins in Egypt, the Euphrates River and the Tigris River, etc. The birthplaces of the world's four major civilizations are all in the great river basin. With its unique living conditions, the river has nurtured human civilization and formed a unique tourism culture. On the other hand, due to the rich natural and cultural resources, rich tourism activities and unique experience, tourism industry in these areas is very developed and has great potential for development. In China, the Yangtze River and the Yellow River have bred China's great river valley culture and each great river basin has become or is becoming a tourist hotspot. These unique river civilizations and their rich natural and cultural landscapes provide the necessary foundations for a series of tourism activities.

2. The Conceptualization of River Valley Civilization Tourism

(1) The Definition of River Valley Civilization

River valley civilization tourism seems to be a concept that people have known for a long time and is an important type of tourism activity. In fact, the value of river valley civilization tourism has long been known. People's appreciation of the natural scenery and cultural experience of the river, as well as the rich and varied tourism activities around the theme have existed for a long time. According to the "Tourism Resources Classification Standards" proposed by the former National Tourism Administration, the

"Landscape River Section" is an important sub-category in the Standards, which includes three basic types: sightseeing recreation, underground river section and the ancient river section. Among the existing 5A-level scenic spots, world heritage sites and national-level scenic spots in China, scenic spots with rivers as the core attraction account for a certain proportion. In the first batch of 66 five-A scenic spots, it accounted for 8 places, reaching 12.1%. By 2015, it accounted for 2 of the 48 World Heritage Lists (the "Three Parallel Rivers" natural landscape in Yunnan, China's grand canal), reaching 4.2%. By 2015, it has accounted for about 36 of the 225 national-level scenic spots in eight batches, reaching 16.0%.[①]

In essence, river valley civilization tourism is a form of cultural tourism. It is a type of tourism that relies on the unique great river cultural resources and natural resources to experience the cultural connotation of great rivers. River valley civilization tourism is an activity that people leave their habitual residences and temporarily go to the remote great rivers basin to get in touch with its natural scenery and experience the river valley civilization. This not only expands people's knowledge and broadens their horizons, but also satisfies people's recreation and spiritual needs. For instance, apart from providing the water source for human survival, great river valley civilization tourism can empower people spirituality in that being near the water has a regulating effect on people's emotions and psychology and this in turn gives people pleasure and relaxation.

(2) The Distinctiveness of River Valley Civilization Tourism

The river valley civilization tourism is an innovative type of tourism concept compared to traditional tourism. It is more a form of experiencing tourism about great river culture and natural landscapes, which helps to understand the cultural and historical background of tourism destinations on the great rivers, and to learn and appreciate the specific human cultural as well as the natural landscapes of the great rivers. The special geographical conditions of the great river basins make its tourism resources with scarcity, specialty and great development potential. The river valley civilization tourism also has the characteristics of inheritance and uniqueness of other cultural tourism, and, besides, it has the cultural connotation and value that can be developed into different types of tourism activities. The unique combination of landscape, culture, folklore, architecture and other resources in the great river areas forms a unique tourist landscape and becomes a special attraction of the great river valley civilization tourism.

---

① Bao Jie, Lu Lin. River Tourism: Origin, Connotation and its Research System——An Ontological Interpretation [J]. Geographic Science, 2017, 37(7) :1069-1079.

Chapter Two Tourism on River Valley Civilization and Development

Tourism industry is known as the sunrise and smoke-free industry of the 21st century. And because of this unique feature, the function of tourism becomes an important feature in the development of modern rivers. In early ages, boat tourism is an important type of river tourism around the world. With the progress of times and market development, the early river tourism is unable to meet tourism needs at present. Therefore, the development of river valley civilization tourism has to be improved. This section first introduces the origin and development of the river valley civilization tourism, then, it comprehensively expounds the present situation of the river valley civilization tourism industry, and finally it analyzes tourist demand and its current market.

Section 1 Origin and Development of River Valley Civilization Tourism

In order to understand the status of river valley civilization tourism industry and the development of tourism market, it is of great importance to identify the origin of the tourism activities. Therefore, this unit mainly explains the origin and development of the river valley civilization tourism. Natural resources such as animals and plants, minerals and so on in the river basin not only have the importance in commercial value, but also in entertainment and tourism value. The river valley civilization tourism activities are developed on the basis of natural, historical and cultural resources accumulated by human beings in the long-term social development.

1. The Origin and Development of Tourism Activities of Amazon Civilization

(1) Characteristics of Cultural and Ecotourism Resources

The Amazon Basin owns the largest tropical rainforest in the world and is known as 'the lung of the earth'. It contains the richest biological resources and the amount of precious animal and plant resources ranks first in the world. Besides, the Amazon basin is abundant in mineral resources, for example coal, metal, oil and so on. The Amazon can be called the largest river in the world whether from its drainage area or the amount of the resources it stores up.

There are some primitive tribes in the Amazon forest. Since the Portuguese landed on the Brazilian continent in the early 14th century, the Brazilian government has discovered 67 Indian tribes in the Amazon, most of which still maintain their primitive living conditions. All follow their different traditions and attract many tourists to visit here. In addition, there are a variety of ecological landscapes in the Amazon basin, such as the most beautiful "black and white river" landscape formed by the confluence of the Black River and Solimance Rivers in the upper reaches, as well as the Amazon tide, a natural wonder of the world. The Amazon tide is comparable to the spring tide of the Qiantang River in China and Brazilians refer to it as "Poboroca". When the tide surges, visitors scramble to go. Such scene is extremely spectacular at high tide.

(2) Origin of Tourism Activities of Amazon Civilization

The name of the Amazon River is related to a Greek mythology. It is said that there is a woman kingdom called Amazon in the Black Sea and the Caucasus, and the women in the kingdom were brave and strong. When the early Spanish colonists came to the current Amazon, they found that the residents of the basin were as brave and unyielding as the women of the Amazon women kingdom in ancient times, and that the river was mysterious and untamed, thus they called it the Amazon.

The earliest owner of the Amazon basin was Indians. As early as 1970, archaeologists discovered more than a dozen caves inhabited by ancient Indians in the basin. Today, hundreds of thousands of Indians still live in the Amazon region, and a considerable number of them known as the "forgotten people," are still in the primitive stage of knife-and-burn cultivation, which has long attracted many tourists to visit. The earliest owner of the Amazon basin was Indians. Brazil was the area where tourism activities were conducted prior to others in the Amazon Basin, but in the early stage, although the Amazon region was rich in resources, it still had been underdeveloped, mainly because of the self-sufficient smallholder production, backward commodity economy, lack of labor force and closed traffic. In order to change the poverty and backwardness of the Amazon region, the Brazilian government initiated the development and governance program of the Amazon River Basin in the mid-1940s. The Amazon Regional Development Authority was established in 1966, and the "National Integration" plan was formulated in 1970. By the 1970s, the development of the Amazon region has accelerated and become a major development area in Brazil.

(3) Tourism Development of Amazon Civilization

Iquitos, a port city in the upper reaches of the Amazon, is the commercial center of the Amazon region. It has a history of more than 130 years. At the beginning of the last century, it was a land of profligacy and entertainment for planters and tycoons, and some European-style buildings with carved and painted walls still retain their style of the year. Since the 1960s, the government of Peru has adopted a special policy here so that now more than 4000 kinds of goods can be imported duty-free and which makes the city a semi-free port and attracts a large number of goods from Europe and the United States. In order to visit and purchase cheap goods, many tourists pour in here every year, and it promotes the development of the local economy.

Manaus, in the middle reaches of the Amazon into which flows the Río Negro, is an emerging industrial and commercial city in western Brazil and also is the first city in the entire Amazon basin. In the 16th century, it was only a small Indian village and has now developed into a famous tourist destination and an important industrial base for machinery, electronics, petrochemical industry and so on. Manaus was the first stronghold for Portuguese to plunder the wealth of the Amazon basin. In 1968, the Brazilian government founded the Manaus Free Trade Area, where imports and exports were free. Now Manaus has become a famous tourist destination in Brazil, and its beautiful natural scenery has attracted tourists from all over the world. In the tourists' mind, Manaus represents a kind of culture. Being old but dilapidated but charismatic, Manaus is large in size with old dock areas, busy business centers and lively nightlife and so on.

Pattins, a small town in the middle reaches of the Amazon River, is an important tourist destination and also the center of jute industry in Brazil. Belém, in the Amazon estuary, not only is the largest port city but a distribution center for agricultural products in the Amazon. In 1978, the foreign ministers of the eight countries in the Amazon Basin signed the Amazon Cooperation Treaty in the capital of Brazil. After more than ten years' efforts, Amazon countries are working together to develop tourism resources rationally, establish and improve the infrastructure and service facilities, maintain ecological balance, improve health conditions constantly, and provide good prerequisites for tourism development in the Amazon region.[1]

(4) Current Tourism Development in Amazon Basin

After years of development, regional traffic conditions have been improved, modern industry has emerged, agriculture animal husbandry and tourism have been developed, and initially changed the economic poverty and backwardness have been initially improved in the Amazon Basin. However, its development process has led to the destruction of rainforest. And it did not achieve the coordinated development of environment and economy, and eventually it led to a great decline in environmental quality. As a result, some improvements need to be made in the development of the Amazon Basin

First, thorough research is needed before development, which includes: formulating authoritative

---

[1] Su Xiawang. The world's largest river -- the amazon [J]. Water Conservancy World, 2006 (12).

laws and regulations, understanding the ecological regulation of Amazon tropical rainforest, considering the ecological sensitivity and vulnerability of rainforest and adapting to local conditions so as to avoid the deterioration of the ecosystem. Second, Attention should be paid to environmental protection in the process of development. The protection and construction of ecological environment should be viewed as the fundamental task and guiding ideology. Environmental and ecological benefits should not be sacrificed in order to avoid the unsustainability of the economy, but the coordinated development of environment and economy should be guaranteed for sustainable development. Third, attention should be paid to scientific research and universal education in the development of Amazon region. How to apply new technology should be studied so as to make comprehensive and balanced use of all kinds of wood resources and reduce the damage to rainforest before using them.

2. The Origin and Development of Nile Civilization Tourism

(1) The Characteristics of Cultural and Ecotourism Resources

The Nile River flows through 10 countries, supporting the livelihood of millions of people. There are diverse kinds of species, especially many unique species, such as tilapia, giant Nile fish, crocodile, soft shell turtle and giant lizard in the basin. The Nile Delta is also the most important route for bird migration in the world. There are beautiful scenery and many historic sites along the either bank of the Nile, the most prominent of which are in ancient Egypt. When it comes to the cultural heritage of ancient Egypt, the pyramids on the banks of the Nile, the paper grass and the mysterious mummies may occur to people's mind. They not only represent civilization development in ancient Egypt within thousands of years, but also are the important forces to promote the rapid growth of tourism in Egypt.

(2) The Origin of Nile Civilization Tourism

The most representative area of tourism development in the Nile Basin is Egypt. Desert with yellow sand occupies the most part of the area in Egypt, and only one washed by the Nile is the green belt. Although Egypt has thousands of cultural relics and its tourism market has been developed very early, in fact, in the early days, for most tourists, their impression of Egypt is only desert, camel and pyramid. They believed that the life of Egyptians is still lagging behind a few centuries ago, and that the tour to Egypt is simply visiting historical monuments. Tourism products of Egypt were all cultural tourism products, and this phenomenon resulted in 80 percent of the tourists came to Egypt at that time only visit the pyramids of Cairo, the temple of Luxor and the mausoleum of Pharaoh. People who have the ability to consume but could not recognize the truc value of it wouldn't choose it as their tourist destination. With the promotion of Egypt by local tourism department, and the arrivals of a small number of tourists, people gradually began to realize Egypt not only has historical monuments, cultural tourism, but also long coastlines, and leisure tourism resources. Since then, people gradually developed a new recognition and the number of tourists to Egypt started to increase.[1]

(3) The Development of Nile Civilization Tourism

Egypt, as an important tourist destination in the Nile River Basin, was the first to develop cultural tourism by means of its historical monuments, however, cultural tourism tends to shrink with the time. Then Egypt began to search for new growth point, promote the "diversity of choices" of tourism products, and it developed leisure tourism and under that condition, a large number of leisure tourism products appeared, so leisure has become the leading direction of tourism in Egypt. Although more than 90% of Egyptian territory is desert, it is on the verge of the Red Sea and Mediterranean Sea. Having a long coastline, Egypt is warm and comfortable all the year round, and it provides resources and conditions for the development of leisure and holiday tourism.

In 2003, Egypt completely liberalized its exchange rate, and the sharp depreciation of the Egyptian pound against the dollar made the price of tourism products more competitive and it led to the rapid growth in the development of Egyptian tourism. A large number of the emerging middle classes in Russia and Eastern Europe have offered a huge supply of tourists because of the desire for leisure. And with the prosperity of leisure tourism in Egypt, it has promoted the investment in this field. In recent years, tourism investment projects account for more than 10% of the total domestic investment projects, and most of the investment comes from private capital.

In the new situation of leisure tourism, cultural tourist towns such as Luxor and Aswan in the upper reaches of the Nile are also trying to scout for their leisure potential. They take advantage of the benefits of where they live, for example, the river is completely unpolluted, and it is even cleaner than the sea, to develop leisure tourism. Tourists are able to enjoy the sunshine, the pure air and sailing on the river without worrying about those heavy monuments.

(4) Present Development of Nile Civilization Tourism

The Nile Basin is the birthplace of ancient human civilization with a long history of development and its rich tourism resources have greatly promoted the development of tourism. In recent years, tourism has become a pillar industry in some countries of the Nile Basin, such as Egypt and so on.

With the development of tourism, some negative effects have followed, such as environmental problems, destruction of cultural relics, etc., whereas the governments attach great importance to these issues and take various active measures to protect cultural heritage and the environment so as to achieve

---

[1] Sun Haiyan, Li Guanyun. Tourism in Egypt: "yellow and blue" of new leisure doctrine [J]. 21st century business review,2005(05) :119-123.

the sustainable development of tourism. However, as far as the river Nile is concerned, due to ethnic contradictions, racial hatred and other reasons, its tourism development is still unsatisfactory, and many scenic spots with great potential have yet to be developed. Many historical relics and monuments are still undeveloped and can not present its attractiveness to people, and even in worse, they have not become tourism products. How to do well in the river management, tourism planning and coordination among various countries in each section of the Nile is still important to develop the potential of Nile tourism resources.

3. Origin and Development of Civilization Tourism Activities in the Rhine River

(1) Characteristics of Cultural and Ecotourism Resources

The Rhine River Basin owns a unique ecological landscape. The middle reach of the river is from Basel, Switzerland to Bonn, Germany, which has winding rivers, overlapping mountains on both sides, countless castles, and a unique landscape. Meanwhile the middle reaches also flows through many large cities and landmarks, such as the old city of Cologne, Dusseldorf, the main commercial center of German coalfields, and so on. The upper reaches is from the source to Basel of Switzerland and the river flows from the south to the north, forming the natural borders between the two countries—Switzerland and Liechtenstein. Liechtenstein attracts tens of thousands of visitors every year with its beautiful natural scenery, ancient castles, exquisite works of art and rare stamps.

The Rhine has a long history and cultural tradition. The Rhine is also the birthplace of Marx, the international proletarian revolutionary mentor, Rembran, the famous Dutch painter, and Beethoven, the music master. In addition, it is the place where the secret of atomic structure has been revealed. Trier, Marx's former residence, is the oldest city in Germany, which is visited by countless tourists from all over the world every year. Bourne Lane, Germany, Beethoven's former residence, was opened as a museum in 1989, where the original works of musicians are displayed. Besides, the Rhine has experienced war for a century, and the long period of war has left many ancient battlefields for today's tourists.

(2) Origin of Civilization Tourism in the Rhine

The Rhine River is not only an important water transport channel in Europe, but also an important source of industrial and domestic water in the basin. It has been famous for shipping and industry for many years, so it has been positioned as a famous navigation canal and industrial river. However, in fact, in addition to its irreplaceable shipping and industrial value, the Rhine is also famous for tourism. In this case, it is also labeled as a scenic, travel and cultural river.

The middle reaches of the Rhine are all in Germany. For hundreds of years, a steep cliff has formed in the middle reaches of the river and under which is a valley between Bingen and Koblenz. Tourists could enjoy vineyards, terraces, green pastures and dense forests. For the reason that beautiful natural landscapes attract more and more tourists, tourism industry has been developed ever since.

(3) The Development of Civilization Tourism in the Rhine

The countries the Rhine River flowing through develop their tourism industry as an effective measure to comprehensively manage the Rhine River, speed up industrial transformation and promote national economic growth. The main measures are as follows: creating compound and pluralistic tourism products, establishing an efficient tourism management model, building a comprehensive water environment management model, formulating a close integrated planning system, building a convenient and unobstructed transportation network, and so on. These measures taken have contributed to the great success of the development of the tourism industry in these countries.

The Rhine was once contaminated by coastal industry in the mid-20th century. In the 1980s, Germany, France, Luxembourg, the Netherlands, Switzerland and the European Union decided to adjust the inland river economic belt. At the end of the 20th century, they jointly signed the Convention on the Protection of the Rhine in Rotterdam. Since then, European countries have also founded the International Commission for the Protection of the Rhine and launched an ongoing campaign called "Save the Rhine". As a result, the Rhine is now clear and sparkling. It can be said that the tourism development of the Rhine River is inseparable from the relevant policies and plans issued by the coastal countries. Although the river basin countries do not have a uniform development plan in tourism industry, every country in the basin has formulated relevant plans tailored to the development of their own tourism industry according to their own resource endowment. Taking Germany as an example, Hesse has formulated a special development plan concerning tourism industry in the whole state economic development plan. Meanwhile, it has also formulated a special development plan in culture and sports in order to support the development of tourism industry. In addition, transportation is the foundation for the development of the tourism industry. From the source to the mouth of the sea, a diversified, unobstructed, convenient and three-dimensional transportation network has been built along the coast and surrounding towns, which includes shipping traffic, water transportation, land transportation and leisure transportation.

(4) Current Development of Civilization Tourism in the Rhine River

In the past two centuries, the Rhine River Basin has gained remarkable benefits in the development of society, economy and environment, and it has become a successful model of river tourism development in the world. The success of the Rhine River has offered valuable experience for other rivers. The achievements of Rhine tourism development are mainly reflected in the aspects as follows.

a. The Development Plan of the Whole Basin

As an international river, the countries within the Rhine basin once lacked uniform planning in the development process, and it was inevitable for each country to conduct their own plans. However, driven by mutual interests, the recognition of economic prosperity has been strengthened, so that all countries have taken it seriously the coordination and cooperation of the whole basin development plan at different historical stages, and to put them into implementation.

b. Strong Awareness of Environmental Protection

Although economic development in the Rhine basin varies, the recognition of implementing sustainable management is the same. The Rhine Basin Management Action Plan requires close cooperation among different countries and departments, as it is not guided by a single local or individual management measure, but with the ultimate goal of sustainable management of the Rhine Basin as a whole. Therefore, the development of the Rhine River Basin is in fact a way of development integrating with protection and coordination of the environment.

c. Complete Infrastructure and Service Facilities

With wharf, airport, coastal roads and railways built, land and water transportation developed, and a three-dimensional communication system formed along the Rhine River, it has laid a solid foundation for the development of tourism industry and industrial agglomeration. In addition, in a variety of guide maps from Mainz to Koblenz Rhine issued by Germany, many campsites and youth hostels are marked, with an average distance of 1.44 campsites per 10 km and 1.11 youth hostels per 10 km, with a higher density of ordinary hostels and holiday hostels in each village and town.[1]

d. Complex and Pluralistic Tourism Products

As an integral tourist area, the tourism products of Rhine River are characterized by integrity and diversification, which can be divided into three types: upstream, middle and downstream. The first type, upstream product is the lake leisure tourism, most of which are mainly in the form of winter skiing tourism and summer tourism; The second, middle-stream product is the historical and cultural heritage tourism, most of which are mainly in the form of cruise tourism, mountain hiking tourism, etc. The third is downstream product, which is industry and industrial heritage tourism.

4. Origin and Development of Civilization Tourism in the Mississippi River

(1) Characteristics of Cultural and Ecotourism Resources

With rich and diverse energy, mineral resources, and convenient shipping resources, the Mississippi

---

[1] Zhai Fudong. A Comparative Study of the Development of Xiang River Scenic Belt and Rhine River Scenic Belt. Journal of Tourism, vol. 03, 2001, pp. 57-59.

River is the longest river and owns the most extensive drainage system in North America. In addition, it is the most important grain producing area in the United States. It possesses unique agricultural resources, an area of about 1.2 million square kilometers of black land, which is one of the three largest black soil areas in the world. Furthermore, it produces the largest amount of wheat, corn, soybeans and cotton in the United States. The United States has become the world's most important producer of agriculture, meat, eggs, milk and etc., which largely contributes to the unique agricultural resources of the Mississippi River Basin.

The Mississippi River is also a treasure trove of national culture, entertainment and leisure. The annual output amounts to more than $20 billion in tourism, fishing and recreation. The Mississippi River is a huge fishing ground with huge dams and backwater areas in the north of the river. In spring, the river is turbulent, where there are many fish species.

(2) The origin of Civilization Tourism in the Rhine River

The Missouri River, which carries a lot of sediment in the middle reaches, accumulates and forms the largest bird-foot delta in the world at the mouth of the lower reaches of the Mississippi River Delta. In the early 20th century, because of historical, ethnic, educational and other problems, the Mississippi River Delta region developed relatively slowly and was one of the poorest places in the United States. In order to change the backward situation and promote the development, the region began to make utmost to develop tourism industry and make full utilization of all resources for its development, such as Oak Avenue and Manor buildings, symbols of the South of the United States. Books such as Uncle Tom's Cabin and Gone with the Wind, as well as blues, jazz and other music resources are popular all over the world. Among them, blues and blues tourism is the most popular, not only occupying a key position in black music, but also becoming an important part of American black culture and even American cultural heritage, which integrates into the ranks of mainstream music in the continuous development and gradually affects the development track of pop music in the world.

(3) The Development of Civilization Tourism in the Mississippi River

The Mississippi River is known for its beauty, grandeur and diversity. The regulation of the Mississippi River began in the 1970s. "Army Corps of Engineering", "Mississippi Committee" and other development and management organizations were founded and the development of specific laws and regulations were made during the time. In the course of the regulation, the government of the United States has chosen a large number of towns on either side of the Mississippi River as the window to the outside world, and promoted the entire Mississippi River as a kind of product. As a result, it attracted foreign funds and tourists and finally improved the income of tourism.

Since the 1930s, with the implementation of comprehensive management and drainage projects, the Mississippi River has basically eliminated floods, and the main stream and tributaries have been controlled according to modern advanced technical standards. With the purpose of conforming to the natural process of the river, establishing a modern shipping network and economic belt, a solid foundation has been laid for tourism on the water in the area.

After the 1990s, in order to protect the precious resources along the Mississippi River and present the attractiveness of the Mississippi River, the government of the United States began to implement the Great River Road National Scenic Road Project, which runs from the north to the south across the whole nation. Therefore, it becomes the longest scenic path in the United States, and becomes the only way to experience the wonders of the river. Because of the different characteristics of the landscape along the Mississippi River, it can be divided into four sections: the source, the upstream, the middle stream and the downstream.

(4) Current Development of Civilization Tourism in the Mississippi River

Environmental awareness keeps the ecological resources of the Mississippi River well-preserved. In the process of river development, environmental protection and ecological balance are taken into careful consideration. For example, after the implementation and completion of the project, special wildlife reserves must be set up, and even appropriate compensation and remedy methods would also be taken into account for mitigating the impact (including noise) on the surrounding residents during the construction process. It is because of many positive and effective environmental measures that the Mississippi River still maintains its beautiful environment and intact ecological resources.

Rational and legally valid planning has laid the foundation for the tourism development of the Mississippi River. The Mississippi River Basin has a clear development and management organization. It is an entity with certain powers and has a more independent management power, whose main purpose is to study the development and management planning of the River. In the course of tourism development of the River, the overall concept, development procedures and implementation steps all play a key role. It is just because of these authoritative planning and strict management that the tourism development of the Mississippi River has got the current achievement.

5. Origin and Development of Civilization Tourism in the Yellow River

(1) Characteristics of Cultural and Ecotourism Resources

The Yellow River Basin is long in history, vast in territory and extremely rich in tourism resources.

There are four ancient capitals, four famous mountains, 105 tourist scenic spots[①] along the river and three grottoes art treasure houses scattering in the Yellow River Basin. Abundant tourism resources have laid a solid foundation for tourism development. Specifically, tourism resources in the Yellow River Basin can be divided into the following types:

First type is the eco-tourism resources characterized by China's famous mountains and rivers. From Mount Tai in Dongyue to Huashan in Xiyue, from Sanmenxia and Hukou Falls in the west to Qingtong Gorge in Ningxia Plain, Liujiaxia in Gansu and the source of the Yellow River in Qinghai. It also includes many famous natural scenic spots, such as Hukou Falls in Shanxi Province of the Yellow River, Shahu Lake in Ningxia, Qinghai Lake tourist area and so on.

Second, the ancient cultural tourism resources centered on cultural relics, monuments and religious monasteries, which include a large number of world-famous places of interest, such as Xiundefinedan, Kaifeng, Qin Shihuang Military Horse Merchant, as well as religious, cultural and artistic shrines left by major religions, such as the Mogao Grottoes in Dunhuang, Gansu, Xiundefinedan Dayan Pagoda in Shaanxi, Famen Temple, Baima Temple in Luoyang, Henan Province, and Wutai Mountain in Shanxi Province.

Last, ethnic customs tourism resources with the religion and customs of ethnic minorities as the focus. The west of the Yellow River Basin is an area inhabited by ethnic minorities in China, and each nationality has formed its unique culture in the process of its reproduction and development, such as the language, clothing and dancing of Xinjiang Uygur, Islamic customs of Hui in Ningxia, "Nadamu" and prairie customs of Mongolian, Tibetan customs and Buddhism of Qinghai and so on. These national cultures not only make the cultural and artistic of China colorful, but also provide conditions for the development of folk culture tourism.

(2) Origin of Civilization Tourism in the Yellow River

The Yellow River Basin is the cradle of Chinese civilization for five thousand years. The development of tourism has its unique advantages, which mainly reflects in the following aspects: first of all, the Yellow River Basin is the birthplace of Chinese civilization, and it retains a complete Chinese cultural heritage. Its cultural background has a strong attraction to tourists, and it provides strong resources and market for tourism development. Second, the natural geographical environment is unique and the ecosystem is complex. There are famous mountains and rivers, desert basins, alpine snow areas within the area, which provides good ecological resources for the development of tourism. Last, the Yellow River Basin has been

---

① Wang Kaiyong, Zhang Pengyan and Ding Xusheng. The Spatio-temporal Variation of Regional Tourism Economy and R/S Analysis in The Huanghe River Basin.Geography science, vol.34, no. 3,2014, pp. 295-301.

a place for many people to inhabit and develop from ancient times to the present. Nomadic and agricultural peoples of different times have left rich and special cultural relics, and their unique folk customs and traditional characteristics are splendid. It has offered opportunity for the development of tourism in terms of special folk culture.

The 1880s was the embryonic stage of the development of tourism in the Yellow River Basin. At this stage, many areas in the basin tried to establish some tourist spots. For example, at that time, a series of social and environmental problems brought about by industrial civilization made urban residents generally had the psychological identity of avoiding noise and returning to nature. Surpassed historic sightseeing tourism, eco-tourism became the first choice for tourists. It happened that the characteristics in tourism resources of Dongying City in the Yellow River Delta coincided with this theme, in this case, Dongying City began to make utilization of the advantages in tourism resources to create eco-tourism at that time, and it identified the five major tourist areas. At the same time, Binzhou City also began to set up a regional tourism bureau, organize and repair some tourist spots and cultural relics, and establish some tourist spots. However, due to the constrains of people's mind, development conditions and other factors, the tourism development in this stage was not matured, but still in the initial stage, and tourism products was low in quality and small in amount. However, there was a lot of space for its development.

(3) Development of Civilization Tourism in the Yellow River

In the 1880s, civilization tourism in the middle and upper reaches of the Yellow River has been unprecedentedly developed with the deepening of reform and opening up. Local governments are fully aware that tourism can not only bring new vitality and growth to economic revitalization and social development, but also play an important role in promoting the region and enhancing international and domestic exchanges in economy and socialization. Therefore, the areas have begun to take actions on tourism, such as one is creating the four tourism characteristics of Henan -- history (history and culture), river (the Yellow River), Kungfu (Shaolin, Chen Taijiquan and Zhengzhou International Shaolin Kungfu Festival), root (ancestors and root searching), flowers (The Peony Culture Festival of Luoyang China); another is creating the "Ancient Culture and Art Festival" of Shaanxi Xi'an and so on.

Since 2000, the overall idea of tourism development in many areas of the Yellow River Basin has basically formed, and the leap-forward development of tourism has basically been realized. After years of continuous development and construction, the tourism industry in the Yellow River Basin has developed rapidly. At present, a series of distinctive tourism products have gradually formed. The scales of tourist reception and tourism income in the basin have also continued to grow. The construction of tourism supporting facilities is fast and tends to be well-furnished gradually.

(4) Present Condition of Civilization Tourism in the Yellow River

The Yellow River civilized tourism is in the ascendant, showing a growing trend of development. Both foreign exchange earnings of tourism and the number of visitors have increased in recent years (Table 1.1). The development of tourist routes and tourist attractions is increasing day by day, the service functions are improving day by day, the regional tourism service facilities are complete, and the transportation and communication facilities are gradually approaching the international level. Generally speaking, the tourism in this area has been changed from the past "reception" to "economic" transformation, and showed a good momentum of development.

Table 1.1 Tourism Income and Number of Tourists in the Yellow River Delta

Year	Number		Income	
	Inbound (thousand)	Domestic (thousand)	Inbound (Hundred Million RMB)	Domestic (Hundred Million RMB)
2010	28.47	4243.70	2.03	324.60
2011	36.92	5189.50	2.57	411.70

Source: Yang Wenjuan, Toursim Development Research on Historical and Cultural Resources of the Yellow River Delta, Jiangsu Normal University, 2013.

Civilization tourism market in the Yellow River has bright prospects, but there is still some gap in the development between the Yellow River and the international tourism industry. Especially, the potential of Northwest China has not been fully utilized. Therefore, civilization tourism development in the Yellow River still needs to be studied significantly and needs to learn from the experience of foreign countries. By doing this, it helps open up the market, so that tourism development accounts for a larger proportion and plays a more important role in the economic development of the area.

6. Origin and Development of Civilization Tourism in the Yangtze River

(1) Characteristics of Cultural and Ecotourism Resources

The Yangtze River Basin is extremely rich in resources and it has been the most important economic zone in agriculture in China since ancient times. There are different geomorphological types, including mountains, hills, plains and lakes (Table 1.2) , all of which form a colorful geographical landscape. In addition, the river basin is big either in longitude or latitude span. The climate is diversified; thus it forms a variety of local climatic characteristics. The complex geological and geographical condition and diverse climatic features have given birth to the biodiversity of the Yangtze River Basin, which not only distributes two thirds biological resources in the whole country, but also provides a huge advantage for tourism development in terms of resources.[1]

Within the years of many ancient dynasties, the Yangtze River Basin has also accumulated a lot of cultural resources. For example, Panlong City, Huangpi District, Wuhan City, the first ancient city Shang Dynasty in the Yangtze River Basin, Daye Tonglushan Copper Mine, the earliest, largest and most well-preserved ancient copper deposit in China. There are also many important sites of the Shang Dynasty in the lower reaches of the Yangtze River, such as the Wucheng site of the Qingjiang River in Jiangxi Province, besides a large number of bronzes, jade, pottery, etc., and as well as the famous and magnificent three Gorges of the Yangtze River, all of which are sufficient to reflect the social civilization of our country. It not only has a very high value for understanding the culture of the Yangtze River Basin, but also becomes a typical resource for tourism development.

Tale 1.2 Ecotourism Resources in the Yangtze River Delta

Mountain	Location	Features and Comments
Wudang Mountain	Hubei Province	the most complete, largest and highest-ranking Taoist architectural complex preserved in China, and listed in the world cultural heritage of the Ming Dynasty
Zhangjiajie	Hunan Province	the first National Forest Park in China, together with Suoxiyu Natural Scenic Spot and Tianzishan Nature Reserve constitute Wulingyuan Scenic Spot, a major national scenic spot and one of the world natural heritages approved by the United Nations
Jiu Shan	Hubei Province	Jiu Shan has the exquisite beauty of the mountains located in Southern China, but also enjoys the same level of magnificence of the Mountains in Northern China; It is magnificent, exotic, beautiful and dangerous.
Mount Lu	Jiangxi Province	In 1996, the UNESCO World Heritage Committee approved Lushan Mountain as a "world cultural landscape" to be included in the World Heritage List.
Sanqing Mountain	Jiangxi Province	One of 72 Taoism temples, one of the national key scenic spots. The predecessors praised it as "the first immortal peak in the south of the Yunhan River in Gaoling, eliminating the dusty world ".
Jinggang Mountain	Jiangxi Province	In 1991, it was rated as the top 40 tourist attractions in China.
Yellow Mountain	Anhui Province	"China's first Magic Mountain", the first batch of national key scenic spots, is also a world-class tourist attraction.
Tianzhu Mountain	Anhui Province	In 1982, it was one of the first 44 key scenic spots in the country, and was praised as the first mountain in the Yangtze-Huaihe region.

[1] Huang Deling and Huang Daoming. Ecological Effects and Countermeasures of Water Resources Development in the Yangtze River Basin. Water Resources and Hydropower Express, vol.18, 2005, pp. 1-4, p. 6.

续表

Mountain	Location	Features and Comments
Langye Mountain	Anhui Province	Since ancient times, it has been praised as "the first scenic spot in East Anhui" and is one of the 24 famous cultural mountains in China.
Boyang Lake	Jiangxi Province	China's largest freshwater lake, the famous island Xiuyu on the lake, Jiujiang Tourism Bureau has linked all the scenic spots on Poyang Lake through cruise boats.
Dongting Lake	Hunan Province	China's second largest freshwater lake, since ancient times, Dongting Lake has attracted tourists with its beautiful scenery, which has been dumped by famous writers of all dynasties. Dongting Lake is the cradle of Chu culture.
Tai Hu	Jiangsu Province	China's third largest freshwater lake, Suzhou Taihu National Tourism Leisure Area, is one of the first batch of national tourism resorts approved by the State Council in October 1992.
Hongze Lake	Jiangsu Province	China's fourth largest freshwater lake, rich in aquatic resources and crabs are also well-known, besides, its lotus root, water chestnut in history enjoys a reputation.
Chao Lake	Anhui Province	Chaohu Lake, the fifth largest freshwater lake in China, is a famous tourist attraction in central Anhui Province.

Source: Chen shengjun. Study on the Development of Yangtze River Waterborne Tourism[D].Wuhan University of Technology, 2003.

(2) Origin of Civilization Tourism in the Yangtze River

Human activities of our ancestors in the Yangtze River Basin started more than 1 million years ago. Because of its profound culture and unique natural landscape, the Yangtze River had always been the focus and become an important place for tourists to visit the mountains and rivers. In history, many famous rioters once traveled to the Yangtze River and left touching works and stories there. At that time, the Yangtze River had been a scenic spot for literati to visit. In other words, it can be said that tourism in the Yangtze River tourism has existed since ancient times.

The Yangtze Gorges represents the tourism development of the Yangtze River Basin in modern times. From October 1978 to July 1979, Deng Xiaoping made a special speech to accelerate the development of tourism. The series of tourism economic ideas by Mr. Deng Xiaoping, such as strengthening tourism promotion, paying attention to environmental protection, constructing relevant supporting facilities, cultivating talents, managing, reforming the distribution system, improving the quality of service, and the development of tourism commodities, have become the guidelines for developing tourism industry in the new period. The Yangtze Gorges of the Yangtze River was approved by the State Council in 1982 as the first national key scenic spots. In 1990, the first cruiseline on the Yangtze River, the Yangtze River Shipping overseas Tourism Corporation, was established, which marked that the Yangtze River tourism has transformed into a professional and systematic stage, and the enterprise form that both travel agencies and ship owners joined in created the forerunner of the great development of Yangtze River tourism.

(3) The Development of Civilization Tourism in the Yangtze River

Since 1990, Yangtze River tourism has turned into a professional stage. In the following ten years, due to the influence of many factors, such as economy, politics, nature and the construction of the Yangtze Gorges Project, the development of Yangtze River tourism does not go smoothly as imagined. However, it is because of this curve development that makes the Yangtze River tourism grow and gradually develop from the preliminary stage towards stability and maturity.

There are several evident changes during the development of Yangtze River tourism: first, tourism service facilities are rich, especially, at the beginning of tourism development of the Yangtze River, there were few ships, which basically did not form a sailing cycle. While at present, the number of cruise ships is increasing, and the construction of various infrastructure is gradually strengthened. Second, the tourist market is becoming more and more diversified through active expansion. In the early stage of its development, in addition to a small number of European and American tourists, the main tourist sources were from, Southeast Asia, Japan and other places, and the companies engaged basically do not have a strong ability in selling and marketing tourism products. At present, Southeast Asian tourists still account for a considerable proportion of the tourist market, apart from this, the European and American markets have increased dramatically, while the Japanese, Korean and Australian markets have also increased. Third, the structure of tourism products is further improved, cruise ship tourism, immigration tourism, historical and cultural tourism, natural ecotourism, urban tourism, festival exhibition tourism and other tourism products are constantly enriched, and the diversified tourism product system is formed.

(4) Current Development of Civilization Tourism in the Yangtze River

Although great progress has been made in tourism in the Yangtze River Basin in recent years, it still needs to be further improved:

First, scientific tourism plan needs to be formulated. Both active tourism market and rational development of tourism resources need to be guided by scientific planning. If tourism is expected to maintain rapid, healthy and sustainable development, it is necessary to formulate scientific and accurate tourism development planning. Planning is placed in the first place in tourism development, which has become the consensus of the tourism industry. Without general tourism planning, the overall development of tourism in the Yangtze River would be restricted, and accordingly the brand can not be formed.

Second, the development of the western region needs further improvement. The Yangtze River runs across China from the west to the east. The lower reaches of the Yangtze River are in the rich eastern part. The middle reaches are in the middle part, while the origin and upper reaches of the Yangtze River are rich in resources but relatively poor in the western part. Although after more than 20 years of development, with the support of national and local policies, the central and western regions have also formed popular international tourist destinations such as the Yangtze Gorges of the Yangtze River and Jiuzhaigou. There are still some gaps in transportation, management, infrastructure construction and other aspects, and further improvement is needed in the future compared with those in eastern areas.

Third, strengthen external marketing and promotion and create an overall image. The Yangtze River runs through eight provinces, two municipalities directly under the Central Government and an autonomous region. Among them, the Yangtze Gorges of the Yangtze River is shared by Hubei Province and Chongqing City. Although the development is relatively matured, its function is far inferior to that of Hangzhou in Zhejiang Province and Xi'an in Shaanxi Province. This is not only the reason for the distribution of tourism resources and the overall development and design, but also, more importantly, the reason lies in the fact that the external marketing and promotion is incomplete.

Section 2   Development of Great Rivers Civilization Tourism Industry

This part will comprehensively elaborate the development of tourism industry of the Great Rivers Civilization at present stage. With the rapid development of economy and society and the changes in tourism market demand, the Great Rivers tourism development is currently undertaking a major transformation and adjustment. People begin to attach importance to tourism planning and construction of regulations, emphasize the effective utilization of space environment and rivers, improve the function of rivers, and constantly adjust the structure of tourism products. Currently leisure holiday is viewed as the tourism theme, more new elements are involved on the basis of early sightseeing, and a new in-depth product development is being conducted.

1. Tourism Planning and Regulation Taking Priority

(1) More Attention to Planning and Guidance of Legal Protection and Authority

Sound legal system and authoritative tourism planning is the top-level design of concrete and visual tourism construction and development of the Great River Civilization. Tourism development should be planned first, so that planned, orderly and reasonable can be achieved. The reason why a complete and authoritative tourism planning is important, is that it is conducive to properly handling the relationship between tourism development and construction and environmental protection, and between tourism development and functional zoning, departmental coordination, and so on. It not only determines the main functions of the river according to the characteristics of the natural and cultural landscape of the river, retains and exerts its characteristics, but also conforms to the principles of ecological protection and overall coordination so that a good regional tourism can be formed. On the other hand, tourism planning is also conducive to reflecting the advantages of regional tourism development, forming complementary characteristics, coordinating the development of coastal countries and regions, and avoiding disorderly development.

At present, the importance of tourism planning in the development of foreign rivers tourism has been highlighted. Before tourism development, clear planning constraints have been formulated, such as Jefferson Paris Master Plan for Entertainment on the Mississippi River. The plan clearly identified the objectives to be achieved within the time limit, including infrastructure construction, environmental protection, natural disaster prevention, etc. Any environmental management department, tourism development and operators must follow and work together to achieve the objectives of the plan. Secondly, the development of tourism projects will be clearly defined in the planning. According to the characteristics of each region, tourism projects will be developed to avoid duplicate development, so as to make great river tourism more competitive and vigorous.[1]

(2) More Attention Paid to Ecological Protection and Regional Cooperation in Tourism Planning

Great River tourism is the tourism developed on the basis of the ecosystem of great rivers. The ecosystem of great rivers has typical fragility. Any disturbance to the natural environment and ecosystem will have serious negative effect on the long-term and stable development of big river tourism. Therefore, the principle of ecological protection should be followed in the development of great river tourism, which has attracted more and more attention in the development of River Tourism in China. In some tourism planning of great river basin, ecological protection receives more and more attention. For example, the ecological management of some river tourist destinations has started from the planning, and environmental impact assessment is carried out during planning, including impact assessment of various environmental factors (atmosphere, water, soil, noise, biological environmental impact assessment), visual landscape impact assessment, socio-economic impact assessment and environmental impact synthesis. At the same time, when allocating and dividing the river shoreline into tourist functional areas, more consideration should be given to the public utilization of all kinds of shorelines, in this case the shoreline for recreation can fully embody the principle of being people-oriented. And the core of the mechanism is to develop

---

[1] Wang Shoushu. Study on River Tourism Function Construction and Products Development. Shanghai Normal University, 2009.

tourism on long-term and orderly development, protect the special environmental characteristics, develop and utilize reasonably and efficiently, and maintain the regeneration of the shoreline.

In addition, regional cooperation in river tourism and the pursuit of mutual development have also reached a general consensus. All countries and cities on the shoreline of the river have fully coordinated, so that they can complement each other in the utilization of the shoreline. Thus, these regions could develop together, and maintain the dynamic balance of the utilization of the shoreline. In the development and utilization of river shoreline tourism, we should coordinate the resources, concentrate marketing, and achieve integrated propaganda and marketing, information sharing and platform co-construction.

Case 1.1

Scientific Development Planning of the Tennessee River Basin

Scientific development planning is the basis of the comprehensive development of the Great River Basin. The Tennessee River Basin has become an example of shaking off poverty in the underdeveloped regions of the world through the formulation and implementation of scientific development planning.

Located in the southeastern United States, the Tennessee River originates from the west slope of the Appalachian Mountains. It is the second tributary of the Mississippi River and the first tributary of the Ohio River. Historically, the Tennessee River has been a "harmful river": vegetation destruction, serious soil erosion, flooding; inadequate water depth, navigation; environmental pollution, the prevalence of infectious diseases in the basin; the decline of the old cotton belt, farmers' debt, per capita income level and per capita crop output is only 2/5 of the national average level.

In order to improve the backwardness of the basin and get rid of the Great Depression, Roosevelt's government decided to carry out the comprehensive development and management project of the Tennessee River Basin. On May 18, 1933, the United States Congress approved the establishment of the Tennessee Valley Agency (TVA), which is responsible for formulating and implementing the comprehensive development plan of the Tennessee River Basin. Planning mainly involves six aspects: ecological protection and flood control, improvement of shipping, development of electricity, improvement of land use along the coast, afforestation in necessary areas of the basin, and improvement of economic and social conditions of the people in the basin.

Scientific development planning has put the economic development of the Tennessee River Basin on a healthy track. Cheap hydropower has provided sufficient power for the country, and improved shipping conditions have attracted the construction of thermal power plants and nuclear power plants. Large power-consuming industries have begun to be distributed in the valley areas. Manufacturing, fisheries and tourism have flourished. Soil and water conservation has achieved remarkable results. Agricultural production has tripled. Tennessee, a former backward state, has grown into an industrial state in the South. Moreover, the results of comprehensive management of the Tennessee River Basin have benefited six surrounding states, thus becoming a milestone in the history of regional economic development in the United States.

It is precisely because of the formulation of a scientific development plan that the Tennessee River Basin got rid of its backward appearance and stepped out of the slump of the past, which fully reflects the importance of planning first for River Basin development.

Source: Xiaji, Xiao Yongqin.Experience in the Development of Mississippi River and its Enlightenment to the Development of the Yangtze River Basin[J].Chongqing social sciences, 2006(5): 22-26.

(The study is sorted from the source)

2. Watershed Management and Functional Positioning

(1) Management of Trans-boundary River Basins in International Rivers Gradually Improved

Generally speaking, cross border areas of great rivers are usually rich in hydropower, forest, mineral, fishery and other resources, which have unique advantages for the development of multiple agriculture, mineral resources and metals. And most of the cross-border rivers hold an important geographical position, which has always been an important resource for countries inside and outside the basin to set their foot and to develop.

For example, the Lancang-Mekong River is the most important cross-border water system in Asia, which originated in China and flows through Myanmar, Laos, Thailand, Cambodia and Vietnam. In recent years, with the assistance of the Asian Development Bank, the six countries have jointly established the Lancang-Greater Mekong Sub-regional Cooperation Organization, which is responsible for coordinating the interests of various countries and seeking common economic development. In addition, there are a number of large rivers that address the development of cross-boarder rivers through the development of spatial watershed planning. It can be seen that the management of cross-border and cross-county rivers can better serve the economic, political and social development of the countries and regions, and this phenomenon has been recognized by many countries. In this field, foreign researchers have more experience in the practice and exploration of trans-boundary watershed management.[1]

(2) Spatial Function of Rivers Being Diversified and Life-oriented

According to different river attributes, River spatial functions can be divided into different spatial functions. River spatial functions are the embodiment of natural, ecological and social attributes of rivers and the beneficial role played by river systems. Clear division of river spatial functions is the basis of regulating and guiding river development and protection. Different countries and regions, in different historical periods, will have different functional zoning for River Tourism development. In the past, the functional zoning of rivers was mostly from the perspective of ecological function, with the main purpose of ecological protection, such as the ecological function division of the main reaches of the Yangtze River in China. But at present, the improvement of living conditions, and the change of tourism demand and other factors have emerged. In the process of tourism development, diversification and activation of spatial functions, construction of public facilities, especially the development of Commerce and tourism facilities are attached more importance. Through spatial presentation of different tourism functions, rivers can meet the needs of different tourism parties.

(3) Functional Orientation of Rivers in accordance with the Development of Cities

The early river function orientation was only the development without special tourism planning, and the product was only simple cruise ship sightseeing. With the acceleration of urbanization in China, to a large extent, river development is a universal reflection of economic and social transformation, spatial form and cultural characteristics reconstruction in the period of economic globalization and rapid urbanization, as well as in the period of development opportunities and challenges brought about by industrialization and information technology. Therefore, formulation of urban development strategy is taken into account in river development, as well as the rapid expansion of cities and other strategic activities. In river functional positioning people also began to consider the overall structure and development of the city. In this case, river development not only undertakes the role of promoting the comprehensive competitiveness of urban rivers and revitalizing the river basin economy, but also undertakes the mission of shaping the image of urban characteristics.

For the waterfront area crossing the city center, more attention should be paid to the integrity of urban life in the function orientation. Commercial facilities and various commercial means should be fully utilized and the revival of urban functions should be focused. For example, the development of Baltimore Port, in the early twentieth century, the shipping and industry of Baltimore Port gradually declined and finally

---

[1] Shen Jiexi, Zhao Youlin and Guo Lidan. Research on Geospatial Information Service Model to Trans-boundary Rivers-a Case to Mekong River. Journal of Wuhan University of Technology (Information and management Engineering), 2017, 39 (03): 330-333.

became a region full of dilapidated wharfs and warehouses. The unemployment and crime rate increased, and the material and social environment was horrible. In 1965, renovation and renewal of the inner harbor began. The goal was to integrate the central area with the inner harbor by utilizing the waterfront conditions in the city center, and to build a city life center with full vitality of business, office, entertainment and other functions. After more than ten years' operation, Money Port has finally formed major functional areas such as World Trade Center, National Aquarium, Inner Port Square, Sports and Entertainment Facilities, Waterfront Walkway and so on. It has achieved tremendous benefits in creating tax revenue, attracting tourists, providing jobs and driving the development of the city center.[1]

3. Resource Development and Product Optimization

(1) Emphasis on Comprehensive Utilization and Development of Water Resources

Water is indispensable to tourism planning and development. Because of the indispensability of water in human life and the inherent hydrophilic characteristics of human beings, water has a strong attraction and affinity for tourists. The planning and design of water resources in tourism planning and development is of great economic and social value. On one hand, water resources are highly inclusive and easy to integrate with other elements and it provides a lot of material for tourism planning; on the other hand, water can be integrated into leisure through bath, recuperation and entertainment. During leisure activities, water offers leisure and recreational space for tourists. At present, more and more countries and regions begin to attach importance to the effective use of water resources. With the help of water resources, various leisure activities are developed to stimulate tourists' enthusiasm to participate in the experience. For the development of river tourism, water is life. If water is well utilized, it will undoubtedly increase the attractiveness to river tourism.

European countries attach great importance to the development of water resources, the comprehensive utilization of water resources, and develop historical and cultural elements related to water, so as to fully tap the potential of water culture. For example, the Delta Plan formulated by the Rhine River Basin aims at comprehensive development and utilization of water resources, including shipping, flood control, water supply, tourism, power generation, irrigation, fisheries, etc., which fully consider the benefits from multi-level and multi-direction, and is also conducive to environmental protection and natural ecological balance. Moreover, all countries in the basin can closely integrate the reality of each section of the river, launch gradual development according to different levels, implement comprehensive development policy of both

---

[1] Gao Yonghong. Research of Development Strategy of Shenyang Hun River's Waterfront. Northeastern University,2005.

main and tributaries, give priority to the development of water energy and transport resources, and provide experience for the comprehensive utilization of river water resources.[①]

(2) Increased Emphasis on Diversification and Functional Optimization in Product Development

Seeking novelty and differences is one of the driving forces for tourists to travel. It is difficult to attract tourists to revisit an area with simple sightseeing function and tourist routes. Therefore, tourism products should be developed and designed as featured and diversified as possible, their own characteristics should be highlighted, and their leisure and recreational functions should also be constantly optimized. Only in this way the area stands out and attracts more tourists from other areas of same type.

River tourism products in China has gradually got rid of being unicity in tourism project development, and people began to pay more attention to diversification and enrichment of products, thus, they started to carefully categorize the product and functional zones of different tourists' needs. By constantly innovating and designing more function-optimized products while increasing interests, participation of tourists was involved to meet the needs of interaction. For example, in the planning of river vacation tourism products, not only tourists' needs for quiet and elegant environment, but also for recreation and sports should be taken into account. Therefore, the reception facilities in the resort area not only reach the standards of being comfortable, private and sense of isolation, but also a number of safe leisure and recreational facilities should be provided for tourists to participate in entertainment.

Case 1.2

Seine River in Paris: Creating a Cultural River of Romance and Leisure

The Seine River is a great river in the north of France. Its tourism development was carried out in 1989 according to the city planning of Paris. According to statistics, the annual tourism income of the Seine River is more than 10% of the total tourism income of Paris. The outstanding concepts and characteristics of Seine River tourism development lie in:

First, effective landscape protection and strong support of cultural heritage. The Seine River links Paris's most elite tourism resources together, while paying attention to the protection of cultural heritage. Perfect legislative protection, detailed survey of cultural

---

① Liu Jian. Development and Construction of Rhine River Basin and its Successful Experience. World Agriculture, vol2, 1998, pp. 3-5.

landscape resources, effective management system, and the participation of the whole people in the protection have all provided fruitful protection.

Secondly, the land-water interaction is well integrated, the cruise ship program is rich, and the river highlights the hydrophilic characteristics. Seine River tourism design is open, land-water interaction is prominent, water, shore all over the leisure places. Its yacht has complete functions and rich programs. Every time it passes through a typical landscape, the yacht's interpretation system will be matched with corresponding commentaries and related literary and artistic works to fully mobilize tourists' senses.

Thirdly, the function of city image which is in harmony with the city temperament of Paris. The Seine River is the spokesman of Paris, France. It radiates a leisurely atmosphere, an artistic atmosphere and a romantic charm everywhere. Functionally, it integrates transportation, tourism, entertainment and leisure; historically, it is the birthplace of Paris, and the Seine River has left a mark of different periods, representing the development of Paris; from the perspective of atmosphere, the Seine River is full of romance and leisure. These are the typical temperaments of Paris, such a fit makes the Seine River a typical representative of the Romantic City of Paris, and has achieved great value-added effect.

Seine River is first and foremost the river of Paris. The success of its tourism development can not be separated from the interdependence between rivers and cities, the effective utilization of water resources, the protection of river ecological landscape and the in-depth development of products based on it.

Source: Shen Hong and Feng Xuegang. Research on Tourism Development of City Cultural River——Taking Suzhou River in Shanghai as an Example. Journal of Guilin Tourism College, vol.05, 2006, pp. 542-545.

(the study based on the above source)

Section 3　Demand and Market of the Great River Civilization Tourism

This part mainly focuses on the analysis of tourist demand and market profile of the Great River Civilization tourism development. The demand of tourists may change because of the change of fashion trend, which will lead to the variation of tourist market. Under present trend of cultural tourism, the market position of Great River Civilization tourism has been upgraded. Countries and regions are also taking advantage of the circumstance, and the enthusiasm of developing the Great River Civilization tourism has increased unprecedentedly.

1. Analysis of Tourist Demand of Great River Civilization Tourism

(1) Changes of Tourism Product Consumption Preference

With the deepening of China's economic reform, the continuous improvement of science, technology and culture, people's life quality, tourists' consumption preferences for tourism products have also changed significantly. Under such conditions, tourists' demands are diversified, tastes are constantly improving, and the interests are transferring from traditional projects to modern entertainment and fashion projects. The traditional development concept of river tourism products obviously can't keep pace with the demand of tourism consumption market which emphasizes individualization, diversification of functions and pursuit of stimulation. On the contrary, some river tourism products with some experiential elements are emerging in the market and are quite popular, such as the experience of foreign folk culture, hot spring convalescence, etc. Compared with traditional fishing and swimming, people show greater interest in performances and entertainment. It can be seen that the theme of in-depth experience is indispensable for future development of high-quality tourism products in Great River Civilization tourism.

(2) Tourists' Recognition of Great River Civilization Tourism

With the arrival of the era of knowledge economy, as well as the change of tourists demand and the improvement of tourism taste, tourists do not constrain themselves to the simple appreciation of beautiful natural scenery at present. Understanding the culture and way of life in different places has become a major motivation to travel, thus promoting cultural experience tourism becomes the focus of tourism. In fact, great river civilization tourism is a kind of cultural and experience tour, which carries the mission and value of experiencing folk culture and humanistic customs in the river basin, and symbolizes the deep integration of river culture and tourism experience. It is consistent with the needs of tourists and the trend of the tourism market, and it has become an important force to attract tourists in the tourism market. Therefore, the position and role of great river civilization tourism is becoming more and more important in tourism market, and the degree of recognition from tourists is also increasing.

2. Analysis on the Supply of Great River Civilization Tourism Market

(1) Expanding the Development Range of Tourist Market

In the early stage, the development of great river tourism market was mainly based on domestic market and supplemented by overseas market. At present, with the popularity of great river tourism, maturity in tourism product design and the increasing convenience of tourism transportation, the great river tourism market began to develop further and the number of international tourists increased gradually. Some countries and regions in the large river basin have begun to expand their tourism market to foreign countries instead of confining themselves to domestic market, such as Egypt's tourism market. In recent years, Egypt has continuously launched transnational tourism routes and vigorously exploited the foreign tourism market, which has resulted in a rapid increase in the number of foreign tourists to Egypt. Simultaneously, the coverage of the source countries has been expanding as well (Figure 1.1).

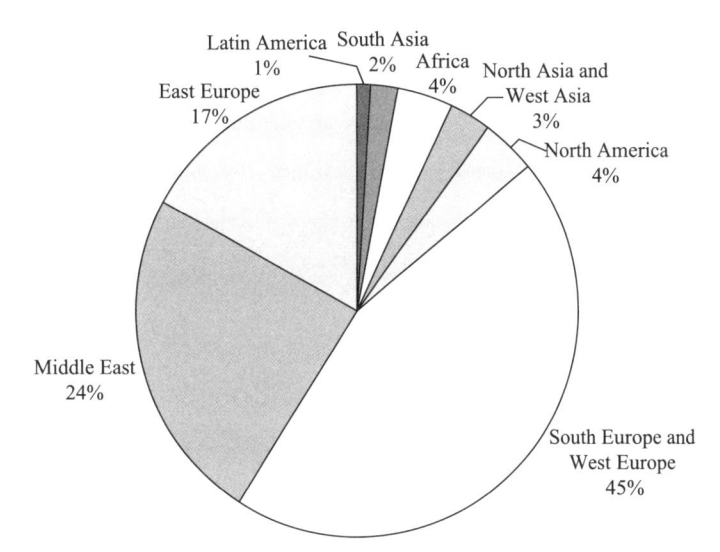

Figure 1.1 The main source of overseas tourists in Egypt's tourism market

Source: Sun Haiyan and Li Guanyun. Tourism in Egypt: 'Yellow and Blue' of New Leisure Doctrine.21st Century Business Review, vol. 05, 2005, pp. 119-123.

However, in the process of developing tourist market, how to attract international tourists continuously and how to improve the market are also signifcant. It requires regional tourism departments to increase their promotion and marketing efforts. Meanwhile, efforts should be made in product development. Only more innovative and attractive tourism products are developed, it can continuously enhance the interest of foreign tourists.

(2) Highlighting the Importance of Classification of Source Market

With the expansion of the scope and scale of great river tourism market, it is particularly necessary to divide the level of the market, because there will inevitably be different types and levels of tourism products in a river basin, such as products concerning sightseeing and leisure, vacation-oriented ecotourism products, as well as professional cultural tourism products. Among them, sightseeing and vacation tourism mainly satisfy people's leisure and relaxation needs by relaxing their mood and mentality, while cultural tourism is a kind of tourism activity with a certain purpose of seeking knowledge. Accordingly, the corresponding target market of different types of tourism products should be different. In the process of marketing, right product is expected in the right target market. For example, for cultural tourism products with higher degree of cultural specialization, the target market should have certain cultural literacy, be aware of the significance of great river culture and civilization, and are also involved in promoting cultural protection and research, rather than the mass tourism market.

Chapter Three Benefits and Challenges of River Valley Civilization Tourism Development

The river valley civilization is one of the important carriers of national spirit and culture. Under the condition of vigorous development of river tourism, the river valley civilization tourism has become one of the important means to protect the environment of water resources, indigenous customs and so on. The revival of river civilization by tourism industry can promote its sustainable development, diversify the forms of regional tourism, and speed up the river basin economy. This chapter will elaborate the benefits and the challenges of the development of river valley civilization tourism.

Section 1 Benefits of Developing River Valley Civilization Tourism

Tourism is known as the sunrise industry in the 21st century. Tourism is also an important function in the modern development of rivers. In the early tourism of the world, river sightseeing by boat is an important type for tourists. With the rapid growth in economy, science and technology, how to make the river valley civilization maintain sustainable development and continue to play its great role, people must give appropriate positioning to the function and development of the river. Developing river valley civilization tourism and forming various characteristic river tourism products are of great value to the development of tourism economy.

1. Social Benefits of Developing River Valley Civilization Tourism

(1) In Line with Industrial Development in the New Era of Cultural and Tourism Integration

In the context of the integration of culture and tourism and the transformation and upgrading of tourism industry, river valley civilization tourism is conducive to integrating the rich cultural and tourism resources along the river basin, meeting the needs of tourists for high-quality cultural tourism products, disseminating extensive and profound Chinese civilization through tourism, and becoming the space carrier of traditional river culture and modern life for the world to know China. Taking the integration of literature and tourism as the core of carrying forward the river culture, the development of tourism products provides a new stage, in which people could explore the effective path of the organic integration of culture and tourism with the help of the historical opportunity for the country to promote the Yellow River civilization tourism belt. It is also in line with the direction of industrial development in the new era of cultural and tourism integration. In addition, through the development of river valley civilization tourism, it will not only help promote the protection and inheritance of traditional river culture, but also promote the coordinated development of cross-regional innovation and integration, and then stimulate the formation of win-win cooperation in the river basin. In the process of the development of tourism economy in the river basin, large range of river tourism products, research and learning tourism products, leisure and vacation products will be gradually formed. The function of culture, tourism, economy and the society of the river can be brought into full use.

(2) Promoting the Exchange of Diversified Cultures in the World and Achieving Coordinated Development

In today's global economic integration, strengthening regional cooperation is the need of the times and the trend of development. Great rivers not only have precious water resources on which people live, but also have formed unique river civilization and culture in the course of historical development. Natural and cultural landscapes with different characteristics in different periods, such as traditional folk customs, ancient buildings and characteristic streets along the river, constitute the unique cultural landscape belt. River valley civilization tourism is carried out in different countries and cultures. Countries with river civilization also attach great importance to the protection and development of water and cultural resources of the river. In particular, river valley civilization tourism has a positive significance in promoting the unity, common prosperity and progress of all ethnic groups in the world, and can further promote the exchanges and coordinated development of multi-civilizations in the world.

First, through the development of river valley civilization tourism, we can not only strengthen the awareness of respect and protection of water resources and culture, but also promote sustainable economic development. Second, through the development of river civilization tourism, cultural exchanges and cooperation among different regions is promoted so that tourists can understand and perceive the life style, folk culture, characteristic architecture and intangible cultural heritage of the people in different river basin areas. River civilization tourism has also become a channel for people to seek cultural enjoyment and strengthen folk exchanges. Third, through the development of river civilization tourism, the linkage of culture and tourism is strengthened, the goal of complementary resources, market sharing, marketing interaction and cooperation can be ultimately achieved.

(3) Promoting Sustainable Development of Tourism in the River Basin

With people's increasing awareness of environmental protection, the great river, as an important environmental factor, will inevitably become the focus of attention and the main body of research. On the other hand, the development and research of river valley civilization tourism lies on its emphasis of the protection of natural landscape, water body, culture, folk custom and other resources according to ecological principles. Environmental protection is taken as the premise and people attach great importance to the integration of human and nature. It provides practical guidance for the sustainable development of great river civilization tourism and thus promotes its development. In China, the Yellow River Basin combines cultural tourism with eco-tourism to enrich the tourism product system and increase new economic growth and diversified tourism modes. And through the river valley civilization tourism, it will guide people to understand the river culture, respect and protect the natural and human resources related to the river.

2. Economic Benefits of Developing River Valley Civilization Tourism

(1) Promoting the Development of Tourism Economy in the River Basin

Tourism is a highly relevant and driving industry. The development of river valley civilization tourism promotes the extensive integration of the primary industry, the secondary industry and the tertiary industry in the great river basin, furthermore, it promotes the economic development of the great river basin, and the tourism economy prosperity of the big river tourism destination. The Great River is a natural and economic union connected by different geographical units linked by rivers. The resources in the river civilization basin have a lot in common, and its resource base, cultural connotation and traffic have become the dominant conditions for people to communicate in the connecting region, and it promotes the development of river civilization tourism. As a result, many large river basins have become developed economic areas. Through the development of the culture and natural resources in the river basin areas, the formation of a perfect and characteristic tourism product system can promote commerce, agriculture and other industries in the basin areas, and help to promote tourism economy, increase employment opportunities, and in turn promote poverty alleviation. Along with the trend of facilitating the development of tourism in China, river valley civilization tourism is also facing good opportunities for development. For example, the Rhine River Basin in Europe, the Seine River Basin, the Amazon River Basin in South America, the Yangtze River Delta and the Yellow River Delta in China are all developed economic circles. The development of these tourism economic circles is increasingly prosperous, and has successively become a hot trend and growing point of world tourism economy.

(2) Providing Reference for Development Model of River Tourism Destination

With the trend of speeding up tourism development in China, through in-depth analysis of the civilization and tourism development in the world's large river basins, and comparison of the development of river tourism at home and abroad, it is helpful to learn from the practices of typical cases, and to construct different development models in various regions of large river basins. It also provides suggestions and solutions for other river-based tourism destinations, as well as the experience of development model. For example, Shanxi Province has made a special development plan for the Yellow River Basin. The river valley civilization tourism in Shanxi Province can not only protect the rich natural and cultural resources in the Yellow River Basin, but also promote the development of tourism economy in the coastal areas, create a global tourism development model, and then facilitate the development of tourism economy in the river basin regions.

(3) Providing Suggestions and Solutions for Governmental Departments

The report aims at providing theoretical guidance for the government to formulate relevant policies and planning services, as well as economic, cultural and tourism development measures in the river basin regions through summary, analysis and comparison of tourism development of river civilization at home and abroad. Furthermore, it tries to find a new tourism development model suitable for China's own river civilization and promote the development of civilization and tourism in the river basin areas. It aims at promoting further integration of culture and tourism, transformation and upgrading of the cultural and tourism industry, and ultimately promote the development of the whole tourism economy.

Section 2 Challenges in the Process of Developing River Valley Civilization Tourism

The ecological environment in the river basin area is often fragile. People's production, life, as well as tourism development, tourism activities might damage the water resources, animal and plant resources, cultural resources and so on. To a certain extent, it has hindered the sustainable development of river civilization tourism. How to develop and utilize the natural and cultural tourism resources of the great rivers, and meanwhile protect all kinds of tourism resources, ecological environment, history and culture, water resources to maintain sustainable development in great river basins is an important challenge to the tourism development of the river valley civilization.

1. Protection and inheritance of Cultural Heritage

(1) Protection of Cultural Heritage

Many famous cities in the world are accompanied by a famous river, and every section of human civilization is inseparable from the breeding of the river. Ancient Babylon, ancient Egypt, ancient India and ancient China, all these successive civilizations are not only the crystallization of human wisdom, but also the achievements of the co-existence with river. The Great River is regarded as the birthplace of ancient civilization, and also the gathering place of cultural heritage. After thousands of years of development, the Great River Basin has conserved rich cultural heritage resources.

The effective development and utilization of cultural heritage resources in the River Basin is related to the sustainable development of human civilization. However, the first step in the development of cultural heritage is the protection of heritage, which is also the top priority of the whole process. Without protection, it can not be well exploited. However, many countries and cities in the River Basin still do not realize the importance of protecting the cultural heritage of the Great River. Therefore, people from all walks of life in the River Basin regions should take active measures to protect the cultural heritage and promote the harmonious coexistence of culture and nature, as well as culture and social development. Specific measures that can be taken include: establishing an international platform for cultural heritage cooperation and innovation; sharing experience in the management, development, protection and utilization of cultural resources in the river basin; building channels for communication and information exchange among cities in the river basin, strengthening intercity cooperation and innovation, promoting the integrated development of cultural heritage, tourism, science and technology, and other industries, promoting the inheritance and protection of the cultural heritage of the river, in order to realize sustainable development of the river civilization.

(2) Inheritance of Cultural Heritage

Culture is the soul of tourism and an important "identification code" to identify different regions. Tourism is the carrier of culture and is an important support to enhance cultural attractiveness. River valley civilization tourism is also a kind of cultural tourism in essence. River cultural heritage is not only the witness of the development of human civilization, but also the crystallization of human knowledge, wisdom and creation. The main characteristics and advantages of river valley civilization tourism are reflected in the inheritance and development of river cultural heritage. Cultural heritage is also the product of history in today's modern society. On one hand, in order to make cultural heritage survive, we need to do well in the process of "transformation" and adapt to the contemporary and innovate ways of the cultural inheritance of the great river. On the other hand, we should also keep the living inheritance of cultural heritage without excessive change, and maintain the authenticity of the cultural heritage on the basis of understanding the value, attributes and characteristics of the cultural heritage in the river regions. We should respect the original appearance of the cultural heritage and ensure the authenticity of the cultural heritage of the river. Only in this way can we ensure the sustainable growth of economic value and social value.

(3) Development of Cultural Heritage

The cultural heritage of the Great River is the crystallization of human civilization, which often represents human civilization and has potential attraction for tourists. Therefore, the cultural heritage of the Great River Basin including the humanistic landscape, natural landscape, folk culture, traditional culture, and scientific and technological culture along its coast should be utilized as different forms for tourism development. These cultural heritage resources have prominent historical, social and cultural values. However, in the process of developing River Cultural Heritage in many regions of the world, the tourism value and cultural value have not been effectively highlighted due to improper development methods, lack of planning and ineffective supervision. River Cultural Heritage Tourism can not be accomplished overnight, thus the development methods should be highlighted so as to meet the current and future tourism needs. People should respect the original cultural connotation and cultural appearance and guarantee they would not be changed at will. On the basis of connotation, we should exploit new river tourism products, such as historical, cultural, literary, artistic, musical and other types of river cultural heritage products for tourists. Only in this way can we widely adapt to market demand and contribute to the prominent economic, historical and intangible cultural values of the river basin.

2. Ecological Environment of the River Valley Civilization

Adhering to the harmonious coexistence between human and nature and protecting ecological civilization is the millennium plan for the sustainable development of mankind. Protecting ecological environment is not only the need for human survival and development, but also the basis of tourism and its prosperity. Therefore, we must establish and practice the idea that green water and green hills are the wealth for human beings; and we must adhere to the aim and principle of sustainable development, implement strict ecological environment protection system, form a green development mode and lifestyle, and implement the sustainable development of great river civilization tourism.

(1) Water Environmental Pollution

For thousands of years, rivers have made great contributions to human civilization, but in the past, human beings often took more than what they contributed to rivers. Due to certain artificial factors, it is not uncommon to see that water environmental pollution is becoming worse, some rivers lose the normal functions, and some river fish are extinct and the rivers lost their landscape value. Such pollution results into the decline of environmental quality, negative effect on sightseeing, entertainment and cultivation and so on. In production and daily life, most of the water pollution substances are caused by the discharge of domestic sewage and industrial waste water. Therefore, it is necessary to strictly control the water from being discharged into the river, strengthen the management of the source of river pollution from the aspects of industrial production, resident life, and agricultural production. In this case, people could ensure that long-term quality of the river can be effectively maintained after environmental control and treatment.

There are also many rivers in the world that have been carefully harnessed and restored to the original clear features. For example, the Rhine River. At first, due to the in-depth development of tourist attractions in the upper reaches of the river, the increasing number of foreign tourists, the adjustment of Alpine animal husbandry and the aggravation of the damage to the natural environment in the Alps, the water quality in the upper reaches has been highly polluted. In order to protect the Rhine River water quality and maintain the original landform, Swiss governments at all levels and professional functional departments have made great efforts. Ten laws and regulations concerning the protection of water bodies have been promulgated, including Forest Law, Environmental Protection Law, Special Waste Recycling and Transportation Regulations, Water Resources Protection Law and Environmental Protection Law. Governments also stipulate that enterprises are not allowed to discharge untreated industrial and domestic water directly into nearby water body. Even rainwater on Riverside buildings must be brought underground through eaves drainage tank, and then discharged into the water body only after treatment. Because of the strict water environment protection law, not only the source of Rhine River, but also the water quality of nearby lakes are improved and return to the clear and transparent conditions all the year round. All the water quality meets the drinking water standard. Nine countries along the Rhine River Basin have formulated an International Convention Center for the daily conservation of the Rhine River, and established a 12-member International Committee for the Protection of the Rhine River. The chairman of the Committee is rotating by the ministers from member countries. For many years, the countries in the Rhine River Basin have basically consciously conserved their respective River sections.

(2) Flood Disasters

Due to the influence of natural factors and human activities, such as the intensity and seasonal variation of precipitation, climatic and hydrological conditions, topographical conditions and other natural factors, frequent natural disasters in river basins have occurred. Floods is one of the most frequent disasters. On the one hand, flood and waterlogging disasters have brought great damage to human production and socioeconomic development, such as destroying houses, directly causing a large number of casualties, resulting in the destruction of farmland, city walls and water conservancy buildings, and bringing about serious refugee problems, causing economic fluctuations and so on. On the other hand, flood disasters also have a great negative impact on river tourism, such as directly destroying tourism landscape and tourism facilities, restricting the demand of river tourism market, hindering tourism traffic, endangering the personal safety of tourists and so on. Therefore, the development of river tourism should establish corresponding measures to prevent flood disasters including improving the flood disaster early warning and prevention system, establishing flood disaster safety shelters, and ensuring the personal safety of tourists. In addition, it is also necessary to do a better job in environmental protection, reducing deforestation, appropriate land reclamation, improving forest coverage, and reducing the frequency of natural disasters.

(3) Forest Degradation

The large-scale development and utilization of the great river basin can endanger the survival and development of the great river system itself. Among them, excessive deforestation which leads to the forest degradation and the destruction of ecosystem stability is a typical example. Forest is an important ecological protection belt and biological habitat in the great river basin. Once it is overharvested, it will lead to the destruction of biodiversity, the deterioration of ecosystem and the decline of ecological function, and even bring a series of natural disasters. Tourism development of the river basin is also inseparable from high-quality forest resources. Forest resources is one of the important ways of river tourism development for tourists to carry out leisure and recreational activities. The degradation of forest resources in the river basin will therefore inevitably restrict the development of river tourism.

Amazon basin is a typical case of forest degradation. Excessive logging has resulted in vegetation destruction, forest degradation, soil and water loss, water reduction, and river siltation. Forest degradation in Amazon also leads to the weakening of the role of tropical rainforest, which has seriously impacted on the earth in the basin areas. In order to protect the Amazon basin, Ecuador has launched a resource conservation project aiming at mitigating deforestation and climate change, protecting the world's most biologically diverse region, and the indigenous peoples who live there.

3. Planning and Development of River Valley Civilization Tourism

(1) The Lack of Cultural Characteristics in Tourism Products

Tourism products should not only be explored and innovated from the external form, but also need to be excavated and created in a cultural sense. Tourism products of the river valley civilization, as the embodiment of human civilization, must be the most coordinated presentation of both external expression and internal cultural connotation. However, in the actual development of river tourism products in a certain extent are limited in category, and lacking regional characteristics and cultural connotation, which directly leads to the decline of the attractiveness of river tourism resources, and reduces the expectations of tourists and affects tourism market demand. River tourism products should not only be a mere formality, but should profoundly present the connotation of river culture, embody the characteristics of river culture, and make tourism products play as a linkage between river culture and the tourists. The cultural attributes of the river will be widely spread to tourists, so that tourists can experience the charisma of river culture and stimulate emotional resonance, so that it could convey sense of identity and pride to human civilization from tourists.

(2) The Lack of Organic Combination in Tourism Product

Although the developing methods of river tourism products at home and abroad have been continuously improved and innovated in recent years, there are still a large number of problems in the fragmented development of the international development for river tourism products. Many river tourism products are still rough, crude, fragmented and lack of organic combination. This kind of scattered and spread product development mode is inefficient and shallow, which is easy to cause many problems, such as inefficient tourism, poor experience of tourists, broken tourism ecological space and so on, which is not conducive to in-depth river tourism. Therefore, it is necessary to put an end to the occurrence of fragmented product development from the source of planning and build a perfect river tourism product system. Based on the comprehensive analysis of the resources, market demand and competitive environment of the great river tourism destination, this paper integrates the great river tourism products, emphasizes the embodiment of the regional cultural characteristics, highlights the positioning of the tourism image, promotes the coordinated development of the great river tourism products. It also forms the product system of the big river basin with the combination of great river tourism which is clear in importance, rich in content and profound in culture.

(3) Low Level of Tourism Product

Great River tourism products bear a heavy river culture, which is its presentation and dissemination. The product development should be strictly controlled and highly valued. At present, there are many problems of the product, such as unitary product, lack of creativity, lack of prominent characteristics of tourism resources and so on. The level product development is quite low, which has little attraction for tourists and does not show the economic and social value that should be presented. In view of this situation, River tourism management departments should pay attention to upgrading the quality and improving the quality of tourism products. With the rapid growth of river tourism market and the expansion of tourism demand, river tourism products need to be innovated according to market segmentation and integration of tourism resources and identification of tourism market, explore the characteristics of resources, and make high-quality tourism products with cultural connotations. For example, products with cultural tourism, water tourism, Eco-sports tourism, folk tourism, heritage tourism and other themes can be developed, which demonstrates quality and diversification, and enhances the attractiveness to tourists.

4. Management and Policies

(1) Management by Multi-departments

There are many international rivers in the world. Because of the richness of the river resources, the interests of strategic parties and the sharing of international river rights, the problems of river development are complicated. In the process of development, multiple stakeholders are involved and the types are quite different, which can be divided into regional sovereign government organizations, foreign government, non-governmental organizations and local people. The roles, rights and responsibilities of each stakeholder within the management process are different, and the external forces often interfere with the watershed planning and management according to their own strategic interests. And the situation leads to management from multi-departments, which makes it very passive for the independent management power of the countries in the region. This pluralistic state of management is not only easy to cause all kinds of disputes due to clashes of interest and hinder the development and construction of tourism in river basins, but also many government functional departments participate in planning and management together, which can easily lead to overlapping of functions and difficult to achieve the complementary benefits from river development.

(2) Resource Allocation

Cross border rivers are often rich in resources, and most of them occupy important geographical positions, so they are important tourism resources for countries inside and outside the basin. However, due to different national strategic between countries inside and outside the basin, the interests of various countries vary, and the demand for resources is different, which leads to the complexity of the environment of cross border river resources. In fact, no matter the problem is the development of river resources or the coordination of the interests of various countries, the distribution of resource ownership is the only cause of the problem. Due to the unclear allocation of cross-border river resources and the ambiguity of resource service objects, the development of resources has become complex, and this phenomenon is hindering the exchange and cooperation among river basin countries, as well as the sharing of river resources. In addition, due to the unclear allocation of river resources, it is difficult to implement management and protection of river resources in an orderly and healthy manner. Some countries in cross-border river basins have made every effort to develop river resources in order to obtain current benefits. What they have done, On the one hand, has caused ecological problems such as abnormal changes in river water level, increased erosion of river embankments and reduction of fish, which is not conducive to the stability of the surrounding environment and the sustainable utilization of water, land and other resources. On the other hand, it also increases the economic cost of river tourism development and affects the sustainable utilization of river resources.

(3) Formulation of Laws and Regulations

The development of international rivers is concerned with national relations in the basin, national economic and social development, as well as the protection of the ecological environment and other issues. If the development of international rivers is not handled properly, it will often lead to international disputes between two or more parties, and even regional instability. Therefore, in order to solve the contradictions and disputes, laws and regulations concerning the construction of international river are necessary, and a sound legal system is the guarantee for its success. Although some international non-governmental organizations and relevant United Nations agencies have begun to explore and formulate relevant laws and regulations on rivers since the beginning of this century, such as the Geneva Convention, the Declaration on the Human Environment, the report of the United Nations Conference on Water Conservancy (Annex) , etc., most of these regulations do not have the legal effect to regulate. During the development and utilization of water resources in international rivers, these international laws and other documents are regarded as a reference only and have not become a common law that basin countries must abide by. Therefore, at present, there is not a uniform international law relating to international rivers. In this case, the construction of international river laws and regulations is still an important issue that countries around the world need to improve. Without restrictions of laws and regulations, the problem of international river development will be difficult to resolve, and the contradictions and disputes among countries will also be difficult to settle.

Part II
Tourism Development Model of River Valley civilization

Chapter One   Integration of Culture and Tourism

Regions along the great rivers contain deep historical and cultural deposits and huge potential for tourism development. Advantages in both natural landscape and human tourism resources of the river promote the new industrial trend of the integration of river valley civilization and tourism. The integration and development of culture and tourism not only shows the inheritance and innovation of the river valley civilization, but also brings about new opportunities for the tourism development in the river region. On the topic of promotion of culture and tourism, many perspectives can be valuable for the analysis of the win-win mode between tourism and river valley civilization, including the brand creation of cultural heritage and tourism, development of museum-based tourist sites, collaborative development in basin areas, etc. This section will analyze the core attraction of river from four perspectives, ancient river valley civilization, water projects, landscape and culture, and regional folk-custom, and further develop a discussion about the integration of culture and tourism of river valley civilization.

Section 1   Integration Driven by the Core Attraction of Ancient River Valley Civilization

This part focuses on the integration model driven by the core attraction of ancient river valley civilization. A wealth of historical sites, legends and events are important carriers of river culture as well as the basis of tourism resources which mainly attract tourists by ancient river valley civilization. The integrative development is of vital importance for the sustainable development of ancient river valley civilization.

1. Archaeological Discovery

Archaeological discovery refers to the material objects or cultural traditions left by ancient human activities found by archaeologists in fieldwork by exacavating and studying the ancient remains, facilitated through historical documents and supplementary means (modern technology). The major objects found in the archaeological process are cultural heritage, including both tangible and intangible ones. Tangible cultural heritage includes all assets of a materialized embodiment of cultural value, like historical towns, buildings, archaeological sites, cultural landscapes, cultural objects, collections, and museums, and intangible cultural heritage includes practices, performances, knowledge, skills and related tools, objects, crafts and cultural sites that are considered as cultural heritage.[①]

(1) Archaeological Discovery and Type of Ancient River Valley Civilization

The archaeological discovery of ancient river valley civilization focuses on the discovery of the historical site because it is the most representative and precious form of cultural relics as well as cultural heritages. Its historical and social value witnesses the long history of river valley civilization. In the process of excavation of the historical site, the evolution of river valley civilization can be deduced, which benefits contemporary generations in understanding the beginning, development, prosperity, and decline of the civilizations in the aspects of agricultural production, political system, military, technology and culture, etc. For example, in the excavation of the Nile Valley, the sites presented how the emerging local dignitaries in southern Egypt used advanced production technology to show their identity by accumulating surplus products, monopolizing luxury goods, and constructing a series of models to represent their status and power with written words and objects.[②] The excavation of the historical sites of Neolithic culture, including Yangshao, Longshan, Dawenkou in the middle and lower reaches of the Yellow River, and Yin relics in Anyang and other former cities in the Shang and Zhou dynasties, proves that the Yellow River Basin is the birthplace of Chinese culture. Tell el-Samara site excavated in the Nile Delta, southern Egypt, is another example, which is the oldest historical site of farming culture ever discovered in the world.[③]

Archaeological sites of ancient river valley civilization can be categorized into ancient city, tomb, cultural heritage, stone monuments, etc. according to their types. From the dimension of movability, cultural heritages found in the archaeological sites can also be categorized into movable and unmovable ones. The movable cultural heritages can be passed on, distributed in the museums in the area of river valley civilization: the Louvre Museum on the North Bank of the Seine River, the British Museum on the Thames River and the Cairo Museum on the East Bank of the Nile River, Egypt, all restore abundant relics

---

① Du Cros, Hilary, and Bob Mckercher. Cultural Tourism. 2nd ed., translated by Zhu Luping, Beijing: The Commercial Press, 2017, p. 83.

② Jin Shoufu. Origins of Ancient Egyptian Civilization: Endogenous and Hybridized Views. Social Sciences in China Press, vol. 12, 2012, pp. 179-200, p. 209.

③ Zheng Ruokui. "The World's Earliest Agricultural Cultural Relics Discovered in Egypt." Agricultural Archaeology, vol. 1, 1987, p. 115.

of river valley civilization. Unmovable cultural heritages can be seen all over the world, like pyramids and the Sphinx in Egypt, the Mehrger Civilization Sites in the Indus Valley, the Hemudu and the Liangzhu Cultural Site, and sites of ancient cities in the Yangtze River Valley.

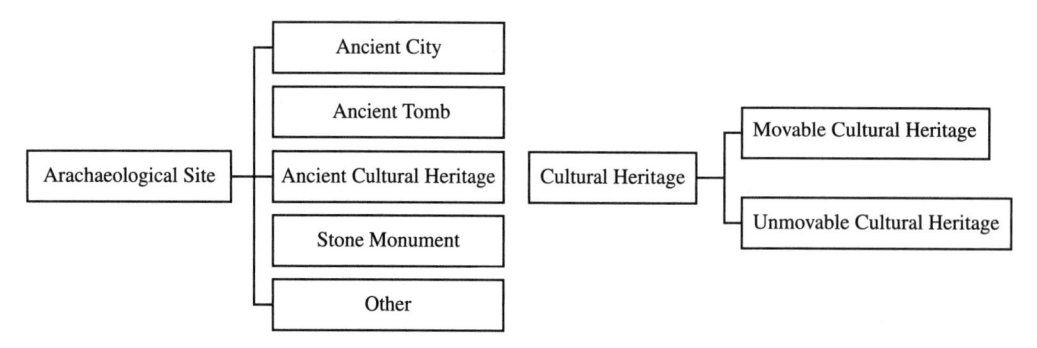

Figure 2.1 Categorization of Archaelogical Site and Cultural Heritage

Source: Concluded from this report.

(2) Culture-Tourism Integration Driven by the Core Attraction of Archaeological Discovery of River

a. Construction of Tourist Sites: Museums or Parks of Ancient Sites

Preservation and development of archaeological sites in the region of river valley civilization are carried out in order to protect the sites, share and spread the culture, and improve the public curiosity and love for the sites. Thus the museums and parks of ancient sites are constructed to display their affluent culture and history. The museums and parks of ancient sites should hold a distinct theme, use diverse ways of presentation, and improve the interaction. Yuanmingyuan Ruins Park, for example, takes the ruin as the theme, having become a unique tourist landscape combining the still history with the lived parks and gardens. The park of the ancient site integrates the comprehensive functions of archaeology, education, and leisure. As a representative of American national park of cultural heritage, Independence National Historical Park of the United States is dedicated to the overall protection and utilization of cultural heritage. Its partnership includes 13 public and private departments, including National Constitution Center (NCC) , Philadelphia Convention and Visitors Bureau (PCVB) , Eastern Naitonal, Greater Philadelphia Tourism Marketing Corporation (GPTMC) , etc. They collaborate for the activities like the preservation of the park, education, tour guide, tourism development, etc. "Discover History" is the core mission of the Park. It aims to make people deeply understand and actively explore American history by protecting and interpreting cultural heritage of great historical significance. The administration of the park defines "Discover History" from four perspectives: "American Stories", "Preserve Places", "Educating & Training", and "Heritage Travel". Taking these as the basis, a comprehensive system with the core of preservation has been formed, covering the functions of research, display, education, leisure, etc.[1]

b. Development of Shared Cultural Background: Cross-regional Tourism Projects

The market value of cultural tourism routes can increase with the expansion of their international geographical scope. The market network formed by integrating tourism products with neighboring countries may increase the number of foreign tourists. As early as in 1987, Council of Europe promoted the route of Santiago de Compostela, which is the first route of cultural heritage of the EU. The route, advocating the travel in the dimension of both time and space, shows how the cultural heritages of different European countries with different cultural backgrounds constitute a whole culture route with shared cultural background. This route is also a network for pilgrims. Pilgrims follow the route guided by signs and maps, and at the end of the journey they can ask for a certificate issued by the Catholic Church to commemorate their journey. The provincial governments on both sides of the border between France and Spain are responsible for tourism publicity. The route is also listed on the World Heritage List. Serbia regards Danube Cultural Heritage as the strategic focus of its national tourism development. In 2009, the Ministry of Culture in Serbia launched the pilot tourism project of "Culture route-Fortresses on the Danube" and established Danube Competence Center - Regional Tourism Cooperation in Belgrade in 2010. Twenty-two members from Republic of Croatia and six countries in the region of the Black Sea joined in. The Center's purpose is to link stakeholders in tourism of the Danube region to strengthen mutual cooperation in tourism and promote the development and utilization of historical and cultural resources of the Danube.[2] Such successful experience can be learned. Since the distribution of river ancient cultural heritages is relatively concentrated, numerous ancient buildings and sites gathered can be regarded as a whole and continuous entity, so that the routes with different themes of cultural tourism can be planned.

c. Construction of the Heritage Corridor of Ancient River Valley Civilization

Heritage corridor is a new mode of heritage protection recognized internationally, which has important value in heritage protection and development. The concept originates in the United States, which refers to the measurements taken to protect the historical and cultural heritages in a large range of the country, especially the resources of rivers, canals, and roads whose shapes are linear and corridor-like. It not only pays attention to the protection of historical and cultural heritages and sites along the corridor and the radiation area, but also focuses on the development and utilization of the resources. Tourism is one of the

---

[1] Wang Jingchuan. Research on the National Historical Parks of America and Their Enlightenments to China, 2018(01): 119-128.

[2] Terzić, Aleksandra, and NevenaĆurĉić. "Culture Resources in Fuction of Regional Development and International Cooperation - Danube Region, Serbia."Geographica Timisiensis, vol. 1, 2016, pp. 45-57.

important functions as well.[1] In the United States, maturely constructed heritage corridor includes John H. Chafee Blackstone River Valley National Heritage Corridor, and Cane River National Heritage Area. In the river region, the resources of large-scale, cross-regional, and linear heritages are abundant. American's practice of heritage corridor is highly practical and applicable to the protection of the ancient river valley civilization's heritages and sites. Some scholars have already proposed to construct the heritage corridor of the Yangtze Gorges to achieve the transformation of archaeological results of cultural relics in the Yangtze Gorges of the Yangtze River into tourism. The proposal also mentions that ancient tombs such as Longgupo Site and Yang Can Tomb can be included in the corridor as important cultural tourism resources.

d. Re-discovery of the Modern Value of Ancient Culture

i. Cultural and creative products. Many movable relics of ancient river valley civilization are restored in the museum. In recent years, many world-known museums combine tourism with culture, developing cultural and creative products with the collection as the model. On one hand, the cultural resource can be turned into economic profit. On another, a health development can be promoted that the revenue can be used for the protection of the relics and the enhancement of exhibition hall. A famous example is the British Museum. Inspired by the ancient Egyptian's Rosetta Stone, one of the most precious treasures in the museum, the museum designed 69 cultural and creative products based on the appearance of Rosetta Stone, including mug, passport holder, mouse mat, etc. It also designed a series of souvenirs of yellow duck combining with the museum's collections, decorating the ducks as Sphinx, Japanese samurai, ancient Roman soldier, viking pirate, and so on. Therefore, the modern value of river culture should be utilized. The diversity of the Internet and other new media should be fully utilized, and the cultural and creative products of the river based on the Internet and mobiles should be strongly developed in order to promote the publicity and presentation of river culture's brand resources on different platforms.

ii. Festivals and great events, including festival activities, sport events, exhibitions, etc. Various cultural and festival events are held in the river region all over the world, traditional ones, like the Seb Festival in Egypt and Chath Puja in India, and newly founded ones, like New Orleans Jazz & Heritage Festival. Since the foundation in 1970, New Orleans Jazz & Heritage Festival, as an inheriting music festival, celebrates the unique culture and heritages of New Orleans and Louisiana every year and holds special cultural and historical activities on the extensive square. The Grandstand gives Festival-goers a chance to take an intimate look at the vibrant culture, cuisine and art of Louisiana. Folk life village displays traditional indigenous native crafts from many Louisiana native tribes, such as the art of basket

---

[1] Gong Daode, Yuan Xiaoyuan and Zhang Qingping. The Analysis of the Operational Mechanism of the American National Heritage Corridor and its Enlightenment to the Conservation and Development of the Large-Scale Linear Cultural Heritage in China. Urban Studies, vol. 23, no. 1, 2016, pp. 17-22.

weaving, wood carving, and beadwork. Visitors can enjoy traditional American food while appreciating the traditional pow wow dancing. Cultural Exchange Pavilion (CEP) was established to honor New Orleans' cultural ancestry. Children's Art Workshop becomes an effective way for children coming from other places to contact the local culture. The festival, besides Jazz performances, also promotes visual arts and local culture.[1]

2. Historical Legends

Historical legend is a charming intangible tourism resource. It takes reality as its prototype, and imagination transcends the reality into art with the narration of the joys and sorrows between human being and God or between people and people to deduce the truth, goodness and beauty in people's hearts. As an ancient cultural genre, historical legends have rich economic and cultural values in today's society. At the same time, because of its extensive connection with the cultural customs of various nationalities and scenic spots, historical legend enriches the cultural connotation of tourist attractions, and is itself an important tourist resource.

(1) Well-known Historical Legends of Ancient River Valley Civilization

Deeply influenced by religion sagas, the ancient river valley civilization's legends form a huge legend system, involving the praise of the Gods, heroes and kings, the creation of the world, the flood, etc., and were popular in the ancient times. Below are two popular legends.

a. Legend of the Danube

On one part of the Danube in Budapest, there are nine bridges, and it is said that when the ship sails under the bridge, the wish of the person on the bridge may come true. The visitor thus can make nine wishes. Among these nine bridges, the Chain Bridge is the most famous one. As the legend goes, in the past, people pushed the Chain Bridge into the channel of Castle Hill when it rained to avoid being wet.[2]

b. Legend of King Yu Taming the Flood

It is said that in the time of King Yao, floods took place frequently in the drainage area of the Yellow River. To prevent the flood and protect the agricultural production, King Yao assembled leaders in the tribes and recruited the expert to manage the water. Jing was recommended and when he accepted the task, he built dams to block the water, but he failed after nine-year attempt. Finally, he was exiled to Mountain Yu and died. When King Shun succeeded to the throne, he employed Jing's son Yu to manage the water.

---

[1] New Orleans Jazz & Heritage Festival. http://www.nojazzfest.com.Accessed 10 Sept. 2019.

[2] Zhao Qiankun, Lu Te, Hong Yi, et al. "River: the Meridian of World Civilization." China Three Gorges, vol. 2, 2009, pp. 71-77.

Yu summarized his father's experience and changed to dredge the channel. The flood was guided to the dredged channels, swamps or lake, then flowed into the sea. Thus, the disaster was solved. To memorize Yu, Chinese called Yu as God and the land of China as "Yu Ji", which means Yu benefited the places to which he had been.

(2) Culture-Tourism Integration Driven by the Core Attraction of Historical Legends of River

a. Construction of Tourism Landscape

Legendary figures left a wealth of sites of activities or commemoration. These sites are not only the carrier of myths and legends, but also indispensable material foundation for developing tourism resource. Historical legends can be a cultural resource today, for instance, they can provide the raw material of folk stories, the temples can be rebuilt, and they can also act as the cultural background of the construction of tourism landscape. Since 1980s, the temples of Yu were rebuilt in a large scale, and the typical ones include the Temple of Yu in Yuzhou and Hejin. A typical case of the construction of tourism landscape is the Pharaonic Village in Egypt. Designed by a famous Egyptian scholar Dr. Ragab, the Village locates on the Jacob Island on the Nile River in Cairo, built totally in accordance with the ancient Egyptian style written in the historical documents. In the Village, people live an ancient life. They are familiar with the history of Ancient Egypt. They wear the clothes in the pharaonic era and hold the replica of the tools used in the ancient Egypt. Men are engaged in farming, grazing, water hanging, pottery making, while women are engaged in harvesting, processing, textile, and waiting on guests and performing and singing for them.[①] Around the island stood many statues, which were restored from Egyptian mythology, including the statue of the Nile God, Osiris and his wife Isis, Bastet, etc. The revival of space with the theme of historical legends and the creation of human tourism landscape provide new resources and ways for the construction of local economy and culture.

b. Artistic Adaption

TV dramas and films are able to promote the cultural tourism of river valley civilization. They are indirect publicity of the place where the historical legends take place. When people are attracted by the dramas/films' stories, images, and narration, they may have the impulse to visit the place. Today many dramas and films are adapted from myths and legends, like India's TV dramas "Devon KeDevmahadev", "Vighnaharta Ganesh", Egypt's TV drama "The Seventh Scroll" and film "Gods of Egypt", and China's TV dramas "The Legend of Deification", "The Foolish Old Man Removed Mountains", etc. In addition, increasing sites actively develop the cultural resources for tourism to spread the local culture and improve

---

[①] Dai Huikun. "Antique Tourist Destination: the Pharaonic Village in Egypt." World Affairs, vol. 22, 1990, p. 21.

the industrial development. They design live performances to convey distinguish tourism theme and images. For example, WeihaiHuaxia Tourism "Huaxia Legend" combines the sound, visual and electronic technologies to give performances of the Chinese classical stories of Nuwa's Legend, Houyi Shooting the Nine Suns, the Goddess on the Moon, and so on. These performances attract the visitors by local dances and special effects, and improve the reputation of the tourist site at the same time.

c. Tourism in the Festival Season (Public Relations)

Good timing matters. The effect of large-scale activities and events should be well utilized to carry out tourism promotion, because the unique festival activities have special attraction for tourists and help tourists to experience the real cultural atmosphere. The cultural connotation of folklore can enable more tourists to participate in the activities, which can improve the popularity of river tourism and expand its influence. Tourism Festival is a popular means of tourism promotion in the industry today. With the help of the extensive influence of "Tourism Culture Festival", it can highlight its characteristics, form a scale-up effect and activate the market.

3. Historical Events

Historical events refer to the ones happened in the history and seen as historically influential by the historians at the time or later. This variety of events, casting important historical influence to the time or the future, always last for a certain period of time in large or small scale, led by several leaderships and responded or participated by mass people.

(1) Types of Important Historical Events in the Ancient River Valley Civilization

In the evolution of ancient river valley civilization in the world, some crucial historical events affected the direction and process of civilization. Shangyang's Reform, for example, enabled the economic and military development in Qin dynasty, which led Qin to become the most prosperous power-concentrated state in the later period of Warring States. Another example is *The Code of Hammurabi*. This code of law published in the climax of the ancient Babylon represents a great achievement of ancient eastern civilization. The principles set in the code, especially the ones about claims, contracts, torts, families and criminal law, all influence the legislation in the future. The historical events of ancient river valley civilization can be categorized as below.

a. Wars

Many wars took place during the evolution of ancient river valley civilization. Some affected the change of the dynasties, and some directly led to the decline or perish of the civilization. In ancient Babylon, wars include the invasion of Amorites and the war with Assyria. The invasions of Persian Empire and Macedonia are famous wars in ancient India. Ancient Egypt were also intruded by Libyans and Persians in addition to the Hittite War. In ancient China, there are more famous wars, like state wars during the periods of Spring and Autumn and Warring States, Chensheng and Wuguang Uprising, the Battle in Julu, and the Battle between Chu and Han in Qin Dynasty, the Battle in Guandu and the Battle in Chibi in the Eastern Han Dynasty, the Battle in Feishui in the Eastern Jin Dynasty, Anshi Rebellion in Tang Dynasty, etc.

b. Reforms and Revolutions

After series of political, economic and cultural reforms, the river valley civilization left an important mark in the human history of civilization. Hammurabi formulated the world's first relatively complete law code –*The Code of Hammurabi*; ancient Egypt established a monarchy system, in which Pharaoh served as a symbol and representative of state power, strictly controlling the national economy. Reform is also an everlasting topic of ancient China: in the 7th Century B.C., Guanzhong's Reform decides the citizen categorization of politician, peasant, craftsman, and businessman as well as the policy of national-controlled trade of salt and metal. In the 4th Century B.C., Shangyang's Reform established land private ownership, household registration system and military title system. The first emperor of Qin founded the system of prefectures and counties, united the currency, measurements and official character's font. Emperor of Wu in Han Dynasty also developed the reforms on industry, trade, currency, financial tax and other core issues. The prosperity of Confucian thoughts is also a part of the reforms.

c. Technology and Culture

Historical events of technology and culture involve the emergence and development of literature, mathematics, astronomy, physics, architecture, etc., as well as the invention breakthroughs of technologies like weaving and ceremics. The cuneiform character is a major invention of Sumerians in Mesopotamia. Ancient Egyptian also reached high achievements in technology and culture. Their mathematicians and geometists were able to calculate the area of isosceles triangles, rectangles, trapezoids and circles. In addition to astronomy, they also invented water clock, sundial, plough, water drawer and channel, even the first paper in the world made by reed. Ancient China's economic and cultural development was also promoted by historical events, such as Zhang Heng's invention of seismogragh, CaiLun's enhancement of papermaking technology, JiaSixie's publishing of *Arts for the People*, and the dredge of the Grand Canal from Beijing to Hangzhou.

(2) Culture-Tourism Integration Driven by the Core Attraction of Historical Events of River

a. Construction of Tourist Site: On the Heritage of Important Historical Events

Important historical events attract the scholars, researchers and visitors. Taking historical events as a source of tourism attraction, the construction of the tourist site with the theme of a certain historical event is also a model of integration. Many tourism programs are established around the ruins of the ancient wars. A typical example is the tourist site of the battlefield of the Battle in Chibi. The ancient battlefield of Chibi locates on the southern bank of the midstream of the Yangtze River, and the golden channel of the River lies here. The Battle itself is one of the seven famous battles that the weak force overcomes the superior one, and the battlefield is also the only ruin of the ancient battles that is preserved as the original, so this place is a carrier of people's memory of the Three Kingdoms.[1] The whole tourist site integrates the ruins of the ancient battlefield with the Han-style architectural complex. In the site, there are statues of historical figures like Zhuge Liang and Zhou Yu, the revivification of locality of historical events, like Chibi Mountain, Nanping Mountain and Jinluan Mountain, and tens of human landscape including the exhibition hall, cultural corridor, tower, etc. The site also develops a camp for research and study, expands "the training base of sailors", and designs the large-scale live performances that represent the characteristics of the Three Kingdoms and the local. With comprehensive functions of sightseeing, leisure, scientific research, and education, the tourist site built with the theme of historical events becomes an efficient practice of the integration of culture and tourism.

b. Innovative Research and Development of Cultural Tourism: With the Theme of Historical Events

Many important historical events took place in the ancient river valley civilization. The representative events can be the source of the innovative R&D, being transformed into abundant cultural tourism products. For example, Fanta Wildlife Adventure in Datong produced a 360° ring-screen 3D film about China's history. Based on the China's history, the twenty-minute film shows many important historical events from the legendary period of King Yan and King Huang to contemporary China. The audience wears special glasses to watch the 3D film. When the film is played, the ring screen embraces the audience and guides them into a vivid world.[2]

c. Construction of Memorial Architecture: In the Name of Historical Events or Celebrities (Tombs, Museums, Monuments, Temples, etc.)

To memorize the historical events and related celebrities, many places in the world build memorial architecture. Visitors may have an immersive experience in the specific site with the utilization of digital technologies, like VR and media. For example, to memorize the historical contribution of CaiLun for the enhancement of papermaking technology, the Temple of Cai in Moyang builds the CaiLun's Museum of Paper Culture and the Memorial Hall of CaiLun. In addition to visit to the exhibition, the visitors can also experience the papermaking technology themselves in the special interactive area. The Mevlana Museum, in front of the tomb of Rumi (Rumi is a poet and mystic living in the 13th Century, the founder of the dance

---

[1] Ancient Battlefield of the Three Kingdoms. http://www.chinachibi.com/intro/1.html. Accessed 10 Sept. 2019.
[2] Fantawild Adventure. http://datong.fangte.com. Accessed 10 Sept. 2019.

ritual of Whirling), holds the dance performance of Whirling to express the memorial for Rumi. If the visitors would like to salute to Rumi, they can also join in the dance.

Section 2   Integration Driven by the Core Attraction of Water Project

This part will briefly introduce the water projects for power generation and of water management at first, then explains the development mode of the cultural tourism based on river projects. River projects have various functions and huge social, economic benefits, and broad application prospects. They also become landmarks and promote the cultural tourism of the basin area due to the excellent architecture, abundant landscape types and rich humanistic spirit and thought.

1. Water Projects for Power Generation

(1) Hydropower Projects

a. Introduction and Present Situation

Water energy is an inexhaustible, renewable and clean energy. However, in order to effectively utilize natural water energy, it is necessary to construct hydraulic structures, such as dams, diversion culverts, which can concentrate the water drop and regulate the flow. Hydropower project requires large amount of investment and long construction period, but it is advanced because of its high efficiency, low cost, fast start-up and easy regulation. Its basic principle is to use the water level difference to generate electricity with the hydro-generator, that is, to use the potential energy of water to turn into the mechanical energy of the hydro-turbine, and then use the mechanical energy to drive the generator to obtain electricity. Scientists take advantage of the natural conditions of the water level drop, make effective use of hydrodynamic engineering and mechanical physics, carefully collocate to achieve the highest power generation, thus cheap and pollution-free electricity can be provided. Low-level water circulates around the earth by absorbing sunlight, thus high-level water sources can be recovered.

As a clean and renewable energy source, hydropower resources have been paid more attention and developed on a large scale in the countries all over world. Under the background of the depletion of traditional energy, such as coal, natural gas and oil, and the huge environmental pressure caused by the consumption of traditional energy, as well as the appeal for environmental protection, clean hydropower resources have been paid more and more attention by all countries. Therefore, hydropower projects are constructed or prepared in many river valleys. As early as in 1878, France established the first hydropower plant in the world before the emergence of Hoover Dam in America and the Yangtze Gorges Dam. The hydropower is built on the upper stream of the Yangtze River and is the largest dam in the world now. It is obvious that the number of hydropower projects is increasing worldwide. Most of today's hydropower projects are modern large-scale water conservancy projects, many of which have the characteristics of comprehensive development and management, so they are often referred to as "comprehensive utilization of hydro-junction projects". It often takes into account the multiple functions of flood control, irrigation, power generation, navigation, river regulation and inter-basin water diversion, and sometimes even includes aquaculture, water supply or other development objectives, optimizing the allocation of water resources, and constituting a comprehensive utilization system of water resources.

b. Significance and Influence

First of all, there is no doubt that hydropower projects bring direct and significant economic benefits in the form of providing electricity, and indirect economic benefits through promoting the development of related industries, stimulating employment and increasing tax revenue. Moreover, hydroelectric power generation uses renewable energy, which has less impact on the environment. In addition to providing cheap electricity and minimizing the impact on the environment, the construction of hydropower projects has other advantages. In terms of ecology, it controls flooding, reduces natural disasters such as drought, improves local climate and reduces environmental pollution; on production and living, it provides irrigation water and improves river navigation; in addition, the project can improve transportation, power supply and economy in the region, especially tourism and aquaculture, etc. For example, the comprehensive development plan of Tennessee River in America is a great hydropower project which promotes the economic development.[1] Spending a billion dollars, the Aswan Dam built by Egypt from 1959 to 1970 controls the annual floods in the Nile, protecting the residents and crops, irrigating tens of millions farmlands, improving the navigation capacity of upstream and downstream, and providing a large amount of electricity. Most importantly, the Aswan Reservoir has effectively prevented drought and flooding in Egypt.[2]

The construction of hydropower projects can bring people a variety of benefits, such as providing clean and large amounts of electricity, and reducing the risk of flood, but it also inevitably causes some negative consequences. The construction of hydropower projects has different impacts on the natural features, ecological environment and even regional climate of rivers, lakes and nearby areas.

c. Requirements for Development

Not every river basin is appropriate for hydropower project construction, so the decision should

---

[1] Chen Xuejun. "Experience and Enlightenment of World Reservoir Dam Tourism Development." Consumer Economics, vol. 29, no. 1, 2013, pp. 71-74.

[2] Luo Meijie. "Cultural Comparison between Three Gorges Project and Foreign Water Conservancy Projects: A Case Study of Hoover Dam, Grand Coulee Dam, Aswan Dam and Itaipu Dam." China Three Gorges Tribune, vol. 2, 2014, pp. 1-8.

be made carefully. Many factors should be considered for the project construction, and below are some requirements.

i. Hydropower generation is an integral part of the comprehensive development, management and utilization system of water resources. Therefore, when planning hydropower projects, it is necessary to take into account the needs of power generation, flood control, irrigation, navigation, drifting, water supply, aquaculture, tourism and other aspects. To meet the requirements of all relevant aspects and to achieve maximum benefits, the full utilization of water resources and a comprehensive river planning is required.

ii. At the same time, social factors must be considered. When developing and constructing hydropower projects, it is necessary to protect multiple interests. To ensure the sustainable development of hydropower projects, the affected local people must be given legal rights and direct benefits. The goal of hydropower project development is to ensure that all individuals and communities affected by it can obtain sustainable benefits. Supporting measures should be taken, such as designing resettlement projects, properly resettling immigrants' lives, and building houses and corresponding facilities elsewhere.

iii. Ecological factors should also be considered. In the early stage of construction, it is necessary to evaluate the possible impacts of the construction of hydropower projects on the ecological environment, and carry on the construction while minimizing the negative ecological impacts.

iv. The impacts involved in the construction and operation of large-scale hydropower projects also include local tourism, flood control, spatial distribution of water resources, and river's shipping conditions etc. It is necessary to comprehensively consider these factors and make overall and coordinated plans for the development.

In general, the construction of hydropower projects can not be separated from the river valley planning. In the development and construction of hydropower projects, the advantages and disadvantages of various aspects should be considered comprehensively. Whether they are economic, social or ecological effects, all these need to be fully estimated. The positive role of hydropower projects should be brought into play as much as possible, while the potential negative effects should be eliminated or minimized as much as possible. In the process of measurement, not only the comprehensive effect of hydropower project construction should be seen, its possible negative impact on the ecological environment and other aspects should also be recognized. In the river development and the design and planning of hydropower project, it is important to adhere to the principle of coexistence of development and protection, implement the concept of sustainable development in the whole process of design and construction, realize the coordinated development of population, resources and environment, and make the hydropower project satisfy the requirements of flood control, irrigation, navigation, water supply, aquaculture, tourism and other aspects of the needs. At the same time, it is also necessary to protect the ecological environment, natural and cultural landscape to reach the win-win development goals.

d. Elements of Resource Composition and its Tourism Value

Reservoirs and hydropower stations (dams) are the main parts of hydropower projects, and they are the combination of artificial architecture and natural landscape. The components of related tourism mainly include water body, aquatic organisms, reservoir bank (basin) and related buildings.[①]

i. Water Body and its Tourism Value

Water body is an important place for water entertainment. As a part of hydropower project, the surface of reservoir water body is long, narrow and dendritic. According to the reservoir's structure and capacity, the water surface of the reservoir can be divided into river zone, transition zone and lake area from the water inlet to the dam. The river zone is located at the water inlet of the reservoir, where the water surface is narrow and shallow, the river water flow rate is the fastest, and the time of hydraulic retention is the shortest. Because the reservoir, stream, harbor and bay are deep and narrow in the river zone, so this area becomes the best place for rowing, swimming, fishing and so on. Compared with the river zone, the transition zone is wide and deep, and the flow velocity is further slowed down. This is the main area of suspended sediment deposition. Here the biomass and growth rate of phytoplankton are the highest, so it is suitable for aquaculture. The lake area is close to the reservoir dam and is the widest and deepest area of the reservoir. Its wide water surface can be equipped with large water recreation activities such as jet skis, seaplanes, water skiing, and paragliding.

ii. Aquatic Organisms and its Tourism Value

Aquatic organisms include a variety of aquatic animals, plants, and microorganisms. Aquatic animals are important attractions in tourism activities because that the beautiful, colorful or exotic fish can be of interest to visitors. At the same time, various aquatic or amphibian animals including fish, crustaceans (eg. crabs, shrimps), turtles (eg. turtles, soft-shelled turtles), and mollusks (eg. clams) provide tourists with entertainments of sightseeing, fishing, and collecting. In addition, large-scale fishing and fish migration are also attractions for tourists. Aquatic plants, such as water lily, lotus and goldfish algae, are also widely praised as traditional ornamental plants, especially in China.

iii. Reservoir and its Tourism Value

As a part of the project, the reservoir bank is one of the important places for outdoor recreational activities. Reservoirs are generally built in river valleys, and the development coefficient of reservoir

---

① Zhang Xilin, Fu Rong and Zeng Xianwen. Exploiting Reservoir-based Tourism Resources. Journal of Central South Forestry University, vol. 6, 2003, pp. 28-32.

shorelines is larger than that of lakes. The reservoir bank includes floodplains of the rivers, bank slopes and mountainous areas around the reservoir. The tourism value of reservoir bank is shown in three aspects. First, it enriches the types of landscape. Mountain and water can complement each other and show the beauty of the nature. Moreover, all varieties of tourism resources around reservoirs, including human landscape, enrich the level and structure of reservoir landscape. Second, it provides a place for tourism activity. The floodplain on the bank of the reservoir includes sand, grassland and so on. It is often the best place for tourists to have various kinds of outdoor recreational activities. Third, it expands the space for tourism activity. The mountainous area of the reservoir bank provides a place for mountaineering, forest tourism and other activities, and completes the expansion of the tourism space from the water to the land.

iv. Artificial Architecture and its Tourism Value

In the hydropower projects, artificial architecture mainly includes river dams, power generation facilities, special buildings and so on. Its huge size and magnificent momentum represent the great achievements of human beings, so the modern buildings have become important tourism resources. Dam is the core building and important symbol of hydropower project, and also one of the important sightseeing objects.

Other hydropower facilities include water inlets, pressure regulating facilities, pressure pipes, power plant buildings and retaining walls. Reservoir drainage structures include overflow dams, spillways, flood discharge tunnels, drain holes of the dam, gates, water flow energy dissipation and scour prevention facilities. When the reservoir discharges the flood water, the roaring water rushes down like a waterfall, which gives tourists unparalleled strong visual impact.

Other special buildings include dam-crossing buildings (for wood and fish), navigation buildings (like gate and lifting facility) and so on. Among them, the operation of gate and lifting facility are new to most tourists, so they can be valuable for their strong attractions.

(2) Culture-Tourism Integration Driven by the Core Attraction of Hydropower Project

a. Ecological Tourism Based on Natural and Ecological Environment

The development of modern industry has caused serious pollution to the urban living environment. The radiation of heat and light, and radioactive radiation, harmful decoration and building materials brought about by the society have caused certain harm to the human body and mind. People's desire for clean air and water as well as a beautiful living environment with natural scenery grows stronger and stronger. In general, the river valleys are rich in ecological resources, with beautiful natural scenery and landscapes. Waters (water bodies) and related natural landscapes, such as coastal land, island, forest and grassland, can also be attractive to visitors. For instance, a wealth of aquatic organism provides tourists with entertainments of sightseeing, fishing, and collecting. Therefore, hydropower projects can combine their own resources with the rivers, and create eco-tourism products based on seasonal and project-specific landscape. The development should adhere to the humane principle, creating a healthy and beautiful ecological environment, and sustainable principle, constructing a low-polluted and ecological environment to attract tourists.

b. Landscape of Hydropower Project Based on Industrial Scenery

While destroying the original natural or cultural landscape, the construction of hydropower projects also creates new tourist landscape and brings profit. The characteristics of the industrial construction can also be used to develop tourism.

Throughout the world, famous hydropower projects have been built or are being built into famous tourist attractions. America's Hoover Dam itself is a famous building and now it is listed as national historical landmark and national landmark of civil engineering. In 1994, it was listed as one of seven modern mirales of civil engineering by American Civil Engineering Society. Since its opening in 1935, more than 35 million visitors have come to the site. Visitors first visit the top of the dam and then take the elevator down 520 feet, directly to the bottom. Inside the dam are some typical architectural styles of the 1930s, various artistic decorations and streamlined modern designs, as well as the floors with unique patterns designed by Native Americans. At the bottom of the dam, visitors can visit a power plant with 17 hydroelectric generating units, which deliver about 3.5 billion kilowatt-hours of electricity per year. Deep down inside the dam, visitors can see the huge diversion tunnels. These diversion tunnels are used to divert water around the dam during construction. Back at the top of the dam, in the part of Nevada (the dam spans the Nevada-Arizona border), the Visitor Center presents the entire Colorado River system and the history of the dam.

Located in Yichang City, Hubei Province, the tourist program of the Yangtze Gorges Dam relies on the Three Gorges Project, the world's largest hydro-junction project. Its unique landscape of hydropower station and the human landscape such as "Lake on the Peak of the Mountains" show the industrial as well as water culture in an all-round way. It not only provides tourists with multi-functional services including sightseeing, scientific education, leisure and entertainment, but also combines modern engineering, natural scenery and human landscape organically and becomes a tourist attraction appealing to both domestic and international visitors.

In addition to the project itself, the completion of the hydropower project can breed new human landscape and promote the development of tourism. The Hoover Dam has bred a new city, Las Vegas. It is fair to say that the Hoover Dam is the mother of Las Vegas. Today, near the Hoover Dam, some small, ruined and desolate villages with the written signs of "Old Las Vegas" (the old city of Las Vegas) can still be found, wherein workers camped during the construction of the dam. It is a village in the desert that Las Vegas grew out of.[①] Thus, the new landscape brought about by the hydropower project itself and its "destructive construction" can both become tourism resources, which can be used for tourism to build sightseeing routes of hydropower projects.

c. Cultural Derivation and IP Development Based on Project's Cultural Resources

The construction of hydropower project itself is a symbol and inheritance of certain spirits. For example, the Hoover Dam and Grand Coulee Hydroelectric Power Station built during the Great Depression of the United States obviously show their value since they are the continuation and embodiment of the spirit of "Western Cowboy" in the western exploitation of the United States. It is self-evident that the construction itself is the best publicity of culture. The tortuous and difficult construction process of Aswan Water Conservancy Project, for instance, has made itself a symbol of Egyptian national culture.

In addition, well-known architecture and landmark can also promote tourism if they are related to the novels created by famous writers and poets, relevant documentaries and books, or they are the shooting sites themselves. Still take the Hoover Dam as an example, Hoover Dam appears in many well-known film and television dramas, such as "San Andreas", "Transformers", "Universal Soldier", "10.5", "Apocalypse", and so on. When the dam is involved in many classic scenes in the films, the dam's reputation and value can be further promoted because it attracts both fans of the films and television dramas as well as other visitors. Therefore, the development of derivative culture and intellectual property (IP) has played a good role in the spreading and promotion of hydropower projects, and to a certain extent led to the development of tourism.

d. Sightseeing Route Based on Project's Functions

The construction of hydropower projects has greatly promoted the development of shipping, which in turns has provided a solid traffic condition for tourism. Therefore, based on the physical condition of the river valley where the project is located, the up- and downstream of the project can be connected and the whole route of one-stop shipping tourism can be developed. For example, the construction of the Yangtze Gorges Dam in the upper reaches of the Yangtze River creates the landscape of "Lake on the Peak of the Mountains", which further improves the navigation of the Yangtze River. This is an excellent condition for the development of shipping and cruise tourism in combination with the resources around the Yangtze Gorges. This naturally has led to the development of leisure cruise tourism. Besides connecting the up- and downstream for the development of shipping tourism, land transportation can be further linked to form a transportation network and a long tourist route.

---

① Zhang Zhihui. "World Famous Dam: An Overview of Hoover Dam in the United States." China Three Gorges, vol. 1, 2012, pp. 69-78, p. 2.

e. Regional (Basin Area) Tourism Development Based on the Integration of Natural and Human Landscape

With the long history and wide coverage, the river valleys are always equipped with a large amount of hydropower facilities, which is advantageous to water tourism. Such advanced regions of water tourism can be integrated with the internal resources of the region to form a linkage effect.

The construction and promotion of the Yangtze Gorges tourism is an example. This region is rich in natural and humanistic landscape. They are not only of great scale, high value and taste, but also of great attraction. The quantity of the attractions is large and tourism industry in this region is strongly monopolistic. At the same time, the landscape of the Yangtze Gorges extends from the central axis Yangtze River to both sides, which enlarges the scope of the tourism resources of the Yangtze Gorges. In addition to the traditional tourism resources on the main channel of the Yangtze River, the accessible scenic spots along the longitudinal and deep waterways of the two wings of the Yangtze River are also increased. Moreover, the construction of hydropower projects, such as the Yangtze Gorges Dam, also brings the landscape combination of "Lake on the Peak of the Mountains" and canyons, the Yangtze Gorges Dam project, culture of the Yangtze River, immigration culture and culture of the hydropower project. Abundant, diverse and high-quality tourism resources provide unique conditions for the development of tourism, leisure and entertainment, eco-tourism, scientific investigation, exploration, traditional and ethnic culture tours, and other special types of tourism in the Yangtze Gorges tourism. Natural advantage is one of the most basic conditions of the development of tourism in the Three Gorges region.[1]

In 2004, the former National Tourism Administration released the *General Plan for Regional Tourism Development of the Three Gorges Region of the Yangtze River*, which is the first plan for cross-regional tourism organized by the national administration in China. In the plan, it is clearly put forward that the tourism of the Yangtze Gorges should be built into a world-class tourism destination with international influence, competitiveness and of sustainable development. Based on natural ecological sightseeing and artificial attraction, the leisure entertainment and folk experience should be the main format of the tourism development, supplemented by scientific expedition and sports competition with the emphasis on the integration of ecology, individualization and thematization.

In the United States, most of the hydropower dams have been built into scenic spots, and the hydropower groups in the Tennessee Valley in the United States have gained tremendous all-round tourism benefits through successful tourism development. The Tennessee River in the United States is 1,050 km

---

[1] Liu Mingjian and Huang Meng. Research on the Construction of Tourism Destination Spatial Structure System: A Case Study of the Three Gorges. Economic Geography, vol. 4, 2005, pp. 581-584.

long and is the fifth longest river in the United States.

Wilson Dam and the hydropower station were built in 1918. In 1933, on the proposal of President Roosevelt, the United States Congress passed the *Tennessee Valley Authority Act*, which established the Tennessee Valley Authority (TVA) . The management has effectively promoted the comprehensive development of hydropower industry, agriculture, forestry, fisheries, especially tourism in the Tennessee Valley, making it one of the richest areas in the United States. At present, 310 scenic spots, 110 camps and clubs and 24 wildlife reserves have been built in the valley. These places attract more than 65 million visitors every year.[①]

2. Projects of Water Management

(1) River's Projects of Water Management

a. Concepts

In river valleys, flood disasters and water pollution can all be associated with water management projects. The development of water management is related to human survival, economic development and social progress. Therefore, water management projects that affect production and life, and even social security, can be found throughout the long history of human society. Water management project refers to the control and allocation of surface water and groundwater in nature to achieve the purpose of eliminating water disasters and promoting water conservancy. Water management projects redistribute water resources in time to prevent floods and develop irrigation, power generation, water supply and other functions. At the same time, the projects also improve the water environment, dredge waterways and build docks to facilitate water transport. In order to prevent water pollution and maintain ecological balance, a series of water conservancy projects should be built according to local conditions.

The concept and functions of water management projects are diverse, and they can be different because of different periods of time or different valleys. With the spread of the thought of comprehensive management of water resources, today's water management projects not only include irrigation, flood control, power generation, shipping and other functions, but also include water resources security, water environment security and water ecological security. It reflects the characteristics of modern management of water resources. The management becomes more advanced in the development level, scientific in the water management strategy, sustainable for the social benefit, highly efficient in the development, utilization and recycle, secured in the risk resistance, fair in the industry service, standardized in the management system

---

① Chen Xuejun. "Experience and Enlightenment of World Reservoir Dam Tourism Development." Consumer Economics, vol. 29, no. 1, 2013, pp. 71-74.

and innovative in the construction.

With the development of human civilization, human beings have exerted their diligence and wisdom to manage, control, and improve water. Numerous large and small water projects have been built, promoting the development of agriculture and economy. Water management project is an inevitable product as well as the carrier of the development of water resources. In ancient times, many large-scale water management projects have been built with exquisite design, of which the level and practical functions were frontier in the world water management projects.

Taking the water management project in China as an example, the measure of water management was initiated by King Yu in ancient time. Other famous projects include the Zhengguo Channel and the Dujiangyan Channel in pre-Qin Dynasty, the channels of Ling, Qin, Liufu, and Bai during the Qin and Han dynasties, and the Tong Channel was built for irrigation during the Three Kingdoms, Jin, Northern and Southern Dynasties. Since Sui and Tang dynasties, the united empire started to construct the Grand Canal throughout the southern and northern China.[1]

All these large-scale water management projects show excellent engineering technology of the ancient working people, and are also excellent cultural heritage reflecting the outstanding wisdom of the Chinese nation. Today, with the development of water management and the progress of science and technology, some water projects used for flood control, irrigation, shipping and other functions in ancient times have lost their functions, while some still play a role by virtue of their powerful functions and the surrounding natural resources, and even in tourism and ornament. For example, the Dujiangyan built by Li Bing during the Warring States Period and the Beijing-Hangzhou Grand Canal excavated by Emperor Yang in the Sui and Tang Dynasties now not only play an important role in the water conservancy function, but also in the tourism of the water management projects, promoting the local economic development.

b. Factors

The differences of water management projects in different river valleys are mainly influenced by two factors.[2] First, natural factors refer to climate, topography, rivers, soil, vegetation, natural conditions, natural patterns, etc. The natural factors such as climate and precipitation are different in different river valleys. Therefore, the water management projects in different river valleys vary from river to river.

The second is social factor, referring to political, economic, and cultural factors. The political factors include the national-released water resources management system and policy of developing water resources,

---

[1] Wu Shiyong. Historical Logic of Water Control, Opening up Waterways and Grain Transport by Water in Ancient China. Journal of Shenzhen University (Humanities & Social Sciences), vol. 35, no. 2, 2018, pp. 152-160.

[2] Han Chunhui, ZuoQiting, Song Menglin and Luo Zengliang. Analysis on the Evolution of Water Control thought in China. Water Resources Development Research, vol. 15, no. 5, 2015, pp. 75-80.

legal system of construction of water resources, safety of cross-border river, etc. It is an artificial controlled factor that conforms to the national development goal and directly relates to the direction of national and social development. In ancient times, channels and canals were built by the state for strategic needs or to drive local economy, while in modern times, they are embodied in strategic deployment, social security, energy development, agricultural security and so on. Economic factors may affect economic system and economic society, such as the balance between the speed of economic development and the supply of water resources, and people's living water consumption. Cultural factors include water culture education, water science and technology, water culture popularization, water-saving concept, customs and habits. The argument of whether there are advanced technology and talents in the area to support the development and construction of water management projects is one example. Therefore, in the development and construction of water management projects, both natural and human factors should be considered comprehensively.

c. Requirements for Development

Water management projects have a long history. It guides us to further explore the natural law and intrinsic attributes of water, helps us to summarize the long history, rich experience and great achievements of water harnessing. It has great significance for promoting the harmony between humans and water, ensuring the sustainable utilization of water resources and development of economy and society, and guiding the development of water management at present and in the future.[①] On the way of exploring the development of water resources, mankind has created and accumulated abundant ideas and methods of water harnessing. Water management projects in major river valleys progress continuously and modern water management projects and concepts are constantly enriched and improved. At the same time, along with the demand for ecological environment protection and sustainable development, in the future construction of water management projects, it is necessary to provide protection as well as carry on development, seek a balance between creating benefits and ecological protection, and comprehensively consider various factors to give full play to the resource, environmental and ecological function of the river valleys.

d. Cultural Resources

In the development of cultural tourism of water management project, the culture that needs to be relied on includes not only the culture of water management project itself, but also the water culture that coexists with the management, and also the regional culture that resources lie in. They together constitute the

---

[①] Mao Chunmei, Chen Yici, Sun Zongfeng, Zhang Pengcheng and Zhu Lixiang. "Connotation of Water Culture in New Period and Relationship between Water Culture and Water Conservancy Culture." Journal of Economics of Water Resources vol. 29, no. 4, 2011, pp. 63-66, p. 74.

cultural system of water resources tourism.[①]

i. Long History of Water Culture

River breeds life and creates civilization. When exploring the origin of world civilizations, it is apparent to find that all civilizations are bound up with water. The civilization of human society originates from and accumulates river culture, the latter of which in turn promotes social development. River civilization is closely related to human civilization, which is the source and birthplace of human civilization. The interaction between rivers and human civilization has created the living culture of rivers. Therefore, the long history of water culture that is owned by rivers is an extremely important tourism resource.

ii. Enriched Culture of Water Management Project

① Solid Material Culture of Water Resources

Water conservancy construction cannot be separated from various forms of facilities. These facilities provide a material basis for the development of water tourism. Ancient facilities such as the Dujiangyan Channel built by Li Bing, a mayor in the Qin State during the Spring and Autumn and Warring States Period, the Zhengguo Channel built by Zheng State (the precedent project of today's Jinghui Channel), the Shaopo Channel built by Chu State and so on. They still exist today and keep benefiting people after expansion, improvement and development. Today more and more forms of water conservancy projects have been constructed to serve human beings and promote the overall development of society. When standing in front of these ancient and modern water resources, visitors may sincerely sigh for these great water management projects.

② Long-history Behavioral Culture of Water Resources

In the history linking with water, China has created many behavioral cultures with Chinese characteristics. According to *Records of Luoyang*, "During the time of King Yu, a Turtle God appeared with scriptures in its shell. The scripture taught King Yu how to manage the water". Because of this story, people then start to make sacrifice of turtle before managing the water by casting a big iron turtle in the water. This ritual means to use the turtle to suppress the evil in water and keep the river valley safe. On the banks of downstream of the Yellow River, states in the Warring States Period built dams to prevent the flood from their states and gullies to attack other states by water. Till 221 B.C. when the first emperor of Qin Dynasty united the whole country, the water attack was ceased, and the water policy of the whole country was uniformed. In addition, as a Chinese folk ritual, people always cast an iron ox on the bank of the river to pray for the avoidance of the flood disaster. This behavior has two possible origins. One is King Yu did so

---

① Ding Shu and Huang Jiangtao. Water-related Tourism Resources: Cultural Inherent and Development Ideas. China Water Resources, vol. 2, 2009, pp. 49-51.

when he tamed the flood. Another is when Li Bing controlled the disaster, he was embodied as an ox and conquered the God of the River. Thus, people started such a tradition. This sort of behavioral culture is also a part of the cultural resources.

③ Advanced Technology Culture of Water Resources

Technology culture of water resources also constitutes a part of water cultural resources. Taking the projects in the ancient China as an example, the plan, design and construction of the Dujiangyan were all highly scientific and innovative. The approach of concentrating the river flow to scour the sludge is a glorious achievement of not only ancient China's but also the world's hydrology, and becomes a theoretical basis for the enhancement of the management and the dam construction of the Yellow River. Baiheliang Stone Inscription in Fuling recorded for the season of low water for 72 years off and on, which is the earliest "gauging station" in ancient China. Because shipping, fishery, salt making, naval warfare and tide disaster prevention activities urgently need to know the time and intensity of the tides, many tide tables were compiled in ancient times, among which Dou Shumeng's "Map of Tides" in Tang Dynasty and the "Map of Tides in Four Seasons" in Song Dynasty were the most famous ones.

Today, from planning, design, construction to operation and management, modern water management project is a comprehensive application of science and technology, including many scientific subjects like construction engineering, mechanical engineering, electrical engineering, management engineering, environmental science and so on. Advanced technology is a common characteristic of excellent water management projects, and also the key point of water resources tourism. For example, a number of important scientific research achievements have been achieved during the construction of Xiaolangdi Water Conservancy Project, including the construction technology of concrete impervious wall of dam, energy dissipation technology of orifice plate in spillway tunnel, etc. It is precisely by virtue of these high tech and scientific design that a large number of water conservancy projects can benefit people.

iii. Colorful Regional Culture of Water Resources

Because of different geographical locations and regional cultures, the water management project of the place can show strong local characteristics. It not only lays a good foundation for the comprehensive development of water-related tourism, but also provides the possibility for the diversification of water-related tourism. The more the culture reflecting the local characteristics, the more it can attract tourists' attention. Combining the water landscape with the local history, culture, customs, food and commodities can create a unique and more attractive tourist site of water management project.

(2) Culture-Tourism Integration Driven by the Core Attraction of Water Management Project

a. Construction of Tourist Site Based on the Water Project's Charm

With the time passing, some early water management projects have lost their functions, but still formed a unique cultural heritage. Meanwhile, some water conservancy projects still play a role by virtue of their powerful functions and the surrounding natural resources. These outstanding cultural heritage resources highlight human's wisdom and diligence. Through later enhancement, like building the museum on the original spot or restoring the ruins, the everlasting cultural and spiritual connotation can attract the visitors.

Moreover, related rivers can also be built into a tourist site, based on the water management project itself as well as the development of the related and attractive natural and human landscape like riverside, island, grassland, architecture, etc. The valley can be developed around the water management project. On the premise of having a certain scale and quality of landscape resources and environmental conditions, the valley can be developed with areas for sightseeing, entertainment, leisure, vacation or scientific, cultural and educational activities. Such a tourist site of water resources should aim at cultivating ecosystems, optimizing the environment, protecting the resources, and realizing harmonious coexistence between man and nature. It should emphasize the organic unity of social, environmental and economic benefits. In the construction of the tourist site of water resources, the existing or newly built water projects and their associated water bodies should be treated as landscape according to the principles of integration of harmony, beauty and practicality. It is necessary to comprehensively analyze the needs of social and economic development, ecology and environment, as well as human and historical demand, so as to form landscape resources with certain cultural and aesthetic connotations. On the premise of satisfying the basic function of production, it is important to give full play to the comprehensive function in a larger space and a wider scope for people to sightseeing, entertainment, leisure and scientific, cultural and educational activities.

One example is the construction of Xiaolangdi Water Conservancy Project. It locates in Luoyang, Henan Province, on the boundary of Mengjin city and Jiyuan city, and is established as a tourist site of water resources. It consists of four areas, which are Xiaolangdi Dam, Jingzishan Mountain, Balixia Dam, Sanmenxia Dam, including 13 scenic areas and 113 scenic spots. In 296-square-kilometer water area, lakes, rivers, islands and peninsulas are densely distributed and become a great gathering of natural beauty.[①]

b. Development of Tourism with Scientific Popularization and Project's Culture

Theme tourism and knowledge-based tourism are important formats of tourism development nowadays. The construction of high-quality popularization has become an important part in the construction of spiritual civilization. When visitors obtain knowledge and learn about the culture during the tour and

---

① Wang Huizhan. A Study of Tourism Sustainable Development of Xiaolangdi Water Conservancy Scenic Spot. 2007. Qingdao University, Master Thesis.

leisure time, the significance of tourism is deepened. Water conservancy project and its basin have abundant resources of education on science, which is an ideal place for carrying out related activities. Therefore, based on the history of water project construction and the popularization of knowledge and culture of water project, the educational function of water project tourism can be brought into play and the spiritual connotation of tourism activities can be extended. Based on water management projects, it is reasonable to build research bases to popularize the education on science, for example, the Water Conservancy Museum built in Dujiangyan and the Yangtze Gorges Project Exhibition Hall built in the Yangtze Gorges Project are effective ones.

c. Diverse Presentation of Cultural Resources of Water

The excavation of cultural connotation of water resources and tourism resources cannot be created out of imagination. It is necessary to combine the water and the culture, and the culture should be related to water. For tourism of water resources, such as water conservancy project hubs and soil and water conservation gardens, which majority of the content is the modern science and technology, the working principle, technological process and overall layout of the project can be displayed by means of words, diagrams and models, so as to enable tourists to recognize and fully understand the meaning of water resources. Thus the tourism can promote the harmonious development of human and water in an all-round way. Special exhibitions can also be an effective way to display the literary and art works related to water in the tourist site and enrich the structure of scenic spots. For instance, Qu Yuan, Du Fu, Li Bai, Wang Wei, Su Shi, Lu You, Ouyang Xiu and other celebrities in the history of Chinese literature have their own stories in the Yangtze Gorges and wrote the poems to praise the place. Thus, the Yangtze Gorges has become a literary landscape because of the poets' emotion, showing a harmonius state of nature and human culture. These poems are always the precious intangible resources of water tourism and should be utilized to deepen the tourists' impression.[①]

d. Development of Derivatives to Show the Spirit of Water Management

Throughout history, persons who managed the water, their thoughts and spirits enlighten, influence and shape the spiritual world of the whole Chinese nation. Their stories also become colorful artitist treasure. King Yu led people to dredge the river course and his methods largely impacted the later understanding of blocking and dredging. Li Bing and his son led local people to dig the Dujiangyan Channel, showing their prominent wisdom and courage. Pan Jixun, a water management expert in Ming Dynasty, experienced ups and downs throughout his life but he never gave up the water management of the Yellow River and the

---

① Ding Shu and Huang Jiangtao. "Cultural Connotation and Development Ideas of Water Conservancy Tourism Resources." Chian Water Resources, vol. 2, 2009, pp. 49-51.

Huai River. His approach of building the dam and concentrating the river flow to dredge the river course is still vital to today's water management of the Yellow River. Other celebrities also include Li Yizhi and Lin Zexu, who regard water management as a way to serve the country. Today the strong spirit of anti-flood and responsible spirit of water management are also passed on to the next generation. The spirit not only enriches the connotation of water culture, but also become an important clue for visitors to learn about and memorize the history and the historical figures. It is a special and local cultural resource, which can become a source of attraction in cultural tourism.[①]

In addition, the historical figures and the spirit of water management in the project construction can also be developed and represented in the artistic forms like films, TV dramas, plays, etc. For example, the legendary story of King Yu taming the flood in the ancient times not only include affluent natural and human landscape, but also embodies deep spiritual and cultural connotation. It is also possible for the development of derivatives that to promote the tourism based on the culture and the legend of King Yu and produce cultural tourism products like the Museum of King Yu Culture, cultural corrido, etc.

Moreover, taking Sanmenxia Dam as an example, the dam is the first large-scale water conservancy project built in the main stream of the Yellow River in China. The scenic spot is a reservoir sightseeing and recreational human landscape built on the basis of Sanmenxia Dam. Sanmenxia Junction has a wide range of visibility and rich Sanmenxia culture of the Yellow River. Excavating its connotation and displaying it through landscape, tourism products and so on can enhance the cultural connotation of Sanmenxia Water Conservancy Project, thereby increasing its tourism visitation.[②]

Section 3 Integration Driven by the Core Attraction of River Landscape

This part will classify and elaborate the natural and cultural landscape of the river, introduce the unique tourism attraction of the magnificent natural landscape and the human landscape with different styles, as well as the inherent cultural connotation of the river landscape created by artists and working people. This part also further explores the integration experience of the river landscape and cultural tourism by excavating the aesthetic value of the landscape, highlighting the education functions of the tourism.

---

① Mao Chunmei, Chen Yici, Sun Zongfeng, Zhang Pengcheng, and Zhu Lixiang. "The Connotation of Water Culture and Its Relation with Water Conservancy Culture in the New Era." Journal of Economics of Water Resources, vol. 29, no. 4, 2011, pp. 63-66, p. 74.

② Li Mingtang. Exploration and Practices on Management of Sanmenxia Multipurpose Dam Project."Yellow River, vol. 39, no. 7, 2017, pp. 1-6.

1. Culture of Natural Landscape

Natural landscape refers to the one that has not changed significantly due to the indirect, slight or occasional human influence, which include the landscape like polar, alpine, desert, swamp, tropical rain forest and some natural reserves. River's natural landscape is surely centered on rivers, especially the river flow. It includes not only the natural landscape formed by the river itself, such as winding rivers, fluctuating river beds, natural shoals, deep pools, sandbanks and aquatic animals and plants, but also the sights along the river, including the vegetation greening projects on the riversides.

The river presents the natural landscape with changeable and magnificent characteristics to people. The natural ecosystem of the river has a strong aesthetic sense and personalized temperament. As a unique tourist attraction, the landscape itself provides a special space for tourism activities. In addition, the mystery of the river makes it an important carrier of aesthetic sentiment for many writers and poets. Artists often imagine beyond the river itself and use their talents to depict the beauty of the ideal river, to express their ideas and give the river an inherent cultural sense of the natural landscape. In ancient China, for example, the Yellow River and the Yangtze River were often places where poets and scholars expressed their homesickness and memorial for the history, and the Rhine River has always been an important place for poets, painters and musicians to seek inspiration as well.

(1) Types of River Culture and Natural Landscape

From the perspective of tourism landscape, the river landscape is often divided into five areas, which are river source, upstream, midstream, downstream and estuary. In the area of the river source, the situation can vary with the different geographical location, which can be lakes, swamps and glaciers; the upstream area is often characterized by mountains, narrow river surface, rich changes in flow patterns such as waterfalls and deep gullies; the river bed in the middle area is often composed of pebbles and sand grains, and sandbanks and braided-style water systems can always be found; the downstream area is characterized by wide water surface and smooth flow, and the scenery along the river is often reflected in the water. In the estuary area, the slope of the river course is gentle, the speed of river flow is slow, the coverage of vegetation is limited and the greening measures are relatively simple.

a. Source of the River

The source of the river is the river's birthplace, which is the most important and ecologically active part of the river. It can be represented in different forms, such as lakes, swamps, glaciers and so on. The natural ecological landscape in the source of the river is the key point to attract tourists. For example, the source of the Yangtze River, the Yellow River, the Lancang River and the Mekong River are covered with snow mountains, swamps and grasslands. The original ecological landscape of the area, like mountains, rivers, grasslands, snow mountains, wetlands and paradise for animals, can all be natural landscape. The source of the Mississippi River is Lake Itaska in the northern part of Minnesota, wherein there are tens of thousands of lakes. These large and small lakes, like natural reservoirs, have important regulatory significance for the water supply of the Mississippi River.

The source of the river is usually the most vulnerable part, which ecological environment can be easily damaged. The changes of natural environment such as global warming, heavy rainstorm, and unreasonable exploitation and utilization of human beings will affect the original ecological balance of the source of the river, thereby affecting the original water quality of the river and some species living around it, reducing species diversity. Thus the original ecological landscape may change or even disappear. Therefore, attention should be paid to the protection of the ecological environment in the tourism development of the source of the river.

b. The Upstream

The upstream of the river is characterized by the river flow's large drop, rapid speed, small discharge and the river's narrow valley. Shoals and waterfalls are often distributed in the riverbed. At the same time, rivers often separate mountains in the upper reaches, and their shape of the tributaries are always braided or winding, thus forming many beautiful canyons. For example, the Colorado River originates from the Rocky Mountains and eventually enters northwest Mexico, cutting out 19 major canyons on the Colorado Plateau, and one of the deepest, widest and longest is the Grand Canyon. The Grand Canyon of Colorado is famous for its unusual appearance and intricate, colorful terrain landscape, which attracts many tourists. The Iguacu River in South America plunges into a canyon from a wide river course before joining the La Plata Parana River in a U-shaped bend, thus forming Iguazu Falls. In 1984, Iguazu Falls was listed as a world heritage site by UNESCO. At present, part of its territory in Argentina has been opened as a national park.

In the upper reaches of rivers, there are affluent tourist resources, rich species and peculiar geological and geomorphological features in the gorges, waterfalls and other landscape zones. It has also become one of the many shooting spots for IP development. The scenes of cowboys shooting as riding horses, galloping and the scene of barren red land in American western films are the portraits of the Grand Canyon. However, due to the steep terrain and inconvenient transportation, tourism development in the upper reaches of the rivers can be difficult because of the limited investment and low level of development. At the same time, natural disasters occur more frequently in canyons and waterfalls, and the living environment is worse, so the total population of the upper reaches of the river is often relatively small.

c. The Middle and Lower Stream

Generally, the middle stream of great rivers flow through low mountains and hilly areas, then the velocity obviously decreases, forming a wider valley plain through the area. The lower reaches of great rivers are characterized by wide riverbed and slow velocity of the river flow, which leaves a large amount of sediment from the upper to the lower reaches. As a result, the sediment is deposited on both banks of the lower reaches, the shoals are distributed everywhere, and the alluvial plains are gradually formed. In addition, because of the river's width and convenient navigation in the middle and lower reaches, compared with the upstream and source areas, the population distribution in these two areas is usually more intensive with urban agglomeration and the agricultural industry is more developed. They are also the birthplace of human civilization's prosperity. The famous plains are the Amazon Plain, the middle and lower reaches of the Yangtze River Plain and so on. But there are also exceptions. The tropical rain forest in the Amazon Plain, located in the middle reaches of the Amazon River, as mentioned above, is densely distributed with a wide range of species of animals and plants. However, the population is limited and the agriculture and industry are underdeveloped.

Most of the middle and lower reaches of the river are gentle and highly accessible. At the same time, the unique water culture of the middle and lower reaches of the river is also a special tourism resource. The lower reaches of the river often cover a wide basin area, spanning provinces, cities, states and even countries. Therefore, in the area of the middle and lower reaches of the river, the water culture of different countries and provinces can also be different. Thus, different regions can carry out various tourism formats by virtue of regional natural river landscape and river culture to different degrees.

d. The Estuary

The estuary is the end of the river and is the place where the river interacts with the ocean. According to its geomorphological characteristics, the estuary can be divided into forms of liman, fjord and sandbank. The liman are generally distributed in mid-latitudes, and are the estuaries of coastal-plain rivers. When more sediment deposits from rivers, it will change the liman's pattern and liman will develop into deltas, such as the Yangtze Estuary in China, the Pearl River and the Mississippi Estuary in the United States; when less sediment deposits, the shape of the limans or estuaries will be totally or partially retained, such as the Thames Estuary in Britain, the Garonne Estuary in France and the Qiantang Estuary in China. The fjords are only distributed in high latitudes. In the region, glacial channels are eroded by the ocean and fjords are formed. It is characterized by a rock dam that is tens of meters above the bottom of the water. The water depth in the rock dam can reach hundreds of meters and extend hundreds of kilometers to the land like Sognefjorden in Norway and Glen Etive in Scotland. Sand-bar estuaries generally distribute in tropical areas or coastal areas with active sediment deposit.

(2) Culture-Tourism Integration Model Driven by the River's Natural Landscape and Cultural Attraction

a. Great Aesthetic Value and High Potential for Expedition Tourism

The most direct cultural value of the river lies in the aesthetic aspect. From the source to the estuary, the river's appearance changes with the geological conditions and forms a wealth of water landscape. With the beautiful sounds, forms and colors, the river becomes a major tourist site for appreciation. Tourists can gain the best tour experience by appreciating the natural beauty of the river. When seeing the same river landscape, visitors may have different aesthetic experience at different time and space. In addition, the steep natural landscape formed on or around the river also attracts many enthusiasts of extreme sports. Some extreme tourism projects, such as kayaking, obstacle swing, river marathon, rafting, kayak ball, etc., can bring different tour experiences to tourists under the condition of ensuring safety.

The special natural landscape of river can be categorized as below:

i. Canyons: eg. Hutiao Canyon at the Yangtze River, the Grand Canyon in the United States, Yarlung Zangbu Grand Canyon, etc.

ii. Rivers: eg. Li River in Guangxi, Fuchun River, etc.

iii. Waterfalls and Streams: eg. Hukou Waterfalls of the Yellow River, Xianglu Waterfalls of Mountain Lu, Hupao Stream in Hangzhou, Qing Stream at Chishui River in Guizhou.

Case 2.1

The Natural Landscape and Exploration Tourism at Hukou Waterfalls of the Yellow River

When the Yellow River flows through the boundary of Ji County, Shanxi, and Yichuan County, Shaanxi, the riversides become steep, and the estuary becomes narrow and looks like a bottleneck. Thus the greatest yellow waterfall in the world, Hukou Waterfalls of the Yellow River, is formed. The Waterfalls is owned by both provinces and is a 4A-level national scenic spot in China. The Waterfall is 50m wide and 50m deep, and the largest area is 30,000 m². The water of the Yellow River roars from afar to the "bottleneck" with thunder like sound and smoke like water fog.[1] In 1992, the Waterfalls was listed as one of the Top 40 China's Tourist Attractions; in 2002, it was listed as National Geopark and Geological Heritage Reserve by China's Ministry of Natural Resources; and in 2008, it was awarded with the qualification of 4A-level national scenic spot.[2]

---

[1] Soul of the Yellow River: the Hukou Waterfalls. Linfen Culture and Tourism Bureau, http://wlj.linfen.gov.cn/contents/1217/364040.html.Accessed 10 Sept. 2019.

[2] The Hukou Waterfalls. Shaanxi Culture and Tourism, http://www.sxtour.com/html/index.html.Accessed 10 Sept. 2019.

The best seasons for visiting the Hukou Waterfalls are spring and autum. In spring, from April to May (which is March in the lunar calendar) , the "March Spring Flood" takes place when the peach flowers blossom all over the mountains and the ice on the riversides melts. In autumn, after the rainy season from September to November, streams gather in the river and the rainbow appears with the autumn breeze. During these two periods, the river flows quickly and the width of the waterfalls can reach 1,000 km. Though it is hard to get close to the major part of the waterfalls, the sight looking from faraway is still miraculous and magnificient. The waves roar like storms on the ocean and crash down from the high. Such a scene can not even be written with words. In winter, the view of the Waterfalls changes. On the icy surface of the waterfalls flows the cool water, rolling with the waves in the river. Different shapes of ice drips also appear on the stones around the Waterfalls. All these are special features of winter in the northern China.

In the tourist site of the Hukou Waterfalls, the main programs include the culture of the Yellow River, canyons of the Shanxi and Shaanxi, natural ecological tour, local customs, geological archaeology, patriotist education, etc.[1] The site focuses on the natural landscape of the riverbed structured by sediment and the erosion of the river. Here the Yellow water and the yellow soil as well as the canyons and mountains complement to each other, showing a local characteristic and the magnificent style of landscape in the northern China. Thus it is the best place to show the customs and culture of the Yellow River. With the road changing on the Jihu part of the national highway No. 309 so that the road can access to the tourist site directly, and the improvement of the construction and management of the site, the site of the Hukou Waterfalls is equipped with better conditions for tourists. According to the statistics, in 2016, the site was visited by nearly a million tourists, and the ticket revenue reached 76 million yuan. In 2017, the number of the tourists surpassed 1.8 million, and on Nov. 25, 2018, the number reaches to 2 million of the year.

In addition, after years of development, the Hukou Waterfalls is more and more favored by the lovers of extreme sports. In 1997, KeShouliang, a famous Taiwan acrobat, drove a car and flew over the Waterfalls successfully. Two years later, Zhu Zhaohui, a local person born in the Yellow River Valley, rode a motor bike to fly over the Yellow River, making the place more popular in the world.

---

[1] The Hukou Waterfalls. Yan'an Local Chronicle Compilation Committee, http://fzbz.yanan.gov.cn/yats/fjmq/yicx/9143.htm.Accessed 10 Sept. 2019.

Sources of the Case:

Soul of the Yellow River: the Hukou Waterfalls (Linfen Culture and Tourism Bureau)

http://wlj.linfen.gov.cn/contents/1217/364040.html

TheHukou Waterfalls (Shaanxi Culture and Tourism)

http://www.sxtour.com/html/index.html

TheHukou Waterfalls (Yan'an Local Chronicle Compilation Committee)

http://fzbz.yanan.gov.cn/yats/fjmq/yicx/9143.htm

(The report summarizes and reorganizes the information from the sources above.)

b. Learning through Tourism to Promote All-round Education and Science

The combination of eco-tourism and science education can be adopted in the source and upstream areas because the unique environmental conditions and the amazing ecological landscape in the river source provide tourists with ideal place for vacation and leisure. First, considering the fragility of the ecosystem in the river source and upstream areas, it is appropriate to adopt the form of eco-tourism with the theme of protecting the natural environment. Second, in the river source and upstream areas, activities of science popularization can be carried out for the tourists travelling for a long distance, focusing on the presentation of the ecological functions and protection of the river source. Such activities are able to enhance the consciousness of the people living in the mid- and lower stream in protecting the river source. For nearby tourists, such tourism activities can enhance tourists' understanding of the origin and upstream of the river from the perspective of its further origin, cultural background and historical myths and legends. The site can also conduct science education on geology and species for all tourists, so that they can understand the cultural ecology of the source and upstream areas of the river, and carry out cross-cultural interpretation so as to make tourists obtain cultural knowledge from all-round perspectives.

The Colorado Canyon, located in Arizona, USA, was opened as the Grand Canyon National Park in 1919. So far, it has become one of the most popular and influential national parks in the United States. The development of the tourism mode of the Park attaches great importance to the function of science and ecological education. In the explanatory boards and tourist brochures introducing scenic spots in the park, attention is paid to the dissemination of scientific knowledge and the education of geology and ecology for tourists. For example, pictures of a section of the rock strata at the site where the visitors are standing are provided. The pictures also highlight the names, characteristics, formation ages and the origin of these specific shapes and colors of the different rock strata in order to help visitors to explore the geological changes, understand the rich knowledge of nature, and acquire historical and cultural knowledge. Training of managing officials also pays special attention to the education of ecological science popularization.[1] In addition, the Grand Canyon Park, based on its unique natural landscape, abundant ecological distribution of animals and plants, natural ecology and exploratory sports tourism, has designed an interpretation system, which mainly focuses on the tourist market of exploration and scientific tourism. The concept of harmonious coexistence between human and nature is the starting point of the construction of the interpretation system of the site of the Grand Canyon, and to a certain extent, has played an educational role in tourism.

c. Promotion of the Cultural Environment to Make the Ecology Alive

The appearance of some famous rivers that feed human beings often plays a subtle role in shaping the national spirit. The characteristics of rivers often complement the spiritual qualities of human beings, such as the Yellow River and the Yangtze River in China, which have been rolling and roaring for millions of years, making people feel the long history of the Chinese nation. The river culture has its own irreplaceable attraction for tourists. Under this premise, the natural landscape of the river is only the basic resource of tourism, and the cultural environment is the core of the river tourism. Each section of the river is rich in tourism resources, but the lack of cultural connotation is often the key to the limited development of most river tourism.

In tourism development, it is necessary to respect the natural ecological culture of each section of the river and activate the culture reasonably. For example, in the Grand Canyon in Colorado, the world-famous tourist site of canyon culture, in order to protect the natural and cultural ecological environment, the scenic area not only does not set up artificial landscapes, strictly controlling the number of tourists to protect the spot, but also provides scenic area vehicles to restrict private cars by hiring local residents as part-time drivers and tour guides. In addition, without destroying the natural landscape of the river, it is possible to use appropriate forms and carriers to show the connotation of the natural ecological culture of the river, highlight the theme of ecological culture, and carry forward the spirit of the river to the tourists. For example, images in the poems or artworks of the natural landscape can be used in the design of the infrastructure for the river valley tourism, so both local characteristics and the original landscape can be saved and protected.

d. Utilization of Intellectual Property (IP)

There are numerous myths and legends, and biographies of historical celebrities carried by the rivers from ancient times to the present. Each river landscape involves rich historical connotations, which cannot be replicated by the others. Since modern times, rivers have been the inspiration for many movies and TV

---

[1] Wan Jinjin, Sha Run and Liu Zehua. Geotourism Management Characteristics of the Grand Canyon in the US and Enlightenments for China. Ecological Economy, vol. 33, no. 10, 2017, pp. 159-162, p.189.

dramas because of their unique natural scenery. Documentaries introducing the natural scenery of the river itself also emerge constantly. All these have become available and potential IP to be used by the river valley tourism. The development and operation of these potential IP can attract the original IP fans, expand the fan base and promote the industrial upgrading and transformation. For example, the documentary project "New Three Gorges" is established in the Yangtze River Basin to record the ecological and humanistic beauty of the Three Gorges. In addition, in the IP construction of the Jialing River, some departments also put forward the idea of building the Jialing River as a cultural and economic industrial belt and a green economic corridor by the means of comprehensive new media platforms.[①]

2. Culture of Humane Landscape

Humane landscape is created by human beings on the basis of natural environment, which is processed by the local natural materials with the combination of human creation. When human thrive in the particular area, special traces of life leave a specific landscape in the place. In addition, such landscape also endows it with intangible meanings such as humanities and culture, forming a landscape different from that of other regions. The riversides have accumulated human landscape of different historical periods, ethnic characteristics, and regional styles.

Since ancient times, human beings have built cities and resided by water. Rivers have provided indispensable and important water resource for human survival, life uses and agricultural irrigation. Most countries and cities have their own "mother river" that feeds their own nation and people and nurtures their own brilliant civilization. For example, along the Seine River in Paris, the Thames River in London and the Nile River in Cairo are the world-famous urban human landscape belts, showing high historical, cultural and tourism value.

(1) Types of River's Culture of Human Landscape

The Types of River's Culture of Human Landscape can be divided into three categories as below:

a. City Landscape on the Riverside

River is a unique and indispensable resource for many riverside cities, which plays a very important role in the development and formation of many riverside cities.

Firstly, the human landscape of a single building and the water mutually reflecting each other. Flowing water can make the scene always in change and bring vitality to the urban architectural landscape along the river. For example, the Seine River, flowing through Paris, has become a unique landscape of the city.

---

① The Opening of Large-scale Documentary 'Jialing River', Issueing Green Declarations in More Than 30 Districts and Counties Along the River. Yuan Rui ,http://www.cyol.com.Accessed 10 Sept. 2019.

There are many amazing bridges in the upper reaches of the Seine River. There are also splendid palaces, ancient churches and elegant sculptures on both sides, such as the Louvre, Notre Dame de Paris and the Eiffel Tower. Drifting down the famous Thames River in Britain, the oldest and most solemn architectural landscapes of the British style are displayed in front of the tourist, including the Big Ben, London Bridge Tower and other world-known spots. At the same time, some aristocratic architectures are historical spots along the Thames River, and some private manors and residences of princes and nobles have been well preserved.

Secondly, the human landscape of flood-control dams on the outskirts of cities. The flood-control dam is an important construction in mountainous cities along rivers. When the river flows through the mountain, the water fluctuation becomes dramatic because of the different heights of the banks, so the flood can be steeply lifted or dropped. Special geomorphological and water conditions cause the city's outskirts to form the human landscape with special flood-control facilities, like riverside path, anti-flood bank, wharf, etc.[1] For the cities with gentle river flows, some projects of river embankment can be built, i.e. planting vegetation at the junction of rivers and cities, increasing greening area, and reducing the extent to which cities are attacked and scoured by river currents and winds. On the basis of increasing the stability and safety of river courses, such greening arrangement forms a pleasant urban green human landscape, such as plant walls. These human landscapes are located at the junction of water and land, near the front of rivers, and are also popular sites for hydrophilic tourism in addition to beaches. Hydrophilic activities such as walking, running and cycling along rivers are usually developed.

Thirdly, the overall cultural vibes of the cities along the river. Generally, in the cities along the river with a long history, the river is often the motive of the city's formation and development. Most of the cities with the richest historical and cultural deposits in the world are built near the river. For example, the cultural image of Qinhuai River in Nanjing is composed of the core historical and human landscape of the riversides of Qinhuai River, the tributary of the lower reaches of the Yangtze River. As a humane landscape, the cultural image of the city as a whole has strong identifying characteristics because of the rivers. The reflection of water can enrich the city's human landscape, and the change of water level also provides a variety of landscape. For example, Hangzhou Bay of Qiantang River in Zhejiang Province is well known for its Qiantang River Tide, which formation is influenced by its shape of the estuary, river bed topography, hydrology, climate and other factors. Every year, around August of the lunar calendar is the climax of the Qiantang River Tide, and a large number of tourists flock to watch the scene.

---

[1] Liu Ping. A Study on the Landscaping of Riverside Flood Control Facilities in Mountainous Cities 2017. Southwest University, Master Thesis.

The humane landscape of the cities on the riverside involves high cultural connotations. Tourists can naturally feel the unique charm of them by walking in the cities, enjoying the beautiful scenery of the integration of the buildings on the riverside and the water and light. Many humane landscape in riverside cities often improves the cultural connotations by building cultural squares and landscape parks. This kind of development needs to pay attention to the invasion and harmony between the development and the original landscape culture as well as the ecosystem. Otherwise it will cause negative consequences. When the cultural atmosphere of a region has reached a certain level, too much artificial construction of cultural signs may have the opposite effect.

b. Village Landscape on the Riverside

River can be used for irrigation and domestic water. The soil along the river is usually fertile and the agriculture is normally well-developed. The excellent water environment is an ideal settlement for human beings who survive mainly depending on farming, fishing and hunting to obtain products from nature. In addition, because of the convenience of land-water transportation of the river, it also provides a driving force for the settlement's location. Therefore, the location of most traditional settlements depends on rivers. The relationship between villages and towns living by rivers has gradually developed from survival dependence to active utilization. In line with people's aesthetic interest, a series of unique humane landscapes of villages and towns are created along the river, including the humane landscapes of public space and private residences.

The humane landscape of public space in villages and towns on the riverside includes river ways, river alleys, pavilions, and gardens along the water.[①] The villages built along the river always take the river course as the main transportation, thus a special landscape is formed, which is river way. It is a special experience for the tourists to travel on the river way with the locals. In Venice and villages on the riverside in Jiangsu-Zhejiang region in China, river ways, river alleys, pavilions, and gardens along the water are both practical and aesthetic humane landscape. They can be used as the places for recreation, places of villages as well as places of the decorative buildings, such as Leifeng Tower and Kuixing Hall. Most pavilions and gardens near the river are built on the edge of the village, accompanied by Wenchang Hall, schools, park and other public buildings, which altogether form a special landscape near water.

The private residence in the villages on the riverside always involves the owner's personal aesthetic tastes, thus the landscape in different residences can be very different. Chinese private residences reflect the thoughts of Fengshui, hierarchy system, harmony of man and the nature, etc. The artificial rocks and

---

① Xiong Haizhen. Discussion and Analysis of Water Chinese and Traditional village Water Environment Landscape. 2008. Southwest Jiaotong University, Master Thesis.

fountains, corridors, and windows all create a sense of beauty to attract the tourists.

c. Other Humane Landscape

Bridge: Bridge is an effective artificial structure to cross rivers. It is the intersection of water and land transportation, as well as a place for rest and sightseeing. At the same time, the bridge landscape attracts many tourists with its fluent form and various shapes. Some bridges also involve historical events or figures, so can be seen as a unique humane landscape. In addition, pavilions, corridors, rooms and buildings extending from bridges are also places for tourists to enjoy the scenery. In some bridge buildings there are also god statues for people to worship and pray for peace.

Temple: From the ancient to the present, religious beliefs are not uncommon elements in the humane landscape. Gods appear in every place or industry, people who live by the river or work in the shipping industry worships the God of Water. In order to express their devotion, people often set up temples along rivers to pray for good weather. For example, since the Shang Dynasty, almost every government in China offered sacrifices, erected temples and conferred titles on the Yellow River and Yangtze River.

Dam and dyke: Dam and dyke are barrier facilities across rivers, which can change the characteristics of water flow. It is often used to divert water into irrigation channels, prevent floods, measure the water volume and increase water depth to facilitate navigation. Dams are barriers built in streams, rivers and estuaries to prevent flooding, generate hydroelectric power, or store water for food supply and irrigation. In addition to the above functions, dams and dykes are easy to become landmarks in their natural environment because of their huge visual effect. The complex feelings and thoughts invested by human beings in the construction will also give them more cultural connotations, and the comprehensive landscape can be easily favored by tourists. The famous dams and dykes include the Dujiangyan in China, the Three Gorges Dam in the Yangtze River, and the Hoover Dam in the United States on the Colorado River.

Dujiangyan is located where the Min River enters the alluvial plain from the valley channel. It irrigates ten thousand hectares of farmland on the Chengdu Plain, east of Guan County. When the Min River flows through the upstream of the steep mountains and rivers and reaches the Chengdu Plain, the water speed slows down suddenly, so a large amount of sediment and rocks are deposited and the river channel is silted up. Every year when the rainy season comes, the Min River and other tributaries surge, often flooding, and when rainwater is insufficient, a drought is formed. In 256 B.C., Li Bing was mayor of Shu County. On the basis of water control by his predecessors and relying on the local people, Dujiangyan was built in Guan County, where the Min River flowed out of the mountains and into the plain. Dujiangyan Water Management Project reflects the superb ancient architectural art and the delicate selection of materials. The original project is basically intact, which amazes the world. After two thousand years, it still stands there for the benefit of mankind, becoming a must-look spot for visitors who travel to the city of Dujiangyan.

(2) Culture-Tourism Integration Model Driven by the River's Natural Landscape

a. Attraction Rejuvenation, Inheritance of Humane Spirit

Rivers with thousand years' history breed humane landscape, which is a condensation of history and a treasure for contemporary generation to explore the future. Through the combination of human landscape in the city and the river flowing across the city, city as the cultural connotation of an integral human landscape can be deeply excavated. Thus, the city's cultural image can be more vivid and more qualified, and legendary culture can also support the tourism. Meanwhile, from the cultural connotation of the various humane landscape, different forms of tourism, like niche tourism, experiential tours, educational tourism, can all be built as good programs with special characteristics and humane spirit.

Case 2.2

The Tourism Development of the Corridor Bridge in Shouning County

Shouning County locates in the north of Fujian Province, which is fully distributed with streams and canyons and the branches flow into Sai River. For the convenient traffic, people in the past built bridges to connect the both sides of the river, especially various forms of corridor bridges. Today in Shouning County, there are more than 40 corridor bridges, among which 19 are timber-arched bridges. From the perspectives of both quality and quantity, the group of the 19 bridges ranks first in China. Shouing County is also praised as the "hometown of world timber-arched corridor bridges" because the corridor bridges there are the oldest and longest in the arch, and the county has the collection of the contracts of bridge construction, which is the only case in China.[①]

Shouning corridor bridges show special culture of Fengshui and sacrifice as well as deep connotation of regional culture. About Fengshui, the choosing of the location of the bridges was in accordance with Chinese Fengshui theory that they are distributed on the upper- or midstream of the river. If they are built on the lower stream, they are used to fill the wind gap formed by the streams to protect the village's Fengshui. The bridges built on the upper stream and the ones on the lower stream show symmetrical style. Now among the 19 corridor

---

① Zhaung Yan, Miu Shuxiu. "Fujian and Zhejiang Jointly Protect the Ancient Corridor Bridge of Intangible Cultural Heritage." Fujian Daily, 2019.

bridges, 4 are on the upper stream, and 8 are on the lower stream.[①]

In recent years, based on the ancient corridor bridge culture, Shouning County streghthened the protection and repair work for the 19 timber-arched corridor bridges and published measures to improve the technical inheritance and protection of the bridges. The County also established a team of corridor bridge construction, enabling the inheritance of the techniques. Fujian and Zhejiang provinces also founded a department to unitedly and coordinatively protect the timber-arched corridor bridges, and applied for the legislation of corridor bridge protection. In order to coordinate the protection and development, implement effective restoration, protect the ecological environment, and scientifically utilize the resources, a special department was established for the application of cultural heritage of timber-arched corridor bridges. The department gathers the related offices and experts in Fujian and Zhejiang and local people who support the application. Meanwhile, to further publicize the culture of corridor bridge, various forms of thematic activities were held to establish the cultural brand of corridor bridge and pass on the regional craftsman spirit. Shouning County also focuses on the development of leisure tourism, health tourism, and countryside tourism to continuously promote tourist products and service innovation, enriching the industry and improving the quality.[②]

In addition, Shouning County is also a key area for Fujian Tourism Investment & Development Group to build up diverse leisure tourism programs and red culture tourism programs. In July 2018, Shouning County and Fujian Tourism Investment & Development Group cooperated and built up Xiadang Tourism Program. The program plans to develop the tourism along with the party construction in Xiadang Village, Shouning County. The program integrates the tourist sites of countryside tourism, leisure agriculture, sports, and culture of Feng Menglong in the area and recombines the diverse tourism products. Opening to the tourism market, the program aims at establishing a new site of China's red culture tourism and national village of learning the party spirit in the new era, integrating the functions of party education, study and learning, ecological leisure, etc.

Sources of the Case:

Zhuang Yan, MiuShuxiu, *Fujian and Zhejiang Jointly Protect the Ancient Corridor Bridge of Intangible*

[①] He Mingchun. The Study of the Timber-arched Lounge Bridge in Zhouning County. Fujian Normal University, Master Thesis, 2014.

[②] Shouning Deepens the Integration of Culture and Tourism and Promotes the Development of Valley Tourism. Zhao Qiaohong and Wu Tonghua. http://cmstop.ndsww.com/p/17875.html.Accessed 10 Sept. 2019.

Cultural Heritage, *Fujian Daily*, 2019.

He Mingchun, *The Study of the Timber-arched Lounge Bridge in Zhouning County*, Master Thesis, Fujian Normal University, 2014.

Zhao Qiaohong, Wu Tonghua, *Shouning Deepens the Integration of Culture and Tourism and Promotes the Development of Valley Tourism*.http://cmstop.ndsww.com/p/17875.html

(The report summarizes and reorganizes the information from the sources above.)

b. Construction of Tourism Public Facilities for In-depth Tourism Experience

The human landscape along the river is normally in linear distribution, the degree of tourism development is different, and the infrastructure of various places can also be imbalanced. Public culture and tourism facilities are indispensable for tourists to stay in the cultural landscape for a long time and experience its cultural charm in depth. For the villages and towns along the river, the human landscape tourism resources of these villages and towns are abundant, and the living habits formed by life on water for years are also primitive. By promoting the comprehensive construction of infrastructure and public service integration as well as expanding the tourism service, the tourist's duration of stay cannot only be increased, the in-depth development of culture and tourism industry as well as local villager's industries of local accommodation and special fishery can also be benefited.

c. Culture-Tourism Integrative Construction of Cities along the Riverside and Construction of Open Museum of the River

When rivers flow through many cities and regions, the humane landscape and culture on the riverside can be similar. By integrating the spatial and regional construction of them, it is possible to avoid repetitive construction, save resources, and maximize the benefits of economic and social development of the regions. For example, Shaoxing city in Zhejiang, advocating the harmony of the nature and human and aiming at inheriting the ancient Yue culture and displaying the charm of river village, strives to build the Grand Canal into a historical and cultural scenic route that integrates history, culture and ecology. Yangzhou city in Jiangsu Province, aims to make full use of those heritage sites connected by the river, to integrate the water-encircling slow-way system and water transportation system, and then to connect the heritage sites in series through the ancient city streets and alleys to create an open Grand Canal Museum.[1]

d. Enrichment of the Cultural Connotations by Art Works

It is necessary to promote the integration of cultural and artistic work creation and the enhancement

---

[1] Jiang Shili. "Integration of Culture and Tourism Creates the Colorful Tourism Belt of the Grand Canal." Chinese Culture, 1 June 2019, p. 7.

of tourism quality, so that cultural creativity can give tourism the most vivid elements, and make tourism have lasting vitality. It is practical to enrich the cultural connotation of human landscape along rivers by means of live performances and artistic reproduction of history events. For example, Tongtian River at the source of the Yangtze River is well known because of the related stories in *Journey to the West*. A famous cultural landscape of the River is Shaijing Stone. When the story of *Journey to the West*is re-performed next to the stone, new vitality can be brought to the site. Thus, the phenomenon of tourist site lacking of cultural background or attraction can be avoided. In addition, in some temples of the God of River, it is feasible to design a sacrifice ceremony at certain times to enrich the cultural connotations of the humane landscape.

Section 4　Integration Driven by the Folk Customs along the Riversides

This part will introduce, classify and elaborate the rich and colorful folk arts and festivals in the river valleys to understand their cultural value and tourism development, and put forward the integration of culture and tourism with the core attraction. The integration of folklore and tourism in the river valleys can not only provide financial support and social attention for the protection of folk customs in the river valleys, but also bring considerable economic revenue to the region. In addition, the use of modern new media to display and promote folk activities in the river valleys is also worth considering.

1. Folk Art

Folk art is proposed to distinguish the styles from academic art and literati art.① Folk art mainly refers to folk paintings and drawings and handicraft in the category of material folk customs, such as folk painting, paper art, utensils, furniture, toys, fabrics and other articles.②

Various folk arts are produced in the river valley, and the ancestors who lived by the river created rich and colorful folk culture. From prehistoric period, these folk cultures, which lasted for thousands of years, were rooted in the daily life of the ordinary people. Along with the changes of life, they grew, developed and disappeared. This is a unique cultural resource. Folk art contains rich historical and cultural heritage, which has natural attraction for tourists. As long as it is reasonably developed, it can become an

---

　　① Liu Xiaozhen. "From Folk Etiquette to Folk Art: The Change and Inheritance of the Cultural Function of GuziYangko in Shanghe, Shandong Province."Journal of Beijing Dance Academy, vol. 1, 2004, pp. 77-81.

　　② Li Mu. "Folklore, Art and Aesthetic Experience, Also an Review of Ji Zhongyang's 'Study on the Aesthetic Experience of Folk Art'."Studies of Ethnic Literature, vol. 35, no. 4, 2017, pp. 120-125.

attractive tourism product. Tourists from all places of the country and even the world often have different cultural backgrounds, and cultural collision and blending will occur in the exchanges, which will promote the spread and development of local folk arts. In addition, various cultural and art festivals, cultural and academic exchanges and other forms of cultural and tourism integration can provides important carriers for cultural exchange and dissemination.

But at the same time, the ancient folk arts are vulnerable to the impact of modern civilization. Only economic benefits are not enough to support their transmission and protection, so the arts require government funding. The development of tourism can not only provide financial support for the protection of cultural resources, but also bring considerable economic revenue and social attention to folk art.[①]

(1) Types of Folk Arts

The rich and colorful folk arts can be classified from various angles. According to the different production techniques, folk arts can be divided into embroidery of dyeing and weaving, sculpture, cutting, carving, folk toys, paintings, knitting, pasting, performance and other aspects (as shown in Figure 2.2).

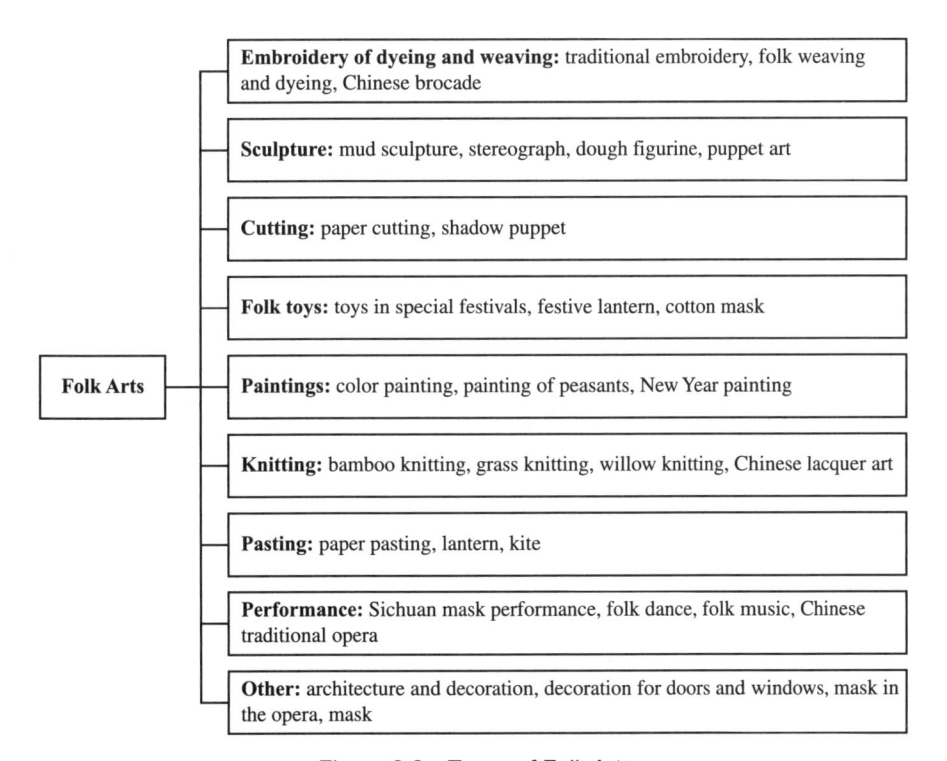

Folk Arts
- **Embroidery of dyeing and weaving:** traditional embroidery, folk weaving and dyeing, Chinese brocade
- **Sculpture:** mud sculpture, stereograph, dough figurine, puppet art
- **Cutting:** paper cutting, shadow puppet
- **Folk toys:** toys in special festivals, festive lantern, cotton mask
- **Paintings:** color painting, painting of peasants, New Year painting
- **Knitting:** bamboo knitting, grass knitting, willow knitting, Chinese lacquer art
- **Pasting:** paper pasting, lantern, kite
- **Performance:** Sichuan mask performance, folk dance, folk music, Chinese traditional opera
- **Other:** architecture and decoration, decoration for doors and windows, mask in the opera, mask

Figure 2.2 Types of Folk Arts

Source: Concluded from this report.

---

① Wang Xia. "Folk Art Integrates into the Development of Cultural Tourism." Shanxi Daily, 3 June 2019, p.10.

a. Embroidery of Dyeing and Weaving, including Folk Weaving and Dyeing, Brocade and Traditional Embroidery

Embroidery of dyeing and weaving expresses and integrates the beauty of textile products with certain creative ways and means of expression. Although folk embroidery of dyeing and weaving is not as efficient in time and cost and accurate as the products produced by modern industry, they have irreplaceable unique charm in skills, smell, pattern and color. The Li people in Hainan Province live in the tropical rainforest area. They have abundant plant resources for dyeing. For thousands of years, ingenious Li women have not only invented advanced textile technology, but also become the best color designer by virtue of a variety of plant dye. The Li people's embroidery of dyeing and weaving, which has survived for more than three thousand years, is known as the "living fossil" in the textile history of China,[1] and has been selected as the first national intangible cultural heritage list.

Case 2.3

The Li People's Embroidery of Dyeing and Weaving

Li is one of the most ancient peoples of China, and they are also the earliest resident on Hainan island. In the long history of laboring, Li people has accumulated abundant traditional culture and created many precious cultural and artistic fortune. The Li embroidery is one of the most colorful Li industrial products. The Li embroidery includes Li people's techniques of spinning, weaving, dyeing and sewing. Today in the Li village in the region of Wuzhi Mountain, Hainan, Li's maidens still use the primitive tools to embroider and make their own beautiful traditional clothes.[2]

As an important part of Li culture, the Li's embroidery's value shows not only in its high techniques, but also in its artistic aesthetic and social culture, which are paid more and more attention by scholars in ethnic culture. In June, 2006, Li's embroidery was listed as a national intangible cultural heritage, which signifies the approval and recognition of the significance of Li's primitive culture. At the same time, because of the attention and promotion of the local government, Li's tourist value is also excavated, developed and popularized. Thus the

---

[1] Fu Shaoling. Research on the Development Strategy of Li Nationality's Intangible Cultural Heritage Resource: A Case Study of Spinning, Dyeing, Weaving and Embroidery Skills of Li Natianality. Art and Literature for the Masses, vol. 4, 2016, pp. 3.

[2] Gao Feng and Gao Chang. "An Overview of Hainan Folk Arts and Crafts." Art & Design, vol. 3, 1999, pp. 4-6.

tourism enables Li people's customs, special boat-shape house, folklore, etc., become the remarkable symbols of Li culture.

The Li embroidery's artistic section and creation features fully show Li people's life, geographical environment, ethnic aesthetic, and special ethnic culture and tradition. For example, the woman's clothes grounding color is either black or composed by different patterns. These patterns are always about the agricultural life or mountains, rivers, animals, planets or clouds. However, they are not pictures of their life, but are abstract lines, figures or geometric designs. The abstraction shows the Li woman's profound observation, imagination, and creation, so the clothes contain high cultural value. In the color selection, because the color selection is limited by the plants for dyeing, the color selection is always simple. But with the special treatment and techniques of the designer, even with just black, red, yellow, and white, the clothes still have the charm to stimulate people's imagination.

The Li embroidery as an advanced technology in weaving and dyeing represents the technological invention and innovation in production. It not only shows the wisdom of the Li people, but also promotes the local economy. Through the protection and promotion of this intangible cultural heritage, the outside world will have a better understanding of the Li region. Thus, the industry of developing tourist products can be formed, the tourism brand of the Li region can be built, and a unique cultural industry can attract the tourist from home and abroad. When they fully learn the charm of the Li culture, the local economy will also be promoted.[1]

Sources of the Case:

Gao Feng, Gao Chang, "An Overview of Hainan Folk Arts and Crafts", *Art & Design,* Vol. 3, pp. 4-6, 1999.

Zhou Guoyao, Wu Xiaowen, "The Artistic Characteristics and Cultural Value of Hainan Li Brocade", *Reform and Opening,* Vol. 8, pp. 196-198, 2009.

(The report summarizes and reorganizes the information from the sources above.)

b. Sculpture

Folk sculpture arts include mud sculpture, dough figurine, stereograph and puppet art. They are mainly the folk artworks produced by the techniques of moulding, piling, and drawing. The origin of dough figurine is the Yellow River Valley in Shanxi. On the dry yellow land, the ordinary wheat-floor buns can be

---

[1] Zhou Guoyao and Wu Xiaowen. The Artistic Characteristics and Cultural Value of Hainan Li Brocade. Reform and Opening, vol. 8, 2009, pp. 196-198.

turned in to delicate artwork and the carrier of Shanxi's abundant and deep cultural connotations. Bun is a symbol of happiness, and the rustic Shanxi people use the good-looking and tasteful bun commonly in the important local activities like wedding ceremony, birthday party and sacrifice. Shanxi bun looks different from the one in other places and has the reputation of the "Top 1 Bun in China".[1] Shanxi's Wenxi Bun was also listed in the national intangible cultural heritage in 2008.[2]

c. Paper Cutting

Folk cutting arts include paper cutting, paper carving, and shadow puppet. This kind of art looks simple with a strong contrast effect and has a high artistic value. The tradition of paper cutting can be found all over China, but they have different styles, quality, themes and materials. The best paper cutting are the single-color paper cutting in Yangzhou, Jiangsu, and Yangliuqing, Tianjin. The paper cutting in these two places is famous for its beautiful design, good quality of paper, and sharp cutting.

d. Carving

Folk carving arts include the carving on jade, wood, stone, and brick. Carving refers to a way of cutting on bamboo, wood, jade, stone, metal and other materials. In this variety, the wood carving in Africa and stone carving in Europe are representative examples. In addition to desert region, African people living in the valleys of the Nile and the Niger also create various forms of wood carving. Besides, stone monument and figure statue are often set up on the banks of rivers.

e. Folk Toys

Folk toys include toys and lanterns for the festivals, cotton toys and toys for intelligent development. In China, there are various delicate folk toys, which are even can be seen as art work. As a special art form in China's folk art, the design of folk toys is also influenced by Chinese culture in the long history. Its functions of entertaining and praying are deeply rooted in Chinese people's life. In the 16th and 17th century, China's folk toys were spread abroad and at the same time, some foreign toys, like "yangpian" (peep show) and some toys for intelligent development, were also imported. Shanxi's folk toys are living fossils of the traditional culture's precious heritage and ethnic artistic development in the Yellow River Valley. Because of the differences in locality, geography, and living environment, the toys vary as well. In the south of Shanxi, which is on the bank of the Yellow River and Fen River, the river courses and gullies are common. With the long history and ancient customs, the folk toys created in this area are always rustic and traditional. The middle of Shanxi has advantages in geographical conditions

---

[1] Xue Xue. A Comparative study on the Decoration characteristics of Dough Modelling: a Comparative study of Gu Jia's Dough Modelling in Shenqiu, Eastern Henan Province and Shanxi Fancy steamed buns. Art and Literature for the Masses, vol. 5, 2017, pp. 93.

[2] Lou Lan. "Jincheng Buns: Eatable Folk Art." China &The World Cultural Exchange vol. 11, 2014, p. 83.

and prosperous economy and culture, so people live an affluent life, and the toys are delicate and smart. The topography of the north Shanxi is mostly mountains and plateau, so the toys are always bold, rustic and primitive.

f. Painting

Folk paintings include color painting, painting of peasant, and New Year painting. Comparing to the paintings of scholars, for palace, with religious purpose, or modern academic paintings, the folk painting dates back to the primitive arts like cliff painting and color paintings on the pottery. They are characterized with strong local and ethnic colors. They are always combined with folk customs with systematic features. Either with strong or light brushstrokes, they look traditional, exaggerate and colorful. The styles of folk New Year paintings are various because of different regional culture. Mainly created in Linfen, Shanxi, the popular wooden New Year painting in the Han people in south Shanxi is one example. The wooden New Year painting is a folk art with a long history in China. It originated from ancient rock paintings and sacrifices. It is a product of popular culture produced along with the folk customs of the New Year, and it is also an art form that the people are very fond of. Pingyang (today's Linfen) wooden paintings have become a unique folk art because of their rigorous style, exquisite workmanship, and simple and beautiful features. It is a comprehensive art, which combines woodcut carving techniques with painting composition, color, lines, and themes. It is the crystallization of the wisdom of folk artists, as well as the image document of folk culture, opera culture, and history.[①]

g. Knitting

Folk knitting arts include bamboo knitting, grass knitting, willow knitting, Chinese lacquer art, etc. In China, the knitting products made of bamboo, grass, vine, willow, and fibre, like other art works, have a long history. The main places of origion of grass knitting are Zhejiang, Henan, Shandong, Hunan, Guangdong, and Guangxi. Lacquer is a kind of natural gum from lacquer tree. It is a precious material given by nature to human beings. After manual treatment, lacquer mud is extracted. Various utensils made of lacquer mud are very firm and light after drying.

h. Pasting

Folk pasting arts include paper pasting, lantern, and kite. Pasting refers to the method of making handicraft products with bamboo, wood, iron wire as the skeleton, silk, paper and other as shell, by binding, fastening, pasting and other methods. Pasting mainly refers to the works made of paper. Broadly speaking, paper pasting works include color doors, spiritual shed, stage, shop decoration, plaque and characters, drama, kite, lantern and so on.

---

① Shi Yu. "Pingyang Wooden New Year Painting and Mr. Zhao Xianyong." Literatures (Theory), vol. 8, 2012, p. 271-272.

i. Performance

Performance includes Sichuan mask performance, folk dance, folk music, Chinese traditional opera, and gong and drum. Many contents in folk art are accomplished through human dancing, acting, singing and other forms. The art categories related to this kind of expression can be called performance art. Sichuan mask performance is a special skill used to shape characters in Sichuan opera art, and it is a romantic technique to reveal the inner thoughts and feelings of characters in Sichuan opera. Folk music is different from professional music in terms of creation methods, techniques, styles and characteristics, including various music genres, such as folk songs and dances, folk instrumental music and so on. Folk dance is a form of dance with distinct regional characteristics and national style, which is popular among the people. Traditional opera is famous in China. It has a long history and has experienced various periods of gestation, formation, development and prosperity. Gong and drum is an indispensable part of folk art, which is very important for the atmosphere rendering of folk dances, operas and so on. Linfen, Shanxi Province, is one of the main birthplaces of gong and drum. The ancient Loess Plateau culture has created enduring folk art of gong and drum. Among the numerous gong and drum art pieces, the Weifeng gong and drum is the most influential and widely circulated folk performing art. It is commonly called as "Jiahuo" or "Weifengjiahuo".[①]

Case 2.4

LinfenWeifeng Gong and Drum

The origin of Weifeng gong and drum, which is short as "gong and drum" or "jiahuo", dates back to the prehistorical period of Yao and Shun. It became popular in Ming Dynasty and reached a peak in Qing Dynasty. With 4,000-year history, the gong and drum performance was very popular in Jinnan region, which centers in Linfen, especially Hongdong Country, Linfen Prefecture, Fenxi, etc. Deeply loved by people, Weifeng gong and drum is characterized by its solemn, unconstrained, aroused, high-range, and varying sound and form and high standards in the instrumental configuration, techniques, team composition, costumes, and performance. In Yao and Shun period, people played gong and drum to create the festive atmosphere. Now it is always performed in January (lunar calendar) and in the

---

[①] Bai Yingfang. "A Preliminary Study on the Origin of Weifeng Gongs and Drums in Linfen." Modern Communication, vol. 11, 2017, pp. 85-86.

competition in the cities. It is also showed in many large-scale national or international galas and gains reputation home and abroad. In 2006, it was listed in the first batch of national intangible cultural heritage.

Linfen Weifeng Gong and Drum consists of an instrumental ensemble of drums, cymbals, gongs and small cymbals, each of which has their own characteristics. When they are played together with mixed parts, the instrument ensemble is characterized by simple, deep and powerful sounds. When playing the gong and drum, the performers stretch and sway their bodies with the rhythm, echoing with the music. The music pieces of Weifeng gong and drum are unique as well, which are always composed in the form of duet. When performers respond to each other, they repeat the rhymes like they are having a dialog. For thousands of years, from Yangxie on the east bank of Fen River to Lishan on the west bank, gong and drum is an indispensable part when welcoming or seeing off the guests. Thus, many tunes are created like "Xihetan", "SimaToutang", "Fengjiaoxue", etc., and each village has their own tunes. Every tune involves a story or special significance, forming a unique and charming local culture of gong and drum.[1]

With the development and inheritance of the Weifeng gong and drum, it has developed from an activity of sacrifice and praying for rain to the best performance during festivals. The form of the performance is varied and carries different social cultural functions, like praying for the good, entertaining, arousing the group spirit, communicating, etc. Through the gong and drum performance, people coordinate with others in the united rhythm, feel the resonance of heartbeat, and communicate the emotions with dance and the high sound of gong and drum. Such communication can be the blessings from friends and family members in the village, or the competition between the villages. In either way, with gong and drum involves people's blessings for others, showing people's emotion and local characteristics.

In the long history of development, LinfenWeifeng gong and drum absorbs the artistic quintessence of eras and enhances the system of performance. Combining with music, dance and other artistic forms, the performance enriches the content and forms a unique artistic style and music. From the sound and music piece to dance and stage settings, the Weifeng gong and drum shows the charm of the instruments and its cultural function and connotations.[2]

---

[1] Zhang Lipeng."Insistence in the Drumbeats."Linfen Daily, 8 May 2019.
[2] Zhang Yue. "Performing Characteristics and Cultural Functions of Weifeng Gongs and Drums in Linfen." Modern Music, vol. 19, 2016, pp. 75-77.

Sources of the Case:

Zhang Lipeng, *Insistence in the Drumbeats*, May 8, 2019, Linfen Daily.http://cnepaper.com/lfrb/html/2019-05/08/content_6_1.htm

Zhang Yue, "Performing Characteristics and Cultural Functions of Weifeng Gongs and Drums in Linfen", *Modern Music,* Vol. 19, pp. 75-77, 2016

(The report summarizes and reorganizes the information from the sources above.)

Other folk arts include architecture and decoration, decoration for doors and windows, mask in the opera, mask, etc. The main themes of architectural decoration are auspicious animals, flowers, or traditional opera paintings, historical stories, auspicious paintings, which are widely used to ward off evils. The cultural connotation of ancient Chinese doors and windows is represented by decorations and patterns. The decoration also reflects the different aesthetic, identity and wealth of house owners, officials, businessmen and literati. Facial makeup can be traced back to the custom of tattoo on the face of primitive people in ancient times. The direct source is costumes of the ancient actors and actresses, which is a part of ancient Chinese cosmetic art. Masks in China have a long history and rich variety. They were first widely used in hunting activities, totem worship, tribal warfare and witchcraft rituals of primitive people. After that, with the development of society, the religious function has weakened, while the function of entertainment has gradually increased, and the appearance of folk-dance masks has greatly enriched the mask culture.

(2) Culture-Tourism Integration Model Driven by the Customs along the Riversides

Folk art is a unique cultural resource. In recent years, with increasing importance of folk art and the rapid development of tourism, folk art has been recognized by more and more tourists, especially those with local characteristics and long history, which have brought strong attraction to tourists. Based on folk art, more creative cultural development and market promotion are carried out in a more diversified form for the tourists.

a. Aesthetic Value of Folk Art

Folk art often reflects the essence of human aesthetic personality, showing not only people's pursuit of beauty of nature, but also mingles with people's ideological feelings of pursuing art, and the expectation of a better life in the future. Take the folk art of our country as an example, the ancient ancestors in folk art often contain good wishes for longevity, auspiciousness, happiness, festivity and so on. The rich and colorful artistic forms of folk art and its great aesthetic value make the experience of folk art activities become an aesthetic activity of people. It covers people's appreciation of beauty, makes tourists feel relaxed and happy, and also cultivates tourists' aesthetic taste.

In addition, folk art also has great research value. There are many domestic and international researchers in folk art, who have been devoting themselves to the study of folk art as a traditional aesthetics for many years. They visit the birthplace of folk arts and initiate deep investigation and deepen the understanding. For example, Yang Xianrang's "The Fourteen Times of Visit to the Yellow River--An Investigation of the Yellow River's Folk Art", which is based on his 30-year investigation. The book not only elaborates on folk arts such as Ansai waist drum, Han stone portraits, woodcut New Year pictures, paper-cut, peasant paintings and stone carvings, but also analyses its artistic style, reflected folk customs and cultural connotations, and records the outstanding folk artists at that time, such as Liu Lanying's and Su Lanhua's paper cutting, Pan Jingle shadow play and so on. The book has left precious pictures and documents for the folk art of the Yellow River Valley.

b. Stage Production of Folk Art

Stage production of folk art is a process of shaping and constructing tourist destinations. It effectively shows the folk art of specific regions and groups to tourists. Stage production of folk art covers all varieties. The most common stage performance is folk music, dance drama and so on. In recent years, with the promotion of protection projects of intangible cultural heritage, more and more intangible cultural heritage has been presented on the stage of folk cultural tourism.[1] The stage exhibition of folk art not only brings enormous economic benefits in tourism, but also promotes the inheritance and innovation of folk art. However, it is also necessary to pay attention to some potential problems, such as in-depth refinement and excavation of historical relics in order to meet the tourists' psychology of seeking novelty and difference. In order to successfully integrate folk art into stage production, first of all, it is important to visit the field to feel the original intangible cultural heritage and understand its historical origin, trigger creative thinking and inspiration in the process of learning and exchanging. Secondly, it is also vital to select the genre that matches the intangible cultural heritage. Finally, it is necessary to conceive and arrange the content and form to ensure that the form of the exhibition is maximized to preserve the authenticity of folk art.

c. Folk Art + New Media in Tourism

Folk art has always been quiet, gentle, small-scale and simple. However, in the days of rapid development of digital media, the conservative mode of market promotion is no longer feasible. With the advantages of the Internet, folk art and new media tourism should be combined, as well as the utilization of image, text, video, sound and other forms of expression, so as to promote a new and comprehensive cultural tourism industry. Many approaches can be effective in improving the promotion of folk arts and tourism destination, such as recording the production process of folk art in tourism blogs, creating a series

---

[1] Li Yu. Inheritance and Innovation: Study on the Stage of Folk Culture. 2013. Guangdong Normal University of Technology, Master Thesis.

of pictures and videos, and promoting them on various social media websites. It is also possible to build an e-commerce marketing platform to realize the combination of the promotion of the folk art in the tourism destinations and the market promotion of tourist products. Thus, an industrial chain of e-commerce of folk art can be developed. Combining traditional folk art with new media tourism is also an inheritance and innovation of excellent traditional culture.

d. Cultural Innovative Product Design in Tourism

At present, tourist souvenirs are repetitive and have few local characteristics, which becomes a major problem in the development of tourist souvenirs. One of the characteristics of tourist souvenirs is that they should contain some unique elements of tourist destinations, which are difficult to buy in other places. Most of the folk art activities drawn from people's daily life have strong national and regional characteristics, such as folk myths like "Eight Immortals Crossing the Sea", "Niulang and Zhinu Meeting on the Milky Way", "Nuwa Mending the Sky", legendary stories of heroes in "Water Margin", Wu Song Killing the Tiger, Yue's Mother Tatooing Her Son, and stories of customs like "Magu Sending Birthday Bless" and "Praying for the Peace All Year Round". These folk arts have tremendous potential to develop into creative products.

When being conscious of the unique cultural value of folk art in tourism development, it is time to integrate folk art with tourism, which can not only promote tourist's understanding of folk art, but also create tourist cultural souvenirs with characteristics of the tourist destination. At present, some areas have used local folk art to develop tourist souvenirs, and are widely popular, such as Suzhou embroidery, Yu County paper-cut, Longdong cloth art and so on.

2. Seasonal and Festival Activities

Seasonal and festival activity is an important part of folk customs. The folk art involved in the seasonal and festival activity reflects people's ideas and emotion in the long-period social development. The river valley is always the region of advanced agricultural development, thus in thousand years of civilization, the agricultural festivals and reglions based on agricultural production during the seasonal and festival activities have tremendous influence on people's life and art creation in the river valley.

(1) China's Seasonal and Festival Activities

Because of the differences in geographical environment and diet, the seasonal and festival customs in the Yangtze River Valley and the Yellow River Valley (north and south of China) are also slightly different. Here are some common seasonal and festival customs in China, as well as the custom differences in the seasons and festivals in the Yangtze River Valley and the Yellow River Valley.

The Spring Festival is the New Year of the lunar calendar, which is also the most solemn and characteristic traditional festival in a year. In the thousand years of historical development, due to the different cultural habits, each region has formed some relatively fixed folk customs and activities. In the north of China, people have dumpling in the New Year Eve, because the pronunciation of dumpling in Chinese is similar to that of "coming of the new year". The shape of dumpling also looks like the currency used in the ancient China, so it also involves the wish of making a fortune in the coming year. In the south, people have rice cakes and sweet dumplings instead because their pronunciation is similar to "good luck" and "family gathering" respectively.

Lantern Festival is the 15th day of January in the lunar calendar, which is also the first night of full moon in the whole year. It is an important traditional festival, during which, people have sweeting dumplings to celebrate the family gathering. In the activities, the northerners have performances of yangko dance and walking on stilts, while dragon and lion dance is popular in the south.

Dragon Boat Festival, May 5th in the lunar calendar, is famous for its custom of making Zongzi. The origin can either be a way of memorial of the patriotic poet Qu Yuan, or to prevent diseases. In the morning of this festival, people hang the Aisong grass or willow on the doors and windows, and children wear colorful weaving bracelets on the wrists. In the Yangtze River Valley, Aisong grass is more popular because it can drive the mosquitoes away, while in the area of Hexi Corridor, willow branches are used to pray for the peace all year round. At the same time, unlike the wide distribution of lakes in the south, most regions are dry in the north. Thus, the dragon boat is not as common as it is in the south. In addition, in the Yellow River Valley, people have the custom of lighting up the torches in the northwest region to ward off the wolves as well as shooting the willow trees and eating Zongzi.

Cizao Festival is on the 23rd, December, in the lunar calendar. It is the day to send the God of Kitchen to the paradise for a God gathering. People value this festival so that it can be seen as a minor Spring Festival. In different regions, the date and the concept of the festival can vary. In the north, the date is 23rd, December, in the lunar calendar, but in some southern regions, the date is one day later. The folk custom is to make "tanggua" by maltose to sacrifice, play fireworks, and paper money to send the God of Kitchen to the paradise.

(2) Seasonal and Festival Activities in Other Countries

a. Paris Plages and Rock en Seine

Beginning in 2002, the Paris Plages was launched by the Paris Municipal Government, which created a beautiful coastal scene along the Seine River with fine sand, palm trees, yachts, folding chairs, hammocks and umbrellas. The festival moves the beach to the streets of Paris. Every year from July to August, along the Seine River, man-made beaches, hundreds of palm trees and various beach sports facilities, as well as stylish small bars are all available. The whole bank of the Seine River becomes a lively and extraordinary

Paris beach, which makes many Parisians who cannot travel far or visitors to Paris feel the unique urban beach. For Paris, a city without the sea, the emergence of beaches brings different beauty to the city. Every summer since 2003, as the closing ceremony of summer carnival, the Rock en Seine has been held by thousands of people for three days in Paris's Saint-Cloud National Park. This is one of the biggest summer music festivals in Paris and one of the most important cultural festivals in Europe. Over the past few days, international pop rock musicians, contemporary music representatives and new musicians have gathered along the Seine River. Participants can devote themselves to the festival at five venues in the park.

b. Carnivals

Carnival is a traditional festival in Europe and America. It originated from the ancient Roman festival of Saturnalia, developed in the Middle Ages and prevailed in contemporary times. The carnival season varies from country to country. Some begin on New Year's Day, others begin on Christmas or other days. But most countries hold it in February and March when the climate is pleasant. The Italian coastal city Viareggio is one of the world-famous carnival resorts. In the Rhine River Valley, such as Cologne, Dusseldorf, Aachen and Mainz, the carnival is called Karneval, while the people who participate in the carnival are called Narr. The most famous carnival in Germany is held in this area, especially in Cologne.

c. Thames Festival

This is London's largest free outdoor art festival, held every September. The Festival is to celebrate the long history of London and the River Thames. It is held in an open-air public venue between the London Eye and Tower Bridge. The food at the feast is all provided by the best sustainable food manufacturer in the UK. "The Great River Race" is a famous water activity during the festival. A fleet of old and new vessels will sail from Tower Bridge to Westminster Bridge. A traditional activity is a display of a collection of classic wooden sailboats at St. Katharine Docks, while the Barge Pulling Race recreates the scene of sailors operating barges loaded with cargo on the River Thames before the Steam Age. During the carnival, music programs and street theatre performances are colorful and eye-catching.

(3) Culture-Tourism Integration Model Driven by the Seasonal and Festival Activities along the Riversides

a. Festival Tourism

Festival tourism refers to the establishment of specific themes on the basis of natural and humane landscape resources in the river valley, and attracting tourists by means of a series of unique folk customs in the festivals. In promoting festival tourism, efforts should be made to set up and enhance the cultural connotation of festival activities, strengthen the cultural construction of festival activities, and form a unique festival culture.

In addition, local college students can also be employed and trained as volunteers during the festival activities to accelerate the development of festival tourism.[1] The cultivation of college students is not only conducive to the improvement of their own abilities, but also benefits the creative thinking of youth groups represented by college students, promoting the overall festival tourism activities, thus attracting more young tourists.

b. Immersive Approach of Cultural Tourism

Immersion experience has emerged in entertainment, education, business and other industries. Festival cultural tourism is a kind of experience economy, which not only meets the material needs of customers, but also brings fresh life experience and rich spiritual enjoyment to customers. In the process of participating in festival activities, tourists integrate into the situation and deeply contact with cultural information on the spot. Such experience makes them form the emotion of identification, acceptance and love for the connotation of cultural activities on the basis of experience, and then spontaneously disseminate it to more people, thus improving the reputation. There are many festival activities in the tourism of other countries, such as Sao Paulo Carnival in Brazil, Christmas in the United States, Bullfight in Spain, Beer Festival in Munich, Germany, Total Thames Festival and so on, which all produce good economic benefits every year.[2]

Case 2.5

Thames Festival

Thames Festival or Thames Carnivals is one of the largest free outdoor festivals in the world. The festival area is on the south bank of the River Thames between the Tower Bridge and the Westminster Bridge. Since the foundation in 1997, nearly 100 countries and regions are attracted to join in the festival to show the cultures, images and charm in various forms.

It is imaginable about the importance of the River Thames to Britain. Flowing through three provinces in England, it is the "mother river" and an important symbol of Britain. With many other London landmarks, it becomes a world known site. To praise this river, every year in London, the UK's largest outdoor art festival, the Thames Festival, is held in London. On this day, nearly 170 exciting art and cultural activities are held on the bank of the River

---

[1] Yang Yuxuan. Festival Tourism Development from the Perspective of Tourist Satisfaction: A Case Study of Qinhuai Lantern Festival. Art and Literature for the Masses, vol. 8, 2019, pp. 247-248.

[2] Zhang Li. "Drawing the Experience Economy of Tourism with Festival Culture." Chinese Culture, 22 June 2019, p.7.

Thames with 2.7-million-people celebration. It is also a ceremony of British to farewell with the summer and to welcome the coming of autumn.

During the festival, a small bottle of river water from the source of the River Thames, Kemble, will be delivered. On the opening day, some traditional ceremonies would be held, especially Morris Dance, a folk circling dance performed by British men. After the ceremony, the water would be delivered to London by thousands of volunteers by swimming, rowing, running, and so on, just like the Olympics Torch Relay. When the "holy water" arrives in London, it would be exhibited in the museum for a few days and time to time during the festival.

Meanwhile, the greatest activity during the festival is the Great River Race. In the race, the audience will see the boats in various forms join the race together, like the dragon boat, Viking pirate boat, Hawaii boat, duck boat, iron-frame boat, etc. More than 300 boats show their own charm. On the bank between Richmond and Ham House, the audience can view the moment of the winner passing through the finishing line and salute and people celebrating the victory. Both sides of the Tower Bridge are also best viewpoints. Visitors who preper to avoid the crowds can also find some food booths on the banks which are not so close to the river, seeing the race while enjoying the cuisine.

In addition to the traditional boat race, tourists have the opportunity to experience the modern entertainment on the water themselves. The high-speed boat launched by London RIB Voyages claims to be the rocket on the River Thames. Taking a boat with 35 friends, the tourists can experience speed and passion on the world's most famous river for 15 minutes. Visitors who love literature, art, and photography can also visit the exhibition held by the London Photo Gallery, which includes photographic exhibitions by cutting-edge photographers from all over the world about London. Their subject is the landscape along the River Thames or Tower Bridge.

Sources of the Case:

"London's Totally Thames Invites Chinese Cities to Sign up for the First Time to Show Their Images", People's Daily (Overseas) www.haiwainet.cn

(The report summarizes and reorganizes the information from the sources above.)

Chapter Two   Spatial Promotion

River valley is a large area, characterized by linear spatial features and zonal distribution, which leads to the need for the river valley to adopt a spatial promotion model for tourism development. This chapter explores three models of river valley development tourism, namely, growth pole model, point-axis model, and linear development. Growth pole model chooses suitable nodes to cultivate the growth pole. Point-axis model links node selection with the construction of axis development. Linear development promotes linear space or corridor. It can be said that these are stages of a progressive development of river valley tourism.

Section 1   Promotion in the Growth Pole Model

Growth pole model is an important model of spatial promotion in river valley tourism, and also the basic premise of point-axis model development. This part first defines the connotation of the growth pole in the river valley tourism and analyses its conditions for cultivation. Secondly, the part elaborates the radiation effect of the growth pole in river valley tourism. Finally, taking the development model of tourism growth pole in the Yangtze River Valley as an example, this part deeply analyzes how to cultivate the growth pole in river valley tourism and promote the radiation effect.

1. The Formation of Growth Pole in River Valley Tourism

(1) Concept of Growth Pole

The concept of "growth pole" was first proposed by French economist Francois Perroux in the "Economic space: theory and applications" published in the "Quarterly Journal of Economics" in 1950. He wrote, "Growth does not appear everywhere and all at once, it appears in points or development poles, with variable intensities, it spreads along diverse channels and with varying terminal effects to the whole of the economy"[1]. Growth pole can appear in industry or in the economic space that has comparative advantages in competition, greater relevance, and broader market prospects. It can also appear in the city, that is, a city

---

[1] AnHusen. "Review of Growth Pole Theory." Nankai Economic Studies, vol. 1, 1997, pp. 31-37.

or a group of cities in a geographical space has strong attraction, agglomeration or polarization effects, or expansion effects and turbulence effects, while having advantages in location, resources, and market.[①]

(2) Concept of Growth Pole in River Valley Tourism

River is a linear space with zonal distribution. Tourism resources can be dispersed and uneven in the basin. Tourism resources can be abundant in some places but limited in others. When the development of river valley tourism is in its beginning phase, it is advisable to adopt the growth pole model. That is to say, the areas with abundant tourism resources should be developed first, and then the development of the areas with general or limited tourism resources can be driven, so that the tourism development in the whole river valley can be promoted in an all-round way. The growth pole model is one of the spatial forms of tourism industry in river valley. Generally speaking, the selection and cultivation of the growth pole in river valley tourism must strengthen the integration of tourism and local industries, enhance the related benefits, and gradually establish the system of growth pole in river valley tourism. Through the constant expansion of the attraction scope of growth pole, the valley's economy can be comprehensively revitalized and the foundation of the point-axis development can be set up.

The growth pole of river valley tourism refers to the tourism center in the river valley, which are always a central town or spot which development scale and potential surpasses other tourist destinations. It shows polarization effect, which can promote the development of river valley tourism. Its spatial diffusion mechanism also exerts a dominant, chain and promoting effect on tourist destinations in surrounding river valleys. When tourists flow and remain in the river valleys, the agglomeration or diffusion of tourism industry emerges and tourist destinations in surrounding river valleys can be developed. In the growth pole model, the main tourism enterprises and reception facilities are concentrated in the center of river valley tourism, which serves as both the distribution center for tourists and the base for tourism activities.[②]

(3) Cultivation of Growth Pole in River Valley Tourism

The formation of the growth pole in river valley tourism can rely on administrative means, directly selecting a place as growth pole, on market's natural selection. The destination with abundant tourism resources and superior traffic conditions in river valley, for example, can be the choice of growth pole. At present, both types of the growth pole in river valley tourism exist in China. The selection and cultivation of the growth pole in river valley tourism is based on certain conditions, and cannot be decided just by subjective will and separated from the practical selection. The tourism growth pole selected is a tourist destination that can realize industrial, talent, capital, information, and technology agglomeration.

---

① Yan Pengfei and Shao Qiufen. "Theoretical Study on Economic Growth Pole."The Theory and Practice of Finance and Economics, vol. 2, 2001, pp. 2-6.

② Fan Xinyou. Study of Spatial Layout of Regional Tourism Planning. 2004. Sichuan University, Master Thesis.

a. Resources

The intensity and characteristics of tourism resources are the preconditions for the formation of tourism growth pole in river valley. When the scale of tourism resources is large, the place will have better development potential. High quality of tourism resources ensures the great attraction for tourists and meeting of the market demand, so that the investment funds can maximize its economic benefits. If tourism resources are unique and have higher degree of importance than similar resources in surrounding areas, they are with strong competitiveness and irreplaceability. They can all be the key factors for a tourist destination to become a growth pole of the tourism industry in river valley.

River valley tourism resources are generally divided into natural and human tourism resources. Natural tourism resources are mainly the natural resources, like the river itself and what river valley tourist spots depend on. Human tourism resources mainly rely on the social environment, people's life, historical relics, culture and art, ethnic customs and material production of rivers, and other things or elements that carry out tourism functions.

b. Infrastructure

Tourist facilities include tourist destination infrastructure and special facilities for tourism in river valley, such as reception facilities, including catering and accommodation. Travel facilities include various means of transport, ropeway in the parking area and communication equipment. Facilities for sightseeing include various signs, tourist distribution points, environmental optimization facilities, etc. Tourist safety and health facilities include the security and emergency services equipped in the scenic spots. The relationship between tourism facilities and tourism development is mutually reinforcing and restricting. Tourist destinations within river valley with sound tourism facilities can produce strong agglomeration capacity, while lagging tourism facilities will restrict the development of growth pole. Therefore, the comprehensively equipped tourism facilities are the basic conditions for the formation of the growth pole in river valley tourism.

Among them, the traffic accessibility of tourist destinations in river valley is particularly important. It includes internal and external traffic accessibility, i.e. high accessibility of tourist attractions which can meet the requirements of "easy entrance, exit and travelling". The task of tourism transportation is to solve the travelers' traffic problems when travelling between destinations, from one destination to another, and among places in the area of the tourist destination. It is not only to solve the problem of spatial distance between different places, but also, more importantly, to solve the problem of time consumption. Tourism transportation is not only a prerequisite for tourists to complete their tourism activities, but also an important source of tourism revenue in river valley.[1]

---

[1] Tao Yun. The Study of the Tourism Industry Growth Pole Theory and its Application. 2006. Anhui Normal University, Master Thesis.

c. Policies

In China, most regions in river valley are remote and the tourism development is limited, so the social awareness of tourism and talents working in tourism are insufficient as well. Thus, the government support is of vital importance to the fast development of growth pole, and the administrative means, selecting and cultivating the growth pole by the administration, should be the dominant approach. From the perspective of promoting tourism development in backward areas and river tourism, the initial development of the growth pole in river valley tourism should mainly rely on the polarization function, with weak diffusion function and small radiation scope. It is necessary for the government to take appropriate and effective measures to support and guide the exchange and cooperation of tourism talents between the growth pole and the surrounding backward areas.

2. The Radiation Effect of Growth Pole in River Valley Tourism

Perroux, French economist and the proponent of growth pole theory, believes that growth is uneven, usually occurs in some growth points or growth poles, and then diffuses outward through different channels. This is the radiation mechanism of growth pole.However, Myrdal, in his book *Economic Theory and Underdeveloped Regions* (1957), examined the radiation ability of growth pole to surrounding areas, using "return effect" and "diffusion effect" to distinguish the two opposite forces of growth pole to surrounding areas.[①]

For the growth pole in river valley tourism, "return effect" and "diffusion effect" can co-exist. On the one hand, the developed tourism areas in the valley may hinder or adversely affect the surrounding areas, so the tourism industry's input and output links and knowledge spillover factors lead to further aggregation of tourism elements into the growth pole in the river valley tourism. On the other hand, agglomeration results in the increase of land cost, urban congestion, saturation of tourism market and excess of local tourism's carrying capacity in the growth pole of the river valley. The tourism elements of the growth pole in the river valley tourism area, including tourism enterprises and tourists, can spread to the surrounding areas, promoting the tourism development of the surrounding poor areas, and gradually narrowing the gap of tourism and economic development between regions. This process shows what "diffusion effect" is.

In the early stage of the development of river tourism, it is necessary to fully mobilize the limited human, material and financial resources on the development of tourist destinations with abundant tourist resources or superior geographical conditions. When all kinds of tourism resources and elements are

---

① Yan Pengfei and Shao Qiufen. "Theoretical Study on Economic Growth Pole."The Theory and Practice of Finance and Economics, vol. 2, 2001, pp. 2-6.

centralizedin the growth pole in the river valley tourism, which enhances the local infrastructure, the tourism industry then can develop rapidly, the talents can gather constantly, and the number of tourists can climb year by year. The growth pole becomes the core area of tourism in the river valley, and the development of tourism economy in the region can be rapid with the polarization effect. At the same time, for the surrounding areas of the growth pole in river valley tourism, return and diffusion effects will also emerge. Only by avoiding the return effect and enhancing the diffusion effect can the radiation effect of growth pole be really brought into play.

(1) Measuring the Surrounding Areas' Capacity for the Growth Pole in River Valley Tourism

After the emergence of polarization effect of the growth pole in river valley tourism, there will be an imbalance between the tourism development of the surrounding areas and that of the growth pole. It is a necessary condition for the application of growth pole model that the surrounding areas can withstand the pressure brought by the increasing gap of tourism development between themselves and the growth pole in a certain period of time. Measures can be taken, such as reducing the trade cost between the growth pole in river valley tourism and the surrounding areas, gradually cooperating with different sectors of tourism, establishing regional coordination mechanism and compensation mechanism, making certain economic compensation for the surrounding areas with backward tourism development, and promoting the exchanges and communication of talents in the field of tourism.

(2) Improving the Traffic Construction between the Growth Pole in River Valley Tourism and Surrounding Areas

Transportation has always been an important factor of tourist activity, and the accessibility can influence the development of tourism in a region. If a growth pole in river valley tourism requires the diffusion effect and radiates the tourism development in surrounding areas, it needs comprehensive transportation and infrastructure. From the diffusion of tourist industry, the flow and communication of talents, the dissemination of tourism information technology, to the influx of tourists, it is the traffic network that is relied on by the diffusion effect to the surrounding areas of the growth pole in river valley tourism.

3. Growth Pole Development of Tourism in the Yangtze River

The Yangtze River originates from the "roof of the world" - the southwest side of Mt. Geladaindong in the Tanggula Mountains on the Qinghai-Tibet Plateau. The main stream flows through 11 provinces, autonomous regions and municipalities directly under the Central Government and flows into the East China Sea at the east of Chongming Island. It is more than 6,300 kilometers long, 800 kilometers longer than the Yellow River. The length of the main stream in the world is second only to the Nile River in Africa and the Amazon River in South America, ranking third in the world.[①]

The Yangtze Gorges is an important section of the Yangtze River Valley. It is about 200 km long from Fengjie, Sichuan to Yichang, Hubei. From west to east, they are Qu Tang Gorge, Wu Gorge and Xiling Gorge.[②] In 2004, the former State Tourism Administration, the Yangtze Gorges Office of the State Council, the National Development and Reform Commission, the West Development Office of the State Council, the Ministry of Communications and the Ministry of Water Resources jointly issued the "Outline of Regional Tourism Development Planning for the Yangtze Gorges Region of the Yangtze River". It points out that in the layout of tourism spatial development, the spatial structure of the Three Gorges tourism development is built up with "two poles, three axes, three districts and four belts", creating Chongqing's and Yichang's urban tourism growth pole. Three axes, taking the main waterway of the Yangtze River and highways and railways alongside as the skeleton, Chongqing and Yichang as two nodes, develops along the axes of all tourist attraction involved in the traditional Three Gorges tourism. Thus there are Hunan-Hubei-Shaanxi axis based on the 209 national highway from northeast to southwest, radiating the regions like Shennongjia, Daninghe, Enshi, Zhangjiajie, Xiangxizhou, Tongren, etc.; and Sichuan-Chongqing-Guizhou axis based on the railways and highways in the region of the lower stream of Wu River and Yuhuai Railway from northwest to southeast, radiating the regions like east Sichuan, west Chongqing, Chishuihe, etc. Three districts are Chongqing Urban and Commercial Tourism District, New Three Gorges Ecology-Culture Tourism District, and Dam-and-Dike Hydropower Tourism District, which are the core area of Three Gorges tourism. Four beltscovers three tourism radiation areasof Chishuihe, Wujiang-Fanjing Mountain, and Qing River, which are sub-zones of the Three Gorges' radiation area.

Jinsha River is an upper stream of the Yangtze River, locating on the west edge of Qinghai-Tibet Plateau, Yunnan-Guizhou Plateau and Sichuan Basin.[③] The lower reaches of Jinsha River spanned Yunnan, Guizhou and Sichuan provinces, covering an area of about 224,712.3 square kilometers. In recent years, the development and construction of national large-scale hydropower projects have greatly improved the traffic conditions in the region. It is particularly important to select and cultivate growth poles to drive the development of the whole region. As a result, Zhaotong and Yibin are divided into the growth polse in river valley tourism selected for the lower reaches of the golden valley of the Yangtze River. The government

---

① Review on the River Valley. Yangtze River Water Conservancy Commission of Ministry of Water Resources, http://www.cjw.gov.cn/zjzx/cjyl/lyzs.Accessed 10 Sept. 2019.

② Yang Dayuan. "Origin and Evolution of the Three Gorges of the Yangtze River."Journal of Nanjing University (Natural Sciences), vol. 3, 1988, pp. 466-474.

③ Xu Changjiang, Fan Kexu and Xiao Tianguo. Analysis of Runoff Characteristics and Trends in Jinsha River Valley. Yangtze River vol. 41, no. 7, 2010, pp. 10-14, p. 51.

and industries pay high attention to and strongly support the development of two regions.

(1) Cultivation of Tourism Growth Pole in Jinsha River

a. Resources

The tourism resources of Zhaotong and Yibin are abundant, so they rapidly become the two growth poles in Jinsha River Valley tourism. Zhaotong is a place having a long history and various tourism resources, and it not only one of the three origins of Yunnan's culture, but also an important node of the China's famous South Silk Road. Zhaoton's Zhuti culture, mountains, grassland, canyon, hot spring, DaguanHuanglian River and other resources all show distinguishing features and complement each other. In Yibin, there are four national 4A-level tourist sites, which are Shunan Bamboo Forest, Xingwen Stone Forest, Xijiashan Ancient Residentce, and Lizhuang Ancient Town. There are also 2 national-level and 5 provincial-level spots as well as 2 provincian-level westland parks. Xiangjiaba Hydropower Station, located at the junction of Yibin and Shuifu City, Yunnan Province, is surrounded by many beautiful tourist resources: canyon, hot spring, Yunnan Dashanbao Mountain, Laojun Mountain in PingshanCounty, Sichuan, Longhua Ancient Town, Shulou Ancient Town, etc. Its reservoir tourism may become a new growth pole of Yibin tourism. Yibin's and Zhaotong's abundant tourism resources enable them to connect with surrounding areas, and cast influence on the market of diversified demands from various aspects.

b. Infrastructure

In the tourism growth poles Zhaotong and Yibin in the lower reaches of Jinsha River, it can be ignored that core traffic location and good transportation play an important role. Zhaotong is famous for its stronghold location, which is in the hinterland of national-planned Panxi-Liupanshui Economic Development Zone. In recent years, the traffic situation in Jinsha River Valley has improved significantly and will continue to be enhanced. Zhaotong, as an important gateway connecting Yunnan, Guizhou and Sichuan provinces, plays an increasingly prominent role as a transportation hub. In promoting the development of hydropower resources of Xiluodu, Xiangjiaba and Baihetan Hydropower Stations, a large amount of construction and resource investment will greatly promote the development of transportation along Zhaotong-related areas and various industries in nearby towns. Traffic facilities and surrounding ecological environment will continue to improve, which will bring a lot of investment opportunities. Therefore, the development and construction of large hydropower stations for more than ten years will be a precious historical development opportunity in Zhaotong.

Yibin is a regional central city in Sichuan Province, which is famous for its comprehensive transportation network of water, land and air. In railways, the Neikun Railway has been built, which is an electrified railway. In 2009, the construction of the Chenggui Railway has been decided to start as a high-speed railway. The expressway has been built and opened to traffic, including Neiyi Expressway and Yikun

Expressway; Yile Expressway and Yilu Expressway are under construction. In aviation, there is already a 4C-class Caiba Airport, and the 4D-class Zongchang International Airport planned for construction in 2009 has been constructed. In terms of water transport, the Xulu waterway of the Yangtze River trunk line was renovated and started in 2007, and will reach the standard of Level 3 waterway.

Zhaotong and Yibin are gradually becoming the core hinterland of tourism development in the lower reaches of Jinsha River and the region with the largest investment because of their superior traffic location and increasingly enhanced traffic facilities.

c. Policies[①]

In 2001, the Yunnan Provincial Party Committee and the provincial government clearly pointed out that the development of tourism in northeastern Yunnan should be accelerated. In 2004, the tourism development plan of northeastern Yunnan tourism area was formally approved. In 2005, Zhaotong explicitly included cultural tourism as an important industry in the 11th Five-Year Plan of the whole city, striving to make tourism a new economic growth point of Zhaotong. In recent years, Zhaotong has taken tourism as a pillar industry. Yibin is one of the four tourism development priority zones and an important node of four excellent tourism routes in Sichuan. The government has put forward the strategy of strengthening tourism development and achieved remarkable results. In 2008, Yibin was confronted with the low temperature and snow disaster in the early of the year, and "5.12"Wenchuan Earthquake. In the second year of the strategy of strengthening tourism development the total tourism revenue was 5.563 billion yuan, an increase of 19.8% over the same period of last year, reaching a new historical high and ranking third in Sichuan Province.

d. Strategies for Cultivation

In addition to the above conditions for the formation of the growth pole in river valley tourism, it is necessary to formulate and implement correct cultivation strategies so that it can truly grow into a tourism growth pole in river valley.

i. Strengthening the Integral Regulation and Establishing a Long-term Cooperation System for Growth Poles in River Valley Tourism

Strengthening the integral management and macro-control of the government can closely link the tourism industry in river valley with other factors of social economy, such as the future economic trend, the change of industrial structure, the conditions of tourism development and environmental changes, so as to make it develop harmoniously with the economic departments, other industries and social groups in the river valley. It can also play a leading role in establishing regional tourism cooperation mechanism in the

---

① Huang He. Research on Cooperation Model of Tourism Circle in the Lower Reaches of Jinsha River Based on Growth Pole Theory. Productivity Research, vol. 12, 2010, pp. 132-133, p. 148.

river valley, making overall planning, formulating policies, coordinating interests and deploying actions, so as to lay a foundation for better cultivation of the growth pole in river valley tourism.

The signing of the agreement between Yibin and Zhaotong provides a framework for tourism cooperation between the two poles of Jinsha tourism circle. How to effectively promote regional tourism cooperation in core areas is a realistic topic. In the process of regional tourism cooperation and development, the two municipalities, as the leading actors, focus on the following aspects: first is to insist the institutional innovation within the core area to promote the quality construction of tourism experience environment. Second, it is necessary to insist on the construction of tourism infrastructure and providing high-quality public services. Third, it is also important to insist on the institutional activities of the community, continuously improving the market cognitive image of the core area, and constructing a mature regional tourism cooperation mechanism. In view of the complexity of the development of regional tourism economic cooperation, the implementation of regional tourism economic policies often requires necessary coordination and unified action among relevant regions, economic departments and social groups to solve the problems of tourism economic development. For this reason, Yibin and Zhaotong can establish coordinating department for compiling regional tourism economic policy, co-regulating "Regional Tourism Marketing Planning", "Regional Tourism Route Planning" and the planning of major projects in key scenic spots. This coordinating body should not only have the corresponding administrative coordinating power, but also have the funds allocated by the two municipalities to solve the problems of regional tourism economic development and their allocation power. Only in this way can it effectively implement the regional tourism economic policy and coordinating work.

ii. Attracting and Promoting the Peripheral Factors into the Growth Pole Area in River Valley Tourism and Setting up Tourism Image of Growth Pole Area

The polarization effect of the growth pole in river valley tourism refers to the process in which the rapidly growing tourism industry attracts and pulls other economic activities towards the growth pole area, which inevitably leads to the geographic polarization in the valley, thus gaining various tourism focuses and further enhancing the polarization of the growth pole area. Developing the growth pole in river valley tourism will produce polarization effect, continuously enhancing the pole's radiation and influence ability, and making it play a demonstration role in the tourism development of surrounding areas.

First, it is necessary to gather the efforts on the socio-economic development of the growth pole in the river valley tourism. Some measure can be taken, such as attracting private capital and external capital to inject funds into local tourism development, expanding investment and financing channels through preferential investment policies, concentrating funds to vigorously develop the social economy of the growth pole in the river valley, improving tourism facilities in the growth pole, and enhancing the quality of local life and tourism attractiveness.

Secondly, it is plausible to create the tourism image of the growth pole in river valley tourism. Building the good tourism image of the growth pole in river valley tourism, expanding tourism advertising and constructing tourism promotion network can well highlight the local characteristics, attract tourist market and promote the river culture. Image is the soul of regional tourism. Building and promoting a good regional tourism image is a most important strategy in regional tourism marketing. A good market image helps tourism regions to highlight their own characteristics, disseminate business ideas, establish customer loyalty, and ultimately achieve marketing objectives. Yibin and Zhaotong co-located in the junction of Yunnan, Guizhou and Sichuan provinces, have carried out extensive exchanges in the long history. According to *Records of History*, after the unification of China, the first emperor of Qin Dynasty excavated the five-foot road, also known as the Shimen Road, which opened the way from the Central Plains Channel to Yunnan and Guizhou. In 122 AD, Emperor Wudi sent envoys to Sichuan to open up the "Nanyi Road" from Yibin through Zhaotong, Kunming, Yunnan, and finally to Myanmar and India, which is known as the "South Silk Road". Yibin is located at the starting point, and Zhaotong is located at the crossroads of Shimen Road and South Silk Road. Thus the historical and cultural ties constitute the resource base for Yibin-Zhaotong to establish the image of regional tourism. The two cities can work together to build the tourism brand of "South Silk Road", and design relevant tourism routes for joint marketing.

Thirdly, it is important to highlight the functional characteristics of the growth pole in river valley tourism. Clarifying the characteristics and strengthening various functions can benefit in concentrating on developing local characteristic tourism resources and tourism products, and enhancing core competitiveness. At the same time, it is necessary to pay attention to tourism innovation to meet the changing and highly personalized tourism market demand.

Finally, it is also vital to train tourism talents and attract tourism enterprises. It is practical to use safeguards and incentives to formulate preferential policies to attract tourism enterprises to the growth pole in the river valley tourism. It is necessary to pay attention to the training of all kinds of tourism talents, provide adequate safeguards and good treatment for the talents coming from other places, and create a good local talent environment. Other measures include establishing tourism colleges and training institutions, strengthening tourism education and training, improving the quality of grass-roots practitioners, enhancing the ability of senior managers, increasing the discussion and exchanges between talents, and becoming the gathering place of tourism talents in the region.

Yibin-Zhaotong growth pole attracts and stimulates the surrounding tourism elements, mainly in the following four aspects. First, it uses safeguards, incentives, both material and spiritual incentives, to attract talents and tourism enterprises. Second, through preferential investment policies, it actively adopts various investment and financing channels, increasing and attracting investment, and promotes tourism capital injection. Third, it concentrates the efforts on the selective development and promotion of Yibin-Zhaotong's most distinctive tourism products, focusing on the production and operation of high-quality tourism products and improving the efficiency of factor allocation. Fourth, it activates and innovates tourism production factors, such as developing special tourism such as ecology and exploration relying on the diverse geographical environment and high-quality ecological resources of Yibin-Zhaotong.

iii. Promoting Tourism Development of Surrounding Areas by the Radiation of the Growth Pole in River Valley Tourism

Yibin-Zhaotong should give full play to its core traffic location advantages, actively contact the cities and states in the region, and construct transportation links with the surrounding areas. It should also take tourism development as a window, expanding the scale of opening-up, strengthen tourism economic links and cooperation among regions, and accept radiation from more developed areas, such as Kunming, to form strategic alliances and expand the scale of its own growth pole. When Yibin-Zhaotong, as regional tourism growth pole, improves its radiation capacity and influence, it can produce external economies of scale and give full play to the demonstration effect of growth pole. Diffusion effect appears on the basis of the formation of Yibin-Zhaotong tourism growth pole, so the surplus and advantageous tourism elements in the city can be exported and allocated to the surrounding areas. Through the export of tourism enterprises and capital, the enterprise's radiation and diffusion effect can be strengthened, especially for large and medium-sized tourism enterprises. They can expand the capital export to the surrounding areas for tourism investment and development by diversified operation, asset restructuring and capital operation. Thus, new economic diffusion effect can emerge and promote the development of the whole regional tourism (The report summarizes from the sources.) [1][2]

(2) Cultivation of Tourism Growth Pole in the Valley of Three Parallel Rivers Where Jinsha River Locates

At the first joint conference of the region of Three Parallel Rivers, delegates from 14 counties (cities and districts) in the four states (cities), the heads of departments of 14 counties (districts and cities) of Nujiang, Dali, Lijiang and Diqing municipalities and relevant tourism experts studied and formulated the "Outline of Tourism Planning for World Natural Heritage Sites with Three Parallel Rivers", and proposed

---

[1] Wang Jing, Luo Mingyi and Du Jingchuan. "On the Selection and Cultivation of Tourism Growth Pole in the Lower Reaches of Jinsha River."The Ideological Front, vol. 4, 2008, pp. 125-126.

[2] Huang He. "Research on Cooperation Model of Tourism Circle in the Lower Reaches of Jinsha River Based on Growth Pole Theory."Productivity Research, vol. 12, 2010, pp. 132-133, p. 148.

that the development of tourism in the region should be accelerated.

The development should be guided by tourism market demand, based on superior tourism resources, led by brand tourism areas, and focus on cultivating new supply power. With the help of the tourism brand effect of Lijiang Ancient City and Shangri-La and the rapid development of industry, the tourism development of the world heritage site should be actively promoted in accordance with the spatial development layout of "one center, three poles, eight circles, ten districts and three belts". The Outline advocates to strengthen the leading and central role of Lijiang tourism, give full play to the tourism brand advantages of Lijiang Ancient City and Yulong County, and strive to build a tourist area of Three Parallel Rivers World Heritage Site, radiating to accelerate the development of the entire regional tourism. The Outline also appeals to create three major tourism growth poles, and turn Shangri-la, Lushui County and Lanping County into tourist distribution centers and tourism growth poles of Jinsha River-Nu River-Lancang River tourism belts. In order to comprehensively improve the accessibility and internal transportation in the Three Parallel Rivers heritage sites, a large tourism transportation network will be constructed.

Section 2 Point-Axis Model

Point-axis model is an extension of model of growth pole, which has a wider scope than model of growth pole for tourism development in the river valley. For example, the valley of the Yellow River, as the mother river of Chinese civilization, takes Yuncheng, Hequ, Hejin and Jixianas important poles in Shanxi Province and takes the Yellow River as the key development axis of valley tourism. It links up the scenery areas of the Yellow River along the meanders of the Yellow River, Hukou Waterfalls, Fenglingdu and Qiaolou, radiating the tourism development of west and south Shanxi, as well as Henan and Shaanxi provinces. This part first defines the concept of point-axis model as well as pole and axis of development in river tourism. Second, using the selection of tourism poles in some branches of the Yangtze River Valley, it explores how to build the valley's key development axis, so as to bring enlightenment for the reasonable construction of point-axis model in the river tourism.

1. The Formation of Point-Axis Model in River Tourism

(1) The Concept of Point-Axis Model

New Economic and Financial Dictionary defines "point-axis model" as an extension of model of growth pole. Because of the increase in the number of growth poles, interconnected traffic lines between growth poles then emerge. When the two growth poles and the traffic lines between them have a higher function than the growth poles, the area is theoretically called the development axis. The development axis has all the characteristics of the growth pole and has a wider scope of action than that.

(2) The Concepts of River Tourism Point and Development Axis

For River tourism, the "pole" in the point-axis model refers to the tourist destination on the "axis" of the river valley, that is, the central city of tourism, the core tourist attractions or their combination. "Axis" is generally the trunk line of transportation, including water and land transportation. For example, the Three Gorges area in the Yangtze River Valley, which relies on the famous cities and scenic spots in the Three Gorges area along the Yangtze River, has led to the development of the whole axis tourism. According to the theory of point-axis model, it is hierarchical for the core tourist destination as a pole and the traffic line as a development axis. Different grades of poles have different status and properties on the development axis, so they need to be positioned reasonably and planned in a coordinated way. The development axis of different grades also has different attraction and cohesion to the surrounding areas. For tourism development in the river valley, it is very important to analyze and determine the location and level of poles and development axis.

(3) The Concept of Point-Axis Model in River Tourism

Point-axis model is valuable for the development of river valley tourism. It can help the river valley to improve the traffic accessibility of tourist spot, let central tourist cities or tourist attractions influence the surroundings, and realize the development of tourism in valley. Here are steps of how river tourism can utilize the point-axis model:

Firstly, according to the distribution of tourism resources and cities, some potential zones of transportation routes can be identified within the river valley, which will be emphatically exploited as "development axis".

Secondly, on each development axis, several poles should be identified as key development towns or tourist spots. Their position, characteristics, development direction and main functions of key development towns or scenic spots on the axis, as well as their service and attraction scope should be clarified as well.

Finally, the grade system of poles and axis should be determined to form a point-axis system with different grades. Within a certain range of valley, priority should be given to the development of high-level poles along the axis and along the line and their surrounding areas. In the future, with the development of the axis and the strengthening of the key development towns or tourist spots, the development focus will gradually shift to the lower-level development axis and poles. Thus, the development axis will gradually extend to the underdeveloped areas, promote the development of secondary axis and poles on the axis, and finally form a point-axis system with a certain hierarchical structure composed of different levels of development axis and its development center, extending the development to the whole region. To a certain extent, the determination of the grade of development axis is also the gradation of tourist routes. The application of point-axis pattern in the development of tourism in river valley should be based on accessibility, and there should be different levels of tourist cities and scenic spots in the river valley.[①]

2. The Development of Point-Axis Model in the Yangtze River Valley

(1) The Construction of Point-Axis Model in Jinsha River

Jinsha River is the upper reaches of the Yangtze River, named for its yellow sandy soil. In the valley of Jinsha River, Yibin and Zhaotong are chosen as two poles, and Neikun Expressway and Railway are taken as the development axes to form the core area of tourism development in the region, and drive the whole region's development in the core area. Each regional tourism layout forms a "market-resource" conjugate tourism destination system in the expanding circles from inside to outside, and realizes the linkage of regions through structural effects.

The construction of Xiluodu Hydropower Station and Xiangjiaba Hydropower Station, located at the border between Sichuan and Yunnan, has promoted the linkage of regional economy between Yibin and Zhaotong. In August 2008, Yibin and Zhaotong became sister cities and signed a cooperation framework agreement. The two cities would cooperate in transportation, resources, tourism and reservoir economy. In September 2008, the tourism departments of the two cities signed the agreement on the construction of barrier-free tourism cooperation zones in Yibin and Zhaotong. In accordance with the principle of "voluntary, equal, fair and win-win", the two cities have reached an agreement on integrating tourism resources, creating excellent tourism products, and jointly building a barrier-free cooperative zone for transportation, services, complaints and a sharing zone of resources, transportation, infrastructure, brand and information. The two cities would jointly carry out tourism publicity, and establish a regional tourism cooperation guarantee mechanism. The point-axis system with the growth pole of Jinsha River tourism has begun its formation. Due to the lack of experience in tourism cooperation in most municipalities in the region, Yibin-Zhaotong tourism cooperation cannot only promote the formation of point-axis system, but also have a demonstration effect, providing a reference for the whole regional tourism cooperation (The report summarizes from the sources.).[②]

(2) The Construction of Point-Axis Model in Jialing River

Jialing River, a tributary of the upper reaches of the Yangtze River, is named for its passage through

---

[①] Fan Xinyou. Study of Spatial Layout of Regional Tourism Planning. 2004. Sichuan University, Master Thesis.

[②] Huang He. "Research on Cooperation Model of Tourism Circle in the Lower Reaches of Jinsha River Based on Growth Pole Theory." Productivity Research, vol. 12, 2010, pp. 132-133, p. 148.

the Jialing Valley in the northeast of Fengxian County, Shaanxi Province. In 1999, for the purpose of channelizing waterways, developing shipping and giving full play to the advantages of Jialing River's water resources, the "Report on the Canalization Development Plan of Jialing River" was compiled by the departments of transportation, water resources and hydropower. The channelized development of Jialing River by combining navigation with electricity is a major project which integrates the comprehensive benefits of shipping, power generation, tourism and flood control. After canalization, the channel mileage can be shortened by 56.2 km. The total 682.8- km channel in the whole valley will reach the level-3 or -4 standards. The 2×500-ton fleet can reach Shanghai directly from Guangyuan. The canalized Jialing River becomes the only artificial canalized inland river shipping line in China. The abundant water resources of Jialing River, the huge transportation channel formed after canalization development and the connected distribution of tourism resources in the valley provide a basis for choosing Jialing River as the key development axis of valley tourism development.

The abundant tourism resources of Jialing River Valley provide the premise and foundation for tourism development, and the potential of tourism development is enormous. With increasing attention paid by governments at all levels in the valley to tourism, the tourism industry of Jialing River Valley has developed rapidly. At present, tourism development has been carried out in a large range, forming a number of attractive and influential tourism hotspots. Taking a spatial view of the comprehensive development trend of Jialing River Valley tourism, tourism hotspots are highly concentrated in Chongqing, Guangyuan and Langzhong, which are the growth poles of valley tourism development. The pole-feature of Jialing River Valley tourism is the objective basis to select points for tourism development in the valley.

Due to the concentration of tourism hotspots, many high-grade and high-quality tourism resources have not been exploited, and the co-existence of both high-quality resources and backward benefits has emerged. To solve the problems, it is a must to optimize the spatial layout of the valley's tourism development. When a rational layout of tourism development is planned, the comprehensive development of the valley's tourism resources can be promoted and the greatest economic, social and ecological benefits can be produced. There are many ways to optimize the spatial distribution of regional tourism. According to the characteristics of poles and axes distribution of Jialing River Valley tourism resources, it is a realistic choice to implement "point-axis" development.

a. The Selection of Points

Chongqing is a famous historical and cultural city in China. It was the capital of ancient Ba State with a long history and profound cultural accumulation. Tourism resources show magnificent natural scenery which integrates mountains, waters, forests, springs, waterfalls, gorges and caves, and rich cultural colors which integrate Bayu culture, catering culture, immigration culture, culture of affiliated capital and urban culture. There are more than 100 tourist attractions in the area, including 4 national and 20 provincial key cultural relics' protection units, 2 national and 3 provincial key scenic spots, 2 nature reserves and 14 forest parks. Chongqing's human tourism resources are mainly composed of cultural monuments, historic memorials, urban gardens and unique buildings, so the diversified characteristics are apparent. Chongqing has abundant tourism resources and high cultural taste. In addition, as a big city in the valley, with good location and developed transportation, Chongqing should become a key tourism development pole in valley. It is necessary to give full play to Chongqing's traffic and geographical advantages, utilize the advantages of cultural tourism resources, promote more influential tourism product combination to market, and make Chongqing become the key growth pole of the valley's tourism.

Nanchong has been striving to build as a regional central city in northeast Sichuan. To build Nanchong as a political, economic and cultural center in northeast Sichuan requires an all-round development of economy and society. Tourism development is an important aspect. The most attractive and influential tourist attractions in Nanchong are Langzhong Ancient City undoubtedly. Langzhong Ancient City is one of the four major ancient cities in China, and it is a highlight of the development of valley tourism of the Jialing River. At present, the tourism development of ancient cities has achieved good economic benefits. Langzhong should be regarded as the key tourism development point of the valley. It is also necessary to speed up the traffic construction between Langzhongand outside the region, forming a stereo traffic network, improving the accessibility of tourism and promoting the rapid development of Langzhong tourism.

Guangyuan is the northern gate of Sichuan Province. Its tourism resources are quite advantageous in the valley and has profound historical and cultural connotations. There are national key cultural relics' protection units like Huangze Temple, Qianfoya Cliff and JianmenShudao National Scenic Spot, Mingyue Gorge, Qingfengxia Ancient Trestle Road, Jianmenguan National Forest Park and other tourist attractions. Guangyuan's festival tourism is also well developed in valley. The annual Daughter's Day attracts many tourists, which greatly improves the popularity and influence of the city. Therefore, there is a solid foundation to consider Guangyuan as a key tourism development point of the valley. However, it must be emphasized that Guangyuan, as a medium-sized city, still needs to be strengthened in urban functions, environmental construction and other aspects to lay a foundation for Guangyuan's tourism development.

b. The Construction of Development Axis

The huge shipping capacity formed after the canalization of Jialing River will undoubtedly greatly promote the development of regional economy. Therefore, as far as valley tourism development is concerned, it is inevitable to take the canalized Jialing River as the key development axis of valley tourism.

At the same time, the national highway 212 passes through Guangyuan, Langzhong, Nanchong, Guang'an, Hechuan and Chongqing in the Jialing River Valley, linking up the central cities of the valley with good regional tourism accessibility. Therefore, in the development of valley tourism, it is necessary take the main stream of Jialing River and the national highway 212 as the main axis, focusing on the development of all levels of growth poles with distinctive resource characteristics, superior development conditions and great impact on the development of all valley tourism resources, and actively developing the secondary development axis (the national highway 318, 210, Nanguang Expressway, and Dacheng Railway) to drive the comprehensive development of valley tourism of Jialing River.(The report summarizes from the sources.)[1]

(3) The Construction of Point-Axis Model in the Yangtze Gorges

The Yangtze Gorges of the Yangtze River is an important part of the Yangtze River Valley. It is about 200 km long from Fengjie in Sichuan to Yichang in Hubei. The cliffs on the two sides of the valley are steep and the flow of the valley is vast. It has a unique geomorphology. The gorges from west to east are Qutang Gorge, Wu Gorge and Xiling Gorge in sequence.[2]

The former State Tourism Administration, the Western Office of the State Council, the National Development and Reform Commission, the Yangtze Gorges Construction Committee of the State Council, the Ministry of Communications and the Ministry of Water Resources took the lead, and the Urban Planning and Design Center of Peking University undertook the formulation of the "Regional Tourism Development Plan for the Three Gorges Region of the Yangtze River" and started to build the "Great Yangtze Gorges Tourism Economic Circle". The actions of the government and various departments greatly promoted the formation of the Yangtze Gorges Tourism Economic Circle.

a. The Selection of Points

In terms of geographic factors and the relations among the Yangtze Gorges of the Yangtze River, the Yangtze Gorges Tourism Economic Circle mainly includes or radiates four provinces and cities, namely Chongqing, Hubei, Hunan and Guizhou, and more specifically, it mainly includes east Hubei, west Chongqing, west Hunan and north Guizhou. To construct the Yangtze Gorges Tourism Economic Circle, it is necessary to first focus on cultivating the growth pole of tourism economy under the leadership of the government, and then, after its gradual maturity, concentrate on the lower-level tourism centers and tourism development axis, thus forming the advantages of comprehensive development network in the regional

---

[1] Zhang Mingchuan. "Study on Tourism Development of Jialing River Basin Based on Point-axis Theory."Science & Technology Economy Market, vol. 10, 2009, pp. 61-66.

[2] Yang Dayuan. "Origin and Evolution of the Three Gorges of the Yangtze River."Journal of Nanjing University (Natural Sciences), vol. 3, 1988, pp. 466-474.

tourism and a point-axis development pattern, and ultimately achieving joint development, mutual benefit and coordinative tourism industry belt.

b. The Construction of Development Axis

The tourism economic development axis of the Yangtze Gorges Tourism Economic Circle can be composed of one main axis and two subsidiary axes. The main axis refers to the axis of the Yangtze River, which is connected by Chongqing and Yichang. The development sub-axes include the tourism development sub-axis of the Yangtze Gorges in Hunan and Hubei and another one in Chongqing and Guizhou. Whether it is the formation of the development of the main axis or the sub-axes, first of all, it is important to strengthen the construction of transportation infrastructure, organize transportation around tourism, and promote the tourism along the transportation lines. In addition to the golden waterway, the Yangtze River, the improvement of land transportation is more important for the tourism routes within the four provinces and cities, especially for the formation of the sub-axes. Due to the influence of topography, geology and funds, the inter-accessibility of highway and railway between provinces and cities is restricted, and the land transportation network has been unsatisfactory for a long time. Recently, however, provinces and municipalities have realized the seriousness of this problem, so the interconnection of provincial and municipal expressways has achieved primary results.In particular, the completion of the Yuhuai Railway (the 625km-long railway starts from Chongqing in the west to Huaihua in Hunan in the east and crosses through Changshou, Fuling, Wulong, Pengshui, Qianjiang, Youyang and Tongren in the three provinces and cities of Chongqing, Guizhou and Hunan) , which is one of the ten symbolic projects for the implementation of the western development strategy by the Party Central Committee and the State Council, has not only ends the long history of lacking of railway in this area, but also plays a decisive role in the formation of the Three Gorges Tourism Economic Circle and the coordinative development of the Circle.

The main axis of the development of the Yangtze Gorges Tourism Economic Circle is the construction focus of the circle. It connects the two most important economic growth poles in the circle. Therefore, the development of the main axis can directly affect the development of the whole economic circle. The two sub-axes of tourism economy of the Yangtze Gorges Tourism Economic Circle, namely, the sub-axes of Hunan and Hubei and of Chongqing and Guizhou, also play an important role in the final formation and perfection of the whole tourism economic circle. (The report summarizes from the sources.)[1]

(4) The Construction of Point-Axis Model in Han River Corridor

The Han River Corridor in southern Shaanxi is located in the upper and middle reaches of the Han

---

[1] Lv Fei. Research on 'Dot-axis' Development in Forming of 'Three Gorges Tourism Economy Circle'. ournal of Chongqing Vocational& Technical Institute, vol. 6, 2006, pp. 52-54.

River, the largest tributary on the left bank of the Yangtze River. It originates from the Hanwangshan Mountain (Gongzhong Mountain) in Da'an Town, Ningqiang County, Hanzhong, crossing Main County, Hanzhong's urban area, Chenggu County, and Huangjin Gorge. It is 110 kilometers long and narrow, and it is ancorridor of ecological landscape. At the same time, the Han River Corridor in southern Shaanxi is the best place on the earth with the same latitude ecology. The valley surrounded by the towering Qinling Mountains and the magnificent Bashan Mountains is nourished by the Han River, the largest tributary on the left bank of the Yangtze River. Although it is located in western China, it shows the same beauty as the south of the Yangtze River. It is a land of geomantic treasure that has the beauty of both north and south China. Because of its warm and humid climate, fertile land, abundant production, good ecological environment, unique tourism resources, and mutual complementary human and nature resources, it has broad potential for tourism development, and urgently needs tourism to drive the regional economic development of the Han River Corridor.

a. The Selection of Poles

Poles in point-axis model are the central towns at all levels that drive regional development. The Han River Corridor tourist area in southern Shaanxi includes three major cities, which are Hanzhong, Ankang and Shangluo. The three cities share similar development level, and are prosperous for the tourism industry in urban areas. Therefore, the urban areas of Hanzhong, Ankang and Shangluo are the basis of tourism development. According to the analysis of tourism development in Hanzhong, Ankang and Shangluo, three key tourism growth poles can be identified, namely, Hantai District of Hanzhong, Hanbin District of Ankang and Shangzhou District of Shangluo.

i. The Selection and Analysis of Level-A Tourist Poles

Hantai District of Hanzhong, Hanbin District of Ankang and Shangzhou District of Shangluo are the political, economic and transportation centers of the three cities in southern Shaanxi Province. Their advantages as tourism location are obvious, the tourism resources are highly concentrated, the tourism infrastructure and service functions are relatively complete, the tourism industry has been formed primarily, and has the most developed transportation conditions in this area. Therefore, it is the level-A growth pole of tourism development in this area. These three primary growth poles integrate the most advantageous traffic factors in the Han River Corridor area of southern Shaanxi Province. They have strong accessibility, thus benefiting tourist gathering and distributing, connecting affiliated counties and districts from all directions. Regional transportation can help tourists to reach all key spots in the cities. Taking Shaanxi Province as an example, tourists must first come to Xi'an, and then to the scenic spots in the counties and municipalities. The development of local tourism must rely on these three poles, which are the necessary places to visit in southern Shaanxi.

ii. The Selection and Analysis of Level-B Tourist Poles

The 25 counties under the jurisdiction of Hanzhong, Ankang and Shangluo cover the key tourism projects in the Han River Corridor area of southern Shaanxi Province. However, due to traffic conditions, some scenic spots have poor accessibility and road conditions, which can only guarantee the basic requirements for entering the scenic spots. The infrastructure construction of the counties and scenic spots is limited. Therefore, although the tourist value of the scenic spots is very high, they all need to rely on Hantai District and Hannin District and Shangzhou District as the backing to attract tourists, so they are the secondary growth poles of the region.

b. The Construction of Development Axis

The Hanzhong and Ankang corridors in southern Shaanxi are located in the valley of the main stream of the Han River and Shangluo in the valley of the tributary of the Han River. In these three areas, the Han River is the most important water system. However, due to its location in the upper and middle reaches of the river, poor navigation conditions, small scale of airports, poor transport capacity and distribution capacity, the external communication of the Han River corridor area in southern Shaanxi is mainly dependent on highways and railways, especially highways. (The report summarizes from the sources.)[1]

Section 3   Linear Development

This part mainly introduces the tourist models developed in the linear spaces (corridor) with rich natural and cultural resources, including the development of corridor of ecological landscape, corridor of heritage protection, and corridor of tourism development. River valley is of the linear characteristics in spatial structure. It has a wealth of function and value, combining functions of landscape ecology, heritage protection and leisure and entertainment. The development of river based on linear space or corridor promotes the tourist development of river valley.

1. Linear Space

(1) The Concept of Linear Space

In landscape ecology, patches, corridors and substrates are usually used to describe the basic spatial structure of landscape. Among them, "corridor" is a special strip element which plays the role of dividing or connecting spatial unit. Forman believes that corridors permeate in all kinds of landscapes,

---

[1] Li Hui. The Study on Tourism Development Model of Hanjiang Corridor in Southern Shaanxi Based on Point-Axis Theory. 2012. Xi'an University of Science and Technology, Master Thesis.

and embody the application value of transportation, ecological protection, aesthetics, and so on.[1] The characteristics of multi-function, complex value and interdisciplinary make corridor research gradually expand from landscape ecology to heritage protection, cultural geography, tourism development and other professional fields. Thus, the study also derives the concepts like ecological corridor, green corridor, heritage corridor, cultural route, cultural corridor, scenic byway, tourist corridor and other similar but also distinctive connotations. These spaces with linear features can be generalized as linear space or corridor. The development of rivers based on linear space or corridor is a model of linear development. This kind of linear space includes natural and artificial space environment around rivers, including rivers, land-water transition area and surrounding on-land space. It carries abundant natural resources and historical and cultural information. It emphasizes the organic symbiosis and sustainable development of natural river resources and human society.

(2) The Categorization of Linear Space

Linear space is a space with many functions such as landscape ecology, heritage protection, leisure and recreation. It is based on rivers (natural and artificial), mountains, ancient roads, traffic lines, parkways, linear structures, thematic historical events and historical figures in time, and links nature preservation sites, scenic spots, historical heritages and other types of human settlements. It includes green way, ecological/green corridor, heritage corridor, culture route, parkway and other concepts.[2]

Linear open space carries abundant natural resource elements and historical and cultural information, and has typical scarcity and non-renewability of resources. It exists in different spatial scales, involving the ones that are beyond administrative boundaries, or the ones more suitable for the scale of natural geographical units to connect or interact with regional and urban areas. Linear open space planning should be a multi-objective integrated complex project on the basis of ensuring sustainable utilization of resources, protecting ecosystem integrity and satisfying other social and psychological needs of human beings. Its success is crucial to the development of large river valleys.

As for the classification of linear space/corridor, according to the emphasis of development, linear spaces can be divided into linear space of heritage protection, of ecological landscape, and of tourism development. Linear space of heritage protection mainly includes cultural corridor, heritage corridor, and cultural route. Linear space of ecological landscape mainly includes green way and ecological corridor. Linear space of tourism development mainly includes parkway, tourist route, tourist corridor and so on. Its classification and main characteristics are shown in Table 2.1.

---

[1] Forman, RTT. Landscape Ecology. New York: Wiley, 1986, pp. 121-155.
[2] Li Xiaojia. Study on Urban Road with Local Characteristic by Linear Space Theory. 2010. Beijing Forestry University, Master Thesis.

Table 2.1 Classification, subdivision and characteristics of corridors

Categorization	Type	Focus
Corridor of ecological landscape	Ecological corridor	protection and sustainable development of ecological environment
	Green way	improvement of human settlement environment and connection between human settlement environment and nature
Corridor of heritage protection	Heritage Corridor	cultural, natural heritage protection and economic development
	Culture route	research and protection of human civilization
	Cultural corridor	value reproduction and development of historical culture route
Corridor of tourism development	Parkway	tourist experience
	Tourist route	development and design of tourism products
	Tourist corridor	focus on the regional distribution of tourism industry

Source:
Wang Fang, Lian Hua, "Research Progress and Development Trend of Linear Space", *Huazhong Architecture*, vol. 7, 2007, pp. 88-91.
QiuHailian, You Yanan, "Definition of Tourism Corridors", *Tourism Form*, vol. 4, 2015, pp. 26-30.

(3) Characteristics of Linear Space

i. As a Dynamic Linear Space[①]

① Transportation: Because of the linear essence, transportation in the linear space is the most fundamental function. Line is the trajectory left by point movement. Therefore, mobility and dynamic traffic attributes constitute the most fundamental characteristics.

② Connectivity: The shape of linear space can be simplified to a line, and this simplified "line" actually has the geometric measurement of two-dimensional geometric figures such as width and area. To connect the functional areas and some important facilities, it is important to construct the "line" to meet the requirements of daily flow of people and spatial transfer of logistics between functional areas.

③ Continuity: Various sequences in linear space form continuity, eliminating the fracture, ensuring that the main body's behavior is continuous and forming the order in motion.

④ Direction and guidance: Visual and psychological continuity constitute the organic wholeness of linear leisure space. Thus, certain directionality is formed, which guides the observer to move towards a certain goal.

⑤ Spatial-temporality: The actor integrates the spatial state of each time point by psychological memory, and obtains the subjective impression of the state of the whole linear space.

---

① Li Xiaojia. Study on Urban Road with Local Characteristic by Linear Space Theory. 2010. Beijing Forestry University, Master Thesis.

⑥ Extensibility: Line "can visually show direction, movement and growth".

⑦ Placeness: People can carry out activities and exchanges in the place. The important conditions that can constitute the linear space of activity place are suitable space form and capacity.

ii. As a Place of Activity for the User

① Diversity: The contingency of human activities and the diversity of life make the linear space as a place for human activities, a place with multi-functions. Linear space attracts people to live together, so it needs to satisfy different functional requirements of people of different purposes and classes through appropriate zoning. The characteristic of multifunction is also manifested in the spatial utilization with a series of changes in time. Diversified activities are interlaced at different times, which makes the linear space full of vitality with high utilization rate and safety.

② Comfortableness: Linear space is dominated by human activities with appropriate scale of space, making people feel intimate and a sense of belonging. The design of facilities in space should conform to ergonomics to comfort the visitor.

③ Accessibility: The accessibility of external traffic encourages various modes of transportation, so that pedestrians and travelers can easily enter the linear space and reasonably organize the multi-level walking system of walkways, squares and gardens. It is also important to emphasize safety, accessibility, comfort and continuity to avoid the impediment of walking system.

④ Culture: Linear space reflects the cultural characteristics of a certain region. Different cultural types can be reflected not only in the form of linear space, but also in the content of people's activities.

iii. As a Growing Space of the Environment

① Landscape: The form, color, scale, texture and detailed design of linear space shape the character of a space of activity and determine the landscape quality of different types of space.

② Ecology: Linear space not only meets the requirements of people's activities, but also balances the ecological environment to a certain extent. Attention to natural ecology includes that to climate, green plants, and water. Linear space based on ecological considerations is a living, sustainable, energetic and natural leisure space.

2. Corridor of ecological landscape

(1) Green Corridor

Green way is a green landscape corridor connecting open space, nature reserves and landscape elements, emphasizing the function of improving environmental quality and providing outdoor entertainment. Taking the management and construction of green way in the United States as an example, thousands of green-way planning and construction projects have been completed in the United States since

1867. In the 1980s, President's Commission on Americans Outdoors released a special report, pointing out that green way brought residents close to nature. Since the 1990s, the green way movement has become an international movement. There are green way projects at the international, national and regional levels in the world.[①]

From the background of putting forward the concept of "green way", it is obvious that green way is a corridor space built by adding necessary leisure service facilities on the basis of natural or artificial corridors. Its main purpose is to provide more natural space for citizens' leisure and recreation. Therefore, compared with the ecological corridor, green way is more artificial and practical. It mostly locates in urban or densely populated areas in spatial distribution, and plays the role of connecting city's life and nature.

(2) Ecological Corridor

a. The Concept and Connotation of Ecological Corridor

Compared with green way, ecological corridor is a type of corridor that emphasizes the function of ecological services. For the construction of ecological corridor, the focus is to use its structural characteristics of dividing landscape pattern and connecting landscape units to realize the protection of ecological diversity. Ecological protection functions can be carried out, like wind-proof and sand-fixing, water and soil erosion prevention and anti-contamination. The concept of ecological corridor is the most original meaning of the concept of "corridor".[②]

Ecological corridor, also known as "green corridor", refers to the ecosystem spatial type that is linearly or zonally distributed in the ecological environment system and can connect more isolated and dispersed ecological units in spatial distribution. It has the functions of protecting biodiversity, filtering pollutants, preventing soil erosion, avoiding wind and sand trapping, regulating flood and other ecological services. The ecological corridor is mainly composed of vegetation, water and other ecological structural elements. The rapid development of economy has caused serious impact on the ecological environment. Thus, ecological corridor emerge as the times require. It is one of the important measures to solve the landscape fragmentation caused by human activities and other environmental problems.

As one of the landscape elements, ecological corridor has the function of connecting landscape patterns and is the channel of ecological flow. At the same time, it also has the negative effect of shielding, filtering and blocking some ecological flows, and other ecological functions. Therefore, according to the needs of the construction of ecological civilization, the construction of ecological corridor for the protection of ecological environment is of great significance to the protection of biodiversity, the promotion of

---

① Sun Shuai. Research on Urban Greenway Planning and Design. 2013. Beijing Forestry University, Master Thesis.
② Qiu Hailian, You Yenan. Definition of tourism corridor [J]. Tourism BBS, 2015, 8(04) :26-30.

ecosystem functions and the maintenance of regional ecological security layout.

Specifically to the ecological corridor of rivers, with the rapid development of economy, human economic activities have carried out a lot of artificial transformation of rivers and riverside vegetation space, which has largely destroyed the ecological function structure of rivers and the natural circulation process of ecosystems. The consequences include crowding up the riverside green space, neglecting the stereo planting of riparian space, homogenizing the green space as landscape, and "breaking up" the landscape corridor. The vegetation ecosystem in some reaches degrades rapidly and the quality of ecological services decreases. Therefore, the construction of river ecological corridor has been promoted. River ecological corridor plays an important role in purifying pollution, improving the quality of biological habitats, maintaining biodiversity and improving the quality of landscape. Based on the principle of ecological corridor, river corridors include the river body itself and the vegetation zones along the river which are different from the surrounding matrix. The landscape ecological service function of the corridor mainly relies on the continuous space of riparian vegetation to be perceived by experience.

b. Functions of Ecological Corridor

In the middle of the 20th century, the function of ecological corridor was mainly to serve aesthetic recreation and connect parks, protected areas, cultural landscapes or historical relics for people to approach nature. At the end of the 20th century, with the emergence of ecological problems such as landscape fragmentation and ecological environment destruction, people began to re-examine the potential and ability of ecological corridor in solving ecological problems. The function of ecological corridor has been extended to other aspects, such as history, culture, entertainment and ecological environment protection. In terms of ecological corridor's ecological functions, they can be summarized as biodiversity protection, ecological environment protection and ecological security pattern construction, and response to global climate change.[①]

c. Categorization of Ecological Corridor

The classification of ecological corridor is diversified. It can be divided into: i. linear corridor (e.g. strip park corridor, scenic forest corridor, shelter forest corridor), ii. strip corridor (e.g. road greening corridor, shade leisure corridor) and iii. river corridor (e. riverside corridor, riverside green belt corridor). Among them, linear ecological corridor refers to the narrow strip dominated by all marginal species; strip ecological corridor refers to the wider strip with abundant internal species; river corridor refers to corridor

---

① Zheng Hao, Gao Jixi, XieGaodi, Zou Changxin, and Jin Yu. "Ecological Corridor." Journal of Ecology and Rural Environment, vol. 35, no. 2, 2019, pp. 137-144.

with the zonal vegetation on both sides of the river, which is different from the environmental matrix, so it is also known as waterfront vegetation belt or buffer strip. From the spatial scale, it can be divided into city corridor, provincial corridor and regional level. In function, the corridors can be divided into natural ecological corridor, entertainment ecological corridor, cultural ecological corridor and comprehensive ecological corridor.

d. Tourist Value of Ecological Corridor

Ecological corridor is one of the most prominent ecological resources, which is also the important tourism resources. Its functions lie in culture, aesthetic appreciation, ecological entertainment, artistic inspiration, establishment of sense of belonging to a place, cultural heritage, knowledge and education, etc. Because of the diversity of functions of ecological corridor, such as ecological protection, entertainment and leisure, historical and cultural protection, the development of tourism is supported by many reasons. On the one hand, the ecological corridor is located in the region, which is based on poles (including nature reserves, forest parks, scenic spots, state-owned forest farms, etc.), axes (rivers, highways, railways, urban and rural roads, green way, landscape forest belts, etc.) and aggregates into a river-lined green way. Natural resources endowment and ecological advantages are obvious in attracting tourists. On the other hand, the benefits of tourism in turn promote the protection of ecological corridor. But attention should be paid to the degree of development and protection, and the principle of "paying equal attention to development and protection, insisting the coexistence of water and land areas, and promoting the coordinated development of upper, middle and lower reaches" should be adhered to.

e. Development of Ecological Corridor

i. Development

In the research of corridors, it is necessary to take into account the interaction and interrelationship among regions, and construct a large-scale ecological corridor system at the regional, national and intercontinental levels. Some international eco-environmental protection organizations recognized the importance of large-scale ecological corridor for landscape connectivity and biodiversity conservation in an early time, and constructed several large-scale ecological corridor systems at the national or intercontinental level. For example, under the background of strong evapotranspiration, fragile ecological environment, reduced biodiversity and serious deterioration of water quality in the Caspian Sea region, key ecosystems were formed. Initiated by the Critical Ecosystem Partnership Fund (CEPF), Russia, Georgia and Iran cooperated to appeal the project of the "Caucasus Biodiversity Hotspot". The project analyzed in detail the main biological species and their habitats in the region. Based on the project, 10 large-scale ecological corridors were delineated, namely Kuma-Manych Corridor, Greater Caucasus Mountain Corridor, Caspian Coastal Corridor and West Small Caucasus Corridor, Javakheti Corridor, East Small Caucasus Corridor,

Iori-Mingechaur Corridor, South Highland Corridor, Arasbaran Corridor and Hyrcan Corridor.[1]

In China, the construction of ecological corridor can be traced back to the project of Green Wall of China in the 1970s. With the increasing prominence of ecological problems, the construction of ecological corridor is constantly emphasized. The report of the Nineteenth National Congress of the Communist Party of China pointed out the need of optimizing the ecological security barrier system, building ecological corridor and biodiversity protection network, and improving the quality and stability of ecosystems. In the practice of river ecological corridor, with the development process, the early construction of cities as the main body gradually developed into the construction of river valley ecological corridor, which shows the strategy of developing from micro-specific planning to a macro-regional one. In February 2010, the "Outline of the General Planning for the Green Way Network in the Pearl River Delta"[2] pointed out that six regional green ways covering provincial, urban and community levels should be built in nine cities in the Pearl River Delta region, which is also the first multi-functional ecological corridor construction project in China at the regional scale (Guangdong Provincial People's Government, 2010). In October 2016, the "Outline of the Development Planning of the Yangtze River Economic Zone" calls for strict protection of the clean water of the Yangtze River and efforts to build a green ecological corridor that coordinates the upper, middle and lower reaches of the Yangtze River and harmonizes the development of man and nature.

ii. Enlightenment

First, the requirements of ecological corridor plans mainly include the following aspects:

① Continuity: It is necessary to strengthen the relationship between isolated patches, because human activities can make the natural landscape fragmented, so the function of the landscape hindered.

② Number of corridors: Corridors are conducive to the movement and maintenance of ecosystems. In most cases, the more ecological corridors, the better. It makes all kinds of ecological flows be flexible in them, forms various radiated areas around corridors, and improves the environment of the surrounding areas.

③ Principle of composition: The corridor itself should be made up of native plant components and be similar to the associated patches.

④ Principle of width: Width has an important influence on the ecological function of corridors. Different types of ecological corridors should be given different widths according to their own characteristics to achieve the ideal function of ecological regulation. Width principle is also one of the most

---

[1] Zheng Hao, Gao Jixi, Xie Gaodi, Zou Changxin, and Jin Yu. "Ecological Corridor."Journal of Ecology and Rural Environment, vol. 35, no. 2, 2019, pp. 137-144.

[2] Approval of the General Planning for the Construction of Greenway Network in Guangdong Province (2011-2015). http://www.gd.gov.cn/gkmlpt/content/0/140/post_140709.html.Accessed 10 Sept. 2019.

difficult principles to grasp.

Second, construction requirements are listed below:

At present, in the construction of some ecological corridors, the various ecological functions of the ecological corridor have not been fully recognized and integrated into the construction, so the ecological functions play a limited role. In view of the existing problems in the construction of the ecological corridor, it is necessary to pay attention to and solve them from the following aspects:

① Focusing on the ecological function of ecological corridor. With the development of industrialization and urbanization, the problems of regional ecological environment have become increasingly serious, and the ecological function of corridors has been paid more and more attention. The construction of ecological corridor should not be limited to urban greening, landscape design and cultural recreation. The construction of ecological corridor based on biodiversity conservation, ecological function improvement and ecological security pattern maintenance can be important research directions in the future.

② Establishing large-scale ecological corridor. Eco-environmental problems gradually reveal the trend of regionalization and globalization, and the decline of landscape connectivity has become a common problem faced by different regions and countries. Therefore, the construction of ecological corridor needs to proceed from regional ecology, carry out large-scale ecological corridor construction at the regional level, national level and intercontinental level of continuous valleys and mountains, strengthen the connectivity and integrity of regional ecosystems, and enhance the overall function of regional ecosystem services. In the process of planning and construction of large-scale corridors, cross-border cooperation and support from provinces, municipalities, autonomous regions or governments are needed.

③ The construction of ecological corridors for ecological protection should be considered as a whole. International large-scale ecological corridor construction often takes into account the existing foundation of ecological protection work. For example, the European Green Belt in the 1990s[①] is an important cornerstone and component of European green infrastructure. Therefore, the existing achievements of ecological land protection, vegetation belt construction and ecological planning can provide support and guarantee for the construction of large-scale ecological corridor. Thus, corridor construction and ecological protection foundation and planning need to be unified, linked and integrated.

3. Corridor for Heritage Protection

(1) Culture route

Culture route refers to a kind of passageway that combines on-land road, waterway or mixed types of

---

① Sun Shuai. Research on Urban Greenway Planning and Design. 2013. Beijing Forestry University, Master Thesis.

roads, which shape and formation are based on its own specific and historical dynamic development and functional evolution. It represents various migrations and flows, people's interaction within or between countries and regions in a certain period of time, multi-dimensional and continuous exchanges of goods, ideas, knowledge and values, and the exchanges and mutual nourishment of the cultures in time and space. They have been constantly reflected through tangible and intangible heritage for a long time.[①]

The selection and identification is strict for culture route. It pays attention to its cultural significance and emphasizes cultural influence, communication and dialogue. It is an objective type of heritage. Those routes which are linked through different heritage and have no historical and cultural significance cannot be identified as cultural route.

(2) Heritage Corridor

a. The Concept and Connotation of Heritage Corridor

From the development of heritage corridor, it originally evolved from green corridor. In other words, it was firstly developed as a regional strategy of heritage protection formed by the combination of green corridor and heritage protection, and then gradually developed into an independent corridor form. Heritage corridor is a combination of landscape belt of cultural resources, pursuing both cultural heritage protection and natural preservation, while taking into account the multiple objectives of economic development, regional revitalization, and residents' leisure and education. Specifically, it refers to the linear landscape with special cultural resources, usually with obvious economic centers, thriving tourism, adaptive reuse of old buildings, entertainment and environmental improvement. Belt-shaped landforms such as rivers, canals, roads and railway lines are all the manifestations of heritage corridor. It is the product of the regional development of historical and cultural protection, and a comprehensive form of heritage protection for green corridors and heritage areas.

Heritage corridor, firstly, is a linear heritage area. It puts cultural significance first, such as river valleys, canals, roads and railway lines, or linear corridors that can connect individual heritage sites in series with a certain historical significance. They are the "works co-created by man and nature" formed in the process of long-period development and interaction between man and nature.

b. Functions of Heritage Corridor

Heritage corridor is implemented in region rather than from a local point to protect heritage, which is a comprehensive protection measure. Thus the natural, economic, historical and cultural factors are combined, and heritage corridor becomes a multi-objective protection system.

---

① Tao Li. "Cultural Corridor and Tourism Development: A New Approach for Tourism Development of Linear Heritage Area." The Ideological Front, vol. 38, no. 2, 2012, pp. 99-103.

Heritage corridor has rich connotations. It not only emphasizes the cultural significance of heritage protection, but also emphasizes its ecological and tourism economic value. Heritage corridor can also become a strategic ecological infrastructure because it not only protects those linear heritage areas with cultural significance, but also restores and protects the ecological environment of the region through appropriate ecological restoration measures and tourism development means. Thus it makes some individual heritage, which were originally lacking in vitality, rejuvenate, become part of modern life and provide recreation, leisure, education and other ecological services for urban and rural residents. This is particularly important for those areas where economic development is backward and the relationship between man and land is in serious crisis.

c. Characteristics of Heritage Corridor

Heritage corridor is a linear landscape. This determines the difference between heritage corridor and heritage area. A scenic spot or a famous historical and cultural city can be called as a heritage area, but heritage corridor is a linear heritage area. It is developed in region rather than from a local point to protect heritage. It can include a variety of different heritages, which can be a linear region of several kilometers long or more.

Scales of the heritage corridor can be large or small, but mostly medium-sized: this is very similar to the green corridor. It can refer to either a river system in a city or a part of a river valley spanning several cities. The Historic Pathway in Pennsylvania is a heritage corridor of 1.5 miles long, while Los Cominos del Rio Heritage Corridor is 210 miles long.[①]

Heritage corridor is a comprehensive protection measure. It values nature, economy, history and culture. Unlike green corridor, it emphasizes the importance of natural ecosystem, but not the cultural characteristics. Heritage corridor puts historical and cultural connotations first, while emphasizing the balance between economic value and natural ecosystem.

d. Development of Heritage Corridor

i. Development requirements. There are difficulties and particularities in the protection and development of linear heritage because of its large span in space and time, complex structure and diverse functions. At the same time, the temporal and spatial characteristics and system functions of linear heritage determine that there should be new perspectives and ways in tourism development, heritage protection and value excavation.

ii. Development practices. In other countries, the Illinois and Michigan Canals were designated the first heritage corridor in 1984. After that, Black Stone River Valley National Heritage Corridor, Delaware an

---

① Sun Shuai. Research on Urban Greenway Planning and Design. 2013. Beijing Forestry University, Master Thesis.

d Leigh Navigation Canal National Heritage Corridor, and El Camino de Santiago in Spain were also listed as heritage corridors.[①] Black Stone River Valley National Heritage Corridor, located in Massachusetts and Rhode Island, witnesses the whole process of settlement industrialization and environmental degradation. In terms of the utilization of cultural heritage system, because Black Stone River Valley National Heritage Corridor has a large number of historical and archaeological resources and industrial relics of the factory buildings, historical industrial buildings are reused to build new factories according to the plan. Meanwhile the plan also decides to integrate the original scattered cultural heritage into a regional whole, and plans for a themed group in the area of heritage cluster. Black Stone River Valley National Heritage Corridor makes full use of its natural ecosystem, utilizes the natural resources of Black Stone River Valley and its tributaries, such as lakes, wetlands, etc. to build ecological parks, and transforms the original farmland into pastoral landscape. It also develops natural terrain such as canyons into forest exploration, rock climbing and other tourism programs, and constructs wildlife protection areas. In addition, Black Stone River Valley National Heritage Corridor has established a comprehensive support system, including recreation system, commentary system, public service facilities system and management system, and encourages celebration activities to be held in the corridor. The tripartite conservation planning system of Black Stone River Valley National Heritage Corridor has greatly promoted the prosperity of culture, environment and economy in the region once again.

Singapore River is the vein of life to Singapore. In the early days, the trade on the ports of Singapore River was flourishing, however, frequent traffic led to serious pollution of the river and the trade gradually declined. In the new round of general planning, the Singapore Canal adopts the method of thematic classification and development for cultural history, natural ecology and other resources. The development is divided into three themes, which are memorial, religion and landmark. According to the characteristics of the themes, the image packaging system is built. The Merlion Park, the Raffles Landing Site, the old Parliament Building of Singapore and the red light code and other representative scenic spots are established. Natural ecological resources are also utilized, the construction of Singapore River Historic Tourist Avenue and green corridor of cycling on the riverside is one example. In addition, the Singapore Canal has a complete supporting system to increase the tourist's sense of experience, for example, a series of tourism resources are connected through a comprehensive walking and recreation system, forming a tourism corridor system. Comprehensive guide boards and interactive experience interpretation system in a variety of languages are also set up. A supporting service system with historical characteristics is

---

① Wang Xiaoyu and Chen Bochao. "Protection of National Heritage Corridors in the United States: A Case Study of Black Stone River Valley." World Architecture, vol. 7, 2007, pp. 124-126.

also established. The introduction of the concept of heritage corridor provides a new way of thinking and method to protect the Singapore River from various crises.

China has rich linear cultural heritage, such as the ancient canal, the Three Gorges of the Yangtze River, the Silk Road, JianmenShudao, etc. At present, some related development and protection measures are also carried out around heritage corridor.

iii. Enlightments

① The combination of conservation and sustainable utilization can promote the revival of regional economy through heritage corridor. Improvement of walking recreation system, construction of interpretation system and effective marketing strategy are the main approaches for heritage corridor to making sustainable use of resources.

② With overall planning and coordination, the establishment of a wide range of partnerships linking with core departments is necessary to achieve common management. The cross-regional and multi-functional nature of heritage corridor determines that its management needs to regularly coordinate with different administrative regions and functional departments. Therefore, only by forming a cooperative partnership with core executive departments and integrating all kinds of government agencies and non-profit organizations, can effective communication and management be truly realized and the smooth implementation of protection and management be ensured.

e. Heritage Corridor and Tourist Development

Heritage corridor is a method of heritage protection originating in the United States. It refers to the linear landscape with special cultural resources. It usually has obvious economic center, flourishing tourism, adaptive reuse of old buildings, entertainment and environmental improvement. As a product of the combination of green corridors and heritage regions, heritage corridor emphasizes not only the cultural significance of linear heritage protection, but also its tourism, ecological and economic value.

i. The Relationship between Heritage Corridor and Tourism Development

Heritage corridor is closely related to tourism development. On the one hand, developing tourism from the perspective of heritage corridor is a new way of linear heritage regional tourism development; on the other hand, tourism development is an important way of heritage corridor development and protection. Some major reasons are shown below:

First, there is a need to use innovate ways of regional protection and development of cultural heritage. There are important natural and cultural resources concentrated in the linear region as well as abundant linear heritage resources along the river. The most common one is the linear cultural heritage based on the channel culture formed by human migration and exchanges in the history. In addition to its inherent historical and cultural value, linear heritage often has social, ecological, economic and even political value, as well as outstanding tourism development value. There are difficulties and particularities in the protection and development of linear heritage because of its large span in space and time, complex structure and diverse functions. It is necessary to innovate the means of regional protection and development of cultural heritage. In practice, tourism is the most direct way to utilize cultural heritage areas.

Second, it is necessary to explore the multiple values of linear heritage areas. The connotation and starting point of heritage corridor not only emphasizes the authenticity and integrity of the route's culture and the protection of cultural heritage, but also puts the overall development of route's region and the relationship between the route and environment and community in an important position. Tourism has dual attributes of economy and culture with strong systematic characteristic. Thus, it is a way to explore the comprehensive values of the route.

Third, heritage corridor is a more profound manifestation of linear tourism products. Line is an important feature of most tourism products. Heritage corridor can be the soul of tourist route, linking the individual scenic spots, facilities and services, urban settlements, roads and bridges, and environmental ecology through stories spanning time and space to form the characteristics of linear, banded and netted tourist destinations. Thus, it is one of the most profound ways of experiencing tourist products. The locality of corridor landscape can be transformed into the locality, symbolity, recognizablity of the destination to attract the tourist and form a strong image.

Fourth, heritage corridor's tourism development can innovate the thinking and mode of tourism development. The temporal and spatial characteristics and systematic functions of linear cultural heritage determine that it should innovate perspectives and ways in tourism development, heritage protection and value excavation. The tourism development of heritage corridor embodies the following innovations. ① It is necessary to integrate the resources on the route within the valley in a broader scope to promote the development of the hot and cold spots of tourism, transitioning from the tourism development mode focusing on scenic spots and areas to the line-centered development. ② It is important to coordinate the relationship among tourism, culture and environment at a higher level, returning from the decision-making-centered tourism planning mode to the cultural-centered planning focus. ③ A brand-new management mode of tourism brand should be developed, focusing on the brand building and management of the route's culture rather than the brand marketing of the destination. ④ Instead of the emphasis on the physical attributes of tourism and transportation, the dynamic and interactive social and psychological layer of "the route's spirit" should be paid more attention to.

ii. The Resource Value of the Tourism Development of Heritage corridor

① Cultural value. Heritage corridor is a special heritage of cultural landscape. Take the Yangtze Gorges as an example, Qutang Gorge is supported by the culture of the Three Kingdoms, Wuxia Gorge takes the history and culture of the Bashu Kingdom as its connotation, and Xiling Gorge focuses on the culture of the Three Gorges Water Conservancy Project. These unique cultural connotations are the soul of the tourism development. For the river heritage corridor, its cultural value as a whole is far greater than the sum of tourism value of each heritage site. Therefore, the evaluation of the overall cultural value based on heritage corridor is of more significance in practice. Creating heritage corridor routes with different cultures is of great significance not only for heritage corridor protection, but also for tourism development within river corridors.

② Ecological value. Heritage corridor of a certain scale can also become a strategic ecological infrastructure project. Heritage corridor not only protects those linear heritage areas with cultural significance, but also restores and protects the ecological environment of the region through appropriate ecological restoration and tourism development. Thus it makes some individual heritage, which were originally lacking in vitality, rejuvenate, become part of modern life and provide recreation, leisure, education and other ecological services for urban and rural residents. This is particularly important for those areas where economic development is backward and the relationship between man and land is in serious crisis. The conservation plan of heritage corridor emphasizes not only landscape ecological process, land coverage, wildlife, species habitat and suitability, but also the organization of cultural protection and tourism development. As far as cultural factors are concerned, it emphasizes the protection of the vegetation with historic value, such as ancient and famous trees, as well as the creation of historical atmosphere.

③ Recreational value. Heritage corridor is often famous for its abundant natural and cultural tourism resources, and the recreational value of ecological and cultural heritage tourism corridors is very prominent. For the river heritage corridor, the design of bicycle lanes and walkways provides a path for recreational activities. The culture and natural resources along the corridor have high-quality recreational value. Heritage corridor constructed for the purpose of ecological protection, heritage protection and tourism development is itself a tourist corridor. The integration of cultural resources, the construction of interpretation system, and the building of recreational routes can not only enhance the tourist experience, but also improve the living standards of local residents. Its comprehensive benefits will affect the areas along the heritage corridor.

④ Educational value. The educational value of heritage tourism corridors can be embodied in the protection of ecological environment, the popularization of historical and cultural knowledge, and the protection and inheritance of intangible cultural heritage. Constructing tourism corridors of ecological and cultural heritage will help to enhance the environmental awareness of the government, local residents and tourists. At the same time, heritage corridor mostly owns brilliant historical culture and rich intangible cultural heritage. Through the interpretation system of core heritage in the corridor, people can understand the historical, cultural and aesthetic value of heritage corridor.

Generally speaking, the construction of heritage corridor will make the scattered cultural heritage become a regional whole. Through systematic interpretation and tourism organization, it can promote the development of tourism, which has been confirmed by a large number of evidences. In practice, tourism brought by heritage corridor in many parts of the United States has become one of the highlights of the local economy. The construction of heritage corridor can make a large number of cultural heritages revitalized and can promote the development of cultural tourism.

4. Corridor of Tourism Development

Corridor of landscape ecology and corridor of heritage protection are respectively based on the perspective of ecology and culture in the corridor study. Both types of corridors inevitably involve tourism and recreation functions. Since linear space with high quality of ecological landscape and high value of cultural resources is itself a tourism resource with high potential for development, so corridor of tourism development emerges therefrom.[1]

(1) Tourist Route

Tourist route is a spatial route that tourists travel from their residence to one or more tourist destinations for recreation and return to their residence. Although the spatial patterns of tourist routes are diversified, the trajectory of spatial displacement of tourists from their residence to their destination must be linear. The concept of tourist route weakens the spatial significance of tourist corridors but emphasizes the combination and overall arrangement of tourism products, and its goal is to achieve the optimal plan of time arrangement for tourists.

(2) Tourist Corridor

Tourist corridor is often understood as a channel for tourism, but its content is more than that. Tourism corridor is a linear corridor that links and aggregates all elements of tourism industry. In essence, it is a linear form of spatial distribution of tourism productivity. Specifically, it realizes the goal by the aggregation all kinds of closely related tourist resource areas on the axis of belt tourism attractions such as trunk lines of transportation or mountains and rivers, and to form a belt tourism system with tourism centers, such as cities and towns, as growth poles. Tourism corridor is the application of point-axis model in spatial organization of tourism industry.

---

[1] Qiu Hailian and You Yanan. "Definition of Tourism Corridors."Tourism Form, vol. 8, no. 4, 2015, pp. 26-30.

(3) Scenic byway

a. The Concept and Connotation of Scenic Byway

Scenic byway is a landscape road which combines tourism and transportation functions. It has multiple values such as transportation, landscape, recreation, history, culture, nature and cultural relics. In the study of scenic byway and related issues, the commonly used concepts are parkway, scenic byway, culture routes, heritage corridors, scenic highway, scenic drive, scenic routes, scenic road, natural beauty roads, historic roads, engineered routes, etc. Generally speaking, these concepts may overlap each other and have slightly different meanings, but they all refer to "beside or within the horizon, the landscape roads with aesthetic scenery, nature, culture, history, recreational value and archaeological value that worth preservation and restoration". The definition of scenic byway can be divided into broad and narrow sense: in broad sense, it refers to a channel with dual functions of transportation and landscape appreciation; in narrow sense, it refers to a landscape road with aesthetic scenery, natural, cultural, historical, archaeological and/or recreational value that is worth preserving, restoring, protecting and promoting.[1]

Scenic byway originated in Europe and America. It is the continuation and development of European and American countries that have paid attention to the protection and management of ecological environment and natural and cultural heritage for more than one hundred years. It reflects the new trend of comprehensive development of engineering technology and ecological protection, history and culture, landscape environment, tourism and recreation, community economy, etc. Scenic byway is a development of ecological civilization. It is the inevitable development of comprehensive transportation in a time of self-driving travel and valley regional tourism.

Scenic byway is playing an increasingly important role in protecting the ecological environment, increasing the attractiveness of natural and human resources, meeting the needs of aesthetic recreation, optimizing the city and road design, and stimulating community economic growth. Waterfront scenic byway refers to the scenic byway that is bordered by rivers, lakes or oceans, and travels through areas with water as the main body. The scenic byway can be divided into three types: the scenic byway of riverside, of lake, and of ocean. These three type takes river, lake, and ocean as the main body of the landscape respectively. People can always get close to river rather than lake or ocean because of the regional area and other factors, so from the perspective of the intimacy with users, scenic byway of riverside should be strongly developed.

b. Spatial Structure of Scenic Byway

The practice and development of corridors show that the spatial structure of tourist corridors is similar

---

[1] Yu Qing, Wu Bihu, Liu Zhimin, Hu Xiaoran, and Chen Linlin. "Research and Planning Practice on Scenic Byway." Geographical Research, vol. 6, 2007, pp. 1274-1284.

to that of general corridors, and has certain spatial elements, such as axis, node and domain surface. The axis is the basic skeleton of scenic byway, which is mainly composed of highway transportation or linear attractions such as mountains, valleys and rivers that have the ability of gathering elements of tourism industry. For example, the Lancang-Mekong River, which flows through China, Myanmar, Thailand, Laos, Cambodia and Vietnam, is the most important tourism corridor in the southwestern border of China. Node is the area where tourism resources, distribution centers and tourism service facilities gather. Domain area is the scope of scenic byway radiation and influence, which centers on the scenic byway axis and extends to both sides to form the scope of scenic byway space. Therefore, scenic byway is an open strip space. The width and coverage of the corridor depends on the agglomeration capacity of the axis and the maturity of the tourism industry along the scenic byway.

c. Development Principles of Scenic Byway

Compared to scenic spots or areas, the biggest difference of scenic byway is that people regard highway corridor as a mixture of broader human values, thus it is necessary to strengthen its functions of landscape appreciation, leisure and recreation, experience education and information guidance during tourists' journey. In the development and construction of scenic byway, following principles should be adhered to:

i. Natural ecology. Scenic byway generally covers a beautiful natural landscape area. Therefore, the planning and design should comply with nature. The newly added landscape and architecture along scenic byway should also be well integrated. At the same time, it is necessary to protect the diversity of ecosystems, the natural environment and original natural scenery, and achieve sustainable development.

ii. Four water activities. Scenic byway with tourism function should develop the activities of riverside entertainment, water appreciation, in-water program and on-water program, providing tourists with ample opportunities to get close to water, and embodying the nature of riverside entertainment in the design of facilities and recreational activities.

iii. Organic combination of land, bank and water recreational activities. The scenic byway of a river is unique in that it connects three types of terrain: water body, coastal zone and land area. Therefore, based on these three types of elements, various types of recreational activities can be developed and combined scientifically and organically. Among them, land elements include waterfront architecture, road and path system, interpretation system, recreational service facilities, etc. Water elements include recreational activities and designs based on water body. Coastal elements include landscape and plant allocation, revetment, bank design, etc.

iv. Historical protection and inheritance. In the process of development and construction of scenic byway, it is necessary to pay attention to the principles of protection and inheritance of historical context, respecting history, inheriting and protecting historical and cultural heritage, and enhancing the cohesion and inspiration of scenic byway in the field of history and culture.

v. Diversification and dimension of transportation. In order to realize the organic combination of recreational activities and enable tourists to experience scenic byway from a dimensional perspective, the construction of transportation should be based on the principle of diversity and stereo dimension, adopt a variety of transportation to meet the diverse needs of tourists, and experience scenic byway from a dimensional perspective.

d. Tourism Characteristics of Scenic Byway

i. Tourist Attractions as Clues

From the perspective of tourism resources, corridor of landscape ecology and corridor for heritage protection are both tourist attractions, which form the basic conditions of tourism corridor in series with a certain spatial order. Depending on the attractions, each scenic byway should have a specific theme to create a unique tourism image. As a series clues of tourist attractions, scenic byway embodies some of the characteristics of tourist routes.

ii. Space of Recreational Activities

Scenic byway is an axis-shaped recreational space which is different from scenic spots or areas. Linear recreational space makes tourist's experience change from static to dynamic, and forms a whole and continuous understanding of tourist attractions. Such linear recreational space allows tourists to get more abundant travel experience and pleasant feeling of various forms of tourism transportation in the traveling, such as self-driving, hiking, bicycle and so on, which are all suitable forms of tourism products for scenic byway development.

iii. Agglomeration of Tourism Industry at the Axis

According to the growth pole theory and the point-axis theory of regional economics, the poles with resource advantages in the region should be given priority of development, and the development potential can extend out of the axis to form an industrial belt, which ultimately drives the economic development of the whole region. The development of tourism industry needs to have tourism attractions, service of tourism enterprises, support and tourist flow. These elements flow and allocate in the corridor area of scenic byway. The corridor's traffic plays the role of convergence axis and development axis, and becomes the passage for tourism cooperation and visitors in the corridor. When each relatively independent tourism space is integrated into a complete belt-like tourism space by means of transportation, the vitality of tourism resources development can be stimulated and the flow of industrial factors can be guaranteed, thus promoting the development and growth of the whole tourism industry in the belt-like region.

e. Development of Scenic Byway

In practice, the United States is the birthplace, main practice and R&D base of scenic byway. According to the National Scenic Byway Program, the official promotion plan for the protection and promotion of scenic byway proposed by the United States, 32 Pan-American scenic byways and 133 national scenic byways were selected in five batches in 1996, 1998, 2000, 2002 and 2005 respectively. Thus the United States established a national scenic byway system composed of national, state and local levels. From the perspective of thematic division, scenic byway in the national scenic byway system includes waterfront, mountain, ecological theme, heritage, sport and leisure, folk culture and so on. Different thematic scenic byway has made great achievements in the practice and theory of scenic byway in the United States. Because of the large proportion of scenic byway, most of which are located in economically and socially developed areas, the research results are remarkable, especially in practice, it has been greatly promoted and developed.

For example, Great River Road in the United States is a famous scenic byway with natural and historical waterfront. Great River Road is located in the Mississippi River Valley in the eastern part of the United States. From north to south, Great River Road passes through Minnesota, Wisconsin, Iowa, Illinois, Missouri, Kentucky, Tennessee, Arkansas, Mississippi and Louisiana in turn. The total length of Great River Road is about 3,000 miles (about 4,800 kilometers). The section of national scenic byway is 2,069 miles long (about 3,329.7 kilometers), which is the very way to experience the wonders of the Mississippi River. The Great River Road (designated as the section of the national scenic byway) can be divided into four sections according to the landscape characteristics of the Mississippi River along the road, namely, the source, the upstream, the middle section and the downstream of the Mississippi River.[1]

The source of the Mississippi River is gentle. The source refers to the Minnesota section of the Great River Road, that is, the section from the source to Sao Paulo. The river flow is cool and gentle. The natural scenery along the Great River Road is beautiful. There are many lakes, swamps and rural lowlands.

The upstream is famous for its natural beauty. Upstream extends from Sao Paulo to the mouth of the Missouri River near St. Louis, Missouri. This section flows between limestone cliffs with a magnificent view. Native American culture in this section is also prominent. This section of the river is called "the father of rivers" by the local Indians.

Mid-stream is the section of metropolitan tourism. From the Missouri River influx to the Ohio estuary is the mid-stream. The flow in this section is turbulent and the sediment content is high. There are many

---

[1] Liu Xiaoxia. Research on Planning and Design of Waterfron Scenic Byways. 2009. Beijing Jiaotong University, Master Thesis.

metropolises along this section with developed industries and prosperous urban tourism.

Lower stream has abundant recreation activities. After the Ohio River joining Cairo, Illinois, it is the section of lower Mississippi River. The river is full and wide. There can be kilometers between the two banks. The landscape is magnificent and recreational activities are very colorful.

Compared with foreign countries, different types of scenic byway have been studied and discussed, and a more mature and enhanced scenic byway system has been formed, the construction of scenic byway in China is at the initial stage and is currently in the process of active promotion. China is famous for its vast territory, numerous rivers and lakes, abundant water resources and dense water networks, especially rivers are always magnificent. It has laid an excellent resource condition for the development and construction of scenic byway in the large river valley. It can be said that scenic byway in the large river valley has great potential and broad prospects for development. For example, on June 25, 2018, Shanxi Tourism Development Committee released the "Shanxi Yellow River Plate's Tourism Development Plan"[①], in which it clearly proposed that a scenic byway of the Yellow River should be built. The scenic byway, a "National Tourism Highway No. 1 of the Yellow River in Shanxi Province", should be built on the basis of the 1225 km highway along the Yellow River. The construction of the scenic byway intends to form a national scenic corridor with smooth transportation between the north and the south, complete tourism service facilities and beautiful scenery.

In a word, scenic byway developed abroad has the complex functions of transportation, landscape, recreation, ecology and protection. It follows the principles of ecological preservation, landscape construction and sustainable development. It conforms to the development trends of traffic planning, landscape design, urban planning and tourism and recreation. It has attracted more and more attention and favor from the government, investors, tourists and community residents. It is playing an important role in transportation, landscape, urban construction, tourism and recreation, environmental protection and local economic development.

---

① Announcement of the General Office of the People's Government of Shanxi Province on the Issuance of the General Plans for Tourism Development of the Yellow River, the Great Wall and the Taihang Mountains in Shanxi Province. Shanxi Culture and Tourism Department, http://wlt.shanxi.gov.cn/sitefiles/sxzwcms/html/xwzx/tzgg/14977.shtml.Accessed 10 Sept. 2019.

Part III
Experience and Strategy of Great River Civilization Tourism Development

Chapter One   Experience and Strategy of Civilization Tourism in the Yellow River

The Yellow River originates from the Qinghai-Tibet Plateau and flows eastward through the Inner Mongolia Plateau, the Loess Plateau and the North China Plain, and finally into the Yellow Sea. In different geographical units, the Yellow River is integrated with the local natural environment and gives birth to a unique regional culture. In recent years, taking the development and utilization of the Yellow River culture as the starting point, the provinces along the Yellow River jointly build the Yellow River tourism development platform the provinces along the Yellow River. It has become a trend within the area that the provinces make great efforts to develop the Yellow River cultural tourism industry and promote the transformation of the local economy. Among them, Shanxi is the most important province along the Yellow River basin, because Shanxi is the birthplace of the Yellow River civilization and the Yellow River culture is also an important part of Shanxi cultural tourism resources. The areas along the Yellow River in Shanxi present themselves a natural landscape with unique attractiveness, and they give birth to the cultural spirit of the Yellow River which represents the national soul. In addition, these areas form a cultural destination image labeled as the Yellow River culture.

Section 1   Experience on the Development of the Yellow River Civilization Tourism

Through a series of cooperation, the provinces and regions of the Yellow River Basin innovate the cooperation mechanism and the content, and issue relevant research reports to analyze the development of the Yellow River tourism. Also they provide suggestions and countermeasures for the future development from different aspects. This section will explain the experience of the Yellow River civilization tourism. Through the analysis of the relevant experience, it would be beneficial to provide reference and give inspiration for market development, product design and marketing campaigns of river valley civilization tourism in other areas.

1. Report on Tourism Development Index of the Yellow River in China

At the China Yellow River Tourism Conference in 2018, "China Yellow River Tourism Development Index report" was released. Combined with qualitative and quantitative methods, the report conducted data collection through online public opinion monitoring, online surveys at home and abroad, in-depth visits, etc. The figure involved 23 countries and regions, including the United States, Canada, Japan, the United Kingdom and the United Arab Emirates, covering more than 90% of source tourist countries around the world. From the Yellow River tourism influence index, dissemination index, quality tourism development index, the report analyzes the sustainable development of the Yellow River tourism. In the tourism dissemination index of the Yellow River, Shanxi Province ranks second in the main provinces and regions along the Yellow River, and the Hukou Waterfall of the Yellow River was shortlisted as the representative scenic spot of "50 Sceneries of the Yellow River in China" and received high attention.[①]

Through studies on professional data, the report pursued a comprehensive analysis on tourism development in the Yellow River Basin, and made a professional and in-depth interpretation from such three aspects as influence index, dissemination index and quality tourism development index of the Yellow River tourism so that more tourism practitioners and relevant government officials could have a better understanding of the present condition of the Yellow River tourism. It also clarified the opinions on the development of the Yellow River civilization tourism industry, all kinds of tourism products, market development and marketing campaigns. By the release of the report, more people learned about the rich cultural tourism resources and products of the Yellow River, which could not only expanded its influence and improve its popularity, but also enhanced the influence of cities and scenic spots along the Yellow River to a certain extent.

2. Holding the Yellow River Tourism Conference to Build a Platform for Exchange and Cooperation

Cities along the Yellow River have held different types of tourism conferences and created a platform for exchange and cooperation in the Yellow River tourism belt, so as to strengthen the exchanges, communication and cooperation within the areas of the Yellow River basin. The aim of holding the Yellow River Tourism Conference lists as follows: first, it is beneficial for tourism experts and scholars, industry practitioners and relevant government officials to study and explore the civilization of the Yellow River, the construction and

---

① 2008 China Yellow River Tourism Congress, "Report on China Yellow River Tourism Development Index" as the Focus http://www.ctnews.com.cn/art/2018/9/21/art_126_25438.html

protection of the human and natural ecological environment of the Yellow River Basin, and the in-depth excavation of different types of cultural and tourism resources of the Yellow River. Second, it shows the achievements of the Yellow River civilization tourism, and it also effectively connects the tourism industry, develops the Yellow River tourism products, expands the scale of the Yellow River tourism industry, builds the Yellow River cultural tourism boutique project, improves the brand awareness and influence and guides domestic and foreign tourists to recognize the Yellow River civilization and enjoy the Yellow River customs. In the end, the Yellow River civilization tourism belt will become a world-famous tourism destination; Thirdly, it promotes the global tourism in the cities along the Yellow River and the construction of a new tourism industry system in the Yellow River Basin, which has become the characteristics in its development and the only way to a new era for China's tourism industry. Fourth, it strengthens the mutual exchange and support among cities along, for example, carrying out the marketing campaigns and promotion, presenting the attractiveness and improving the brand awareness of the Yellow River civilization tourism; Fifth, it has further expanded the scope of participation and cooperation among cities, increased integration viscosity, formed greater joint forces to serve the tourism industry along the Yellow River. It has created an international experience line for tourists to get access to Chinese civilization. It aims at offering quality tourism products and good services. Sixth, through the exchange and cooperation platform, it is helpful for the cities to learn and share with each other, exchange their experience and practices in tourism development of the Yellow River, enhance development ability as well as management ability of the Yellow River tourism in the whole region, and promote the formation of high-quality tourism in cities along the Yellow River.

In a word, it is of great importance in promoting the development of civilization tourism and industrial prosperity of the Yellow River by means of discussing the cooperation and development of tourism on the occasions of different conferences on the Yellow River tourism and building a variety of communication and cooperation platforms for the tourism industry along the Yellow River.

3. Promoting Mutual Development by Establishing Tourism Industry Development Fund along the Yellow River

The Development Fund of Tourism Industry Alliance of the Yellow City was jointly set up by the Shaanxi Provincial Tourism Development Committee and the Hancheng municipal government. The fund has attracted a number of well-known investment institutions, such as the overseas Chinese Town Group Company and HNA Group Co., Ltd., and it has also facilitated the cooperation with Ping An Bank, CITIC Bank, Pudong Development Bank and other banks to build a capital platform for the success of the projects to be invested. The total amount of the fund is 20 billion yuan, with an initial contribution of 2 billion yuan, mainly investing in high-quality tourism and cultural projects along the Yellow River, such as regional tourism facilities along the Yellow River, tourism and sightseeing projects, cultural and tourism industry projects so as to play the leading role of government funds. Investment projects involve "tourism + poverty alleviation", "tourism + culture", "tourism + sports", "tourism + science and technology", "tourism + recreation" and other industrial integration projects. It effectively speeds up the transformation from traditional tourism to industrialization in the cities along the Yellow River, enriches the tourism product system, innovates the form and content of tourism products, realizes the integration of culture and tourism, and builds a river tourism destination with the Yellow River civilization tourism as the core. The purpose of this fund is to provide major support for the development of tourism industry alliance and product development of the Yellow River basin in the era of global tourism, and to vigorously push industrial integration, so as to upgrade tourism quality and brand of the Yellow River basin.

4. Innovative Cooperation Mechanism of Tourism Industry Alliance along the Yellow River

In order to push the development of civilization tourism of the Yellow River, the cities in the Yellow River Basin break through the boundary of administrative division, the constraints among the industries and found the Tourism Development Community along the Yellow River Basin, in which the Yellow River is acted as the link, cities as the carrier, products as the core, market as the guide, and the mutually beneficial cooperation as the premise. Tourism cities of 9 provinces along the Yellow River have founded the alliance, and it has built a win-win cooperation platform to serve member units, realize complementary advantages, promote resource sharing as its own responsibility, and work together to create a new model of tourism cooperation among rivers in China. The launch of the tourism industry alliance along the Yellow River innovates the cooperation mechanism so that the cities could work together to create a new exploring spot of the Yellow River civilization tourism belt, and build a world-famous tourism brand and cultural tourism belt as well. The members of the alliance will carry out more interactive cooperation in policy consultation, tourism industry, tourism product, boutique tourism route design, marketing campaigns, Yellow River tourism image building, Yellow River civilization brand packaging, cities and enterprises, experience sharing. And the alliance promotes the product serialization, service quality and market standardization, regular exchanges so as to present the Yellow River tourism belt to the world.

Section 2   The Development Model of the Yellow River Civilization Tourism in Shanxi Province

Among the provinces in the Yellow River Basin, Shanxi Province is rich in Yellow River civilization tourism resources, and it is a province with distinct characteristics and outstanding image. Linfen, Shanxi province was the capital of Imperial Yao in ancient times. Yao culture was the culture in the transition period from late primitive society to the first class society. It was the main source of the traditional Chinese culture. It played an important role in the development of Chinese civilization. Inheriting the primitive social culture and enlightening the Chinese civilization, Linfen, Shanxi province is not only the birthplace of the Yellow River civilization, but also gains its fame as "Travel to Shanxi to know five thousand years' culture, the soul of the Yellow River lies in Shanxi". Shanxi Province contains rich resources and distinctive characteristics, which forms the priority of the Yellow River civilization. Shanxi is known as the "theme park" of Chinese civilization, the museum of ancient Chinese architecture, the treasure house of ancient Chinese oriental art, the cradle of ancient Chinese opera, and the laudatory name of "think tank" of Chinese social change. In the section of the Yellow River in Shanxi, the natural and cultural resources in Linfen are the most diverse. Linfen, known as "the first capital of China" and one important birthplace of Chinese national culture and the cradle of the Yellow River civilization has created a unique development model.

1. The Yellow River Civilization Tourism Resources of Linfen

The Yellow River in Shanxi flows 1081 kilometers through Shanxi, including 19 counties and 4 cities, from Guanlaoniuwan in Xinzhou to Yuanqu County in Yuncheng to the south. Among these 19 counties and 4 cities, 11 counties are national key ecological functional areas and ecological management belts at the same time. Four counties are the main producing areas of state-level agricultural products. Shanxi Yellow River is rich in tourism resources and there are many magnificent landscapes, for example, more than 30 traditional tourist attractions, natural and magnificent landscapes of Hukou Waterfall, and a large number of beautiful natural villages. Along the way, there are Yao, Shun, Yu and other prehistoric imperial relics, which has become one of the birthplaces of the ancient civilization of China. It has a long history of Yellow River civilization and the rich and colorful folk culture, farming culture, red culture and famous mountains and rivers, which has laid a solid cultural and natural landscape foundation for the development of Shanxi Yellow River tourism. Among them, in the Yellow River section of Shanxi, Linfen with the most abundant tourism culture and natural resources is one of the birthplaces of China. "Emperor Century" said: "Yao capital Pingyang", that is, now Linfen. In Yugong acient China was divided into nine states, Pingyang was Jizhou. Jizhou was located in the central part of Jiuzhou, so it was called "China" and the word "China"came from it. In Linfen, Yao culture, Jin culture, Yellow River culture, folk culture, red culture and other high-quality cultural tourism resources was formed in Linfen in 5000 years' history.

Linfen is the earliest city in Shanxi Province to develop Yellow River tourism. Yellow River tourism is one of the two major tourism brands of "Chinese Root Yellow River Soul" in Linfen, and it is the main and core area of the Yellow River plate in Shanxi Province. Hukou Waterfall, Qiankun Bay and other scenic spots are not only the most valuable tourist attractions, but also the core of the Yellow River civilization and the landmark of Chinese spirit. A sentence "all travel is to set out, but to Linfen we are home" arouses the homesick of many tourists. The development goal of Linfen City is clear, the pace is steady. "Pingyang Memory", "Impression Linfen" forges new business cards of the city, "Yellow River, Taiyue, Genzu", these three major tourism plates are called "China's Root and the Soul of the Yellow River".

(1) Survey of Linfen

a. Superior Geographical Position and Convenient Transportation

Linfen is located in the southwest of Shanxi Province, the middle reaches of the Yellow River and the lower reaches of the Fenhe River. It now covers 1 district, 2 cities, 14 counties and two economic and technological development zones with a total area of 20.275 million square kilometers. Linfen City is located in the middle of Beijing-Tianjin area, Taiyuan, Zhengzhou, Xi'an and other popular destinations. It has convenient transportation and superior tourism location conditions. There are two railway stations in Linfen, Linfen Station and Linfen West Station (Daxi High-speed Railway) . In Linfen, national railway artery Tongpu Railway and Daxi High-speed Railway lay from the north to the south, besides, Houxi Line and Houyue Line cross its east-west region. There are four main railway lines in Linfen within the framework of the railway system, 1835 km in length and Linfen Qiaoli Airport in the city. Linfen is the second major artery in east-west direction of China and an important section of the Eurasian Continental Bridge. The city of Houma under its jurisdiction is one of the four major railway transportation hubs in North China and one of the four major freight center stations in China.

b. Pleasant Climate and Suitable for Tourism

Lifen is located in semi-arid and semi-humid monsoon climate zone, whose climate type belongs to temperate continental climate. It has abundant sunshine, heat resources. Rain and heat at the same period is its climate characteristic. With pleasant climate and rich humanistic culture, it is an ideal area for tourism. The city has four distinct seasons in the year, with rapid temperature rise in spring, hot and rainy summers and heat and rains in the same season, pleasant autumn, dry winter with little snow. April to October of the year are the seasons suitable for tourism. Although March and November are bridging months of season exchange, and the climate of most counties (disricts) is comfortable and suitable for tourism.[1]

---

[1] Gaoming, Jia Haiyan, Shencunliang, et al. Linfen Tourism Climate Comfort Characteristic Analysis [C]// S5 of the 33rd Annual Meeting of the Chinese Meteorological Society to cope with climate change, low-carbon development and ecological civilization construction. 2016.

c. Good Social Environment

In December 2017, Linfen was shortlisted for the top charismatic cities with Chinese characteristics in 2017. Charming city brand with Chinese characteristics is not only a comprehensive representation of the charm of city production, life and livability, but also an important symbol of city integration into modernization, internationalization and sustainable development of intelligent city. The selection is mainly a comprehensive evaluation of the city by the world famous brand conference (WFBA), focusing on the city characteristics in nine aspects: historical style, ecological civilization, development quality, people's livelihood happiness, regulation level, innovative vitality, real economy, Internet +, regional culture. At the same time, it focuses on 15 indicators: quantity of international tourists, ecological environment quality, community safety index, per capita public green space area, disposable income of residents, satisfaction of people's livelihood, efficiency of government management, proportion of real economy, forest coverage, proportion of new Internet economy, soft and hard environment for investment, construction of large data platform, proportion of e-commerce logistics, tribute for technological progress Rate of contribution and number of patent applications. According to the performance of each index of the candidate city, the comprehensive evaluation is carried out through the procedures of independent public questionnaire survey, statistical data analysis, on-the-spot investigation and authoritative expert letter evaluation. The fact that Linfen has been shortlisted as a charming city with Chinese characteristics shows that Linfen has a high score in all the evaluation indexes, and it also shows that its social and economic condition is good.[1]

In addition, Linfen was awarded Excellent City in Toilet Revolution, November 2017 on World Toilet Day and China Toilet Revolution Campaign Day. It was another highest honor in construction public toilet civilization after the titles of "China Habitat Environment Model Award", "Dubai International Best Model Award", "China Public Toilet Model City". Linfen City also integrates the concept of green, environmental protection, recycle and high-tech into future toilet planning, and it combines the development needs of the aging society and special care for infants and young children to design the "third toilet". Furthermore, it adds automatic deposit machines, newspaper kiosks, convenient bookstores and new energy car charging piles to urban toilets, and wireless networks which promotes the rapid development and upgrading of tourist toilets.[2]

---

[1] 2007 Top 200 Charming Cities with Chinese Characteristics http://china.cnr.cn/gdgg/20171224/t20171224_524073802.shtml

[2] Du Chunchun, Linfen won the National Excellent City Award for Toilet Revolution" http://www.xinhuanet.com//local/2017-11/24/c_129748314.htm

(2) Diversity of Cultural and Natural Tourism Resources

As early as 4,000 years ago, the ancient emperor Yao established his capital here, so it is known as "the First Capital of China", besides, it is the cradle of human multiplying and living in China. Linfen has abundant natural and cultural landscape, intangible cultural heritage and so on, it is characterized by the famous mountains and the river, Root and Ancestor culture and a variety of tourism resources in folk customs. Linfen has the largest yellow waterfall in the world. Hukou waterfall, which is known as "the heart of the Yellow River", "the soul of China", and the famous relocation site of Ming Dynasty in China, the root ancestor cultural tourism marked by Hongtong Dahuaishu. Linfen is also one of the birthplaces of Chinese ancient culture, such as the middle Paleolithic culture represented by Xiangfen Dingcun site. "Dingcun people" and Dingcun culture reflect the development of human culture in the middle Paleolithic period about 100,000 years ago. Dingcun Folk Museum also enables people to appreciate the variety of Han culture and folk customs. Other culture includes Jin culture represented by Quwo Jinguo Museum, Houma Jinguo site and so on.

In addition, there is the famous Taoist shrine Yunqiu Mountain which is as famous as Wudang Mountain in ancient China. The Huozhou State Department is the only existing ancient state office in the country, what's more, the Qiliyu Taiyue Mountain National Forest Park, which is known as "Green Lung in North China", and so on. It can be said that if we grasp a handful of soil here, we can feel the civilization, and most of the history of Chinese civilization is concentrated here. At the same time, there are many kinds of intangible culture in Linfen, including Puzhou Bangzi, Wei Feng gongs and drums and other folk arts, thus the city is known as "hometown of plum blossoms", "hometown of paper-cut" and "hometown of gongs and drums".

In 5000 years of historical development, Linfen has formed high-quality cultural tourism resources, such as Yao culture, root and ancestor culture, the Yellow River culture, folk culture, red culture and so on. It has formed three high-quality routes: roots and ancestor worship tour in the middle line, the Yellow River customs tour in the west line, ecological leisure tour in the east. The first two lines have been included in the six top-quality lines in the province. At present, Linfen has a total of 56 tourist attractions (districts), including 1 national 5A tourist scenic spot, 12 national 4A tourist scenic spots, 11 3A tourist scenic spots and 2 2A tourist scenic spots. And it has 2 national nature reserves, 2 geological parks, 1 scenic spot, 2 forest parks, 10 national and provincial eco-agricultural tourist attractions and 3 provincial scenic spots. Due to its long history and culture, the Linfen Museum has a collection of more than 46000 pieces of cultural relics. In addition, there are 43 national key cultural relics protection units, 58 provincial key cultural relics protection units, more than 3000 cultural relic units of all kinds, and the number of intangible cultural heritage ranks first in the province. Linfen's cultural essence and folk characteristics are worth visiting and appreciating step by step.

a. Natural Tourism Resources

In terms of natural landscape resources, Linfen has 4 national 4A tourist scenic spots, which are Hukou Waterfall Scenic spot, Fenhe Cultural Ecological Scenic spot, Yunqiu Mountain and Renzushan, 4 national 3A scenic spots: Quwo Jin Garden, Qu Shijing, Mopanling, Yicheng Foye Mountain, 1 National 2A tourist Scenic spot: Quwo County Lotus Pond Moonlight Scenic spot; and other natural scenic spots, Gushe Mountain, Huozhou Qiliyu, Tao Tangyu, Xiangfen Longshu Valley, Pu County Wulu Mountain, Yicheng Lishan Shunwangping, Yonghe Qiankun Bay, Fushan Yaoshan Forest Park and so on.

Table 3.1 Natural Tourism Resources of Linfen

Type	Name
National AAAA Tourist Scenic Spot	Hukou Waterfall Scenic spot, Fenhe Cultural Ecological Scenic spot, Yunqiu Mountain Scenic spot, Renzushan Scenic spot
National AAA Tourist Scenic Spot	Quwo Jin Garden, Shijing Landscape Scenic spot, Mopanling, Yicheng Foye Mountain
National AA Tourist Scenic Spot	Quwo Lotus Pond Moonlight scenic spot
Others	Gusheshan Scenic Area, Qiliyu Scenic Area of Huozhou, Taotangyu Scenic Area, Longmaoyu Scenic Area of Xiangfen, Wulu Mountain of Puxian, Lishan Shunwangping of Yicheng, Qiankun Bay of Yonghe and Yaoshan Forest Park of Fushan

Source: Summarized by this Research

b. Human Landscape Resource

In the aspect of cultural landscape resources, there are 1 national 5A tourist scenic spot, that is, Hongdong Dahuaishu tourist spot, 8 national 4A tourist scenic spots, which are Yao Temple, Huamen scenic spot, Jin Museum, Xiaoxitian scenic spot, Chinese Pear Expo Garden, Peony Culture Tourism Area, Dongyue Temple, former residence of Peng Zhen. There are 7 national 3A tourist scenic spots, namely Quwo Shiqiao Castle, Spring and Autumn Jinguo City, Jixian Kenanpo, Hongdong eighth Route Army Memorial Hall, Guangsheng Temple, Chaoyanggou, Anciet Yicheng, 1 national 2A level tourist scenic spot, which is Hongdong Ming Dynasty prison, as well as other cultural landscapes, such as Yao Ling, Yao Ju, Niu Wang Temple stage, Huozhou Department, Tiefo Temple, Dingcun site, Dingcun residence, Tao Temple site, Shijiagou ancient architectural complex, Puxian Dongyue Temple, Great Mercy Temple and so on.

Table 3.2 Human Landscape Resources

Type	Name
National AAAAA Tourist Scenic Spot	Hongdong Big Sophora Tree Scenic spot
National AAAA Tourist Scenic Spot	Yao Miao-Huamen tourist Scenic spot, Jin National Museum, Xiaoxitian Scenic spot, Huaxian Chinese Pear Boyuan Scenic spot, Guxian Peony Cultural Tourism area, Dongyue Temple Scenic spot, Peng Zhen former residence
National AAA Tourist Scenic Spot	Shiqiao Castle, Spring and Autumn Jin State City, Ke Nan Po, Ji County, Hongdong eighth Route Army Memorial Hall, Guangsheng Temple, Chaoyanggou, Yicheng Ancient City
National AA Tourist Scenic Spot	Hongdong Ming Dynasty Prison
Others	Yao Ling, Yao Ju, Niu Wang Temple stage, Huozhou Department, Tiefo Temple, Dingcun site, Dingcun residence, Tao Temple site, Shijiagou Ancient Building Group, Puxian Dongyue Temple, Great Mercy Court, etc.

Source: Summarized by this Research

c. Intangible Cultural Heritage

Linfen is a city with plenty of intangible cultural heritages in Shanxi Province. Up to now, Linfen City has 21 national "non-heritage" projects which accounts for 20% of the total number of national "Intangible Cultural Heritage" projects in Shanxi Province, 136 provincial "Intangible Cultural Heritage" projects and 300 municipal "Intangible Cultural Heritage" projects. The national projects mainly include Jinnan Weifeng gongs and drums, Xiangfen Tianta lion dance, Yicheng flower drum, Puzhou Bangzi, Legend of Yao, Pingyang wood painting, Houma cloth tiger, Hongdong Taoqing, Yicheng Qinshu, Quwo bowl cavity, Yunqiu Mountain Zhonghe Festival, Weicun running drum, Jinnan Meihu, Houma Qilin Qinbabao, furniture production technique of Jin style, among which, Linfen Weifeng gongs and drums is the representative.

Weifeng gong and drum is a kind of traditional percussion of Han nationality, which is played by gongs, drums, cymbals and drums. Because of its performance, the gongs and drums are called Wei Feng gongs and drums. During the lunar New Year and festivals, harvests, gatherings and processions, Weifeng gong and drum is played in public. Weifeng gong and drum is an ancient folk art form of Han nationality. It began in the era of Yao and Shun and has a history of more than 4000 years. Weifeng gong and drum integrates with music, dance and other techniques, showing the depth of the Yellow River culture, reflecting the rough and bold, indomitable character of the northern men living on the Loess Plateau. It is a fine traditional art among the treasures of Han nationality.

Drama has a long history. Its prosperous stage dated from the Jin Dynasty to the Yuan. Greatest characters in Chinese drama, for example Dong Jieyuan, Guan Hanqing, Zheng Guangzu, Wang Shifu,

Bai Pu, Shi Junbao all once lived here. According to historical records, as early as the Yuan Dynasty, ancient Pingyang has become as famous as Beijing, the Yuan capital Beijing being one national drama center. In Mural painting of Yuan Dynasty in Shuishen Temple of Guangsheng Temple, Sheng, Dan, Jing Mo and Chou were drawn. The characters in the painting were eye-catching, complete, and vivid, which shows that the development of opera in Pingyang area at that time had been much matured. According to historical records, the prosperity of Linfen opera was 30 years earlier than that of Beijing, the drama center. Among the eight Yuan Dynasty stages existing in the country, there are five in Linfen. Court music and dance in the stone carvings of the Tang Dynasty, the dramatic brick carvings unearthed from the tomb of Hou Ma Jin, wooden carvings of Xiangfen Ding Village, wooden pictures of the Ming and Qing dynasties, folk embroidery and paper-cut are all historical witnesses of the evolution of Chinese opera.

There are Puzhou Bangzi, Jinnan Meihu, Quwo bowl cavity, Hongdong Road situation, Yicheng Qin book, Fushan music cavity, Houma shadow show, Fushan puppet show, 8 kinds of drama in total. There are 25 opera groups, and the number of opera practitioners has reached 1042. Since the new period, 598 dramas have been staged and 273 new dramas have been produced. The heavy history and culture has demonstrated the lasting artistic charm of the local opera culture in Linfen. Among them, Pu opera (Puzhou Bangzi) is the oldest opera in Bangzi, known as the ancestor of Bangzi drama and the first of the "four Bangzi" in Shanxi. In 2006, it was included in the first list of national intangible cultural heritage protection. In 1984, Linfen won the first Plum Blossom Award for Chinese Drama for twice. Ren Jixin, a famous master of Pu opera, won the honor again in 2002. Today, 64 people who won plum blossoms award are competing in Pingyang. In order to recognize Linfen's great contribution to the development of opera, the Chinese dramatists Association specially awarded Linfen the title "Hometown of Plum Blossoms" in 2005.

d. Festival Cultural Resources

In addition to cultural, natural landscape and intangible cultural heritage, Linfen is also rich in festival cultural resources. At present, Linfen has formed more than 10 tourism brands, such as Hongtong Dahuaishu Ancestor Memorial Festival, Hukou Cultural Tourism Festival of the Yellow River, Yaodu Cultural Tourism Festival, Cultural Tourism Festival of the Ancient Capital of Jin Dynasty and so on. Tourism festival activities with their own characteristics of traditional culture and humanistic and natural resources with different carriers fully explain the diversity of Linfen festival activities, multi-level humanistic essence and they are conveying the spirit of Chinese civilization, while people are publicizing the long history, culture and civilization of the China, meanwhile, they are excavating the traditional culture, carrying forward the spirit of the times, and promoting the prosperity and development of Linfen cultural tourism through festival tourism.

Table 3.3 Linfen Festival Cultural Tourism Resources

Brand	Activity	Details
Seeking roots and offering sacrificing for ancestors	Root worship Festival	In 1991, Linfen held the first Hongdong locust tree root worship festival. It was held at the site of immigrants in Hongdong County. During the festival, the main sacrifice ceremony, immigrant culture seminar, calligraphy and painting meeting, folk art exhibition, folk custom performance, literature and art performance, etc., were held. At the same time, a material exchange conference was held, and a meeting for attracting investment and investment was held.
Tour of the Yellow River	Hukou International Tourism Month of the Yellow River	Activities including Waist drum, Suona, Weifeng Gong and drum and other local literary and artistic programs, painting ,calligraphy and photography exhibition, the Yellow River Cultural Seminar, rural leisure experience activities and etc.
Tang Yao Cultural Tour	Yao Miao Root and Ancestor Tourist Month	Visiting temple fairs, scenic spots, worship ancestors, appreciate folk customs, awards, delicacies, entertainment, various literary and artistic show, theatrical show, cultural exhibitions, Mid-Autumn Festival Moon Festival, star concerts, prestigious gongs and drums selection contests.
	Yaodu Cultural Tourism Festival	Ten activities including traditional cultural performances such as Weifeng Gong and drum, Yicheng Huagu, Suona in Jixian County, Yao Culture Summit Forum, Baijia Travel Agency Promotion Meeting, Baijiazong Family Exchange Meeting, 100 business elites joining hands with Yao Du, Yao Culture Development Achievement Exhibition, Taosi Archaeological Achievements Exhibition, etc.
Cultural Tour in Jin Dynasty	Ancient Capital Culture Festival	Cultural studies of the ancient Jin Dynasty, folk art exhibitions, chrysanthemum exhibitions, famous commodities exhibitions, economic and trade negotiations, literary and art evenings, opera performances, gongs and drums contests, art exhibitions and auctions of the ancient capital of Xintian in Jinbaozhai, etc.
Other Cultural Tourism	Rural Peach Blossom Club	Colorful activities include flower sightseeing, art exhibition, opera, specialty exhibition, calligraphy, tea ceremony, photography contest, farm delicacies and so on. Activities extends from simple garden flower sightseeing to many items such as folk display, children's games, mass cultural and sports activities.
	Guxian Peony Culture Tourism Festival	Guxian has the reputation of "the first peony in the world". Tourism activities including cultural exchange activities, opera evenings, folk cultural performances, inheritance of intangible cultural heritage, food exhibitions, etc.

续表

Brand	Activity	Details
Other Cultural Tourism	Yunqiu Mountain "Zhonghe Festival"	Yunqiu Mountain "Zhonghe Festival" is a national intangible cultural heritage and a traditional carrier of Chinese cultural spirit. The main activities include sacrificial ceremonies, Yunqiu Zhonghe Huaguo Exhibition, Yunqiu Mountain Zhonghe Festival Temple Fair, Yunqiu Mountain Traditional Folk Customes Show (Wedding Customs, Shadow Show, etc.), and Yunqiu Mountain Organic Eco-agriculture, Yunqiu Mountain Ancient Village, Yunqiu Mountain 24 Festival Culture Academy, Yunqiu Academy, Wuhou Huajing Avenue and other tourist attractions.
	"Pear Blossom Festival" in Xixian County	Including the opening ceremony, cultural exhibition, bonfire evening, the "Yulu Xiangli" Development Expert Forum, fruit tree customization and adoption symposium, agricultural products exhibition, tourism promotion, calligraphy exhibition and photo competition, etc., . Expand and strengthen the cultural tourism industry with pear blossom as the medium, culture as the connotation, and a series of activities as the carrier
Other Cultural Tourism	Anze Xunzi Cultural Festival	During the festival, the lasting charm of Xunzi culture is displayed in a panoramic way through activities such as offering sacrifices to Xunzi, forum of Xunzi culture, National Photography Contest of "Xunzi's hometown, ecological Anze" and painting and Calligraphy Festival of Xunzi culture.
	Anze Huanghua Tourism Festival	The main activities include the opening ceremony of the cultural tourism festival, the singing of Xunxiang, folk dance, Huanghualing photography contest, lectures on health preservation of traditional Chinese medicine, and Shangdang Drum Book and Bayinhui Concert.

Source: Summarized by this Research

2. Linfen Yellow River Cultural Tourism Development Model

(1) Natural Scenic Spot-driven Development Model

The natural scenic spot-driven development model mainly refers to relying on the unique scenic spot in Linfen, regarding it as the kernel and the source so as to push the development of the neighborhood areas. Specifically speaking, improve tourism public service system and infrastructure construction from leading scenic spots, planning tourism products, scenic spots layout, tourism routes. On the basis of the radiation-driven role of leading scenic spots, promote the integration of regional tourism industry and related industries, and realize economic cooperation among regional cities. Cooperative development with economy. Make full utilization of the leading role of scenic spots in tourism brand building, tourism spatial structure optimization, tourism campaigns, Tourist Distribution Center construction and other fields to promote the development of surrounding villages, folk culture, tourism commodities and so on. Linfen City has already taken the advantage of the Hukou Waterfall of the Yellow River to promote the tourism industry of the surrounding areas and played a leading role in tourism. At present, it has formed a development model driven by the scenic spots of "the soul of the Yellow River+Huaxia root+rural tourism", with Hukou Waterfall as the leading factor so as to drive the surrounding rural tourism, highlight the Huaxia civilization of the Yellow River. A top-quality tourist area of the Yellow River has been built, which embodies the local characteristics and combines the culture of the Yellow River, Chinese civilization, natural landscape and folk culture.

a. Overview of Hukou Waterfall

Hukou Waterfall of the Yellow River, known as the "Wonder of the Yellow River", is both a national AAAA tourism scenic spot and a national geological park. Hukou Waterfall was selected as the national practical education base for primary and secondary school students in 2017 and the "50 Sceneries of the Yellow River in China" at the 2008 China Yellow River Tourism Conference. Hukou Waterfall is located in Hukou Town, Jixian County, Linfen City, Shanxi Province. Hukou Waterfall is the second largest waterfall in China and the largest and the only yellow waterfall in the world. The Yellow River runs to this point, with steep stone cliffs on both sides and narrow estuaries, so it is called Hukou Waterfall. The Yellow River in the upper reaches of the waterfall is 300 metres wide. Within a distance of less than 500 metres, it is compressed to a width of 20-30 metres. It flows straight down and waves roll over. It is known as "it is difficult to see the true face of the Yellow River without looking at Hukou Falls". The 1000 cubic meters per second of river water pours down from the cliff of more than 20 meters high, forming the atmosphere of "a pot swallows the Yellow River". The river bed here is like a huge teapot, which harvests the water of the rolling Yellow River, hence it is named the mouth of the pot. Hukou Waterfall is very spectacular, with torrential yellow water pouring down. The height of the waterfall can reach 15-20 meters in dry season and 45 meters in summer and autumn.

Hukou Waterfall is the only latent, mobile waterfall, and the one with varied and changeable scenery and rich cultural connotations in China. With the magic of nature, Hukou Waterfall has created two magnificent spectacles, vibrant and moving, which make the world shocked. It is Qiankun Bay, winding and beautiful, Hukou Waterfall is an important symbol of the spirit of the Chinese nation, and Qiankun Bay is the perfect interpretation of Chinese civilization. Hukou Waterfall has dreamlike changes in different seasons, different times and different currents, which forms ten spectacular scenes of Hukou Waterfall: Mengmen Night Moon, Huzhen Rampant, Shili Longgou, Tianhe Suspended Flow, Thunderstorm of the Yellow River, Smoke at the Bottom of the Hukou Waterfall, Rainbow Ferry, Ice Waterfall Galaxy, Shiwo Baojing, Dryland Shipping. As the center of the scenic area, Hukou Waterfall integrates the Yellow River valley, the Loess Plateau and the ancient plateau villages, which shows the magnificent natural landscape and rich and colorful historical and cultural accumulation of the Yellow River Basin. Hukou Waterfall, with its profound philosophical connotation, attracts the descendants of Yan and Huang Dynasty. People regard it as the spiritual symbol of the nation's constant self-improvement and vigorous struggle, and this spirit is the "national soul" of the China.

The tourism of the Yellow River is one of the two major tourism brands of Linfen "China's root and soul of the Yellow River". It is the main and core area of the Yellow River Plate in Shanxi Province. Hukou Waterfall, Qiankun Bay and other scenic spots are not only the most ornamental scenic spots on the Yellow River Plate, but also the core of the Yellow River civilization and landmark of Chinese spirit.

b. Representative Tourism Projects and Scenic Spots

Linfen takes Hukou Waterfall as its core and it drives the rapid development of tourism around it. It concentrates on building two small tourism circles, namely, the Great Circulation of Tourism in Jixian, Hukou and Renzushan in Linfen. It strives to build six-in-one tourism circles, namely landscape tourism, historical and cultural tourism, folk custom tourism, archaeological root-seeking tourism, agricultural tourism and leisure vacation tourism. The diversified development will promote the integration of Hukou scenic spots and rural tourism. In addition to Hukou Waterfall, the core scenic spot of the Yellow River, Hukou scenic spot also plays a leading role, joins together with Kenanpo and Renzushan scenic spot in order to shape and highlight Chinese spirit of struggle and hard work.

i. Yellow River Cultural Tourism Festival

The Yellow River Cultural Tourism Festival takes the "original ecological experience of Hukou culture of the Yellow River" and "sightseeing the social customs and apple picking" as its core, concentrates on displaying the four tourism cultural brands such as "Yellow River culture, ancestor culture, United Front Culture and apple culture", and creates the "three-colored brand" of red apple, green ecology and yellow waterfall. The event launched "outdoor experience, economic and trade negotiations, rural tourism" three major sections, held "opening ceremony, featured agricultural products exhibition, persimmon beach unearthed cultural relics exhibition in Renzushan, good calligraphy and painting exhibition in Qin and Jin Dynasties, apple picking tour, self-driving tent conference, economic and trade negotiations, tourism promotion, national singing and dancing invitation contest" ten themes. Move to show the elegance of "Jinshan Jinmei Damei Hukou".

ii. Develop Rural Tourism on the Basis of Apple Industry

In accordance with the global rural tourism development pattern "driven by Hukou Waterfall, supported by apple picking", Ji County of Linfen has formed an apple picking garden, folk experience garden, farming sightseeing park, characteristic snacks and other comprehensive flowering, and it gradually developed its own distinctive characteristics and unique advantages. Ji County, with high altitude, large temperature difference and sufficient light, is the best eugenic area for apples in China determined by the Ministry of Agriculture, and it enjoys the reputation of "the hometown of apples in China". Jixian apple with correct high pile, bright and delicate fruit surface, bright red color, crisp and sweet taste, rich nutrition, green and safety, excellent quality, repeatedly won the grand prizes including gold medal on the first China Agricultural Expo, the third China Agricultural Expo famous brand product and so on, which accounts for more than 20 international and domestic awards, and it is known as "Chinese famous fruit." At present, there is 280000 mu apple planting area for tourists to pick. In Ji County the forest coverage rate is 47.2%, and the beautiful ecological environment has created a pleasant "natural oxygen bar", known as the "green pearl on Luliang Mountain", and "leisure park", "beautiful home", "fictitious land of peace" for tourists are located everywhere within the area .

At present, Ji County has created a collection of agricultural production, farming experience, culture and entertainment, food culture, fruit picking, agricultural products sales in one of the folk villages, tourism resorts and leisure agricultural parks. Shangdong Village Leisure Agricultural Park attracted the attention of children by setting up cartoon characters, simulated apple tree shape, windmill promenade, and "second generation of gardeners" bar made young people linger and linger. Taidu Folk Village cuisine street, farm music attracted "foodie" people, villagers perform eye-catching literary with local flavor, artistic and marriage shows. The educated Youth Cabin in Xiling Village seems to take people back to the 1960s by setting up hiking trails in the forest, allowing hikers to experience the pleasure of walking in the "Natural oxygen Bar." The happy farm in the kiln canal village provides people living in cities with the experience of farming, returning to the countryside, leisure and entertainment.

iii. Ancestor Worship Tour in Renzu Mountain

Renzu Mountain, located in Ji County, Linfen City, Shanxi Province, is the only mountain named after "ancestor" in the country. It is in the neighborhood of Ancestor Shanxi and Hukou Falls, with 1742.4 meters above sea level, scenic area of 203 square kilometers, the core area of 45 square kilometers, and it is a straight and majestic mountain. The beautiful legend of "the ancestor of human roots, born in Jizhou" comes out here. There are 132 species of animals and more than 400 species of plants in Renzu Mountain, which maintains a good primitive ecology. Here, with profound historical and cultural heritage and dotted with cultural relics, the main peak has built ancestral temples surrounded by more than 200 temples either large or small size, and the bunkers, trenches and fortifications during the Anti-Japanese War are well preserved. The development goal of the scenic spot is to create a tourist scenic spot with natural resources as the basis, human resources as the support, human ancestor culture as the soul and tourism resources as the leading factor. Known for its beautiful scenery, Renzu Mountain is an excellent place for natural sightseeing and leisure.

Ancestor culture refers to the sum of prehistoric material and spiritual civilization accumulated in the process of forming new cognitive consciousness in the period from the end of the Paleolithic Age to the early Neolithic Age, that is, Nuwa Fuxi era, in which human beings created new ways of life continuation and living conditions, such as marriage and fertility, settlement and fire, farming and livestock raising, watching and measuring days, etc., Nuwa Fuxi era extendes from the end of the Paleolithic Age to the early Neolithic Age and accordingly it includes two different type of culture: Nuwa culture and Fuxi culture. The core of ancestor culture embodies the profound patriarchal consciousness of China and the traditional concept of seeking roots and ancestors, the great changes, the fearless spirit of seeking survival, the exploring spirit of seeking development and the stale livelihood, the dedication spirit of seeking harmony, and the spirit of sacrifice for well-being.

There are more than 100 temples and niches in the mountains, especially the ancestral temples, Xuantian God Temple, Kongshan Temple and Beidou Qixing Temple. There is still a living fossil of prehistoric civilization. All kinds of stone tools and pottery pieces used ten thousand years ago were unearthed in Shizitan, Taohuaping and other sites; the oldest carving existing in China "Nuwa rock paintings" and "Fuxi rock carvings"; the "emperor bones" found under the statues of Nuwa in the Imperial Palace of the people's ancestral Temple 6200 years ago, the bones of cattle and sheep sacrificed from 2100 to 900 years ago, famous places and villages, such as Fengshan, Roll Grinding ditch, piercing Needle Beam, Dongfang Valley, Gaohuaping, etc. The local custom of offering sacrifices to ancestors lasted for a long time; and the beautiful legends about the creation of ancestors have made a new interpretation of the mythological figures of Nuwa and Fuxi: Nuwa and Fuxi are human beings, not gods. As a result, Zushan has become the birthplace of Chinese civilization and a well-deserved ancestral mountain of the China. Main natural scenery includes: Renzu Temple, stage Temple, Anti-Japanese Martyrs Mausoleum, Anti-Japanese War Cultural experience Park (Real person CS Playground), Glass Rainbow Magpie Bridge, sacrificial Square, Cai Jiachuan Forest Park and so on, among which the Ancestral Mountain is an excellent place for sightseeing and leisure.

The Ancestral Temple, the earliest site in China to offer sacrifices to Nuwa and Fuxi, is the key scenic spot of Renzushan, which was built at the top of the main peak of Renzu Mountain at an altitude of 1742.42 meters. There are Fuxi Temple, Kui Imperial Palace, Dizang Temple, Tang Dynasty Stone tablet, etc.; Fuxi Rock under the cliff of the Imperial Palace is built with 18 Luohan corridors, and the mountain wall is embedded with 18 Luohan reliefs. According to the mountain wall, a small temple was built, which was dedicated to Xuanwu and Guanyin. There is a natural boulder in front of the gate of the imperial palace, which is known as "lying marble", "mending roof" and "moulding stone". There are two layers in the above and below, and there is a group of square stone nests. Some scholars believe that Fuxi could look up at the sky and look down on the earth, which leads to the expression of the concept of "Heaven and Earth".

iv. Yonghe Qiankun Bay

Located in the middle of Jinshan Canyon, Qiankun Bay has a huge river landscape with a shape of "S". The mountains are cold and the Yellow River is circuitous. It stands on the bank and overlooks the cliffs. It is magnificent and has beautiful Zhong Lingxiu. It resembles the "Taiji Yinyang Map" in Chinese traditional culture. Each of the "S" bays has an ancient history. In general, the villages are like the two "eyes" of the Taiji Pisces. According to the records of Qingxian County, "Fuyi" is the transliteration of "Fuxi". There are Fuxi Temple in Fuyihe Village. There are two thousand years old cypress trees in front of the temple. There is a Niangniang Temple in Hehui Village. The ancestor of Niangniang Temple is Nuwa, so many villages on both sides of the Taiwan Strait are named "Wa". In Qingxian Chronicle records: there are no jujubes in the past dynasties. According to textual research, jujubes are female Yin, and Wa is the transliteration of Wa, which should be Nuwa. This unique landform of mountains and rivers and exquisite place names, which spread thousands of years of old legends in the local area, as well as the investigation and demonstration of some experts in recent years, show that Yonghe County is closely related to Fuxi and Nuwa.

In January 2005, it passed the examination of Shanxi Yonghe Yellow River Shequ Geopark by the Department of Land and Resources of Shanxi Province, and was submitted to the Ministry of Land and Resources of the People's Republic of China In August 2006. The Ministry of Land and Resources of the People's Republic of China formally approved the establishment of the Yellow River Shequ (Shanxi Yonghe) National Geopark. The Yellow River Shequ (Yonghe, Shanxi) National Geopark is located in the southwest of Shanxi Province and the west wing of the southwest end of Luliang Mountain. The area of the park is 210 km^2. The main geological relics distribution area is 152.64 km^2. The Yellow River Snake qu (Yonghe, Shanxi) National Geopark is located in the southern part of the Shanxi-Shaanxi Gorge. The main tourist landscape in the park is the river snake meandering landscape. There are other geological tourism resources and relics formed by river geology, such as Hexin Island (Shoe Island), terraces, lateral erosion caves, steep valley slopes and fossil relics. In addition, the cultural tourism resources left over from the history of the park can be found everywhere, which provides rare and valuable information for the investigation and study of Yellow River culture, loess customs, modern revolutionary war history and so on.

The Yellow River Shequ (Yonghe, Shanxi) National Geopark is rich in tourism resources. In particular, geoscience tourism resources are precious macro and micro landscape relics, with high teaching, scientific research and tourism ornamental value. The textual research on the Geopark here can help us to deeply understand the development and evolution of the crust in the middle reaches of the Yellow River, the changes of the loess environment, and the hydraulic erosion model of the Yellow River valley.

v. Qiliyu Scenic spot in Huozhou City

Qiliyu Ecotourism Scenic spot, located in the hinterland of Huoshan, northeast town of Huozhou, Linfen City, Shanxi Province, is an important part of Taiyue Mountain National Forest Park. The scenic spot is only 5 kilometers away from the Huozhou exit of the Dayun Expressway, 90 minutes' the Dayun Expressway to Taiyuan Airport. National Highway 108 and South Tongpu Railway across the city north and south, which makes traffic convenient.

The scenic spot has a long history and rich natural landscape resources, and it is the best primary vegetation area with the largest number of ecotourism resources, more than 90% of vegetation coverage, air quality up to the national first-class standard, 800-2504.5 meters above sea level, the annual average temperature of 10 degrees, more than 670 species of rare plants, more than 70 species of precious wild animals in Shanxi Province, which can be described as natural botanical gardens and wildlife zoos.

Qiliyu Scenic spot is divided into three areas, including Huo Hongzhao, Sanyanyao, Heilongjiang Gorge, with 28 scenic spots in total. The main scenic spots are "five dragon gully, Liushuiya Waterfall, Shuangru Peak, South Tianmen, Shirengou, Niulaogou, Shiyaqifeng, Baxian Cave, Hongzhao Martyr Pavilion, Jingou Manmu Larix plantation, Heilong Gorge" and so on. At present, the construction Qiliyu Scenic spot is stepping up, which will become a resort for traveling, vacation, leisure, scientific research and teaching, and so on.

vi. Yicheng Shunwangping

Shunwangping is located in Lishan Nature Reserve at the junction of Yicheng, Yuanqu and Qinshui in Shanxi Province. It is said in the legend that it was the place where Emperor Shun cultivated in ancient times. Shunwangping is the main peak of Lishan Nature Reserve about 2358 meters above sea level, and it is the highest subalpine meadow in North China. Surrounded by mountains and luxuriant trees, the lawn is the only well-preserved primeval forest in North China and the middle and lower reaches of the Yellow River.

Shunwangping has more than 5400 mu of grassland. According to local villagers, Shunwangping grows more than a dozen kinds of Chinese herbs. If cattle eat the herbs, it is both disease-proof and to gain weight for them. After the busy spring every year, the farmers in the surrounding villages send cattle to live freely on the grassland. In the evening, each herd gathers on one side, with the bull in a circle, double horns sticking out, acting as a guard to protect the cows and calves in the enclosure overnight from wild animals. During the busy autumn season, the villagers drive the cattle down the mountain and harvest autumn seeds.

Shunwangping has more than 100 scenic spots, including Shunwangping Yagao Meadow which is about 260 hectares. The legends and scenic spots of Shun began here. In the north of Shunwangping, there is a row of uneven stone walls made of natural stones on the grassy slope, among which a monkey-shaped stone is very conspicuous, and known as "Qun Hou Wang Yue." In the counties around Shunwangping, there are still many ancient stories about Emperor Shuni planting millet and so on, as well as the Wangxian Village of Yao Wang's visit to Xianxian.

(2) Development Mode Health and Wellness Tourism

In May 2016, the State Forestry Administration highlighted the development of forest tourism, leisure and rehabilitation in the 13th five-year Plan for Forestry Development, that is, it is necessary to vigorously develop forest rehabilitation. In September 2017, Lou Yangsheng, the Governor of Shanxi Province made it clear for the first time that efforts should be made to build the "Xia Yang Shanxi Health and Wellness Brand". Lou Yang Sheng, the Governor pointed out further in the "2018 Shanxi Provincial Government work report", "the implementation of health care industry ". To nourish the heart, health, pension as the development direction, the development of the whole life cycle of health care products, tourism, housing, health care, medical care, nursing is one of the industrial cluster. Encourage the development of rural health, forest health, hot spring health, traditional Chinese medicine and real estate and other new business type. We will speed up the construction of a number of recreational tourist cities, towns, industrial parks and resorts. This fully shows that recreational tourism has been an important way of tourism, and has been paid attention to by government departments. The development mode of health tourism is the sum of all kinds of tourism activities, such as raising beauty and health, nourishing diet, cultivating the mind, caring for the environment and so on, so that people can achieve the excellent state of natural harmony in body, mind and spirit. The connotation of health tourism includes three levels: phenomenological basis, health needs and poetic habitation. As a new type of tourism, health tourism is the product of the combination of health products, resources and leisure vacation tourism, to meet people's pursuit of healthy life, so that people can obtain physical and mental health in tourism, which can also promote the transformation and upgrading of tourism.

As one of the birthplaces of the Chinese nation, Linfen has a long history and culture. The scenic spot represented by Yunqiu Mountain is rich in culture and recreational tourism resources. Yunqiu Mountain is characterized by the local unique Genzu culture to create a recreational cultural experience, recreational education and leisure resort. At the same time, because of the "healthy and sustainable" characteristics of recreational tourism, the development of recreational tourism can not only promote the development, upgrading and transformation of tourism in Linfen City, but also coordinate the development of related industries. Yunqiu Mountain Recreation Tourism drives the development of local ancient village tourism, forest tourism, agricultural planting, characteristic culture and so on.

a. Overview of Yunqiu Mountain

Yunqiu Mountain, a national AAAA tourist scenic spot, is the core scenic spot of Genzu tourism in southern Shanxi. It is one of the birthplaces of Chinese agricultural civilization, and the geographical indication of Chinese local culture, the inheritance of neutralization culture-intangible cultural heritage, and it conveys strong hometown affection. Yunqiu Mountain is rich in natural resources, cultural landscape and cultural heritage. Yunqiu Mountain is a rare comprehensive tourism scenic spot in southern Shanxi, which integrates the functions of tourism, leisure and entertainment, vacation and health preservation, folk experience, cultural exchange and so on. Yunqiu Mountain is surrounded by special karst landforms and stone mountain forests.

Yunqiu Mountain is not only a unique natural landscape, but also has a profound cultural heritage. It is a travel place of Taoist fairies for thousands of years, and it enjoys the reputation of "shooting the most beautiful peak" and "the first place of interest in Hefen". First, ecological environment in Yunqiu Mountain is excellent. Second, Yunqiu Mountain carries heavy human resources and cultural heritage. The cultural context of Yunqiu Mountain can be traced back to the ancient civilization, where Fuxi and Nuwa were said to breed Chinese descendants; Xi and Guantian set up 24 solar terms here; Houji inherited farming skills here, and the farming civilization of the Central Plains began. Third, Yunqiu Mountain brings together the three religious cultures of Confucianism, Buddhism and Taoism. The ancestral court of the Longmen School of Taoism originated from here, and Wudang, Wulong Palace, Babao Palace and other Taoist temples and Yunqiu Academy, Duobaolingyan Temple and other Confucian and Buddhist cultures blend and coexist harmoniously. Fourth, Yunqiu Mountain is also completely preserved with 11 thousand-year-old villages, which is a rare group of ancient villages in the south of Shanxi Province. Today's Talpo, inherited the local folk customs, instantly let you feel the kind of male ploughing and female weaving, self-sufficiency, marriage and funeral of Xanadu life. Here you can also see the local unique flower bun, a kind of Han folk art in Shanxi Province.

b. Development Strategy

In 2018, the Shanxi Provincial Tourism Development Committee issued the "Master Plan for the Tourism Development of the Yellow River Plate in Shanxi Province." The plan points out that it is necessary to make full use of the natural environment of Yunqiu Peak and Mountains, explore its cultural connotation of original ecological health and neutralization, and build outdoor sports, recreation and vacation, ancient village leisure, self-driving tourism, expansion experience, mountaineering and praying for blessing, Confucian, Buddhist and Taoist cultural experience and farming cultural experience. Upgrade and build a 5A ecological recreation tourist area. Regarding Yunqiu Mountain Scenic spot as the core, promote the rapid development of ancient villages, folk culture, characteristic planting and other tourism. By building Yunqiu Mountain Recreation Tourism Resort, promote the diversified development of Yunqiu Mountain.

First, expand the existing international cultural and creative base, carry out the original cultural and artistic activities beloved by international tourists, so as to form a destination for international tourists in Shanxi. Second, with the purpose of maintaining health, protect and utilize five traditional villages, develop mountain recreation and health vacations, and create characteristic outdoor recreation centers, traditional Chinese medicine, organic vegetable planting areas, flower beds, and so on. Third, enhance the construction of the existing folk culture experience blocks and increase the areas of art commodities and native products in the mountains. Fourth, construct Fuxi, Nuwa reproduction culture, Xihe observation of the sky and earth to sets the 24 solar terms, and Houji inherit farming technology and other culture in one of the farming culture park. Fifth, develop and preserve more complete ancient villages, create authentic thousand-year dwellings and courtyards, and create folk prints and New Year painting art villages in southern Shanxi. Sixth, enhance the popularity of the Zhonghe Cultural Festival held in March every year, expand the scale of performances and performance projects, and turn it into the most important folk sacrifice festival in Shanxi Province.

c. Representative Tourism Projects and Scenic Spots

i. Theme Recreation Activities

Around the origin of Chinese civilization, local culture, Taoist culture and other cultural excavation, protection and inheritance, the development of tourism products. At present, Yunqiu Mountain Scenic spot has formed four major theme activities: folk year, Zhonghe Festival, Art Festival, Red Leaf Festival. Through the activities to convey the impression of Yunqiu and folk feelings, attract tourists to participate in it, and harvest happiness and satisfaction in the experience.

Yunqiu Mountain has a variety of entertainment projects. Among them, the most popular is the tallest and longest Yuanyang Bridge (Glass suspension Bridge) in Shanxi Province. Yuanyang Bridge hangs between the two huge peaks of Yunqiu Mountain and reaches the bridge. You can swim the fantasy Yunqiu Mountain Fairy World in all directions, overlooking the thousands of mountains and ravines that are "close at hand." Yunqiushan high-altitude glass bridge has an overall length of 219 meters, a height of 195 meters and a width of 2 meters, which is the longest + highest transparent high-altitude glass bridge in Shanxi Province. When the wind is fine and sunny, step on the glass bridge, take a panoramic view of the canyon cracks under your feet, walk on it as if against the wind, breathtaking; when the clouds are deep and foggy, enjoy the sky on the bridge such as walking in the clouds, such as "overpass in the clouds."[①]

Yunqiu Mountain Ice Cave Group is one of the three major ice cave wonders in the world, and it is also the largest natural ice cave group found in China at present. The age of the surrounding rock strata

---

[①] Recreation Project-Shanxi Yunqu Mountain Website http://www.yunqiushan.cn/about/?31.html#menuSub

is about 400 million years, and the geomorphology of the region was formed 3 million years ago. The wonders of ice caves in the world are mainly divided into three types: the first type is glacier type ice hole, the second type is climate type ice hole, and the third type is geothermal negative anomaly type ice hole. Yunqiu Mountain Ice Cave Group belongs to the geothermal negative anomaly ice cave with the most complex refrigeration mechanism, and the global authoritative experts have so far been unable to decipher its formation principle. Because of its complex causes, the largest scale and 356 days of ice throughout the year, Yunqiu Mountain Ice Cave Group has also become a natural ice cave group with scientific research value and ornamental value. At present, the ice cave has been developed and opened to tourists.

ii. Tourism Route

First, find the root and the ancestor (two-day tour) . Yunqiu Mountain is a geographical indication of Chinese local culture, which inherits the local context of China and conveys a strong feeling of hometown. You may come from afar, but this is our common hometown. Find the root to find the ancestor line to take you to appreciate the Yunqiu Mountain-to feel the solid ring in the root vein of Chinese civilization. The route includes visiting local cultural specimen villages in southern Shanxi, visiting ancient villages, watching folk performances, experiencing the life interest of Taoist symbiosis, climbing through Yulian Cave, one / two / three days Gate, and enjoying the most beautiful scenery of Yunqiu Mountain. The next morning, I climbed to the top of the mountain to feel the neutralization culture, wish culture and fertility culture handed down from Yunqiu Mountain for thousands of years. Finally, you can choose to experience gliding, high-altitude gliding, dry land skiing and other events. (source: official website of Yunqiu Mountain Scenic spot, Shanxi Province)

Second, travel around Yunqiu (one-day tour) . How can the beautiful scenery and cultural wonders of Yunqiu Mountain be completed in one day? Travel around the Yunqiu line series scenic spots, take a look at the flowers will not miss the beautiful scenery. The ferry bus and cable car ropeway in the scenic area can not only facilitate tourists to travel between scenic spots, but also enjoy other kinds of scenery along the way. The route includes the quintessential scenic spots of Yunqiu Mountain, experiencing the blessing culture of the integration of the three religions in Yunqiu Mountain, challenging the heartbeat and stimulation of the extreme project, feeling the indigenous life of Taoist symbiosis, and after the hustle and bustle and agglomeration, will experience spiritual satisfaction. (source: official website of Yunqiu Mountain Scenic spot, Shanxi Province)

Third, the most beautiful peak (one-day tour) . Yunqiu Mountain is famous for its Taoist culture and can be on a par with Wudang Mountain. The most Xiufeng peak tour line, focusing on the characteristics of "praying for blessing and worship, mountaineering to visit immortals", through the Wulong Palace, Jade Lotus Cave, ancestral Master Ding, Jade Emperor Ding and other Taoist caves, you can also visit the 2500-year-old Tarpo ancient village and appreciate the unique "Taoist symbiosis" culture of Yunqiu Mountain. This route is the most beautiful route along the way to the summit of Yunqiu Mountain. The route can listen to the swallow warbler singing in the echoing mountain stream, and it is better than the sea of clouds in Penglai. (source: official website of Yunqiu Mountain Scenic spot, Shanxi Province)

Fourth, explore the secrets of the ancient village (one-day tour). Yunqiu Mountain has more than 10 ancient villages and towns, known as "Huaxia ring local context." The ancient village brand-new experience tour line selects the Tarpo ancient village which has a history of more than 2500 years for tourists to visit, as well as Yunqiu mountain brand-new experience project glass bridge, gliding wing, rope gliding and dryland skiing. You can not only experience time travel in the vicissitudes of stone kiln caves, but also taste the local water mat, feel the inheritance of thousands of years of marriage customs, farming culture, but also experience a variety of extreme recreational projects. Go to the ancient village of Tarpo to listen to the gurgling streams and gentle winds, taste Shanxi snacks, and then personally make a Yunqiu mountain flower bun to feel the charm of the local culture of southern Shanxi; and then participate in the Yunqiu mountain limit project challenge, across cliffs, water glides, gliding wings overlooking beautiful peaks. (source: official website of Yunqiu Mountain Scenic spot, Shanxi Province)

d. Yunqiu Mountain and Cultural Festival

In the Master Plan for the Tourism Development of the Yellow River Plate in Shanxi Province, the Yunqiu Mountain Zhonghe Culture Festival is one of the ten key festival activities in the Yellow River Canyon and the Red Cultural Tourism area. Yunqiu Mountain Zhonghe Culture Festival is an ancient festival that has been handed down for thousands of years. Tang Zhenyuan five years (AD 789) Tang Dezong Li Shiqin point, the Zhonghe Festival was officially identified as an important national legal festival, the imperial court performed the ceremony of the field, the hundred officials went to the peasant books to persuade the peasants, and the folk had customs such as offering sacrifices to the awn to pray for the New year Valley. For more than 1200 years, only Yunqiu Mountain has completely preserved the tradition of the Zhonghe Festival, known as the "living fossil of the Zhonghe Festival." In 2011, Yunqiu Mountain Zhonghe Culture "Zhonghe Festival" was included in the third batch of national intangible cultural heritage list published by the State Council. The festival project inherited the local spring festival ceremony in southern Shanxi in 1227. After the careful creation and inheritance of Yunqiu Mountain Scenic spot, as one of the grand traditional folk festivals, Zhonghe Festival has become an influential cultural festival and tourism festival. It has become an important window for Linfen Shanxi to show its unique cultural charm and an important platform to promote the integration of tourism and culture.

In ancient times, Yunqiu Mountain was an official and folk place for offering sacrifices to heaven and earth, and people were in awe of heaven and earth. Through offering sacrifices to heaven to express gratitude for all things given by heaven, in order to pray that the emperor God bless the Chinese people without natural and man-made disasters, national peace and well-being, good weather, grain abundance, meaning "harmonious symbiosis, inheritance and continuation." As the most important activity of the annual Zhonghe Festival, the blessing method is for all the people who come to Yunqiu Mountain to pray for the gods of Yunqiu Mountain to bless their health, the happiness of their families, and the good luck of the year. The Zhonghe Festival of Yunqiu Mountain is different, which is not only a ceremony, but also the inheritance of Yunqiu people to the Zhonghe Festival. Yunqiu Mountain, as the last inheritance of the Zhonghe Festival, has a deep sense of responsibility and mission to carry forward the Zhonghe culture.

Sacrifice ceremony is the most exciting part of the Zhonghe Festival, offering sacrifices to ancestors, primitive witch operas, parades of gods to carry pavilions, large-scale literary and artistic performances, splendid. During the festival, dozens of folk cultural activities will be held, including "praying for neutralization-sacrifice ceremony and opening ceremony of the Neutral Festival", "wishing Tiancheng-10,000 people praying for neutralization Festival", "signing on the nine frontiers of Yunqiu-Yunqiu", "Fuzhao Yunqiu-receiving blessing tree". Planting blessing ","Yunqiu Zhonghe Old Temple Fair", "Yunqiu wedding ceremony-whip stick pick flower basket", "Yunqiu Zhonghe Wufu porridge", "Yunqiu Zhonghe Hua bun exhibition", "Yunqiu Mountain Ice Cave Group-freezing Point Challenge", etc., bring tourists and the masses to feel the charm of neutralizing culture.

The blessing will keep you safe. Yunqiu Mountain as a famous Taoist mountain, Quanzhen Longmen School opened the ancestral court, during the Zhonghe Festival, held Taoist law meetings in the Wulong Palace and the Babao Palace, through a series of Dharma meetings to honor heaven and worship ancestors, understand the natural truth of heaven and earth, and at the same time pray for the common people, eliminate disasters and bless peace.

e. Tarpo Ancient Village

Yunqiu Mountain Tarpo Ancient Village, has a history of more than 2500 years, formerly known as taerpo, because Laozi Li Er traveled to the world has stayed here and got its name. Then, Taoism famous, and the local mountain people living next to each other, gradually formed a village. The ancient village of Tarpo is also known as "living fossils of thousand-year-old residential buildings". The whole village of Talpo rests on the mountains and water, hidden by ancient trees. In front of the village, there are clear springs flowing down from the Shenxianyu on the mountain, and the back of the village is in the main peak of the high and straight Yunqiu mountain and in the belly rock above the ancient village of Guanxiong, Jade Lotus Cave.

All the courtyards of Tarpo ancient villages are built according to the mountains, and the building materials are mainly stone. The village has a stone vault cave construction, now Tarpo, inherited the local folk customs, instantly let you feel the kind of male ploughing and female weaving, self-sufficiency, marriage and funeral of Xanadu life. Local villagers also continue the ancestors of reproductive worship, marriage and childbearing, social sacrifice, blessing and other local cultural customs, began in the Tang Dynasty "Zhonghe Festival" as a national intangible cultural heritage to this day. Here you can also see the local unique flower bun, Yunqiushan flower bun is a kind of Han folk art in Shanxi Province.

(3) Tourism Development Model of Humanistic Scenic Spots

The tourism development model of humanistic scenic spots mainly refers to the development of tourism by making use of the cultural resources such as sites, relics and ancient buildings of tourism value in the Yellow River Basin in Linfen. Hongdong County has a long history, splendid culture, ancient and unique human resources, colorful folk customs. For more than 600 years, "ask me where my ancestors were?" The ballad of "the big locust tree in Hongdong, Shanxi Province" makes the big locust tree in Hongdong become the "root" of most Chinese people. Hongdong relies on the great locust root ancestor culture to develop cultural tourism, at present has formed a more mature big locust tree tourist scenic spots and big locust tree root worship festival.

Hongdong Dahuai Tree Scenic spot is the key scenic spot of "Middle Line Genzu Culture Tour" in Linfen City and the industry driving core in the layout of Hongdong County cultural tourism industry "one core, four belts and six major areas". In order to better build the brand of family affection and build a new pattern of root ancestor tourism, Hongdong Big Sophora Tree Root worship Park has won a good reputation for the scenic spot by means of brand-driven service, brand-led management and brand-driven development. We will promote the high-quality development of the tourism industry of Sophora japonica.

a. Overview of Hongtong Dahuaishu Ancestor Memorial Garden

A history of emigration in the Ming Dynasty made the big locust tree in Hongdong become the "root" haunted by most of the Chinese people. Behind a unique and lasting cultural phenomenon, there must be a unique spirit to support, this spirit is the spirit of the big locust tree. Hongdong Huai Tree Root-seeking ancestor worship Garden is a national AAAAA tourist scenic spot and a key cultural relic protection unit in Shanxi Province. It is not only the only sacred place of folk sacrifice with the theme of "root-seeking" and "ancestor worship", but also a sacred place for Chinese to seek roots and ancestor worship all over the world. For centuries, it has been regarded as "home", as "ancestor", as "root". The scenic spot is composed of four theme plates: "Immigrant Monuments area", "ancestor worship activity area", "Fenhe Ecological Zone" and "Fenhe Ecological Zone". There are more than 60 scenic and cultural attractions. Hongdong locust tree root-seeking ancestor worship garden is the national intangible cultural heritage. It has also won many honors, such as "Ten Scenic spots in Shanxi Province", "Ten Brand Enterprises in Shanxi Tourism Industry", "Standardization pilot Unit of National Tourism Service Industry" and so on.

Hongdong Huai Tree Root-seeking ancestor worship Park has always adhered to diversified development, and has developed from a single scenic spot to a comprehensive tourism service area with the three major business sections of scenic spots, folk hotels and travel agencies as the main body, integrating food, housing, transportation, travel, shopping and entertainment, which not only embodies the profound cultural connotation of immigrants, but also creates an atmosphere for the descendants of great locust immigrants. At the same time, it also meets the needs of the majority of descendants of immigrants to seek roots and worship, tourism, sightseeing, rest, catering and shopping, which is the best choice for the majority of descendants of immigrants to carry out in-depth cultural experience and understand the folklore of their hometown.

b. Representative Tourism Project and Scenic Spot

First, the main scenic spots in the immigrant historic area are archway, the first generation of big locust tree sites, teahouse, the second generation of big locust tree, three generations of big locust tree, stone building, ancient post road, Guangji temple and so on. Among them, the Stone Sutra Building is the oldest cultural relic in the ancestral sacrifice garden, and it is also the only historical witness of the extant migrants in the Ming Dynasty. Sutra is a kind of ancient Buddhist stone carvings, founded in the Tang Dynasty, made of a number of stone carvings built into columns, covered with plates, column carvings of Tharoni scriptures and Buddhist statues, built by Guang Ji Temple Dafa Hui in Jin Chengan five years (1201 years), more than 200 years earlier than immigrants, is the only relic of Guangji Temple, but also a typical classic building works, more than 800 years of history. It is made of bluestone, the plane is octagonal, four layers and fifteen levels, 9.4 meters high, carving art simple and profound, calligraphy vigorous and smooth, relief lifelike, is a treasure of carving art in the Jin Dynasty.

Second, the main scenic spots in the ancestor worship activity area are root carving gate, "root" shadow wall, Lianxin bridge, Huaixiang bridge, stork bridge, sacrifice hall, sacrifice square, ancestor worship hall, Wangxiang pavilion, tracing source pavilion and so on. Ancestral worship hall is the core of the whole scenic spot, the hall is dedicated to the 1230 confirmed immigrant ancestor surnames, is the country's largest civilian ancestral hall, so it is called "the first hall of people sacrifice in the world." "Root" character shadow wall shape is unique, beautifully carved, is the landmark landscape of the scenic spot. Shadow wall, commonly known as Zhaobi, can often be seen in folk buildings in our country, such as the general courtyard or the courtyard of large families. The root shadow wall is the landmark building of the big locust tree scenic spot, it is not the general plane structure, but the unique eight-shaped structure. The carvings above are also very exquisite, all of which are auspicious folk patterns.

Third, the main functions of the folk tourism area are sightseeing and rest, including Lianhuatang, Huai Shu Zhuang, Hongya Ancient Cave and other scenic spots. Among them, "Hongya Ancient Cave" is the origin of the present "Hongdong" county name, taking the south of the county seat "Hongya" and the north "ancient cave". "Lianhuatang" is the alias of Hongdong County-the symbol of Lotus City. For thousands of years, Hongdong City has been surrounded by water and planting lotus, summer lotus flowers blooming and full of interest, so Hongdong City is called "Lotus City". Huai Shu Zhuang is located in the middle of the folk experience area on the west axis of the scenic spot. The main buildings include characteristic folk houses, local vegetable gardens, ancient well platforms, old tea shops, traditional workshops, and so on. In the village, there are private schools, ploughing and reading gardens, water mills, local special products workshops, threshing fields, entertainment facilities and other activities, and there are a variety of activities for tourists to participate in, including cultural exhibitions, tourism, folk experience, etc. So that the root ancestor cultural charm of the hometown has a panoramic view.

Fourth, the Fenhe Ecological Zone is a new project in the overall planning of the national AAAAA-level scenic spot, which was opened free of charge in 2015. Fenhe Ecological Zone is not only beautiful but also a collection of humanities, which can fully meet the leisure and entertainment needs of tourists and local residents.

c. Hongtong Dahuaishu Cultural Festival

"Hongdong Big Sophora Tree Cultural Festival", with Ching Ming Festival as the main sacrifice day, each cultural festival has tens of thousands of descendants of the big locust tree immigrants gathered here, expressing strong love and deep feelings for the hometown of the big locust tree. The holding of Hongdong Great Sophora Tree Culture Festival has promoted the integrated development and high-quality development of cultural tourism industry in Linfen City. Through the holding of the Great Sophora Tree Culture Festival, we can carry forward the feelings of the Chinese nation in thinking of filial piety, tracing back to the source of the newspaper, and respecting and loyal to the country, and can carry forward the excellent traditional culture and the national intangible cultural heritage "the custom of offering ancestor worship to the great locust tree." promote the integration of literature and tourism, and strongly create a "Hongdong hometown" cultural tourism brand with local characteristics and national standards. At present, the ancestor worship Garden holds ancestor worship ceremonies every year in Ching Ming Festival, Ghost Festival, Hanyi Festival and other festivals to attract tourists to participate in the sacrifice. The custom of offering ancestor worship to the great locust tree in Hongdong has also been included in the list of national intangible cultural heritage protection.

Hongdong locust tree root worship garden as the vanguard of cultural and tourism integration and development, has always been to inherit non-heritage, carry forward culture as its own responsibility, in order to further deepen the integration and development of literature and tourism, and strive to launch the "hometown" brand. Since the first Hongdong Great Sophora Tree Cultural Festival was held, the scenic spot has not only preserved and inherited the "Hongdong Great Sophora tree ancestor worship custom" intact, but also set off a "root-seeking craze" and "ancestor worship fever" throughout the country, polishing the gold-lettered signboard of the 5A-class scenic spot of the great locust tree. During the cultural festival, Hongdong famous snack festival, traditional opera performance, Hongdong locust tree cultural festival root worship ceremony, Hongdong locust tree immigrant culture seminar, memorial revolutionary martyrs, 100 gold medal tour guide competition and other activities will be held to carry forward the ancestor worship culture, sing the "hometown" brand, and take the road of integrated development of cultural tourism. Hongdong big locust tree, has been deeply rooted in the common spiritual home of the Chinese people, bearing the rich connotation of excellent Chinese traditional culture.

d. Education Base of Hongtong Dahuaishu Ancestor Memorial Garden

In October 2018, Hongdong Huai Tree Root-seeking ancestor worship Garden was named by the Ministry of Education as the national primary and secondary school students' research and practical education base. At present, combined with the advantages and characteristics of the existing resources in the scenic spot and the plan of research and learning projects throughout the year, and adhering to the principle of "education, practicality, safety, and public welfare", the Hongdong locust Tree Root worship Park has formulated the "implementation Plan for the Promotion of the work of the National Primary and Middle School students' Research and practical Education Base," and comprehensively deployed the development of research courses and the development of research and learning activities to ensure the steady progress of the tasks of the base construction project. The scenic spot has determined that four research courses and research activities will be developed, and the curriculum design is arranged in Table 3.4 below.

Table 3.4 Courses of Hongtong Dahuaishu Ancestor Memorial Garden

Name	Content	Place
Understand the Root of Huaxia and Express Patriotic Love	Red Educational experience (nostalgia, perception, inheritance)	Martyrs Pavilion Academy of Cultural Revolution
Promoting Genzu Culture	Chinese Root-ancestor Sacrifice Culture (non-legacy, inheritance, experience)	Empirical Exhibition Hall of Immigrants in Stele Pavilion, Temple of Sacrifice and Ancestral Hall
Beautiful Chinese Roots Charming Baijia surnames	Chinese Genzu Name Culture (Family traditions, family precepts, inheritance and promotion)	Ancestor worship hall and Chinese family name garden
Multiple practice Comprehensive experience	Combining Education with Comprehensive Practice (Inquiry Spirit, Practical Ability)	Peach Garden and Folk Village Research cultivated land Dahuashu Folklore Hotel

Source: Website of Hongtong Dahuaishu.

e. Relics of Tao Temple

Tao Temple site is located in Xiangfen County Tao Si Township Tao Si Village South, a distribution area of about 3 million square meters, in 1988 was announced by the State Council as the third batch of national key cultural relics protection units. Tao Temple site is not only the national "Eleventh five-year Plan, 12th five-year Plan" large site protection project, but also the "Southern Genzu Culture Tourism" the most valuable brand, is the "Genzu culture" straight root, the total root. The protection, utilization and development of Taosi ruins are of great significance to the realization of transformation and development. It is a sacred place for Chinese children at home and abroad to seek roots and ask ancestors, and is the most potential project for the development of cultural tourism industry in Shanxi Province. It is an important carrier to carry forward the "long-standing culture of a clean and honest government". Its"Yao du" and "China" brands have unlimited value and are unique in the whole country.

Since 1978, after 40 years of archaeological excavation and research, it has been preliminarily revealed that Taosi site is the most complete prehistoric functional division in China, and its construction and use date is 4300-3900 years ago. Here, we found unprecedented urban sites, magnificent palace areas, image sacrifice areas, independent warehousing areas, handicraft areas under the management of foremen, royal cemeteries, civilian residential areas, and so on. Unearthed pottery, bronze, wood, jade ritual vessels and other cultural relics more than 5500 pieces. Among them, the discovered drum is the earliest drum ritual instrument in China, and the bronze bell is the first metal musical instrument in China, indicating the formation of the earliest etiquette music system; the observation platform discovered is the earliest observation platform in the world; the earliest words and wooden ritual vessels in China have been discovered.

On June 18, 2015, the Chinese Academy of Social Sciences, the propaganda Department of the Provincial CPC Committee, and the Linfen Municipal Party Committee and Municipal Government held a press conference in Beijing, confirming that the Tao Temple site is an important node for archaeological exploration of the formation of the core of Chinese civilization in time and space and the birth of China at first. It is the main pulse of Chinese civilization. According to the existing excavation data and research results, from the age, the earth, the grade, the connotation and the nature of the site, the Tao Temple site is the capital site of Emperor Yao.

On May 28, 2018, the "Comprehensive study on the Origin and early Development of Chinese Civilization" was held at the Information Office of the State Council, pointing out that the discovery of the site of Xiangfen Pottery Temple in Shanxi Province is one of the empirical examples of 5000 years of civilization in China. Taosi sites play an extremely important role in the formation of Chinese civilization. The state, provinces and cities attach great importance to the protection and utilization of Taosi sites.

They have been listed by the State Administration of Cultural relics as the "11th five-year Plan large site Protection Project" and the "Special Plan for the Protection of large sites during the 12th five-year Plan (150 sites)". It has also become the support of the "philosophy and Social Science Innovation Project" of the Chinese Academy of Social Sciences, the "Source Exploration Project of Chinese Civilization" and the "National Archaeological Plan of large ruins".

f. Jin Guo Museum

Jin Guo Museum, located in Qucun Town, Quwo County, is the first ruins museum with Jin culture theme built by the national key cultural relics protection unit "Qucun-Tianma site". It was officially opened to the public on National Day in 2014. The Jin Museum is the first large-scale ruins museum in Shanxi Province, which integrates the collection, protection, research and display of cultural relics, and it is also the only platform in the country to completely display the historical and cultural features of Jin. it is of great significance to inherit and carry forward the traditional culture, highlight the regional civilization characterized by Jin culture, and perfect the tourism industry structure of Shanxi Province.

Jin Guo Museum is located in the "Qucun-Tianma site" on a large scale, from Tianma Village in Yicheng County in the east to Qucun Town in Quwo County in the west, riverbank in the south and hillside in Beida Bridge. The site is 3800 meters long from east to west, 2800 meters wide from north to south, and covers an area of nearly 11 square kilometers. More than ten large-scale exploration excavations have been carried out by Peking University and Shanxi Institute of Archaeology, with a total area of 100 square meters and more than 1000 tombs excavated, including more than 800 tombs in the Zhou Dynasty. Especially in the core area of the site, nine groups of 19 tombs of the early monarchs and wives of the State of Jin, ten chariot and horse pits, and more than 12000 precious cultural relics were excavated. The excavation results provided support for the solution of the chronological subject of the Western Zhou kings of the Xia, Shang and Zhou dynasties in China. It was listed as one of the top ten new archaeological discoveries in 1992 and 1993, and in 2001 it was appraised as one of the 12000 major archaeological discoveries in China in the 20th century.

Jin Guo Museum, with Jin culture as its theme, has created three highlights of Jin history, excavation history and ruins exhibition. The historical and cultural exhibition hall takes the history of Jin as a clue, through a large number of precious cultural relics unearthed in the graveyard of Jin princes, it shows a series of important events that can influence the historical process of ancient China, such as the change of Jin Dynasty from Shuyu to Jin, Wen Hou Qin Wang, Xian Gong Tujiang, Wen Gong domination, Liuqing dictatorship, and three separate Jin dynasties, etc., through a large number of precious cultural relics unearthed in Jin Hou cemetery. The exhibition hall of site excavation history shows a series of great achievements made by three generations of archaeologists from Peking University College of Archaeology and Shanxi Institute of Archaeology. The exhibition hall of the site adopts a way of display of a site, focusing on the tombs of four groups of Jin princes and their wives and three chariot and horse pits, showing the audience a panoramic picture of the tombs of the kings of the state during the two-week period.

g. Pu Xian Dongyue Temple

Dongyue Temple, located at the top of Mount Baishan 2.5 kilometers east of the city, is the palace of Huang Feihu, the Great Emperor of Dongyue Tian Qi Ren Sheng. Surrounded by dozens of miles of luxuriant trees, Nanchuan at the foot of the mountain, and the scenery is very beautiful, which is the first tourist attraction in Puxian County. Dongyue Temple in the ring courtyard, two-story porch, kiln building, character stage, known as "the temple in the four unique", but also to the millennium Liriodendron, eight Immortals celebrating birthday, the Jin Dynasty stone carvings, magnolia slow, music building inscription and sunny monument, eight sound bell known as "temple seven treasures." In 2001, it was listed as the fifth batch of national key cultural relics protection units.

Dongyue Temple has a long history, Tang Zhenguan has a scale, the Yuan Dynasty Yanyou five years, that is, 1318 AD reconstruction, has a history of more than 700 years. There were also repairs and additions in the Ming and Qing dynasties, and the architectural style of Tang, Song, Jin, Yuan, Ming and Qing dynasties became great. Dongyue Temple is a mixed Buddhist temple, a rectangular combination of groups, courtyard court architecture, covering an area of more than 10,000 square meters, construction of more than 7,000 square meters, a total of 280 halls and pavilions. The building takes the main hall of the palace as the center, with the paradise building in front and the underground mansion in the back. Four corners corner tower towering, courtyard week porch surround, form a large-scale, majestic palace-style buildings, mainly by the Taiwei Temple, Huachi Palace, Palace Hall, 72 Division, hell five parts, especially the Ming Dynasty built hell, the internal sculpture of the five Yue Emperor, the Ten Temple Yan Jun, six Cao judges and the underworld all kinds of torture, a total of more than 150 statues, the size is similar to the real person, in fact, it is a masterpiece of mud painted sculptures in the Ming Dynasty.

(4) Development Model of Rural Tourism

The development model of rural tourism mainly refers to the development of tourism by making use of the characteristic agriculture, farming culture and other resources of tourism value in the Yellow River Basin of Linfen. The farming areas of the Great River Basin are located in beautiful environment, beautiful mountains and rivers, which can meet the needs of tourists for the pursuit of natural and healthy rural cultural tourism. According to the local culture and natural characteristics, we can develop various forms of tourism activities, such as rural tourism, thematic tourism and so on. Linfen City strengthens the local agricultural characteristics, integrates the local pear industry, natural resources and national culture, innovates and develops a number of "tourism +" industries, leads the development of rural tourism industry, and constructs characteristic rural tourism destinations. For example, the representative county relies on the local unique pear fruit industry, holds the pear flower festival, develops the rural tourism, promotes the development of the local tourism industry.

a. Overview of Pear Flower Festival in Xixian County

Xixian County is rich in tourism resources, pure and beautiful pear orchard scenery, Zijingshan, Shimagou scenery pleasant, Wulu Mountain natural scenic spots mountains, Xiao Xitian hanging art exquisite, the Ming Dynasty Daguanlou extraordinary momentum, attracting tourists from all directions. The most famous scenic spot is Qianfo nunnery, also known as Xiao Xitian, located at the top of Fenghuang Mountain in Xiyi County, Shanxi Province. It is a Buddhist Zen monastery founded by Dongming Zen Master in Ming Dynasty in the second year of Chongzhen in Ming Dynasty (1629). At first, it was named because there were thousands of Buddhas in the main hall, and then it was renamed Xiaoxitian for the sake of distinguishing another Ming Dynasty monastery in the south of the city. The whole temple is stacked and integrated according to the mountain, especially the wooden bone and mud hanging art in the hall of the main hall has its own characteristics, which can be called the "hanging last song" in the history of Chinese sculpture art. The color sculpture of the hall of the main hall alone accounts for more than 4% of the colored sculpture works of the Ming and Qing dynasties in Shanxi province, and these masterpieces are only molded in the small hall with an area of only 169.6 square meters, which can be called the treasure of Buddhist colored sculpture art.

Jiaxian County has a long history of planting pear fruit, which is famous as "the hometown of Chinese golden pear", "Chinese Damei pear" and "the hometown of Chinese crisp pear". Yuluxiang pear produced in Yuluxiang County has many advantages, such as large fruit, high edible rate, high sugar content and so on, which is recognized as "the first pear in China" by experts in the national pear industry system.

In addition, Linfen also has Anze Huanghua Festival, Guxian Peony Festival, Yaodu Peach Blossom Festival, Quwo Global Tourism Promotion, Renzushan Tent Music Festival, Puxian Siqiao Chaoshan Festival and so on.

b. Representative Tourism Project and Scenic Spot

Yixian County every year in the county Wu town Yangdeyuan ten thousand mu pear orchard held pear blossom festival, for a period of one week. Through the holding of the Pear Flower Festival, the new leap from simply selling pear fruit to watching pear blossom, promoting culture, strengthening industry and enriching the people has been realized, and the process of increasing farmers' income and becoming well-off has been accelerated. The Pear Flower Festival usually includes the opening ceremony, literary and artistic performances, non-heritage cultural display, bonfire party, investment promotion negotiation and concentrated signing ceremony, "Yulu fragrant Pear" development expert forum seminar, fruit tree custom adoption special meeting, characteristic agricultural products exhibition, tourism promotion meeting, calligraphy exhibition, photography and sketching competition, etc., in order to take pear blossom as the medium, culture as the connotation, and a series of activities as the carrier to integrate tourism resources. Create a pure and beautiful pear garden scenery, from simply selling pear fruit to watching pear blossoms, promoting culture, strengthening the industry, expanding and strengthening the tourism culture industry, calling the county jade dew fragrance brand, speeding up the process of increasing farmers' income and becoming well-off. At the same time, through omni-directional and diversified publicity to show the pear fruit industry and tourism resources in Jiaxian County, to be famous, to make friends, to live the county, to further highlight the charm of the county, and to strive to build the hometown of China's Golden Pear, the green state of Shanxi, the livable place in the west of Shanxi, and the beautiful and happy capital.

The Fifth Pear Flower Festival in 2019 identified Yuli Village as one of the rural tourism demonstration villages. The first is to create characteristic farm tourism. Around farm tourism, planning and construction of peach, grape, mulberry, jade dew fragrant pear, apple-based picking garden; leisure-based fishing area; farm food-based farm music; to the original ecological agricultural products-based "agricultural exhibition platform", the formation of rural tourism with individual characteristics. The second is to form a pilot project for integration and development. Comprehensive construction should be carried out around the development of industrial integration. Take the jade dew fragrance industry as the foundation, build the base, do the demonstration, extend the chain, strengthen the leading industry; adhere to "Green Water and Green Mountain is Jinshan Silver Mountain", take "Stone Mill" as the title, record, dig culture, engage in special topics, form humanistic effects, expand the scope of propaganda, build Yuli Village into a miniature pastoral complex, and become a demonstration village for industrial integration and development of the whole county.

(5) Development Mode of Integration of Culture and Tourism

As an important part of cultural protection and inheritance, it has become a consensus that intangible cultural heritage can inject vitality into the development of tourism. In order to promote the in-depth development of the integration of literature and tourism, and fully display the excellent traditional culture and tourism resources of Linfen City, Linfen City innovative development ideas, let "non-heritage" hand in hand "scenic spot", start non-legacy scenic spot activities, create a cultural and tourism integration demonstration base, so that the scenic spot becomes popular.

Linfen City, combined with the environment and location advantages of Lotus Town in Xiangfen County, through the establishment of non-heritage site experience area, non-heritage project exhibition area, folk activity demonstration area, commodity exhibition area, non-heritage project propaganda area, etc., focus on the display of Linfen excellent intangible cultural heritage, regularly carry out a series of non-heritage exhibition activities in the town, and truly achieve the common inheritance and development of non-heritage and scenic spots in the integration of literature and tourism. And take this as a non-heritage and tourism integration demonstration park to build, promote Linfen city to carry out non-heritage scenic spot work, gradually build a number of cultural and tourism integration demonstration base, comprehensively promote the integration of culture and tourism development, and promote the development of related cultural and creative industries.

The non-heritage scenic spot is a concrete action for Linfen City to actively practice the non-heritage protection concept of "seeing people, seeing things and seeing life". It is of great benefit to display and publicize the rich and colorful intangible cultural heritage of Linfen in an all-round way, enhance the cultural connotation of tourism industry, and promote the development of deep integration of culture and tourism. Through the non-legacy scenic spot to let "non-heritage" and "tourism" hand in hand, let cultural and tourism activities and publicity and marketing meet, through the perfect combination of "poetry" and "distance", let non-heritage "live", let scenic spots "fire", let tourists "stay", let the brand "light up", accelerate the development of deep integration of cultural and tourism in Linfen City, and innovate the development mode and path of the integration of cultural and tourism.

Section 3 Experiences and Countermeasures of Tourism Development of the Yellow River in Linfen, Shanxi Province

Taking the development and utilization of the Yellow River culture as the starting point, Linfen City has made great efforts to develop the cultural tourism industry and promote the development of local tourism in the direction of high quality and high quality, which has not only promoted the economic transformation, but also formed a cultural tourism destination with the cultural label of the Yellow River. This part will make an in-depth exposition of the experience, suggestions and countermeasures for the future development of the Yellow River tourism in Linfen City.

1. Experience in the Development of Yellow River Civilization Tourism

This part will give an in-depth explanation of the development experience of the Yellow River civilization tourism, through the analysis of the relevant experience, it is helpful to provide reference and inspiration for the market development, product design and marketing publicity of the river civilization tourism in other areas.

(1) Government Attention and Creating Three Plate Planning

At the Provincial Tourism Development work Conference in 2018, Sheng Xianqing, director of the Shanxi Provincial Tourism Development Commission, pointed out: Shanxi Province is guided by meeting the growing needs of the people for a better life, with the development of global tourism as its strategic requirement, and with promoting the structural reform on the supply side of tourism as the main line, insisting on the scenic spots as the king, giving priority to the road network, deepening the integration of culture and tourism, and implementing large projects, large enterprise operations, and large activities to detonate. Efforts have been made to forge the three new tourism brands of the Yellow River, the Great Wall and Taihang, speed up the construction of the upgraded version of the general pattern of the development of cultural tourism in Shanxi, and formulate the tourism plans of the three major plates, namely, "the Master Plan for the Tourism Development of the Yellow River Plate in Shanxi Province (2018-2025)", "the General Plan for the Tourism Development of the Great Wall Plate in Shanxi Province (2018-2025)" and "the Master Plan for the Tourism Development of Taihang Plate in Shanxi Province (2018-2025)". Through the planning, we can further clarify the uniqueness of the three major tourism resources in Shanxi Province, highlight the theme characteristics of the integration of literature and tourism, further clarify the specific development ideas and work objectives, and plan and implement a number of key projects to improve product quality and service function. Further scientific analysis and prediction of tourist market, the introduction of customized design to meet the multi-level consumption needs of global tourism. The systematic, scientific, pragmatic and effective planning of the three major plates is bound to coruscate the unparalleled unique charm of the three great articles of the Yellow River, the Great Wall and Taihang.[①]

The tourism planning years of the "three major plates" are the near 2018-2020 and the long-term 2021-2025, with the core areas along the Yellow River, the Great Wall and Taihang as the main areas, radiation and related areas as the related areas, covering the whole province. The planning content mainly includes planning background, tourism resources analysis and development status, goal orientation and overall thinking, functional zoning and spatial layout, tourism destination public service system, tourism image and brand, market expansion and promotion, tourism resources protection, social sharing and integration development and so on.

a. Plan for Tourism Development of the Yellow River Plate in Shanxi Province (2018-2015)

The tourism development of the Yellow River plate takes showing "the soul of the Yellow River in Shanxi" as the strategic focus, creating the Yellow River tourism scenic corridor with all-round

---

① Consideration and Approval of General Planning for Tourism Development in Three Major Plates of Shanxi Province-Portal Website of Shanxi Provincial People's Government http://www.shanxi.gov.cn/yw/sxyw/201806/t20180625_457038.shtml

development of water, land and air, and constructing tourism projects with great influence at home and abroad, which fully embody the integration of literature and tourism, unique creativity and great influence at home and abroad. on the basis of the Yellow River plate tourism out of the mountain driving, the formation of the plate global tourism development pattern, the general trend, the great prosperity of the leapfrog development trend.

b. Plan for Tourism Development of Taihang in Shanxi Province (2018-2015)

The main body of Taihang Mountain is in Shanxi, Shanxi Province Taihang plate scenery is magnificent and beautiful, history and culture is thick, folk customs are rich, but also the holy place of the Anti-Japanese War. Taihang plate tourism resources abundance, high density, strong combination of good integrity, the value of global tourism resources is great. Tourism resources have distinct characteristics, high grade and high concentration of dominant cultural heritage in China. Wutai Mountain, Pingyao ancient city of two world cultural heritage, Wutai Mountain Scenic spot, Imperial City Xiangfu Scenic spot, Yanmenguan Scenic spot and other national 5A tourist scenic spots, with monopoly and international. The tourism development of Taihang plate is supported by the "Taihang No. 1 Tourism Highway in Shanxi Province", which runs through the north and the south, and forms a national demonstration corridor connecting scenic spots, key counties, tourist towns and key tourist villages, and forming a national demonstration corridor integrating tourism traffic corridor, cultural landscape corridor, tourism economic development corridor and tourism experience corridor along the north and south of Taihang Mountain.

c. Plan for Tourism Development of the Great Wall in Shanxi Province (2018-2015)

Shanxi retained the sites of the Great Wall from the warring States to the Ming Dynasty, and witnessed the gradual integration of Xiongnu, Xianbei, Dangxiang, Shatuo and other ethnic groups in history. Shanxi is the historical symbol and cultural landmark of Shanxi as a national melting pot. It is not only the precious heritage left by its ancestors, but also the carrier of Chinese civilization and the symbol of Shanxi's heavy cultural heritage. The Great Wall of Shanxi includes many kinds of architectural relics, such as wall, Guanbao, enemy building, horse face, horse wall and so on. Many of these architectural relics are distributed in the precipitous and magnificent geographical environment, solidifying a variety of historical and cultural elements, such as military culture, border trade culture, folk culture, regional culture, and so on. Through in-depth excavation of the historical and cultural connotation of the Great Wall of Shanxi, scientific protection, maintenance, management and rational use, condensing the theme of patriotism and national integration, Combined with the existing world-class cultural heritage of Wutai Mountain, Pingyao Ancient City and Yungang Grottoes in Jinzhong and Northern Shanxi, the Great Wall of Shanxi is gradually built into a world-class cultural heritage tourism destination.

Based on the brand image of the Great Wall Expo in Shanxi, the Great Wall plate tourism investigates the resource distribution and cultural characteristics of the Great Wall in Shanxi from the perspective of the global development of Shanxi Province. According to the ornamental and research value of the Great Wall, the primary and secondary regions are divided; through the classification of the background, history, culture and resources of the Great Wall in Shanxi Province, the service core, the Great Wall Road, the theme area and the development axis are taken as the key development elements; through the re-planning and organization of the existing traffic network, the tourist scenic spots are connected as a whole; through the improvement of the service system, the tourist experience is enhanced.

(2) Policy guidance and Optimization of Environment

The policy guarantee and implementation measures for the tourism development of the Yellow River are clearly defined in the Master Plan for the Tourism Development of the Yellow River Plate in Shanxi Province. First, strengthen organizational leadership. Shanxi Province has set up a system of joint meetings of cities on the Yellow River plate led by the Shanxi Provincial Tourism Development Committee to communicate regularly on the tourism development of the Yellow River plate, so as to realize the sharing of information and experience, and solve the difficulties and problems encountered in the tourism development of the Yellow River plate in a timely manner. The establishment of Shanxi Yellow River plate city view alliance, that is, by the plate county (city) level tourism and development committee and the person in charge of important scenic spots established a permanent joint meeting. The Alliance holds a large-scale tourism activity and festival coordination meeting of the Yellow River plate once a year. The aim is to hold joint consultations on dislocation in large-scale events and festivals, so that there are all kinds of activities and festivals in the Yellow River plate all the time and everywhere, so that tourists can play and have fun everywhere and all the time in the 1000 km zone from north to south, so as to strengthen the overall tourism attractiveness of the Yellow River plate. The second is to strengthen the guidance of planning. In the basic principle of "integration of multi-rules and regulations", in view of scenic spots, tourism projects, characteristic tourism villages and towns, etc., it is necessary to formulate corresponding special or detailed plans to implement the control of specific construction space, especially in characteristic tourism villages and towns. We will comprehensively promote the coordination and connection between tourism planning and urban and rural areas, land use, road traffic, cultural relics protection and utilization, environmental protection, forestry, agriculture, water conservancy, sports, and so on, so as to enhance the maneuverability and landing of the planning.

In recent years, Linfen has made great efforts to improve the infrastructure, environmental hygiene, product development, service level and development model of tourism development. First, in terms of infrastructure, all counties and cities under Linfen City have begun to develop, expand and renovate roads, and have ranked first in the province, with a total length of more than 10,000 kilometers. Second, in terms of environmental protection, Linfen actively carried out environmental control, changing the traditional situation of environmental pollution. Third, attach importance to tourism development, pay more and more attention to the cultural connotation of scenic spots, and vigorously create tourist scenic spots with rich cultural heritage and obvious regional characteristics, and issued a series of policies, plans and schemes, including "Linfen Tourism Development Master Plan", "Linfen Tourism incentive method" and so on. All these are the concentrated embodiment of Linfen's attaching importance to the development of tourism.

(3) Planning First and Conducting Scientific Development

From the central government to the local government, they attach great importance to the development of the Yellow River civilized tourism, including the corresponding tourism industry planning. At the level of the national government, the 13th five-year Plan for Tourism Development, issued in 2016, points out that it follows the principles of landscape continuity, cultural integrity, market brand and industrial agglomeration, relying on linear natural and cultural corridors and traffic channels such as rivers, rivers and mountains. Series of key tourist cities and characteristic tourism functional areas; It is clearly put forward to focus on building the Huaxia civilized tourism belt of the Yellow River, which has opened up a new situation for the Yellow River tourism with worldwide characteristics. At the local government level, the Shanxi Provincial Tourism Development Committee formulated the "overall Plan for the Tourism Development of the Yellow River Plate in Shanxi Province" in 2018, and made a detailed plan for the Yellow River tourism plate in Shanxi Province. Combined with the cultural characteristics of the resources of the Yellow River tourism plate in Shanxi Province, create the brand image of "the soul of the Yellow River in Shanxi Province", and carry out the overall positioning of the Yellow River tourism plate in Shanxi Province, and determine the overall development goals.

a. Construction of Fine Tourism Belt of the Yellow River

Shanxi Province will rely on the unique natural resources of the Yellow River, coastal human resources, as well as the unique Yellow River spirit and Yellow River culture, to build a fine tourism belt of the Yellow River in Shanxi, China. To implement the development requirements of the National 13th five-year Plan for Tourism Development, taking the Yellow River No. 1 National Tourism Special Highway under construction as the axis, connecting the brand scenic spots and tourist lines built by fine products, expanding new products, enriching new business type, developing characteristic tourism villages and towns, and strengthening the support of solid elements, the tourism plate of the Yellow River in Shanxi Province has been built into a "excellent tourism belt of the Yellow River in Shanxi, China."

b. Constructing Tourism Destination of the World River Civilization in Shanxi Province

Shanxi will rely on the rich cultural tourism resources of the Yellow River to create a world river civilization Shanxi tourism destination. The five thousand years of historical and cultural development in

Shanxi has fully demonstrated the only remaining and continuous Huaxia River civilization in the four major river basins in the world, as well as the soul and pulse of the Chinese spirit. Combined with the current development strategy of "Belt and Road Initiative" in China, make full use of the heavy culture nurtured by the Yellow River, build the selling point and brand of world cultural tourism, and build it into "Shanxi tourism destination of world river civilization". In particular, the convening of the Great River Civilization Tourism Forum, on the one hand, set up a high-end tourism platform for Shanxi and global exchanges and mutual learning, win-win cooperation, and create a high-specification and influential tourism conference brand for Shanxi; on the other hand, with the "big river civilization" as the carrier, help Shanxi seize the cultural tourism value highland of the Yellow River and further enhance the image of world-class cultural tourism destinations. The holding of the forum can not only promote the integration and development of Shanxi tourism and cultural industry, show China's cultural self-confidence, cultural prosperity and cultural soft power, but also help Shanxi speed up the creation and launch of tourism products, promote the in-depth excavation and innovative marketing of "Yellow River IP", so as to speed up the construction of the upgraded version of the development pattern of Shanxi cultural tourism and create the golden business card of "World Great River Cultural Tourism destination".

c. Creating a National Yellow River Cultural Tourist Area

In the Master Plan for the Tourism Development of the Yellow River Plate in Shanxi Province, the cultural development goal of the Yellow River tourism plate is clearly put forward, which highlights the Shanxi provincial government's attention to the Yellow River civilization. The plan points out that the cultural development of the Yellow River plate should build a national cultural tourism area that tells the story of Shanxi and deduces the Chinese spirit in the process of innovation, integration and characteristics. These include planning and performing three national famous and world-influential real-scene performing arts and ceremonial performances, vigorously protecting and developing the intangible cultural heritage of the sector, and making efforts in the aspects of folk opera, song and dance, music, characteristic food, characteristic handicrafts, characteristic tourism commodities, etc., key scenic spots, tourist towns and villages should be used as the main display places of intangible cultural heritage. Excavating the history and culture of the Yellow River plate, using modern scientific and technological means to activate, manifest and interesting historical and cultural stories, so that it has become an important part of the development of tourism, study tourism, so that the Yellow River plate tourism highlights the history and culture of Shanxi and rich and colorful folk culture advantages.

The overall goal of the tourism development of the Yellow River plate in Shanxi Province is to take the No. 1 national tourism special road and related roads of the Yellow River in Shanxi Province as the skeleton, to integrate and upgrade resources and exquisite construction as the means, to build the tourism industry into a strategic pillar industry affecting economic transformation as the starting point, to build the national tourism boutique routes of the mother Yellow River, Longteng Yellow River, colorful Yellow River and Ecological Yellow River. Promote the overall uplift and development of plate tourism, build a new highland of Shanxi tourism, a new benchmark of Yellow River tourism, and a new perspective of world cultural tourism.

(4) Adapt measures to Local Conditions and Create Diverse Products

According to the relevant contents of the Master Plan for the Tourism Development of the Yellow River Plate in Shanxi Province, and according to the natural and cultural resources of different regions of the Yellow River, the Yellow River plate is divided into four functional areas: "Xikou Culture and Yellow River Castle Leisure area, Yellow River Canyon and Red Culture Tourism area, Luliang Mountain Ecological Recreation and Recreation area, Yellow River Wetland and Ancient Chinese Culture Leisure area". Second, the main area of the Yellow River will construct the spatial pattern of "one Yellow River corridor, four major tourism cores, four famous tourist counties, six major theme tours and eight characteristic scenic spots". The third is to build two leading projects, ten key projects, ten characteristic projects and 55 key projects at the county level. Two of the leading projects are the No. 1 National Tourism Highway Project of the Yellow River in Shanxi Province and the World River Civilization Expo Park project.

a. National Tourist Special Highway Project along the Yellow River in Shanxi

The Yellow River, which flows through Shanxi Province, is about 1008 kilometers long, and the planned construction of the Yellow River No. 1 National Tourism Highway is about 1225 kilometers long, from Wanjiazhai in Xinzhou to the west of Yuncheng, running through four cities (Luliang Linfen Yuncheng, Xinzhou) , connecting 14 Grade A and above scenic spots and 75 non-Class A important tourism resources. With the construction of Shanxi Yellow River boutique tourism belt and Shanxi tourism destination of world river civilization as the starting point, the main highway along the Yellow River will be built into a scenic corridor with smooth north and south, complete tourism service facilities and beautiful scenery. The special highway will be built into a national first-class scenic road integrating mother Yellow River, Longteng Yellow River, colorful Yellow River and ecological Yellow River, well-known cultural sightseeing and leisure corridors of the Yellow River at home and abroad. series scenic spots and a variety of activities of the characteristic route tourism complex. Along the way, the innumerable wonders of the Yellow River Canyon and countless historical and cultural relics have become the road of tourism, the way out of poverty and the road to prosperity. Relying on the "Yellow River No. 1" tourist highway to create four areas: Xikou Culture and Yellow River Castle Leisure area, Yellow River Canyon and Red Culture Tourism area, Luliang Mountain Ecological Recreation and Recreation Resort area and theme area, Yellow

River Wetland and Ancient Chinese Culture Leisure area.

Among them, the Yonghe section of Linfen, with a main line of 104 kilometers and a branch line of 56 kilometers, is connected with more than 20 scenic spots, including ancient villages, ancient ferries, ancient temples, and the Red Army Eastern Expedition Memorial Hall. There is also the largest and densest river snake song group in the country, Qiankun Bay. The 99 corners of the Yellow River in the world turned seven turns in Qiankun Bay. The Qiankun Bay experimental section is a branch of the tourist highway, forming a bay connecting, scenery connected, fast forward and slow swimming. In addition, Linfen City has also made every effort to create Linfen poverty alleviation tourism highway along the Yellow River, which takes "Jiuqu Yellow River Soul, Canyon amorous feelings Line" as its theme and integrates "Traffic + Tourism + Poverty Alleviation + Culture + Internet of things". It will connect Qiankun Bay along the Yellow River in Linfen City, the Red Army Dongzheng Memorial Hall, Ji County Renzushan, Hukou Waterfall, Daning Erlang Mountain, Xiangning Yunqiu Mountain and so on, which will promote the development of tourism along the Yellow River.[1]

b. World River Valley Civilization Expo Park Project

Relying on the manifestation of the ancient civilization of the great rivers in the world and combined with the development strategy of "Belt and Road Initiative" in China, the World Great River Civilization Expo Park is built in the Shanxi section of the Yellow River Basin, which mainly highlights the Yellow River civilization and integrates the civilization of the four ancient river basins. Shanxi is one of the important birthplaces of Chinese civilization. Wanrong County post-soil culture fully shows the dawn of Yellow River farming civilization and the characteristics of the mother of China, and is a typical representative of ancient civilization in the Yellow River basin. Therefore, we choose to build the World River Civilization Expo Park on the bank of the Yellow River in Wanrong County to create a 5A tourist area.

c. World River Valley Civilization Tourism Forum

Shanxi stands courageously in the spring tide of the integration of culture and tourism, ploughing resources, innovating products and forging brands to further enhance the image of world-class cultural tourism destinations. The first World River Civilization Tourism Forum was held in Linfen in 2018, which enhanced the international popularity of Yellow River tourism and Linfen tourism in Shanxi Province. The "Master Plan for the Tourism Development of the Yellow River Plate in Shanxi Province" clearly points out that it is necessary to build the brand of the World River Civilization Forum, specifically to plan and hold

---

[1] Linfen, Shanxi, Invested 7.68 Billion Yuan to Build Poverty Alleviation Tourism Highway along the Yellow River [J]. Urban Roads, Bridges and Flood Control,2018,(2) : 10.

the World River Civilization Forum and build a permanent venue for the World River Civilization Forum. The forum focuses on the study of the civilization and culture of the four famous river basins in ancient times, and widely invites scholars who study the civilization of the world's major river basins and young students majoring in history and culture. The main theme of the forum is discussion, research, academic exchanges and the development of civilization tourism in the world's major river basins. It is devoted to the study of the protection of the ecological environment of the big river basin and the establishment of the cooperation mechanism of the sustainable development of economy, society and environment, and the relationship between the continuation and development of the ancient civilization of the four river basins and the strategy of "Belt and Road Initiative" in China.

Through the World River Civilization Tourism Forum, Linfen will further enhance the visibility and influence of the tourism brand "China Root Yellow River Soul", integrate Hukou Waterfall, Yunqiu Mountain Scenic spot, Hongdong Dahuai Tree, Qiankun Bay and other scenic spots, plan and build an eco-cultural tourism belt along the Yellow River, create a Yellow River cultural corridor and ecological corridor full of cultural characteristics and spirit of the times, and promote the rapid development of Yellow River cultural tourism in Linfen City.

(5) Creating the Brand and Image of the Soul of the Yellow River in Shanxi Province

"The Soul of the Yellow River": the Jiuqu Yellow River in Shanxi Province is one of the most outstanding landscapes in the Yellow River Basin, and it is also the most representative area with 5000 years of Chinese culture in the Yellow River Basin. By making the heavy culture conceived by the Yellow River and the roots and veins of the Chinese nation the selling point and brand of world cultural tourism, tourists entering the Yellow River plate in Shanxi will deeply experience and realize that "the soul of the Yellow River is in Shanxi".

"Shanxi sentiment": Shanxi Yellow River plate tourism can provide tourists with multiple emotional perception and imagination. The construction of Shanxi Yellow River plate into Shanxi Yellow River boutique tourism belt can not only make tourists get the psychological hint that "traveling to Shanxi Yellow River plate can experience friendship and hospitality" and "honesty-based Shanxi tourism" in the process of tourism, but also experience the friendship, hospitality and tourism enjoyment of Shanxi people in the actual process of tourism.

The propaganda slogans of "River pregnant Huaxia, Caiping Shanxi", "the Yellow River of Jin Dynasty, Beautiful Landscape" and "thousands of miles of scenery of the Yellow River, Shanxi Province" have been formed. One of these slogans is to show that the Yellow River in Shanxi is the core area of China's civilization. Second, it is directly pointed out that the natural scenery of the Shanxi section of the Yellow River is beautiful, highlighting that the landscape scenery of the Shanxi section is different from that of other places, and it is worth visiting and visiting. Third, it shows that the Shanxi section of the Yellow River is more than 1,000 kilometers long, and the scenery along the way is unlimited, which shows that the cultural and natural characteristics of the Yellow River in Shanxi are distinctive and colorful, and it is worth seeing and traveling.

(6) Developing Cultural Innovative Products to Promote Poverty Alleviation in Rural Areas

Linfen City in addition to rich natural resources, human resources, intangible cultural heritage and other tourism resources, Linfen City has also developed a series of unique cultural and creative products. Linfen City promotes poverty alleviation in rural tourism through the development of rural cultural and creative products, through skills training for farmers, encourages and supports them to make use of rural raw materials, and through creative design and processing, to become tourism commodities with local cultural characteristics to help rural farmers find employment and increase their income.

Shangyao Culture and Art Company, a subsidiary of Linfen Culture and Tourism Bureau, launched "Rural memory, Wenchuang Poverty Alleviation", and the "rural memory" series of cultural and creative products were welcomed by the market. Shangyao Culture and Art Co., Ltd. combined with non-heritage protection units and art college students to experience life in rural areas, adopt style research, targeted design and launch of the "Rural memory" series of nearly 20 kinds of cultural and creative products, with practical actions to retain rural memory, to promote Wenchuang poverty alleviation. These cultural and creative products include tea tables, flowerpots, incense inserts, inkstones, cultural games, futon, storage boxes, mud prints and so on nearly 20 kinds, are drawn from the vast rural areas are waste old bricks, old wheat straw, old door panels, old wall mud, old weathered wood and some waste production materials, the processing of these cultural and creative products do not need complex professional technology, local farmers can be completed with a little training.

2. Suggestion and Recommendation for the Future

At present, tourism has become an important part of the daily life of the people. Self-help tours and self-driving tours have become the main ways to travel. The demand of tourists for tourism products shows a trend of quality. The demand of tourists has changed from traditional sightseeing tours to leisure vacations, and the travel mode shows the development trend of liberalization, individualization and retail, and the demand for high-quality holiday tourism products is increasing rapidly. the demand for transportation infrastructure, public service and ecological environment is getting higher and higher, and the demand for personalized and characteristic tourism products and services is getting higher and higher, and the trend of quality and medium-and high-end tourism demand is becoming more and more obvious. In this context, Linfen in the development of river civilization tourism to do the following aspects.

(1) Integrating Culture and Tourism and Highlighting Characteristics

Culture is the soul of tourism, and tourism is the carrier of culture. With the development of cultural tourism industry, culture is no longer the accessory of tourism, but the key factor to determine the success or failure of tourism industry. It is necessary to make full use of and display the culture of local characteristics in the design and development of tourism products. The essence of tourism product development is to visualize the cultural connotation, so that tourists can experience the cultural connotation, so that more tourists can understand the Yellow River civilization, identify with the Yellow River culture, and produce a sense of cultural pride and identity. Highlight the cultural value and social value of tourism. With the continuous improvement of tourists' economic income and education level, the pursuit of knowledge, innovation and difference is bound to become an important tourism motivation, and their requirements for the cultural quality of tourist destinations are getting higher and higher. In this regard, in-depth excavation of the connotation of cultural tourism in the Yellow River needs to explore both tangible and invisible cultural tourism resources on the basis of field investigation, create a cultural atmosphere, have both form and spirit, and fully meet the tourists' desire for aesthetics and knowledge.

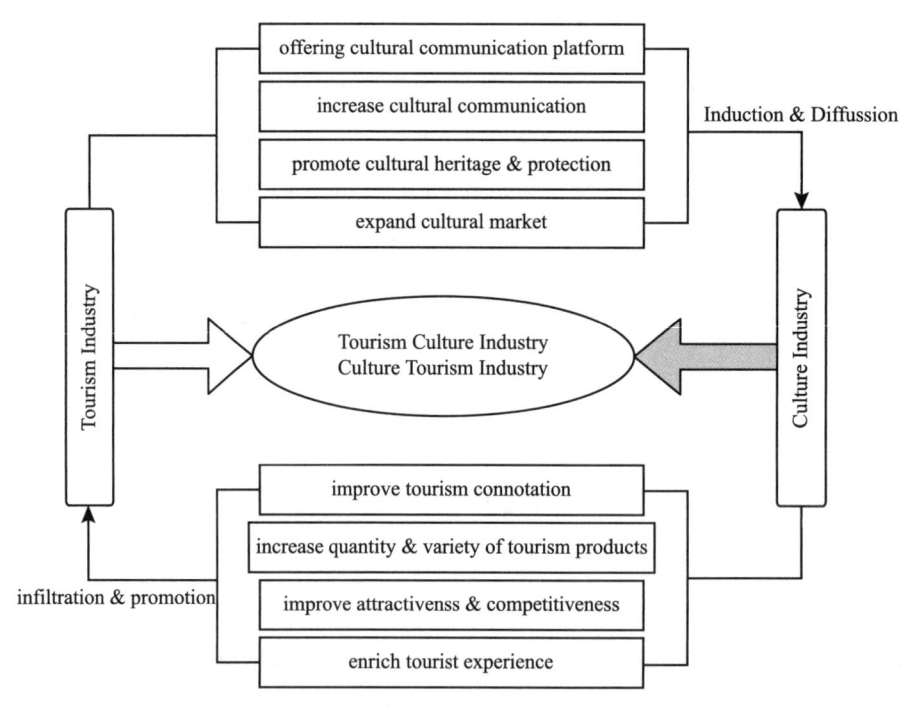

Figure 3.1　The Integration Development Mechanism of Tourism and Culture Industry

Source: Liu Chuchu .Research on the Integration Development of Cultural Industry and Tourism Industry in Shanxi Province[D].Shanxi University of Finance and Economics, 2018.

Therefore, when developing tourism projects and products of the Yellow River civilization, we must fully excavate the culture, the spirit of the Yellow River, together with the historical, folk, religious culture and intangible cultural heritage formed in the Yellow River basin. With the unique culture and spirit, it enhances the competitiveness of tourism for the reason that the characteristics of culture and tourism resources in Linfen basin of the Yellow River are distinct. It is necessary to fully tap the cultural characteristics of the Yellow River, do enough water articles, and integrate tourism resources such as culture, natural scenery, wetlands, folklore, and intangible cultural heritage. Specifically, based on the intangible cultural heritage, the hometown of celebrities, historical relics and characteristic buildings along the Yellow River Basin, we should develop tourism products or activities such as cultural leisure vacation, folk experience and so on. Planning and holding a series of Yellow River civilization tourism and cultural festivals to fully demonstrate the profound historical and cultural heritage of the Linfen Yellow River Basin. We will actively create a cultural theme tourism brand, rely on the history and culture of the Yellow River, build the Yellow River civilized tourism corridor route, and build a famous river tourism product system. In particular, it is necessary to fully tap the high-quality resources of the famous mountains, rivers, humanities, history, and cities in Linfen, and strengthen the integration of resources and regional coordinated development by relying on the Hongdong tree and Hukou waterfall in the Yellow River basin. Efforts should be made to create natural scenery and eco-tourism belts in the Linfen River Basin of the Yellow River.

(2) Innovate Products Oriented by Tourist Needs

According to the "China quality Tourism Development report 2018" released by the China Tourism Research Institute, tourists pay more attention to leisure, lifestyle, business environment and public services. About 70 percent of some tourists choose non-scenic spots and non-core urban areas, and the living space shared by hosts and guests has gradually become an attraction for tourism. At present, the demand of domestic tourists is changing from sightseeing to leisure vacation. The core value of leisure tourism lies in the extensive participation and in-depth experience of tourists in the process of tourism. Tourists for the quality of travel content has been raised, in the process of travel is not only to take pictures, to visit here, they also want to experience some of the details of the destination, be able to experience the feelings of a group of locals, get a high-quality tourism experience. Therefore, the development of tourism products of the Yellow River in Linfen should be guided by the needs of tourists, enrich the cultural connotation, strengthen the tourism experience and prolong the tourism industry chain. Therefore, Linfen City should increase the supply of leisure tourism products, enhance product characteristics and attractiveness, form a reasonable supply structure, sightseeing products and high-quality leisure vacation products that can attract tourists to meet the demand of tourists for the leisure function of tourism products.

a. Product Differentiation and Balance

First, Linfen City in the development of Yellow River civilized tourism products should avoid product homogeneity, only product differentiation in order to achieve characteristics. In the product system, product lines, product services to form their own characteristics, enhance the attractiveness of products, efforts to create river tourism products, Genzu tourism products, rural tourism products, cultural tourism products, leisure tourism products. Second, Linfen City in the Yellow River tourism product development should highlight the hierarchy, form from the point (scenic spot), line (tourism route) development to the face (tourism destination) development, the development of global tourism. The development of civilized tourism products of the Yellow River should be based on water tourism, take the creation of high-quality tourism area as a breakthrough, form diversified development, and create a global tourism destination. Third, tourism product design adheres to people-oriented. The relevant tourism enterprises should adhere to people-oriented in product design, regard tourist satisfaction as the fundamental purpose of the development of river civilization tourism, and promote people's all-round development through tourism. Dahe civilization tourism has become a happy industry to improve the quality of life of the people.

b. Highlighting Advantages and Emphasizing Characteristics

In the existing tourism development, Linfen should highlight the cultural characteristics of the Yellow River and the ecological characteristics of pastoral, rural, landscape and other ecological characteristics, develop in-depth experience cultural tourism products and leisure vacation products, combined with the initial mature root worship tourism, create tourism brands and products with Linfen characteristics, Yellow River customs and root ancestor culture, and promote the all-round development of ecology, culture and economy through the development of tourism. Speed up the development of the Yellow River civilization tourism in Linfen, take a leading position in the pattern of tourism development in the Yellow River basin, and grow into an important destination and demonstration area of the Yellow River civilization tourism with compound culture.

The supply of Dahe tourism products should effectively meet the needs of tourists for the diversification, quality and characteristics of tourism products, and improve the hierarchical structure of Dahe tourism products. Therefore, in the process of tourism development, it is necessary to carry out more in-depth development and interpretation of personalized and leisure vacation products, focusing on the development of characteristic tourism and deep tourism products. On the basis of highlighting advantages, emphasizing characteristics and consolidating tourism, we should develop research tours, ecological tours, folk tours, leisure vacation tours, outdoor, modern fashion and other characteristic tourism products.

c. Explore the Cultural Connotation of Products

In the aspect of tourism product innovation, Linfen City should deeply excavate the cultural characteristics of tourism products and improve the quality and cultural connotation of tourism products. Make full use of the national cultural characteristics in the basin, break through the single form of tourism, deeply excavate the cultural connotation, promote the development of cultural tourism, perfect combination of national culture and tourism creative development, develop the Yellow River tourism products with national characteristics, create cross-regional and transnational tourism routes, and promote the transformation and upgrading of Yellow River cultural tourism products.

d. Special Tourism Routes and "Route package"

Open up the "water + land + air" tourism route, connect the counties within the Yellow River plate in Linfen, and display the brand image of "Huaxia Root and Yellow River Soul" from a 360 °perspective. Through the organic connection of tourism routes with important scenic spots, characteristic towns, tourist attractions, folk culture, rural scenery, former homes of celebrities and all kinds of tourism service facilities, through "tourism +" to form a "tourism route package" system with outstanding characteristics and multi-products and forms, To provide tourists with a variety of tourism products, including sightseeing, leisure and vacation, folk entertainment, recreation, scientific research, business meetings and life supply, so as to meet the various needs of tourists and establish a three-dimensional tourism product system.

(3) Building Brand and Strengthening Marketing

At present, Linfen City relies on its natural and cultural landscape of the Yellow River and takes "Chinese Root and the Soul of the Yellow River" as its brand image to build Linfen into a golden eco-cultural tourism belt with green ecology, cultural heritage, modern agriculture and tourism. The Yellow River is not only the "mother river" of the Chinese nation, but also the main birthplace of the Chinese nation and East Asian civilization. We will strengthen the integration of resources and regional coordinated development, and strive to create natural scenery, cultural tourism and eco-tourism belts in the Yellow River civilized watershed. The Yellow River Linfen Basin will be built into an internationally well-known Yellow River civilized tourism destination with diverse tourism functions, distinctive cultural characteristics, superior ecological environment, perfect infrastructure and high quality tourism services. In addition, it is necessary to constantly improve the service and marketing level of modern tourism, and strive to promote the construction, management and promotion of the tourism brand of "China Root and Yellow River Soul", so as to achieve the actual effect of the tourism image propaganda of "China Root and Yellow River Soul". Specifically:

The first is to carry out network marketing publicity and promotion. With the development of network mobile information technology, consumers can receive information through a variety of network electronic devices, so Linfen should make full use of all kinds of network marketing channels to publicize and promote tourism products, tourist routes, tourist attractions and so on. If you can make full use of the current popular WeChat, Douyin, webcast and other self-media platforms to create topics for promotion.

Second, advertising media publicity and promotion. Through the television, radio broadcasting, network, newspapers, magazines and other media advertising on Linfen tourism products, tourist attractions for vigorously publicity.

Third, attach importance to the promotion of festival tourism image. For example, through the Yellow River Cultural Tourism Festival, the Great River Civilization Tourism Forum, the Great Huai Tree Cultural Tourism Festival, etc., to create a bright tourism image, such as "Chinese Root, the Soul of the Yellow River", "Guyao Capital, New Linfen" and so on, to create Linfen tourism brand.

Fourth, all regions of Linfen City should cooperate in planning publicity and promotion system, build destination network publicity and marketing platform, share sales teams and sales channels to reduce advertising costs and sales costs, accurately locate the customer source market, and implement network accurate marketing.

(4) Protecting Ecological Environment and Achieving Sustainable Development

Firmly establish the idea that "Green Water and Green Mountain is Jinshan Silver Mountain", run through the whole process of tourism planning, development, management and service, and form a new pattern of modern tourism development in harmony between man and nature. The ecological environment is the foundation of the Yellow River civilization tourism development, the ecological environment is related to the survival problem, is the most fundamental problem of tourism development. In the tourism development, we should pay attention to the protection of the ecological environment in the Yellow River basin. According to the actual situation of the Linfen basin of the Yellow River, we should achieve the organic combination of moderate development, sequential development and protection and development.

(5) Training Talents and Establishing Guarantees

The development of civilized tourism in the Yellow River has put forward higher requirements for the quantity, service ability and service quality of tourism practitioners in Linfen City. Tourism service talents are important support for the development and management of cultural tourism products of the Yellow River in Linfen. They improve the overall quality of employees through cooperation with well-known tourism colleges and universities, tourism enterprises, training, learning and other ways to meet the requirements of the market for talents. Such as tourism resources development and tourism product development needs tourism planning and product design personnel, high-quality service personnel, scenic spot management personnel and so on.

First, tourism enterprises should carry out regular vocational training, cultivate employees' professional skills, professional knowledge and professional literacy, and then improve their service ability, service quality and service level, so as to create a good tourism service experience for tourists. In the process of training, we not only pay attention to the teaching of experts, but also arrange the on-site operation experience, which not only provides space for the speakers, but also sets up a platform for students to participate in interactive exchange and dialogue.

Second, we should carry out school-enterprise cooperation and the integration of production and education to explore the mechanism of training high-quality tourism talents. According to the demand for talents in Linfen tourism market, we can cooperate with local colleges and universities to develop tourism curriculum system, teaching standards and teaching materials. At the same time, schools and enterprises can also cooperate to develop talent training or staff training programs to provide mutual support for students' practical training, staff training and so on. Through the above ways to provide high-quality talents for the development of Yellow River civilization tourism in Linfen City.

Third, establish a flexible talent policy system, attract more high-quality, understand the operation and management of high-level tourism talents to Linfen to start a business, and provide a strong talent support system for speeding up the development of the Yellow River cultural tourism industry in Linfen.

(6) Taking Advantage of "One Belt and One Road" and Strengthen Regional Tourism Cooperation

At present, many countries and regions regard river tourism as an industry to stimulate domestic demand and promote national economic growth. The competition of river basin tourism between regions and countries is an unavoidable problem for tourism enterprises and companies. For example, the cities along the Yellow River Basin are making great efforts to develop the Yellow River civilized tourism resources, create the Yellow River civilized tourism belt, and develop diversified Yellow River civilized tourism products. To a certain extent, the cultural and natural tourism resources in the Yellow River Basin are similar, and some areas are also competing for the same main target tourist market. Under this background, Linfen City should highlight the resource characteristics, product characteristics and cultural characteristics of the tourism area of the Great River Civilization Basin, and realize the cooperation with other areas and scenic spots so as to complement each other's advantages.

"Belt and Road Initiative" has also brought great opportunities for the development of Linfen tourism, especially the development of inbound tourism. Linfen City should seize this opportunity. First, it should establish a linkage mechanism for tourism development in the Yellow River Basin with other cities along the Yellow River and improve the tourism market system. The areas along the Yellow River basin should follow the development concept of "protecting the ecological environment and carrying forward the Yellow River culture", make overall planning, and cooperate in the development and utilization of the superior resources in the Yellow River basin. To achieve cross-administrative cultural and tourism ecosystem development, linkage development, improve tourism supporting services. Second, we should further strengthen urban cooperation and establish a cooperation mechanism for the coordinated development of tourism. Linfen City should strengthen cooperation with the coastal areas of the Yellow River in Shanxi Province, expand the space for tourism exchange and cooperation, establish a regional tourism cooperation alliance, and realize regional tourism prosperity. Third, strengthen regional administrative cooperation, through the formulation of policies, break down the spatial restrictions and administrative barriers in the development of cultural tourism products of the Yellow River, fully combine the culture and tourism resources of the Yellow River basin, speed up the introduction of diversified high-quality tourism routes integrating leisure and vacation, rural tourism and cultural tourism, and build a cultural tourism product system of the Yellow River with Chinese characteristics and cultural connotations, so as to enhance the international competitiveness of tourism products. Fourth, we should properly handle the distribution of interests among regions, mobilize positive factors in all aspects, promote the coordinated development of tourism among regions, and achieve mutual benefit and win-win results. Joint establishment of regional coordination organizations, specifically responsible for the completion of various cooperation matters. A typical representative in this respect is the "Guangdong, Hong Kong and Macao Pearl River Delta Tourism Promotion Agency". Fifth, in improving the quality of tourism services and tourism market order, to achieve different regions, different departments of joint law enforcement, common supervision, to jointly ensure the quality of the Yellow River tourism products, standardize the tourism market order, build a community with a shared future for tourism.

In the process of strengthening regional cooperation, we can build a tourism cooperation mechanism led by the government, tourism enterprises and other multi-stakeholders. As shown in figure 3.2, under the leadership of the government, all stakeholders cooperate together, that is, to strengthen communication, exchange and cooperation between the government and the government, between the government and enterprises, and between enterprises to achieve information sharing. Promote the exchange of information, capital and talents in the Linfen Yellow River Basin, build a benefit distribution and compensation mechanism, coordinate the interests of all parties, and ensure the healthy development of cultural tourism in the region; the government provides the corresponding infrastructure and tourism public service system, and enterprises provide all kinds of tourism products according to the needs of tourists.

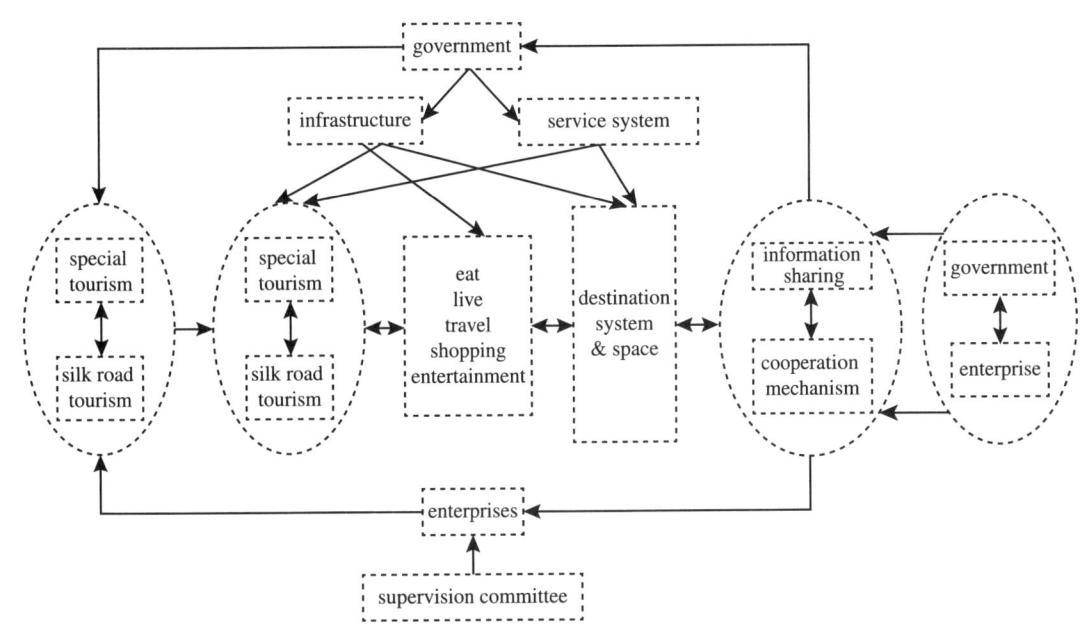

Figure 3.2 Contents and Mechanism of Cooperation in Tourist Areas along the Yellow River

Source: Liu Min, Ren Yapeng, Wang Ping. Shanxi Yellow River Culture: Connotation, Symbols and Tourism Development: Based on the Comparative Study of the Scenic Spots along the Yellow River in Western Shanxi [J].Journal of Jinzhong College, 2018, 35(4) : 39-43

(7) Industrial Linkage and Innovative Development Model

In the process of developing the civilized tourism of the Yellow River in Linfen, the industrial linkage should be achieved. Give full play to the industrial driving function of tourism, integrate with modern service industry, agriculture, industry, forestry, commercial and cultural industries, form a "tourism +" industrial development system, and create a tourism economic belt in the Yellow River civilized basin of Linfen. To help Linfen tourism economy transformation and development. For example, relying on 10 national and provincial eco-agricultural tourism spots, we should vigorously develop the characteristic tourism and leisure agriculture in Linfen City, and give full play to the advantages of cultural resources, natural resources and agricultural resources in the Yellow River Basin of Linfen City. Create the rural tourism brand image of ecological leisure agriculture, actively declare the geographical indications of characteristic agricultural products, well-known trademarks, etc., and speed up the formation of rural tourism brand effect and scale effect. We will vigorously develop characteristic agricultural products on the Loess Plateau and form tourism products with local characteristics through cultural and creative development.

Especially in the context of cultural and tourism integration, speed up the integration of Linfen local cultural industry and tourism industry, and explore the linkage development model of river culture and river tourism industry. As shown in figure 3.3, the government should take the lead, with the participation and coordination of enterprises, consumers and communities, so as to provide protection and support for

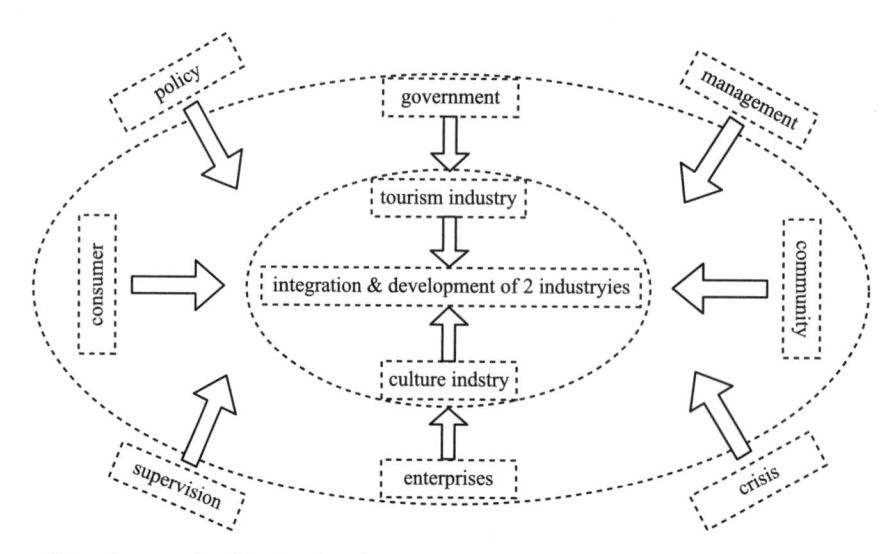

Figure 3.3 Cooperative Mechanism for Linkage Development of Culture & Tourism Industry

Source: Liu Min, Ren Yapeng, Wang Ping. Shanxi Yellow River Culture: Connotation, Symbols and Tourism Development: Based on the Comparative Study of the Scenic Spots along the Yellow River in Western Shanxi [J].Journal of Jinzhong College, 2018, 35(4) : 39-43.

the linkage development of the cultural tourism industry, shape tourism image brands with distinctive characteristics, launch products with compound characteristics of cultural tourism, adopt multi-channel publicity methods, and properly control policy implementation, system management, crisis management, social supervision and other issues in the process of joint development. To provide internal driving force for the joint development of the two major industries. For example, with the joint development of cultural industry and modern science and technology industry, the intangible cultural heritage can be integrated into other landscapes by means of modern science and technology, through the protection of ecological folk villages, the construction of related theme parks and large-scale live shows, it not only achieves the purpose of the overall protection of the intangible cultural heritage, but also provides it with the space carrier and the consumer market, and attracts the attention of more youth groups. Through the integration and development with other industries, it is possible to make the sustainable development of intangible cultural heritage possible.

(8) Improving Tourism Supporting Service Facilities

Linfen City is located in the Loess Plateau, surrounded by mountains, the whole territory is mainly mountainous, hilly, basin three major topographic units. First, it is necessary to strengthen the tourism traffic construction of scenic spots, make it more convenient for tourists to enter the road environment of scenic spots, and improve the accessibility of tourists such as free travel, self-driving tours and so on. Second, strengthen the overall planning and construction of the infrastructure within the scenic spot, such as tourist center, tourism marking system and other tourism public service facilities layout to improve the tourism experience of tourists. Third, the through train system from the urban area to the scenic spot is not perfect, most of the scenic spots in Linfen are far from the city center, so it is necessary to strengthen the improvement of the tourist public transport system and open more tourist bus lines. Fourth, improve the level of intelligent tourism construction, so that the scenic area of the internal free Wi-Fi to achieve full coverage, improve the scenic spots at any time positioning intelligent voice explanation system, upgrade electronic ticket checking.

Linfen has formulated and issued relevant policies to improve tourism supporting service facilities. First, enhance the reception capacity and level of tourism hotels, strengthen the comprehensive renovation of the tourism market, and promote tourism to benefit the people one card. Second, the infrastructure construction part, including the implementation of tourism highway construction project, tourism toilet construction project, river ecological construction project. Third, the improvement of human settlements, including increasing environmental sanitation construction, garden city construction, ecological environment management, urban facilities protection, Fenhe scenic spots to improve the quality of five contents. Fourth, the part of improving the quality of civilization, including deepening the creation of civilized cities, civilized tourism series theme propaganda, Linfen image overall publicity, "small hand holding big hand" civilization co-construction four contents.

Chapter Two Development Experience of The World's Typical River Civilization Tourism

Section 1 Experiences of Rhine River Tourism Development

As one of the great arteries connecting the north and south of Europe, the Rhine was once the source of European cultural inspiration, gave birth to the splendid culture along the river, and is one of the long rivers in Europe with historical significance. The Rhine River flows through the country as an important way to develop tourism as an important way to comprehensively control the Rhine River, speed up industrial transformation and promote national economic growth. Through combing and summarizing the experience and practice of tourism development in the Rhine River Basin, it has important reference significance for the management and development of the big river basin in our country.

1. Scenery along the Rhine River

The total terrain in the Rhine River Basin slopes from south to north, and the southern part of the river (Upper Rhine reach) passes through the Heshan forest, characterized by alpine mountains, snow peaks, meadows, lakes, wetlands, forests and waterfalls, including the famous Alps, Lake Tomas, Lake Geneva, Lake Constance, Rhine Falls, Black Forest, etc. The middle (middle Rhine section) is the hilly area, is the most magnificent section of the river scenery, mainly canyons, hills, the Rhine River flows between steep slopes, forming a tortuous and profound canyon, both sides of the hillside is full of vineyards and pastoral villages and towns, and distributed with different styles of ancient castles, ancient city sites, the famous four lakes are also located here; The north (Lower Rhine) is a coastal lowland, where water is plentiful and industrially developed, and Ruhr, the famous industrial center, is located here.

Thanks to the rich cultural environment and beautiful natural landscape along the Rhine, the towns along the Rhine attract many tourists every year, especially the tourism industry. In addition to ancient castles, ancient city sites, estates, there are large sleigh slopes, German Cape, Rat Tower, Franco Prussian War Monument, Dutch windmill and many other tourist attractions. The most famous port city along the river, Cologne, has more than 3300 bars, cafes and restaurants, and a large number of galleries and museums fully showcase the city's history and civic life to tourists. In addition, various festivals are held every year in the Rhine River Basin, including the Basel Carnival and the Cologne Oktoberfest in Germany.[1]

2. Development Model of Rhine River

On the basis of the key development and protection of water resources, the Rhine River has promoted the overall development of the river basin through urbanization and scientific and technological innovation, and has accumulated and formed industrial belts such as chemical industry, iron and steel machinery manufacturing, tourism, finance and insurance, etc. The economic development of the Rhine River Basin follows the evolution law of the economic spatial structure, giving priority to the development of port cities as the core of economic growth, regulating the river courses, excavating artificial canals and building dykes, so that the Rhine shipping has become the inland river with the highest freight density in the world, which has led to the sustainable development of the inland economy. Then the layout of the shipping network, connecting the edge of the river hinterland and connecting the upper reaches of the river to form an economic spatial network structure. With the development of ports and node cities, nearly 50 medium-sized cities have been built only on the main stream of the Rhine, and have their own leading and characteristic functions and positioning, such as Amsterdam as the financial center, Strasbourg and the Hague as the administrative center, Cologne as the media center, perfume capital and chemical center, Essen, Dortmund and Constance as the education center. The functions of cities complement each other, the urbanization rate has increased rapidly, and Germany has become an economic power without "big cities" and one of the countries with the highest urbanization rate in the world.[2]

3. The Spatial Distribution of the Rhine River Tourism Industry

The Rhine flows northwest from the Alps. Based on the characteristics of its geomorphological types, it has gradually formed the spatial structure of tourism industry with its own characteristics in the upper, middle and lower reaches.

---

[1] Xu Haifeng, Nie Zhen and Li Mei. Research on the Development of Rhine River Basin." Sichuan Architecture, vol.36, no. 1, 2016, pp. 10-13.

[2] Ma Jing and Deng Hongbing. The Enlightenment of the Yangtze River Belt's Development Based on the Mode of Typical River Basins' Development in the World.Regional Economic Review,vol. 2, 2016, pp. 145-151.

(1) Upstream: Leisure Tourism

The upper reaches of the Rhine are mainly alpine, subalpine, middle and low mountain landforms, a large number of lakes, such as Boden Lake, Zurich Lake and so on. These lakes have become the main resources of winter ski tourism, summer tourism and various forms of sightseeing tourism in the upper reaches of the Rhine River, it forms the spatial layout of leisure tourism in the upper reaches of the Rhine River. Take Boden Lake as an example, this area is located at the junction of Germany, Switzerland and Austria. It covers an area of 540 square kilometers and is a natural reservoir in the upper reaches of the Rhine River. Its unique geographical location, beautiful and pleasant scenery, the formation of water, land, air and other resources, a wide range of tourism products enables the region become a well-known tourist resort in Europe.

(2) Middle Reaches: Historic and Cultural Heritage Tourism

The middle reaches of the Rhine River is dominated by low mountain canyon landforms, and the core part is the World Cultural Heritage site of the "Middle and Upper Rhine Valley", which is recognized as the most beautiful section of the Rhine River scenery. At the World Heritage Conference held in Budapest in 2002, the Middle Rhine Valley was one of the most important transport routes in Europe, which has been promoting material and cultural exchanges between the Mediterranean region and northern Europe. As a model of the outstanding and spontaneous cultural landscape of mankind; As well as a typical representative of the continuous evolution of traditional lifestyles and communication methods located in narrow river valleys, these three points have been included in the World Cultural Heritage list.[1]

The World Heritage Committee rated it as the 65km Middle Rhine Valley, with its castles, historic towns and vineyards along the way, vividly describing a long human history entangled with the changing natural environment. There have been many historical events and legends that have inspired countless writers, painters and musicians over the centuries.[2] The main tourism resources in the middle reaches of the Rhine are the medieval castle landscape, thousands of years of grape farming culture, wine brewing technology and the natural scenery of ancient towns and canyons along the river.

a. Rhine Castle

About 40 ancient castles are scattered over a distance of about 65 kilometers from the Central Rhine Valley, where the number and density of castles are among the highest in Europe, most of them built between the 11th and 13th centuries AD. Today, these castles have lost their original military defence and

---

[1] Zhang Danming. Central Rhine Valley: Sonata of Vineyard-Castle-Town-Mountain and River. China Cultural Heritage, vol.2, 2007, pp. 102-107.

[2] Dong Bo and Du Yuchen. Enlightenment of Foreign Canal Heritage to the Construction of Grand Canal Cultural Belt in China. Development Planning Study, vol.5, 2019 .

tax collection functions, and most of the better protected or renovated castles have been converted into hotels, youth hostels and restaurants, etc., as living and in-use cultural heritage.

b. Vineyard

The Central Rhine River Valley is one of the four major wine producing regions in Germany. The ancient Romans brought grape planting and wine-making techniques to the banks of the Rhine in the 2nd century BC. Since then, the scale of grape cultivation has gradually expanded, and vineyard terraces have become the main scenery of the valley by the 12th century AD. Eighty-five percent of the vineyards in the middle Rhine region are on the terraces on the hillside. The vineyard on this steep slope and extremely steep slope is a very important and indispensable factor for the human landscape in the middle reaches of the Rhine River. More than 2000 years of grape planting history has influenced and shaped the landscape in many aspects. It is the result of people coordinating and adapting to the complex man-land relationship in the long-term production practice.

c. Towns along the River

There are more than 30 towns along the Central Rhine Valley, including Bingen, Poppard, Braubach, Kobrenz, etc., some of which can be traced back to ancient Roman settlements before 2000. Bingen and Braubach are typical Rhine towns that still retain the living environment of ancient Rome and the Middle Ages. They used to be representatives of the earliest towns and commodity trading places that established fortresses and fortresses in Roman times. Many of the walls and defenses have been fully preserved, and the town center of Braubach still retains the market square of the year. Located at the confluence of the Rhine and Mosel rivers, Colenbuz belongs to a larger town in the middle Rhine valley, leaving a large number of cultural relics and historical buildings in the city. One of them is the German Cape, on which stands the state flag and emblem of 13 states and three cities symbolizing the peaceful reunification of Germany, as well as the riding statue of Emperor William I, who completed the great cause of German unification.[1]

The main forms of tourism in the Middle Rhine Valley are cruise ship tourism, mountain hiking, mountain cycling and so on, and it forms the regional characteristics in tourism space of the historical and cultural heritage tourism in the middle reaches.

(3) Downstream: Industry and Industrial Heritage Tourism

The tourism resources in the lower reaches of the Rhine are mainly the industrial heritage of the Ruhr Industrial Zone in Germany, which was formed in the Rhine River and its tributary Ruhr River Basin after

---

[1] Zhang Danming. Central Rhine Valley: Sonata of Vineyard-Castle-Town-Mountain and River. China Cultural Heritage, vol.2, 2007, pp. 102-107.

the industrial revolution.

The Ruhr Industrial Zone is located in western Germany and is named after the Ruhr River (a tributary of the Rhine) flowing through the area. In the first half of the 19th century, large-scale coal mining, iron and steel production made Ruhr area one of the most famous heavy industrial areas and one of the largest industrial areas in the world. After more than 100 years of prosperity and development, Ruhr began to experience economic decline in the early 1960s, that is, the so-called "anti-industrialization process," especially in the coal, iron and steel industries. For example, in 1957, there were 141 coal mines and 490000 coal miners, with an annual output of 120 million tons of raw coal; by 1995, there were only 13 coal mines, with less than 70, 000 coal workers, with an annual output of 40 million tons of raw coal. In the process of anti-industrialization, a large number of workers were unemployed, tax revenue was reduced, pollution can not be controlled, regional image deteriorated, and it was urgent to change production and implement transformation.

In the face of various problems caused by the development of industrialization, Ruhr District breaks the conventional mode of thinking and rediscovers the historical value of a large number of abandoned industrial and mining industries, old factories and huge vacant industrial buildings and facilities retained in the process of industrialization. Regard it as an industrial and cultural heritage and carry out strategic development and renovation of industrial heritage tourism and regional revitalization. After three stages of "negation and exclusion", "confusion" and "cautious attempt", it has finally entered the strategic stage of "the road of industrial heritage tourism". With "museum", "public recreation space", "combined with shopping tourism" and other three modes to implement. At that time, the factory building became a creative design center, the workshop became a large theater, the former industrial workers became tour guides and narrators, and formed the Rhine River tourism industry spatial structure of the industrial and industrial heritage tourism area. At present, the Ruhr region of Germany, located on the banks of the Rhine, has become the best example of industrial heritage tourism in the world.[1]

4. Main Forms of Tourism products of the Rhine River

From the above spatial layout of the Rhine tourism industry, it can be found that the tourism products with different characteristics are formed due to the different resource of the upper, middle and lower reaches, but as a whole tourism area, the tourism products of the Rhine River also have its integrity.

---

[1] Tong Qianming. Industrial Heritage Tourism, Another alternative to transformation. Land & Resources Herald, vol. 7, 2012, pp. 17.

(1) Aquatic Tourism Products

The aquatic tourism products of the Rhine are mainly inland cruise ships in addition to the sailing boats, windsurfing and short-distance cruise boats around the lake in the upper reaches of the lake. The difference between these cruise products lies in the length of the trip and the combination of waterway tourism. Generally, the Rhine River cruise ship boarded from Amsterdam and passed through Cologne, Heidelberg, German Black Forest, Alsace Wine Township, and finally reached Basel.

(2) Land Tourism Products

With the application of information technology and the development of economy, the consumption habits of consumers have changed, and more people choose to travel by themselves and travel freely. In its planning, the government has fully taken into account the tourism and holiday needs of individual tourists, and a sightseeing railway has been built on both sides of the Rhine, each with a high-grade highway, and pedestrian (bicycle) lanes have been set up on the side of the road. Therefore, in addition to participating in regular team sightseeing products, tourists can also choose self-driving tours, RV tours, cycling, hiking and wine cultural experience tours in small towns. Vehicles are mainly cars and trains, bicycles and other means of leisure transport.

(3) Urban Tourism Products

There are many important cities on both sides of the Rhine, such as Mainz, Koblenz, Cologne and so on. Therefore, the urban tourism products of the Rhine River Basin are very popular with tourists, and the related products mainly include two aspects: on the one hand, it is the combination of urban tourists and Rhine short-distance cruise ships; On the other hand, it is through the Rhine traffic, finance, commerce, logistics as the main support of large and medium-sized cities to develop urban business, mice, such as Cologne, Dusseldorf and other cities.

(4) Air Tourism Products

Air tourism products mainly refer to low-altitude tourism, in other words, it is the entertainment and sports in which people fly in low-altitude airspace by general air transport, general aircraft and low-altitude aircraft. Helicopters, hot air balloons, paragliding, aircraft skydiving, light and small unmanned aerial vehicles all belong to this category. The low-altitude tourism products in the Rhine River Basin are mainly developed in some key tourist towns. It also includes hot air balloons overlooking the Rhine Valley, paragliding and private customized trips, such as flying on a private jet.

5. Experiences in the Development of Rhine Tourism

The river is the cradle of human civilization, and the river valley civilization flows with the richest humanistic feelings. Every river has its own story. The Rhine River in Europe flows through the hinterland, so the Rhine River Basin has also become an important tourist destination in Europe. Especially for Germany, the Rhine River Basin is one of the most important tourism resources and tourism has become the second largest industry after the manufacturing industry in the German Rhine River Basin economy. The tourism development of the Rhine River has important referent significance for other areas to carry out river tourism. By analyzing their success, it can be found that the following measures have been taken.

(1) Constructing Comprehensive Management Model of Water Environment

For decades, one of the main problems in the Rhine has been water quality. Over the years, a large amount of waste water from cities and industry has flowed directly into the Rhine without treatment and destroyed the river ecosystem. Most of the species which lived in rivers 70 years ago have disappeared. In order to control the water pollution of the Rhine River, in 1963, the countries of the Rhine River Basin and representatives of the European Community signed a convention on cooperation within the scope of the International Commission for the Protection of the Rhine River, and the International Commission for the Protection of the Rhine River. It also formulated corresponding laws and regulations to impose harmless treatment of industrial waste water discharged into the river; which strictly controls the discharge of solid pollutants from industry, agriculture and life into the Rhine River, and imposes heavy penalties on violators. On 23 October 2000, the European Parliament and the Council of the European Union issued the EU Water Framework Directive on the institutional basis for all activities in the regions of the Rhine Basin; the Rhine Basin Management Plan and the Plan of Action was drafted and implemented. Through decades of governance and development, the Rhine has become a drinking water source for 20 million people, the most important tourism resources in neighboring countries, and a famous international tourism destination.

(2) Formulating a Closely Integrated Planning System

In addition to the unified formulation of relevant policies such as the Berne Convention, the Convention for the Prevention and Control of Chemical pollution and the Rhine Action Plan by the International Commission for the Protection of the Rhine, various localities have formulated tourism development plans according to their own reality. First, state planning. Take Germany as an example, the state of Hesse, through which the Rhine River flows, has formulated special tourism plans and travel-related plans, such as the Hesse Tourism Policy Action Plan, the Hesse Tourism Industry Strategic Impact Plan, and the Tourism Cooperative Enterprise Task and structure-Local level Action funding Program. The second is interstate planning. Hesse, Rhineland-Pfarce and North Rhine-Westphalia jointly planned a 320-kilometer hiking trail along the east bank of the Rhine and a cycling trail along the Rhine Valley. Third, international planning. Along the river, the six countries have also developed a unified cycling lane system from the source of the Swiss River to the Rhine estuary of Rotterdam, the Netherlands, which realizes cross-border connectivity and a unified marking system.

(3) Building a Convenient Traffic Network

One is air traffic. From upstream to downstream, international famous airports such as Zurich and Amsterdam have realized the air connection and convenient transit between the Rhine region and the whole world. The second is water transportation. A water passenger and freight system from Basel, Switzerland to Rotterdam and Amsterdam, the Netherlands, was constructed. Third, land transportation. The whole coastal area has formed a convenient connection from railways and highways to urban transportation and small towns and tourist attractions. In particular, many land transportation modes are built along the river, which makes land traffic not only both a passenger flow, logistics channel and a landscape channel. Fourth, leisure traffic. The cycling lane system and hiking route system along the river are constructed.

(4) Creating Compound and Diversified Tourism Products

Based on the history, culture and natural resources, the Rhine River has basically formed a reasonable product structure in the upper, middle and lower reaches: first, leisure and vacation tourism in the upstream lake. The main forms of tourism are winter skiing, summer tourism and various forms of sightseeing. Second, historical and cultural heritage tourism in the middle reaches. The main forms of tourism are cruise, mountain hiking and mountain cycling. Third, industry and industrial heritage tourism in the downstream. At the same time, as a whole tourism area, the Rhine River mainly includes four categories: water tourism products, land tourism products, urban tourism products and air tourism products, which fully embodies the characteristics, differences and integrity of tourism products.

(5) Establishing an Efficient Tourism Management Model

The management of the Rhine tourism industry is realized in official and semi-official forms. Take the German state of Hesse as an example, its tourism industry management function belongs to the Hesse Promotion Bureau under the Ministry of Economic Affairs of the state government. Tourism industry policy is formulated by the Ministry of Economic Affairs, Hesse Promotion Bureau performs government functions, and is responsible for the implementation of tourism industry policy, tourism destination marketing and industry norms by means of a state-owned limited company. At the same time, information service is an important function of government management of Rhine tourism industry. Functional departments provide tourism investors and operators with relevant information about tourism destinations through exhibitions and networks, and directly provide tourism public service information for tourists.[①]

[①] Yang Guangrong. The Enlightenment of Rhine River Tourism Development in Europe to Hunan Province. China Tourism News, vol.11, 2011.

Section 2 Tourism Development Experience from the Thames

The Thames is the second largest river in the United Kingdom (UK), flowing through more than ten cities across the whole country. It is the busiest city river and one of the landmarks in London. Having nourished the resplendent civilization and long-standing history, the Thames is recognized as the most precious innate asset to the city with delightful environment and well-developed recreation facilities.[1] Tourism development along the Thames is relatively mature and can shed light on other river valley regions in the world.

1. Landscape along the Thames

The Thames is originated from the Cotswold Hills in the Southwest of England with a length of 346 kilometer and running out of more than ten cities across the UK. It is a golden waterway for regional trade and economic development in the process of industrialization.[2] Along the river, it epitomizes the essence of British culture and nourished the resplendent civilization. The major historical buildings of London are located along the Thames through the ages, including the grand Westminster Abbey, Statue of Admiral Nelson symbolizing victory, St Paul's Cathedral with Renaissance style, the Tower of London, Tower Bridge with lifting bridge body, The Houses of Parliament and Elizabeth Tower. Going through all the vicissitudes in history, all these buildings are the masterpieces of art and are still kept in their original designs and characteristics. Apart from the long-standing historical buildings, there are a range of contemporary architectures along the Thames, such as the skyscraper of The Shard with a height of 309.6 meters, and the London Eye which the so-called the highest skyscraper in the northern hemisphere. These modern buildings along the Thames add up a sense of contemporary fashion vibe to London.

2. Tourism Development along the Thames

River basins areas are the origins for human civilization and the ideal space for human settlements. Most of the famous cities in the world are built and thrive over the river regions. Over the ages, river banks have gradually become the central axis for urban expansion and have offered delightful recreation spaces for tourists and residents.

---

[1] Lu Jingyi. The design idea in the renovation of the Thames – The construction project in Millennium year. Foreign Science, vol.1, 2000.

[2] Gao Jing. A Study on the Regeneration of Recreationalization of Waterfront in Metropolises: A Case-based Comparison between London and Shanghai. Shanghai: Southern Normal University, 2015.

The development of recreation activities over the Thames has a long history. There are several reasons for its well-developed recreational facilities. First, the city of London originates from the banks of the Thames. At the outset, the Thames was already a place for residents to product, to live and to recreate. Second, later urban expansion of London also revolved around the Thames. Third, in medieval times, the municipal construction of London took advantage of the Thames and was built and expanded along the river. This made the Thames enjoy a strategic geographic location in urban municipal service and municipal management. Forth, royal buildings, royal gardens and other political centers were also constructed along the Thames. This further strengthens the strategic position of the Thames. Lastly, amusement parks have entered into UK since 16th century. Between 17th-18th centuries, the most iconic amusement parks in London were both located along the Thames, namely, Vauxhall at the south side of the Thames and Keansburg at the north side of the Thames.

However, with the progression of the industrial revolution, the Thames had become a death river in London. On June of 1858, the Thames was polluted and became highly smelly that the House of Parliament over the river had to put up many bed sheets soaked by disinfecting liquid. In 1878, the "Alice Prince" cruise sank into the Thames with more than 640 casualties. However, majority of those 640 casualties didn't die of drowning but die of sewage poisoning. In fact, the pollution of the Thames was still severe even after the World War II. During the national festival of UK in 1951, due to the river pollution, foreign ships which anchored alongside the Thames got their lead layer of the ship body corroded. This caused an international uproar back that time. It was until 1955 that large-scale pollution control was finally taken place on the Thames. After 1985, government started to realize that tourism development alongside the Thames has great potential to offer job opportunities, generate economic benefits and stimulate the development of local small medium enterprises.

Because of the agglomeration effect of the attractions and hotels, in 1990 s, most of the sightseeing activities happened in the City of Westminster, Kensington and Chelsea district, and Camden district, in the north side of the Thames. The iconic attractions include the House of Parliament, Westminster Abbey, the Tate Gallery, Madame Tussauds, The Downing Street, Oxford Street, Leicester Square, Convent Garden, the British Museum, Buckingham Palace, National Gallery and St Paul's Cathedral. Compared with the north side, the south side of the Thames was relatively less-developed. However, after 1993, government took effective measures to develop and promote tourism industry in the south side. For example, billions pounds was invested into the infrastructure as well as attraction constructions in the south side. A cultural center was also built to stimulate tourism demand.

In order to promote recreation and tourism development alongside the Thames, in 1990, the company Dockland introduced some artistic activities at the quayside areas. Such artistic activities aimed at attract visitor arrivals and maintain the stay of artisans. These activities include regular artistic programs, public art, visual art, music, performance art and art education. The building of footpaths, shopping malls and water activities made the quayside areas more attractive and comprehensive. Meanwhile, public water bus and sightseeing cruise also stood out.[①]

3. Tourism Spatial Layout alongside the Thames

The physical forms of the attractions layout alongside the Thames have typical leisure characteristics. The spatial layouts of architectures are attractive, the spatial layouts of the waterways are various and the visual landscape of the corridors are controllable.

The Thames flows through the urban center of London and epitomizes the essence of the British Empire over the river. The north side of the Thames serves as gathering points for culture exchange. Many landmark architectures of medieval designs together with the Thames comprise the dynamic and attractive landscape. These landmark buildings cover the House of Parliament, Trafalgar Square, Buckingham Palace, Westminster Abbey, London Bridge, Tower Bridge, London Docklands, Covent Garden and Regent's Park. Meanwhile, The Thames enjoys a range of branches which connect different parks, wetlands, and lakes. Such spatial layout becomes the important ecological corridor in London and enhances leisure opportunities over the river.

In order to protect the visual effect of the ecological corridors, London government have made several master plans. For example, "Guidelines for spatial planning" published in 1991 specifies the protection of strategic gazebo points; and "Draft for Landscape Management in London" published in 2005 includes the House of Parliament, Westminster Abbey, Buckingham Palace, Greenwich Museum and St Paul's Cathedral as the newly strategic gazebo points. With the assistance of such protection measures, waterways centering on the Thames have become high-quality corridors.

4. Major Tourism Products over the Thames

(1) Tourism Activities in the Field of General Aviation

Travelling via general aviation is one of the emerging travel format that combines tourism with aerial transportation. Tourism activities via general aviation help to turn around a homogeneous tourism market and promote the tourism industry upgrading and transformation. Tourism activities through general aviation are the important carrier for the Thames to enhance river-tourism experiences and enrich tourism

---

① Gao Jing. A Study on the Regeneration of Recreationalization of Waterfront in Metropolises: A Case-based Comparison between London and Shanghai . Shanghai: Southern Normal University, 2015.

resources. For instance, traveling across the Thames in helicopter has become one of the most popular activities for visitors in London.

Travelling via general aviation can connect different attractions in the city as a whole, and meanwhile involve outdoor adventure in the trip. It is convenient, adventurous, less limited by the geological constraints, and with a bird's eye view of the whole river basin regions of the Thames. Such experience meets the needs of the high-end customers as well as the young travelers. The flight route of the helicopter trip stresses cultural components with several heritage attractions included, such as St Paul's Cathedral, London Bridge and Buckingham Palace.

(2) Cruise Tourism along the Thames

The Thames flows through the whole city of London. By cruise travel along the Thames, tourists can enjoy the nearby attractions on the shores. There are 24-hours and various types of cruises offering for the tourists. A range of services are also provided on the cruise such as breakfast, working luncheon, romantic dinner, selective sightseeing and overnight dancing party.[1] As such, cruise is the most favorite tourism product by tourists when traveling along the Thames. There are several famous docks on the Thames including Westminster dock and St Katharine Dock.

(3) Cultural Festivals

Along the Thames, there are several themed festivals famous in the world. They are normally the sports, entertainment and political events which oftentimes were held at the sites of the historical buildings, parks and bridges over the Thames. These events include the following:

a. Oxford and Cambridge University Boat Race held every spring on the Thames: As the largest boat race in the world, there are 420 participants from eight teams joining the race each year.

b. Mayor's Thames Festival: Mayor's Thames Festival is also known as Thames Cultural Festival. It is the largest free outdoor festival in the world. It aims at celebrate the long history of the Thames and the city of London. Each year, various programs will be held during the festival including music, dancing, choir, carnival, feasting, river competition, street art and so on. Since 1997 when it was first established, Mayor's Thames Festival every year attracts more than 100 countries and regions to participate and it also serves as a great platform to showcase various cultures, images and charms from different nations.

c. Royal Ceremonies: British royal family hosts a range of ceremonies along the Thames. Such royal ceremonies embody local cultural history and are of solemnity and holiness, which enrich the connotation of the Thames.

---

[1] Shu Xiaoming. Experiences of Aquatic Tourism Development in Famous Waterfront Cities Overseas. Ningbo Univeristy Journal, vol.21, no. 3, 2008, pp. 94-96.

The above cultural festivals link the Thames and its coastal resources together as a whole and provide visitors an integrated experience of both sightseeing and participation. This not only stimulates cultural tourism along the Thames, but also enrich destination image of London.[①]

5. Tourism Development Experiences of the Thames

The Thames flows through the urban center of London and epitomizes the essence of the British attractions over the river. Tourism development based on this river has become a unique model for London, it not only generates sustainable economic returns but also develops into the core component of the city image.[②] However, 100 years ago the Thames used to be highly polluted by industrial revolution that massive pollutants filled up the water body and aquatic lives were endangered. The large-scale environmental protection of the Thames started after the World War II. After more than 30 years' effort, the Thames gains back to the original beauty and vibe. Meanwhile, with the further development of coastal attractions, the Thames has become one of the well-known landmarks in the world. In retrospect, there are several effective measures that the Thames has adopted:

(1) Keep the Integrity Harmony of the Attractions along the River

There are various buildings, parks and bridges along the river with historical, cultural and sightseeing values. These buildings are part of the city history and are the representations of London and even UK. London government has committed to the protection of the historical buildings and ensure the harmonious integrity of the new buildings.[③]

(2) Continuous Improvement on the Legislations of Heritage Protection

In 1882, the British Parliament approved the first "Heritage Protection Law", but this law only applies to castle-related buildings. After World War II, the British Parliament further enacted "City Planning Law" (in 1947) and "Protection Law of Historical Building" (in 1953). Moreover, government registered and repaired all the historical buildings which had been damaged during the World War II. In 1967, British government enacted "Protection Law of Historical Blocks" which bought about the issue of protecting buildings in historical blocks for the first time. Since October 3rd 1967, Stamford became the first block under the protections. Afterwards, the Parliament Square and St Paul's Cathedral district have all become

---

[①] Gao Jing. A Study on the Regeneration of Recreationalization of Waterfront in Metropolises: A Case-based Comparison between London and Shanghai .Shanghai: Southern Normal University, 2015.

[②] Shu Xiaoming. Experiences of Aquatic Tourism Development in Famous Waterfront Cities Overseas. Ningbo Univeristy Journal, vol.21, no. 3, 2008, pp. 94-96 .

[③] Yan Shuiyu and Wang Xiangrong. The positioning of the Thames in the city of London. Foreign City Planning, vol.1, 1999, pp. 34-35, p. 42.

the historical blocks under protection.

(3) Encourage the Active Participation of the Stakeholders

The balance of power relationship of all the stakeholders of the Thames has positive effect in tourism development of the Thames. Taking tourism functional management committee at the south side of the Thames as an example, the committee is comprised of multiple stakeholders including transportation and administration department, tourism development department, marketing department, employer committee, heritage committee, chamber of commerce, residents forum and tourism government officials. Among them, marketing department focuses on how to advertise and market relevant tourism infrastructures, large-scale events and how to design tourism promotion brochures; employer committee is mainly responsible for attracting governmental investment and host city-wide event; transportation and administration department offers managerial suggestions to the cooperation of all the departments. Meanwhile, although small and medium enterprises are the outliers of certain policy makings, chamber of commerce helps them in building communication channels between small enterprises and other governmental departments.[①]

(4) Subarea Protection and Developing Cultural Attractions along the River

Although UK is the origin place of modern city planning, it has never made a single master plan for cultural attractions. Instead, government oftentimes enacts planning criteria. Then each subarea plans, renovates and re-develops certain cultural sites to meet the planning criteria. As a result, there are totally five subareas centering on the Thames currently under protection in London. First is the old town district. From Buckingham Palace to Trafalgar Square, there are classical buildings neatly line up including the palace, the House of Parliament, Elizabeth Tower and other commercial and cultural buildings. Second is the religious and historical district. Represented by the St Paul's Cathedral, this district extends from London Tower to Waterloo Bridge. Third is Southern modern subarea. Typified by the Royal Festival Hall, this district is comprised by modern architecture. Forth is the technological district. This district covers Greenwich Observatory, national Maritime Museum and Military Science Museum. Fifth is the Dockland modern water-front landscape. The old obsolete dock was transformed to the modern commercial and residential zone while preserving the old dock facilities such as tower crane and pier.

(5) Government Establishes Protection Funds and Attracts Private Investment

The protection of cultural attractions in certain degree belongs to social welfare which require large-scale investment and long payback period. UK government uses the approaches of establishing governmental funds and attracting private investment. As long as the project is related to the protection

---

① Gao Jing. A Study on the Regeneration of Recreationalization of Waterfront in Metropolises: A Case-based Comparison between London and Shanghai . Shanghai: Southern Normal University, 2015.

of historical blocks and heritage, all the departments and social groups and even individual can apply for protection funds.

Looking at the past funding cases, the funding of 100 thousand ponds for 27 districts has been increased to 1490 thousand ponds for 81 districts. The accumulated governmental funds are 2.4 hundred million ponds. Above this, a total of 10 billion ponds have been attracted from private investment. Most of these funds were invested to the districts along the Thames.[①]

Section 3 Tourism Development Experiences from the Mississippi

The Mississippi is located in the south-central of North America. It is the fourth longest river in the world covering areas of South and Central US. It is a geopolitical center for US and is a key foundation for economic development in the early US. Meanwhile, it is also a long-standing livable place as well as a treasury for national culture and recreation.[②] This section will summarize tourism development experiences from the Mississippi and shed light on other river valley regions in the world.

1. Tourism Development in the Mississippi

The Mississippi is the longest river in US which serves as the artery of transportations between the North and the South. The management of the Mississippi starts from 1870s when specific laws and management organizations were established including "the US Army Engineer Corps", "Committee of the Mississippi" and "Administration of River Management". Since 1930s, there were comprehensive environmental programs that govern the main stream and branches of the Mississippi. Modern high-tech was introduced to ensure the natural geomorphological structure of the river. The promotion of green shipping, construction of attraction landscape and building a standardized shipping network and economic belt were put forwarded. Meanwhile, the Mississippi fully leveraged well known films and Jazz to develop tourism. It has become a treasury for national culture and recreation.[③]

---

① Zheng Bohong and Tang Jianzhong. Experiences of developing coastal attractions in London. City Issues, vol. 1, 2002, pp. 71-74.

② Wang Shoushu. Study on River Tourism Function Construction and Products Development. Shanghai Normal University, 2009.

③ Wang Shoushu. River tourism function construction and product development research [D]. Shanghai normal university, 2009.

2. The Development Model of the Mississippi

The Mississippi is developed in a point-axis approach. In US, there are almost 150 cities have a population of more than one hundred thousand. Among them, 131 cities are located along the Mississippi. Such allocation enhances trading chances among cities, strengthens the usage of water resources, and stimulates a close connection by water transportation. As a result, a bunch of port cities emerged and various medium and small cities were further built around each port city. Facing with the new opportunities brought by technology, these port cities have upgraded their industrial structures and developed new manufacturing and service industries.

In management level, Committee of the Mississippi was launched. This committee is fully independent in its revenue and profit. Under the committee, there are more than 10 departments including water resources and hydropower, finance, industrial development, environmental protection, engineer, agriculture, chemistry, fishing, tourism and so on. It has the authorized power and legal effect but managed in a private corporate approach. In line with the notion of integration development of the Mississippi, this committee promotes the integrated planning, flexible management and high-quality economy of the Mississippi.[1]

3. The Main Forms of Tourism Products

(1) Aquatic Tourism Product

The Mississippi a treasury for national culture and recreation. There are green ecological corridors and industrial towns along the river. Many types of aquatic tourism products can be found over the Mississippi including fishing, drifting, water skiing, cruise and houseboat. The major cruise routes of the Mississippi are from New Orleans to Memphis, and from St. Louis to Saint Paul.

(2) Tourism Products onshore

Along the Mississippi, there is the Number 61 highway running through the North and the South. The Number 61 highway has a length of 2252 kilometers and connects the state of New Orleans and Minnesota. This road is also named as "Great River Road" and "Blues Road". It is recommended by National Geographic as "one of the must-drive roads in life". Tourists who do the self-driving tour on Number 61 highway can enjoy heritages, lakes and wild life reserves along the road.

(3) Urban Tourism Products

The Mississippi has a large basin area and its branches connect more than half of the American

---

[1] Ma Jing and Deng Hongbing. The Enlightenment of the Yangtze River Belt's Development Based on the Mode of Typical River Basins' Development in the World. Regional Economic Review, vol. 2, 2016, pp. 145-151.

economic regions. Therefore, urban tourism products such as urban leisure tour, business travel and MICE tourism are always available. For example, New Orleans is the port city of the Mississippi. It is the most important industrial city in the South of the US. Tourism is the second largest industry in the city, second only to the transportation industry.

4. Tourism Development Experiences from the Mississippi

Same to the other river valley in the world, the Mississippi also goes through the times when its ecological environment is highly deteriorated. As one of the top ten endangered rivers in US, the Mississippi gradually returns to the original beauty and becomes a treasury for national culture and recreation after more than 100 years water management. Its tourism development experiences and the effective management of the Mississippi can shed light on the river valley regions of China.

(1) Continuous Improvement on the Law System

A comprehensive law system is the foundation to the success. Back to 1820, US congress started to discuss the legislations of developing inland river navigation. After this, many relevant regulations and laws have been enacted to manage water resources, hydropower and water transportation including "Water Resource planning" and "Water Cleaning Laws". For instance, the "Water Cleaning Laws" established in 1972 regulates the quota of certificates on pollutant discharge. Through such certification, water quality was highly improved.

(2) Establishing the Integrated Management Committee

In 1879, US congress established the Committee of the Mississippi. Through the integrated planning, the whole river basin becomes a standardized inland navigation network that offers multiple functions including transportation, flood control, hydropower, water supply, irrigation, and recreation. In 1928, "Law of Flood Control" specified that Department of the Army Engineer is responsible for flood control and waterway improvement. In 1997, agriculture working group was launched with agriculture departments from 12 states involved.

(3) Formulating Strategic Management of the River Basin

In 1980s, US Environment Protection Agency started to recognize that water management based on river unit is an effective measure with the cooperation of different stakeholders in the region. In 1996, US Environment Protection Agency enacted the "Framework towards the Protection of River Basin" and dealt with the water pollution through the joint effort from multiple subjects, multiple departments and multiple communities. In the process of fulfilling this Framework, efficiency of environmental protection was finally improved.

(4) Dynamic and Comprehensive Water Monitor

Dynamic monitor of the natural resources is the foundation to success. There are four missions: first is to have an in-depth understand the natural system and resource of the Mississippi; second is to monitor the resource change in the water eco-system; third is to seek alternative plan for managing the river system; forth is to offer appropriate information management. The aim of such dynamic monitoring is to offer effective information and policy support for the Mississippi.[1]

---

[1] Zhang Wanyi, Cui Minli and Delong Jia. Implications of river management in the Mississippi. China Mining Industry Journal, vol. 1, 03 JUL, 2018.

参考文献

[1] 张雷，鲁春霞，李江苏. 中国大河流域开发与国家文明发育[J]. 长江流域资源与环境，2015，24（10）：1639-1645.

[2] 张永秀. 论古印度文明的特性[J]. 潍坊学院学报，2011，11（01）：86-89.

[3] 刘健. 苏美尔文明基本特征探析[J]. 外国问题研究，2016（02）：43-49+118.

[4] 王东. 中华文明的文化基因与现代传承（专题讨论）中华文明的五次辉煌与文化基因中的五大核心理念[J]. 河北学刊，2003（05）：130-134+147.

[5] 鲍捷，陆林. 河流旅游：缘起、内涵及其研究体系——一个本体论的诠释[J]. 地理科学，2017，37（7）：1069-1079.

[6] 王素霞. 世界第一河——亚马逊河[J]. 水利天地，2006（12）：34-35.

[7] 孙海燕，李关云. 埃及旅游业：新休闲主义的"黄与蓝"[J]. 21世纪商业评论，2005（5）：119-123.

[8] 翟辅东. 湘江风光带开发与莱茵河风光带对比研究[J]. 旅游学刊，2001，16（3）：57-59.

[9] 王开泳，张鹏岩，丁旭生. 黄河流域旅游经济的时空分异与R/S分析[J]. 地理科学，2014，34（03）：295-301.

[10] 黄德林，黄道明. 长江流域水资源开发的生态效应及对策[J]. 水利水电快报，2005，26（18）：1-4+6.

[11] 王守书. 河流旅游功能构建与产品开发研究[D]. 上海：上海师范大学，2009.

[12] 夏骥，肖永芹. 密西西比河开发经验及对长江流域发展的启示[J]. 重庆社会科学，2006（5）：22-26.

[13] 沈皆希，赵又霖，郭利丹. 跨界河流空间信息服务模型研究：以湄公河为例[J]. 武汉理工大学学报（信息与管理工程版），2017（3）：330-333.

[14] 高永宏. 沈阳市浑河滨水区开发战略研究[D]. 沈阳：东北大学，2005.

[15] 刘健. 莱茵河流域的开发建设及成功经验[J]. 世界农业，1998（2）：3-5.

[16] 沈虹，冯学钢. 都市文化型河流旅游开发研究——以上海苏州河为例[J]. 桂林旅游高等专科学校学报，2006（5）：542-545.

[17] Hilary, Du Cros, Bob Mckercher. Cultural Tourism[M]. 第二版. 朱路平译. 北京：商务印

书馆，2017.

［18］金寿福. 内生与杂糅视野下的古埃及文明起源［J］. 中国社会科学，2012（12）：179-200+209.

［19］郑若葵. 埃及发现世界最早的农耕文化遗迹［J］. 农业考古，1987（1）：115.

［20］王京传. 美国国家历史公园建设及对中国的启示［J］. 北京社会科学，2018（1）：119-128.

［21］Terzić, Aleksandra, and NevenaĆurĉić. "Culture Resources in Fuction of Regional Development and International Cooperation−Danube Region, Serbia." Geographica Timisiensis, 2016（1）：45-57.

［22］龚道德，袁晓园，张青萍. 美国运河国家遗产廊道模式运作机理剖析及其对我国大型线性文化遗产保护与发展的启示［J］. 城市发展研究，2016，23（1）：17-22.

［23］New Orleans Jazz & Heritage Festival. http://www.nojazzfest.com.Accessed 10 Sept. 2019.

［24］赵乾坤，鲁特，洪毅，等. 大河：穿行世界文明的经络［J］. 中国三峡，2009（2）：71-77.

［25］戴惠坤. 仿古旅游地——埃及"法老村"［J］. 世界知识，1990（22）：21.

［26］Ancient Battlefield of the Three Kingdoms.［EB/OL］. http://www.chinachibi.com/intro/1.html. Accessed 10 Sept. 2019.

［27］Fantawild Adventure.［EB/OL］. http://datong.fangte.com.Accessed 10 Sept. 2019.

［28］陈雪钧. 世界库坝旅游开发的经验与启示［J］. 消费经济，2013，29（1）：71-74.

［29］罗美洁. 三峡工程与国外水利工程的文化比较——以胡佛、大古力、阿斯旺、伊泰普为例［J］. 三峡论坛（三峡文学. 理论版），2014（2）：1-8.

［30］张西林，傅蓉，曾宪文. 水库旅游开发研究初探［J］. 中南林学院学报，2003（06）：28-32.

［31］张志会. 世界经典大坝——美国胡佛大坝概览［J］. 中国三峡，2012（01）：69-78+2.

［32］刘名俭，黄猛. 旅游目的地空间结构体系构建研究——以长江三峡为例［J］. 经济地理，2005（4）：581-584.

［33］吴士勇. 古代治水、开河与通漕的历史逻辑［J］. 深圳大学学报（人文社会科学版），2018，35（2）：152-160.

［34］韩春辉，左其亭，宋梦林，罗增良. 我国治水思想演变分析［J］. 水利发展研究，2015，15（5）：75-80.

［35］毛春梅，陈苡慈，孙宗凤等. 新时期水文化的内涵及其与水利文化的关系［J］. 水利经济，2011，29（4）：63-66+74.

［36］丁枢，黄江涛. 水利旅游资源的文化内涵及开发思路［J］. 中国水利，2009（2）：49-51.

［37］王会战. 小浪底水利风景区旅游可持续发展研究［D］. 青岛：青岛大学，2007.

[38] 李明堂. 三门峡水利枢纽工程管理探索与实践 [J]. 人民黄河, 2017, 39 (7): 1-6.

[39] 黄河魂——壶口瀑布. 临汾市文化和旅游局 http://wlj.linfen.gov.cn/contents/1217/364040.html

[40] 壶口瀑布. 陕西文化旅游网 [EB/OL]. http://www.sxtour.com/html/index.html

[41] 壶口瀑布. 延安市地方志编纂委员会 [EB/OL]. http://fzbz.yanan.gov.cn/yats/fjmq/yicx/9143.htm

[42] 万津津, 沙润, 刘泽华. 美国科罗拉多大峡谷地质旅游管理特色及对我国的启示 [J]. 生态经济, 2017, 33 (10): 159-162+189.

[43] 刘平. 山地城市沿江防洪设施的景观化研究 [D]. 重庆: 西南大学, 2017.

[44] 熊海珍. 中国传统村镇水环境景观探析 [D]. 重庆: 西南交通大学, 2008.

[45] 庄严, 缪淑秀. 闽浙联手保护非物质文化遗产古廊桥 [N]. 福建日报, 2019.

[46] 何明春. 闽东周宁县木拱廊桥研究 [D]. 福州: 福建师范大学, 2014.

[47] 赵巧红, 吴通华. 寿宁深化文旅融合推进全域旅游发展: 秀外慧中开新景. 闽江日报网. [EB/OL]. http://cmstop.ndsww.com/p/17875.html

[48] 姜师立. 文旅融合打造大运河缤纷旅游带 [N]. 中国文化报, 2019-06-01 (007).

[49] 刘晓真. 从乡俗仪礼到民间艺术——当代山东商河鼓子秧歌文化功能的变迁与传承 [J]. 北京舞蹈学院学报, 2004 (01): 77-81.

[50] 李牧. 民俗、艺术及审美经验——兼论季中扬《民间艺术的审美经验研究》[J]. 民族文学研究, 2017, 35 (04): 120-125.

[51] 王霞. 民间艺术融入文化旅游业发展 [N]. 山西日报, 2019-06-03 (010).

[52] 符少玲. 黎族非物质文化遗产资源开发对策研究——以黎族纺染织绣技艺为例 [J]. 大众文艺, 2016 (4): 3.

[53] 高丰, 高昌. 海南民族民间工艺美术概述 [J]. 装饰, 1999 (3): 4-6.

[54] 周国耀, 吴晓雯. 海南黎族织锦的艺术特点与文化价值 [J]. 改革与开放, 2009 (8): 196-198.

[55] 薛雪. 面花装饰特色的比较研究——豫东沈丘顾家面花与山西花馍的比较研究 [J]. 大众文艺, 2017 (5): 93.

[56] 楼兰. 晋城花馍: 可以吃的民间艺术 [J]. 中外文化交流, 2014 (11) 11: 83.

[57] 石瑜. 平阳木板年画与赵大勇老人 [J]. 文学界 (理论版), 2012 (8): 271-272.

[58] 白英芳. 临汾威风锣鼓溯源初探 [J]. 现代交际, 2017 (11): 85-86.

[59] 张玥. 临汾威风锣鼓的表演特色及文化功能 [J]. 当代音乐, 2016 (19): 75-77.

[60] 李毓. 传承与创新: 民俗文化的舞台化研究 [D]. 广州: 广东技术师范学院, 2013.

[61] 杨宇轩. 游客满意视角下的旅游节庆活动开发——以秦淮灯会为例 [J]. 大众文艺, 2019 (8): 247-248.

[62] 张力. 用节庆文化牵引旅游体验经济 [N]. 中国文化报, 2019-06-22 (007): 7.

［63］安虎森. 增长极理论评述［J］. 南开经济研究，1997（1）：31-37.

［64］颜鹏飞，邵秋芬. 经济增长极理论研究［J］. 财经理论与实践，2001（2）：2-6.

［65］樊信友. 区域旅游业空间布局研究［D］. 成都：四川大学，2004.

［66］陶云. 旅游产业增长极理论与应用研究［D］. 芜湖：安徽师范大学，2006.

［67］杨达源. 长江三峡的起源与演变［J］. 南京大学学报（自然科学版），1988（03）：466-474.

［68］徐长江，范可旭，肖天国. 金沙江流域径流特征及变化趋势分析［J］. 人民长江，2010，41（07）：10-14+51.

［69］黄河. 基于增长极理论的金沙江下游旅游圈合作模式研究［J］. 生产力研究，2010（12）：132-133+148.

［70］王静，罗明义，杜靖川. 试论金沙江下游流域旅游增长极的选择与培育［J］. 思想战线，2008（4）：125-126.

［71］张明川. 基于"点—轴系统"理论的嘉陵江流域旅游开发研究［J］. 科技经济市场，2009（10）：61-66.

［72］吕飞. 论"三峡旅游经济圈"构建中的"点—轴"式开发［J］. 重庆职业技术学院学报，2006（6）：52-54.

［73］李慧. 基于点—轴理论的陕南汉江走廊旅游开发模式研究［D］. 西安：西安科技大学，2012.

［74］Forman RTT. Landscape Ecology［M］. New York, USA：Wiley, 1986, 121-155.

［75］李晓佳. 以线性空间理论解读富有城市特色的道路景观［D］. 北京：北京林业大学，2010.

［76］孙帅. 都市型绿道规划设计研究［D］. 北京：北京林业大学，2013.

［77］邱海莲，由亚男. 旅游廊道概念界定［J］. 旅游论坛，2015，8（4）：26-30.

［78］郑好，高吉喜，谢高地，邹长新，金宇. 生态廊道［J］. 生态与农村环境学报，2019，35（02）：137-144.

［79］关于广东省绿道网建设总体规划（2011~2015年）的批复［EB/OL］. http://www.gd.gov.cn/gkmlpt/content/0/140/post_140709.html.

［80］陶犁. "文化廊道"及旅游开发：一种新的线性遗产区域旅游开发思路［J］. 思想战线，2012，38（2）：99-103.

［81］王肖宇，陈伯超. 美国国家遗产廊道的保护——以黑石河峡谷为例［J］. 世界建筑，2007（7）：124-126.

［82］余青，吴必虎，刘志敏，等. 风景道研究与规划实践综述［J］. 地理研究，2007（6）：1274-1284.

［83］柳晓霞. 滨水型风景道规划设计研究［D］. 北京：北京交通大学，2009.

[84] 山西省人民政府办公厅关于印发山西省黄河、长城、太行三大板块旅游发展总体规划的通知_通知公告_新闻中心_山西省文化和旅游厅政务网［R/OL］. http://wlt.shanxi.gov.cn/sitefiles/sxzwcms/html/xwzx/tzgg/14977.shtml.

[85] 2018中国黄河旅游大会,《中国黄河旅游发展指数报告》成焦点.［R/OL］. http://www.ctnews.com.cn/art/2018/9/21/art_126_25438.html.

[86] 高明,贾海燕,申存良,等. 临汾市旅游气候舒适度特征分析［C］// 第33届中国气象学会年会S5应对气候变化、低碳发展与生态文明建设. 2016.

[87] 2017中国特色魅力城市200强出炉［EB/OL］. http://china.cnr.cn/gdgg/20171224/t20171224_524073802.shtml.

[88] 杜春春,临汾荣获全国"厕所革命优秀城市奖"［EB/OL］. http://www.xinhuanet.com//local/2017-11/24/c_129748314.htm.

[89] 游乐项目. 山西云丘山旅游景区官网［EB/OL］. http://www.yunqiushan.cn/about/?31.html#menuSub.

[90] 山西三大板块旅游发展总体规划审议通过. 山西省人民政府门户网站［EB/OL］. http://www.shanxi.gov.cn/yw/sxyw/201806/t20180625_457038.shtml.

[91] 山西临汾投资76.8亿元打造沿黄扶贫旅游公路［J］. 城市道桥与防洪,2018（02）：10.

[92] 刘楚楚. 山西省文化产业与旅游产业融合发展研究［D］. 太原：山西财经大学,2018.

[93] 刘敏,任亚鹏,王萍. 山西黄河文化：内涵、符号与旅游开发——基于晋西沿黄旅游景区比较研究［J］. 晋中学院学报,2018,35（4）：39-43.

[94] 涂海峰,聂真,李媚. 莱茵河流域发展研究［J］. 四川建筑,2016,36（01）：10-13.

[95] 马静,邓宏兵. 国外典型流域开发模式与经验对长江经济带的启示［J］. 区域经济评论,2016（2）：145-151.

[96] 张丹明. 中莱茵河谷：葡萄园-古堡-城镇-山河的奏鸣曲［J］. 中国文化遗产,2007（2）：102-105.

[97] 董波,杜雨辰. 国外运河遗产对中国大运河文化带建设的启示［J］. 发展规划研究,2019（5）.

[98] 童潜明. 工业遗产旅游 另一种转型选择［J］. 国土资源导刊,2012,9（07）：17.

[99] 杨光荣. 欧洲莱茵河发展旅游业对湖南的启示［N］. 中国旅游报,2011（11）.

[100] 陆静依. 泰晤士河河岸改造工程的创意之作——新千年广场建设工程［J］. 国外科技,2000（1）：51-55.

[101] 高静. 大都市滨水区游憩化更新研究——基于伦敦与上海的比较案例［D］. 上海：华东师范大学,2015.

[102] 舒肖明. 国外著名滨水城市水上旅游开发的实践与经验［J］. 宁波大学学报（人文科学

版），2008，21（3）：94-96.

［103］阎水玉，王祥荣. 泰晤士河在伦敦市规划中的功能定位、保证措施及其特征的分析［J］. 国外城市规划，1999（01）：34-35+42.

［104］郑伯红，汤建中. 伦敦巴黎河岸景观带建设的实践与经验［J］. 城市问题，2002（1）：71-74.

［105］张万益. 美国密西西比河流域治理的若干启示［N］. 中国矿业报，2018-07-03（001）.

［106］杨文娟. 黄河三角洲历史文化资源的旅游开发研究［D］. 江苏师范大学，2013.

［107］陈胜军. 长江水运旅游发展研究［D］. 武汉理工大学，2003.

［108］冯天瑜. 中国大河文明探略［J］. 地域文化研究，2018（03）：1-4+153.

［109］高晨旭，李永乐. 我国遗产廊道研究综述［J］. 昆明理工大学学报（社会科学版），2018，18（03）：101-108.

［110］潘华琼. 苏丹的古王国遗址［J］. 中国投资，2018（18）：89-93.

［111］张艳彬. 黄河流域经济空间开发模式［J］. 时代金融，2018（26）：97.

［112］CIPRA会长吴红波出席首届大河文明旅游论坛并发表演讲［J］. 国际公关，2018（05）：40-42.

［113］孔华. 非物质文化遗产文化旅游开发对策研究——以安徽池州为例［J］. 黑河学刊，2018（06）：65-67.

［114］白庚胜. 寻访文明：行走在大河流经的地方（下）［N］. 中国社会科学报，2011-08-02（019）.

［115］吴传清，孙智君，许军. 点轴系统理论及其拓展与应用：一个文献述评［J］. 贵州财经学院学报，2007（02）：30-36.

［116］汪芳，廉华. 线型空间研究进展与发展趋势［J］. 华中建筑，2007（07）：88-91.

［117］冯景云. 神话传说与历史文化名城旅游形象策划——以宜宾为例［J］. 宜宾学院学报，2007（04）：77-79.

［118］伏尔加河流域：俄罗斯的历史摇篮［J］. 重庆与世界，2014（02）：86-87.

［119］李国栋，刘雨潇. 麦作文明与稻作文明——释读《大河文明的诞生》［J］. 贵州师范学院学报，2014，30（01）：34-38.

［120］葛颖. 论黄河水利旅游发展策略［J］. 现代经济信息，2014（15）：386.

［121］周瑞雪，王露瑶，陈玉英，杨含. 黄河沿线旅游资源"点—轴"开发模式研究——以河南省黄河旅游开发为例［J］. 旅游纵览（下半月），2014（08）：222-223.

［122］付奇峰. 水的文化记忆［J］. 水利发展研究，2015，15（01）：98-104.

［123］刘昌玉. 科尔德威与巴比伦城的考古发掘［J］. 大众考古，2015（03）：33-36.

［124］段友文，张小丁. "长城文化遗产廊道"：边关古村镇整体保护之构想［J］. 山西大同大

学学报（社会科学版），2015，29（03）：1-7.

［125］乔晓光.《沿着河走——黄河流域民间艺术考察手记》［J］.中华手工，2015（09）：105.

［126］陈娟，王洋.水利风景区水文景观规划设计研究［J］.科技创新导报，2015，12（17）：13+15.

［127］令狐若明.古埃及天文学考古揭示的辉煌成就［J］.大众考古，2015（06）：72-76.

［128］何志印，齐晓玉，郭晓宁.滨水生态文化廊道景观设计分析［J］.河南科技，2015（10）：98-100.

［129］王新文，毕景龙.大西安"八水"遗产廊道构建初探［J］.西北大学学报（自然科学版），2015，45（05）：837-841.

［130］张雷，鲁春霞，李江苏.中国大河流域开发与国家文明发育［J］.长江流域资源与环境，2015，24（10）：1639-1645.

［131］张敬秀.交通工具和五大文明的对应［J］.内蒙古大学学报（哲学社会科学版），1996（06）：66.

［132］郭大顺.《两河流域史前时代》评介［J］.考古，1996（07）：95-96.

［133］吴涛，张巍.汇聚大河文明 共谋未来可持续的高质量发展——"2018大河对话"国际论坛综述［J］.文化软实力研究，2019，4（01）：64-71.

［134］张瑾.尼罗河流域的水政治：历史与现实［J］.阿拉伯世界研究，2019（02）：62-75+119.

［135］胡春良.垣曲——大河之曲的文明皈依［J］.铸造设备与工艺，2019（02）：57-61.

［136］张小军.黄河：不朽的大河文明［J］.民主与科学，2019（01）：57-59.

［137］王渔.文旅融合下文化遗产与旅游品牌建设探讨［J］.现代商业，2019（12）：45-46.

［138］李玉臻，刘璐.三峡遗产廊道空间构建及优化研究［J］.重庆理工大学学报（社会科学），2019，33（05）：62-71.

［139］苏晓萍，江金兰.线性文化遗产与文化旅游业协同发展路径——基于东阳古道资源开发的思考［J］.江苏经贸职业技术学院学报，2019（03）：21-23.

［140］胡文瑞.大河文明谈［J］.中国石油石化，2008（16）：34.

［141］张红贤."点—轴—网络"理论与长三角旅游区一体化的空间发展模式研究［J］.特区经济，2008（08）：49-50.

［142］贾淑芬.伏尔加河沿岸的历史文化名城［J］.俄语学习，2001（02）：35-40.

［143］王志芳，孙鹏.遗产廊道———一种较新的遗产保护方法［J］.中国园林，2001（05）：86-89.

［144］刘建国，王霞，张蕾.洹河流域区域考古信息系统的建设与探索［J］.考古，2001（09）：78-81.

[145] 祁玲, 朱自强. 都江堰水利工程旅游深度开发初探 [J]. 智能城市, 2016, 2 (11): 261–262.

[146] 余熙. 武汉融汇世界大河文明——"2016大河对话"国际论坛纪实 [J]. 对外传播, 2016 (12): 68–69.

[147] 井娟. 汇聚陶器精萃 传承灿烂文明——"大河上下·黄河流域史前陶器展" [J]. 文物天地, 2017 (01): 52–54.

[148] 文国繁. "点-轴系统"理论下的丝绸之路经济带旅游空间结构研究 [J]. 金融经济, 2017 (02): 41–43.

[149] 李容全. 黄河、永定河发育历史与流域新生代古湖演变间的相互关系 [J]. 北京师范大学学报 (自然科学版), 1988 (04): 84–93.

[150] 丁四保. "增长极"模式与不发达地区经济发展——意大利南部的教训及启示 [J]. 经济地理, 1989 (04): 297–301.

[151] 张敬秀, 田建平. 东亚大河文明系统论略 [J]. 内蒙古大学学报 (哲学社会科学版), 1995 (01): 47–58.

[152] 刘锡诚. 旅游与传说 [J]. 民俗研究, 1995 (01): 19–26.

[153] 唐际根, 荆志淳, 徐广德, 瑞普·拉普. 洹河流域区域考古研究初步报告 [J]. 考古, 1998 (10): 13–22.

[154] 前伟超. 淮河的光芒: 黄河与长江的联结——《舞阳贾湖·序》[J]. 东南文化, 1999 (01): 28–29.

[155] 汤晓敏, 王云. 滨水景观的规划设计模式探索 [J]. 上海农学院学报, 1999 (03): 182–188.

[156] 阎同生, 郑天然. 旅游发展增长极研究 [J]. 合作经济与科技, 2006 (08): 41–42.

[157] 阚如良, 汪胜华. 长江三峡·清江水利旅游开发研究 [J]. 特区经济, 2006 (01): 203–205.

[158] 李瑞, 曲扬. 旅游走廊: 概念、动力机制、发展模式研究——以宁西铁路旅游走廊为例 [J]. 南阳师范学院学报, 2006 (03): 65–68+79.

[159] 万先进, 刘亚玲. 三峡旅游产业竞争力的现状分析及对策 [J]. 经济地理, 2006 (03): 516–520+537.

[160] 袁学勇, 杜毅志, 李红斌. 话说传统水利与现代水利 [J]. 水利天地, 2006 (09): 26–27.

[161] 蔡婵静, 周志翔, 陈芳, 郑忠明. 武汉市绿色廊道景观格局 [J]. 生态学报, 2006 (09): 2996–3004.

[162] 吕飞. 论"三峡旅游经济圈"构建中的"点——轴"式开发 [J]. 重庆职业技术学院学

报，2006（06）：52-54.

［163］严建伟，任娟. 斑块、廊道、滨水——居住区绿地景观生态规划［J］. 天津大学学报（社会科学版），2006（06）：454-457.

［164］孙开泰. 论三晋古文化对春秋战国诸子百家争鸣的影响［J］. 邯郸职业技术学院学报，2006（04）：7-11.

［165］李娟. 发挥优势，做好水利旅游大文章［J］. 陕西水利，2002（06）：16-17.

［166］咸蔓雪. 湄公河流域：一条大河串起的文明［J］. 世界知识，2002（23）：14-15.

［167］陆玉麒. 论点-轴系统理论的科学内涵［J］. 地理科学，2002（02）：136-143.

［168］杜俊涛，陈迅，雷森，王亚娜. 增长极理论的模型化研究［J］. 重庆大学学报（自然科学版），2002（04）：103-106.

［169］杨先让，杨阳.《黄河十四走》［J］. 中华手工，2012（08）：94.

［170］于媛媛. 印度北部的大河流经长2700多公里 印度的古老河流孕育出"恒河文明"印度人心中的圣河看做女神的化身 观览印度恒河［J］. 中国地名，2012（04）：61.

［171］张玲玉，任志平. 乌江——一种大河文明［J］. 当代贵州，2012（18）：22-24.

［172］徐江伟."血色曙光——华夏文明与汉字的起源"之八 西域文明、两河流域文明与华夏文明之源［J］. 社会科学论坛，2012（08）：128-158.

［173］付飞，董靓. 基于生态廊道原理的城市河流景观空间分析［J］. 中国园林，2012，28（09）：57-61.

［174］余凤龙，黄震方，尚正永. 水利风景区的价值内涵、发展历程与运行现状的思考［J］. 经济地理，2012，32（12）：169-175.

［175］张镒，柯彬彬. 我国遗产廊道研究述评［J］. 世界地理研究，2016，25（01）：166-174.

［176］张定青，王海荣，曹象明. 我国遗产廊道研究进展［J］. 城市发展研究，2016，23（05）：70-75.

［177］高吉喜. 构建国家生态廊道 保护生物多样性［J］. 中国发展，2016，16（03）：87.

［178］赵希玉. 博物馆文化创意商品的开发设计研究——以大英博物馆为例［J］. 美术教育研究，2016（13）：61.

［179］伍开云，张丹丹. 基于全域旅游视角的三门峡大坝旅游发展路径研究［J］. 教育教学论坛，2016（39）：87-88.

［180］娜仁图雅，和金生. 基于"一带一路"倡议的沿黄河沿交通干线经济带区域物流发展空间布局实证分析［J］. 内蒙古财经大学学报，2016，14（05）：24-31.

［181］Zhokhov A E, Pugacheva M N.［Parasites-invaders of the Volga river basin: history of invasion, perspective of dispersion, possibility of epizootic］.［J］. Parazitologiya, 2001, 35（3）.

［182］李敏纳，蔡舒，覃成林. 黄河流域经济空间分异态势分析［J］. 经济地理，2011，31

（03）：379-383+419.

[183] 青分，周魁一. 从治水社会到水利社会 [J]. 国学，2011（08）：17-20.

[184] 赵丽华. "点——轴系统"理论在环青海湖旅游圈开发中的应用 [J]. 青海师范大学学报（自然科学版），2011，27（03）：76-79.

[185] 赵林，韩增林，石迎春. 基于"点—轴系统"理论的鲁南旅游长廊建构 [J]. 云南地理环境研究，2011，23（05）：32-37.

[186] 行龙. 从"治水社会"到"水利社会"[J]. 读书，2005（08）：55-62.

[187] 岳隽，王仰麟，彭建. 城市河流的景观生态学研究：概念框架 [J]. 生态学报，2005（06）：1422-1429.

[188] 田至美. 山西旅游地域系统结构及其优化布局 [J]. 资源·产业，2005（04）：61-63.

[189] 汪德根，陆林，陈田，刘昌雪. 基于点—轴理论的旅游地系统空间结构演变研究——以呼伦贝尔—阿尔山旅游区为例 [J]. 经济地理，2005（06）：904-909.

[190] 张西林. 水库功能调整与旅游开发 [J]. 水利渔业，2005（01）：80-81.

[191] 张成岗，张尚弘. 都江堰：水利工程史上的奇迹 [J]. 工程研究-跨学科视野中的工程，2004，1（00）：171-177.

[192] 李伟，俞孔坚，李迪华. 遗产廊道与大运河整体保护的理论框架 [J]. 城市问题，2004（01）：28-31+54.

[193] 汪波，白彦壮，杜俊涛. 增长极理论在西部开发中的应用研究 [J]. 西北农林科技大学学报（社会科学版），2004（02）：40-44.

[194] 阚如良. 论大三峡旅游圈的构建与发展 [J]. 地理与地理信息科学，2004（06）：87-90+103.

[195] 宋忠升. 旅游经济增长极 [J]. 招商周刊，2004（Z2）：24.

[196] 朱尖，姜维公. 黄河故道线性文化遗产旅游价值评价与开发研究 [J]. 资源开发与市场，2013，29（05）：553-556.

[197] 奚雪松，陈琳. 美国伊利运河国家遗产廊道的保护与可持续利用方法及其启示 [J]. 国际城市规划，2013，28（04）：100-107.

[198] 鲁婉婷. 基于生命周期理论的城市滨水区旅游开发模式研究——以武汉汉江为例 [J]. 中小企业管理与科技（下旬刊），2013（07）：137-139.

[199] 李飞，宋金平. 廊道遗产：概念、理论源流与价值判断 [J]. 人文地理，2010，25（02）：74-77+104.

[200] 江小蓉. 基于"点—轴"系统理论的鄱阳湖旅游开发研究 [J]. 农业考古，2010（06）：34-36.

[201] 王薇，李传奇. 河流廊道与生态修复 [J]. 水利水电技术，2003（09）：56-58.

[202] 肖星，王生鹏. 甘肃旅游点轴开发模式探讨［J］. 西北民族大学学报（哲学社会科学版），2003（02）：36-40.

[203] 罗坤，蔡永立，郭纪光，左俊杰. 崇明岛绿色河流廊道景观格局［J］. 长江流域资源与环境，2009，18（10）：908-913.

[204] 侯文静. 美国国家风景道对中国的启示［J］. 才智，2009（30）：139-140.

[205] 凤晓.《恒河之流》研究［D］. 呼和浩特：内蒙古大学，2013.

[206] 沙田. 史前遗址展示与阐释的景观途径研究［D］. 重庆：重庆大学，2018.

[207] 王殿民. 唤醒古文明浩瀚记忆展现大河东壮美画卷［N］. 运城日报，2017-11-28(003).

[208] 王文慧. 山、陕、豫大禹神话传说的文化意蕴与当代展演［D］. 太原：山西大学，2017.

[209] 王晓. 三江并流区多元生计的历史人类学考察［J］. 西南边疆民族研究，2015（1）.

[210] 张雷. 中国大河流域开发与国家文明发育［C］// 河南大学黄河文明与可持续发展研究中心黄河文明与可持续发展（第九辑），2014.

[211] Belgrade, Serbia. Cultural Resources in Fuction of Regional Development and International Cooperation. –Danube Region, SERBI Geographica［J］. Timisiensis, 2016,（45-57）.

[212] Martin Schletterer, Leopold Füreder. The Volga River: Review on Research History and Synthesis of Current Knowledge［J］. River Systems, 2011, 19（2）.

[213] Gomanenko Olesya Aleksandrovna, Bulatov Vladimir Viktorovich. To the History of Financial and Economic Activity of the Volga River Transport During the NEP and the First Five-Year Period［J］. Vestnik Volgogradskogo Gosudarstvennogo Universiteta. Seriâ 4. Istoriâ, Regionovedenie, Meždunarodnye Otnošeniâ, 2016, 21（1）.

[214] Paul Josephson. Rivers, Memory and Nation-Building: A History of the Volga and MississippiRivers［J］. Technology and Culture, 2016, 57（3）.

[215] G. Isachenko. Geographic roots of ancient civilizations（on the 120th anniversary of L. I. Mechnikov's Civilization and Great Historic Rivers）: Part II［J］. Regional Research of Russia, 2011, 1（2）.

[216] Tristram R. Kidder, Haiwang Liu. Bridging theoretical gaps in geoarchaeology: archaeology, geoarchaeology, and history in the Yellow River valley, China［J］. Archaeological and Anthropological Sciences, 2017, 9（8）.

[217] Lei Gao, Hao Long, Ping Zhang, Toru Tamura, Wenli Feng, Qinqin Mei. The sedimentary evolution of Yangtze River delta since MIS3: A new chronology evidence revealed by OSL dating［J］. Quaternary Geochronology, 2018.

[218] Tianyuan Li, Shenglian Guo, Lu Chen, Jiali Guo. Bivariate Flood Frequency Analysis with Historical Information Based on Copula［J］. Journal of Hydrologic Engineering, 2013, 18（8）.

[219] 王奥. 论大禹治水传说在武汉旅游开发中的应用［D］. 武汉：华中师范大学，2017.

[220] 郝丽利. 水利风景区的科普教育功能研究 [D]. 郑州：河南大学，2013.

[221] 王松. 水库型水利风景区景观规划研究 [D]. 福州：福建农林大学，2011.

[222] 孟秋莉. 我国水库旅游开发研究 [D]. 上海：上海师范大学，2007.

[223] 宋建平. 小浪底水利枢纽工程旅游开发与管理研究 [D]. 南京：河海大学，2007.

[224] 张西林. 水库旅游开发与规划研究 [D]. 长沙：中南林学院，2003.

[225] 杨成华. 加快构建茅岩河峡谷经济产业带 鼎力打造张家界全域旅游增长极 [N]. 张家界日报，2017-10-24.

[226] 李凤霞. 图们江增长三角旅游产业集群发展研究 [D]. 沈阳：东北师范大学，2005.

[227] 邓丽娟. 基于点—轴系统理论的环洞庭湖旅游空间结构优化研究 [C]// 湖南省农业系统工程学会. 湖南省农业系统工程学会2012年年会论文集，2012：9.

[228] 刘宇楠. 探索江河流域旅游目的地规划 [N]. 中国旅游报，2012-08-01.

[229] 覃成林，马芳芳. 黄河流域经济空间开发模式研究 [J]. 黄河文明与可持续发展，2012（2）.

[230] 周杜辉. 渭河流域经济空间分异及其优化对策研究 [D]. 西安：西北大学，2011.

[231] 周二黑. 黄河流域经济空间分异规律研究 [D]. 河南大学，2007.

[232] 张守艳. 黑龙江省三江地区旅游开发模式研究 [D]. 青岛：青岛大学，2005.

[233] 胡碧玉. 流域经济论 [D]. 成都：四川大学，2004.

[234] 蒙倩彬. 基于生物多样性保护的城市生态廊道研究 [D]. 北京：北京林业大学，2016.

[235] 段秋岑. 线性文化遗产廊道的保护研究 [D]. 昆明：云南大学，2014.

[236] 黄静. 城市水景观体系规划研究 [D]. 南京：南京林业大学，2013.

[237] 刘宇楠. 探索江河流域旅游目的地规划 [N]. 中国旅游报，2012-08-01.

[238] 付飞. 以生态为导向的河流景观规划研究 [D]. 重庆：西南交通大学，2011.

责任编辑：谯　洁
责任印制：冯冬青
封面设计：中文天地

图书在版编目（CIP）数据

大河文明旅游报告：汉英对照 / 世界旅游联盟编
. -- 北京：中国旅游出版社，2019.11
ISBN 978-7-5032-6376-7

Ⅰ.①大…　Ⅱ.①世…　Ⅲ.①滨海旅游—旅游业发展—研究报告—中国—汉、英　Ⅳ.① F592.7

中国版本图书馆 CIP 数据核字 (2019) 第 242419 号

书　　名：	大河文明旅游报告
主　　编：	世界旅游联盟
出版发行：	中国旅游出版社
	（北京建国门内大街甲 9 号　邮编：100005）
	http://www.cttp.net.cn　　E-mail:cttp@mct.gov.cn
	营销中心电话：010-85166503
排　　版：	北京中文天地文化艺术有限公司
印　　刷：	北京工商事务印刷有限公司
版　　次：	2019 年 11 月第 1 版　2019 年 11 月第 1 次印刷
开　　本：	889 毫米 ×1194 毫米　1/16
印　　张：	25.75
字　　数：	506 千
定　　价：	128.00 元
ＩＳＢＮ	978-7-5032-6376-7

版权所有　翻印必究
如发现质量问题，请直接与营销中心联系调换